W9-BYK-468

1866-1991
125th
ANNIVERSARY

BY THE SAME AUTHOR

This Wild Abyss:
The Story of the Men Who Made Modern Astronomy

In the Presence of the Creator:
Isaac Newton and His Times

FOX AT THE WOOD'S EDGE

A BIOGRAPHY OF LOREN EISELEY

GALE E. CHRISTIANSON

HENRY HOLT AND COMPANY
NEW YORK

Published by Henry Holt and Company, Inc.,
115 West 18th Street, New York, New York 10011.
Published in Canada by Fitzhenry & Whiteside Limited,
195 Allstate Parkway, Markham, Ontario L3R 4T8.

Library of Congress Cataloging-in-Publication Data
Christianson, Gale E.
Fox at the wood's edge : a biography of Loren Eiseley /
Gale E. Christianson. — 1st ed.
p. cm.
Includes bibliographical references.
1. Eiseley, Loren C., 1907–1977—Biography.
2. Authors, American—20th century—Biography.
3. Anthropologists—United States—Biography.
4. Naturalists—United States—Biography.
I. Title.
PS3555.I78Z63 1990
306′.092—dc20
[B] 89-24714
CIP

ISBN 0-8050-1187-0
ISBN 0-8050-1858-1 (An Owl Book: pbk.)

First published in hardcover by
Henry Holt and Company, Inc., in 1990.

First Owl Book Edition—1991

Designed by Ann Gold

Printed in the United States of America
Recognizing the importance of preserving the
written word, Henry Holt and Company, Inc.,
by policy, prints all of its first editions
on acid-free paper.∞

1 3 5 7 9 10 8 6 4 2
1 3 5 7 9 10 8 6 4 2
pbk.

TO LAURIE

Measure for measure, beat for beat.

UNPUBLISHED BEGINNING OF AUTOBIOGRAPHY

It is the ruse of the fox; I learned it long ago. In the pages which follow I will show you fear, I will show you terror. But huntsman, let us have one thing clear: I am a man, in flight. Though I am an archaeologist by profession, there are tombs that for my life I would not enter, vaults through whose doorways I would not descend, silences that on my deathbed I will not break. Though I sit in a warm room beneath a light and compose these lines, they are all of night, of outer darkness, and inner terrors. They are the annals of a long and uncompleted running. I set them down lest the end come on me unaware, as it does upon all fugitives. There is a shadow on the wall before me. It is my own. I write in a borrowed room at midnight. Tomorrow the shadow on the wall will be that of another. Very well, huntsman, let the hunt begin.

Loren Eiseley
June 20, 1963

CONTENTS

FOX AT THE WOOD'S EDGE

1

PROGENITORS

I

The boy's first memory was of time. Held aloft in the strong, reassuring arms of his father, he gazed into the midnight sky of a chill and leafless Nebraska spring. It was 1910, and Halley's comet was fast closing on the sun to keep its only rendezvous in the normal life span of a man. Still, the boy, who was not yet three, had a good chance of beating the odds.

"If you live to be an old man," his father whispered, "you will see it again. It will come back in seventy-five years."

"Yes, Papa," the boy replied dutifully. Tightening his hold on his father's neck, he promised that when he grew old he would gaze on the comet a second time and remember the person from his childhood he would always care for more than any other.[1]

Had it not been for the gnawing class discrimination and economic deprivation suffered by his restless European forebears, the boy's earliest memories might have been of a rather different sort—of martial music and spiked helmets, of strident speeches and cheering throngs, the anthem of German militarism nearing its crescendo, conducted by a headstrong demigod called the Kaiser.

Charles Frederick Eisele, Loren's grandfather, was born on July 3, 1838, on a farm near Stuttgart, capital of the Kingdom of Württemberg. According to the family history, he decided to emigrate rather than risk conscription into the army of his sovereign, William I. Charles left Germany at age fifteen and made his way to the Belgian port of Antwerp. From there he sailed for America, arriving in New York harbor on a Sunday morning. A few days later he was in Pittsburgh, where he was reunited with his brother, Gottlieb Frederick Eiseley, and two sisters, whose names are unknown. Charles moved in with his brother, who, as a new member of a less formal social order, had exchanged his Christian name for his middle name, Frederick, which was further shortened to Fred. The older brother had also anglicized the family name by adding a *y* at the end, and Charles, now Charley, immediately followed suit.

Of the time Charles spent in Pittsburgh, which encompassed his transition from late youth to early manhood, very little is known. He worked three years as a baker's apprentice and was later employed as a pastry cook by a steamboat company whose packets plied the waters of the Ohio and Mississippi rivers. In St. Louis, in 1858, Charles said good-bye to his fellow crew members and struck out for Iowa. He settled for a time in the village of Tipton in Cedar County, not far from Iowa City, the former territorial capital, supporting himself by teaching school and farming on the side.

It was not long before the mustachioed young bachelor, who was slight of build with hazel eyes and dark hair, became attracted to a local girl of English descent. Born in Medina, Ohio, on July 24, 1842, Josephine Whitney had moved with her family to Iowa in the late 1850s. No early photograph of her survives, and little is known of her relatives, except that she had at least one sister and one brother.[2]

Charles did not have a great deal to offer a prospective bride, and when he fell in love with seventeen-year-old Josephine, they agreed to postpone marriage until their future together seemed more secure. Bidding his fiancée farewell, Charles headed westward once again, this time bound for the newly created territory called Nebraska.

II

In 1842 Lieutenant John C. Frémont led an expedition through the country lying between the Kansas and Platte rivers. Frémont then attempted to expedite the long return of his party by descending the Platte in a makeshift boat. After dragging the vessel over the sandy bottom for three or four miles, the Great Pathfinder abandoned the effort in disgust, noting in his report to the government: "The names given by the Indians are always remarkably appropriate; and certainly none was ever more so than that which they have given to this stream—the Nebraska, or Shallow River!"[3]

Whatever one called it—the Oregon Trail, the Mormon Trail, or the California Trail—the route through the Nebraska Territory was about the same for all overland emigrants. Whether they went along the north side of the Platte or the south, the river was their guide. If, on leaving Iowa in 1859, Charles had also planned to pass through Nebraska and penetrate even deeper into the great frontier, something caused him to reconsider his decision. The mind-numbing vastness of the region had already stopped many a traveler. Willa Cather evoked it trenchantly in her autobiographical novel of pioneer life, *My Ántonia*: "I do not remember crossing the Missouri River, or anything about the journey . . . through Nebraska. Probably by that time I had crossed so many rivers that I was dull to them. The only thing very noticeable about Nebraska was that it was still, all day long, Nebraska."[4]

Charles Eiseley followed the Platte to a point some thirty miles beyond the newly established settlement of Omaha and then turned north. After traveling another dozen or so miles, he found what he was looking for. The young pioneer purchased a quarter section of land from the federal government at the going rate of $1.25 per acre and, three years later, exercised his right under the new Homestead Act to acquire an additional eighty acres. His farm, composed of fertile silt underlaid by deep loess soil, was located on Logan Creek, at the boundary of Dodge and Washington counties. Within less than a year, Fred acquired land next to that of his younger brother.

Like thousands of other young German males, Charles had fled his homeland out of uncertainty rather than cowardice. On October 23, 1862, Charles arrived in Omaha, where he enlisted in Company A, 2nd Regiment, of the Nebraska Cavalry Volunteers. The unseasoned horse soldier probably would have been ordered south to some theater of the Civil War had not the Sioux recently gone on the warpath in Minnesota. Fearing that the violence might spread across the northern plains, the authorities ordered Company A to proceed northwest to Fort Randall on the Missouri, just inside the southern boundary of what is now South Dakota. Many years later Charles described the place to a reporter as "miserable country where we traveled the prairie for weeks. Evenings hot winds would scorch us and even in June and July there was no grass."[5] Saddle sore and weary, Charles was mustered out of the cavalry on September 21, 1863, eleven months from the date he'd enlisted. As far as is known, he had not taken part in so much as a skirmish with the Sioux, let alone a significant battle.

The holiday season of 1864–65 was one of the happiest Charles Eiseley ever knew, for he spent it by keeping the promise he had made five years earlier. On January 2, 1865, Charles wed Josephine Whitney in a service performed by the Reverend Samuel Pancoast at the local hotel in Tipton, Iowa.[6] Ready now to shoulder the responsibilities of a frontier wife, the twenty-two-year-old bride crossed the Missouri with her husband and entered the Nebraska Territory for the first time. She would not leave that land for the remainder of her eighty-one years.

Josephine became pregnant by midspring and gave birth in January 1866 to a son named Francis. The couple's joy was multiplied by the knowledge that Charles, together with one E. H. Clark, had been chosen to represent Washington County in the Territorial Legislature at Omaha. This historic session, convened on January 4, was to be the last of its kind. A committee composed of Charles's fellow Republicans and rival Democrats met in secret to draft a state constitution, which was ratified by the full House the following month. The voters themselves approved the document by a narrow margin—3,938 to 3,838—in a special June election. As one historian later observed, "The results . . . were determined by those who counted the votes rather than by those who cast them."[7] Political chicanery notwithstanding, Nebraska was admitted as the thirty-seventh state of the union in 1867.

III

By the mid-1870s Charles Eiseley owned 320 acres—twice his original claim—half of it under the plow, the rest in grassland, of which thirty acres were fenced-in pasture, an unmistakable sign of frontier prosperity. Sensing that the moment was right to pursue additional economic interests, in 1874 Charles settled a few miles to the southwest in the newly platted village of Hooper and opened a hardware store.

Shadows, however, cast themselves over Charles and Josephine's private life. A second son, Clyde Edwin, had been born on December 29, 1868, and a third, Horace, in July 1871. But between Clyde and Horace, a daughter named Mary died shortly after her birth in April 1870. A second daughter, Lydia, followed her sister to the grave early in 1873, as did another son, Homer, in 1874. Josephine's final pregnancy resulted in the birth of twins, namesakes Charles and Josephine, on June 2, 1876. This time the fates proved even crueler than before. Little Josie clung to life nearly a month before dying on June 26. Then, like a blow on a bruise, Charley, who lived nine months, becoming the darling of the family, passed away on March 31, 1877. All the infants were buried in Logan Valley Cemetery, northeast of Winslow, the last three sharing the same marker.[8]

In 1882 Charles decided to move once more. He sold both farm and hardware store for the impressive sum of $9,000 and, with his family, set out for Norfolk, a village of some six hundred residents located forty miles northwest of Hooper on the Elkhorn River. Charles had scouted the community well and come away impressed. During 1878 Norfolk's local implement dealers had sold $55,745 worth of farm machinery, including more than three hundred harvesters and reapers. The discovery of gold in the Black Hills by an expedition under the command of General George Armstrong Custer brought a stampede of whites into the Dakota Territory. Once the Sioux were pacified, Norfolk became a main source of supply on the way west. The railroad reached the community in September 1879, and in May 1880 the Flynn brothers began manufacturing brick out of the excellent clay deposits in the region. A new brick bank, general store, newspaper office, and other buildings were completed in 1880 and 1881. In sum, it was the story of Hooper all over again, except on a larger scale, and Charles was not about to pass up the opportunity to become part of another frontier boom.[9]

The town's newest businessman chose to locate at Second Street and Norfolk Avenue. Here he built his second brick establishment, but on a grander scale than the first. The three-story structure, which still stands, was christened the Eiseley Block and served the community and surrounding area in a variety of ways. The first floor was for hardware sales. The second was commonly referred to as the City Opera House. Here itinerant stock companies put on plays, the Republicans held conventions to select candidates for local offices, and young people came to dance on Saturday evenings. The third floor was set aside as an armory and drill room for Company L of the Nebraska National Guard, better known locally as the Moore Rifles. Nor did Charles stint when it came to his family's comfort. He built a lovely home on West Norfolk Avenue, to which he walked every evening, reflecting on the day's events while puffing contentedly on a good cigar. He was a respectable if not distinguished figure, in three-piece suit, narrow-brimmed hat, mutton chops, and walrus mustache.[10]

IV

Of the three Eiseley sons, whose prospects looked so bright given their father's business acumen, only Clyde would have children of his own. He was thirteen when the family moved to Norfolk. Clyde completed grade school and then, as was common at the time, quit school at age sixteen, before earning a high-school diploma. Like his father, he took an active interest in civic affairs. Clyde became a member of the Norfolk Volunteer Fire Department and the Nebraska National Guard. His name was often mentioned in the local paper in conjunction with business he conducted on behalf of the Sons of Veterans, which took him across the state.

Something of a dreamer, Clyde possessed the perfect vehicle with which to bring his fantasies to life. At some point after he dropped out of Lincoln School, Clyde was entrusted with the management of the Opera House. Eastern Nebraska was then doing a lively business in the theater, as evidenced by the April 1888 appearance at Omaha's Boyd's Opera House of Edwin Booth and Lawrence Barrett, two of the nineteenth century's greatest Shakespearean actors. Performing on four successive nights, Booth and Barrett alternated leads in *Julius Caesar*, *The Merchant of Venice*, *Hamlet*, and *Macbeth*. While such distinguished thespians rarely set foot on stage in towns the size of Norfolk, they inspired the formation of numerous stock companies that made the circuit of local opera houses throughout the state. Not only did Clyde book these performances, but he sometimes joined the players. A caption from an old family scrapbook reads: "When Clyde played in 'Stock Co.' on stage, *East Lynn*, *Over the Hills Poor House*, *Count of Monte Cristo*, etc." Having grown a mustache for his role, perhaps that of the count himself, Clyde, with his dark features, high forehead, and Roman nose, reminds one of a young Errol Flynn. On December 29, 1888,

Clyde's twentieth birthday, Charles Eiseley presented his son with an inscribed one-volume edition of *The Complete Works of William Shakespeare*. Within six months, he had finished most of the tragedies, committing to memory long passages, which he would one day recite to entertain his son.[11]

Norfolk continued to attract new citizens of predominantly German descent. Among their numbers were Christian and Mary Catherine Enderly, parents of eleven children, who arrived with their family in 1889. A butcher by trade, Christian ran a meat market and established a vegetable farm on the six acres he purchased a mile and a half east of town. Among the Enderly children was a daughter named Anna Barbara, who was born on December 11, 1869. Although Anna could not be described as pretty, she possessed a number of admirable physical traits, including high cheekbones, a delicately formed mouth, and a radiant complexion.

When Clyde Eiseley first came courting is not known, but because he was the son of one of Norfolk's most respected citizens, his suit was strong. And, like Charles Eiseley, the Enderlys had immigrated from Germany in 1853. Clyde and Anna married on August 25, 1892, when she was twenty-two and he twenty-three. They spent their honeymoon at Omaha's fashionable Millard Hotel on Douglas Street, and then went on to Des Moines for a visit with Anna's older sister, Mary Catherine Handley. On returning to Norfolk, the couple moved into the house Clyde had purchased for his bride at 409 South Third Street. Anna settled cheerfully into her domestic duties and, like her mother-in-law, became active in the affairs of the Methodist Church located nearby on Fourth Street. She conceived the following year, giving birth, on September 30, 1893, to a nine-pound son named Leo.

On August 25, 1898, the sixth anniversary of her marriage to Clyde, Anna gave birth to the couple's second child, a daughter named Esther. Anna never fully recovered her strength after the birth. The following winter she contracted pneumonia; then consumption set in. In April 1899 a desperate Clyde, hoping that his wife might be saved by a change of climate, accepted a position in a hardware store in Gordon, in the western part of the state, but by this time Anna was too ill to go with him. No longer able to care for herself, let alone the baby, she was carried to her in-laws' home, where Josephine maintained a constant vigil. Anna, who was not yet thirty, died in the early morning hours of June 12. Her body was taken back to the home Clyde had purchased for her for last rites. A devastated Clyde buried his first and only love next to her mother in the Enderly family plot in Prospect Hill Cemetery.[12]

More grief was soon to follow. Esther, not yet ten months old, had been infected by the fatal tubercle bacillus her mother carried. The infant's tiny lungs were quickly overwhelmed, and she, too, died of consumption, six weeks after Anna.

Besides having to deal with his overwhelming personal grief, Clyde had the interests of six-year-old Leo to consider. He turned to Mary Catherine Handley, Anna's widowed sister, who, along with her two daughters, moved into Clyde's modest home. Finding Norfolk and its poignant associations more than he could endure, Clyde took a job as a hardware clerk for Holloway and Company in Fremont, some thirteen miles southeast of his old hometown of Hooper, and rented a room on West Sixth Street. He returned to see Leo at least once a month, and sometimes the boy was put on the train to visit his father. This arrangement continued for nearly three years, until Clyde became involved in his father's business interests once more. But by this time Charles Eiseley's fortunes had undergone a catastrophic reversal, the result of a deadly economic contagion best characterized as sugar beet fever.

During the 1880s and 1890s certain civic-spirited activists, who had not yet formed local chambers of commerce, as had their fellows back East, were known by the colloquial but apt name of "boomers." By 1888 Norfolk, Nebraska—the Queen City—had surpassed the 1,000 mark in population and was in the throes of a modernizing campaign that for a time made her the envy of the state. That year alone saw the opening of a mule-drawn street railway, a municipal waterworks, an electric generating station powering fourteen new streetlights, and the installation of the city's first sixteen telephones, one of which was in Charles Eiseley's hardware store. There were grandiose visions of a great metropolis on the Elkhorn, and the boomers were desperately seeking an investment opportunity to bring major industrial development to their community.

Following aborted attempts to secure a large packinghouse and a starch factory in 1889, the breakthrough came. "A GREAT VICTORY WON!" read the banner headline in a special industrial edition of the *Norfolk Daily News*, dated November 1, 1890. "Norfolk Secures the Second Sugar Beet Factory in Nebraska, to be Twenty-five Per Cent Better Than the One at Grand Island. THE LARGEST SUGAR FACTORY IN THE WORLD!" It had taken more than a year of public meetings and intensive fund-raising before the contracts could be signed with Henry T. Oxnard, the millionaire president and hard-bargaining owner of the factory in Grand Island. Twenty local businessmen, including Charles Eiseley, were required to sign a $400,000 bond to run for three years, guaranteeing that at least 2,500 acres of beets would be planted, harvested, and delivered to the proposed factory by the autumn of 1891. The first $100,000 immediately changed hands.[13]

The huge plant was constructed on fifty acres of land, also provided by the boomers, two miles outside the city limits. Operations began on October 15, 1891, and the following week proud Norfolk merchants began selling sugar processed in the plant. Labor was so scarce during the beet harvest that it was necessary to run three trains out of Omaha each day. The factory itself employed about 250 men and produced 1,320,000 pounds of beet sugar during the first year. The *Daily News* summed up the great venture in a single, boastful phrase: "Twas a famous victory!"[14]

A Pyrrhic victory as it turned out. In 1893 Norfolk was gripped by the financial panic that swept over most of the nation's cities and towns. Investment in new business came to a halt, while long-established enterprises failed by the thousands. Drought came to Nebraska in 1894 and again in 1895, causing a drastic shortage of beets, even as Congress debated elimination of the annual bonus awarded to beet producers. Though he managed to hang on longer than most, Charles, too, was forced into bankruptcy well before Norfolk's last beet was processed in 1903. Following a court-ordered auction of his property, which included the stately home on West Norfolk Avenue, Charles walked away with a few hundred dollars, some unsold merchandise from the store, and a Civil War pension of $22.50 a month. Having nowhere else to go, the Eiseleys moved into the house Clyde had purchased for Anna.[15]

Charles, though sixty-five years old, could not accept the fact that he had been beaten. His thoughts returned to the "miserable country" on the Nebraska–South Dakota border, which he had patrolled as a young horse soldier. The Northwestern Railroad had recently extended its tracks from Verdigre, Nebraska, to Bonesteel,

South Dakota. As a result, a new town site called Anoka had been platted in Nebraska's northern Boyd County, just below the South Dakota state line.

Anoka's main street, indeed its only street, was of dirt; its buildings were wooden. But what mattered most about it to Charles was the opportunity to win back a measure of his self-respect, and possibly some money as well. Leaving Josephine at home, he shipped his leftover hardware to Anoka, where he saw it placed on rough-hewn shelves in a small frame building next to the post office. Satisfied that he had done everything he could, Charles returned to Norfolk to assume the modestly paid but respectable position of municipal court judge, leaving Clyde, who had come north from Fremont, to manage the store.

The widower had been in Anoka only a short time before he met thirty-one-year-old Effie "Eva" Cearns, a singularly unattractive woman who came from the nearby village of Butte. Little of her background is known, except that she is reported to have been a divorcée. Clyde and Eva took out a marriage license on May 4, 1903, and were wed that evening. The couple set up housekeeping in the so-called Toler Building and were given a warm welcome by the newly established *Anoka Herald*: "Mr. Eiseley is well known in this community as the Anoka hardware man, and the lady of his choice has recently located here and comes as a stranger amongst us. We wish them many happy days in the village of Anoka."[16]

The marriage lasted little more than two years, ending abruptly amid a swirl of gossip and public humiliation. Clyde filed for divorce on July 22, 1905. According to his petition, Eva "regardless of her marital duties and obligations, on the 25th day of January, 1905, in the city of O'Neill . . . Nebraska committed adultery with one Frank T. Welton, without the consent or connivance of the plaintiff, and the plaintiff has not cohabited with the defendant since the discovery of such offense."[17] Eva neither answered the petition nor entered a plea before the court, and the cuckolded Clyde received his divorce on January 8, 1906.

Soon another woman took Eva's place. During the summer of 1906, Daisy Corey, who lived with her mother in Lincoln, visited Anoka for a week, lodging at the local hotel. She came at the invitation of Clyde Eiseley. They had most likely become acquainted during one of his occasional business trips to the state capital. Daisy met Leo, visited the family hardware store on Main Street, and earned the good graces of the townspeople. In September Clyde left Anoka to attend the state fair at Lincoln. He also took this opportunity to propose to the thirty-one-year-old Daisy, and she promptly accepted. In early November the couple boarded a train for Sioux City, Iowa, where they exchanged vows before a justice of the peace.[18]

V

Clyde's new wife had grown up in the small Mississippi Valley town of Dyersville, Iowa. On her mother's side Daisy descended from one Robert McKee, whose six days of service as a minuteman during the Lexington alarm entitled her to membership in the Daughters of the American Revolution, a privilege she chose not to exercise. By the time the wagons bearing the mostly German immigrant founders of Dyersville arrived in Dubuque County in 1846, Appleton Hollister McKee, Daisy's grandfather, was well settled on a claim he had staked by Hewett's Creek, five miles northeast of the future town site.[19] He married twice and fathered at least one son before taking his third wife in June 1839, twenty-four-year-old Permila (or Permilia) Shepard, daughter of Sarah and Levi Shepard from New York. Almost thirty years her husband's junior, Permila gave birth to at least five children, including a daughter, Malvina, who arrived on the auspicious day of July 4, 1850.

After leading an apparently normal existence, Permila went quite mad, displaying what were described in the family as "homicidal tendencies."[20] One sees hints of this disturbance in the photograph of the granitelike countenance that stares back, unflinchingly, from the Eiseley family Bible. The fixed eyes, the most dominant feature, are too large to be contained by the wire-rimmed spectacles perched on the bridge of Permila's broad, masculine nose; the wide, downturned mouth, which crowns a resolute lantern jaw, seems never to have smiled, let alone laughed. Never institutionalized, Daisy's grandmother lived out her days under the watchful eyes of nervous family members.

Malvina wed in December 1866, at the early age of sixteen. The groom, Milo Franklin Corey, was a master carpenter almost ten years her senior. Like Malvina's father, Milo had already been married twice, although nothing is known of his past or his family roots beyond the fact that he came from New York. The couple established their home in Dyersville, which boasted a population of over eight hundred. Malvina gave birth to her first child, a daughter named Grace, on October 6, 1870. Another daughter, Bertha, was born in March 1874, but she died a year and a half later. The Coreys' third and last child, Daisy, arrived on August 26, 1875. A lifelong Methodist, Malvina saw to it that the infants were baptized in the new brick church on South Fourth Street.[21]

Daisy was a pretty child, with long, dark hair and the penetrating eyes of the McKees, but an attack of some unknown malady had left her with degenerative hearing loss. When she spoke it was in a high-pitched monotone accompanied by exaggerated gesturing of the hands and head as a way of emphasizing her point. Still, Daisy possessed the eye and the hand of an artist. Her father, hoping to nurture this gift, fashioned a box for the pigments and brushes purchased during occasional visits to nearby Dubuque, on the Mississippi. If there were to be no man in Daisy's life, if she could not teach school or work behind the counter of a dry goods store, maybe she could sustain herself by decorating plates in the Victorian manner and turning out modest canvases at modest prices for the art-starved citizens of the prairie.

Daisy was fifteen when the Coreys moved to Lincoln, Nebraska, in 1890. Milo pursued his trade as a carpenter, and little else is known of the family during this period except that Grace, who had inherited her grandmother Permila's lovely singing voice, quickly won the heart of a young attorney, William Buchanan "Buck" Price, a newly minted member of the Nebraska bar. The son of a prominent Lynchburg, Virginia, physician named Abner Clopton Price, Buck was almost literally born in the ashes of the Confederacy, three months after the end of the Civil War, in which his father had served as an officer. Rich in heritage but financially strapped, the Prices eventually moved west. Possessed of Old World charm and manners to match, an agreeable disposition, and an irrepressible sense of humor, Buck wed Grace in her parents' home on June 23, 1891.[22]

Among the few surviving objects Daisy painted after her arrival in Lincoln is a china plate bearing the rather whimsical portrait of a young girl seated at the dinner table. She has been distracted momentarily by something unseen in the room, and a large dog at her side is taking advantage of the situation by licking her platter clean. On the opposite side, the artist painted her name, then later attempted to conceal the last part of it with a second application of paint. When the translucent china is held up to bright light, the surname *Myers* becomes fairly visible—Daisy Corey Myers.[23]

According to the Lancaster County Court records at Lincoln, the marriage license was issued on October 14, 1895, and the wedding took place later that day, before John Doane, pastor of Plymouth Church. The bride was twenty-one, the groom, Frank E. Myers, two years her senior. Neither of the local papers carried an account of the service, although the *Lincoln Evening Journal* did publish the routine notice that a license had been issued.[24]

All that can be said of Frank Myers is that he was a jack-of-all-trades, and a less than prosperous one. At the time of his marriage to Daisy he was listed by the *Lincoln City Directory* as a driver for one R. B. Suter. The following year he entered the horseshoeing business with T. W. Rolofson; the year after that saw Frank in business with his equally peripatetic brother James, after which he disappears from the local scene altogether. Daisy, in the meantime, turned to dressmaking, unable to earn enough as an artist to compensate for her husband's meager pay. Frank was last heard of in 1900 in Humphrey in Platte County, where he had taken up barbering. When Daisy finally sued for divorce in September 1902, he made no attempt to answer her petition, which alleged him to be "a healthy, robust, able-bodied" man who has "wantonly and grossly neglected to provide a home and suitable maintenance for the said plaintiff," compelling "her to rely upon the charity of her friends and relatives for the necessaries of life." The judge had no choice but to rule in favor of the petitioner, granting the requested divorce and restoring her maiden name of Corey a month after the case was filed.[25]

By the time Daisy met Clyde Eiseley and consented to become his wife, both desperately yearned for lasting companionship, and each bore individual wounds. Daisy had had to face the terrifying realization that she was becoming deaf. More than anything, she may have been drawn to Clyde by the reassuring timbre of his rich baritone voice, still audible when he placed his lips next to her cocked and eager ear. For his part, Clyde had been marked forever by the death of the one he loved most: Daisy's face reflected the lost Anna—high cheekbones and forehead, gently arched brows, sculptured chin, and dark, expressive eyes.

Daisy became pregnant with her first and only child about a month after the wedding. Shortly thereafter the railroad, Anoka's lifeblood, became the town's mortal enemy when it was extended into northwestern South Dakota. The wagon traders and settlers, who had regularly stocked up on goods at the hardware store, literally disappeared overnight, marking the end of an era whose dawning Charles Eiseley had helped bring about. Other merchants soon began to close up their shops and move on. Clyde, who held the unenviable position of chairman of the village board—the equivalent of mayor—was faced with the same decision, which took on an added urgency because the dying town was without a doctor to deliver his child. It was decided that Daisy should return to her mother and sister in Lincoln, where proper medical care could be had. Meanwhile, Clyde contacted his old employer, now Holloway and Fowler, in Fremont, requesting that he be rehired as a clerk. The company agreed, telling him to report for work as soon as his affairs were in order. Clyde and Leo left Anoka for the last time in 1907. They arrived in Fremont, where Clyde rented a house at 716 Military Avenue. With Daisy's time of delivery almost at hand, Clyde received permission to take a brief leave of absence and with his son boarded the train for Lincoln, where, in Leo's words, they waited "until it was all over."[26]

2

"A HOUSE OF GESTURE"

I

Loren Corey Eiseley was born on September 3, 1907, after a long and apparently difficult labor. The hour of his arrival was not recorded on the birth certificate. We know only that he was named for a distant cousin, Loren V. McKee, a Methodist minister.[1] He would one day write of his own nativity in the haunting and melancholy style for which he is especially remembered: "I was born in the first decade of this century, conceived in, and part of the rolling yellow cloud that occasionally raises up a rainy silver eye to look upon itself before subsiding into dust again. That cloud has been blowing in my part of the Middle West since the Ice Age."[2] So traumatic was the ordeal for Daisy, who had celebrated her thirty-second birthday twelve days earlier, that her physician kept the mother and child in the hospital for two weeks. After their release, Daisy and Loren were taken to her sister Grace's home. Not until November did Daisy, accompanied by Grandmother Corey, arrive in Fremont with her two-month-old son, whose most robust cries barely penetrated the expanding wall of silence enveloping his mother's world.[3]

As before, Clyde remained with Holloway and Fowler for about three years. Leo, who was fourteen years older than his infant half brother, graduated from the eighth grade and entered high school in January 1909. The following September an epidemic of spinal meningitis forced the Fremont Board of Education to close the schools for several weeks, and the youth, who was interested in all things electrical, got a job in an appliance shop. Thoughtful yet happy-go-lucky, Leo was occasionally a source of consternation to his mild-mannered father. The boy had a penchant for practical jokes, especially those that allowed him to display his skills as a novice electrician. His favorite prank consisted of wiring the family chairs when company was expected, then waiting for the propitious moment to turn on the current.[4]

The meningitis epidemic ran its course and the schools were reopened, but Leo did not return to the classroom. He had celebrated his sixteenth birthday on September 30, 1909, reaching the lawful age for quitting school. Shortly thereafter he was offered the position of messenger boy with the Western Union Telegraph Company and promised that he could practice telegraphy and study advanced communications in his spare time. Clyde opposed Leo's plan, citing the usual parental arguments about the importance of education. It was Leo who prevailed, however, arguing that the family needed the extra income and that he would be joining an excellent firm. Having finally given his consent, Clyde accompanied Leo to the Western Union office, where he saw to it that his son "got the best they had to offer." Leo continued to live in his parents' home for the time being, and, true to his word, contributed to the family finances by paying room and board.[5]

In 1910 Clyde moved his family to Lincoln, leaving his younger son with but a single memory of the Fremont years—that of the cold, star-filled night when his father had held him aloft, the better to see the flaring Halley's comet. They made their home at 1318 C Street, and Clyde began clerking downtown for Frank E. Lahr, one of Lincoln's pioneer hardware merchants, who specialized in stoves and furnaces. Leo, who would soon strike out on his own, went to work as a messenger for the Postal Telegraph Company. He passed the evenings practicing Morse code until the dots and dashes flowed from the round black key at his fingertips.

A year later, after Leo had received his first position as telegraph operator in Sioux Falls, South Dakota, Clyde, Daisy, and four-year-old Loren moved into a bungalow at 1811 South Street. It would remain their home for the next six years. The small frame house had an earthen cellar, which occasionally filled with water after a hard rain; the parlor was kept perpetually shuttered against the stinging Nebraska sun. Electrical service was not yet available to the scattered residents of Lincoln's far south side, so evenings were spent in the dim glow of kerosene lamps.

Loren's possessions were few. His favorite, a tawny stuffed lion with shoe-button eyes, accompanied him to bed each night. There was also a teddy bear and toy soldiers cast from lead, glass marbles that he kept in an old candy tin, a tiny U.S. flag of the kind given out at Fourth of July parades, and a toy hammer with a spent cartridge attached to the end of its handle—a reminder that his father had once stood at faro tables where professional gamblers still played with derringers concealed beneath their sleeves. Clyde told his son he had given up carrying a gun only after accidentally shooting himself in the leg. "You can't depend on the things," he lamented. "Familiarity breeds contempt."[6]

Loren sensed that something was seriously wrong shortly after the family moved to Lincoln. It was a time of hushed and troubled voices: "The whispering, always the whispering of Grace, grandmother and the rest. [Ours] was a house of whispers."[7] It was also a house unto itself. Visitors rarely came, and those few who crossed the threshold were not encouraged to remain long. The shuttered and curtained windows not only kept the sun at bay but discouraged curious neighbors from establishing contact with those who dwelled within. The Eiseleys were dismissed as peculiar, though harmless and unimportant, social outcasts of their own making.

Daisy's deafness would have been a barrier to social contact in the best of circumstances. Clyde, who worked six days a week, rarely returned home before dusk. But the source of the problem went beyond these matters. Whether because of her hearing loss or because of a combination of more complex psychological factors, Daisy had moved dangerously close to the precipice of mental breakdown, provoking Aunt Grace and Grandmother Malvina to speak in whispers of the mad Shepards. Loren searched the pictures in the family Bible in an attempt to understand, but all he saw were the stern visages of bewhiskered patriarchs and their equally dour wives. He realized after a time that he was being watched carefully for the slightest sign that something might be amiss, that he too might embody the dread legacy.

In contrast to the actions of Great-grandmother Permila, the wounds inflicted by the paranoid and neurotic Daisy were of the spirit. From the time he was four years old, Loren recalled his parents' endless pacing after midnight, the quarrels Daisy initiated over matters both important and trivial. The child especially dreaded Saturday evenings, when Clyde brought home his weekly pay envelope only to have its slender contents ridiculed by a scornful wife. Once, after being awakened by their shouting, Loren climbed from his bed and took both parents by the hand, pleading wordlessly for quiet. Touched by her son's eloquent gesture, Daisy relented. Yet only rarely was she so tractable. Many was the night Loren's beloved stuffed lion soaked up the tears of its young master as he cried himself to sleep.[8]

Loren grew to loathe his mother's increasingly alien tongue. He remembered her discordant jangling, which was frequently unintelligible, her daylong facial contortions accompanied by erratic waving of her arms and hands; the stamping of her feet to create vibrations on the floor; and a score of other exotic signals that the family alone could understand. Years later, after becoming an anthropologist, he likened the experience to the first attempt of the australopithecines to establish a primitive language. In another instance, he was reminded of a "household of the stone age, a house of gesture."[9]

The hearing child of a deaf parent is often forced to accept greater than normal responsibility at an early age, a requirement that, in turn, stimulates precocity.[10] Acting as interpreter and go-between when no other family member was around could have reinforced Loren's consciousness of language. But it was Clyde's sonorous voice and rich vocabulary that left the deepest impression on the boy. He shivered when his father recited passages from Shakespeare:

> *Put on my robes, give me my crown, I have*
> *immortal longings in me.*

As were other children his age, Loren was introduced to literature in the form of fairy tales and nursery rhymes. One incident in particular, recounted many times in his later writings and correspondence, he believed to have been a turning point of his childhood. Leo had come home for a visit when Loren was five years old, bringing a copy of *Robinson Crusoe*. He began reading the book to Loren, who was entranced by the story of the marooned Englishman, as any boy might be. They had just reached the point where the astonished hero discovers unfamiliar footprints on the beach when Leo had to leave. Loren had already learned the alphabet and was reading from little primers, containing mostly single-syllable words. But the book Leo left behind was the adult version of the Defoe novel. Loren sat down alone with a dictionary and, as he observed many years later, "proceeded to worry and chew my way like a puppy through the remaining pages." He remembered reading insatiably after this experience, losing the little that remained of his fear of adult books.[11]

II

Robinson Crusoe was an accidental castaway, an unwitting victim of chance and circumstance. But Loren soon learned that there were other kinds of castaways—real men with whom he would identify for the rest of his life. Whereas Crusoe's saga unfolded on an uncharted tropical island in the limitless South Seas, these men's life-and-death drama played itself out in his own state amid a raging blizzard, ending just days after it began.

On Thursday, March 14, 1912, three convicts, armed with smuggled pistols and a quantity of nitroglycerin, left their work stations at the Nebraska State Penitentiary, some two miles south of Lincoln. They broke into the office of Deputy Warden Charles Wagner, killing him before he could rise from his desk. After wounding the cell-house keeper, the trio blew the lock off the barred steel door leading to the main corridor, where they were met by Warden James Delahunty. During the resulting exchange, the warden was hit twice and left on the hallway floor, mortally wounded on this his fifty-fifth birthday. Delahunty's clerk, who rushed out of his office to assist his fallen superior, also paid with his life. Less than a minute later, the three prisoners, all clad in gray convicts' garb, ran out of the prison's main entrance and disappeared into a violent snowstorm, which had reduced visibility to little more than arm's length.[12]

The lead conspirator was Convict Number 5672, a gaunt, dusky-complexioned expert in the use of firearms and explosives named Charles Taylor, alias Shorty Gray, Tom Murray, Harry Forbes, Dublin Shorty, James Rogers et al. Taylor, a forty-four-year-old Irishman by birth, had served previous terms in the Nebraska, Iowa, and Minnesota state penitentiaries. He had been in

Lincoln since August 22, 1911, sentenced to twenty-eight years for blowing up the safe of the Citizens Bank in Giltner and making off with $1,400 in cash. John Dowd, Taylor's cell mate and coconspirator, was twenty-five years of age and a fireman by trade. Dowd had been arrested in Omaha and sentenced in Plattsmouth, where he was convicted of blowing the safe of a jewelry store in Louisville, Nebraska. The third member of the trio, a thirty-eight-year-old barber named Charles Morley, was serving a fifteen-year sentence for what the newspapers described as "highway robbery."[13]

That night, after struggling home from work through blowing and drifting snow, Clyde read the account of the shootings to Loren from the evening edition of the *Lincoln Daily Star*. When he had finished, he tossed the paper on the table with a sigh and remarked, "They won't make it."

Why did it matter, his son wanted to know. "The papers say they are bad men. They killed the warden."[14]

True enough, but Clyde tried to explain that the papers cannot always be counted on to report everything. What Clyde had in mind was something else he had read in the papers during the weeks before the violent escape. Part of it involved a convict named Albert Prince, a Negro, who, on the morning of February 11, had calmly walked up to Deputy Warden Edward Davis during Sunday chapel and stabbed him through the heart. Prince, already convicted of one murder, eventually hung for this deed, but not before his enterprising attorney trotted out a host of witnesses, most of whom were convicts like his client, who testified that they had been systematically beaten, hosed, and otherwise abused by the penitentiary staff.[15]

If the testimony of convicts was not to be believed, there was other evidence of official misconduct that the public found less easy to dismiss. Five days before Warden Delahunty was cut down by Taylor, Dowd, and Morley, six men from Lincoln, all members of the Prison Reform Association, had demanded that Governor Chester H. Aldrich fire the prison head. Only an hour before receiving this party, Aldrich had held a brief but highly animated session with the young penitentiary chaplain, P. C. Johnson, who complained bitterly about the manner in which the facility was being run.[16]

While Clyde's reservations were understandable in the circumstances, there was not the slightest evidence to suggest that any member of the fugitive trio had been subjected to physical abuse of the type that Albert Prince and others claimed to have endured. Theirs were simply the vicious acts of desperate men.

After arming themselves with Winchester rifles and revolvers, the members of a posse set out in sleighs and on horseback to scour the countryside south and east of Lincoln. They found footprints leading from the prison toward the Burlington Railroad's Kansas City line, but these soon vanished beneath the swirling snow.

Everyone feared that the convicts would want to hole up until the weather improved. Rudolph Umland, a farm boy Loren's age and a future friend, remembered how his older brothers got their shotgun and rifle ready and took the almost unheard-of precaution of locking up the house before the family went to bed.[17] Rumors flew like the very snowflakes, the worst proclaiming that thirteen men had been killed at the penitentiary while two hundred others had joined in the escape.

By Friday morning the state had posted rewards totaling $2,100, the maximum allowed by statute. At least six posses were in the field, examining every vacant house and barn, peering into culverts, beneath bridges, under woodpiles, combing clumps of brush and leafless woods. Most of the country roads remained blocked by six-foot snowdrifts, a circumstance which supported the theory that the three were still in the vicinity. The tempers of officials and citizens alike grew shorter, creating a panic that resulted in a number of ill-considered incidents. A tramp, who bolted in fear from beneath a railroad viaduct, was fired at and nearly killed. Mistaken for Morley, he was dragged to the sheriff's office, where his pockets were emptied. All they contained were two clean handkerchiefs and a prayer book. During the afternoon a posse searched a house that had been "marked by peculiar behavior." Nothing was found but two men, a boy, and a pair of talking parrots.[18]

The breakthrough the authorities had been hoping for finally came on March 17. Flushed from their hiding place in a farmhouse within two miles of Lincoln, Taylor and his friends had been spotted making their way northward on foot along the Burlington tracks. They got as far as bordering Sarpy County before combined posses from Lincoln, Springfield, Louisville, Gretna, and Papillion cut them off. After burglarizing a Gretna hardware store for guns, ammunition, and knives, the three had commandeered a horse-drawn wagon and forced its owner, a young farmer named Roy Blunt, to drive them northward at a gallop. The posse soon picked up their trail, and a running gunfight erupted. Blunt's team was visibly tiring, and his relatives, who had joined in the chase, begged the officers not to shoot for fear the innocent victim would be hit. "To hell with Blunt" was the alleged reply. Moments later the farmer was shot in the back and died instantly. Some thought the bullet had been fired by one of the pursuers, but it was later determined that Blunt was probably shot by Taylor as the hostage attempted to jump from the careening wagon. When the posse was within seventy-five yards and closing in from three sides, Sheriff Gus Hyers of Lincoln, who had been leading the search and pursuit ever since the prison break, reined in his horse and rested his Winchester against a telephone pole, taking aim. He struck Taylor with a single shot close to the heart, and the ringleader keeled over, dead. Dowd then put his own pistol to his temple and pulled the trigger. Only a whimpering Morley survived.

The bodies were carried to Gretna, where a loose-tongued Sheriff Hyers sickened most of the crowd that had gathered to witness his bizarre conduct. A special train arrived from Lincoln, and, as the corpses were being loaded aboard, Hyers held them up in turn so that everyone could see. "This is Gray [Taylor], the man I killed. How do you like him?" Then Dowd was hauled up "like a dead dog," blood still flowing freely from the gaping wound in his head and forming clots on what remained visible of his ashen face. "This is Dowd. How do you like him?"[19]

Clyde had kept his son abreast of this tragic adventure by reading him the lengthy newspaper accounts, remarking that "Someday when you are grown up you may remember this."[20] Loren took his father's words to heart, vowing never to forget what had happened to the convicts in 1912. He would one day reenter that year of snow and arctic wind to join Charles Taylor, taking the place of Morley and Dowd. Together they would flee in his imagination and dreams through the howling blizzard, their ammunition running desperately low, Death's posse closing fast.

III

Loren became eligible to begin kindergarten in the autumn of 1912. He remembered an unusually tempered conversation between Daisy and Clyde during which they decided to wait another year before sending their son off to school. "Let him be free to play just one more time," one of them had said. "There'll be all his life to learn about the rest."[21]

By the time Loren entered school the following year, he had long been master of the alphabet and was reading as much as he could on his own. He read through his primer the first day of class despite warnings from his teacher that the book was supposed to last the entire year. And although he succeeded in masking his ability for a time, he grew increasingly restless as his classmates moved along at what seemed to him an agonizingly slow pace. Other aspects of his education, however, did not come so easily. The children played store once a week, an exercise designed to teach them to count and make change. Loren always had difficulty working the simplest math problems in his head, and even when they were allowed to use paper and pencil he made mistakes of the most elementary kind. He was also teased for his innocent use of grandiloquent words, which he committed to memory from Clyde's recitations. What he remembered most about this first year of school were the nodding yellow buttercups of the only picnic he was ever taken on as a boy.[22]

Dark eyed, broad shouldered, and unusually tall for his age, Loren did everything except write with his left hand. As was common at the time, his teachers forced him to change to his right hand, an adjustment he apparently took in stride. One of his earliest compositions is a small "book," probably written in 1913, when the author was six. He printed the misspelled title—ANIMAL AVENTURES—in bold letters and pasted on the cover an idealized magazine photograph of a small girl with blond tresses standing beside a seated collie who gazes lovingly into her eyes, a scene reminiscent of the one Daisy had painted on the plate during her previous marriage. The third and fourth chapters of the book are the most revealing. "Animal Kindness" relates the story of a large dog that had once lived next door to the Eiseleys. The animal barks at the boy each time he passes by on his way to school. "But instead of hurting him I petted him and he did not bark anymore." Already the empathy for animals that became an integral element of Loren's later poetry and prose was present. In "The Cunning Fox" a man watching wild ducks on a pond notices that when a seemingly harmless branch floats in among the fowl they all take flight. But the ducks soon return, and the pattern is repeated many times until they are no longer frightened. Looking up to the far end of the pond, the man observes that a fox is responsible for sending down the branches. When the clever beast sees that the ducks are no longer wary, he jumps on an even larger branch and silently floats down among them. "Then he seized one and . . . guided the branch to shore where he ate the duck."[23] No other animal fascinated Loren to the degree that the fox did. He admired its talent for watching silently from the underbrush, allowing others no more than a fleeting glimpse of its protective coloration.

Except for the make-believe fox, whose real-life counterpart Loren had not yet seen in the wild, the animals he wrote about were all of the domestic variety—and for good reason. Daisy's deafness caused her to look upon the world as if it were a conspiracy directed against herself and her son. She rarely let Loren venture out on his own, and when he did, he was not allowed to wander more than a block or two in any direction.

Most of his days were passed in solitude, a book in his lap for company. Loren read about insects and turned over the bricks of the front sidewalk to see if the ants and crickets beneath would react to the light as they were supposed to. He started collections of grasshoppers, beetles, and butterflies, then abandoned them, only to begin anew. The boy cast a longing eye at the natural ponds in the distance, where dragonflies, spotted frogs, minnows, and crayfish abounded. He dreamed of building and stocking his own aquarium, but for the time being these tantalizing reaches were strictly off limits, for he had not been taught to swim.

Occasionally nature came to his very doorstep. He awoke one morning to find the seemingly lifeless form of a woodpecker next to the front porch. He laid it out on the railing and was startled when it began to quiver. Soon, the bird was not only back on its feet but hammering away on a wooden post as if nothing had happened. Loren finally realized that the woodpecker had been plucking insects off a utility line when its long tongue had chanced to touch the wire. The bird had been knocked senseless by the current, and Loren had arrived on the scene just in time to see it revive. How curious, he thought, that a creature could come so close to dying yet harbor no memory of the event.

Loren's first knowledge of what it means to die came late one summer afternoon at a place known locally as Green Gulch. Despite Daisy's admonitions, Loren had wandered away from home and begun following a group of older boys until they came to a large sandstone basin of dark water surrounded by green ferns and tall trees. The boys started to play, and one of them discovered a huge old turtle, asleep in the ferns. Suddenly the youths were swept by a nightmarish frenzy. First one, then another, then all except Loren picked up stones, with which they pounded the trapped reptile to death. Angered by Loren's refusal to join in their primitive rite, the other boys roughed him up and sent him running home crying. Only much later was he able to articulate his feelings about the event: "I had discovered evil."[24]

His was not a moral judgment based on any type of formal religious training. He claimed to have attended church only once during his childhood, although it was an experience he never forgot. Malvina Corey took her grandson to an evangelical tent service during which he remembered being stuck with a pin wielded by a restless youth in the row behind him.[25]

Loren attributed his absence of religious training to the fact that the family was not agreed upon any mode of worship: "I merely wondered as I grew older how it was that things came to be."[26] This explanation, though, is not easily reconciled with what we know of the Eiseley and Corey family histories. Different in many ways, the families, particularly the women, shared an almost identical religious heritage. Clyde's mother remained a dedicated Methodist all her life, and Clyde himself had been very active in church affairs as a young man living in Norfolk. The roots of Methodism were equally deep on Daisy's side. Malvina had raised her two daughters in the faith back in Iowa. In October 1891, within a year of moving to Lincoln, all three had had their letters of membership transferred to Trinity Methodist Church. They were still enrolled in the same adult Sunday school class three years later.[27] Unfortunately, the church membership records for 1900–1914 are lost and with them the possibility of determining whether Loren was baptized or whether the family attended services after returning to Lincoln from Fremont. Only Malvina appears on the membership rolls after 1914. If Loren did not enter a house of worship as a child, his absence probably had more to do with personal suffering than with any disagreement over creed. Clyde was permanently wounded by the death of Anna, and this grief may have resulted in a loss of faith. Daisy could not have distinguished a single word uttered from the pulpit or sung by the volunteer choir.

IV

Clyde's fortunes took a further turn in 1917, when his employer, Frank E. Lahr, became terminally ill. He secured yet another position as a hardware salesman in Aurora, Nebraska, some eighty miles directly west of Lincoln, and moved his family into a white frame house at 915 Q Street in time for Loren, who was now ten, to enter the fifth-grade class of Alma Grosshaus in September. For the most part, he was an excellent student. His marks in reading, spelling, history, and writing averaged in the nineties, while those in geography, language, and physiology were almost as high. Arithmetic, however, was still proving difficult for him: he received a 72 the first semester but improved sufficiently to end the year with an overall mark of 79 in the subject. Music, which never interested Loren, almost proved a disaster: after receiving a 45 in the subject the first semester, he achieved a passing grade of 73 by the end of the year. Loren earned high marks in deportment, and his attendance record was good, except for the month of November, when he was present only thirteen days because of illness. This period took on a special significance for him, for during this time he saw his father weep: "I was young and very ill; I looked up in astonishment as a tear splashed on my hand."[28] Loren soon recovered and completed the fifth grade, the only year of his elementary schooling for which records are available, with a creditable average of 86.5.[29]

It was in Aurora that Loren developed one of his few childhood friendships, with a youth known only as the Rat: "He was deceptively slight of build, with the terrible intensity of a coiled spring. His face, even, had the quivering eagerness of some small, quick animal." The Rat was the undisputed leader of a little gang whose initiation rite consisted of uttering a series of swearwords, which Loren, anxious to gain acceptance, dutifully repeated, though he had never heard most of them before and had no idea what they meant. But there was more. "You gotta go down under the ground. You ain't afraid of the dark are ya?"[30]

The Rat's domain was a thirty-six-inch storm sewer, which still runs under Aurora's railroad tracks between Fourteenth and Sixteenth streets. The youths secretly scrounged candles, smuggled food into the abyss, and ambushed members of rival gangs who encroached on their territory. Like cavemen they scratched signs and crude pictures on the water-stained walls of their narrow sanctuary, always using pointed stones rather than metal because, as the Rat observed, "Cavemen didn't have no chisels."

Although the boys were always clever enough to scan the western horizon before venturing underground, once beneath the city streets they had no way of protecting themselves against a sudden shift in the weather, a frequent occurrence on the windswept plains. One cloudless summer morning after eating breakfast, Loren met the Rat, and together they worked their way deep into a side tunnel partially filled with sand. Suddenly the Rat, who was leading the way, stopped dead. From a distance came the faint sound of dripping water. The dripping soon gave way to a pouring noise, muffled yet unmistakable. Loren panicked and was about to cry when the Rat took control. Moving as quickly as their cramped surroundings would allow, they retraced their path on hands and knees, searching for a larger pipe. The water was moving with them now, soaking and fouling their clothes as it began to rise. By the time the two reached the main chamber, where it was possible to walk, their hands and knees were scratched and bloody, their pants legs shredded by the rough surfaces of the brick and tile. They staggered toward a faint halo of light in the distance. When they finally emerged through the manhole cover, the boys were blinded by sunlight on a street so hot it nearly burned their palms. Incredulous, they looked down the road and noticed that a city employee had opened a fire hydrant for routine flushing. A stern voice spoke to them from behind, and a startled Loren turned to face his father, whose rare fury could hardly be suppressed. The boy was marched firmly away to the razor strap and the narrow confines of home.[31]

It was not long, however, before Loren rejoined the Rat's little gang. They now contented themselves with digging caves in the bank of a creek and exploring the surrounding countryside. Yet the greater Loren's yearning for independence, the more fanatical his mother's desire to control her son's every movement. Daisy exercised arbitrary judgment, driving certain boys away merely because they seemed too large while encouraging Loren to associate with smaller youngsters, no matter how scheming or uncouth. She often pursued her son and his friends through the streets and into the farmland, shouting at Loren in her eerie voice and embarrassing him in front of his playmates.

It was on one such occasion that the normally obedient youth took a stand. Daisy followed Loren and his friends to a pasture on the edge of town and ordered him to come home at once. He glanced in humiliation at the other boys, who were waiting to see what he would do. Loren thought of his father's words: "Your mother is not responsible, son. Do not cross her." He had promised to obey, but this time he turned and ran, his gleeful companions close on his heels. From over his shoulder he caught glimpses of Daisy in futile pursuit; suddenly the image came together—the shrill wailing, the tortured gestures, the disheveled dress and windblown hair—witch, he thought, my mother is a witch!

Walking home alone in the twilight, the ten-year-old fugitive felt bitterly ashamed of himself. He had broken a promise to his father, and a woman who loved him just as deeply had suffered additional anguish for which he was in some part responsible. And what would the already suspicious neighbors think when the story of his disobedience got around, as it surely would? Still, Loren would never again look on Daisy in quite the same light. The horrific image he formed of her that wild summer day was too powerful to dissolve.[32]

Though they had abandoned the sewers at the insistence of their parents, Loren and the Rat laid plans for one last subterranean venture. It was occasioned by Loren's discovery of an ancient drain that was not a part of the system they had previously explored. The tunnel was brick and large enough to permit the boys to stand upright. Thick moss circled the weed-covered entrance, giving it the aspect of a green door; the air flowing out of the large opening was cool and tantalizing. The boys had gone almost one hundred yards when they picked up the vibrations of cascading water. Loren suggested that they come back later with the rest of the gang, but the Rat demurred: "We'll keep it for our own." Promising each other that they would soon return to complete their mission, they retraced their steps and took care to cover the entrance with brush. But it was not to be. The Rat became ill a few weeks later and died of some childhood disease, leaving Loren alone as before. One day he returned to the green door, but the magic had vanished along with his clever friend.

Chance was to play yet another part in Loren's childhood. On a solitary ramble after school he followed a road he had not taken before to an abandoned farmhouse whose windows were smashed and whose fallen plaster lay thick on the sagging floors. Old school papers were scattered about, and he picked one up out of curiosity.

What he saw made the hair on the back of his neck stand on end, for the name Eiseley was written on it. He picked up another, and it too bore his surname, written in a child's hand not unlike his own. The date was from the last decade of the nineteenth century.

Besides the papers all that remained in the room was a pair of dice. Loren began casting the ivory cubes, making up his own rules as he played against himself. How long he played he could not remember, but all at once he became aware of the gathering darkness and the chill wind blowing through the empty window casings. Seized by panic he fled, abandoning the papers but clutching the dice, one of which still lay in a drawer of his desk almost sixty years later.[33]

V

The Eiseleys spent a little less than a year in Aurora before moving back to Lincoln in the summer of 1918. Clyde had secured a position as a traveling salesman for the Chicago-based firm of Hibbard, Spencer and Bartlett, covering the territory west of the capital. From a purely geographic perspective, Aurora appears to have been a better location for him than Lincoln, but that advantage was outweighed by the fact that he did not wish to leave his wife and son alone for extended periods of time. The family purchased a four-room bungalow at 2116 South Twenty-second Street, only two blocks from Daisy's sister, Grace. Loren's tiny bedroom was just a few steps away from that shared by his parents, close enough for him to hear every insulting remark and acrimonious exchange. The child believed that he was the only reason Clyde did not leave Daisy. "He stayed for me. He stayed when his own closest relatives urged him to depart."[34]

In 1918 Clyde became a victim of the great influenza epidemic, which claimed more than 20 million lives worldwide. He returned home ill one afternoon and went directly to bed, lying for days without medical attention, his eyes roving the ceiling and oak woodwork as he waited to see which way the dice would fall. It did not seem to Loren that his father really cared very much whether he lived or died.[35] Clyde recovered, but the few pictures taken of him at this time are those of a besieged and haggard soul. He had come a long way from the days when "Clyde Eiseley," as the *Norfolk Daily News* had reported, "made a still hunt for the clerkship and captured it." Balding and shrunken, he now represented the antithesis of the American dream, a second-generation son who failed to rise above the foothold left him by his self-made father.

Although Loren was an isolated child of the middle border, he was not unaware of the cataclysmic forces that were grinding a generation of young men into dust on the far-off battlefields of Europe. He remembered it as the time of the gold crosses. Loren discovered a bottle of gilt Daisy used on picture frames, and it gave him an idea: he would honor the fallen by creating a mock cemetery. After whittling several small markers out of wood, he gilded their surfaces and set them up in a vacant lot beyond the Eiseley backyard. Most of them stood over newspaper clippings of war heroes, which Loren placed in little boxes before covering them with earth. One day he returned to discover that the gold crosses had been carried away by the man who mowed the lot with a scythe. The boy wept bitterly but could not bring himself to tell anyone of his sense of loss.[36]

One of the few places Loren could go without his mother's protest was the home of his aunt and uncle, on South Twenty-third Street. Buck Price always had a dog to play with and an interesting story to tell his adoring nephew, and there was steak and other good things to eat for dinner. An imposing figure if not a handsome one, Loren's attorney-uncle, who was affectionately dubbed the Colonel by his closest friends, had a large head and kindly face; thick, well-groomed hair, which he parted on the left; and soft eyes accentuated by heavy, dark brows. Though he weighed 220 pounds, his ample girth was elegantly contained in tailor-made frock coats, which he continued to wear decades after they had gone out of fashion. The high collars that circled Buck's thick neck were heavily starched; the knot of his silk tie was always adorned with a golden stickpin. He never appeared in public without a boutonniere; the flowers, like the imported cigars he smoked nonstop, were special-ordered by the dozen. Generous to a fault, Buck contributed to every worthy cause in the city. At Christmas he loved to don a Santa Claus suit and visit the houses of his neighbors, seeing to it that every child received at least one gift, sometimes two or three.[37]

It was the affable Colonel who introduced twelve-year-old Loren to a tall red-brick building on the University of Nebraska campus known simply as the Museum. The undistinguished-looking structure contained extensive exhibits on anthropology, zoology, geology, and archaeology, including more than four thousand Indian relics. The first label the boy read so stirred his imagination that he never forgot it: "Shoe from horse given by the Sultan of Turkey to General Grant."[38] He wondered what had become of the other three shoes—indeed of the horse itself.

Loren returned whenever he got the chance, roaming the marble corridors for hours on end. He studied drawings of early human skulls, mostly slope eyed and primitive, and persuaded his reluctant grandmother to join him in a minor conspiracy. Loren modeled skulls of clay, taking special care to get the hollow eye sockets and heavy mandibles just right. Some of them were given teeth fashioned out of matchsticks or bits of mother-of-pearl scavenged from discarded buttons. When they were alone in the kitchen, Malvina placed the skulls on pie or cookie tins and baked them in the oven until they hardened. Occasionally the old woman, pricked by her Methodist conscience, protested by tapping her grandson on the shoulder with a roasting fork. "Mind you, this is getting out of hand. There's no ordinary heads in there and no young'un can tell me so. They've got that *look*, they have. That Darwin look. You've got to stop it 'fore the Devil gets you by the feet."[39]

Despite her scoldings, Malvina never betrayed her grandson's trust. Yet neither would she allow Loren to keep his primitive creations in the house. He carried them down the block to a place called Hagerty's barn, a sagging, unused stable where the October light filtered in between the shrunken siding to create a kind of warm, golden secrecy. Gripping the bag of heads between his teeth, he climbed on wooden crosspieces to the rickety half loft above and set his unique treasure in little rows along the ancient beams. Hagerty's barn became Loren's museum, a boyish imitation of the redbrick one that had so impressed him.

VI

Now that he was older, Loren could no longer be kept from exploring the countryside. During periods of heavy rain, the Russian or "Rooshen" Bottoms, in the southwestern part of the city, were covered by several inches of fresh water. When the floods receded the area became a giant sunflower forest, taller than a man. Neighborhood children roved this great yellow and green wilderness in gangs, ambushing one another with sunflower spears from secret positions near the meandering trails. Loren occasionally joined in such campaigns, but he preferred the more solitary activity of collecting insects and small animals, which he placed in jars and tin lard buckets for the journey home.

One day, while visiting the Lincoln City Library, he came across a little volume by one Eugene Smith titled *The Home Aquarium: How to Care for It.* Smith's work contained step-by-step instructions for building a tank of one's own. Loren got the glass and cut it himself; he also made a bottom and sides of wood and waterproofed it all with boiled tar to prevent decay and leakage at the joints. When the aquarium was ready for occupancy, he mastered Smith's simple account of how to find and identify freshwater flora and fauna.

The only problem lay in the fact that the author assumed the collecting would take place during the spring or summer. Loren, however, had encountered the book in midwinter, when the world he planned to enter lay dormant under thick pond ice. Undaunted, he hung his skates around his neck, picked up his homemade net along with a lard bucket or two, and set off. On reaching the pond, he chopped a hole in the ice near the shore and began dredging the opaque bottom for signs of life. Despite the adverse physical conditions, his net yielded a small assortment of water boatmen, dragonfly larvae, whirligig beetles, and other more diminutive animalcules.

Before leaving he decided to celebrate by strapping on his skates for a turn around the pond. He was out over the deeper water when the ice suddenly gave way, leaving one of his legs dangling below the surface. His head shot forward and struck the ice with such force that he was momentarily stunned. He lay motionless after regaining his senses, fearful of extending the ice fracture by struggling. Slowly he slid forward, arms spread, and gradually extricated his leg, which was soaked to the hip. A deeply shaken Loren jogged all the way home with his covered buckets, taking great care to hide his condition on arriving. "After such an event there was no one's arms in which to fall at home. If one did, there would be only hysterical admonitions, and I would be lucky to be allowed out. Slowly my inner life was continuing to adjust to this fact. I had to rely on silence."[40]

Although Loren succeeded in creeping away from death in an ice hole, both of his grandfathers succumbed during the winter months of that year. Charles Frederick Eiseley, who had reached the venerable age of seventy-nine, was the first to go; he died on February 2, 1918. The old judge's declining years had been fraught with financial worries and plagued by ill health. Josephine Eiseley's condition was little better, and, though the proud couple disliked taking what they called "charity," both were almost totally dependent on the assistance of friends and neighbors at the time of Charles's death.[41] A picture of the family was taken on the day of the funeral. Clyde and Leo were present, as were Clyde's brothers, Francis and Horace. Curiously, Loren, who was going on eleven, does not appear in the photograph. Neither do references exist in any of his extensive autobiographical writings to visits to Norfolk while his Grandfather Charles was living.

By contrast, Loren saw his Grandfather Corey almost daily at the home of his aunt and uncle. The old master carpenter in his declining years ruled a small room where dried sweet corn hung among the rafters for planting in the spring. Milo was "brimful with a Viking rage" that fell upon everyone around him, most especially children who tracked up his garden. He took a brand of snuff called Copenhagen, sneezed into red bandanna handkerchiefs, cursed his grandson for picking his blackberries, and ate dried cod shipped in boxes from the East Coast. Loren was so terrified of him that he always tiptoed by his door, yet watched spellbound as the craftsman's gnarled hands poked endlessly through a giant tool chest in search of something he could never seem to find.

Malvina once asked her husband to make their grandson a birdhouse for his birthday. Loren remembered that he rumbled like a cyclone and spent two days considering whether to comply. He went at last to his workbench and, after two more days of measuring, sawing, planing, and pounding, came up with a miniature Victorian house, porticoes, windows, and all. He placed it gruffly in the boy's hands and quickly turned away without uttering a word. It was one of the last things Milo ever built. The seventy-nine-year-old Viking died in his daughter's home three months later, during the late afternoon of December 12, 1918, possibly a victim of the same influenza epidemic that had nearly claimed the life of Loren's father.[42]

In addition to the birdhouse, Loren received at least one other gift for his twelfth birthday, Jules Verne's little volume of science fiction *From the Earth to the Moon*. The youth had become an insatiable reader once he had mastered *Robinson Crusoe* and, though his parents were poor, they helped him acquire a respectable little library of his own. Each of his books, which numbered in the dozens, was inscribed with his name, age, address, and date of purchase. They often bore the name of the giver as well, which in the majority of cases was Clyde. Loren's constant dreams of fleeing his oppressive environment were at least partly nurtured by his father's taste for adventure stories: *The Motor Boys Across the Plains*, *The Motor Boys on Blue Water*, and *Tom Swift and His Aerial Warship*.

Loren was equally attracted to stories of animals. *Black Beauty* sensitized him to animal suffering, particularly that inflicted on horses, since they were still an important part of the world in which he grew up. He also became a lifelong friend of the much reviled wolf after reading James Oliver Curwood's *Baree, Son of Kazan* and Charles G. D. Roberts's *Haunters of the Silences: A Book of Animal Life*. Robert Louis Stevenson's *Treasure Island* drew him into the enthralling world of the Spanish Main, which led him on to read Lionel Wafer, William Dampier, and other great buccaneer navigators. *Before Adam* by Jack London and Stanley Waterloo's *Story of Ab* made Loren privy to the concept of evolution a decade before the celebrated Scopes trial.[43]

The books Loren received on special occasions were but a small portion of the scores he read each year, for he frequented the Lincoln City Library, a gift of the steel magnate and philanthropist Andrew Carnegie. The library was located at Fourteenth and N streets, some two miles from the Eiseley home, and Loren pedaled there regularly in his red coaster wagon, which he filled with volumes of every description. This he could not have done without Daisy's acquiescence, an indication that Loren and Clyde were not the only readers in the family. Indeed, at least three books containing Daisy's signature survive, including a copy of *The Roughneck* by the Klondike writer and correspondent Robert Service. As Loren grew older, he took refuge in the stacks for hours on end and had to be chased out at closing time by Head Librarian Lula Horn.[44] He lived among the creations of his own mind, which were in many ways more real to him than anything he encountered outside. The energy he might have put into developing lasting relationships with family members and children his own age was turned protectively inward, producing a desire to understand intellectually a world that remained unresponsive to his emotional advances.

Besides the Rat, whom he had known but briefly in Aurora,

Loren remembered having only one close childhood friend, a youth named Jimmy Dawes. They met in grade school and became members of a secret order whose clubhouse was an old piano box in the backyard. Another of the initiates was a dog named Mickey, who endeared himself to the boys by trying to act like a human being. The two also visited the public library together, and Loren took Jimmy with him when he walked to the surrounding ponds in search of additional specimens for his aquariums. Yet the more their friendship deepened, the greater became Loren's awareness that something was terribly wrong, something he was powerless to change.

Lincoln in those days was a sharply divided city: the north side was mainly working class and poorly educated, while the south side was home to the college-trained professionals and old money. It was the Eiseleys' misfortune to be living on the "right" side of town, but without financial resources or social standing. In contrast to Clyde, Jimmy's father was a prominent and financially secure businessman. "He ruled a healthy, well-directed household in which one knew that because of the wisdom of father everyone would marry well, be economically secure, and that each child was bound to live happily ever after."[45] Loren sensed that Mr. Dawes had bent the rules by allowing his son to associate with a boy who belonged on the other side of the tracks.

Everything went well until the youths graduated from the eighth grade at Prescott School. Loren saw nothing of Jimmy the following summer. When school resumed in September, he walked the corridors of the huge building, vainly searching for his friend. It was possible, of course, that Jimmy had been sent elsewhere to complete his education, but if so, why hadn't he taken a few minutes to stop by and say he was leaving? Looking back, Loren realized the separation had been handled so deftly that it must have been orchestrated by an adult hand. The father had decided that the time had come for his son to relinquish the last vestiges of childhood and get on with the business of becoming a properly respectable young man. Loren, as yet, had no idea what the future might hold for him, but he realized beyond the slightest doubt that Jimmy Dawes was destined to become something he would never be.

3

T.C.H.S.

I

Little is known of Loren's early adolescence, except that these normally traumatic years were made even more painful for him by a shyness born of social deprivation. So embarrassed and hurt was the youth after Jimmy Dawes severed their childhood ties that no friend of his ever again received an invitation to visit the Eiseley home and meet his parents. For the time being, the barren spaces in his life were filled by long walks in the countryside, occasional visits to the Museum, and countless hours of reading in the public library, which had literally become his home away from home.

Meanwhile, his restless father had changed jobs once again. In 1921 Clyde began selling storage batteries manufactured by the local firm of H. C. Wittman. Coincidentally, Leo returned to Lincoln during this period with a family of his own, much to Loren's delight. The young telegrapher had moved in 1916 to Norfolk, where he met and courted Mamie Harms, whose father operated the Norfolk School of Business. They were married in December of that year and moved into the home Clyde had purchased for Anna a quarter of a century earlier. In November 1917 Mamie gave birth to the couple's only child, a daughter they named Athena. For the holidays that year they presented Leo's half brother with a copy of Captain Wilbur Lawton's *The Ocean Boys and the Naval Code*, which bears the inscription "A Joyous Christmas and Glad New Year, Loren, Your brother and sister, Leo and Mamie."

After brief stints with Western Union in Florida and New York, Leo was promoted to chief night operator and assigned to the Lincoln office in May 1920. He rented an apartment on South Twenty-ninth Street, to which Loren frequently came. Mamie, who was in her early twenties, seems to have been particularly sympathetic to her lonely brother-in-law and encouraged the normally reticent youth to talk freely about his many problems. A strong bond developed between them, and Loren was deeply saddened when Leo sought and was granted a transfer to Colorado Springs during the summer of 1922.[1]

The youth's social awkwardness was accentuated by the fact that he had reached physical maturity more rapidly than most boys his age, giving him the aspect of one much older than his years. Loren was large boned and attained his full stature of five feet eleven inches within a year or so of entering high school. Though on the thin side, he had a broad chest and powerful, well-developed shoulders and forearms. His chiseled head, even at this early age, bore an uncanny resemblance to the most intimidating of all his forebears. The broad, prominent nose, downturned mouth, lantern jaw, and high forehead are strangely reminiscent of Permila Shepard's physiognomy. And like his great-grandmother, Loren wore wire-rimmed glasses to compensate for extreme nearsightedness. He oiled his dark hair and combed it straight back in the fashion of the day, taking special care to keep it trimmed above the ears.

Having just turned fifteen, Loren entered Lincoln High School in September 1922. Despite an affinity for nature writing, he had little idea of what he wanted to do or to be; nor, as he later recalled, were his parents, neither of whom had gone beyond the eighth grade, of any help to him in this regard: "Unconsciously, they had arrived at the philosophy that foresight merely invited the attention of some baleful intelligence that despised and persecuted the calculating planner."[2] Still, they shared the simple working-class faith in the importance of education and even hoped that their son might go on to college. It was up to Loren to choose his lifework, however, so long as he "made something of himself."[3]

In truth, nothing could have been further from his mind at the time, for he felt besieged on all sides. Conditions in the Eiseley household had deterioriated so much that the youth had been forced to move in with his aunt and uncle. He was equally estranged from his classmates, and his poor performance in Latin and algebra raised the unsettling prospect that he might fail both subjects.

He held on for the time being and made it through the first semester of his sophomore year without failing a course. Indeed, he did superior work in a number of subjects, earning 90 or above in civics, European history, general science, and zoology. In English he received an 89, but he just squeaked by in Latin, with a lackluster 74. His recovery in algebra proved somewhat more impressive; he managed to raise his grade to an 80 by semester's end.[4] Yet during this period Loren was not only rudderless but inwardly defiant and seemingly on the verge of open rebellion. Several weeks into the semester, he wrote a soulful and bitter letter to his only confidante:

October 22, 1922

Dear Mamie:
I am sorry I didn't write to you before but I have been studying so much the last week or so that when I did have time I wanted to get outdoors.

I became real ambitious and have been studying Latin (think of it!) so hard that though I failed in my six weeks test; I haven't rec'd a failure notice yet. Maybe its' because the old bird has'nt recovered from her astonishment yet.

Just between you and I, however, it was'nt any more than a sudden spurt and all I got out of it was a case of permanent spring fever. I have relapsed into my old condition and in algebra and Latin much of my time is spent day dreaming and longing for the open fields.

Take it from me, boy, I know how that guy must have felt when he wrote:

I never new sad men who looked
with such a wistful eye
Upon that little tent of blue
We "prisoners" call the sky.

Still, I suppose I shouldn't kick for a fellow can't appreciate nature, poetry and junk till he has some education.

As you know I'm staying over to Grace's. They're enough to make you want to chew your fingers and howl sometimes. "They trust me so. You never tell a lie." but just the same I guess they believe in safety first from the way they keep on my heels. They even ran me out of one of the rooms so I wouldn't see where they were ditching their dough. They think the woman across the street is a "perfect disgrace" because she wears knickers and plays golf! When they are trying to talk and not have me hear; they converse in stage whispers that you can hear through the whole house and yet they seem to think their putting something over on me.

Quite a list of woe, eh?; but don't worry I'm still living, and hope to be when they're dressed in wooden kimonas.

Having a good time? Be sure and get it while you got a chance and remember you must gain *fifty lbs.* so you can lay us all out when you get back. . . .

I sure miss you lots. If everybody had a sis like you heaven would be an unnecessary institution.

I'm kinda runnin down so I guess I'll hit the hay.

So long
Loren[5]

The lines of verse Loren quoted are from Oscar Wilde's best-known poem, *The Ballad of Reading Gaol* (1898), which Wilde composed after being imprisoned for having been found guilty of homosexual behavior. The trenchant and deeply melancholy work was inspired by the case of Wilde's fellow prisoner, Charles Thomas Wooldridge, a trooper in the Royal Horse Guards who was condemned to hang for cutting his young wife's throat in a fit of jealous rage. It is not known whether Loren read sanitized excerpts of the lengthy work from a textbook or came across an unexpurgated edition. In either case, the alienated adolescent committed Wilde's haunting metaphor to memory, as if it had been written for him alone.

II

When second-semester classes began in late January 1923, Loren did not return to the sprawling, yellow-brick school building at 2229 J Street. He could no longer cope with its impersonal environment and what he viewed as "the snobbishness" of students who came from Lincoln's upper middle class. They had a future; he did not. Hoping to assuage the anger and disappointment of his parents—not to mention Grace and Buck, who seem to have nurtured even higher ambitions for their troubled nephew—Loren took a menial job to help pay for his room and board. Because he was not yet sixteen, he had to keep a wary eye out for the truant officer, but doing so made him feel like a criminal when all he claimed to want was to be left alone.[6]

His conduct, however, appears to have been that of an extremely sensitive youth in search more of guidance than of isolation. His love of books and ideas had deepened during his adolescent years. Despite certain difficulties in the classroom, he had never given up when it would have been easy to accept lower marks in some courses and simply fail others, thus foreclosing on the future.

Even his distaste for affluence was belied by a secret dream of becoming wealthy. The fantasy dated from childhood, when he had been attracted to a great Romanesque house he called the Rudd mansion, a pseudonym for A. C. Zimer, a Christian Science practitioner who built the thirty-three-room estate on Euclid in 1909. The red stone used in its construction was shipped from Colorado and cut by hand on the site. Moss-green cedar shingles covered the roof and upper portions of some exterior walls. Sixty twenty-dollar gold pieces were molded into the kitchen windows, while a cast-iron lion head, chains in its mouth, stood guard over the back porch. The boy had often scavenged for burned toys in a stone incinerator outside the fence at the edge of the property. One frosty night in early autumn he had found a metal wheel the color of gold and pretended that the gold was real. "To me it represented all those things—perhaps in a dim way life itself—that are denied by poverty."[7] He carried the little treasure around with him like a talisman and returned many times over the years to gaze wistfully at the mansion from the street, dreaming of what it would be like to be fenced in rather than fenced out.

Long after he dropped out of high school, Loren came across a letter written by Clyde during his years on the road. Addressed to Buck and Grace, it seems to be a plea for understanding in behalf of the traveling salesman's wayward son: "Remember, the boy is a genius, but moody."[8] While there is no way of knowing for certain when these words were written, the fact that Loren was living with the Prices between 1922 and 1923 makes it possible that they date from this troubled time. Buck was in no mood to give up on his nephew at such an early age, but he also sensed that it would be unwise to put additional pressure on the youth at that moment. The attorney had a plan, but he waited awhile before broaching it with Loren, giving him time to ponder the consequences of life from the perspective of an unskilled laborer.

Buck knew nearly everyone there was to know in Lincoln, including Charles W. Taylor, the affable principal of Teachers College High School. Located on the University of Nebraska campus at Fourteenth and S streets, Teachers High had been founded in 1908 as a laboratory school for university seniors who were about to graduate with teaching degrees in secondary education. It was here, under the supervision of the regular faculty, that they completed their student practicum. In contrast to Lincoln High School, where the grades often numbered over three hundred students each, at Teachers High they averaged between thirty-five and forty-five pupils, making it possible to place a premium on individualized instruction. Academic standards were high, as they had been in the beginning, when the student body was composed largely of the children of university professors and administrators.

Charles Taylor, an educational progressive, was determined to make the institution more representative of the community as a whole. During his administration the sons and daughters of the professoriat were joined by those born on farms and into Lincoln's rapidly expanding working class. Taylor personally screened each candidate for admission and was particularly interested in the troubled but promising student, a natural extension of the humanistic credo that made him, along with William Buchanan Price, one of the main supporters of the local Salvation Army. It is not known whether Buck, having made prior arrangements with Taylor to accept his nephew, encountered any difficulty in persuading Loren that he should return to school. In any event, the sixteen-year-old paid his four-dollar fee to cover registration and incidentals, and became a member of the junior class of Teachers High on September 19, 1923.

Loren had some catching up to do, especially since his schedule of courses—which included English, geometry, botany, and medieval history—had no soft spots. English had always been his first love. It was not long before his nascent ability as a writer came to the attention of Miss Wyman, his student teacher. He composed an essay about a dog named Whiskers he claimed to have owned. The animal had allegedly been attacked and killed by a pack of hounds belonging to a neighboring farmer, an event that caused its youthful master to undergo a crisis of conscience: "I remembered what the big folks said about heaven and was content until I learned that church people didn't seem to think animals went to heaven. I was terribly hurt at this and I don't believe I've ever had as good an opinion of God's judgement since." While the facts of the story bear little resemblance to the facts of his life, the story does evidence its author's future beliefs. He earned high praise for his effort. "I like the informal air of this," Miss Wyman wrote at the bottom.[9] His semester mark of 92 in English V was exceeded by 96s in medieval history and botany. Only mathematics still gave him serious difficulty.[10]

For Christmas 1923 Loren received a copy of Henry Fairfield Osborn's *Origin and Evolution of Life*. The inscription contained some thoughtful advice from a steadfast hand: "Get knowledge but get it with understanding. From your 'buck', W. B. Price."

During the only semester he attended Lincoln High School, Loren had longed to join the debating team. But when a teacher, attracted to his powerful baritone voice, asked him to try out he was simply too self-conscious.[11] Finding his new surroundings more congenial, he decided to try his hand at dramatics during his second semester there. Small though it was, Teachers High had a football team, which suffered from a chronic shortage of able-bodied recruits. Since Loren was among the largest youths in the school, he soon caught the eye of the coach, who turned him into a somewhat reluctant lineman. He recalled later, "I was not very handy with mathematics, and I must say in all seriousness, that I fear I only graduated from high school because I was playing football."[12]

Yet Loren's most vivid image of this period did not take the conventional form of a game-saving tackle, classroom achievement, or awkward first date. He was leaning from a window on the school's second floor. A block away he saw a broken-down horse plodding before a cart piled high with the flotsam of modern civilization—scrap metal, worn-out furniture, cast-off clothing. The horse's harness was in keeping with the load it pulled, having been fashioned from discarded pieces of leather and rope. The bearded, ill-clad man perched high in the driver's seat also looked as though he had been compounded from the junk heap in the cart bed. What seemed even more curious to Loren, however, was the street sign and the year: R Street and 1923. It suddenly dawned on him that the junk man was the symbol of all that is disappearing or already gone. "He is passing the intersection into nothingness. Say to the mind, 'Hold him, do not forget.' " Immortalize the fleeting moment. Loren vowed to remember what no other would, just as he remembered the dice, the gold wheel, the slain turtle, the blood of the escaped prisoners on the snow. One could never tell when these mental artifacts might work their way to the surface again and come in handy. He would keep them for use another day.[13]

III

Mamie Eiseley returned to Lincoln with her daughter, Athena, in July 1924. Ordinarily, it would have been cause for celebration, but her visit on this occasion brought Loren little joy. Mamie had been discontented with her marriage to Leo for some time. In fact, she had requested a separation two years earlier, before her husband's transfer to Colorado Springs, which he had sought in the hope that new surroundings might cause her to undergo a change of heart. When they did not, Leo decided to stand in her way no longer. Mamie obtained her divorce a few months later, although she agreed to bring Athena south to Montgomery, Alabama, so that the child could be near her father, who had decided to move once again.[14]

Loren, meanwhile, continued to spend much of his time under Buck's roof. Daisy had grown increasingly belligerent and, when challenged on the most trivial point, screamed uncontrollably until she got her way. An insomniac, she stalked the tiny bungalow until the small hours, depriving Loren and his father of their sleep and straining tempers to the limit. In a snapshot taken in profile during this period, Daisy's eye—dark and mischievous—reflects the glint of family madness. It was an image Loren never forgot, and he dreamed about it more than once: "There was an eye that seemed torn from a photograph, but that looked through me as though it had already raced in vision up to the steep edge of nothingness and absorbed whatever terror lay in that abyss. . . . I knew the eye and the circumstance. . . . It was my mother."[15] Clyde was visibly withering under the strain; he began to suffer intense abdominal cramps and an unexplained loss of weight. The condition was finally diagnosed as stomach ulcers, the eternal baggage of the traveling salesman.

Loren, much to his dismay, found that the shadows of his ancestral past pursued him wherever he went. At Buck's he was periodically awakened by Malvina, who cried out desperately in her sleep. Upon being roused, his grandmother refused to reveal what she feared, as if to do so might spread the curse to other members of the family.[16]

In contrast to his Uncle Buck, who despite his aristocratic bearing was as warm and friendly as an old wood-burning stove, Loren's Aunt Grace was outwardly reserved, rarely given to any display of emotion. Though she was short and grew somewhat stocky, her imperious countenance gave her the aspect of studied gentility. Grace thought highly of her nephew, but she never seemed able to put her deepest feelings into words, leaving it up to her husband to speak on her behalf. Even the inscription in the only book she ever gave her nephew, *The Motor Boys on Blue Waters*, is completely devoid of sensibility: "Loren C. Eiseley From Aunt Grace."

As a boy Loren had sometimes slipped into his aunt's silent Victorian bedroom, crowded with knickknacks and curios. He was especially attracted by a beautiful iridescent seashell on the dressing table, a gift from some wandering relative. Loren held the large, cool object up to his ear, mistaking the vastly magnified whispers of his own coursing blood for the rhythmic murmur of the sea. He also remembered a lovely silver-backed hand mirror, the twin of one given to Daisy by Milo Corey. Whereas Grace had treated her father's gift with great care, Daisy's mirror had been marred by petulant violence, its handle broken off. The mirrors had marked the difference between the sisters, their treatment of things, their very lives.[17]

IV

September 1924 marked the beginning of Loren's senior year at Teachers College High School. Like the other members of his class, he was required to take the Freeman IQ test early in October. His score of 109, a little above average, ranked him twenty-third out of thirty-eight and bore little relationship to his academic performance the previous year, except perhaps in mathematics. Neither was the test designed to measure creativity.

Having established himself as a writer of some promise, Loren did not disappoint his latest student teacher of English, Agnes Graham. He wrote a short story concerning the heroic exploits of a dog in Alaska, which she urged him to enter in the annual writing contest sponsored by the prestigious *Atlantic Monthly.* When Miss Graham's class was selected to appear before a college class taught by Frederick A. Stuff, chairman of the Department of English in the Teachers College, Loren was asked to read his story aloud. The reaction was anything but expected: several members of Stuff's class, thinking the work too professional for a high-school senior, accused him of copying it from some magazine. Agnes Graham was furious, for she had seen the story evolve from little more than an idea into a polished composition. She came to Loren's defense, but to no avail. Later that semester, however, both teacher and pupil enjoyed a measure of revenge. A letter from the *Atlantic Monthly* arrived informing Loren that his story had received honorable mention in the category of short fiction.[18]

The essay and the short story had to compete for Loren's attention with an even more alluring literary form. One day during class he found himself writing verse on the back of a theme. "I was about seventeen at the time, and can still remember the mild shock I experienced upon discovering what I was doing. From then on I took poetry as though it were a drug, reading it intensively and continuing to write a bit."[19]

This newly awakened interest was also nurtured in the classroom, largely through a method of instruction pioneered by Dr. Lucius Adelno Sherman, professor of English Literature at the University of Nebraska. A realist when it came to undergraduates and classical literature—especially poetry—Sherman observed that in the average class hardly more than half the students have any taste for verse beyond a burlesque *Aeneid*. The fault, he insisted, lay in the practice of requiring them to memorize long passages rather than appealing directly to their sensibilities. Like their classmates in the sciences, students of literature should learn by doing. Sherman's method, which was employed at Teachers High, required students to write something almost every day. During class concepts such as Truth and Beauty would be studied in the works of Tennyson or Browning. Students then composed verses of their own containing examples of the ideas being discussed. On some occasions a sentence or two sufficed; on others they were required to hand in a paper several pages long. This practical experience taught Loren not only how to express himself better but also how to distinguish between an ode and a sonnet, a sonnet and a ballad, free verse and rhyme.[20]

The teacher who most deeply influenced Loren's writing rarely saw him in a formal classroom setting. She was Letta May Clark, assistant professor of methods of instruction in English. As the supervisor of all student teachers in her discipline, Miss Clark began to receive enthusiastic reports concerning young Eiseley's unusual way with words. They piqued her curiosity, and she was soon reading almost every important assignment he handed in.

While Loren blossomed as a writer in these sheltered surroundings he also achieved a degree of social acceptance far beyond anything he had experienced in the past. Not only did he captain the football team during his senior year but he was elected class president. Still, although his classmates numbered fewer than forty, Loren did not mix with everyone. Faye Munden, a close acquaintance and fellow lineman on the football team, characterized him as "selective" in his friends. He associated mainly with a dozen or so seniors who commonly referred to themselves as "The Crowd." Although the group was made up of both boys and girls, there was relatively little, if any, serious dating because most were planning to continue their education. On weekends they often went to one another's homes for parties. Dancing, which underwent a revolution during the twenties, was among their favorite activities, but Loren, who was somewhat awkward when it came to the opposite sex, almost always sat on the sidelines. He preferred to get out the Ouija board and try his luck with the spirits. A natural with the planchette, he entertained his friends by the hour, spelling out messages ostensibly emitted from beyond. While some of Loren's friends came from well-to-do families, the majority, like himself, had little extra money to spend on entertainment. They sometimes went to the movies on Saturday nights, but most of their spare change found its way into the cash register of the old Central Cafe on P Street in downtown Lincoln. A popular hangout among university students, the establishment was also frequented by those from the high schools who harbored similar ambitions.

Other than the fact that he was usually short of spending money, Loren's straitened circumstances were not readily apparent. His clothes were of the same style and quality as those worn by others, and he seems never to have lacked the basic supplies required to complete his assignments. The deep strain of melancholy that dominates so much of his poetry and prose, both early and late, was also little in evidence. Sixty years later Loren was still remembered for his wry wit and endearing mischievousness. Georgia Everett, a fellow senior who sat next to him in class, recalled that "he seemed to delight in making people laugh." Although he was neither a prankster nor a disruptive influence, "there was always something going on where Loren was concerned." Classmates Leah Dale and

Faye Munden had similar memories.[21] Indeed, he was nicknamed Bozo by some of his best friends. Those not a part of his inner circle were encouraged to call him Larry, Loren's own masculine substitution for his troublesome Christian name, which was sometimes mistaken for that of a girl.

The unofficial title of senior class jester was claimed by John Alfred Cave, Loren's best friend. Jac, as he was known to everyone, moved to Lincoln with his family in the fall of 1924, just in time to begin his senior year at Teachers High. Classically tall, dark, and handsome, he sported a carefully groomed mustache, which made him the envy of the boys and the object of much deep sighing among the girls. A natural athlete, Jac joined Loren and Faye on the football team, shunning the lineman's ignominious lot for the glory of the backfield. A great wit and inveterate practical joker, Jac kept the seniors in stitches and his nervous student teachers on the edges of their seats. Helen Hopt, a member of The Crowd, succinctly but affectionately described Jac as "that rascal."[22]

The second youngest of seven children, Jac was the son of W. Alfred Cave, an Episcopal priest. The Caves were a fun-loving, gregarious clan and treated Loren like another member of the family. Jac's kid sister Alice recalled that Loren, whom she considered at heart a lonely and rather moody young man in spite of his fey sense of humor, inquiring mind, and adventurous spirit, was "as dear to us as any brother or son could be."

Alice remembered once tearing into the house with the news that two big tarantulas "or something" were hanging on the bushes outside. After a brief look at the creatures, Loren assured her that they were not deadly spiders but harmless polyphemus moths, no doubt blown to earth by high winds the night before. Alice warmed to this display of erudition from a youth still in high school. "Perhaps this marked the beginning of my 'crush' [on him]; he seemed to know everything!"[23]

Loren, Jac, and Faye were often seen in the company of another member of the senior class, LeRoy Stholman. A victim of some debilitating childhood disease, LeRoy required crutches to move about. The four thought it would be fun to try their hand at acting, and each landed a part in the senior class play, *Kicked out of College*, a farce penned by one Walter Ben Hare. The plot concerned the marital exploits of Bootles Benbow, a popular college senior who took a different wife in each of the play's three acts. None of the four friends got the lead. Loren played Mr. Gear, owner of the Speed Motor Car Company; Jac was cast as Sandy McCann, coach of the Dramatics Club; LeRoy played Shorty Long, a member of the Glee Club; Faye took on the dual roles of Scotch McAllister, "a hard student," and Officer Riley, a cop from the Emerald Isle. The play itself was only mildly amusing, but the cast was royally entertained by the antics of the fun-loving quartet. One member of the production recalled that if the public had been allowed to attend rehearsals, the play would still be running.[24]

If Loren did not exactly conform to the description of a melancholy loner, it was nevertheless evident to his more perceptive friends that he was holding something back. Realizing that his family situation was "peculiar," they politely overlooked the fact that he never took his turn inviting The Crowd to his home on a Saturday night. Only Faye and Jac managed to meet any of his relatives: both were introduced to the Prices when Loren was staying at their house, but neither ever set foot in the Eiseley home, although Faye harbored vague recollections of once being introduced to Clyde. Leah Dale, who sat next to Loren in senior English, remembered that he vowed never to have any children of his own.[25]

Loren was also recognized for his unusual abilities, especially what one classmate called "his grasp of subject matter." Having taken refuge in books even before he entered school, Loren was far better read than anyone else in his class and was treated more as a peer than as a student by the faculty. Arthella Gadd, another of his student teachers, remembered that "he looked older than his age—very studious and intellectual. . . . He always had the answer, which I liked very much. . . . He seemed as though he should be in college."[26]

Faye Munden was impressed by Loren's excellent memory and vocabulary; Georgia Everett simply described him as "brilliant." She was somewhat shocked, however, when the class honor roll was published and Loren's name, in contrast to her own, was not on it: the grades he earned as a senior did not measure up to his previous year's performance.

Although his lower grades may be partly explained by the fact that his social life and extracurricular activities were making unaccustomed demands on his time, other factors suggest that Loren also realized he could be quite charming and could get by with a minimum of effort. Those who composed the class will and prophecy knew him better than he might have suspected: "Loren Eiseley bequeaths his English ability to Carl Mayer, provided he does not vamp the teachers." And what would the senior class president be doing ten years hence? "Loren Eiseley [is] now head of the college of applesauce feeding or how to get through college without knowing anything. His most famous book is the science of teacher vamping in two volumes."

On Friday, May 1, the classes of 1925 and 1926 gathered at 6:30 P.M. in the Grand Hotel for the Junior-Senior Banquet. Beside each plate lay a homemade program whose dark brown cover bore the ink sketch of an endearing mongrel puppy and the senior class motto: "It's better to be a live scrub than a dead Thoroughbred." Before taking their seats the students joined in the school song, "Cheer to Old T.C." A "musical prelude" followed, which included a saxophone solo, a flute solo, a reading, and yet another solo—this one on the piano. After dinner Richard Oades, president of the junior class, offered the traditional toast to the seniors. Loren Eiseley then took the floor to perform his last official act as senior class leader:

> At first I had half a notion to change this title to "Release from Slavery" or something on that order but on 2nd thought I remembered Mr. Taylor would be here. I was afraid he might take offense and we've got to watch our step because the final emancipation proclamation hasn't been signed yet. . . .
>
> This banquet brings home to the Seniors the fact that it won't be long until the only evidence of our having attended T.C. will be a few photographs on the wall accumulating dust and fading into oblivion. And the funny part of it is that we're glad about it. . . .
>
> But seriously folks, this is a gladness not unmixed with regret. . . . Those of you who have attended other schools of the snobby sort . . . know what I mean. Old T.C. may not be the largest school in the world, but it has what is worth more—the friendly homey feeling that seems to be dying out. So we're glad to be here, glad to be graduating from a real school.[27]

A month later, the seniors came together for the last time. Graduation exercises took place at eight o'clock in the evening of June 4 in the Temple Theater on the University of Nebraska campus. Following the invocation and two vocal solos, the commencement address—"Forces That Build Mental Fiber"—was delivered by Dr. Charles Fordyce, of the university faculty. Principal Taylor then presented the class, and Chancellor Samuel Avery awarded the certificates of graduation. The ninth student in line, Loren marched across the stage to receive his diploma, something no Corey or Eiseley had ever done before.

V

Some weeks before their graduation, "Mr. Gear, Mr. McCann, Shorty Long, and Officer Riley" hatched what was later described as a "harebrained scheme," but what at the time seemed the quintessence of common sense—if only to the players themselves. They would pool their modest resources and strike out for the West Coast, ostensibly in search of summer employment. With their diplomas in hand, the four acquired a 1919 Model T Ford dubbed Old Purgatory. Other than its extremely modest purchase price, the vehicle's main appeal lay in the fact that its previous owner had altered the front seat so that it would lie flat and make a "pretty respectable" bed for two. A pup tent, in which Loren and Jac had often slept when camping on the Boy Scout grounds, provided shelter for the others. Before departing Lincoln the four took special care to stock up on motor oil, since test drives through the nearby countryside revealed that they were burning at least one quart of oil for each five gallons of gasoline. Lacking an oilcan of their own, they improvised with a container whose bottom and sides were still thickly coated with the residue of its previous contents—wild honey. Thus supplied, the four high-spirited pilgrims started out on what Faye Munden remembered as "a fine June morning."[28]

The first leg of the trip, from Lincoln to Denver—nearly five hundred miles over mostly dirt and gravel roads—took them ten days but was completed without serious incident. On reaching the Colorado capital, they camped overnight in the yard of Faye's uncle before heading south to the Garden of the Gods, a region of colored sandstone hills and ridges eroded by wind and water into grotesque shapes. They chose to spend the night in the 770-acre park, a decision that nearly resulted in the kind of tragedy long since legendary in the West. Loren woke Jac very quietly the next morning and told him to roll, as carefully as possible, out of the blanket the two were sharing. After they gained their feet, Loren cautiously lifted the cover to reveal a large rattlesnake, which had been stretched out between them, basking in the warmth of their bodies.

Following a visit to the Royal Gorge, whose near-vertical walls rise more than one thousand feet above the Arkansas River, the four resupplied in Canon City before turning southwest. The easy miles were behind them now: ahead lay the San Juan Mountains, part of the Southern Rockies, and primitive Wolf Creek Pass at an elevation of nearly eleven thousand feet. The rock-strewn track—for one could hardly call it a road—snaked its way up the granite escarpment for mile after harrowing mile. According to Faye, it was built for one-way traffic only; "if one met another car and were going up hill it was advisable to find a wide place and put your hub caps right against the rock wall because . . . that fellow . . . needed everything he could muster to get by." They finally made the summit and, thinking the worst was over, began the steep descent in a light-hearted mood. It quickly became clear to all that they had congratulated themselves prematurely. The old Ford's brake bands began to squeal and smoke in protest, forcing the driver to shift repeatedly from forward into reverse as a means of slowing the downward momentum. Soon the transmission bands also began to give out, and the four breathed a collective sigh of relief when, late in the afternoon, they limped into the little town of Farmington in northern New Mexico.

LeRoy, who had grown up on a farm, served as the mechanic: he spent most of the following day stretched out on his back replacing both the transmission and the brake bands. Their oil reserves were also fast disappearing, and each time the can was tipped, a little more honey flowed into Old Purgatory's fouled crankcase. To make matters worse, the tires had taken such a beating that flats had become routine. For some unexplained reason, no one had thought to bring along a jack, and there was too little money left to justify the purchase of such a "frill." A simple but effective system was devised: "Loren . . . would back up against the wheel, take hold of the wooden spokes, and lift that quarter of the car high enough so we could [put a] block under the axle and change the tire." Even gasoline proved a problem, because the petroleum industry was just beginning to ship refined fuel into this still remote part of the Southwest.

Nevertheless, the undaunted quartet pushed on and connected with Route 66, then known as Old Trails Highway. The honey finally caught up with them in Peach Springs, on the Walapai Indian Reservation in Arizona. They camped in a park by the railroad tracks, where LeRoy undertook a major overhaul of the motor. This was not their only problem: they were flat broke. Faye, whose father and grandfather were railroad men, persuaded the local Santa Fe agent to let him catch the California Limited to Kingman free of charge. "I got the agent at Kingman to wire my Dad (free again). Dad was so pleased to know I was still alive he sent money and a day or so later we had Old Purgatory going with fresh parts and clear oil."

They had driven only about one hundred miles when disaster struck in the Mojave Mountains near the California line. Faye was behind the wheel and heading down the side of a mountain. "At first I was able to handle the grade pretty well." But in the distance the road made a sharp turn to the right, which required that the car be slowed almost to a stop. Faye stepped on the brakes; nothing happened. Unable to negotiate the hairpin, he had two choices: either drive straight ahead into a towering wall of rock or angle left on a strip of upgrade littered with massive boulders.

> By that time the boys could see what was going to take place and they started to unload. Loren jumped off the right side and slid on his stomach with his hands ahead of him. He skinned his palms and hands pretty badly. Jac got off without injury as I recall but LeRoy [who was crippled] rode with me as I turned to the left up the grade and into the boulders. Well, after we negotiated three or four of these 4 foot boulders we came to a halt wedged between 2 good sized ones. All tires blown out and the car a complete wreck. LeRoy and I were scared but all in one piece.

The four walked the remaining distance into Oatman and stopped at the town's only garage. They asked the owner what he would give them for Old Purgatory, sight unseen. "I guess because he felt sorry for us he offered $5.00 cash. We took it and got something to eat."

Later that day they hitched a ride into Needles, California, with two miners who were driving an old Jordan touring car. Only after they set out from Oatman did it become apparent to the youths that their benefactors had been drinking. The boys were taken for what Faye described as "a merry ride through the winding dirt roads of the desert." It was midafternoon when the six finally rolled into Needles. The boys wasted no time heading for cover: "We found shade down by the Harvey House [Hotel] and the temperature was away over 115°."

Toward evening they hopped a freight and rode to the first water tank, where the brakeman put them off. When the next westbound train came through, they got down inside the compartment of a refrigerator car that still had a little ice in it. Although it was dark as "billy hell," the welcome break from the stifling desert heat made the temporary sacrifice of sight well worthwhile. Several hours later found them "yarded" in the isolated town of Barstow, some eighty miles north of San Bernardino. When it became evident that the train was not going anywhere, they climbed out of their hiding place. As Faye was emerging through the roof, the hatch door came down on his head, leaving a nasty gash above the scalp line. It bled profusely, forcing the weary quartet to find a water hydrant so Faye could wash up.

It was apparent to everyone that LeRoy's disability was incompatible with jumping freights. They wired home for more money and, when it arrived, reluctantly put their boon companion and star mechanic on an eastbound passenger train. Loren, Faye, and Jac made it the rest of the way to Los Angeles, where one of them rented a single room for four dollars a week, concealing from the landlady the fact that all three were living together. Money remained tight, and the trio took whatever work they could find. Faye remembered that he and Loren were employed by a contractor to dig ditches, while Jac, a more genteel sort, clerked in stores. Still, they could not make ends meet, and the telegraph lines stretching back to Lincoln were kept humming with further requests for financial aid. Faye decided to call it quits after a short while and used the last of his money from home to purchase a ticket back to Nebraska.

Little is known of Loren's and Jac's movements during what remained of the summer, except that they stayed on in California a while longer. According to Alice Cave, they may have moved down the coast to Long Beach so that Loren could be nearer the ocean, whose shores he had envisioned walking ever since he'd first tiptoed into Grace's bedroom and held her mysterious, iridescent seashell against his ear. All that is known for certain is that he persuaded Jac to undertake one final journey before heading back home. They walked and hitchhiked most of the day to reach the famous Mount

Wilson Observatory northeast of Los Angeles. According to the guidebooks Loren had read, the public was allowed to visit the complex on certain nights and look upon some remote object through the giant reflecting telescope. They arrived, exhausted but hopeful, and not a little naive. Loren wrote later, "We thought, though we were poor, that we would be welcome upon the mountain because of our desire to learn. There were reputed to dwell in the observatory men of wisdom who we hoped would receive us kindly since we, too, wished to gaze upon the wonders of outer space."

The two waited through the cold night, the guard eyeing them and their disheveled clothing with "sullen distaste." Busload after busload of tourists arrived from the better hotels in the valley to be greeted by uniformed guides. The youths purchased some chocolate and then dozed until the glint of the rising sun pierced the eastern horizon, confirming what both already knew. They would not be allowed to see the men of wisdom after all. The two looked at each other and then, without saying a word, turned and began their long descent through the early morning dark.[29]

4

"SOME DESTINY NOT DECIDED"

I

Loren and Jac returned to Lincoln at summer's end, in time to begin classes at the University of Nebraska on September 15, 1925. It was the heart of the Jazz Age, and the campus population had climbed above ten thousand during the so-called return to normalcy following World War I. Housing proved a serious problem, spurring the growth of fraternities and sororities and exacerbating the traditional rivalry between "Greek" and "Barbarian." The administration received an increasing number of complaints from concerned citizens: many more students were smoking, it was said, and large numbers of coeds were blighting their natural, God-given beauty with liberal applications of rouge and other unwholesome cosmetics. Even more scandalous was the new style of female clothing. Story Harding, editor of the student newspaper, the *Daily Nebraskan*, reported: "knee-length dresses of the modern girl have cast modesty from the dictionary."[1]

Standards of propriety in student publications had also undergone a revolution. Forty-two undergraduates were severely ridiculed by name in the student life section of the 1921 *Cornhusker*, the university annual. One unkempt female was singled out for never having had friendly relations with Pepsodent toothpaste or Woodbury soap. Dean Carl C. Engberg, whose office bore the brunt of the widening criticism, was inclined to attribute most of these problems to labor unrest and the tremendous craze for amusement: "Students don't get down to business. . . . People are just wild over movies, dancing and other forms of entertainment."[2]

The university administration did try to contain some of the "radical" new social developments. Early in 1924 the regents specifically charged Dean Engberg with enforcing the rule against alcohol consumption among students. When the leaders of a campus organization asked for a referendum on the question of prohibition, Chancellor Samuel Avery countered: "It is possible that some other schools have permitted a referendum among their students as to whether or not they favor upholding the Constitution of the United States and the enforcement of the law. Such a proposal, however, in the University of Nebraska is preposterous." Of almost equal concern was the proliferation of automobiles on campus and their presumed negative effect on student morals. The used Model T Ford was especially popular. In the fall of 1927 William P. Warner, president of the Board of Regents, announced a new policy severely restricting the use of cars on and around campus. "There is too much diversion from the real purpose of attending the University," Warner was quoted as saying. "Whether all are here for a legitimate purpose is questionable."[3]

Automobiles and campus high jinks aside, most students were enrolled in the university for a legitimate purpose. The average expense for the school year was $725, and, according to a poll conducted during Loren's freshman year, nearly 80 percent of the student body held down a job. The Board of Regents, mindful of these statistics, struggled to keep fees at a minimum. Tuition was $1 per credit hour in the arts and humanities, $2 in the sciences.

Although it was a less than ideal arrangement, Loren was able to save on expenses by shuffling between his parents' home and that of the Prices. Since it does not seem that he held a job nor that he received an academic scholarship, it would appear that Buck was covering the cost of his books and tuition. In any event, the myth of Jazz Age prodigality found no substantiation in Loren's case, as Jac Cave would verify in a letter to his friend some fifty years later: "I was not so good at studies so drifted to other things, but you continued on with study and books your main love."[4] So it was; yet the scales could easily have tipped in the opposite direction. "I had never known anything to last so long," Loren later wrote of his undergraduate education. "Eight years and in them death, illness, boredom, uncertainty, at a time when others went straight to their careers, or to whom doors were opened. Eight years that might as well have been a prison. Perhaps they were in that I could not get outside the ring, the ring of poverty."[5] For some the twenties were a decade that roared, for others a time of heavy squalls.

Loren entered the university with the intention of majoring in science, not because he was particularly adept in the laboratory, for he was not, but because he was automatically drawn to the environment that had sheltered him since childhood—Nature.[6] His intellectual interests had never been narrowly channeled, and he soon realized that he was temperamentally ill-suited to operate within the confines of a technical curriculum. Besides geology and zoology, he took courses in sociology and philosophy, including ethics, logic, and cosmology. A semester rarely passed without an English or literature course appearing on his schedule. Curiously for a scientist in the making, he succeeded in avoiding mathematics, not to mention chemistry and physics. He did try his hand at foreign languages, another chronic academic weakness, albeit to little positive effect. Loren was permanently excused from ROTC. No cause was noted, but it seems likely that poor eyesight kept him out of the ranks.[7]

Though Loren had been a class leader in high school, he was intimidated by the impersonal nature of his new and less protected surroundings. He did not see his old friends as often as before and withdrew increasingly into a world of his own. Neither a fraternity man nor a social campus figure, he confessed to a lack of nerve when it came to seeking this kind of status.[8] His academic performance during this first semester was a mixed bag. English composition, in which he scored a 95, was his best subject by far. He also did well in zoology, earning a solid 85. Geology was another matter; he scored a very weak 62. He failed Spanish, a blot on his record that would haunt him in years to come.

His overall performance the second semester was little better, except that he failed no courses. Matters were made worse by the fact that he suffered the consequences of an unprofessional act over which he had no control. Buoyed by his excellent showing in English 3, he had enrolled in the second half of the course, only to be confronted by the incensed professor after submitting his first assignment. "You didn't compose this," he was told. "It is too well written."[9] Loren was catapulted back into his high-school nightmare. While the professor could not prove his charge of plagiarism, neither could Loren, who was easily threatened, summon up the courage to defend himself. He was living with the Prices at this time. Buck, sensing that something was amiss, finally persuaded his reticent nephew to tell him what had happened. Loren concluded his story by asserting that he was not about to continue his studies. No more willing to let the youth squander his future in this instance than he had been when Loren had dropped out of Lincoln High School, Buck went to the university to discuss the situation with the supervisor of Loren's high-school English teachers, Letta May Clark. Miss Clark was deeply sympathetic, but she had some serious reservations about the wisdom of approaching Loren's professor directly. Nevertheless, she assured Buck that she would see what could be done. She encountered Frederick Stuff, chairman of English at Teachers High, while walking across campus and relayed the story to him. He immediately recognized the situation for what it was: "Don't think anything more of it" was Stuff's purported reply. "I'll take care of it."[10] He proved as good as his word; Loren returned to the university, if not to the class of his accuser, having withdrawn from English 4 without earning any credit but with his reputation intact.[11]

Because he had failed Spanish and withdrawn from courses in English and philosophy, Loren completed his first year with only twenty-one hours of credit, some nine hours less than he needed to be classified as a sophomore. He made up this lost ground by attending both summer sessions in 1926, earning the maximum twelve hours' credit in zoology (evolution and genetics), geology (elementary paleontology), sociology (social psychology), and applied physiology. His grades, the equivalent of an A and three B's, were much improved, a seeming indication that he had righted himself at last.

Loren enrolled in but two courses during the fall of 1926, English literature and French 2. He made a 90 in English, but, as before, a foreign language proved his undoing. Instead of earning five hours of credit in French, he received a C, which stood for "conditional," a polite way of saying that he had failed. According to a university regulation, any student who did not pass more than half his hours in a given semester was subject to automatic suspension for a minimum of one academic term. Loren was thus forced to withdraw after the first semester of the 1926–27 academic year.[12] Looking back on some of the "mad irrevocable thing[s]" one does in youth, he mused, "We set clocks working in a future still not gained, persuade some destiny not decided, to be ours."[13]

II

Exactly when Loren hopped his first freight train is impossible to say, but he had been riding the boxcars for at least three or four years, both alone and with his friend Jac Cave. His niece, Athena, remembered that he paid more than one visit to her parents, Leo and Mamie, while they were living in Colorado Springs. Mamie sometimes packed a picnic lunch, and the four of them would climb aboard a lineman's handcar, Loren and Leo working the dual-handled pump. "We didn't even know the train schedules," Athena laughingly recalled. "We'd go through tunnels and all over."[14]

Though vague as to both his whereabouts and the chronology of his wanderings, Loren traveled through much of the American West. "If you are young and there is speed in your blood," he wrote in 1933, "you begin as a passenger stiff. . . . Going is the business of your class, and as a young novitiate you grit your teeth on the decks of passengers hurtling through mile-long tunnels and strive to equal the time records of paid fares." The times to beat were chalked on water tanks as much as a thousand miles apart. "It does not matter that there is no place for you to go and only yard bulls to greet you upon your arrival."[15]

It was not until after sundry encounters with aggressive railroad detectives that Loren began to take notice of the older and still relatively healthy members of the wandering brotherhood, who showed no particular concern for timetables and matters of speed. "When this fact was first brought home to me I considered it, with the usual cockiness of youth, to be a loss of nerve due to advancing age. I pitied these elderly stiffs and was moved to sighs." Fast freights were plentiful; hence he saw no good reason to jump the slow trains making all the local stops—trains known scornfully in the jargon as "peddlers."

One day, however, in a little town below the Sierra Nevada, Loren missed the afternoon's last highballing freight. Too impatient to linger, he jumped a peddler, which labored forward under the combined efforts of three throbbing engines. Hobos by the score lined the roofs of the boxcars. They chugged for miles through the stifling heat of the Sacramento Valley; the rhythmic clicking of steel on steel finally lulled Loren to sleep. Toward evening he awoke. "The scene that presented itself might have been some modern evangelist's dream of the last train arriving in Paradise. There were dreary faces, mad faces, happy faces, evil faces. The wise were not with us."[16] Apple orchards, redolent of the great harvest to come, spread out on either side, as far as the eye could see. The hungry men began climbing down off the undulating cars to fill their ragged pockets and dingy caps with nature's unexpected bounty. They swung back aboard, the scene repeating itself for miles along the steep grade. In the late sunlight with the pine scent of evening already in the air, it seemed to Loren that he and his nameless companions "had slipped tunnel-like through time," phantom travelers on a phantom track, running from the past, the present, and the future.

During the time Loren was forced to withdraw from the university, his parents sought their own reprieves from their baneful existence. Clyde, his stomach ulcers flaring up with increasing frequency, continued to earn a small living as a traveling salesman. Jaundiced and drawn, he spent most of his spare hours alone in stark rooms or among the artificial palms in small-town hotel lobbies. In the end, he preferred this way of life, which provided him with some measure of peace, coming home only to check on his unbalanced wife and exchange his soiled shirts for freshly laundered ones. Daisy, too, sought her own form of escape from the blighted affection and Victorian dinginess of South Twenty-second Street. She read adventure stories such as *The Black Pirate* by Mac Burney Gates and *The Roughneck* by Robert Service.[17] She occasionally disappeared for weeks, sometimes months, hiring herself out as a domestic on the farms and in the small towns of eastern Nebraska. Loren preferred not to know the details of his mother's peregrinations.

III

The running man always finds his way home somehow. Loren was readmitted to the university in the summer of 1927. He enrolled in both six-week terms and earned eleven hours of credit. Strangely, the only course in which he performed indifferently was English 137: Browning. It was offered by none other than eighty-year-old Dr. Lucius Adelno Sherman, whose "scientific method" of teaching literature, used in Loren's high school, is alleged to have caused the iconoclastic H.L. Mencken to snort, "God help the poor yokels!"[18]

He eked out a 70 but scored in the high 80s and 90s in everything else.

Loren's lackadaisical showing in Browning may have had little to do with the pedagogical techniques of his Victorian professor. The mature-looking but awkwardly shy young man had recently become infatuated with another member of the class, an older woman whose acquaintance he had made during his senior year at Teachers High. He scribbled lines of poetry to her on pages in his notebooks. Although she could not help but be flattered, she also felt it her duty to remind Loren that his studies must come first. "Remember," she wrote next to some verse he composed in another of his classes, "this is a history course."[19]

These were not the first words that Mabel Langdon, a somewhat frail, dark beauty, wrote in the margins of Loren's papers. They had met two years earlier, in 1925, after Mabel was placed under the supervision of Letta May Clark for the purpose of completing her student teaching requirement in English. She began reading Loren's work and responded by drafting notes of encouragement on virtually every one of his written assignments. Thinking that Miss Clark would surely be interested in a student possessed of the young Eiseley's literary ability, Mabel approached her supervisor, only to learn that she had already compiled an extensive file on the youth. It seems that every one of his English teachers had told Letta Clark a similar story and, as Mabel later quipped, "They'd all like to claim him."[20]

The eldest of three children, Mabel was born on July 9, 1900, in Hastings, a bustling community in southeastern Nebraska. The Langdons had come to the state as homesteaders but went broke trying to wrest a living from the intractable prairie sod. Unable to pursue his dream of becoming a lawyer, Mabel's father, George, taught in several country schools.

An Irish Catholic, George married Edith Bingaman, a Methodist farmer's daughter with a high-school education. He stopped teaching after the birth of his first child and joined the Burlington line as a brakeman about 1902. He worked on the line for forty-four years. Mabel recalled that money was always scarce when she was young, yet the family was never without sufficient food and clothing and the wry sense of humor that her parents shared. Her pleasant childhood was marred only by her parents' insistence that she serve as a model for her younger sister, Dollie, and brother, Charles.

By the time Mabel was ready to begin high school in 1914, the Langdons had moved to Fairfield, a small town southeast of Hastings. Despite her school's small numbers, Mabel seems to have received an excellent education. In addition to seven semesters of English, she took two years of Latin and one of German, as well as American and European history, algebra, and geometry. Her work in the sciences was not as extensive, but she completed one semester each of botany, chemistry, and physics. After graduating in 1918, Mabel found herself in the same financial position as her father had when he was her age. Yet George, who "believed that every woman ought to know how to support herself," sent his daughter back to Hastings to attend the local business school while living with her grandmother. An excellent student, Mabel completed her course of study in less than the prescribed academic year and received several job offers. She liked Hastings and, after considerable deliberation, accepted a position with the Gaston Music and Furniture Company.

Mabel was hired as a secretary, but she had other duties, which occasionally allowed her to leave her desk. The young woman had taken piano lessons since the age of eight. According to those who heard her play, she performed exceptionally well. She loved Scott Joplin as well as classical music, and her proficiency enabled her to demonstrate sheet music to Gaston's customers on Saturday evenings, when the girls with more seniority were off work. Reflecting on this period of her life, Mabel thought that the three years she spent in Hastings were "very informative and good for me, because they taught me how to do a job. . . . I learned my lessons that way."[21]

In the meantime, the railroad transferred George to Lincoln. The Langdons' standard of living had improved to the point where the family was able to purchase a modest but comfortable frame home at 2435 D Street. It was here that Mabel came to spend her vacation in the summer of 1921. Her father, finally in a position to provide his eldest child with the higher education he had been denied, persuaded Mabel to quit Gaston's and move to Lincoln in time to enter the University of Nebraska in mid-September.

Mabel possessed a reserved elegance. Her slender frame and long legs made her appear taller than her five feet, five inches. Her high, sculptured cheekbones, delicate mouth, and penetrating blue eyes might have taken her far as a model had she chosen to leave Nebraska for a center of high fashion. As one lifelong friend remarked,

"Mabel looked like she came from Sheridan Boulevard," the most fashionable part of Lincoln in those days.[22]

Mabel graduated from the University of Nebraska in June 1925 with a major in English and a minor in French history. An honors student, she had been elected to Phi Beta Kappa that spring.[23] She left Lincoln in September to undertake her first and only teaching position in Arnold, an isolated village in the central part of the state. Though the young woman had not seen her most promising pupil since the last day of classes at Teachers High, Loren was still very much on her mind. Hoping to encourage him as a writer, she purchased a collection of plays by the Norwegian dramatist Henrik Ibsen, which she took to Loren's home before leaving the city. Loren had not yet returned from California, so Mabel left her little gift, with a note. She did not know it at the time, but her visit, on September 3, coincided with Loren's eighteenth birthday.[24]

Mabel departed without realizing just how deeply attached she had become to life in the city. The starkness of central Nebraska's treeless autumn landscape soon made her homesick. She sought to overcome her melancholy by devoting as much time as possible to her classroom duties. The few hours that she had to herself were spent reading the novels of Charles Dickens, Henry James, Jane Austen, and William Makepeace Thackeray. She also wrote poetry, indeed admitted to harboring "suppressed ambitions" as a writer, and was deeply pleased when a few of her works were later published. Her tastes in this field ran to the then emerging poets Edwin Arlington Robinson, G. K. Chesterton, Archibald MacLeish, Robinson Jeffers, Carl Sandburg, and Nebraska's own John G. Neihardt. Mabel was equally certain about her dislikes. For her graduation from college a well-meaning aunt and uncle had presented their niece with a leather-bound volume by the folksy, sentimental bard Edgar Guest. Mabel promptly hid the book in the attic.[25]

Although Loren and Mabel first met while he was a student and she was a teacher, they came to know each other mainly through the letters they exchanged during Mabel's year in Arnold. Touched by her gift of Ibsen's plays, Loren initiated the correspondence, which concentrated on their favorite works of poetry and literature. "Some may think Loren gave me my love for poetry," Mabel once wrote. "Not so. I used to spend my spare hours memorizing poems that I liked. At the time Loren and I met I was avidly collecting 'new' poetry from such magazines as then existed: *Bookman—Harper's—*

Atlantic & others." These works she copied and sent to Loren in Lincoln; he reciprocated by forwarding works that caught his eye. "Early in our acquaintance Loren said delightedly, 'You're the only person I've found who likes the same kind of poetry that I do.' "[26]

Despite the fact that her students and an appreciative administration hated to see her go, Mabel gave up teaching with no regrets. She returned to her parents' home in the early summer of 1926 and immediately began taking courses toward a master's degree in English. She saw Loren quite often, albeit discreetly, for the difference of seven years in their ages—which they went to great lengths to conceal—made them both uncomfortable when in the company of others. The couple spent much of their time together in private, reading favorite works, including their own, aloud. When they did venture out, it was usually to walk the winding banks of Salt Creek hand in hand, or to survey the woods now known as Wilderness Park at First Street and Van Dorn. Loren later evoked one of these fondly remembered days together in a touching inscription to Mabel in *Cavender's House* by the reclusive Edwin Arlington Robinson:

> This to Mabel, so that when life is somewhat more dusty than it is now she may remember the wood-lilies—and how we hid above Salt Creek when it was all dappled sun-gold and leaf shadow. And having remembered that far she will think kindly of Glitter Wing, the blue dragonfly so generous that he allowed his dinner to escape alive—probably because its taste was singularly unedifying! Remember Glitter Wing, like us betrayed by summer, his destiny to forsake the sun-paths and shiver to a pinch of jeweled dust at the first touch of frost. Remember Glitter Wing—his dust was jeweled.
>
> Larry[27]

IV

In October 1926 a dozen or so University of Nebraska undergraduates, all males, founded the Wordsmith Chapter of Sigma Upsilon, a national literary fraternity. Meetings were usually held once a month, either in the homes of individual members or in the basement of the local YMCA. Students brought manuscripts of their essays, short stories, and poetry to read aloud. They then sat back to listen to the critical comments of their small but dedicated audience. The honorary fraternity's influence was so negligible in the beginning that it received no mention in the university catalog under the heading of recognized societies.

The only faculty member of Sigma Upsilon was its adviser, Assistant Professor of English Lowry Charles Wimberly, a newly minted Ph.D., son of a Presbyterian minister, and grandson of a former slave owner and Confederate soldier. His mother, May Lowry, was a pioneer schoolteacher whose father, a cotton grower, had also owned slaves and fought for the South in the Civil War. Although Wimberly had spent most of his adolescence and young manhood in the Midwest, he retained something of his aristocratic ancestry in both his looks and his bearing. Angular to the point of gauntness, the sharp-featured young academic possessed a high forehead and deeply knit brow, penetrating yet sad, dark eyes, an elongated nose, and pursed lips, which curled outward beneath his brush of a mustache as he spoke. His laugh was closer to a snicker, for the burden of being a minister's son had stifled his spontaneity. While Wimberly could be as "common as an old shoe," his humility masked a deep strain of fierce pride and enduring melancholy.

Members of Sigma Upsilon had been attracted to his witty, incisive lectures punctuated by the waving of bony hands and flying elbows. Wimberly incited his students to probe more deeply than they ever had before. Yet he sometimes expressed profound disappointment at the questionable rewards of having worked his way up from the position of desk clerk and general handyman in a Nebraska hotel. "Intellectuals lose the capacity for happiness," he confided to a friend. "The deeper the mind probes, the less spontaneously it reacts to enjoyment." He didn't believe he had known true happiness after reaching the age of thirty and had come to detect a hollow ring in his own laughter. The only people who succeed in clinging to their illusions, he thought, are those who have not opened a book since third grade. Marx, Darwin, Freud, and Einstein had changed how men of his generation—and all generations to come—would look at the world and the universe.[28]

A student of coincidence, which he thought was seldom accidental, Wimberly was disdainful of all modern science with the exception of anthropology, which was crucial to his area of scholarly interest and had not been reduced, like physics and chemistry, to a series of passionless laws. Indeed, he believed that scientists were destroying the only things that give life fundamental meaning: myth, religion, folklore, literature, and music. He loved the Lorelei cry of the wild prairie winds, the creak of heavy tree branches, lightning and driving summer rains, the purr of a contented cat resting against his thigh. Of all the twentieth-century novelists, he believed that only Faulkner, the student of decadence and subnormality in the Deep South, would stand the test of time. Barely pausing to draw a breath after completing his Ph.D., he plunged into additional research on witches, ghosts, goblins, fairies, changelings, and other supernatural forms. The resulting manuscript, *Folklore in the English and Scottish Ballads*, was published by the University of Chicago Press in 1928 and immediately hailed by experts as a classic of its kind.

Despite his academic accomplishments, Wimberly had been unable to write the fiction and poetry of which he constantly dreamed. Scholarly publication had taken precedence; besides authoring several articles and two lengthy monographs, he had coedited a book of essays on agriculture. Still, the young professor found the time to compose a few poems, which were published anonymously in the *Daily Nebraskan*. Writing under the nom de plume Merus Andritt, he also contributed a number of short stories and some poetry to *The Sunshine State and Progress Magazine*. The young men of Sigma Upsilon were well aware of their frustrated adviser's sympathy toward anyone who shared the compulsion of putting words on paper in the hope of one day seeing them in print. When V. Royce West, a fraternity member, thought of a way to facilitate that process, he hastened to Wimberly's office in Andrews Hall, where he tried out his idea on "the Doc."

Would it not be possible, West wanted to know, for Sigma Upsilon to sponsor a campus literary magazine? Everyone realized how difficult it was for unknown midwestern writers to publish in the established popular periodicals, most of which were headquartered in the eastern cultural bastions of Boston and New York. After all, Harriet Monroe had succeeded in 1912 in starting her famous *Poetry: A Magazine of Verse*, the first of the so-called little magazines. Scores, eventually hundreds, followed. West and the other members of Sigma Upsilon were particularly drawn to John T. Frederick's *Midland*, published in Iowa City; *The Frontier*, out of the University of Montana; and the *Southwest Review*, published on the University of Texas campus. If Wimberly would agree to become involved, West would present his idea at the next fraternity meeting. The Doc's normally sad eyes began to twinkle.

Aware that additional faculty support was essential if the fledgling enterprise was to have any prospect of success, Wimberly approached Lucius Sherman, the octogenarian head of his department. Although Wimberly and Sherman held polarized views on the teaching of literature, Sherman was sympathetic toward the project and agreed to serve on the two-man advisory board. He was joined by Robert Douglas Scott, a dyed-in-the-wool grammarian and no-nonsense director of Freshman English.

By November 1926 the magazine had taken shape and after considerable discussion was dubbed *Prairie Schooner*. The editors then commissioned a logo: a pioneer walking alongside a canvas-covered wagon drawn by a yoke of straining oxen. A full-column front-page story announcing the literary magazine's approaching publication appeared in the *Daily Nebraskan* on November 10. Sigma Upsilon's days of obscurity on campus were at an end.[29]

V

The biographer and critic Leon Edel once observed that Concord, Massachusetts, was a place where one could hear "a great scratching of pens" during the mid–nineteenth century: those of Nathaniel Hawthorne, Ralph Waldo Emerson, Louisa May Alcott, Henry David Thoreau, and Margaret Fuller, among many others.[30] Rudolph Umland, a gifted writer and a longtime friend of Lowry Wimberly, described Lincoln, Nebraska, in much the same way after the *Prairie Schooner* was born. "From every nook and cranny in the city poets and storytellers crawled. Scribble, scribble went their busy pens. Tap-tap-tap went the keys of their typewriters. From that single decade [1927–1937] came three geniuses and a dozen other writers of books," not to mention countless journalists, essayists, publishers, and editors. The geniuses, as Umland saw it, were the dauntless western novelist and historian Mari Sandoz, the dispirited, ultimately suicidal poet Weldon Kees, and the melancholy literary naturalist Loren Corey Eiseley. Nearly all got their start in the pages of what quickly became known as Wimberly's *Schooner*. "Such a literary fervor as this had never prevailed before in the dull little city lying amidst the cornfields, sunflowers, and cocklebururs and shall probably never prevail again."[31]

As yet Loren had taken no courses with Wimberly and knew him only by sight. Mabel, by contrast, had, during her senior year in 1925, enrolled in Wimberly's Poetics 109, a class intended to teach an appreciation of poetry through the study of metric form and to provide assistance in the writing of original verse. After entering graduate school, Mabel enrolled in Wimberly's seventeenth-century literature course. He approached her after class one day to ask whether she had any poems of her own that might be suitable for publication in the *Schooner*. "No, I don't have any," she replied, "but I know a young man who is very talented and writes lovely poetry; you might be interested in him." Wimberly told Mabel to have her friend stop by his office. "Loren went over and introduced himself and they got along famously; and in a short time Wimberly did take some of Loren's poetry."[32]

In truth, the first of Loren's poems Wimberly accepted had been previously published in *The Freshman Scrapbook*, a recently defunct little campus magazine sponsored by the English Department. The fourth and final issue of the *Scrapbook*, containing two poems by Loren, was reprinted as a supplement to the July 1927 *Schooner*, whose editors were desperately in need of quality writing to fill the early issues. The longer of the two, "There Is No Peace," is particularly noteworthy, for it contains many of the elements that would dominate Loren's later writing—deep snows, wailing wind, deserted roads at midnight, burial places, fleeting time, shadows, tears, and death:

Through the cold light of the moon before me and behind me
Was the Fall of tears, the awful sound of time upon the wing,
Cold laughter, and the fall of shadowy feet.
This is the iron harvest of the years;
There is no peace.[33]

This bleak narrative poem was followed by an equally somber offering called "Cinquains," a series of five-line stanzas bearing the following titles: "Fear," "Despair," and "Night in a Graveyard."

Men die
Grass crawls over
Cities and builders. Why
Should I be glad a child is born
Tonight?[34]

By October 1927 Loren had joined the *Schooner* staff as an associate editor and three more of his pieces appeared in the magazine. The most interesting of these is an impressionistic prose sketch titled "Autumn—A Memory." Based on a visit to the Aztec Ruins National Monument near Farmington, New Mexico, where Old Purgatory had been fitted with new brake bands, the sketch, like his early poetry, evokes the major concepts and attitudes that informed the author's lifework. Although he was barely twenty, the eloquent literary style makes it difficult to distinguish Loren's elegiac meditation from the longer essays composed decades later:

> The round stone pits of the kiva were deserted and the walls were crumbling. It is a lonely thing to look on men's broken handiwork and muse wide-eyed over their disappearance. . . . Still, perhaps it was their dust that floated in a slight breeze over the ruined wall. . . .
>
> There may have come a time when the offended god turned his face away, when prayers and the gay-colored prayer stones and the holy medicine lost power and men died in gasping heaps. . . . Or maybe the harvests burned. Did any live to go . . . ?
>
> Starlight and dust in starlight. . . . Does it matter now at all . . . ?[35]

Loren's two other pieces in this issue, "Death in Autumn" and "Graveyard Studies," appeared under the pen names Eronel Croye (an anagram for Loren Corey E.) and Silas Amon, a necessary ruse first employed by Wimberly to disguise the fact that publishable material remained scarce.

Wilbur "Bill" Gaffney, an elfin young man of dark features, dancing gray eyes, and puckish wit, also joined the editorial staff of the *Schooner* in 1927 and found that Wimberly and his student editors cared nothing about one's social and economic background. It was here that he met Loren, "who was not a proper southsider but a working man's son. That gave us a certain amount of kinship."[36]

Loren and Bill loved to take long walks together in the countryside surrounding Lincoln. Their more ambitious excursions took them southwest of the city to the bucolic village of Denton, a distance of some ten miles as the crow flies. Their standard fare on these expeditions was a bar of German chocolate—nourishing but not so sweet as to arouse thirst. The high hills gave them an unobstructed view of the city skyline, which was dominated by the state capitol. Near Denton they crossed three or four miles of unfenced land, which the two fancied was the closest thing to moors they might ever see. They quoted stanzas by Tennyson, Coleridge, Wordsworth, and Yeats from memory.

On other occasions the pair ventured north of town to the old military academy on Belmont Hill, then back along the Northwestern tracks bordered on either side by deep blue ponds and ringed with gleaming deposits of salt.

Although they agreed on many things, the two sometimes differed in their opinions concerning the new generation of poets. Whereas Bill was tepid when it came to the works of Robinson Jeffers, Loren waxed enthusiastic over the alienated master of Tor House—the personification of Wimberly's twentieth-century man who knew too much. Jeffers had moved so far west that he came to the end of the land. In Carmel, California, on the Monterey Peninsula, he built a granite house and observation tower with his own hands. There he worked in splendid, albeit tortured, isolation, the mountains and sea his backdrop. Man, Jeffers asserted in his poem "Contrasts," is inferior to animals and natural objects: "There is not one memorable person to stand with the trees, one life with the mountains." Bill recalled of Loren: "As to his pessimism, he had the same sense as Jeffers had [that] the world is gradually going down hill and we will all wind up in the grave, forgotten except for a few inscriptions."[37]

All was not gloom and doom on the "moors" and salt flats of eastern Nebraska. Loren was also interested in certain of the more popular humorists, such as A.A. Milne, the creator of the immortal Christopher Robin and Winnie-the-Pooh, and Don Marquis, the protégé of Joel Chandler Harris, author of the *Uncle Remus* stories. Loren and Bill both followed the syndicated adventures of Marquis's characters mehitabel, the alley cat who believed she had been Cleopatra in a former incarnation, and archy, the cockroach poet and storyteller who typed all of his manuscripts without punctuation and in lower case because, according to a well-known law of physics, no cockroach could hop on two keys at the same time. Bill and Loren sometimes made up risqué limericks, which they recited back and forth, but these hardly approached the vulgar. Another friend who spent considerable time with Loren during the thirties observed: "I never heard him use a dirty four-letter word but he occasionally said goddam and called certain individuals he didn't like bastards."[38]

The two always carried notebooks in their shirt pockets in case their muses should chance to pay a call. At times these blank pages were put to less exalted use. Like schoolboys, they would sit down on the bank of a pond or stream and fashion little paper boats. The young bards especially loved the north side of Capital Beach Lake, located on a salt flat. They walked the gently sweeping arc of rimed shore, occasionally bumping shoulders, Loren pointing out flora and fauna that Bill "wouldn't have begun to recognize." The prevailing summer wind blew salt spray into their deeply tanned faces, while an inland species of gull darted and cried in the distance. For a brief while it seemed to them that Nebraska was partly covered again by the great sea that had once washed over everything from central Mexico to the southern border of Canada. Short man and tall, light of foot and heavy, they turned homeward reluctantly, Tennyson's lines, which Bill was fond of quoting on occasions such as this, wafting on the freshening breeze:

In the afternoon they came into a land
in which it seemed always afternoon.[39]

VI

Rudolph Umland got his first glimpse of Loren Eiseley while walking across campus one chilly morning with Bill Gaffney. Loren stood alone in front of the Temple Theater, bareheaded, wearing a leather jacket, apparently lost in thought. Umland never forgot the impressive brow, "soaring up with a glacial whiteness. There was a quality of bleak aloofness in him and in his poetry you couldn't put your finger on."[40]

Loren was not the only campus persona to whom a certain air of mystery clung like a shroud. Lowry Wimberly trudged the streets of Lincoln in a dark overcoat and black Confederate-type slouch hat, his sallow face turned into the wind, a partly smoked cigar hanging from his thin, bloodless lips. Some saw him as a tragic, Poelike figure, not only in looks but in thought. Loren was fascinated by Wimberly from the moment they met; the sad-eyed editor of the *Prairie Schooner* rubbed off on the drifting young poet like lampblack.

Loren soon found himself assisting Wimberly in reading freshman themes for twenty-five cents an hour. Contrary to Loren's claim that "I never had a single course under Wimberly," he took English III, the Doc's two-hour term paper course, in the spring of 1928.[41]

He soon drew close enough to Wimberly to begin addressing him by his first name. With Bill the two visited a number of Lincoln's new "spiritual churches," an outgrowth of the resurgent postwar interest in the supernatural. The three quickly determined that most of those connected with the movement were "utter quacks" and "charlatans," but Wimberly refused to be completely dissuaded, no matter how asinine the performances. "Coincidences aren't meant to be scorned," he was fond of saying. "There is some force putting the patterns together."[42] As editor of the *Schooner*, he found it difficult to reject a well-written piece concerned with telepathy, precognition, clairvoyance, or any other branch of parapsychology. His own early *Schooner* stories, "Dispossessed" and "The Red Gentian," were based on certain of these very themes.

There is no question that Loren was very much interested in the paranormal as well, especially as represented by the more scholarly English school. He purchased many volumes on the subject over the next several years, including Frederic W.H. Meyers's *Human Personality and Survival of Bodily Death*, T.C. Lethbridge's *Ghost and Ghoul*, J.W. Dunne's *An Experiment with Time*, G. N. M. Tyrell's *Apparitions*, and Henry James's *Psychical Research*. He and Mabel, encouraged by Wimberly, began to experiment with the Ouija board. Loren had grown fond of the largely forgotten San Francisco poet George Sterling, an intimate of Robinson Jeffers and Jack London. Tall and thin, with a lock of gray hair crowning his elongated, Dantean face, Sterling had committed suicide by poisoning himself in November 1926. According to Bill, Mabel began receiving spirit messages in the form of poetry from Sterling a year or two later. Loren wrote down the lines and may even have incorporated some of them into his own early writing. He could never quite decide whether he believed in the messages or not, but they certainly had a ring of authenticity.[43]

Accounts of violent deaths, the gorier the better, also fascinated Wimberly. He purchased almost every issue of *True Detective*, *Master Detective*, *Inside Detective*, and *Startling Detective* and conjectured that if Shakespeare, Browning, and De Quincey were alive they too would be reading the crime magazines. On Saturday nights, though, the Doc was forced to settle for a more controlled form of mayhem. Accompanied by Loren, he attended illegal boxing matches, betting a dollar or two on the outcome of each fight. "They were the shabby little back street affairs of the depression," Loren recalled, "generally held in some local garage or something of that kind."[44] Men drank illegal hooch from amber-necked bottles wrapped in brown paper, puffed on cheap cigars, and turned ugly and vulgar when the fighters they backed hit the blood-splattered floor and failed to rise. Among the several books Loren purchased during this period was Alexander Johnston's *Ten and Out! The Complete Story of the Prize Ring in America* (1927).

Wimberly liked to go about town in threes. Bill remembered that the Doc and Loren were joined at the fights by Preston Holder, a physically rugged youth who rode the freights with reckless abandon and extolled the virtues of the classic boxing lithographs of George Bellows. Having crisscrossed the country by boxcar, Preston harbored fewer illusions than most young men of his generation and delighted in shocking his less worldly companions with spontaneous declarations such as "I lost my virginity in Amarillo." When Bill learned that Preston was also a Robinson Jeffers devotee and had thoughts of becoming a writer, he introduced him to Loren, and the two became good friends. Preston, like Loren, eventually turned to anthropology and rose to become sometime chairman of his department at Nebraska. This mutual interest may well have been stimulated by Wimberly, who had also thought of taking such a turn while writing his dissertation.

VII

In the three years that had passed since Loren had enrolled in the university, he had earned only sixty-one hours of credit, which meant that he was now a full year behind. He likened himself to a wolf attached to an invisible chain, padding endlessly "around and around the shut doors of knowledge. I learned, but not enough. I ran restlessly from one scent to another."[45] Some of the black marks on his lengthening transcript were the product of indifference; others were spawned by the same fear of the world shown by his deaf mother. When Loren's fellow students found themselves in the wrong course or were faced down by the occasional hostile professor, they went through the proper channels and dropped the class. Instead, Loren wrote, "I simply walked away and there the record stands. Bureaucracy intimidated me."[46] While his academic adviser was "a good man," he was unable to reconcile Loren's seemingly contradictory interests in the sciences and literature. An admitted underachiever, Loren was later to admonish his fellow educators: "I feel it so necessary not to lose sight of those late-maturing, sometimes painfully abstracted youths who may represent the Darwins, Thoreaus, and Hawthornes of the next generation." The good teacher should never grow indifferent to their possibility—"not, at least, if there is evidence even in the face of failure in some subjects, of high motivation and intelligence in some specific field."[47] Loren had looked back into time's mirror and seen his own reflection in the visages of his nineteenth-century heroes.

Only his writing and the enduring confidence of Mabel, the Prices, and a few professors such as Wimberly kept him from dropping out of the university for good. His poetry continued to reflect the tortured thoughts of an alienated young man overlooking a bleak prospect. In the spring of 1928 the *Schooner* carried what was the longest Eiseley poem to date, a haunting work titled "Spiders":

> *Time is a spider*
> *the world is a fly*
> *caught in the invisible, stranded web of space.*
> *It sways and turns aimlessly*
> *in the winds, blowing up from the void.*
> *Slowly it desiccates . . . crumbles . . .*
> *the stars weave over it.*
> *It hangs . . .*
> *forgotten.*[48]

The young author of "Spiders," who never sounds young, had only recently purchased the new English translation of Oswald Spengler's *The Decline of the West*. Loren's entry into this world of Germanic thought could have done nothing but strengthen his developing sense that mankind is part of a pattern of events and behavior independent of anyone's control. Lowry Wimberly put the matter less philosophically but more succinctly one day while gazing out his office window. He saw a bleak-faced Loren in the distance, plodding stoop-shouldered across campus. "Poor devil!" the Doc muttered. "He looks just as if he has been kicked off a freight train."[49]

5

DEATH OF A SALESMAN

I

Standing beneath a switch light in Sacramento, Loren opened the letter he had carried in his pocket since leaving San Francisco. He was already moving east on the freights in response to the summons he knew it contained: "Your father is dying, come home." It was March of 1928, but later he chose to enhance an already tragic event by setting it in the Great Depression, more than a year and a half in the future: "All over America men were drifting like sargasso weed in a vast dead sea of ruined industry. . . . Like thousands of other aging, unaggressive salesmen [Clyde] was expendable. His dismissal had been abrupt and brutal. He came home yellow and cadaverous."[1]

Clyde had resigned his position as a traveling salesman in the spring of 1927 and moved to his old hometown of Norfolk, where he took a job as store manager for the Thomsen Hardware Company. His ulcers continued to flare up, making it impossible for him to eat solid food and maintain his weight. After several months his light skin gradually turned yellow, a telltale sign of liver disease. Finally, in early March 1928, the hardwareman was diagnosed as having cancer. He resigned his position the following week and returned home to die.[2]

By the time Loren arrived in Lincoln, Clyde was confined to the living-room couch, unable to eat, a black exudate of blood trickling from the corners of his mouth. He showed his son the strange growth that had recently sprouted from his side. "Christ," Loren thought to himself, "he's done for." Loren left the house long enough to send a wire to Leo, who had remarried and recently moved from Florida to Newport News, Virginia. He stepped into the garage alone, where he put his head against a beam and wept.[3]

Clyde was admitted to St. Elizabeth's Hospital. Since the malignancy was too far advanced to contemplate surgery, there was nothing to be done but await the inevitable. The patient lay back among the pillows, racked, jaundiced, and emaciated, beyond speech, his heart unwilling to quit. Drugs were few and largely ineffectual against the intense pain. Looking back, Loren sometimes asked himself if he should have accepted the consequences and shot his father. In Clyde's ravaged body, only the hands remained unchanged. As one of his last conscious acts, he lifted them up, flexed his fingers, and looked at them curiously. Then he smiled softly, as if to say, "The hands [are] playthings and [have] to be cast aside at the last like a little cherished toy."[4]

Leo made his appearance in the final scene of the last act. For hours there had been no outward sign of consciousness. A nurse shouted in Clyde's ear, "Leo has come home." Slowly, to what Loren described as his boundless surprise, the dying man's eyes opened. "There was an instant of recognition between the two of them, from which I was excluded." Loren walked out into the white hall unnoticed. Leo, he reminded himself, was the offspring of his father's early manhood, of a first love who had perished in the springtime and of whom Clyde could never bring himself to speak. "I was loved, but I was also a changeling, an autumn child surrounded by falling leaves. My brother who had been summoned was the one true son, not I. For him my father had come the long way back, if only for a moment."[5]

Fifty-nine-year-old Clyde died at 3:30 in the afternoon on Friday, March 31. Carcinoma of the liver and stomach was listed as the official cause of death.[6] The body was taken to Norfolk on Sunday, and the services were held the following day at the Wolt Funeral Home. One Mr. Beels, a reader in the Christian Science church, officiated. Clyde was buried next to his parents in Prospect Hill Cemetery, not far from Anna Barbara and baby Esther. Mabel Langdon, who had met Loren's father only once, did not attend the services; for some unknown reason, neither did Buck, although Grace was there to comfort her widowed sister and bereft nephew.

So poor was the family that twenty years were to pass before Loren could afford to put a stone on his father's grave.[7] This bitter memory was made even more distasteful by the fact that the one person Loren had hoped would acknowledge his loss never did. "Jimmy Dawes was still in my home town, a few blocks from where I lived, but no note of condolence ever came."[8]

The death of one's father is one of life's crucial events. It is a deliverance as well as a blow. The surviving son, who often experiences a new sense of freedom, is also filled with dread. He begins to contemplate his own mortality: all at once, there is no more becoming, everything is being, unwinding.[9] When the vigil at Clyde's hospital bed finally ended, Loren noticed that he could no longer stand the ticking of the alarm clock in his bedroom. At first he tried to smother it with a blanket, but the ticking persisted as though it were coming from his own head. He lay for hours staring into the blackness of the slumbering house, his arms and legs invisible, like those of some disembodied spirit. Finally, out of desperation, he abandoned the attempt to sleep and passed the small hours trying to read. He did not know it at the time, but he had entered a new realm, from which there was no exit—a place he was later to call the Night Country.

This place had long been familiar territory to another member of the family, his aging grandmother Malvina. She watched for the light coming from beneath Loren's door and came to sit quietly at his side. He credited her with bringing him back from the precipice by retying the thread of his life to the world of the living: "I knew she had saved my sanity." Yet from this hour onward there remained in the back of his mind the nagging thought that the unlit bedroom door is the entrance to the tomb.[10]

Only rarely had Loren felt compassion for the deeply disturbed Daisy. Now that Clyde was gone and he was left alone with her scolding, raspy voice, his resentment solidified into a cold and calculated hatred. "Her conduct," he wrote, "was one long persecution of father. My mother was a woman who invited murder."[11] As if the emotional wounds of a harsh and solitary childhood had not been enough to last a lifetime, Loren was appalled by Daisy's conduct while Clyde lay dying. "I had heard her speak words to my father on his deathbed that had left me circling the peripheries of a continent to escape her always constant presence." She had leaned across Clyde's almost lifeless form, "asking harshly about his insurance."[12] From this moment on her image as an acolyte of Satan was forever fixed in Loren's mind's eye. In the seventeenth century one of the common superstitions about witches was that they did not weep, for empathy was a virtue alien to the Devil's disciples. "Daisy," Loren scrawled in a notebook, "was a woman who never wept; she made others weep."[13]

That Loren had endured much is certain, but Daisy also had her story to tell. Clyde had been an honest but meager provider at best, forcing her to work as a seamstress and part-time domestic. Her able-bodied son was still living at home or with relatives nearby, making painfully slow progress toward a university degree. Loren, who would soon be twenty-one, had never held a steady job and disappeared for weeks at a time. Clyde's small insurance policy represented all the money Daisy had. The little house on South Twenty-second Street, which was still heavily mortgaged, had to be rented out because she could not afford the monthly payments. A widow at age fifty-two, deaf and without options, Daisy soon joined Loren at her kindly brother-in-law's, becoming a member of what Buck's people in the South would have called "the poor relation."

II

Loren now found himself working in a strange, indeed macabre, place at midnight, not because he wanted to be there but because Daisy demanded that he contribute something to the family finances.[14] One of the Eiseleys' few friends had introduced him to the owner of a chicken hatchery. Following a perfunctory interview, he was put on the payroll as a combination night watchman and general attendant. He reset the alarm clock in the hatchery office every hour on the hour. When it rang, he awoke from a fitful slumber to walk up and down the long rows of huge, kerosene-fed incubators filled with sleeping embryos. During each round he read the temperature gauges, rotated trays containing hundreds of eggs, and checked the level of fuel in the heat lamps.

The late hours, the lack of uninterrupted sleep, and the psychic trauma of Clyde's recent passing combined to create an almost palpable air of menace and doom. "One had the feeling that something, someone not human, was walking down the aisle beyond, keeping pace with one's own steps, challenging even one's thoughts in the great humming hive."[15] The lifelong student of evolution also got his first sustained look at nature's darker side. In the hissing life machines of the factory the genetic road map sometimes blurred. Among the many perfect chicks were cheeping mutants, pitifully trying to stand on one leg or attempting to avert starvation by picking at feed with grotesquely twisted beaks. On seeing them, Loren shivered and thought of human wrecks hidden from sight in the attics of shamed households.

While it is not certain why Loren left the university for a second time in January 1928, indications are that his decision was based on his intense feelings for a vibrant young woman who had graduated from Nebraska in the spring of 1924 with a bachelor's degree in education. Having distinguished herself in the classroom, she, along with twelve of her peers, was initiated into the prestigious Order of the Black Masque, the university chapter of Mortar Board, a national senior honor society for women. Facial coverings in place, their hands ostentatiously hidden in the loose-fitting sleeves of their academic robes, the thirteen coeds posed for their official picture, which appeared in the 1924 *Cornhusker*. Another photo reveals a dark-haired, dark-eyed, sensuous woman clad in the open-collared chemise of a flapper.

Her special place in Loren's affections would never have been known were it not for a chance occurrence. A librarian discovered the rough, partially missing draft of an undated letter, written to a woman identified only as Lila, folded inside the young Eiseley's book on the history of boxing, a work purchased in 1927. Further evidence that the letter was written during the late twenties is provided by Loren's cramped pen strokes, which gradually broadened over the years. It seems that he had heard nothing from her for several months and was growing more anxious by the day. Hoping to pierce this vacuum of silence, he had written asking if anything was the matter. Lila had finally replied, telling him she had married a Mr. Graves the previous autumn. Loren responded in turn, and it is the draft of this letter that survives.

Although no one, including Mabel, Bill Gaffney, and Rudolph Umland, had ever seen Loren so much as put on a boxing glove, he created the illusion—doubtless inspired by his weekend outings with Lowry Wimberly—that he had taken several beatings in the ring of late, but nothing to compare with this withering assault on his emotions. Even worse, he had been bedridden when he'd received Lila's devastating announcement. Still, he lamely agreed that they should remain friends in spite of what had happened and even promised that he would pay her a visit:

> Your letter arrived when I was very ill with influenzal heart neurosis—hence my belated (and very envious!) congratulations. You're a real sport Lila, I'm going to take advantage of your invitation. Though first I've got to get well—I'm a very scrawny sight at present and don't know whether I'll ever be able to put on a glove again. Oh well, there are compensations, if not I'll be quitting while my nose is still in its usual prominent position. But I'm coming, yes indeed.
>
> Late last autumn—maybe about the time you were married—I went on a picnic with some friends down to a secluded spot in the hill country near Weeping Water—which if you've been down there you'll remember as one of the loveliest spots in this rather uninteresting State. I had taken a nice lacing from a fast man a day before and was properly bruised up and disgruntled. It was growing dusk when I and a friend went back up the winding road through the hills to get some dishes from the car. I walked wearily along nursing a battered eye when suddenly the utter silence of the place aroused me.
>
> . . . At that moment Lila, I saw you for one ecstatic instant clothed in a white dress walking toward me in the twilight down that hill.
>
> I stopped and gasped so audibly that Shorty asked me what was wrong.
>
> Do you understand Lila? I don't think for a moment there was anything supernatural about it. The place and the hour . . . combined with my overstrung mood made me the momentary victim of an hallucination I suppose. But that is a little of what I think of you. And there is no beautiful thing that doesn't make me lonely for your presence.
>
> I have read a few books—I have called myself a realist—I have no philosophy except the belief that the universe is indifferent and blind. And so believing why has one voice—your voice—and a few brief memories weight enough to drive me restless out of class rooms to the wasteland and the high white solitude of autumn stars? Why should I who believe that at the moment of my death I am as utterly obliterated as the torn leaf or the crushed ant be troubled by something out of reach when the years are passing and there is so much that is "sensible" to be attained and enjoyed?
>
> What is it you psychologists would call it a "fixation" a "monomania" or something?
>
> . . . I have been something of a failure I expect—I have taken

more beatings—physical and mental—than are respectable for any man and yet I think perhaps after all I am very lucky—and I know that I am proud.

To have loved something fine and high and lovely enough to make oneself forever unsatisfied and driven is a satisfaction even when one stumbles and fails.

I have that pride and the sweet fine gesture of your letter made sure it would remain.

So you see I shant need to shatter my last illusion. If anything it is reborn. The fact that someone else is a very lucky man alters nothing in my attitude. It makes you forever remote and unattainable, but it doesn't stop me from loving you. That's impossible. You will always be the ghost in the dusk on the road to Weeping Water, the suntanned little lady who was to tell me about silence up on the Navajo.

And you may expect me at the unexpected time.

Loren[16]

Loren had met Lila, or Miss Wyman as she was known to her pupils, when she was assigned to Teachers High School to begin student teaching in September 1923. It was for Miss Wyman's English V class that he had composed his essay about the fictional dog named Whiskers, the animal that was supposedly killed by a neighbor's pack of hounds. He would save the paper containing her praise of his writing for over fifty years.

To what degree, and under what circumstances, the romance blossomed is impossible to say. Although Lila may have been the first teacher Loren "vamped," one cannot be certain of her feelings for the youth, who was five years younger than she. In the letter he speaks only of the day when "we are all grown old and respectable," a day when he can call upon her "without exciting the neighbors' comment!," a possible sign that their assignations had turned some heads.

According to a niece and nephew, from whom most of Lila's story has come, their aunt fell in love with some unknown man while bound for India. He jilted her, and the resulting emotional trauma was so great that she was institutionalized in California after her return. It was probably there that she met the handsome, soft-spoken Robert Graves, a hotel manager, whom she may have married on the rebound, in 1926. Loren apparently saw little, if anything, of his first love after this, and he soon began to focus his attentions on Mabel.[17]

III

"Be something better than a hardware salesman," his father had said.[18] After Clyde died, Loren vowed that he would honor that final wish: "I tried to make whatever dream father had had of me into a reality."[19] He returned to the university in the summer of 1928 and completed one three-hour course during each of the two sessions. His schedule for the fall consisted of five courses: primitive religions, social economy, criminology, aesthetics, and the history of philosophy. At semester's end Loren had earned the highest overall marks of his undergraduate years, the numerical equivalent of four A's and a B-plus.[20]

Although the memory of his father motivated him academically, it was his father's death that caused Loren's mind to wander. He thought of Herman Melville, who, like himself, had been born into a poor family of distinguished colonial descent and was young when his father passed away. The great writer left school at fifteen, worked at many jobs, and in 1839 signed aboard as a cabin boy on a ship bound for Liverpool, an experience chronicled in his autobiographical romance *Redburn*. With an old map in hand, the title character wanders the streets in a doomed search for his vanished father. The map fails him, just as had the man who slipped into the void where his son could not follow.[21]

So closely had the son identified with the father that he attempted to fulfill one of his father's ambitions. Faye Munden, who had not seen Loren since their excursion to California the summer after high school, received a letter asking him to join his old friend in a commercial venture. They would go to Florida, where land was cheap, and open a chicken ranch, something Clyde had always dreamed of doing. Faye, who had married and started a family, reluctantly declined.[22] This illusion dashed, Loren created another. In 1928 or early 1929, he composed a sentimental poem titled "Deserted Homestead." The dedication—"For My Father"—that appears in holograph on the manuscript was omitted on publication. The salesman who had never owned any farmland was placed there in the memory of a grieving son:

His standing corn with mildew rusts
Forsaken on the hill.
The wild will cover up the road
Now his hands are still.[23]

Loren continued to search for parallels between their lives. Just as Clyde had lost his Anna, Loren lost his first love, Lila. It was a coincidence to be sure, but one that Loren turned into an imitative plaint. He had seen Clyde weep but twice: the first time when Loren was young and very ill, the second over the marriage partner of his father's early manhood. After Loren had grown up, he remembered weeping only twice himself: once alone in the garage as Clyde lay dying on the sofa, and once afterward over a woman.[24]

The physician who had ordered Clyde taken to the hospital was described by the son as a "callous" man who had infrequently visited his father's bedside. Now it was Loren's fate that hung in the balance. He listened while two of the university's doctors discussed his condition on the other side of a loose-fitting office door. " 'Tuberculosis,' the bellow came through the paneling. 'Advanced. Not much chance. . . . Prescription? All the milk he can drink. Maybe four quarts a day.' " The illness had come on suddenly while Loren was working in the chicken hatchery. He began to stagger under the burden of feed sacks he had once handled with ease. Shuddering at the thought that he might be accused of malingering, yet unable to help himself, he crept off to hide from the owner in an unlit shed, where he could lie down on the bags of stacked grain. His skin turned gray; his heart pounded and fluttered; his weight dropped from 170 to 140 pounds. "Basically what I needed was a graveyard. I put my hands over my ears to shut out the noise."[25]

Whether these events actually took place as Loren described them is open to question, for he habitually spun fact and fiction into a captivating but mingled yarn. He restructured and embellished this memory until it was transformed into the romantic tragedy of the disease that had killed many of his poetic forebears. He claimed that he sought the second opinion of a skilled private physician, who referred to his condition as one of incipient tuberculosis: "It's here, the rales, I mean, but faint, dubious." In point of fact, even this diagnosis was probably exaggerated, something the patient himself later indicated in a document scarcely meant for public scrutiny. Loren had contracted influenza, which developed into a pulmonary infection. The onset of secondary anemia posed some threat of tuberculosis, but little more.[26] The doctor told him to get as much rest as possible and also recommended that he leave Lincoln for the less humid climate of the West.

Loren asked Daisy for some of Clyde's insurance money, but she refused. A small sum had been left directly to him; he now withdrew it from the bank. "My mother never expected to see me again. Among the Coreys . . . no one went away except to die."[27] Grace insisted on accompanying her nephew west. She considered it not only her family duty but a Christian one in the literal sense, stemming from her testing experiences as a young wife. Buck had become a severe alcoholic after their marriage, downing between one and two quarts of whiskey a day. As a last resort he had turned to the teachings of Mary Baker Eddy, founder of the Church of Christ, Scientist. Not only was he cured of his alcoholism but a chronic lung disorder vanished and he discarded the glasses he had worn since law school.[28] To the Prices Buck's cure verged on the miraculous. Grace severed her Methodist ties and embraced her husband's newly found faith. This conversion also explains why Clyde's funeral, arranged with the assistance of his in-laws, was conducted by a reader in the Christian Science church.

According to Loren, he traveled with his aunt to the central Colorado town of Manitou (Manitou Springs), in the rugged foothills below Pikes Peak. There they rented a cabin and waited to see if the supposed lesion in his lung would calcify. As Loren explained later, "If it did you won; if it spread you lost."[29] Feeling claustrophobic, he occasionally wandered down to sit in the town square. His unoccupied mind raced endlessly; he did not even remember having had a book to read. The summer came and went. Finally the money ran out.

Loren returned to Lincoln in the fall of 1929. A visit to the doctor proved inconclusive. "Holding," was all he said. It would be better if Loren stayed out of school and returned to the West. By this time word of his illness had circulated among Loren's professors. One of them, a flamboyant poet named Orin Stepanek, came to see him. Stepanek's cousin, a wealthy widow, owned a vast tract of undeveloped land in the Mojave Desert east of Los Angeles, near Lancaster. She needed a caretaker there. Loren would have his own cabin and a Model T pickup. The desert air would do him a world of good. Stepanek had already written to his cousin about Loren; all he had to do was agree to go.

For the first time Loren traveled by Pullman to the West Coast. He then took a streetcar to Pasadena, where he waited for his new employer to pick him up. "Mrs. Lockridge," as he called her, finally arrived in the backseat of a Pierce-Arrow. The brown-haired widow of "distinct cultivation" was accompanied by a hulking chauffeur whose face was scarred and whose front teeth had been replaced with gold. Loren gave this largely fictional character the unlikely name of Nelson Goodcrown and claimed that he had once been an enforcer for the Detroit underworld.[30]

What Loren really wanted was to be left completely alone—freed from all responsibility—to think, to daydream, and to write. Mabel came out to visit for a few weeks, boarding with a nearby rancher. To the best of her recollection, all Loren had to do was keep an eye on the irrigation machinery, since the more productive grazing land was rented out. Mabel also met the pseudonymous Mrs. Lockridge, who seemed warm and kindly. Unlike Loren, Mabel had no reason to think that his employer, who spent most of her time in San Diego, was even remotely associated with the criminal element. As far as Nelson Goodcrown was concerned, she neither met nor saw anyone who so much as resembled the ponderous bodyguard of Loren's account.[31] Neither was Loren condemned to live in the ramshackle, pack rat–infested cabin of his writer's memory. Deeply tanned and looking surprisingly fit, he was photographed with Mabel, standing arm in arm next to what he described in a family album as "the house I lived in," the Model T in the background. The structure is not only solidly built but freshly painted, its one visible window topped by a gaily striped canvas awning.

Loren ended the story of his sojourn in the Mojave more dramatically than he began it. One night while his employer was away, a drinking party took place in the kitchen of the main house. "The men involved were part of an indeterminable underworld that seemed to circulate far out in Mrs. Lockridge's shadow." Someone, in a moment of drunken passion, fired a shotgun through the ceiling. Loren found out later that Mrs. Lockridge held him responsible for the vandalism, even though she knew that he owned no firearm and had no keys to the damaged residence. His health had improved in the dry, cloudless environment, and it seemed a good time to leave: "October is a traveling month for both birds and men."[32]

After his return to Lincoln, Loren ran into the professor who had arranged for his stay in the desert. "Mrs. Lockridge thinks you are mad," Stepanek fumed. "She wrote me that you had fired a shotgun through her roof." Since there was little Loren could say, he made no attempt to defend himself. "That was the last time I saw him."[33] So he wrote, but in fact he enrolled in Stepanek's Slavonic literature class in the fall of 1930.

IV

"On this perfect day, when everything has become ripe and not only the grapes are growing brown, a ray of sunlight has fallen on to my life: I looked behind me, I looked before me, never have I seen so many and such good things together."[34] So wrote Friedrich Nietzsche in his fanciful little autobiographical work, *Ecce Homo: How One Becomes What One Is*. Loren, who read the German philosopher, also wrote of a perfect day severed from time and reality—"the most perfect day in the world." It was among the last of his drifting days on the rails, and he could not remember the month or the year. Somewhere in the wheat fields of northwestern Kansas he had joined three others on the edge of a town. They pooled their meager change, bought some grape soda, and stretched out in the shade beneath a water tank. They drank the refreshing liquid slowly, with relish. Time seemed suspended: "We were just there. Birds of passage with no past, no future, no desires."

The thing that made this, of all days, so special to Loren was the company he kept; three nameless men who became metaphors for his yet undetermined lifework as an anthropologist and prose poet. The first, an Indian, looked like a warrior who might have ridden with the Chiricahua Apache leader Geronimo. His wild Tartar face, by some strange genetic twist, had floated down from the glaciated wastes of the Pleistocene. Then there was *homo universus*, a slight, brown figure of aristocratic bearing who could have flourished in any century and should have been carrying an ancient scroll of papyrus instead of a pair of soot-streaked goggles. "Ever heard of Atlantis?" he asked an astonished Loren. "The books are wrong. The location is wrong. They knew better in Egypt but that is all gone, too."

Loren dubbed the fourth member of the group, who sounds suspiciously like his friend Preston Holder, "the boxer from Olympus." While riding the tender of a locomotive the night before, Loren had watched him creep forward over the roof of a speeding passenger train. The youth then rose to his feet and clambered down into the coal car. He was the only man Loren had ever seen with the guts and agility literally to dance with death atop a hurtling express. After drinking their fill, the contented quartet of drifters stretched out to take a nap. "We had no destination. It was the perfect day, the centuries had finished their work, while we dreamed there in the shade of the water tower."[35]

Few of Loren's memories of his days on the rails were suffused with such nostalgia. He once claimed that he was nearly killed while returning from California to Clyde's bedside. The mail train was "hitting sixty" when the brakeman unlocked the car door next to where Loren was perched. " 'Get the hell off. Jump, you bastard,' he roared, shouldering me and trying to push me out above the pounding wheels." He struck Loren across the face and pushed him again. This half-crazed worker out of his father's time was trying to kill him for no reason other than the sheer pleasure of it. Loren assumed a boxer's crouch as the blows rained down. Suddenly a hot wire, "like that in an incandescent lamp," began to flicker in his brain. Gripped by an animal savagery, he had but a single thought: " 'Kill him, kill him,' blazed the red wire. 'He's trying to kill you.' " At that moment the train began to lose speed. Loren's adversary turned and rushed inside as suddenly as he had appeared. The railroad bulls would be alerted the moment the train rolled to a stop. Loren climbed onto the steel ladder, took a moment to steady himself, then jumped. He rolled over once and came up running.

Hours later he wandered into a hobo jungle in Provo, Utah, where he washed his bruised face and bloodstained clothing. He traveled with a grizzled drifter for the next several days. Before they parted company Loren's companion gave him a piece of advice. "Remember this: The capitalists beat men into line. Okay? The communists beat men into line. Right again?" He gestured toward Loren's still swollen face. "Men beat men, that's all. That's all there is. Remember it, kid."[36]

While his stay in the Mojave cured Loren of his pulmonary infection, it also left him restless, at odds with himself and his environment. Yet when he departed the great desert by freight in 1930, he emerged into an even harsher world than the one he was leaving behind. Along the rights-of-way were countless signs of the type posted by one local chamber of commerce: "Jobless men keep going. We can't take care of our own."[37]

He also entered a new social dimension: the "great underground world," someone once called it, peopled by tens of thousands of American men, women, and children of all ages, races, and descriptions. By day they sunned themselves on flatcars; by night they cooked their meager fare in blackened tin cans, then slept with one eye open, wrapped in old newspapers in nameless hobo camps. Many begged their way across the country; others stole anything that was not nailed down. They fought with bare knuckles, straight razors, and switchblade knives, had intercourse under dirty blankets in the dark corners of crowded freight cars, converged into pairs and small groups, then dispersed again, only to repeat the ritual down the line. Most were anxious for the next town but tired of it within a day and knew contentment only when the steel wheels were clicking beneath them, the fence posts hypnotically slipping by. Some worked, but rarely for long; the jobs did not last, and the pay was always too low to kindle hope. There were strange characters among them and ordinary ones, criminals and misfits, too many fools and sinners to count, an occasional genius or saint. It was a time of hatred, a time of love, a time of hunger, a time of sharing. In sum, it was all that every generation encounters, but on a scale previously unknown in the United States. No one quite understood how it came about or who was responsible, let alone how to get out of it. Yet all agreed that there was only one name for this vast and seemingly endless trail of human misery—the Great Depression.

It seemed to Loren that half of America was on the move. Like leaves in windrows, the dispossessed gathered beside the Union Pacific, the Rock Island, the Santa Fe, the Katy. At night their fires blinked like the bivouacs of great armies on the outskirts of cities under siege. There were no more apple orchards of the kind he remembered in the foothills of the High Sierras; no more dreams of nirvana in the big rock candy mountains.

In 1935 the *Prairie Schooner* published a second piece based on Loren's days as a drifter. It recounts the meeting of two young men on a freight bound for Kansas City one chill autumn night. The narrator, a robust and ruggedly independent sort, has just stolen an overcoat before swinging aboard a gondola, where three other men sit huddled in some straw in the forward end. A slender youth, blackened with coal dust, is standing alone to one side. The two strangers strike up a conversation.

As the narrative unfolds, it becomes evident that Loren has projected himself into the character of the kid, who is desperately trying to reach Leavenworth in the hope of spending the winter with a former employer. There are hollows under his frightened eyes; his mouth moves in a sick tremble; beads of sweat cover his fevered brow despite the cold; and he sometimes speaks "like he [is] a little off." He is returning from Rochester, Minnesota, and the famed Mayo Clinic. He hands the reluctant narrator the doctors' report, but there is no need for him to strike a match and read it. The symptoms are unmistakable: the pitiful young man is dying of tuberculosis.

"But you'll make Leavenworth all right. You live there don't you?" his companion asks him.

"I ain't got no home" is the reply. "I'm just goin' there. I ain't never had no home."

"Poor devil," the narrator muses just before they part company, "running from himself, I suppose."[38]

Loren's stories of the rails are many and almost always filled with high drama. Once, somewhere in Colorado after sunset, he caught a freight on the fly after a mad dash from behind a lighted signboard. They crossed over into Kansas, and he moved to an iron ladder behind the tender, determined to ride the express into another dawn. Fatigue set in. He recounted later, "I was starting to fall asleep in the most dangerous spot in the world, the spot from which others had never awakened." His hands became numb; he was too weak to climb up onto the coal or back to the relative safety of the blind. When the train finally stopped his muscles were so cramped he could scarcely walk. He asked a switchman where they were and was stunned to find out that Kansas City lay just ahead. "Good God, I thought. I've crossed a state almost in one run. You fool, you utter fool . . . you could be dead."[39]

Many of these journeys were products more of Loren's imagination than of firsthand experience. Whereas Melville had gazed out on billowing wheat fields from his second-story window in rural Massachusetts, transforming them into giant swells on which men risked their lives amid the rigging of tall ships, Loren's imaginary characters bobbed and weaved with death atop the boxcars of hurtling freights. Stimulated by his father's repressed wanderlust, he read the pulp magazine *Railroad Stories* and listened attentively while others, like Preston Holder, related their experiences on the rails. Bill Gaffney put the matter quite simply: "Eiseley was rather shy and physically frail; he traveled inside cars. Holder was physically rugged and often 'rode the rods,' or hung precariously between cars, or, in the countryside with no tunnels, rode the running boards that topped boxcars."[40]

Rudolph Umland, who did little but ride the freights from coast to coast between 1929 and 1931, echoed Bill's impressions.

> He could not have survived a long period of "drifting." The longest stretch he probably accomplished was the week or ten days during August–September 1930, when his mother wouldn't or couldn't send him any money and he had to beat his way back from California. He arrived back "in a dreadful state" according to Mrs. C. R. Hasskarl, who was secretary to Prof. A. J. Pool of the Botany Department of the university. He had no money and Viola [Mrs. Hasskarl] and Mabel Langdon brought him meals. . . . I don't believe Loren could have spent more than six weeks altogether in his life as a hobo. I suppose to him, thinking back on it, it seemed years.[41]

Before graduating from Harvard College, Henry David Thoreau asked his mother what he should do with himself. Her reply, though well intended, was not what her son expected: "You can buckle on your knapsack and roam abroad to seek your fortune." Tears came to his eyes and rolled down his cheeks. His older sister Helen, who could not bear the pain, rushed to his side, tenderly put an arm around him, and kissed him, saying, "No, Henry, you shall not go, you shall stay at home and live with us," which is exactly what Thoreau did while creating the grand illusion that the wilderness was his natural abode.[42] Loren had no older sister, but he had Mabel Langdon. She saw to it that he returned to the university, and, as Umland sagely observed, she made a famous man out of him.[43]

6

"THE TEARSTAINS OF REMEMBERING"

I

In September 1930 Loren found himself back in familiar yet unsettling surroundings. The tree-shaded walks, formally landscaped flower beds, and neoclassical buildings of the University of Nebraska campus were the same. What had changed drastically were the faces. Most of the students with whom he had started college in 1925 had either entered professional schools or begun their careers and started raising families. But after five years of drifting Loren still lacked a sense of direction. Although English was his first love, he wished for no part in the classroom beyond the role of student; the stultifying task of reading freshman themes had convinced him of that. Writing verse for a living was a dream he shared with Bill Gaffney and other aspiring bards, yet the stock of self-supporting poets, which had never been high, had plummeted to almost nothing as a result of the widening depression. And though science was his declared major, he had taken no courses in physics, chemistry, or mathematics.

Loren had taken several classes in sociology, but it was only now that he decided to enroll in his first two anthropology courses, Introductory Anthropology and Field and Museum Techniques. Three of his examination papers from the introductory course have survived.

Of particular interest is a test he took in November 1930 on the deeply controversial subject of race. He scored a 91 and wrote the following at a time when the Ku Klux Klan flourished nationwide and Hitler's rise to power in the Weimar Republic through popular elections seemed prefigured by historic events:

> An analysis of the three main races [Caucasoid, Mongoloid, and Negroid] as regards evolutionary advancement leaves, as far as physical characteristics go, no conclusions of any importance to be drawn. . . . The results are simply that in some characteristics one race would be farthest removed from the ape, another closer. But in the end it all balances up rather evenly in the matter of averages.

He then addressed himself to the emotionally charged question of why Negroes seem, to the uneducated eye, to be inferior to whites.

> His [the Negro's] unfortunate environment may have handicapped him. Today in America there are many Negroes with high cultural achievements to their credit. Especially in literature where they can be less ostracized than in other fields. All in all it would seem [that] if there is any difference it is only in the matter of the number of geniuses produced. The great mass of the three peoples is on a level, but the Caucasian and Mongoloid seem to have produced more genius[es] per population. That the Negro can adjust himself to his acquired white culture seems obvious, ostracized as he has been by the dominant white.[1]

Having earned a 92 in Introductory Anthropology and a Pass in Field and Museum Techniques, Loren enrolled in the second half of both courses in January 1931. During spring vacation he joined his first scientific expedition under the direction of Dr. William Duncan Strong, professor of anthropology. The dozen or so researchers drove northwest out of Lincoln and established a camp next to the site of an early Pawnee Indian village on the Loup River in central Nebraska. More than sixty mounds, still discernible in spite of periodic cultivation and centuries of erosion, were surveyed and mapped. Averaging some sixty feet in diameter and sixteen inches in height, these manmade hillocks proved to be refuse heaps containing a rich store of broken pottery, implements, and animal bones. The village had once contained an equal number of houses.

Because time was short, the party concentrated on excavating one particularly promising lodge site.

The structure in question had been hastily abandoned and burned, perhaps because of an attack or accidental fire. On the collapsed altar was a charred buffalo skull decorated with a few glass and sheet copper beads, the only traces of white contact. Neither were any horse bones found, a fact that persuaded Strong to place the date of habitation at about 1600. Glass beads of European origin could not have reached these plains dwellers through trade with the Indians of the Southwest much earlier than this, and horses were known to be present in Pawnee villages by the 1680s. Several beautifully incised pots—indeed the best examples of the craft discovered anywhere in Nebraska up to this time—were found on the lodge floor, where they had been broken by the falling beams of the burning structure. Contrary to what anthropologists had first expected, the earlier pottery and tools were far superior to those of later design.[2]

Loren was justifiably proud of his association with such an important expedition. On Sunday, May 10, the *Lincoln State Journal* ran an eight-column article under the headline "Anthropologists Uncover Remains of Sixteenth Century Pawnee Home." He received mention, as did each of the other party members, and clipped the article for safekeeping. John Champe, who later became chairman of anthropology at Nebraska, was also a member of the expedition. Champe retained vivid memories of the unintentionally comic adventures of the greenhorn Loren Eiseley and his equally callow friend, whom someone dubbed the "Russian poet."[3] The party encountered almost every type of bad weather imaginable, including half a foot of snow. Everyone came prepared except Loren and the poet, who were without blankets and winter clothing. Luckily, Champe had carried some extra gear in his bedroll, which he shared with the shivering pair. It grew so cold at sundown that the party abandoned its tents for the protection of a nearby barn. In the middle of the night Strong was awakened by the meek protests of Loren and his friend: "Dr. Strong, Dr. Strong, there are mice in here." Strong's amusement turned to exasperation a few days later, after he sent the young men to town on a routine errand. The road was icy, and whoever was driving lost control of the pickup, which slid off the shoulder and into the ditch. Little if any damage was done, but the two violated a cardinal rule by leaving valuable equipment unattended. Instead of trying to get the truck back on the road, they chose to walk the remaining distance into town, a decision that earned them a humiliating reprimand from their leader.[4]

II

Dr. Erwin Hinckley Barbour had long been regarded as a legend. A gentleman of the old school, the renowned paleontologist was already in his early sixties around 1919, when William Buchanan Price had taken his nephew on a visit to the University of Nebraska Museum, where Barbour was director. His high forehead, a Vandyke beard, dark, bushy brows, and well-trimmed mustache contributed to his air of absolute authority, as did a pair of pince-nez, which were connected to a gold chain and guard to keep them from escaping into space when their wearer became overly animated, a not infrequent occurrence. Though he moved constantly amidst the dusty fossilized remains from ages innocent of human presence, the director was equally fastidious about his dress: dark three-piece suits and starched collars were the order of the day, while a smoke pearl stickpin adorned the perfectly executed knot of his matching silk tie. He expected the museum's employees to follow his example, with one exception. Those working on fossil materials were allowed to remove their suit coats, roll up their sleeves, and don protective aprons. However, their neckties were to remain in place at all times.

Barbour had come to Nebraska in 1891, shortly after taking his Ph.D. at Yale under O. C. Marsh, one of the founding fathers of American paleontology. Together they had traveled by wagon through the still untamed land west of the Mississippi, collecting fossils and mapping the terrain for the U.S. Geological Survey while cajoling the suspicious Indians into letting them work there. Barbour prized old bones—the bigger the better—including those of the mastodon, mammoth, saber-toothed cats, and *Hyaenodon horridus*, a wolflike creature about the size of the black bear. In Nebraska and the adjoining states of the Great Plains he found a rich and largely untapped field for his research.

Barbour's activities piqued the interest of the wealthy Nebraska landowner and financier Charles H. Morrill, who had come to the state shortly after it was admitted to the Union in 1867. In 1893 he donated his first thousand dollars to assist Barbour in excavating fossils for the museum. When the initial funds were exhausted,

Morrill gave Barbour more, and he kept giving for decades, urging his friend to make haste lest scientific expeditions from other institutions forge into the lead. When the final tally was made, Morrill's gifts amounted to some $100,000.

By the mid-1920s the red-brick museum had outgrown its usefulness. Its great overflow of material was either stored in the basement of the Lincoln Sanitarium or sequestered beneath the campus in the huge steam tunnels connecting the various buildings. The museum possessed a towering skeleton of a mammoth, which the director was itching to put on display. There was no room in the building for a complete exhibit of the giant fossil, but Barbour had a brilliant idea à la P.T. Barnum. On one of the upper floors, at the head of the stairway, Barbour had the forelimbs, associated vertebrae, and ribs set up to form an arch under which all who ascended the steps had to pass. This and similar feats of showmanship eventually proved their worth; in 1925 the state legislature, with considerable prodding from Morrill, long a university regent, decided that Barbour's unique treasure deserved a new home. Morrill Hall, constructed on what was then the far north side of campus, was completed and ready for occupancy in the late spring of 1927.

The regular museum staff was bolstered by a number of student assistants, including an affable, easygoing undergraduate named C. Bertrand Schultz. Bert, as he was known to almost everyone, was born in June 1908 in Red Cloud, namesake community of the great Oglala Sioux chief. Beginning on his grandfather's farm, Bert passed much of his youth building an impressive collection of Indian artifacts, many of which eventually wound up in the Webster County Museum, within two blocks of his childhood home. When he was not out searching for relics, Bert frequently engaged in rough-and-tumble games with his friends near the house where Willa Cather stayed on her return visits to Red Cloud. Bert remembered how she sometimes came out on the porch, exasperated, and told the children to "shush!"[5] Not until several years later, after the publication of such widely acclaimed works as *Death Comes for the Archbishop* and *One of Ours*, did Bert realize why the seemingly dour woman demanded peace and quiet. By the time Bert was ready to graduate from high school in 1926, he had not only collected hundreds, perhaps thousands, of artifacts but built almost a score of model Indian villages, concentrating on the locally dominant Pawnee, who had once lived in considerable numbers along the nearby Republican

River. At the university Bert opted for a geology major, with a minor in anthropology. By 1927, his freshman year at Nebraska, he had already become a familiar face at the museum.

In 1925 two young men from western Nebraska, Morris Skinner and James Quinn, made a spectacular discovery on the Quinn farm, near Ainsworth. The two unearthed several fossil mastodons, the forest-dwelling predecessors of the modern elephant. They also found the remains of other large mammals associated with these great beasts. Barbour was stunned when he learned that the skeletons had been purchased by the Denver Museum and the American Museum of Natural History in New York. Childs Frick, who was associated with the New York museum, had engaged Skinner and Quinn to collect for him.

Totally preoccupied by the construction and furnishing of Morrill Hall, Barbour could do little but wax envious. Not until the spring of 1928 was the director able to outline a plan of action. He decided that two museum parties—to be underwritten by yet another infusion of Morrill funds—should go into the field and do what Skinner and Quinn were doing. In theory, one of the two-man teams would cover the northern half of the state and its counterpart, the south; in practice this idea was soon found to be unworkable. What mattered most were the results. The four men were instructed to collect anything and everything of potential scientific value, with the unwritten proviso that the quest for big game should always take precedence.[6]

Bert Schultz and fellow student John Dewey LeMar were the original members of the South Party, whose formal designation was the Morrill Paleontological Expedition. By the time Bert met Loren in 1930, he had spent three summers in the field and was already coming to know the geographic and geologic features of his native state with unequaled intimacy. The two became acquainted in anthropology classes and accompanied Duncan Strong on weekend digs to fulfill their Field and Museum Techniques requirement. They worked mostly along the Missouri palisades south of Omaha, frequently taking over the supervision of inexperienced students. Loren admired Bert not only for his winsome manner and constant good cheer but because the self-confident young scientist seemed to know exactly what he wanted out of life. "He was," in Loren's words, "one of those fortunate people who knew his course and did not wander."[7]

It was to Bert that Loren turned for help in July of 1931. He also wrote to Dr. Barbour, asking that he be permitted to join the South Party. Barbour did not know Loren well, but he was favorably impressed by his writing ability and sincere interest in the history of the Earth. When Bert next returned to Lincoln from the field, it was decided that Loren should be given a chance. Bert picked him up at the Prices' in early August, and together they headed for the Henry Arthaud farm north of Cambridge, where the party, now six in number, had discovered some promising signs of mastodon remains.

III

As were others new to the field, Loren was paired with an experienced member of the expedition, a short, robust, and ruggedly handsome young man named Emery Blue. The former Iowa farm boy loved to handle and identify old bones, but he found the laboratory of Morrill Hall too confining. Intrigued by life in the field, he had persuaded Barbour to let him join the South Party in 1930. Emery was thus completing his second season of collecting when Loren arrived, and he cheerfully made room in his tent for the shy newcomer. Frank Crabill, one of Bert's childhood companions, was also a member of the team and, like Emery, befriended Loren from the outset.

Satisfied that all was well, Bert, who had more urgent matters on his mind, headed for Omaha. On Saturday, August 8, while the other members of the party worked the quarry on the Arthaud farm, he wed Marian Ruth Othmer, his college sweetheart, in an early-morning ceremony at her parents' home. The couple left immediately on a fossil-collecting honeymoon in the Black Hills of South Dakota. Bert had told the boys that he was especially anxious to explore an ancient fish quarry in a glacial deposit southwest of Highmore, provoking some good-natured ribbing about his pursuit of these and other Cenozoic delights. Bert had the last laugh, however. Not only did he return with a pretty bride but the trunk of his old Chevy was laden with the fossil remains of the very fish he had promised to seek out.[8]

Meanwhile, the boys had not done too badly themselves. Working with Henry's Arthaud's team of horses and a metal scraper, they had unearthed two complete lower mastodon tusks and substantial portions of two others, along with a scapula, several vertebrae, and numerous leg bones. Their treasure, which weighed over four hundred pounds, was packed and shipped to Lincoln by rail on August 15, the day after Bert's return.[9]

In late August the party moved from the sandhills of the southwestern corner of the state to a campsite near Redington on the High Plains. First explored by the Spanish in the 1600s, this scarred and broken land of little rain was considered part of the Great American Desert until well into the nineteenth century. At first pioneers bypassed the region in the belief that it could grow neither trees nor crops, leaving the native Indians and the buffalo in relative peace. Then came the railroads, bearing an indomitable generation of European immigrants. Cattle ranches soon occupied much of the grassland, while the more fertile soils were planted in corn, sorghum, wheat, and flax where water was available. The buffalo disappeared and with it, the Indian. Yet to the trained eye the land had another, far more ancient, story to tell.

Some 40 million years ago, at the beginning of a geological epoch known as the Oligocene, the Earth's poles cooled and new global weather patterns developed. The Oligocene, which lasted some 15 million years, was marked by the appearance of the true carnivores and other direct ancestors of modern mammals. Rain-bearing clouds relentlessly poured their burden onto Nebraska and the Dakotas, while mud and silt from swift-flowing streams mixed with ash that had drifted eastward on the winds from the volcanically active Rockies. After 3 or 4 million years the rains finally subsided, bringing a virtual end to the archaic mammalian life-forms of the preceding epoch, the Paleocene. Out of this level, grass-covered landscape new rivers incised and fluted sandstone and clay into scarped cliffs hundreds of feet high. Mazes of waterless gullies, which flooded without warning during seasonal downpours, formed deadly traps for the unwary animals that inhabited their lengths. Once the waters receded many of the carcasses sank into the drying mud, often hardening into stone. Shell, tooth, hoof, bone, horn, and beak turned to mineral, creating happy hunting grounds for the paleontologist.

While Emery and Frank worked a region in the Wildcat Hills called Redington Gap, Bert and Loren ranged farther afield, searching for possible quarry sites in the company of a rancher named S. R. Sweet. Although prospects looked very good, the two were quickly disappointed. A party from Chicago's Field Museum had already obtained the local landowners' permission to dig in the area. Thus it was decided that Emery and Loren should follow the Pumpkinseed Valley westward into Banner County, on the Nebraska-Wyoming border, where elephant remains had been reported.

On arriving in the small ranching community of Harrisburg in early September, the two headed for the local newspaper office in search of information. They were told of an aging farmer named George Bennet who possessed a giant elephant bone, supposedly the only impressive fossil specimen of its kind in the county. Bennet was a dyed-in-the-wool fundamentalist and would have nothing to do with "modern geological heresies." Feeling that they had little to risk but some time and the prospect of an evangelical tongue-lashing, Emery and Loren followed a twisting gravel road up into the pine-covered Wildcat Hills east of town. Passing through a ramshackle gate, they encountered a horde of screaming children, who broke and ran toward the sod house in the distance. Pa Mullens, Loren's fictional name for George Bennet, soon appeared at the door. "The moment I saw him I felt a great sense of relief. He had the merry, wondering, wandering eye of the born naturalist. Poor, uneducated, reared in a sect which frowns upon natural science, some wind out of the Pliocene had touched him." He had been touched in another manner as well. Bennet's straw yellow mustache contrasted oddly with his blue-tinged countenance, a telltale sign of advanced heart disease.

The "elyphant" bone, as Bennet referred to the huge, brown femur he kept in his living room, had been in his possession for twenty years. He had made no map of the valley where he found it and had not returned to the site since the day of its discovery. Countless others just like it, he said, were spread across the land, bleached white by the blinding heat of a thousand summer suns. Moreover, this was hallowed ground, for God in his infinite wisdom had chosen this particular place to deposit the residue of the mightiest flood of all—the Noachian deluge of Genesis. "The marvel of it struck me," Pa confided reverently to the strangers. "I was scared green, but I wanted [the bone]. I wanted to bring it home."[10] And so he had.

The search began on the late-summer morning of September 5. With Bennet in the front seat giving directions, the party drove across sandbanks, up dry arroyos, through withered prairie grass—

lowering fences and startling cattle so far removed from human contact that they might never go to market. Finally, after coming to a barrier of steep, rocky hills, the fossil hunters abandoned their cars and pressed forward on foot, the stout Bennet inclined toward the horizon like an obsessed conquistador. Emery recollected: "Although he had had a heart attack, [Bennet] outwalked all of us who were much younger than he. We just could not keep up with him; he'd lead us one place, and that wasn't the right one so he'd go somewhere else. He really led us on a wild chase."[11]

Hours passed and the prospects got no better. Bennet seemed to be turning bluer by the minute, prompting a worried Loren to urge that the search be abandoned. They were now some nine miles due east of Harrisburg, on a fork of Pumpkin Creek called Indian Springs. The land was owned by a sociable rancher named Emerson Faden, whose father had settled there in the 1880s. The party had worked its way to a site on the far side of a high mesa. Suddenly, their frenzied leader gave a yell and pointed down the slope. Directly below where they stood were scores of bones, tusks, and teeth, encapsulating millions of years of the planet's history, just as old man Bennet had remembered them. The ecstatic guide rushed forward to point out some exposed mastodon molars: "See those great agonized teeth; well that beast used them to domesticate his food with."[12]

While the unlettered Bennet murmured rhapsodically over the remains left behind by the Great Flood, Loren committed the surrealistic panorama to his scientist's memory, knowing full well that he would probably never see anything like it again: "I saw the ivory from the tusks of elephants scattered like broken china that the rain has washed. I saw the splintered, mineralized enamel of huge unknown teeth. I saw, protruding from an eroding gully, the jaw of a shovel-tusked ambelodont [mastodon] that has been gone twice a million years into the night of geologic time." Adrenaline pumping, he walked stooped over for hours along the eroded hillsides, picking up one tantalizing object only to discard it for another moments later. He stuffed his pockets, emptied them, then stuffed them again while indecision reigned. "We were rich at last—as the bone hunter reckons riches."[13]

The discovery of the Faden Ranch occurred one month to the day after Loren joined the South Party. Twenty-four hours later he was back on the long road to Lincoln in the company of fellow students Frank Denton and Eugene Vanderpool. Reluctant though the three were to depart, they all faced registration and the beginning of fall classes in little more than a week. Emery and Frank Crabill followed them in two days later, leaving only Bert and his bride in the field. The collecting season of 1931 officially ended on September 19, when Bert penned the following entry in his field notes: "Shipped bones, broke camp late in P.M. and started to Lincoln."[14] The saber-toothed cats and shovel-tusked mastodons would be allowed to slumber undisturbed for one final winter before being roused by the jar of the bone hunters' dynamite.

IV

Shortly after she began her graduate studies in 1926, Mabel Langdon started working for Paul Grumman, a tall, gloomy, and somewhat sinister-looking Ibsen scholar who had been serving as director of the School of Fine Arts since 1912. As assistant curator of the art gallery, she typed letters, hung exhibits, prepared gallery catalogs, and in between wrote publicity releases, which the newspapers usually printed without a single editorial change. Mabel was rewarded for her efficiency in 1929 with a promotion to curator and a raise in pay from fifty to sixty dollars a month. Meanwhile she continued to take courses toward a master's degree in literature and drama, earning the same high marks that had gained her a Phi Beta Kappa key as an undergraduate.

Earlier in the year, before Loren went into the field with the South Party, Mabel's literary constancy finally began to have its intended effect. On the evening of May 3 the poet laureate of Nebraska, John G. Neihardt, appeared before the spring meeting of the Nebraska Writers' Guild to read from several of his works, including "The Death of Crazy Horse." Officers of the Poetry Society, a division of the guild, were elected earlier in the day and announced at the banquet. Loren C. Eiseley was named president; Mabel Langdon gained a seat on the board of directors.[15]

Yet the bond between Loren and Mabel was soon put to its severest test. Paul Grumman resigned the directorship of fine arts and was replaced by Dwight Kirsch, a quiet, unassuming watercolorist and printmaker who had been on the university faculty for several years. Since Loren hoped to be in the field, Mabel decided to take a leave of absence and study elsewhere for two or three months. But mostly she wanted to reflect on her relationship with Loren from a distance—and she urged him to do the same.

As was typical of her reserve, Mabel did not share her feelings with anyone but Loren. Nevertheless, a careful reading of the poetry she composed during their long courtship offers some intriguing clues to the doubt, pain, and struggles masked by a placid exterior. In "The Cathedral," her first published work, she imagines herself in a black mourning dress kneeling before a high altar, candles flickering in the background.

A small breeze stirs the dead
Air heavy with incense . . . Nothing
Stirs me.[16]

"Autumnals" speaks of her wounded soul, marked by the "tear-stains of remembering—and Dark pain."[17] In "Twilight Musing," Mabel projected the theme of self-mourning into old age. Arrayed in a gown of softest rose, white hair waved and knotted at the neck, she goes to bed alone, wraps herself in silk covers, and lies

So deep in sleep that I shall never know—
Girl with brown hair and youth so dear to her—
If you stand quietly without my door
And whisper of your love—and pity me.[18]

The story of Mabel's doubts and their parting was told by Loren to an attentive, sympathetic young woman whom he had met in the fall of 1924, when both were seniors at Teachers High. After graduating from the university in 1930, Helen Hopt—a petite, dark-eyed brunette—accepted the dual position of high-school teacher and principal in the village of Ruskin. She was attending summer school in 1931 and living at her parents' home in University Place, a sedate, upper-middle-class suburb of Lincoln, when Loren paid a call sometime in June.[19]

Loren was both lonely and out of a job; he told Helen that he felt free to date whomever he wished. She was deeply flattered by his attentions: the former class president and captain of the football team was also "the outstanding scholar of our class. He seemed older than most of us and had a certain glamour because of his hobo days riding the rails." Helen's parents, especially her father, an intellectual and a member of the university faculty, liked Loren almost as much as she did. Loren rode the streetcar out to University Place almost every day. He loved the Hopts' huge old home on Holdrege Street, with its sweeping lawn and well-manicured tennis court in the back. The couple sometimes took long walks in the nearby countryside, returning to play a set or two before retiring to the shaded porch with a large pitcher of lemonade and chipped ice. There they talked for hours, often in the company of Helen's parents, Loren savoring the material comfort and gentility so alien to his youth.

In early July the two left Lincoln in a Ford for an extended trip through the Indian reservations and national parks of the Southwest. They were joined by a second couple and a girlfriend of Helen's, whose parents owned the car. They existed on sandwiches and slept outdoors rolled up in a blanket or two, nestling together for warmth under the vault of desert stars. "Occasionally we rented an inexpensive room and luxuriated in a warm bath," Helen recalled. "Sometimes we girls shed our clothes to bathe in an irrigation ditch or in a quiet river, while the fellows kept watch [to make certain] that we weren't disturbed." By the time their travels were over, they had traced a huge circle through Colorado, New Mexico, Arizona, and Utah. Within this circle another had been drawn.

> Loren and I recognized that we loved each other and wanted to marry, but the prospect of soon doing that seemed out of the question. It was important that Loren get at least his bachelor's degree before attempting to support a family. That meant that for several years I would need to be the main support for the two of us—and married women teachers simply were not being hired at that point during the Depression.
>
> And then he received the shattering letter from Mabel! Probably unaware that Loren had found a new romantic interest, her summer away from him had enabled her to evaluate how she felt about him. She was eagerly looking forward to their reunion and resumption of their close association.
>
> It was a heart-breaking situation for Loren. I was his love and the one he wanted to marry. On the other hand, he felt an obligation and strong loyalty to Mabel and did not want to hurt her, either. He had to make a decision and make it soon, for Mabel would be returning in a few days.[20]

This, however, was something Loren could not bring himself to do. He began showing up at Holdrege Street in the evenings, but only after having taken a few drinks, much to Helen's alarm. The more they talked, the more obvious it became that she was the one who would have to make the decision: "I reluctantly arrived at what I felt to be the only feasible solution. I would step out of the picture. . . . I feared that Loren would have strong feelings of guilt which might damage his self-esteem and might also erode our life together." Another factor also entered into her deliberations. "Neither Loren nor I was adept at practical matters. If we were to make a life together, I believed that of necessity I would have to assume dealing with the practical matters. . . . Actually, I felt there were other aspects of my being which it was more important that I cultivate."[21] Finally, she believed that she could not rise to Loren's intellectual level, something that Mabel, whom Helen knew and admired, had proven herself capable of doing.

Helen bid Loren an emotional farewell one early August evening and soon returned to Ruskin. Loren left Lincoln with Bert at about the same time. He was haunted by the failure of their summer romance and his lack of personal resolve, and wrote to Helen from Lincoln after returning from the field in September. Fall term had just begun, and his genuine sense of loss stirred poignant memories of an old grief suffered at the hands of Lila, his lady in white:

> For three days I have walked through a parade of men and things that are supposed to matter. But the voices are small and inconsequential and the faces blur. I have blundered off a peak where the stars were close enough to touch and now it is very hard to see and I am a frightened child in an empty house. There is pain, too—of a kind and a quantity I have only experienced once—and so long ago that I had dreamed myself safe from ever being hurt again.
>
> There was a glass you drank from on a certain night—and afterwards a parade of moments in which I hated and loved you by turns and never, for one moment, was the master of myself any more than one masters air. I do not think I should be writing this, but I am writing it. . . . Just as, in the office, when we pore over maps and my duties in the north are pointed out to me I am looking at Ruskin.[22]

He wrote to Helen for the last time in October, toward midnight: "I think . . . I shall remember the smell of sage till I die. Everything grows too clearly in the mind—our lost fires in the dark, the places where we slept—or looked at stars—or felt the immense loneliness of earth—they are in my brain. I walk among them when I hardly wish to. . . . God bless you my dear. How funny for me to be using that old fashioned phrase."[23]

V

One of Bill Gaffney's fondest memories of Loren was of a warm spring night in early 1932. Instead of going for a walk alone, the two had joined a "mildly roistering group" on a late ramble in the country. Sometime after midnight they all wound up at the house of a total stranger. The conversation turned to writing, and Loren asked if any of those present had seen what he considered perhaps the greatest modern poem after G. K. Chesterton's *The Ballad of the White Horse*. No one had. He left immediately to fetch the latest issue of *Harper's*, which contained the prologue to Archibald MacLeish's *Conquistador*—soon to win a Pulitzer Prize. Although no more than half the group of twenty or so were "poetry-reading types," Loren held them spellbound with his recitation. When he finished, "We paid what some have called the highest possible tribute to any work of art: a few minutes of absolute silence. Fifty years later, I remember vividly that silence."[24]

Others shared Bill's admiration for Loren's oratorical skills, inherited from Clyde, which he frequently displayed before a small circle of friends on Sunday afternoons. Mabel often hosted the readings in her parents' home. Loren recited from his own works and those of the more popular poets. Dorothy Thomas, a frequent guest and one of Lincoln's brightest literary lights, remembered that when Loren read aloud "you felt it clear to your kneecaps."[25]

Just as the indelible imprint of the performing father was left on the son, so was that of the afflicted mother. One snowy December evening Dorothy visited the public library downtown. At first glance the large reading room, its long oak tables illuminated by a row of green lamps resembling an avenue of trees, appeared deserted. But as her eyes adjusted to the soft light, Dorothy saw Loren and Mabel gesturing to her to come and sit with them. Loren, his tones muffled, began reading a short story, "Silent Snow, Secret Snow," by Conrad Aiken. The story concerns a young boy who is losing his hearing but is not aware of it. His parents chide him for day-dreaming, while he mentally berates himself for behaving stupidly. As Loren read, "his voice began to shake and really to quiver; at last his voice broke; he could read no farther, and he began to pat his pockets for a handkerchief."[26] Loren then excused himself and read the rest of the story in silence. Dorothy did not learn of Daisy's deafness until many years later. When she did, she could never quite decide whether Loren's display of emotion was in sympathy for his mother or whether he had projected himself into Aiken's tragic character.

As a writer Loren was never taken lightly. Mari Sandoz, who lived at the time in an eight-dollar-a-month room and subsisted on stale cinnamon rolls, presided over an enthusiastic circle of artists and would-be writers at the all-night restaurant in the old bus depot. She recalled that for the price of a cup of coffee one could talk endlessly about the *Dial*, James Joyce, John Dos Passos, D. H. Lawrence, Sherwood Anderson and *Winesburg, Ohio*, or *Spoon River Anthology*, *Babbitt*, and *Main Street* and the outrage of H. L. Mencken on being arrested for selling a copy of the *American Mercury* in Boston. Mari also remembered long discussions involving the work of local writers: poems by Loren Eiseley, Mabel Langdon, and Weldon Kees, short stories by Pan Sterling, Dorothy Thomas, Lasalle Gilman, and Lowry Wimberly, essays by Rudolph Umland. They talked technique and the remote hope of publication. Professor Louise Pound occasionally took one or more of them into Lincoln's better homes, where they read their original works to polite, if not always comprehending, upper-class matrons.[27]

Loren liked nothing so much as to be surrounded by a protective nest of femininity. Women were more drawn to him than were men. He was physically attractive and vulnerable on the one hand, charming and worldly on the other. By the time he reached his early twenties, he had already professed his love to at least three women, all teachers, and was adored by several others. When his spirits flagged he drove over to Nebraska City on the Missouri to be alternately teased and praised by an engaging bevy of young females who laughingly referred to themselves as "Loren's Harem." The group was composed of sisters, girlfriends, and in-laws of Jac Cave, whose father had been chosen to head the local Episcopal congregation in 1926. Loren usually visited on weekends and loved to pose for photographs with the ladies. On one occasion he donned a long apron and shaped his dark hair into a formidable spit curl; the harem lined up four on either side, paying court to their zany lord and master. Jac's sister Alice, now a fetching high-school sophomore, was smitten by her brother's best friend.

Jac lost contact with Loren a year later. The minister's son drifted through the long depression, taking whatever job offered itself—insurance salesman, truck driver, hotel desk clerk. Before leaving Nebraska for good, he dreamt up the publicity stunt of floating down the Missouri, from Omaha to St. Louis, in an inner tube. While the gimmick made him no money, he was given a full-page spread, complete with pictures, in the Omaha paper. Loren almost certainly read the story and doubtless smiled to himself: the senior class jester was still living up to his reputation. Then the handsome young man drifted quietly down memory's river, not to be heard from again until Loren published his autobiography more than half a lifetime later.

VI

Loren was a student in Kenneth Forward's 1932 class The Nineteenth-Century Essay, and he had turned in a paper describing the houses in which he had lived while growing up on Lincoln's south side. All three homes were within a few blocks of one another; each held painfully vivid memories of his mother's presence. Loren's essay so touched Forward that he talked his student into taking him on a tour of the neighborhood. Five or six years later, Forward retraced the route he had taken with Loren for the benefit of Rudolph Umland. When they paused in front of the Prices' house, the curtains parted, as if on cue, and a gray face peered out. The embarrassed pair quickly turned away and resumed their walk. "The stone-deaf woman and her sister were still living in that house."[28]

Although Loren's reputation as a writer was largely that of a poet, time would one day reveal that verse represented his passport to prose. Forward's course, which provided the disciplined setting in which to experiment with the essay form, dealt exclusively with the English masters: Hazlitt, Macaulay, Lamb, De Quincey, Carlyle, Ruskin, Huxley, Newman, and Stevenson. Lectures covered the biography of each essayist, their differences of style, and analysis of their finest literary endeavors. Students were required to compose at least five essays a semester, adopting the prose style of the figures assigned to them. Though Forward was a precisionist when it came to language and punctuation, he was no pedant. Loren was told to write a piece in the manner of Walter Savage Landor, a little-remembered poet, literary critic, and prose writer known for the severity and intellectual aloofness of his style. Instead of an essay, he submitted a poem titled "Lizard's Eye," the tale of an abandoned lover adrift in the alkaline basins of the Mojave. He appended the following note, dated January 28, 1932, to the bottom of the page: "I had something crawling up and down in me last night—and this is the result. I thought you might not mind it in place of the Landor essay."[29] Instead of failing the paper or making Loren do it over, Forward gave him an A.

Of the essayists whose literary style Loren was required to imitate, none seems to have left a more lasting impression on him than Thomas Henry Huxley, whose advocacy of evolutionary theory earned the memorable Victorian the nickname Darwin's Bulldog. His essay "On a Piece of Chalk" was first presented to the laboring men of Norwich in 1868. "Huxley," in Loren's words, "understood instinctively how to take simple things—in this case . . . a piece of chalk in a carpenter's pocket—and to proceed from the known, by some magical doorway of his own devising, back into the mist of long-vanished geological eras."[30] Huxley told his rapt audience that when placed under a microscope, a thin slice of chalk presents a totally different appearance. One sees that it is composed of innumerable bodies less than a hundredth of an inch in diameter, each having a well-defined shape and structure. These granules, or *Globigerina*, were once living organisms, which drifted, like microscopic rain, from the surface of the world's great oceans to the dark, muddy bottom. Thus did the layers accumulate, time out of mind, while great geologic catastrophes intervened between one epoch and another. In the days before the chalk broke through to form the familiar cliffs of Albion, "the beasts of the field were not our beasts of the field, nor the fowls of the air such as those which the eye of man has seen flying." As some species vanished, others took their place. "The longest line of human ancestry must hide its diminished head before the pedigree of . . . insignificant shellfish."[31]

It was writing such as this that pointed Loren in the direction of the popular scientific essay, that helped him shape his own grand metaphor of limitless change in limitless time. As Rudolph Umland wrote, Huxley's essay "must have sent [Loren] musing and pondering under the stars. . . . Thirty years later [he] became the Huxley of his time but a Huxley with more poetry in his soul."[32]

7

LES MAUVAISES TERRES

I

Bert Schultz was hard at work on Sunday, May 1, 1932, spending all that afternoon and most of the following day at Morrill Hall, packing supplies and camping gear in preparation for his fifth season as leader of the South Party.[1] Other than an occasional weekend foray, Bert had never gone into the field so early in the year. His thoughts were on the weather, and his concern deepened when he pondered the party's destination—an isolated ranch on Nebraska's nearly mile-high western rim, within sight of the snowcapped Rockies. It was Loren's idea, Bert remembered. He had spent the winter dreaming of those great beasts whose remains lay mostly buried beneath thick deposits of gravel and clay on the Emerson Faden Ranch. Indeed, Bert had never seen his normally reserved friend so excited about anything, which made his pleas that they head west, without waiting for Emery Blue and the party's student workers, that much harder to resist. Though the academic year would not end for another month, Loren made arrangements to take Incompletes from Kenneth Forward and a second professor.[2] He breached Bert's not very formidable defenses and secured his surrender with the approval of Dr. Barbour, who was only slightly less enthusiastic about the summer's prospects.

On Tuesday, May 3, Bert, Marian, his wife, and Loren left

Lincoln in the early-morning hours, a new trailer constructed by the museum staff in tow. Its freshly painted sides incorporated the name of their benefactor—"Morrill Paleontological Expedition"—but gave no hint of their provenance. "In those days," Bert laughingly recalled, "we didn't dare to have 'University of Nebraska' on anything out in western Nebraska, because it wasn't very popular."[3]

The trio reached Banner County and the Faden quarry on Friday evening. Their host told them that they were welcome to stay in an abandoned stone cabin on the slope of a pine-covered hill near the excavation site, about a mile from the ranch house. But the structure could accommodate no more than two and had other problems as well: the roof leaked, and the rafters had long since become a favorite roosting place for coyote-wary birds. Still, it provided protection from the weather and promised the Schultzes, who had been married only nine months, a measure of privacy incompatible with tent life.

Weary from their long day's journey, Bert and Marian turned in early, only to discover that their squatters' rights had been preempted by others. A pair of young sparrow hawks had claimed the cabin as a spring nesting site. The male soon left through a hole in the roof, but the female, her maternal instincts aroused, refused to give in so easily. Bert and Marian had barely dozed off before the hawk swooped menacingly over their heads, forcing them to cover their faces in self-defense. The couple nodded off again, only to have their winged terrorist make another sortie. When, shortly after dawn, Loren heard what had happened, he went to the trailer and returned with a stepladder and gunnysack. With Bert's help the female hawk was cornered and placed in the bag without incident. After the hole in the roof was repaired, she was taken outside and released.[4] Although its source is nearly unrecognizable, Loren eloquently retold this story in "The Bird and the Machine."

"We came into the valley through the trailing mist of a spring night," he began. "It was a place that looked as though it might never have known the foot of man, but our scouts had been ahead of us and we knew all about the abandoned cabin of stone that lay far up on one hillside." Loren and his companions were supposedly after not only bones but animals: "The word had come through to get them alive—birds, reptiles, anything. A zoo somewhere abroad needed stocking. . . . My job was to help capture some birds and that is why I was there before the trucks."

Loren entered the cabin alone; it was pitch dark except for the faint light of a few stars visible through the decaying roof. Having climbed atop a ladder, he carelessly reached for a roosting bird without first determining its species. "I snapped on the flash and sure enough there was a great beating and feathers flying, but instead of my having them, they, or rather he, had me." The hawk gave a sharp, metallic cry before sinking his hooked beak deep into Loren's thumb, enabling the female to whisk neatly through the roof to freedom. "The little fellow had saved his mate by diverting me, and that was that." Loren put his perfect specimen in a cardboard box for safekeeping until morning.

He rose at first light and looked furtively around camp to make certain no one else was stirring. Then he opened the box and carefully picked up the wild bird. He "lay limp in my grasp and I could feel his heart pound under the feathers but he only looked beyond me and up." Loren scanned the cloudless sky, thinking that perhaps the bird's mate had kept an all-night vigil. There was no sign of her. "Probably in the next county by now," he thought to himself as he eyed the waiting trucks. "I suppose I must have had an idea then of what I was going to do, but I never let it come into consciousness." He reached over and placed the hawk gently on the ground. For a long minute the disoriented bird of prey remained motionless, his piercing eyes fixed on the blue vault above. In the next second he was gone, like a flicker of light—"gone straight into that towering emptiness . . . that my eyes could scarcely bear to penetrate." Then came a cry that made Loren's heart turn over. It was not that of the hawk he had captured but of its mate, who came diving straight out of the sun's blinding golden eye: "I saw them both now. He was rising fast to meet her. They met in a great soaring gyre that turned to a whirling circle and a dance of wings. Once more, just once, their two voices, joined in a harsh wild medley of question and response, struck and echoed against the pinnacles of the valley. Then they were gone forever somewhere into those upper regions beyond the eyes of men."[5]

Work in what was commonly called "the elephant quarry" began in earnest on May 9. Within hours the party found several leg bones and numerous smaller specimens, including mastodon teeth, vertebrae, and toe bones by the score. Similar remains of extinct rhinoceros and camel were unearthed later in the week, along with those of a saber-toothed cat. Frank Denton, who had recently arrived and set up camp with his wife and child near Redington, spent most of May 18 helping Bert and Loren ready the season's first collection of bones for shipment to Lincoln. They also discussed whether to hire a dynamiter. Since the quarry had already yielded several hundred pounds of material with a minimum of digging, the consensus was to hold off.[6]

Even though June was not far away, the nights seemed to be getting no warmer, and the spring rains brought a chill damp that penetrated spleen and marrow. "Continued rain and cold," a glum Bert wrote in his log on May 28. "Obtained a stove in P.M. from Redington store."[7] Loren had no similar luxury in his tiny abode, an umbrella tent located about one hundred feet north of the stone cabin. He usually stayed up late reading by the light of a Coleman gas lantern, which also provided a little heat. One night Bert and Marian were awakened by a sharp rat-a-tat-tat on the cabin door. It was Loren, who beseeched them in a low voice, "Marian, Bert, let me in quickly!" Bert, a flashlight in hand, went to the door and could tell immediately by the expression on Loren's face that his friend was deeply frightened.

"I think somebody's been murdered in the woods behind the tent!" Loren exclaimed. "I heard a bloodcurdling, humanlike scream; then it was all quiet."

The next morning they set out to solve Loren's mystery. A telltale clue—some fur splattered with blood—lay near the tent. Bert speculated that a great horned owl, which roosted near the cabin, had swooped down on a rabbit silhouetted in the light from the tent's lantern. The doomed creature had uttered a death scream, which Loren mistook for that of a stricken woman. When asked what he had been reading when the incident occurred, Loren sheepishly admitted that it was a murder mystery.[8]

Loren was occasionally given over to wildly theatrical gestures. One night he burst into the cabin yelling, "I'm a pyromaniac!" and began pouring kerosene on the floor. He then lit it while Bert tried to calm Marian, who began to scream. Loren quickly doused the flames, saying it was only a joke. This was not the sort of "humor" the Schultzes were used to, and they puzzled over Loren's behavior for a long time to come.[9]

Such incidents were clumsy ploys for attention by one who felt like the odd man out. Bert and Marian had each other to lean on, while Mabel was working in an office hundreds of miles away. The self-styled loner gave more than a hint of his true feelings in a haunting, existential letter written to Bill Gaffney less than three weeks into the season:

> Here where there are only bones asleep in their million-year long rotting, where the events of the Pliocene seem more real than those of civilization—that overnight fungus—you may take it as a compliment that I was genuinely moved by these sonnets. Love is a faint far cry along the wind here—an old troubling lament from the world's edge that came to me in your letter. Not real. Something suffered a long time ago before I stepped out of time. That is the way it is here. Or was. Yesterday a pretty young gypsy waved at me from a camp by the road. It took me a whole day to forget—not very successfully. Why? I don't know except that she was young and beautiful—and I was young—and we would never see each other again and never speak. And she was one of the outcast people among whom I should have been born—the people who have no ties but a duty to horizons, who never grow old as we do squatting by the little fire of memory that goes out and leaves us to freeze alone in the end.[10]

It was about this time that Loren asked Bert if Mabel could visit the camp. The Schultzes were delighted at the prospect, and Mabel arrived by train around Decoration Day. Hardly what one would describe as an outdoor person, she nevertheless accepted the primitive living conditions in good cheer. The interests of propriety were also served: Mabel took over Loren's tent, while he moved his bedroll into the trailer, where he spent the nights for the duration.[11]

II

Work in the elephant quarry was growing more tedious by the day. Fewer and fewer of the larger bones yielded themselves to pick and shovel, while myriads of camel toes, rhino anklebones, and mastodon vertebrae became the bane of the diggers' existence. The South Party acquisition records for 1932 contain hundreds of entries similar to number 113: "Very small toe bone." Eventually even Bert, the person in charge of record keeping and a stickler for detail, was forced to streamline his entries in the interest of sanity: "wrist bones 37, phalanges 33, ulna 3," and so forth.[12]

For diversion the trio began working the eastern terminus of the Wildcat Range. On June 1 Bert did some geologic work at Courthouse Rock and at the somewhat taller Jail Rock. "Not any good prospects," he jotted in his field notes, but all was not lost. Pioneers streaming west through nearby Birdcage Gap had carved their names and accumulated wisdom on the pliant limestone faces of the buttes. These, together with the migrants' still discernible wagon tracks, are things Loren never forgot. The barefoot children, the lined brown women with sunbonnets, the fathers who became forest cutters and wheat farmers passed eternally across the rutted landscape of his inner eye. "I back off reluctantly," he wrote in "Oregon Trail," a nostalgic tribute to these High Plains pilgrims,

and out of some shamed courtesy
slip my spectacles
into my pocket
and raise my hand
saying a wordless
goodbye.[13]

III

Emery Blue drove into the Faden Ranch on the evening of June 14. Beside him was a novice student worker from Cowles, Nebraska, named Robert Long, who possessed both the rangy build and the elongated facial features of a young John Updike. Frank Crabill and Eugene Vanderpool were also in the field, camped at Redington with Frank Denton. The party, which rarely assembled as a group, gathered at the Faden Ranch on June 17 to celebrate Bert's twenty-fourth birthday. Hopes for the season were high, not least because of a discovery made the previous afternoon. As luck would have it, Bob Long, who was spending only his second day in the field, found a perfectly preserved Pliocene bear dog skull in the much cursed elephant quarry. The specimen was later shipped to Childs Frick at the Museum of Natural History for exact identification.[14] The quarry held renewed promise, and now, with the full team assembled, bison remains found near Scotts Bluff could be claimed. Frank Denton topped the evening off with an additional piece of good news. A farmer named J. H. Brubaker had approached him concerning some bones found on his property, ten miles north of Bridgeport. Denton had driven out to the Brubaker place on June 10 and liked what he saw. "No articulated [intact] material, but plenty of variety: horse, pig, rhino, dog."[15] The bones were present in such quantity that plans for opening yet another quarry began taking shape.

Emery and Loren had gotten along so well the previous summer that they were paired off once again. Operating largely as floaters, they worked at whatever site most needed their services. Bert, who subscribed to what he termed Barbour's "the grass is always greener theory," also made certain that the two spent part of every week scouting the terrain for new prospects.

The young men were usually in the field by 8:00 A.M., after a spartan breakfast. Almost never returning to camp for lunch, the two took sandwiches, coffee, and a large canvas water bag with them. Whoever was scheduled to prepare the evening meal usually quit work about 5:00 P.M., to be followed in by the other an hour or so later. Their mutual distaste for washing the dinner dishes quickly became known to all, and the Schultzes teasingly charged them with sharing the same plate, something both emphatically denied.[16] The pair joined the Redington camp on June 18 to assist Frank Denton in the removal of oreodont, camel, and deer remains.

Mineralized bone, although hard, is as brittle as glass. Depending on the type of material in which a fossil has been encased, the specimen might literally begin to disintegrate upon coming into contact with the air. In contrast to the practice of the early days of paleontology, when fossils were picked and pried out of rock and clay in countless fragments to be carted back to the laboratory for tedious reassembly, the South Party made every effort to recover the bones in as few pieces as possible.

The complicated, sometimes nerve-racking, process began with the clearing away of any gravel or soil resting atop the fossil deposit, an operation that might take anywhere from hours to days. After shoveling the "overburden" aside, the team discarded their spades and picks for more delicate hand tools, including awls, whisk brooms, soft brushes, and old dental instruments, which worked almost as well on fist-sized mastodon teeth as on the molars of *Homo sapiens*. As bone became exposed, they sealed it with a mixture of white shellac and denatured alcohol. After uncovering more of the specimen, they mapped out the fossil floor into "blocks." The underlying matrix was then cut into squares, in preparation for removing each block as a unit. For more important remains, photographs were usually taken while the object was still in situ.

Before the fossils could be hauled away, rolls of toilet paper were dipped in a pan of water and wrapped around the shellacked bones to act as a separator. (The party used so much that it had to be purchased by the gross, prompting one curious storekeeper to inquire as to the nature of their diet.[17]) Like physicians setting broken limbs, they dipped strips of burlap in plaster of Paris, encasing the top and sides of each block in a pristine cast of white. Once the plaster dried, the block was ready for undercutting, an especially tricky operation. If it held together, it was gingerly turned over for plastering on the bottom, each man uttering a silent prayer that it would not crumble, destroying hours of painstaking labor.

If the procedure was successful, all that remained was the crating and shipping of the refossilized bones. On occasion ready-made boxes could be obtained in town, but more often than not nails and wood had to be purchased at a local lumber yard. Bales of hay or straw for packing were procured from a nearby rancher. Since the South Party drove no trucks, arrangements also had to be made for hauling the larger fossil blocks to the freight yards in Bridgeport or Scotts Bluff. From there the cargo was shipped under a category in the railroad manuals called "Fossils-in-Rock," a reduced rate first granted to the collectors of the late 1800s. Once the material arrived in Lincoln, it was trucked to the laboratory at Morrill Hill, where it awaited the field-workers' return. During the long Nebraska winter several members of the expedition, including Loren, reversed the process that had begun on the High Plains. Working with a handsaw and small chisels, they gingerly removed the protective coverings from their securely wrapped packages, enabling them to grasp the full range of their discoveries for the first time. "It was," as someone remarked, "a bone hunters' Christmas every day."

During their trips to the freight yards, Bert noticed that Loren went out of his way to strike up conversations with members of the transient population. One day he asked his friend if he was lonely for his days as a drifter. "No," was the reply. "Just curious why these men are doing what they do." With Loren, Bert mused, it was always "the why."[18]

Camp morale soared near the end of each month in anticipation of payday. When their checks caught up with them in some nearby town, the expedition members all piled into cars and drove to the bank together. Emerging with cash in hand, they stood on the curb and exchanged their currency for IOUs written during the preceding weeks. Then it was off to the local merchants to square individual accounts for everything from groceries to automobile repairs. Loren earned about sixty dollars a month and, like the others, received a food allowance of fifty cents a day. At first, both he and Emery tried to live on a little over half that amount, vowing to pocket the rest. When the two next joined the Schultzes and the others in camp, they ceremoniously announced that they would continue to do their own cooking rather than contribute their full daily allowance to the common fund. Sitting off to one side with their tin utensils and meager fare, they watched enviously while Marian served up thick cold cuts, boiled potatoes and onions, coleslaw, canned pineapple, and green beans in white enamel bowls. Banana cream pudding, chilled to perfection in a nearby stream, followed; so did Loren and Emery. Taking their lumps good-naturedly, they joined the others at dinner, and even washed the dishes with only minor complaints.[19]

IV

Their latest shipment of bones safely on its way, Loren, Frank, and Emery began working a canyon named Black Hank on the north side of the Wildcat Range. They blocked out an oreodont skeleton and sighted another protruding from a cliff face beyond their reach. After considerable discussion the three reluctantly decided to borrow a heavy fourteen-foot ladder, which they took turns lugging deep into the narrow chasm. Emery tersely recorded what happened next. "June 24. Used ladder to get to nice specimen which later fell and rolled down 150 ft. slope. Negative Results." The rest of the month went little better. Emery closed it out with a chilling reminder of why everyone was required to wear high-top boots while in the field: "Killed first rattler."[20]

In the meantime, things were going well at the new bison quarry below Signal Butte, where digging had begun on June 8. Using a combination of pickaxes, shovels, and a horse-drawn metal scraper, or fresno, the workers had pushed aside portions of the massive overburden to reveal a great Pleistocene ossuary. The two- to four-foot vein of compacted bone was thirty feet long and yielded hundreds of pounds of material every week. Although most of the huge skulls were badly crushed, ten were obtained in restorable condition, along with enough fibias, femurs, vertebrae, ribs, pelvises, and scapulae to fill several rooms. As word of the major find spread, Bert found himself hosting a growing list of distinguished visitors, including the South Party's steadfast patron, Charles H. Morrill.

Loren and Emery worked at the bison quarry on occasion, but Bert preferred to keep them moving. His thoughts returned to the many bones that Denton had examined north of Bridgeport in early June. On July 9 Bert, Loren, Emery, and Frank Denton returned to the area to explore further. They quickly determined that the prospects were mixed. It was true that hundreds of bones lay scattered over the surface, but most of these were either very small or fragmentary. Nevertheless, Bert thought the site promising enough to order the others to make camp and open a new quarry the following day.

While they camped on the J. H. Brubaker farm, the Bridgeport Quarry was located on the land of Jim Lister, about a mile or so to the north. Loren and Emery separated from Frank and began digging just below the sparse sod on top of an eroding hill. By July 20 they were picking up over one hundred bones a day, most of which came from the feet of some lost Tertiary species of rhinoceros.[21] "It was useless," Loren recalled, "to ask why we found only foot bones and why we gathered the mineralized things in such fantastic quantities that they must still be stacked in some museum storehouse. Maybe," he conjectured, "the creatures had been immured standing up in a waterhole and the . . . carcasses had eroded away from the hilltop stratum. But there were the foot bones, and the orders had come down, so we dug carpals and metacarpals till we cursed like an army platoon that headquarters has forgotten."[22]

At the Brubaker farm Loren and Emery encountered the retarded daughter of a sod house–dwelling tenant from whom the bone hunters purchased their fresh milk and eggs. Loren preserved a studied image of her in one of his most evocative essays, "The Last Neanderthal." Short, thickset, and massive, her body was not that of a typical peasant woman. "Along the eye orbit at the edge of the frontal bone I could see . . . an armored protuberance that, particularly in women, had vanished before the close of the Würmian ice." When she walked, her head swayed like a giant muzzle beneath its curls; thick golden hair covered her powerful forearms. "We are out of time, I thought quickly. We are each and every one displaced. She is the last Neanderthal, and she does not know what to do. We are those who eliminated her long ago." Yet to Loren's surprise, he was swept by a compelling sexual urge when he gazed across at her in the camp firelight one evening. "I saw through the thin dress, the powerful thighs, the yearning fertility going unmated in this lonesome spot." They broke camp not long afterward. Loren stood by the running board, letting his eyes wander over that massive "yet tragically noble head" one last time. He bid her farewell. "The motors started. *Homo sapiens*, the energy devourer, was on his way once more."[23]

Emery's old Chevy had a top speed of fifty-five miles an hour. Whenever they were headed for Lincoln and Loren was at the wheel, he drove the dust-choked gravel highway with the gas pedal hard against the rattling floorboards. With Eugene Vanderpool, Loren and Emery left Bridgeport for the capital on Saturday, July 23, at 7:00 P.M. After driving all night on bad roads, they wheeled into the city just past noon the following day, a record run. Even though the collecting season was far from over, Loren had recently decided to call it a summer. "Eiseley leaves party for trip to California," Emery had jotted in his field notes just before they headed in.[24]

The West Coast may have been Loren's ultimate destination, but it was not his immediate one. "An opportunity has suddenly come my way to do archeological research for the next two months or so among the pueblos of the Southwest," he had written to Dr. Barbour from Redington on July 16. "As it is a chance I have long hoped for—and since such chances come but rarely—I thought it possible you would not mind too greatly if I obtained my release on the 25th." Loren went on to say that he did not have the money to return to school in the fall and that he wanted to avoid spending the next few months in idleness.[25]

The old gentleman may have been even more solicitous than usual because of a keen disappointment Loren had suffered earlier in the year. Writing on April 23 to Bill Gaffney, who was in New York, Loren mentioned that he "didn't get the scholarship to C. Better go hoboing with me."[26] The "C" he referred to was Columbia University. In February, Barbour had written a letter of recommendation in his behalf, which concluded: "[Eiseley] is exactly the type of man that such institutions as Yale, Harvard, and Columbia seek."[27] Loren's uneven and prolonged undergraduate career had probably tipped the scales against him. His rejection, which had come in the spring, doubtless contributed to his desire to get into the field far earlier than before. Had Columbia's decision been favorable, he would have taken no Incompletes and graduated in June 1932. As matters now stood, he was soon to enter his eighth year as an undergraduate.

For an aspiring anthropologist, Loren's timing could hardly have been worse. The digging proceeded in his absence, with most of the manpower now concentrated at the Scotts Bluff Bison Quarry. On August 4, shortly before the noon break, a volunteer high-school student named Gordon Graham called attention to a dart point exposed by the intentional carving off of a bank containing fossil bones. The artifact's position was well toward the lower layer of the fossil bed, about ten inches above the floor of Brule clay. Before the removal of the overburden, it had been buried at a depth of some fourteen feet.

Bert was summoned immediately. When, without thinking, their leader reached down to pick up the point, his arm was firmly pushed away by the quick-witted Graham. "Leave it in situ," the youth cautioned. Bert had become highly suspicious by now and accused several in the camp of planting the artifact as a practical joke, then using the callow Graham as their goat. By the time Bert was convinced that the discovery was indeed genuine, the dart point had begun to slip from its precarious position. Someone ran to fetch his camera so that pictures could be taken in the presence of the expedition team. Within minutes a slight jar caused the specimen to dislodge from the fine gravel, but the impression left in the bank was itself venerated like a holy relic. During the next few days numerous influential pilgrims of science, such as Childs Frick and Duncan Strong, who was now excavating Indian relics on Signal Butte for the Smithsonian Institution, visited the site. Meanwhile, Bert wired Dr. Barbour, who arrived on August 6 in the company of Earl Bell, Loren's first professor of anthropology. Five more weeks of digging among the extinct bison bones yielded seven other flint artifacts: three knives, two scrapers, and two broken dart points.[28]

Finds of this type were rare and inevitably gave rise to more questions than answers—not to mention a whirlwind of scientific controversy. Ever since 1839, when several arrowheads, stone axes, and a spearpoint had been uncovered among some mammoth bones in Minnesota, a few heretics within the anthropological profession had believed that man had been an inhabitant of North America for at least ten thousand years, perhaps longer. According to this theory, he had migrated from northern Europe via Alaska while the planet was held in thrall by massive sheets of ice. Recent discoveries had given the harried exponents of the Ice Age hypothesis even greater reason to hope. At Folsom, in extreme northeastern New Mexico, a number of beautifully executed spearpoints had been found in undisputed association with the remains of an extinct species of bison—the same species, it later turned out, being excavated at Scotts Bluff. Then, 150 miles to the south, near Clovis, similar yet distinct spearpoints of what appeared to be Pleistocene mammoth hunters were recovered from the bluish gray sands and hearths of butchering grounds. And even as the South Party was unearthing what were eventually proven to be Paleo-Indian artifacts, the anthropologist J. D. Figgins, working in nearby Dent, Colorado, was excavating the remains of at least twelve mammoths, along with fluted spearpoints and numerous large stones that had been carried by early human predators to their kill site. Indeed, the list of such locations was growing by the year, but the traditionalists, who remained in the majority, staunchly clung to their beliefs.

At least some of their reservations were admittedly difficult to dismiss. Perhaps, as many of them argued, the mammoth and ancient bison had persisted later into prehistory than anyone realized. And why, if they once existed, had no one found so much as a tooth from one of the mysterious slayers of these great shaggy beasts? What was more, most of the available evidence was too recent and scattered to support the revolutionary shift in dating revisionists demanded.

As far as Bert was concerned, the data were already more than sufficient to prove that man had been an inhabitant of North America for much longer than the conventional estimate of two thousand years. From their private conversations, he knew that Loren also held this view. Yet when Bert later bemoaned the fact that his friend had not been present to share in the greatest discovery of all, Loren was not so much disappointed as relieved. He told Bert of his ambition to continue his anthropological studies on the graduate level. Becoming associated with such a highly controversial discovery might ruin his chances of entering a reputable institution. Bert understood and promised not to link the Eiseley name to the Scotts Bluff discovery when writing up his findings.[29]

V

On the morning of April 24, 1930, twelve years of planning and construction, undertaken at a cost to Nebraska's taxpayers of $10 million, were brought to a spectacular conclusion. A nine-and-a-half-ton bronze statue, heavily coated with beeswax to protect it from the elements, began its final ride to the top of the newly built state capitol tower, four hundred feet above the city. Within thirty minutes the metal giant, measuring nineteen and a half feet from head to toe, rested on its side atop the massive limestone structure; it was righted a week later and set upon a twelve-and-a-half-foot pedestal of sculpted wheat and corn.[30]

The Sower, as the figure became popularly known, was the work of Lee Lawrie, the renowned New York architectural sculptor and former pupil of Augustus Saint-Gaudens. The barefoot colossus, portrayed in the ancient custom of hand-casting seed, wears an Egyptian hood and peasant's tunic; from his waist hangs a cloth sack bulging with grain. Yet as Lawrie was quick to point out, it is not oats, corn, or wheat that this bronze giant is metaphorically casting to the four winds. Rather, he sows the seeds of life—the promise of bringing a finer, more noble existence to all Nebraskans.

The statue, which had been commissioned during the boom times following World War I, immediately became an object of mockery in the eyes of many Cornhuskers, especially those who sought to wrest a living from the dying land. By the time Loren returned from his time in the Southwest late in 1932—a sojourn about which nothing is known—the state's basic industry was virtually moribund. Oats were selling for ten cents a bushel, corn and barley for only three pennies more; wheat topped the grain market at twenty-seven cents.[31]

Drought recurs in twenty- to thirty-year cycles on the Great Plains. The years 1931 through 1933 brought less than normal rainfall; in 1934 Nebraska received only fourteen inches, the lowest amount in seventy years. Conditions were even worse in states to the south, where the high price of wheat during World War I had encouraged farmers to plow and seed areas that had formerly been used only for grazing. After years of high yields, surplus grain flooded the market, causing prices to tumble. Cattle were returned to the traditional grasslands, where their hooves pulverized the thin, moisture-starved topsoil. And always there was the wind—in summer dry and sear, withering the limp leaves of the stunted corn, wailing around the corners of the farm buildings; in winter frigid and biting, piling snow into ten-foot drifts.

Suddenly, it began. The prairie winds swept up tons of powdery soil, carrying it from Oklahoma to the Dakotas and beyond, blotting out the sun, creating darkness at noon. When the winds temporarily died down, their burden settled in multicolored drifts against sheds and fencerows, red soil from Oklahoma, yellow from Kansas, other hues from other states. Abandoned cattle walked knee-deep across these new landmasses, only to find that they were bridges to nowhere. Thirst and starvation waited on both sides of the fence and sometimes claimed their victims halfway, front quarters and hind neatly divided by barbed wire. Only the coyote and the buzzard made out.

Like their crops, people became straws in the wind. Sheriffs' auctions on Lincoln's courthouse steps put cattle, horses, machinery, and household possessions on the block to satisfy mortgages held by the banks that were themselves foundering. As things got tougher, the county hired those on relief to pick water grass from the courthouse lawn on their hands and knees.[32] Echoes of the Populist Revolt, kindled by the drought and depression of the late 1880s, reverberated across the land. Although William Jennings Bryan, the Lincoln lawyer whose silver tongue won him fame as "the boy orator of the Platte," had died in 1925, many Nebraskans, including William Buchanan Price, an old Bryan protégé, were still imbued with the three-time presidential candidate's fighting spirit. A frequent and previously disappointed candidate for various public offices, Buck rode the massive Roosevelt landslide to victory in the November elections of 1932 as the new state auditor. Loren, who had moved back under Buck's roof upon returning to Lincoln, could not help but be proud of his dauntless uncle. Yet so far as his friends could recall, he shared none of Buck's political fervor or shirtsleeve passion for social justice. When asked if Loren was political in any sense, Bill Gaffney responded: "Nohow!"[33]

Loren did, however, possess a "capacity for tremendous visual memory."[34] Though loath to admit it, the son gradually came to realize that it was from his mother, a skilled freehand drawer, that he inherited the eye, if not the hand, of an artist. He experimented with paper and colored chalk in 1932 or 1933. His two surviving works present a strange contrast between the whimsical and the macabre. In one drawing a seemingly playful mammoth rears up on its hind legs, frightening away stick men who want no part of the frolicsome beast. In the other the forward-leaning figure of Death, his hideous red skull highlighted in green, appears to be leading the headlong charge of the Book of Revelation's accursed Four Horsemen.[35]

Yet for the time being, the poet held sway. Loren's themes—desolation, loneliness, autumn winds, cold, and death—had changed little during the previous eight years, although his style reflected a greater maturity. Sensitive to the criticism of those who thought him overly preoccupied by the tragic, he gave his subtly disguised reply in a review of Robinson Jeffers's "Music of the Mountain," which appeared in the New England quarterly, *Voices*:

> Jeffers' celebration of death . . . is only a paradoxical substitute to hands reaching for the moon. It is the only gift that quite overwhelms and destroys the consciousness that our puny and limited bodies cannot long endure nor satisfy. . . . [His] are not the words of a complacent pessimist who has already set up housekeeping in his tomb. There is a greater pride of life in them than in the words of many optimists. They shine the brighter coming as they do from a man who has known full the depths of the "night side of love."[36]

Appreciative of Loren's sympathetic reading, Jeffers sent his young champion a letter of thanks.

However much Loren was drawn to the haunted works of Jeffers, Browne, Donne, Poe, Melville, and Yeats, it was the abiding melancholy of Lowry Wimberly that gave the stamp of legitimacy to his unshakable sense of alienation. That imprimatur lay heavy upon the *Prairie Schooner* as well. "Dog in the Manger," a regular section for comments from readers, ran a letter from a Mrs. H.M.W. of Chicago, whose copy of the little magazine arrived one morning just after breakfast. "I sat down immediately, as I always do, and read it through. Heavens! what a morbid affair! I felt so happy when I got up this morning; the sun was shining—a rare event in Chicago—and now I feel as if the Yoke of the Oxen were around my neck."[37]

In 1933 the university's board of regents was forced by the legislature to adopt a draconian budget. All salaries over $1,500 were reduced by 22 percent, in addition to a 10 percent cut ordered the previous year. The School of Fine Arts was closed, although Mabel's services were retained. All tuition awards, save the 150 Regents Scholarships, were eliminated, along with forty-two major and twenty minor faculty positions.[38] "The time was now," Loren wrote. "One more impediment and I knew what would happen." There would be no diploma, no future as a writer or much of anything else.[39] Having removed the Incompletes from his record before the beginning of spring semester 1933, Loren had at last cleared the way for his graduation in June. During the few months that remained, he took introductory German, which he would need in the pursuit of an advanced degree. A second course, Archeology of North America, rounded out his schedule and was credited as graduate work.[40] He chose not to participate in the graduation ceremonies with those who were four years his junior and total strangers. Both his name and picture were absent from the *Cornhusker*.

VI

Bachelor of arts in anthropology and English in hand, Loren began his third summer with the South Party a week or two after graduating. Writing to Wimberly from near Bridgeport on June 22, he struck the same melancholy chord he had in his letter to Bill Gaffney while in the field the year before:

> The work progresses but all in all it is lonely here and the days pass slowly. An occasional coyote met in the hills, the heat and quiet and the bones of dead beasts make up our day. I'll try and send you a picture or so later.
>
> Yesterday a flood came down the canyon from a rain in the hills. We had to scamper for higher ground. It is night now and outside the darkness is filled with the cries of some peculiarly mournful type of frog brought out by the floods. My back is blistered from the sun and I think I shall brave the frogs and go down and splash around in the darkness. There is a whole heaven full of stars and I can only repeat again inarticulately that it is lonely . . . lonely. You can't believe civilization exists here. I write to the *Schooner* office but it is only a myth somehow that the senses refuse to acknowledge. And by the way—have we become a myth?[41]

But things in the field were not always dull. Emery, with whom Loren was digging again, remembered well the terrifying incident of the flood. The sky had suddenly opened up and rain pelted the arid land. The deluge, which lasted for hours, had no sooner begun to subside than a horseman came galloping down the valley where the fossil hunters were camped. "There's four foot of water coming; get your gear and head for higher ground!" The two succeeded in moving their belongings just as the water surged. Loren, who loved to be photographed, climbed out onto the limb of an old willow, hollering over the din to Emery to take his picture. "It was really roaring by this time." Emery fetched his camera and was just bringing his companion into focus when the limb Loren was standing on snapped, throwing him into the torrent. Realizing that his friend couldn't swim, Emery put the camera down and raced for the tree. But by the time he reached the water's edge, Loren had somehow managed to pull himself back onto the willow, exhausted but unscathed.[42]

While Loren and Emery continued to dig north of Bridgeport, the rest of the party set up camp at the base of Scotts Bluff National Monument, the first of the great buttes pioneers encountered while traversing the Oregon Trail. With one exception, the faces were all familiar. T. Mylan Stout, a fine-featured, shy geology major whom Barbour dubbed "my walking encyclopedia," had joined the expedition early in June. Mylan possessed a keen eye for detail and became Bert's closest associate next to Marian, a relationship that would continue throughout their lives.

Few in the party took so much as a single day off during their first month in the field, not even the Fourth of July. The Schultzes headed for Denver on July 8, while the rest of the party drove south through Colorado and into New Mexico, where they visited the Paleo-Indian kill site at Folsom. There they viewed an arresting display of the mysterious Pleistocene points. Many were several inches long with beautifully fluted edges whose makers had been inspired to transcend simple craftsmanship, creating art. Afterward they drove over to Santa Fe, where Loren promised that a friend would be pleased to put them up. They soon learned, however, that their prospective host was out of town.

Night was fast coming on, and the young men were dead tired, having driven straight through on several hundred miles of washboard roads. After blundering around in the dark for some time, they arrived at what Mylan described as "a big expanse that seemed all right." They pitched their tents, tumbled into their blankets, and quickly nodded off, taking little notice of the pungent odor permeating the night air. "The next morning we got up and found we were in the middle of the city dump." No one suggested that they hang around to prepare breakfast. Sighting a building in the distance, they decided to drive over and ask for directions. Several uniformed men appeared, their rifles and pistols pointed at the startled faces behind the windshield. The guards of the New Mexico State Penitentiary were taking no chances, especially with two carloads of unshaven, rather desperate-looking characters with Nebraska license plates. After answering a few questions, the frightened bone hunters were told to scram in language Mylan described as less than polite.[43]

Loren and his companions headed north for Taos. Cultural life there was presided over by Mabel Dodge Luhan, the American heiress known for her salons in Paris, Florence, and New York. A friend and patron of leading artists and writers, she regularly entertained Gertrude and Leo Stein, Alice B. Toklas, John Reed, Pablo Picasso, Henri Matisse, Max Eastman, Isadora Duncan, and D. H. Lawrence. Loren was determined to introduce himself, having read much about life in the famous Luhan compound, which was modeled after ancient Indian communal dwellings. Only Frank Crabill remembered anything about the July afternoon spent there. "Mabel Dodge Luhan had a very lovely house. . . . Trees were a rarity and she had this place surrounded with trees of all kinds; it was a real oasis."[44] Loren, the only one in the party with literary ambitions, was left to talk in private with Mrs. Luhan while the others explored the surrounding sights. The young men were back in the field only three days after having set out for the Southwest, about to enter a land forgotten not only by the twentieth century but by time itself.

VII

The region where the boundaries of Nebraska, South Dakota, and Wyoming now meet figured prominently in the history of several Indian tribes. In the earliest days the Crow, who called themselves the Absaroka, or bird people, controlled the land; later the Cheyenne took possession by force, only to be pushed out in turn by the Dakota Sioux. The people of the Dakota believed that Wakan Tanka, a powerful spirit of nature, had rent the earth during a great storm, thus protecting them from invasion by fierce tribes living in the western mountains. According to legend, nothing could grow on the sprawling, barren swath left by the cataclysm: to the Sioux this would forever be the *mako shika*, "land bad." Eighteenth-century French traders and trappers, probably the first of their race to cross this part of the continent, took the Sioux at their word. On what represented the western boundaries of their hand-drawn maps, the voyageurs scrawled *les mauvaises terres a traverser*—"bad lands to travel across." But to early settlers, who had no intention of moving on, this great wilderness of rock and grass, incised by water and sculpted by wind, was simply the Badlands.

In mid-July the South Party began to explore the southern flank of the White River Basin, the most spectacular and dramatic stretch of land sculpture in northwestern Nebraska. Giant boulders of red granite, hundreds of miles from their point of origin, litter the sparse terrain as far as the eye can see. Stratified layers of corpse blue volcanic clay, five hundred feet thick in places, are juxtaposed against cream, pink, red, and green bands of sand crystals and brittle scoria. Caves filled with stygian shadows abound, while thin drifts of sterile earth conceal bogs that can swallow up the unwary.

Temperatures fall to 40 degrees below zero in winter, and sometimes hit 110 above on a late summer's afternoon. General Alfred Scully, the craggy old Sioux baiter, coined the classic description of the Badlands when he called them "Hell with the fires out." In the shimmering distance, certain formations take on the overwhelming presence of lost civilizations: domes, towers, minarets, and spires adorn cathedrals, mosques, and palaces, creating skylines never dreamed of by the architects of old. Such visions fade quickly, however, for the land inevitably reasserts its claim on the incongruous and the grotesque. Cathedrals dissolve into runneled, sunbaked ridges, while turreted castles are overrun by the anarchy of rocks. Never ceasing, the wind whips across the peaks and down into the narrow ravines, mocking the birds who fly into it by flinging them back beyond the point where they took wing.

Loren claimed that he had almost eidetic recall of his "solitary years" in the Badlands and that the place "enchanted" him.[45] One of his most extensive passages on the subject suggests that his true feelings were otherwise:

> In the last glow from the west one gets the impression of a waste over which has passed something inhumanly remote and terrifying—something that has happened long ago, but which lies close to the surface. Crows circle above it like disturbed black memories which rise and fall but never come to rest. It is a barren and disordered landscape, which remembers, and perhaps again anticipates, the cold of glacial ice. It has nothing to do with man; its gravels, its red afterglow, are remnants of another era, in which man was of no consequence.[46]

In actuality Loren spent only a month in the Badlands—and less than six months with the South Party altogether. He and Emery joined their colleagues on July 24 at the Paul Zerbst ranch, ten miles north of Harrison in Sioux County, virtually within sight of the Wyoming and South Dakota borders. From there they fanned out to work the Miocene deposits atop Pine Ridge. At its base, eight hundred to one thousand feet below, Oligocene deposits also beckoned.

By ten o'clock the morning chill had vanished; shirts were discarded, but still the sweat ran down the diggers' arms in small rivers that petered out in the thick dust coating their wrists, like freshets in desert arroyos. The dust settled just as thickly in their hair and, after mixing with their sweat, gradually hardened, forming a peculiar kind of plaster of Paris. They took turns dizzily searching the sky for signs of relief, but all anyone ever saw were a few scattered clouds that taunted them by assuming the exotic shapes of the very creatures whose bones they hunted.

During rest periods they scrambled for shade of any kind. Munching on a sandwich, Loren could see miniature cattle and horses grazing on distant, grass-rich flats, where little more than a generation before buffalo had covered the land like a moving robe. To the northeast lay the Pine Ridge and Rosebud Indian reservations, territory once patrolled by a blistered and saddle-sore Charles Frederick Eiseley. There the mysterious and gifted Crazy Horse rose to prominence, later to help lead the crushing assault on a headstrong Custer at the Greasy Grass, or what the whites called the Little Bighorn. Loren and the others purchased supplies at nearby Fort Robinson and visited the place where, in 1877, the defiant chief, a bluecoat hanging on either arm, was stabbed to death for allegedly resisting his captors.

The Sioux had not suffered alone. One day Loren came upon a long-deserted cabin, with a sand dune just beginning to swallow its far side. Whether the vanished occupants had been shot, run off, or simply left in despair was impossible to tell. He remembered a wash-pan with cast-iron handles hanging under the eaves, a long-laced woman's shoe, a Sears, Roebuck catalog dated 1900.[47] He had been reading Oswald Spengler and would soon discover Arnold Toynbee, whose theories of numbing beats and sweeping cycles matched perfectly his own vision of the prehistoric past. In the end, it mattered little whether one was contemplating the fate of the giant mastodon or some forgotten nester in cattle country, for it was all of a piece: neither amounted to more than a shrug of eternity.

Despite the considerable physical hardships, the work went well. The party uncovered its first carnivore remains, a saber-toothed cat skull, on July 21. Later in the day Bert was randomly poking around on the surface when he noticed large numbers of tiny rodent jaws, bleached white by the sun. He picked up thirty or so of the better Miocene specimens, which he showed to Mylan and Bob Long. Bob thought the find was a fluke and wagered Bert a malt that he could not duplicate his effort. The next morning Bert, accompanied by Bob and Mylan, gathered another forty jaws in short order.[48]

With much greater exertion, the Oligocene yielded equally important treasure. *Hyaenodon horridus*, the heavy-fanged, wolflike giant, put in an appearance during the last week of July, as did the burrowing beaver paleocastor. The remains of mesohippus, the small, graceful, three-toed horse, were only slightly less plentiful than those of the oreodonts, whose skulls and leg bones were uncovered by the score. On August 1, some thirteen miles north of Harrison and about three miles from Pine Ridge, Loren and Emery struck bone hunters' gold. Working along a road, they spotted fossils protruding from sandstone near the top of the so-called Chadron formation. It took but a few minutes to identify the remains, for there was nothing like them anywhere else in the world. Standing in a light rain the two might well have reached out and shaken hands; titanothere, the legendary Thunderhorse of the Sioux, who had first discovered its bones, had finally been run to earth.[49]

The giant measured as much as ten feet at the shoulder, fourteen feet in length, and weighed upward of ten thousand pounds. Its massive body was made all the more impressive by huge, shovellike horns that extended beyond an elongated snout. The fossils of more titanotheres surfaced during the next few weeks, as did those of most other members of the Oligocene bestiary—giant pigs, rhinoceroses, camels, deer, turtles, and an occasional mineralized egg. Many of the finest specimens were obtained northwest of Crawford in a vast, eerie field of gigantic stone mushrooms now known as Toadstool Park. Loren and Emery arrived there on August 3 and were joined by the rest of the party a few days later.

One afternoon, while Emery was busy elsewhere, Loren made what he looked back on as his single most memorable discovery. Working with Frank Crabill, he unearthed the skull of a saber-tooth. Further digging revealed that one of the predator's elongated canines, "beautiful as Toledo steel," pierced the leg bone of another cat of the same species. The excited collectors conjectured that these beasts had died in mortal combat. In a poem recounting the events of some 25 million years ago, Loren dubbed them "The Innocent Assassins," a name that also became the title of his second book of verse.

I wondered why
such perfect fury had been swept away, while man,
wide-roaming dark assassin of his kind,
has sprung up in the wake
of such perfected instruments as these.[50]

The skull and pierced tibia were placed on permanent exhibit in Morrill Hall, where they remain to this day.

The notebook Loren always carried in his shirt pocket was something of a mystery; he was forever taking it out, jotting down a line or two, then resuming work without comment. Yet unlike Bert and Emery, he was not required to keep a permanent set of field notes. Bob Long, who was only eighteen, considered Loren "a man of the world" and would have given a lot for a peek at those writings. "I had the very strong feeling that he was not keeping the kind of notes [the others] kept and that he was indeed recording things that he observed—whether it was mountains, flowers, stones, or whatever—and that he was writing down some of his deep thoughts. . . . The notebook was ever present."[51] Emery, who spent more time in the field with Loren than anyone, remembered only that his friend kept "some special notes" and that he never discussed their contents—nor did Emery ever inquire about them. "I just felt that he was meditating on something I was not familiar with or was not involved with."[52] Mylan realized what was going into Loren's notebooks, as did Frank and Bert. "We were very pleased that [Loren] was writing his poetry." Yet Mylan never thought of Loren as someone possessed of special gifts: "He was just one of us. That he would ever amount to anything as a writer was beyond our grasp at that time."[53]

In the evenings the party gathered around a small fire, repeating a ritual first enacted while man was still a dubious experiment in the highlands of East Africa. Sometimes they listened to depression-era ballads on Bert's old wind-up Victrola, but mostly they talked of the day's work and of what tomorrow might bring. Then, in this country of grandeur, immensity, and loneliness, silhouetted against sunsets so beautiful that one unconsciously reaches out to touch them, the campers listened as Loren recited some new poem for the first time. Shadows lengthened and disappeared; the moon drifted low in the silver chill; countless in their shimmering numbers, the stars reclaimed the night sky.

8

MASKS

I

Philadelphia's Woodlands Cemetery, which sits atop gently rolling hills overlooking the placid Schuylkill River, is a monument to Victorian sensibilities. Fronted by a great fence of black iron spears, the sprawling graveyard is rich in obelisks and marble crosses. Statues of angels, both guardian and avenging, stand among chiseled stone tablets of every description, while mock cathedral spires rise high above the earth. Amid this Poelike setting, meandering old pathways of sunken bricks convey the living to the dead, some of whom were born when the frontier still lay east of the Appalachians. The most dominant feature is a sixty-foot obelisk commemorating Dr. Thomas William Evans, the nineteenth-century founder of a museum and dental institute, both of which bore the philanthropist's name. Woodlands was only a ten-minute walk from the room Loren Eiseley had just rented in a five-story, red-brick apartment building at 4514 Pine Street. The "Pride of the Bad Lands," as he printed beneath his name in a student notebook from this period, sometimes came to ruminate at the base of Evans's towering memorial.[1]

Loren had left the South Party in early September 1933 and headed east two or three weeks later to begin graduate study in anthropology at the University of Pennsylvania. He had saved a little money while working in the field but not nearly enough to cover tuition at an Ivy League institution, let alone pay his room and board for the academic year. Having lived more or less under Buck's roof for the past decade, he could not bring himself to ask his uncle for additional financial support; still, he did not object when Mabel offered to approach the flamboyant Buck. Penn, she argued, would be a good thing for Loren; graduate education was the way of the future, and once the terrible depression was over an advanced degree from a top-notch university would open up numerous possibilities. Buck, who considered the pretty yet practical-minded Miss Langdon a good influence on his nephew, waited politely until she had finished, then gave her a reassuring wink.[2]

Had Loren not been befriended by an influential figure at Penn, his spotty academic record would probably have elicited another letter of rejection. Edgar Billings Howard, a transplanted millionaire from an old and distinguished New Orleans family, had grown restless in the Philadelphia-based export-import business. In 1929, at age forty-two, he obtained an appointment as research associate at the University of Pennsylvania Museum. A 1909 graduate of Yale, Howard completed a master of science in archaeology at Penn in 1930 and went on to earn his Ph.D. five years later. Loren had first met the wan, bespectacled Howard in Lincoln when he came to consult with Dr. Barbour and Bert Schultz on various scientific matters. He was especially interested in the Paleo-Indian artifacts Bert and the others had unearthed at the Scotts Bluff Bison Quarry, for Howard had a dream of proving the existence of Folsom man by excavating his skeletal remains. He had been working in New Mexico and Arizona when Loren had struck out for the Southwest during the summer of 1932. How much time Loren may have spent with Howard is unknown, but Mabel later stated that Loren went to Penn because of his contacts with the Philadelphia patrician.[3]

Loren had developed a reputation as a writer and literary intellectual at the University of Nebraska, but this counted for little at Penn, where he was an outlander starting anew. His classroom debut was so disastrous that he gave serious thought to catching the next train west.

Fall classes began on October 6. A nervous Loren climbed the four flights of stairs to 400 College Hall, the combination office, library, and seminar room of Dr. Frank Gouldsmith Speck, chairman of the three-member Department of Anthropology. He took a seat among the handful of students enrolled in Ethnology of the American Indian and waited for the professor to appear. The stocky, dark-complexioned Speck strode to the seminar table and pulled up a chair, a little cigar of the brand Between the Acts protruding from the corner of his mouth. To Loren he appeared surly, but when he began speaking the ideas poured forth like rain. Loren, who was shy and absorbed in taking notes, said nothing; when class was over he promptly departed, and this pattern continued for weeks. One day Speck emptied a small container of square-cut metallic objects onto the table and barked: "What are these? Any of you know?" He eyed Loren, the experienced archaeologist, like a hunter about to spring a trap.

"They are not Indian at all," Loren replied. "They are eighteenth-century gun flints for flintlock rifles." He could hear the other students tittering in the background. They were certain "the old man" had tripped up the silent newcomer.

"What makes you so sure?" Speck shot back.

"Sir," Loren answered, "I just know. They're square-cut European flint. I've seen them on the guns themselves."

"You are right," Speck growled without changing expression. The tittering ceased. "Class is dismissed."

"Jeez," whispered Richard Faust, the student seated next to Loren. "The old man will make you pay for that. He likes to win those games."[4]

Not yet knowing how to read his future mentor, Loren thought back on the letters he had exchanged with the feisty chairman before coming east. It seems that neither he nor Mabel had quite told Buck the whole truth concerning his prospects. Loren was welcome to come to Penn if he wished, Speck had written, but jobs were few and far between. A student of his limited resources would probably starve in a city like Philadelphia, and there would be absolutely no possibility of any financial support until he had completed at least one year of graduate work. If, after considering these factors, Loren was still determined to enroll, Speck would do what he could for him.[5] Reflecting on the day's harrowing encounter, it is hardly surprising that Loren considered disappearing, yet he settled instead for a lonely stroll through Woodlands Cemetery before sunset.

Word of the incident quickly made the rounds of the small department. A few days later Loren was hailed on the street by a ruggedly handsome young man with the shoulders and easy carriage of a natural athlete. Although the smiling stranger was not a member of the seminar, Loren had seen him browsing in Speck's library as if it was his own. He introduced himself as Lewis "Lou" Korn, a graduate student in the department, and confessed, somewhat sheepishly, that he had been watching Loren's sincere but awkward attempts to win Speck's favor. "Loren needed some help," he recalled. "He was kind of boyish for his age."[6]

According to Lou, who had studied under Speck at nearby Swarthmore College before following him to Penn, Speck was not as put off by Loren as the newcomer had talked himself into believing. Both the straight-from-the-shoulder correspondence and the rough initiation before the class were his way of separating the wheat from the chaff, of seeing who would stick up for himself and who would back down under pressure, a fatal flaw in an anthropologist. By holding his ground and not falling for the old gunflint trick, Loren had secretly pleased his inquisitor: "Proved you're from the West" is how Lou put it. At the same time, Lou faulted Loren for being impervious to his surroundings and always leaving right after class: "The old man doesn't like it. He thinks if you're a true anthropologist, not just a student, you should stick around. It's part of his way of judging people." There was one more thing; if Loren should ever see Speck on campus, he must never forget to "sing out." "Just remember the old man hates formalities and he's spent time in the north woods."[7]

II

The north woods to which Lou Korn referred were mainly those of Canada's great Labrador Peninsula, home of the Naskapi Indians, skilled hunters and trappers who covered their wigwams with the skin of the migrating caribou. Among Speck's few surviving personal papers is a letter from a member of the tribe. Its author, the owner of a three-foot bow and several arrows, thinks the weapons a bit too dangerous for his young son and wishes to know if Speck might find a buyer for them. He also possesses a "Dream Mask," which he is willing to sell. Finally, he wonders if the Philadelphia professor can obtain some eagle feathers for use in an upcoming ceremony.[8] To anyone who knew and understood Frank Speck, this letter is not what it might at first seem—a testament to the degradation of a once proud people. On the contrary, it is a communication not only from one man to another but between a Naskapi and a fellow member of his tribe.

Frank Speck was the elder son of Frank Gouldsmith and Hattie L. Saniford Speck, born in Brooklyn on November 8, 1881. When the boy reached the age of seven, his health, which had never been good, deteriorated rapidly. Frank's parents decided to place him in the care of an old friend, Mrs. Fidelia A. Fielding of Mohegan, Connecticut. A widow who had already raised a family of her own, Mrs. Fielding also happened to be a full-blooded Indian and one of the few remaining speakers of her native tongue in southern New England. Speck's health underwent a marked improvement within weeks of his leaving home. He attended a local grammar school and quickly made friends among the Indian children, a transition aided by his own claim to Indian ancestry. Meanwhile, the youth began mastering the Mohegan language under the watchful eye of Mrs. Fielding, an avid gardener and herbalist. The love of natural history she instilled became one of his great passions, as did the nonconformity and social rebellion that made up an important part of her heritage. In her home Speck developed a deep sense of irony toward white society and its culturally narrow view of the past.

At age fourteen the youth returned to live with his family in their new home in Hackensack, New Jersey. A lover of water and wildlife, Speck purchased a dugout canoe and spent much of his free time paddling alone through the yet unspoiled salt marshes of the eastern shore. He graduated from high school and entered Columbia University at the turn of the century. Uncertain about his future, he embarked upon theological studies without any specific objective in mind.

During his sophomore year, Speck immersed himself in the study of classical languages and enrolled in a course on philology taught by the eminent linguist and polyglot John Dyneley Prince. Prince was lecturing one day on the peculiarities of certain Hebrew words when a hand shot up in the back of the room.

"I believe I can understand that, sir. It is very similar to what exists in Mohegan."

Prince paused and adjusted his glasses before answering. "Young man, Mohegan is a dead language. Nothing has been recorded of it since the eighteenth century. Don't bluff."

"But sir," came the impassioned reply, "it can't be dead so long as an old woman I know still speaks it. She is Pequot-Mohegan. I learned a bit of vocabulary from her and could speak it with her myself. She took care of me when I was a child."

"Young man," answered the intrigued but dubious Prince, "be at my house for dinner at six this evening. You and I are going to look into this matter."[9]

Within months the first of three articles, "The Modern Pequots and Their Language," appeared under the joint authorship of the professor and his student in the prestigious journal *American Anthropologist*. Before Speck received his B.A. in 1904, ten other papers were published under his name alone.[10]

A natural prankster who chafed at the formalities of academia and the pretensions of polite society, Speck was more than merely eccentric. He lived a simple, uncluttered life and was most at home when paddling a canoe down an unspoiled river or camping out in the mesmerizing silence of the north woods. The chairman's graduate classes rarely lasted to the end of the academic year. Speck grew increasingly restless as spring advanced, until he finally vanished with the migrating geese. The professor exchanged his rumpled, ill-fitting suit for the garments of a trapper of the Canadian forests, some of Indian, some of white manufacture. Heavy fur mittens protected his large hands while knee-length mukluks, bound by thin strips of caribou hide, kept his feet warm and dry. From under the wolf fur circling the massive forehead peered the steady, dark eyes and formidable countenance of the voyageur and mountain man who had preceded the great rush of whites into the High Plains.

III

By November Loren had moved from the apartment building on Pine Street to 4619 Cedar Avenue, a private residence in the same prosperous West Philadelphia neighborhood. Built shortly after the turn of the century, the three-story brick duplex had a large front porch overlooked by matching bay windows facing south. The twenty-minute walk to College Hall took him by block after block of stately homes on wide, undulating streets. Even though money was tight, Loren was living amid surroundings that were materially better than those he had known in Lincoln.

"I've been busier than a flea on a hairless dog," Loren wrote to Bert Schultz the second week in November. "I have seen Howard a good many times. He has been very kind and gracious to me and very much interested in the activities out there."[11] Lowry Wimberly also heard from him: "This is a *real* Anthropology department—a keen brilliant set of men that can't be bluffed. . . . Things are running quite nicely now though I despair of being able to get my degree in the one school year. Degree or not, however, the experience has been very worthwhile."[12] Busy as he was, Loren found time to visit New York City, where he finally met Harold Vinal, the editor of the poetry journal *Voices* with whom he had corresponded for over five years. The urbane New Englander charmed his guest by showing Loren the town and then treating him to his first Broadway play, Christopher Morley's *Thunder on the Left*. "Vinal is a very sophisticated handsome appearing man of forty," Loren gushed to Wimberly. "I'll tell you about him at more length later." He closed with a plea for the Doc to pay him a visit: "Don't think I haven't yearned for the old armchair in the office. God!"[13]

Contrary to the upbeat tone of these letters, Loren would have only glum recollections of the period:

> When evening fell I looked out upon rain falling endlessly under the street lamps at the nearby corner. I was homesick. The high plains are cold in winter but they were sunny and unpolluted in that time. There was little in the way of diversion in Philadelphia because funds had to be husbanded carefully. I was just barely getting by; furthermore, I was not adjusted to the climate. Colds assailed me. The rain seemed never to cease in that autumn of 1933.[14]

Loren had been away from Mabel many times before, though never for quite so long. She wrote to him every day; he reciprocated but not as often because of his heavy workload. He never failed to write on Sundays, however, and sent each letter special delivery.[15] None of them was destined to survive: "I burned all of my precious letters because they were much too personal ever to be read by anyone but me," Mabel confided to a friend.[16]

One Philadelphia diversion Loren never mentioned was his close proximity to family. His half brother, Leo, who was now forty, had remarried in 1927, three years after his divorce from Mamie Harms. His second wife, the former Beatrice Howie, gave birth to their only child, a son they christened Leo Maurice Eiseley, Jr., in March of 1929, while the couple was living in Newport News, Virginia. Following a brief move to Pittsburgh, Leo, a repeater attendant with Western Union, was transferred to Philadelphia in the wake of the stock market crash. The Eiseleys lived in a number of apartments before settling down at 4504 Pine Street, just a door or two from Loren's first place of residence.[17]

The brothers had seen little of each other since Loren was a child; the difference in their ages and background prevented them from ever growing close. Nevertheless, Loren became a frequent guest at Sunday dinner and often turned up, restless after a solitary evening of study, to share a cup of coffee at Bea's kitchen table. By living so near to Leo he was assured of a helping hand should anything go amiss.

Loren also began to share confidences with Richard "Ricky" Faust, one of the dozen or so graduate students in the Anthropology Department. Ricky had been born in Japan to American missionary parents. He later attended the American School in Tokyo, then returned to the United States to take his B.A. in 1933 from Catawba College in Salisbury, North Carolina. Ricky boarded with family friends on Warrington Avenue and usually met Loren for lunch at some inexpensive campus restaurant, such as the Greek's or Pop Heller's. Afterward the two walked over to the decrepit university dormitory annex on Locust Street to play blackjack until it was time for class.

One of the dorm rooms was occupied by Takashi Francis Tachibana, an undergraduate biology major variously nicknamed Sir Francis Drake, Drake, Tachi, or, as Loren preferred, Duke. An American citizen, Duke had been born and spent his boyhood in Yuma, Arizona, where his immigrant father had grown wealthy in the grocery business. The Tachibanas had returned to their native Japan during the 1920s, and Duke had been enrolled in the American School, where he met and became fast friends with Ricky. It was Ricky who introduced Duke to Loren in October 1933. Impressed by the tall, deep-voiced westerner, Duke never addressed him by anything but his last name.

Heeding Lou Korn's advice, Loren and Ricky began to hang around Speck's cluttered office between seminars. Loren browsed the book-lined walls and kept track of the old man out of the corner of his eye, marveling at his powers of concentration. Speck sat at a small desk answering his correspondence and preparing final drafts of articles in a bold hand while his students conversed or plied him with questions. At another desk, near the door, sat his pretty Indian graduate assistant, Gladys Tantaquidgeon, a lineal descendant of an aide to Uncas, the chief made famous in James Fenimore Cooper's *The Last of the Mohicans*. Box turtles, collected by Speck on weekly forays into the countryside, wandered sedately over the littered floor, while nonpoisonous snakes writhed in mud-stained gunnysacks. Scattered everywhere were headdresses, leather breeches, rattles, hunting implements, cooking utensils, and Speck's most prized acquisitions—two birchbark canoes fashioned by the Montagnais of Lake St. John in northern Quebec.

Thinking Speck was away from the office one day, Loren donned an Indian bonnet and began an impromptu buffalo dance for the amusement of his friends: "*haiya, haiya, haiya.*" Speck had entered the room and stood, arms folded, watching the performance, but Loren did not catch the subtle hand signals of his audience. Finally he turned and froze in midstep, the blood rushing to his cheeks. Speck said nothing for several moments, then burst into laughter.[18] The mischievous professor was not above such conduct himself. As a way of getting his students "into the spirit of things," he began his introductory class in anthropology by walking into the room and issuing a resounding war whoop.

Both Lou and Ricky noticed that Speck had developed a particular liking for Loren, who began to spend an occasional day in the field with the chairman. Speck often took the morning train over to the New Jersey Pine Barrens, some three thousand square miles of swamp-edged streams, cranberry bogs, and stands of second-growth fir. During one such visit, Speck told a rapt Loren of how he had sat around campfires with "Pineys" whose ancestors had lured his grandfather's ship to destruction on the nearby coastal shoals.

On another occasion the two visited a taxidermist's shop at the edge of the barrens. Rough-hewn men with weather-worn faces were seated next to a wood-burning stove, talking of hunting and trapping. The smell of fox skins permeated the air; on the floor lay a pile of legs from freshly killed deer. "Saved 'em for you, Frank," the proprietor gestured. "Know how you're always takin' 'em to those Indians for rattles." Some adolescent boys gathered around Speck and listened eagerly to his Indian stories while he cut up the deer legs with the nonchalance of a master woodsman. Nobody said

"Doctor." Nobody said "Professor." When the time came to go, the youths tagged along behind the amused object of their veneration, eager to carry part of his load.[19]

Loren, whom Florence Speck considered "an essentially jealous individual" in matters concerning her husband, began to see himself as the master's apprentice.[20] He longed for the day when he, like Speck, might be "as close to earth as the fox's tail," at one "with the [timeless] men who dream the game" in the totemic dark, where animals speak and their skins are easily shifted.[21] Harold Vinal, who was always writing Loren in the hope of obtaining some new poems for *Voices*, received the following verse late in 1933:

> *Though I meekly pass*
> *Where you plow and fire,*
> *Everywhere I leave*
> *Fox fur on the wire—*
>
> *And a fox's face,*
> *Masked in human skin,*
> *Sometimes wild and sharp,*
> *Holds its laughter in.*[22]

Dream though he might, the shaman's apprentice must wait reverently for the moment when his master is no longer of this world before assuming his mantle. "I was fifty years old when my youth ended," Loren was to observe many years later.[23]

IV

With his first semester at Penn drawing to a close, Loren faced the intimidating prospect of making a seminar presentation, which the entire department would attend. As the fateful day neared, he came down with a severe cold, which soon spread: "I found myself trapped, over a long week-end, with a throbbing ear, in which the drum finally broke. It was a wonder that my mastoid did not become infected." Loren gave his lecture but supposedly failed to hear the questions directed at him from the back of the room. "I was not heartened to learn later that Speck had remarked in his gruffest manner, 'He's deaf as a post.' Coming from him this could only mean impending doom."[24]

Harboring visions of the shabby little dispensary in Lincoln,

Loren was taken by Duke to the university medical school, ignorant of the fact that it was one of the best in the country and that his student fees entitled him to treatment. A young intern cleaned out the ear's wax and hardened discharge, then gave Loren some oil to soften what remained of the interior mass. "I never inquired [about] the precise degree of my hearing recovery. The point was, I could hear. Speck and the others quit eyeing me dubiously," he recounted.[25] There would be many such crises and countless lesser complaints in the future brought on by periods of intense emotional strain.

Loren's flair for the dramatic also followed him to Penn. In February 1934 Virginia Wilkins Tomlin, a recent graduate of Penn, was hired by Edgar Howard to help compile the bibliography for his controversial dissertation on Paleo-Indian man in North America. One winter day the door to Howard's office in the University Museum opened and in stepped what appeared to be a detective right out of the movies. "He [was] wrapped in a black overcoat and had the collar up around his neck and a black slouch hat way down over his eyes. He slipped in and out very silently and very stealthily, a tall man and rather impressive figure." But the enigmatic stranger's physical appearance is not what Virginia Tomlin most remembered about him; rather, it was his deep, cadenced speech, which bordered on oratory: "It seemed as though he was playing a part."[26]

Loren's main reason for visiting Howard's office was money. The wealthy research associate had contacts with almost every private foundation awarding grants to anthropologists. With summer only a few months away, Loren was anxious to find employment. However valuable his experiences with the South Party, the time had come when he needed to work at some sites involving human habitation. On June 19, 1934, the *Daily Nebraskan* announced that Loren C. Eiseley, a former student, had been awarded the Harvard Fellowship for Anthropology, calling for a summer of study in the area around Carlsbad, New Mexico. According to Edgar Howard, the expedition leader, attempts would be made to prove the existence of Pleistocene man through his association with prehistoric animals. A second graduate student, Joseph B. Townsend, Jr., a future architect, and a local guide would round out the four-member team.[27]

A product of the Main Line, the Quaker City's posh surburban enclave built along the westward route of the Pennsylvania Railroad, Joe belonged to the same social circle as Edgar Howard. Although the youth had no background in anthropology, he prevailed upon the longtime family friend to allow him to join what was officially termed the Carnegie Expedition to the Southwest in Search of Early Man. As part of the arrangement, Joe agreed to pay his own expenses and to drive both himself and Loren Eiseley to New Mexico, where they would spend the summer excavating the floor of a limestone cave in the Guadalupe Mountains.

The two, who had not known each other at Penn, left Lincoln around June 20 and arrived in Carlsbad a few days later. Rather than camp in the field, where the heat was relentless and water difficult to obtain, they each took a room at a tourist park for $1.25 a night.[28] At Carlsbad they met up with their local guide, a crusty, hard-swearing sheet metal company owner named R. M. P. "Bill" Burnet. An amateur archaeologist with a particular fondness for prehistoric Indian pottery, Burnet knew the surrounding mountains and their myriad caves better than any man alive.

Williams Cave, in which Loren and Joe were to spend nearly six weeks, is now part of Guadalupe Mountains National Park. Located in Culberson County, Texas, just south of the New Mexico state line, the property was then owned by J. Adolphus "Dolph" Williams, a gaunt, hollow-eyed sheep rancher whose baggy overalls and floppy straw hat gave him the aspect of a malnourished scarecrow. The cave itself is situated southwest of Signal Peak, a massive limestone pyramid rising 8,400 feet above a semidesert landscape rich in cactus, yucca, and scrub oak. The nearly mile-high entrance, which faces east, looks onto a rugged canyon 200 feet below.

When Edgar Howard first visited the cave in 1930, it was apparent that he had been preceded by others. Billy the Kid, the hero-bandit of the Southwest, once roamed these slopes, and tales of his violent career and hold-ups fired the imagination of treasure hunters. Rumors of Spanish bullion also abounded, the occasional discovery of a silver stirrup or wrought-iron bit lending renewed zest to the search. Matters were made worse by the recent proliferation of pothunters like the craggy Bill Burnet. Thus it was almost impossible to find a cave whose floor had not been disturbed by random diggers.

Excavation began in late June or early July. Plans called for Loren and Joe to dig a trench along the north wall from the front to the back, a distance of forty-eight feet. They immediately ran into large rocks, which were hauled to the entrance and sent crashing down into the echoing canyon below. Tons of dirt had to be moved with the aid of a ponderous wheelbarrow that had nearly given them hernias when they dragged it up the steep canyon wall. Each powdery shovelful of earth had to be screened for artifacts before following the discarded rocks into the abyss. Joe, who had never before been subjected to such exhausting labor, suffered terribly at first: "Hottest damned weather you ever felt," he remembered. The youth marveled at Loren's stamina and physique: "He was very strong physically; the most beautifully built guy you ever saw."[29]

Evidence of human habitation soon turned up. The sifted earth yielded bits of cord, basket fragments, pottery shards, projectile points, and bone implements. On July 24 the field party discovered an Indian burial site twenty-three feet from the cave entrance.[30] The first remains unearthed were those of two children, one lying on top of the other, eighteen inches below the surface. The upper skull was covered by an inverted coiled basket in perfect condition, while the lower was adorned with a necklace of pink shell beads. Below the children were fragments of a large basket that had once held the charred remains of several adult cremations.

A second burial, that of an infant six to twelve months old, was found close to the north wall during later trenching operations. The baby had been placed in a triangular-shaped cradle, a practice common among the Basket Makers, who may have inhabited the region as early as 1500 B.C. Its body was swaddled in a soft, red-painted hide, the leg holes sewed up and fastened on top with a pin made of thorn. This wrapping was covered by a second hide with the fur still on. Over the whole was a rabbit-skin blanket, badly disintegrated. A bag of charms—containing a chert scraper, the remains of seed, some needles, and a small animal leg bone—was also attached to the cradle. Next to the child, in the insulating dust, lay a grooved rabbit stick, which had been "killed" (broken) and sent along with the deceased to the next world, possibly as sustenance.[31]

Thinking back forty years later on that moment of discovery, Loren remembered experiencing mixed emotions: "I stood silent and was not happy. Something told me that the child and its accouterments should have been left where the parents intended before they departed, left to the endless circling of the stars beyond the cavern mouth and the entering shaft of sun by day. This for all eternity." He realized that, sooner or later, treasure seekers would discover the infant's resting place. "Eventually all would be crushed, broken, or sold for antiquity in the valley below."[32] Perhaps they were doing a service by rescuing what would otherwise be destroyed. Yet in both cases the result was desecration—the equivalent for these simple people of the fate that had befallen the pharaohs.

Howard was summoned: the man who was largely responsible for bringing Loren to Penn now became the villain in his eyes. The expedition leader decided that most of the materials should go to the Archeological and Historical Society of Carlsbad, which was establishing a museum. When Loren started to protest on the ground that the local facilities were inadequate, Howard supposedly cut him short: "We don't want to bother with this stuff. . . . We've got to go deeper, much deeper."[33]

While it is true that Howard seemed unwilling to settle for anything less than the skull of Folsom man, he was hardly the insensitive opportunist Loren portrayed. "The material we recovered is a duplication of what we already have," he wrote to Horace Jayne, director of the University Museum, "and I am therefore leaving it in Carlsbad for the time-being, . . . bringing home only such specimens as we have not represented in the Museum and which I wanted to study further."[34] The artifacts and human remains were well cared for and today constitute one of the major exhibits at the Carlsbad Municipal Museum. But Loren hung on to the wistful, moralistic ending he so favored: "What eventually became of the contemplated museum I never knew, nor of the child carefully wrapped in a rabbit-skin blanket and the tools intended for its after existence. Wasted, really, wasted because the man in charge had a driving mania for one thing alone—the people of the ice."[35]

V

While the son of the middle border and the Main Liner did enjoy each other's company, Joe remembered that they did not agree on many things because of their diverse backgrounds: "Loren was an entirely different breed of cat. He wrote these fantastic poems which he called poetry and I didn't consider poetry at all at that age in my life. He'd recite these at night, and I couldn't have cared less." Loren also had his "dour moments; he was not always full of fun by any means."[36] Loren later told Lou Korn that Howard had not been entirely pleased with his performance in the field. In Korn's words, "Howard thought Loren was doing too much communing with the spirits—like Speck always talked about—instead of digging." This did not come as much of a surprise to Lou, who had gotten to know Loren pretty well: "Loren was not concerned with spending a whole lifetime on Folsom man and a few Folsom points."[37]

Further digging yielded a third and last burial, that of an adult whose charred bones had been sewn into a finely crafted deerskin bag. Although they excavated to a depth of seven feet in places, no evidence of human occupation before the Basket Makers was found. If, as Howard believed, Ice Age man had once lived at this southern extreme of the Guadalupes, it now appeared all but certain that Williams Cave had not sheltered him for any significant period of time.

Before the summer came to an end, Loren and Joe were given the assignment of checking out another cave on El Capitan, a massive, cliff-flanked sentinel visible from fifty miles away. A troop of Boy Scouts from Carlsbad had visited the cavern and reported finding a large hole in the floor. Lowering themselves with the aid of ropes, Loren and Joe discovered a second cave, whose surface was strewn with ancient camel bones. Whether the animals had blundered to their deaths or had been trapped there by early hunters was unknown. Deferring to Loren's expertise, Joe waited while his companion determined that the beasts had not died at the hands of prehistoric man.

Three years later, unbeknownst to Joe, Loren published a fictionalized account of that day. "There were three of us," he wrote in *The Nebraska Alumnus*, "including a fat, two-hundred pound priest whose hobby was archeology and who had volunteered to show us the place. Joe, my co-worker, carried a blue print." Too obese to descend the rope ladder, the collared Buddha promised to maintain a vigil until the other two returned. Instead of finding a single chamber at the bottom of the rope, the explorers discovered multiple passages that veered off in several directions. Choosing what they thought was a promising tunnel, the pair set off single file through the dark.

The footprints they were following soon disappeared. From walking upright they shifted to a half crouch, then wormed their way forward on hands and knees. "We writhed over knife-sharp crystals on our stomachs—dripping with sweat, our shirts torn to ribbons. . . . Lying so, one could make a choice of myriad directions. If one looked backward one could scarcely choose the way one had come. We crawled on." The air grew worse, finally forcing Joe to stop. Loren's heart contracted sickeningly. Neither ventured to utter that terrible word: "Lost!"

They debated whether to sit tight and wait for the priest to summon help or to try to find their way back through the daunting maze of stifling passages. Joe had an idea. They must be the first human beings ever to have come this far. The tiny stalagmites shredding their clothes and skin had been broken off by the thousands, leaving a bizarre trail of their progress. "Maybe we can follow our path out of this place," he ventured.

"There followed long minutes like hours, interrupted only by protesting bats pouring past into the dark, or gibbering from the walls." The two made frequent stops to extinguish the dimming flashlight and listened in the blackness to the tinkle of water dripping from the stalactites. After a long period of tracking boot and knee scratchings, they were able to regain their feet and peer at the map. In possession of their bearings at last, the two reached the chamber containing the bones and hailed the priest. "Where you been?" he queried. "It's lonesome up here without any light. Makes time go slower I guess. I got to thinking you'd been gone a long time. You get funny ideas in the dark."[38]

When he was revising this piece for inclusion in his autobiography many years later, Loren expunged the last vestige of evidence that linked it to the one person who might read about the mythical expedition and know better. Having recently written the Philadelphia architect to ask about some old photos taken in Carlsbad, he took no chances and dropped Joe's name from the tale.[39]

Their summer's work over, Loren and Joe decided to celebrate before going their separate ways. Lured by the romance of old Mexico, they drove west to El Paso and crossed the border into Ciudad Juárez, where they were promptly arrested for "doing something ridiculous," the specifics of which Joe could not remember. Loren tried to smooth things over by addressing the authorities in his faltering Spanish, but to no avail. The two were finally allowed to contact the American consul, who, "with a little doing," obtained their release.[40] Loren rode with Joe as far as Santa Fe, where they shook hands and said good-bye, promising to get together back at Penn in the fall. They never did.

VI

Mabel, accompanied by two friends, had left Lincoln by car on August 8 to join Loren in Santa Fe. On the morning of the fourteenth, the couple drove down El Camino del Monte Sol (The Road of the Sun Mountain) and pulled up in front of a sprawling adobe building with a broad terrace of brick facing north to the Sangre de Cristo Mountains. At first they puzzled over the seemingly inordinate amount of activity, then dismissed it as normal for the residence presided over by the grande dame of the local artists' colony. Only after the two located their transplanted Lincoln friend Dorothy Thomas, who had been renting an apartment in the ten-room dwelling since April, did they learn that something was indeed amiss: Mary Hunter Austin, the writer and owner of La Casa Querida (The Beloved House), had passed away in her sleep the previous day. The author of *The Land of Little Rain, Starry Adventure,* and *Earth Horizon* had died of a heart attack after suffering another of her bouts of hallucinations and occasional tantrums, which Dorothy called "Mary's mads."

A steady stream of poets, painters, and craftspeople came to pay their respects, some standing, some kneeling to cross themselves in front of the wooden casket before merging into small groups to recall the deceased in hushed tones. Loren, who had spent the summer working among death's most poignant reminders, wandered the premises in a contemplative mood, taking in everything from the handmade tin light fixtures on the ceilings to the multicolored Indian rugs covering the floors. On impulse, the afternoon before the memorial service, he wrote a poem, "Requiem for Mary Austin," and showed it to the subject's niece, Mary Hunter. Touched by Loren's sensitivity, Miss Hunter asked him to read it at the nonsectarian service, which he did.[41]

> *The fiercer body and the too-proud fingers*
> *None of these keep*
> *The fire in the crucible has over-run them.*
> *They will not sleep.*[42]

Other commemorative poems were read by John Gould Fletcher, who was to win a Pulitzer Prize in 1938, and Witter Bynner, an intimate of D. H. Lawrence. One of Loren's childhood heroes, the naturalist and animal-story writer Ernest Thompson Seton, reminisced about his long association with the deceased. Seton's *Biography of a Grizzly, Two Little Savages,* and *Wild Animals at Home* had been partly responsible for Loren's grade-school declaration: "I want to be a nature writer."

After the funeral, Loren and Dorothy's brother Macklin spent several days roaming the Indian remains in the encircling mountains. At Pecos Pueblo, once the largest Indian settlement in the Southwest, Macklin reached into a limestone cleft and pulled out several obsidian points, which had been untouched by human hands for at least five hundred years. The two also drove over to Chaco Canyon, whose thousand-year-old ruins represent the highest level of prehistoric Pueblo civilization. From a barren horizon the sun rises and sets like a crimson balloon, while beneath it Chaco lies cracked and empty—a great discarded pot. Sage, yucca, and saltbrush dot the alkaline surface, and lizards, who seem to have inherited the earth, dart furtively across decaying walls. Juniper, ponderosa, and piñon pine were once plentiful, but the race of men who built these adobe apartments ravaged the land, hastening the ecological disaster that sealed their fate.

The explorers talked of books and writing and quoted their own poems from memory, for Macklin was also a contributor to *Prairie Schooner.* "There was a hidden presence to Loren," he observed, "which you were always more or less aware of, depending on how well you knew him. This came out in the melancholy of his writings." At the same time, the social Loren was always "pleasant, considerate, and lively," which to Macklin's way of thinking made him "about the sweetest guy who ever lived."[43]

At age thirty-six Dorothy Thomas, a fetching brunette with dancing eyes and a ready smile, was just coming into her own as a writer. Her short stories had recently appeared in *Atlantic Monthly, Harper's,* and the *American Mercury.* The crusty, often vitriolic H. L. Mencken had been charmed by her tales of Ma Jeeter, a blonde with an enormous bosom that oozed down over the belt of her dress and rested flat on her broad belly. At Mencken's urging, Dorothy had written more vignettes about the harried, one-eyed widow and her ne'er-do-well progeny, which publisher Alfred Knopf snapped up and printed as *Ma Jeeter's Girls* in 1933.

Still, the going had not been easy. When Dorothy left Lincoln to pursue her career as a writer in Santa Fe, she was accompanied to the depot by an embittered Mari Sandoz, who had not published much of anything after more than a decade of impoverished devotion to her art. Marguerite Lewis, another friend, was also present and remembered Mari's parting comment to Dorothy as she boarded the train: "You are going to be sorry; Mary Austin will kick you out in no time at all."[44]

With even minor distractions few in number, Dorothy spent most of her time alone at the typewriter. She began to dream "very interesting" dreams and decided to write them down the minute she arose. "Each morning my dream record was longer and longer. It got to be so long I found myself going to sleep to dream, and the time came that it got in the way of my making a living." When Dorothy told Loren what had happened, he became very excited and asked to see her writings on the subject. Fearful of her growing obsession, she had already wadded up the dream manuscript and consigned it to the flames in her corner fireplace. "Loren really deplored this; he felt that I should have kept it; it was an experiment, an unfinished one."[45] Loren then told Dorothy that something similar had happened to him when he was out in the desert, attempting to recover his health. However, unlike Dorothy's dreams, Loren's had been self-induced.

"Shepherd's madness, Loren?" Dorothy queried.

"No, not exactly," he replied. "An idea comes like a gift, and one must pursue it no matter its source."[46]

He went on to discuss the animal in man, that "something else" one rarely encounters in books, a lurking, evasive something that rustles and runs, yet insists on being noticed. It is this element, a kind of primal consciousness, that dreams might well supply. Like Mary Austin, Loren was to seek this elusive communion all his life, and his finest writing would reflect an awareness of presences and powers unsensed by the casual observer. "I have become," he wrote, "my own fox at the wood's edge."[47]

9

THE HUNTERS AND THE HUNTED

I

Before scattering for the summer, Loren, Duke, and Ricky had entered into an agreement. The trio enjoyed one another's company so much they decided to room together when classes resumed in the fall. Duke, who worked part-time at Penn's International House, a Victorian mansion at 3905 Spruce Street, had been offered the former master bedroom on the third floor. As a result of the depression, the number of foreign students had declined precipitously, making it possible for Loren and Ricky to move in with him for a monthly rent of only ten dollars apiece. The facility, which was managed by a former missionary family, also housed four Chinese, two Indian dental students, two Filipinos, a Haitian, and two or three other Americans.[1]

Besides the camaraderie and proximity to campus, the new living arrangements provided an unexpected benefit. According to the editors of the student newspaper, *The Pennsylvanian*, the true son of Penn "shall have a man's physique; clean, strong, graceful in posture and action; with a steady nerve and red blood and a facility for skill, and the enjoyment of physical power and prowess in work and play."[2] It naturally followed that the Penn physique must be properly attired. The undergraduate who wore anything other than a suit and tie to class found himself the object not only of arched brows but of occasional editorial ridicule.[3] The standard applied even more rigorously to graduate students, working a particular hardship on those, like Loren, with little money. "To our delight," Duke recalled, "our wardrobe tripled in size! We were almost the same . . . build [and] could wear each other's suits. Now we could wear a different tie for every day of the week, and of course the first one up in the morning had the first choice of the suit he was to wear. You can imagine we never had a late sleeper."[4]

Loren's financial difficulties had also eased. Having proved himself in Frank Speck's eyes, he had received word that he was the recipient of the Harrison Scholarship in Anthropology for the 1934–35 academic year. The prestigious award provided for a waiver of tuition and a stipend of two hundred dollars, payable in eight monthly installments.[5]

The rambles with Speck resumed. In addition to tramping the pine barrens and canoeing nearby rivers, the two sometimes made their way down to the waterfront along South Street, the center of Philadelphia's Negro culture. There the old man spent hours chatting with the proprietors of Negro herb shops and street vendors of sugarcane and blackstrap molasses. Loren stood by in a kind of dazed wonder:

> Around us swarms the black world of the metropolis—credulous, naive, wicked—a hint of the barbaric still clinging like a scent in the air. . . . We enter a Negro church and the organist, proud of his fine instrument, lets us climb into the body of the organ to see the huge pipes. We emerge, dusty but impressed. . . . Later we sit dreamily in the darkened church lulled by the organ music. The organist with slender brown hands and the sensitive hurt face of a between-world dweller, leans over to me in the dark. "That man—that Dr. Speck—he's a nice man. A very fine gentleman." He pauses inarticulate. "Yes," I say. The barrier between our worlds seems to lessen. We try, shyly, to talk.[6]

Speck must have been watching Loren out of the corner of his eye, perhaps even smiling to himself as his student struggled to square textbook theory with the reality of everyday life on the streets. Another of his professors, D. S. Davidson, had commented on Loren's naiveté, calling him "a boy from the backwoods."[7]

At age twenty-seven, Loren was living the life of a freshman in a dormitory and loving it. "The year was one of the happiest in my life," he fondly recalled.[8] Ricky Faust echoed his friend's sentiments; the Loren Eiseley he had known the previous year "tended to overdramatize relatively minor incidents in his life—or what might well have been minor incidents in the lives of others—and dwell upon them." At least for the time being, "he felt he had friends; the sense of gloom which seemed to pervade him actually tended to fade and he allowed himself to relax."[9]

Ricky characterized their social life, which centered on places to eat, as "rather prosaic." He remembered that Loren was especially fond of a student hangout called Cohen and Kelly's, which served superb ham and cheese sandwiches on freshly baked rye bread with good draft beer. They were also regulars at Pop Heller's Cafeteria, whose owner Loren described as a "wily old huckster." One never knew quite what to expect when biting into a mouthful of Pop's food, which contained everything from strands of boiled rope to fragments of tin can. Still, the meals were inexpensive—ranging from twenty-five to fifty cents, even cheaper if one bought a week's ticket in advance.

Their favorite spot, which they visited in their "more affluent periods," was the Nanking restaurant, located farther away on Market Street. They generally went as part of a larger group in order to share the excellent dishes more economically. Loren remembered the restaurant as epitomizing what a paradoxical time it was to be alive: "As we all dined amicably together—black, white, yellow—terrible forces were at work beneath the surface of things. Jobs were few, yet I could walk after midnight from the homes of friends and pass safely through neighborhoods from which I would not now expect to emerge alive." Violence had begun to stalk the wider world. Educated refugees from Nazi terrorism came to Speck, hoping that his academic connections might help them establish new lives. A prescient Ricky had remarked, "Never make the mistake of underestimating the Japanese Navy." At the Nanking's tables sat gifted intellectuals whose lives would be forfeited on obscure Pacific atolls or in the postwar convulsions that engulfed a festering China. As student onlookers they sensed that something was wrong but possessed no power to alter their course. Later, as he tried to match vaguely remembered names with long-vanished faces, Loren wrote: "I was never again to encounter the genuine peace I experienced among these individuals whose national governments were already making the first moves on that chessboard whose pawns were to be swept away in millions."[10]

Until he went to Philadelphia, Loren had not seen Mamie, his former sister-in-law, for several years, but he had never forgotten their long, therapeutic talks during his troubled adolescence. She had married a southerner named George Lawhon in 1926 and was now living near Jamaica Bay on Long Island. Athena remembered that her uncle often came up from Penn to visit on weekends. At other times the high-school senior was allowed to catch the train to Philadelphia, where she stayed with her father and stepmother in their Pine Street apartment.[11]

Athena spent many hours in Loren's company. Their favorite pastime was strolling Woodlands Cemetery, where they teased each other about having the large Eiseley nose and paused among the stones to speculate about those who lay beneath the gently contoured earth. Such occasions always brought back one of Athena's earliest memories, from when she was no more than five and Loren about fifteen. The two were walking one morning, and Loren was telling her about insects. "You should never ever hurt a ladybug," he cautioned, "because they do an awful lot of good."[12] A year or two later, after Athena and her parents had moved to Colorado Springs, Loren showed up with a shoe box full of lizards he had caught while hitching his way west. He deposited the container in the bathtub and incurred Mamie's extreme displeasure when one of the creatures got away, leaving its expendable tail in her trembling hand.

Since their last times together, Loren had developed a strong puritanical streak. Athena was at the age when young women were beginning to wear cosmetics and had darkened her eyebrows with a pencil. Loren took one look at her and rubbed off the makeup with his thumb. On another occasion he became "terribly upset" and snatched a book from her hands. Athena forgot its title but remembered that it was about native life in Samoa and had been written by a young anthropologist named Margaret Mead.

Even more curious was an incident that occurred while Loren was living at International House. There was to be a formal dance at the university, and he asked Athena to accompany him. "I did not have the proper clothes or the proper anything. Bea tried to outfit me; we shopped all one day for a pair of shoes and she loaned me a dress. When the time really came to go after all this was done he did not take me, and I never did find out exactly why."[13] Athena spent the evening at the brick mansion on Spruce Street, playing Ping-Pong with a sympathetic Duke Tachibana.

Although there had been no money with which to purchase an engagement ring, Loren and Mabel had supposedly reached an understanding before he enrolled at Penn.[14] She dated occasionally during his long absences but made it clear to potential suitors that their relations were to remain platonic, and it appears that Loren had not violated her trust in the past. Athena had been going out with a young man named Robert Whitlock, the son of one of her father's co-workers at Western Union. Robert's sister, an eighteen-year-old brunette named Eleanor, became friends with Athena, who, knowing nothing about her uncle's fiancée, introduced the young woman to Loren. The two were attracted to each other and began spending a good deal of time together. Bea was quite upset over this development, believing that Miss Whitlock's background and education were not good enough for her up-and-coming brother-in-law. Loren, who was obviously in love, or thought he was, asked Athena her opinion. "I told him that [what Bea thought] didn't matter; it depended on what his feelings were—and hers." Athena never knew for certain why the two finally decided to go their separate ways: "Somebody won out; I think it was himself."[15]

II

On his way back to Lincoln from Santa Fe the previous summer, Loren had stopped off in the northeastern Colorado town of Yuma to visit with Perry Anderson, an amateur collector whose name was becoming well known in anthropological circles. As early as 1913 Anderson had been making regular rounds of the nearby sand blowouts, securing fine examples of Indian points similar to those fashioned in Ice Age Europe. In contrast to the Folsom points, most of which are distinctively grooved or fluted, the "Yuma points," as Anderson's specimens came to be designated in the literature, are as straight edged as a knife blade and heavier in the keel. While some experts thought it likely that both types of points were fashioned by nomadic peoples ranging over a partially icebound North America, there was considerable debate as to which had been developed first.

Of the eight artifacts Bert Schultz and his fellow workers had discovered at Scotts Bluff in 1932, one was a finely chipped example of the Yuma type, another of the Folsom variety associated with northern New Mexico. What was more, the two objects had been found together in situ, leaving no doubt as to their equal age and contemporary existence. Loren presented this evidence in a well-received seminar paper, which became the basis of his thirty-nine-page master's thesis, "A Review of the Paleontological Evidence Bearing upon the Age of the Scottsbluff Bison Quarry and Its Associated Artifacts."[16] Ironically, he had decided to write on Paleo-Indian man, the very subject he had made Bert promise never to link with the Eiseley name. However, that had been before he was accepted for graduate study at a distinguished university and became associated with Edgar Howard and Frank Speck.

Speck was not about to allow Loren's thesis to languish in the dimly lit stacks of Furnace Library. As an associate editor of the prestigious journal *American Anthropologist*, he was in an excellent position to smooth the way for publication and urged Loren to ready a manuscript as quickly as possible. Since much of the research was based on data and advice supplied by Bert, it was decided that the paper, which was drawn almost verbatim from chapter 2 of the thesis, should appear under both their names. When the manuscript was accepted by the *Anthropologist* in January 1935, Loren was elated. "The first issue of the [year] is just out and looks very fine indeed," he wrote to Bert. "The next number will contain our paper and I can assure you that we can be very proud of appearing in so scholarly a journal."[17]

Bert and Loren proposed an earlier date for the Scotts Bluff site—and Folsom culture—than other scholars had previously set forth: "To pronounce that the site seems definitely Pleistocene and at least late Wisconsin [12,000 to 15,000 years old] may be branded as bold in the eyes of many authorities. . . . Nevertheless, when it is remembered that the number of deeply buried and genuinely authenticated finds of this nature appear to be growing yearly, it would seem that to propose a late Pleistocene dating for this site is not too radical."[18]

Many issues were still to be resolved, but the authors felt "content" that their dating of the bones and associated artifacts was near accurate. Replying to their critics a year later in "An Added Note on the Scottsbluff Bison Quarry," the two wrote more forcefully in support of their position, claiming that if they had erred, the dating would almost surely have to be extended downward rather than upward.[19] As it turned out, they overestimated the antiquity of Scotts Bluff by a minimum of three thousand years.

With Leo, Bea, and Athena looking on, Loren received his A.M. degree during the commencement exercises of February 9, 1935. It was a proud moment for all but one tinged in the graduate's mind with the knowledge that his days at Penn were numbered. Though Loren hoped to remain in school and complete a Ph.D., the prospects of his obtaining the necessary financial support seemed remote. According to the rules governing the Harrison Scholarship, no individual could hold the award for more than one academic year. The Harrison Foundation had also established fellowships for "men of exceptional ability," but in order to qualify the candidate was required to possess a reading knowledge of both French and German, something that Loren did not have.[20] He wrote Bert that Speck would be able to come up with some money, but "I couldn't get by on that alone and anyhow I need to clear the languages far more than the course credits of which I have a large number beyond the M.A."[21] All things considered, it would be better if he returned to Lincoln in the fall, where it would be cheaper to live and easier to face his old nemesis on familiar ground.

Loren was back in the classroom only two days after graduation, but the hectic pace that had marked the previous semester had slackened considerably: "Everything [is] slow here and drifting along," he wrote to Wimberly in the spring.[22] His mood became more melancholy as the end drew near, and with it the realization that his friends would soon scatter over the face of the globe. During a final gathering at the old Nanking one evening, the group presented him with a Modern Library edition of Thomas Mann's *The Magic Mountain*. Inscribed between its covers were some fifteen names. Aside from Ricky and Duke, he was to hear from only one of them again, a fellow anthropology student named Chou Li Han. Han survived the Second World War in his native China but was forced to seek refuge in the Tibetan highlands during the Communist Revolution, only to fall prey to a rampaging tiger. In the years to come Loren would often envision Han trudging relentlessly forward through the Himalayan solitudes, the great yellow-eyed beast padding toward him in the snow.[23]

III

Roughly twenty-eight miles due north of Fort Collins, Colorado, within sight of the Wyoming state line, lies a small, seemingly inconsequential valley, only a quarter of a mile wide and two miles long. Virtually flat over most of its surface, the depression slopes gently upward at its western edge to overlook Box Elder Creek, an ephemeral tributary of the Cache la Poudre River. A serpentine arroyo also cuts through the grass-covered terrace, exposing deep deposits of black earth rich in organic matter.

Thousands of years ago spring-fed meadows and broad marshes attracted herds of *Bison antiquus* from the plains not far to the east. Pronghorn antelope were also plentiful, along with jackrabbit, coyote, fox, and wolf. The surrounding vegetation was equally rich and varied; juniper, piñon, spruce, and ponderosa pine dotted the horizon; wild berries of several varieties abounded. It was only natural that as the ice retreated another species of some significance should be attracted to this site. Its skin-clad members camped sporadically for centuries on the valley's upward slope at a place now called Folsom Man Hill.

The first artifacts in the area were discovered in 1924 by Judge Clyde C. Coffin and his son, who had received permission to explore the property of William Lindenmeier, Jr., a Larimer County horse rancher. The judge and his brother, Major Roy G. Coffin, had been collecting relics for years, and both had extensive knowledge of the prehistoric Indian remains commonly found in Colorado and Wyoming. Although the Coffins were aware that their so-called Lindenmeier collection represented a type of projectile different from most others found in the region, it was not until they learned about the Folsom discovery that they recognized the valley's importance as a site of early human occupation. Major Coffin, a professional geologist and dauntless correspondent, spent years trying to interest members of the U.S. Geological Survey and the staff of the Smithsonian Institution in Lindenmeier, but to no avail. Then his letters somehow came to the attention of Frank H. H. Roberts, Jr., a young Harvard-trained archaeologist in the Smithsonian's Bureau of American Ethnography. Acting against his better judgment, Roberts visited Lindenmeier in the summer of 1934. His first day in the valley did nothing to temper his skepticism: "not encouraged by what [I] have seen," he noted in his journal. On the second day, however, his opinion was reversed after a series of test holes yielded charcoal, ash, and a quantity of animal bone. Roberts remained at the site for several more weeks and was to return for at least two months during each of the following six summers.[24]

The academic grapevine sprang to life. Bert wrote to ask Loren if he was privy to any information about the Roberts find. "I . . . will tell you what I know," he replied. "I've just heard stray gossip lately, but I think it is to be opened this summer. I expect it is too early to tell just what may come of it, but if it is as extensive as they say, it may really be possible to define the people's culture at last and thus end that more or less academic argument."[25] His information seems to have improved during the following weeks: "I strongly urge you," he cautioned Bert in early February 1935, "to be extremely careful, as the abundance of the material sure to be gotten from the new Roberts site is liable to explode many of our preconceived theories."[26] Loren added that he hoped to join the South Party during the coming summer and coauthor another paper with his friend.

Four months later found him not in the Badlands of Nebraska but setting up camp with seven other young men and a cook near the arroyo at Lindenmeier. Like Frank Speck, Roberts was an associate editor of the *American Anthropologist.* Impressed by the joint article on the Scotts Bluff Bison Quarry, he thought Loren would make an excellent addition to his field party. Having tentatively identified certain of Lindenmeier's artifact-bearing deposits the previous summer, the leader was anxious to begin excavating on a much larger scale. In a hastily drafted letter to Dr. Barbour dated June 14, Loren, who functioned poorly under pressure, described the scene as one of "general uproar" and "complete confusion."[27]

Things did not remain chaotic for long. Frank Roberts was one of the best field men in the business, and his camp quickly assumed the appearance of a marine platoon on extended bivouac. A double row of white canvas tents, anchored against the stiff prairie winds by shoulder-high stakes, faced each other across an open space devoid of everything but some scattered tufts of parched grass. On the raised wooden floors inside were sawbuck pallets, each containing the bedding of an individual worker. Among scores of surviving photographs is one labeled "How to keep a tent" and another "How not to keep a tent." Subtle forms of protest were allowed. Loren was photographed, cigarette in hand, standing before a tent with "Boar's Nest" carved in wood above the entrance; in another picture the 1935 crew is self-consciously posed before "Bison's Roost." Overhead, against the inspiring backdrop of a pine-covered ridge, flew Old Glory, adding to the general esprit de corps. According to Roberts's journal, the summer's effort produced but one sour note, and it was not struck until August 7: "Cook went to town. Fell off curb and broke his ankle. Not in line of duty."[28]

Roberts's objective for the season was to establish the exact geologic position of the artifact-bearing sediments and, if possible, to determine their age. The archaeologist also hoped to unearth skeletal remains of Folsom man and find evidence of the types of shelters he used. The strategy was straightforward and ambitious: two broad trenches would be dug across the terrace, to converge at the arroyo 270 feet to the north. Trench A, by far the larger, was begun in early June and excavated in 10-foot-square sections. Detailed drawings were made of the north face and sidewalls of each square as the workmen advanced. Trench B, approximately 75 feet west of Trench A, was excavated in the same manner, but it was abandoned after Roberts determined that its stratigraphic information duplicated that of its twin.

The abandonment of Trench B made it possible to begin a third excavation. Bison provided the inhabitants of Lindenmeier with the bulk of their meat, and the butchering was done next to where the Coffins had made their original finds. While working in the "Bison Pit" one morning, Loren spotted several bones, including a cranium, that were beginning to erode out of the surface. He dug down a little way and uncovered a Folsom point driven deep into the matrix of two neck vertebrae, providing indisputable proof that the weapon and animal were of the same period. Not wishing to appear "presumptuous," he thought Roberts should have the honor of announcing the discovery in print, although this concession deprived a rueful Loren of a direct scholarly connection with the history of Pleistocene man.[29]

When she was in camp, Linda Roberts, Frank's winsome spouse, assumed all responsibility for cataloging specimens. As the season wore on, the bone and mineral artifacts piled up at an exponential rate: fluted projectile points of chert and quartz; bone scrapers, needles, and awls; grinding stones and flat rocks on which meat was cut and energy-rich marrow extracted. So many animal bones were found that hundreds, perhaps thousands, were eventually discarded, to the chagrin of later scholars.

The Colorado Museum of Natural History also carried on excavations at Lindenmeier during the 1935 season. Its three-member crew was led by John L. Cotter, who had just received his M.A. in anthropology from the University of Denver. A gregarious young man with a ready smile and incisive wit, Jack was headed on a Harrison Fellowship for Penn, where he would become Frank Speck's office assistant. He remembered Loren as a "dark, rather well-built, fairly heavy-set" figure, "somewhat retiring although . . . fun to be with." Every now and then Loren would go off by himself. "We would nudge each other and say, 'I guess he's out writing another poem,' because it was bruited about that he had a poem in the *American Mercury*, which . . . was the be-all and end-all of avant-garde literary progress."[30]

Loren regularly packed up his gear at the end of the week and headed for parts unknown, presumably to be by himself in the surrounding hills where a thinker could go about his business undisturbed. It turned out that the poet was "roughing it" in a modern cabin on Big Thompson Canyon, near the entrance to Rocky Mountain National Park. The property was owned by relatives of Mabel's boss, Dwight Kirsch, and his wife, Truby, with whom Mabel had come out to spend part of the summer.

Lindenmeier meant more to Loren than just another summer's work: he needed to begin thinking about a dissertation topic. In the unpublished conclusion of his master's thesis, he had entered into a brief discussion of invertebrate life-forms found at the Scotts Bluff Bison Quarry and in the Yuma blowouts haunted by Perry Anderson. Mainly mollusks such as gastropods and tiny shellfish, these seemingly insignificant creatures might well provide important clues in the dating of Pleistocene kill sites, a promising subject for further study. Upon arriving at Lindenmeier, Loren told Roberts of his interest in the problem and was given responsibility for collecting and identifying the appropriate specimens, which he placed in bottles for safekeeping. Most of the gastropods were gathered from the Bison Pit; the aquatic species were dredged from Brannigan Springs. "I had intended to secure more and then dry them," he wrote apologetically to Roberts on September 9; "I had also intended, before leaving, to clean all of the invertebrates."[31] Loren had been unable to complete these tasks through no fault of his own. An urgent message had reached him in camp on Tuesday, August 20: Buck was dead; he had to return home.

IV

The end had come without warning. Though troubled by a chronic heart ailment, the flamboyant state auditor, who had recently turned seventy, worked all day Monday at his desk, where he was overheard telling his deputy, "I've never felt better in my life." That evening, while preparing to retire, Buck suffered a massive heart attack and died before Grace could get to the telephone. His passing made the front page of the *Lincoln Journal*, along with a photograph of the wrecked plane that had carried Will Rogers and Wiley Post to their deaths along the bleak coastline of northern Alaska.[32]

Buck's gray steel casket was taken to the capitol Thursday morning to lie in state in the rotunda. Two of his Masonic brothers kept a vigil as several hundred mourners passed by to pay their final respects. As always, the Colonel was dressed like a southern gentleman of the previous century: dark frock coat, white vest, and high starched collar, while a fresh flower—his lifelong trademark—graced the buttonhole of his wide lapel. G. S. Ferguson, a reader in the Christian Science church, presided at the funeral. Among the many flowers was a spray purchased with pennies and nickels collected by the children of South Twenty-third Street, who wanted to say goodbye to their neighborhood Santa Claus.[33]

With Governor Roy L. Cochran serving as honorary pallbearer, the cortege of black automobiles wound its way slowly toward the eastern edge of the city and a beautifully wooded site the Sioux chiefs had called Wyuka—"Place of Rest." The casket was carried from the hearse to a grave in the cemetery's Masonic section, where members of the Lancaster Lodge conducted a brief ceremony while Grace, flanked by Daisy and Loren—the new head of the family—looked on.

This moment of recognition in the public eye faded quickly. Loren's nightmares returned, as they almost always did when he suffered prolonged mental stress or increased responsibility. He had dreamed of his father twice in the years following Clyde's death, seeing him for the last time through a windowpane in the night: "then he was gone forever, to be replaced by something far more terrible than the gentle dead—death itself the secret agent dogging every alleyway of my dreams." Buck's demise stirred old memories of the chicken hatchery and the dark presence lurking just beyond the dancing shadows, which appeared to Loren now in another guise. One night he dreamt of sitting in the parlor of his uncle's home, rocking gently and waiting. A laugh came from behind a curtained door, followed by the sound of a snapped lock. The laughter resumed, deep and vibrating. The lights suddenly went out, and then he heard the mocking voice of Death emanating from Buck's favorite chair: "We are alone now. Isn't that what you have always wanted?" Loren hurled himself at the chimera, only to be met in midair by an equally violent force. The mortal adversaries twisted and rolled across the floor like Saturday-night saloon brawlers, smashing every piece of furniture in their path. Loren gradually gained the upper hand; he had his foe by the throat and could feel something collapsing between his constricting fingers. The lights blinked to life again; in his hands was the unrecognizable form of a crumpled puppet, a papier-mâché creature "murdered" in an imaginary moment of blind rage. "It was a mask, a mask for the escaped invincible intruder. . . . I sat down and thought weakly, clearly, for the first time: perhaps that's all there is, an emptiness."[34]

Virtually penniless once more, Loren had no choice but to move back in with his mother, aunt, and grandmother. Mabel, who had been giving him money almost from the time the two began dating, helped him reenter the University of Nebraska in the fall.[35] He served as a research assistant in sociology and signed up for three courses in the department, as well as a noncredit class in German for graduate students.[36] With so much riding on his performance in the foreign language, Loren was taking no chances; he arranged for Mark Thomas, Dorothy's younger brother, to tutor him on the side.[37] Back in Philadelphia, Frank Speck was pulling some strings in behalf of his star pupil. Despite Loren's dismal undergraduate record in Spanish, his mentor somehow persuaded the registrar's office to substitute it for the catalog requirement of French.[38]

Things were even less settled by the end of the year. Writing to Bert, who was in New York working as a research associate at the Museum of Natural History, Loren described his plans as shifting and uncertain. He had all but given up hope of returning to Penn the second semester; still, he was thinking of taking a "running trip" east to discuss this and other matters with Speck. His efforts to achieve proficiency in German would make little difference if he failed to win a Harrison Fellowship. With the application deadline fast approaching, he asked Bert not to reveal his ambitions to anyone: "There are probably about forty million other guys . . . with the same idea."[39]

The new year brought no resolution of his personal problems, only additional ones. Grace became ill in February and protested her nephew's plans to visit Philadelphia, even for a short while. When her condition worsened, she was hospitalized for surgery. Loren wrote Bert that the resulting bills had left him with little to count on from his recuperating aunt: "This whole thing has cut me down to an awful shoe-string." Nor was he sure that his German professor would support his fellowship application before he passed the qualifying exam.[40] As if this weren't enough, a paper read by Dr. Barbour at a recent paleontological meeting in St. Louis had been subjected to bitter scholarly attack. The shattered old soul had turned to Loren for solace, which only added to his deepening gloom. To a missive to Bert, he appended the postscript: "Better destroy this letter."[41]

V

After dropping out of the University of Nebraska in 1932, Rudolph Umland had spent three years bumming across forty states, Canada, and Mexico. He eventually returned to his hometown of Eagle, but husking nubbins soon made him restless for the open road, so he decided to turn hobo once more. Before departing he stopped by Andrews Hall to tell Wimberly good-bye and give him a manuscript for the *Schooner*. The Doc stared in perplexity at the stocky, redheaded figure before him and finally exclaimed, "You can't leave Lincoln just now. It's too damned cold to ride a boxcar!" He then told Umland about the Works Progress Administration and the need for a state editor to manage the newly established Nebraska Writers' Project, which was headquartered in the Union Terminal Warehouse, only a few blocks away. Although Umland had never done any editorial work, he was hired on the spot and soon found himself in charge of publishing *Nebraska: A Guide to the Cornhusker State*. Wimberly had launched him on a government career that would keep him forever out of boxcars and cornfields.[42]

Instead of returning to Penn second semester, a strapped Loren signed on with Franklin Roosevelt's New Deal. In February 1936 Wimberly arranged for him to join the local staff of the National Youth Administration, which in turn placed him on loan to the WPA. As editor of the Nebraska guidebook, Umland assigned Loren the task of writing introductory essays on the geology, paleontology, and prehistoric Indian culture of the state.[43]

During the following months, the two discovered many parallels in their lives, yet as Umland came to know Loren better, he realized that they were separated by a vast gulf of experience—and maturity. In contrast to his campus reputation as a stoical, self-sufficient drifter, Loren projected a youthful shyness combined with the overly polite manners of a poet. "Most boys in Lincoln got their first work experience mowing lawns, delivering newspapers, washing windows, scrubbing floors, hoeing weeds, spading gardens, but Loren did none of these. His was a case of prolonged adolescence and as he approached maturity he seemed actually fearful of making his own way in the world."[44] He had almost no confidence in his ability to earn a living, partly because, at age twenty-eight, he had never held a steady job. He questioned Umland again and again about his future plans. "When I told him that I had no intention of ever resuming any studies at the university to obtain a degree he couldn't believe it. He was incredulous. The WPA would end one day! What would I do then?"[45] If Loren didn't finish his Ph.D., Umland thought to himself, there was little hope that his friend would lead a successful life.

Loren's ingrained paranoia was also much in evidence. "To him," Umland wrote, "the world was full of two kinds of living things—the hunters and the hunted. He believed he was one of the hunted, a Steppenwolf figure." This image, which became an accompaniment to Loren's poetry, "persisted and grew to blossom strangely in the books he wrote. There is that startling picture of himself as prisoner of a Mexican guerrilla with a submachine gun [in] *The Immense Journey*. There are other pictures he made up to conceal his anxious self and he called it 'symbolical' writing."[46]

Loren also appeared to Umland to be less fit than he did to others who knew him at the time; somewhat frail with thin wrists and muscles that did not bulge is how his new editor remembered him. But above all, Loren was plagued by crises: "He always seemed to be between two of them."[47] If none existed, he had no difficulty torturing the facts to satisfy his psychic needs. "His suffering spilt over into little spells of madness at times and revealed itself in books like *The Night Country* and *All the Strange Hours*."[48]

Loren informed Wimberly that he was going to marry Mabel, but the Doc stunned his protégé by telling him that he considered this unwise. Mabel was not one of the outcast people that Loren felt a special kinship with but rather someone who could resolve his immediate problems—a safe, secure anchorage. It would be not only unfair but extremely selfish of him to spend a lifetime drawing on her strength while offering so little emotional sustenance in return. Wimberly and Loren drifted apart, and Loren began palling around with James M. Reinhardt, a Georgia-born sociology professor. Frank Speck became Loren's sole model, although he owed every bit as much or more to the sardonic, sad-eyed editor of the *Schooner*. There is no evidence that Loren ever told Mabel of his conversation with the Doc, but the master's thesis she had arranged to write under Wimberly's direction in 1933 was never completed—the only requirement left unfulfilled toward her graduate degree.[49]

Mabel's younger sister, Dollie, remembered meeting Loren during the twenties: "He came out to the house—a very shy boy; he was a loner, very moody, very ill at ease." He sat on the davenport with Mabel, and they read to each other by the hour, a pattern that continued throughout their long courtship. While always discreetly polite, Mabel's parents were baffled by this attraction. Sensing their uneasiness, Mabel grew increasingly defensive of Loren, who "was very awkward and inclined to be a bit abrasive to people. . . . He got so dependent upon her he would call all the time for her opinion about any little thing in his life or he'd come over if he'd had a disagreement with his family. . . . It was a strange relationship of almost a mother looking after someone." Mabel also took charge of Loren's future. Dollie remembered that "she was very aggressive in getting him on with his work and into school . . . getting scholarships and . . . getting people to notice his work."[50] Whenever she was removed from the picture, Loren could scarcely cope. His brief affairs with Helen Hopt and Eleanor Whitlock were the product less of romance than of the need for constant emotional reinforcement. Loren hated his mother, but he could never get enough mothering.

At times Mabel's devotion created family friction and hurt feelings. "We had a lot of arguments about religion," Dollie recalled. "I was really frightened to hear them talk. In those days it was considered very sophisticated and very smart to not believe in God.

They made several remarks that hurt me very much. . . . At that time he and Mabel both made fun of . . . my rather fundamental beliefs." Neither could Dollie understand Loren's uncompromising breach of the Fifth Commandment: "Honor thy father and thy mother." Daisy used to visit the Langdons quite frequently, usually around mealtime. Dollie thought her a "beautiful lady," if a bit bizarre. She wore her dark hair in tight curls like a young girl, sported frilly, outsized hats, and wore clothing that rarely matched. Daisy seemed fond of Mabel, who tried hard to conceal her distaste for the person she blamed for Loren's suffering. So far as mother and son were concerned, Dollie remembered, "There was no apparent love between them at all. . . . I tried to talk to him one time about his mother and see if he could understand what may have caused this, but he had no feeling but a hate—a cold hatred."[51]

In spite of their differences, Dollie loved both Loren and her sister and observed an important facet of their relationship to which neither Wimberly nor Rudolph Umland was privy. Near Christmas one year the couple had gone downtown to view the department store windows. Mabel spied a beautiful Spanish shawl with long purple fringe, which she later described to Dollie in detail. When Dollie asked her what she planned to buy Loren, Mabel replied, "Not very much because he can't afford to get me anything." He came over that same evening to visit; before departing he left a paper bag containing the unwrapped shawl and forgotten sales slip. Mabel wept over the awkwardly tender gesture. Their affections for each other deepened after that: "It was a very real relationship," Dollie mused, "very beautiful."[52]

The news Loren had been hoping for arrived by letter in April. The executive committee of Penn's graduate school had awarded him another Harrison Fellowship, which provided for a waiver of tuition and a stipend of six hundred dollars, money enough to see him through the final year of his Ph.D.[53] A second letter arrived a few weeks later, informing him that his short story "The Mop to K.C." was to be included in the Distinctive Index of Edward O'Brien's *Best Short Stories of 1936*. Following the volume's publication, Loren received an exhilarating note from Jacques Chambrun, the head of a major New York literary agency. Chambrun had just finished reading about Loren's work in O'Brien and wondered if he had any other stories he might wish to sell. "May I say that I represent H. G. Wells, Bertrand Russell, Hendrik Willem Van Loon, Rupert Hughes, Irvin S. Cobb, William McFee, Thomas Burke, and Andre Maurois."[54] The contents of Loren's reply are unknown, but this was a letter to cherish during those moments when he daydreamed of communing with the great.

In the meantime, his struggle with the language of his Teutonic forebears continued. While German troops occupied the Rhineland and the electorate rewarded Hitler with 99 percent of its vote, Loren completed a second semester of noncredit German and some additional course work in sociology. Still lacking confidence in his ability to pass the qualifying examination, he remained in Lincoln to study throughout the summer, postponing the day of reckoning until the last possible moment. When the ordeal was over, he left, with Mabel and her parents, for the Colorado Rockies and the cabin where they had stayed the previous summer. "Have just completed passing my German examination," he wrote to Bert on August 18. "I was so wound up with [it] for weeks that I could do little else."[55]

Wishing to put the distasteful experience behind him, Loren sometimes told the story of an even more hapless student who made a fool of himself in German class one day. Asked by the professor to translate a passage concerning the futility of man's efforts to create lasting monuments to himself, the tongue-tied fellow finally spoke up in a hesitant voice: "No man's erection lasts forever." There was a brief moment of silence before everyone went into hysterics, Loren's deep laugh reverberating off the classroom walls.[56]

VI

Loren entered the crowded New York-to-Philadelphia passenger express feeling tired and alone. Aside from his three professors, most of the faces familiar to him had vanished from the Penn campus by the fall of 1936. Lou Korn had accepted a government job and was working among the Indians in New Mexico; Ricky Faust, who had married the previous autumn after earning his M.A., was teaching high school in North Carolina; Duke Tachibana, an American citizen, had returned to Japan to face an uncertain future during the oncoming war. Scanning the coach for an empty seat, Loren discovered that the only place left was next to a huge, powerfully built man who seemed lost in slumber. As the train pulled out of the station, the conductor gradually made his way to their seats. Loren handed over his ticket to be punched, then sat back to see how the giant would behave when roused.

The conductor was about to tap the inert hulk on the shoulder when he suddenly straightened up and whipped out his ticket. When the conductor moved on, the large man turned to Loren with a glimmer of amusement in his fathomless blue eyes and said, in a booming voice, "Stranger, tell me a story."

Taken aback, Loren put down his book and replied, "You look to me as if you were the one to be telling *me* a story. I'm just an ordinary guy, but you, you look as if you had been places. Where did you get that double thumb?"

With no sign of embarrassment, the traveler turned his freakish right hand over to reveal another surprise: nails that were raised and thickened like the claws of a predator. The vision of a tiger flashed through Loren's mind; in a fight such a hand could be almost as lethal as a Bengal's slashing paw.

The stranger introduced himself as Tim Riley, a merchant seaman born and raised in San Francisco. As a teenager he had quarreled with his widowed father, a brawling police captain who beat men into line while patrolling the city's crime-ridden waterfront. Tim had shipped out as a deckhand at age fifteen, learned the ropes from bottom to top, and was now an engineer on a ship immobilized by a strike. "The company wants me to get . . . the freighter out to sea. I'll get through the picket line all right, but we're mighty short of hands. . . . Look, do you like what you're doing? 'Cause if you don't, you can come with me. I'll get you signed on." Memories of Loren's adolescent literary discoveries came flooding back—*Moby-Dick, The Nigger of the Narcissus, Twenty Years Before the Mast.* "A torrent opened in my head, the thunder on a thousand beaches. 'Go now.' "[57]

Whether there ever was such a curious specimen as Tim Riley is open to question. He may have been no more real than the fictional policeman of the same name portrayed years earlier by Faye Munden in the class play at T.C.H.S. Yet Loren alluded to Riley elsewhere, when he recalled being sorely tempted to give up the academic life on three separate occasions: "once at the urging of an oil man with whom I had shared a drink on a shoddy coach in Wyoming, and who proffered me a job with his crew; again when a local newspaper editor in desperation offered me a cub reportership in a little town in the Sandhills; the third time when a marine engineer, also with a bottle, offered to run me through a blockade of strikers to help take a freighter out of Philadelphia."[58]

Thinking of his uncle's faith in him and the office atop College Hall where one of the country's great maverick anthropologists held forth, Loren bade Tim Riley a reluctant farewell and returned to Penn. Speck, who was engaged in a wide range of projects, both new and ongoing, could not have been more pleased to see him. The old man had always admired Loren's literary gifts and immediately put him to work reading a stack of manuscripts being readied for publication. Quick to anger, the stocky Dutchman roared in protest whenever Loren offered advice. However, once his vanity had been appeased, he would "graciously accept a suggestion" as if nothing had happened.[59] When their day's work was over they hit the streets of West Philadelphia, to add yet another chapter to the old man's never-ending quest for the quintessential bowl of oyster stew.

It was not long before Loren's role was expanded from editor to collaborator. Speck's classic *Naskapi* had been published the previous year, but his material on the Algonkian Indians of northern Quebec was so extensive that much of it had had to be excluded from the monograph. This material became two coauthored articles on the hunting territories of the Naskapi and their closely related neighbors, the Montagnais.[60] Having convinced Loren of the necessity of getting his research into the scholarly journals, Speck was to remain deeply disappointed on another score. He could never talk his student into accompanying him on one of his annual migrations into the depths of the Canadian wilderness.[61]

Speck's love of publishing was coupled with a strange aversion to libraries and professional meetings. "If he had to consult a file of journals," Loren wrote, "he preferred to send an emissary, which in my later graduate years turned out to be myself."[62] Once, when the American Anthropological Association was meeting in Philadelphia, Speck refused to attend any of the sessions, while distinguished scholars from all over the country drifted into his office to be received. Like a child afraid of the dark, he asked Loren to stay with him. "There're more brains in Philadelphia this week than there is sewage in the Delaware River," Loren recalled him growling.[63] To avoid making lame excuses, the two headed over to the pine barrens for a day of tramping the cranberry bogs.

What may have been Loren's most profound experience with his mentor took place during one of their occasional visits to the Philadelphia Zoo. They came upon a wood duck, paddling serenely about a small pond. Mesmerized by its brilliant plumage, neither man said a word. Speck finally broke the spell: "Loren," he asked in an unusually soft voice, "tell me honestly. Do you believe unaided natural selection produced that pattern? Do you believe it has that much significance to the bird's survival?"

Loren turned around in astonishment, for the very thought had been occupying his own mind. "Frank, I have always had a doubt every time I came out of a laboratory. . . . Sometimes it seems very clear, and I satisfy myself in modern genetic terms. Then, as perhaps with your duck, something seems to go out of focus as though we are trying too hard, trying, it would seem, to believe the unbelievable. I honestly don't know." Darwin himself had occasionally wobbled in the face of such numbing complexity. Only his disciples had been sufficiently proud of their powers to forsake all doubts. "Perhaps," Loren concluded on a wistful note, "the scope is too vast for us. . . . We trick ourselves with our own ingenuity. I don't believe in simplicity."[64]

VII

In mid-December Loren found himself peering warily at falling snow from the window of a taxiing airplane. The craft rumbled into the leaden sky, slowly gaining altitude as it turned westward. Loren sat back, half dazed and troubled. His thoughts returned to the seemingly endless months following the death of his father and to the old woman who had comforted him during his midnight grappling with the world. He remembered touching his Grandmother Corey's white hair before leaving home three months earlier and sensing that this would be their last farewell. He had been away no more than two or three weeks when the eighty-six-year-old widow fell, fracturing her hip. Ten agonizing weeks of hospitalization had seen her condition deteriorate to the point of death, and the summons for Loren had arrived too late. Malvina died at 3:30 A.M. on December 17, only hours before her grandson's plane touched down at Lincoln Municipal Airport.[65]

Loren faced his final deadline as a student upon returning to Penn after the holidays. According to university regulations, his completed dissertation had to be in the hands of the graduate school's Group Committee by April 1 if the degree was to be conferred in June. "The time is short," he wrote to Bert in early March 1937, "but I still have hopes of finishing it. . . . I've completed the pollen chapter and am now turning to the vertebrates."[66]

On April 30, 1937, Speck wrote to H. L. Crosby, dean of the Graduate School, to certify that he had accepted Eiseley's dissertation: "Three Indices of Quaternary Time and Their Bearing on the Problems of American History: A Critique." The monograph was not in final form, as evidenced by Speck's careful choice of words, "as now completed." He also informed the dean that arrangements had been made to publish the study in three separate installments—publication being a requirement. The first part of the work would soon appear in the twenty-fifth anniversary volume of the Philadelphia Anthropological Society; "the subsequent material," as Speck termed it, would be published at a later time in the Daniel Garrison Brinton Centenary volume, to be edited by the department chairman himself.[67] Speck's letter must have satisfied both Dean Crosby and the Group Committee he chaired, since there is no indication that any of its members asked to see the completed monograph. It is highly unlikely that Speck ever set eyes on it either, for Loren had not complied with the letter of the law, something the old man was willing to overlook in the hope of getting his student, who had a solid job offer, to embark upon his long-delayed career.

When, after gaining fame as a writer, Loren was belatedly asked to provide the Penn library with a copy of the work, he did not respond.[68] Two articles remain; the third, although researched, was never actually written, perhaps because the volume in which it was to be published never appeared.[69] It was Loren himself who informed Bert that, with the deadline less than a month away, he had finished only the chapter on pollen analysis, making it difficult to believe that he could have polished off two others during the few remaining weeks. No dissertation was found among his papers after he died. Mabel, who had read almost everything Loren wrote, confessed to never having seen one.[70]

The concept of Quaternary time was first advanced in 1759 by Giovanni Arduino, an Italian natural philosopher who thought that the great flood described in Genesis was responsible for most deposits of fossils and other ancient debris. The term now denotes all geologic time from the end of the Tertiary period to the present—some 2 million years—and the period it encompasses is divided into the Pleistocene and Holocene (or Recent) epochs. At the time Loren was working on his dissertation, scientists from several disciplines were struggling with the problem of establishing an accurate chronology for these glacial and postglacial periods. Some had turned to pollen analysis and faunal successions, both invertebrate and vertebrate, in an attempt to improve the measurement of Quaternary time and its many climatic changes. Loren planned to examine the journal literature in each of these areas to determine the reliability of the new dating techniques and to suggest whether the disparate findings could be drawn together. His was to be a work of synthesis as opposed to original research, a characteristic of almost every one of his numerous scientific papers.

The less than startling conclusions he reached in the article on mollusca were identical to those pertaining to pollen analysis and vertebrate remains: "If we are now to summarize the possibility of mollusca as indices of late Pleistocene or post-glacial time," he wrote, "the effort is hardly testing. The fact is, briefly, that this approach is suggestive but requires further development."[71] Speck, who as Loren's official presenter extolled these findings as "critical," was also forced to admit that his student's evaluation of the existing evidence had led to "essentially negative conclusions."[72] Nor, as it turned out, would matters change dramatically until the advent of radiocarbon dating.

On Wednesday, June 9, at 10:30 A.M., without friends or relatives, Loren stood up to receive his doctorate. "I knew a good deal of ethnological lore from the Jesuit Relations of the seventeenth century," he later wrote, "about divination through the use of oracle bones. I knew also about the distribution of rabbit-skin blankets in pre-Columbia America and the four-day fire rites for the departing dead. And mammoths gone ten thousand years, I knew them, too."[73] Yet in Loren's case it was not so much the formal instruction as the inclination of the spirit that mattered: the poet walked off the stage—diploma in hand—wearing the fox skin of a scientist.

10

MOUNT OREAD

I

Prolonged violence had earned the territory the nickname bleeding Kansas well before it was admitted to the crumbling Union in January 1861. Its settlement had been spurred not so much by natural westward expansion as by an ill-conceived concept called Squatter Sovereignty, which stiffened the resolve of both proslavery and antislavery factions to achieve a majority. Towns were established by each party during the strife-ridden 1850s—Lawrence and Topeka by the abolitionists, Leavenworth and Atchison by the advocates of bondage.

At dawn on August 21, 1863, Confederate Captain William Clarke Quantrill and his company of 450 Missouri Bushwhackers approached a slumbering Lawrence in a gray haze and rode up to the high ground overlooking Main Street. The raiders cocked their pistols and were reminded a final time of their orders to "burn every house and kill every man" they could find. The command was given: "Rush the town!" The sounds of revolver shots, rebel yells, and echoing hoofbeats soon gave way to the screams of the wounded and dying, who had run, terror stricken, into the streets, wearing only their nightclothes. When it was over four hours later, the bloodstained marauders, their mounts laden with booty, formed a ragged column and headed eastward out of town, the fading wails of widows and orphans signaling their retreat. Some 150 innocent people lay dead in the yards and streets, while the entire business district and 200 houses were either destroyed or burning to the ground.

Eiseley visited the first log cabin built by the Free-Staters and occasionally paused to muse over the burial place of Quantrill's victims, but his earliest memory of Lawrence went back to his own days as a drifter. The freight on which he was riding had just crossed a tributary of the Missouri River called the Kaw, or Kansas, which he then knew nothing about. The train stopped in Lawrence to uncouple a few cars; when he stepped down to stretch his legs, a cinder-throwing cop forced him to move on. "That was a historic moment, although I didn't realize it at the time. Some six or seven years later I would begin my teaching career in that same town. I didn't even know then that the state university was located there."[1]

Eiseley had accepted a position as assistant professor in the Department of Sociology a month before he received his Ph.D. Negotiations had been going on since February 19, when Frank Speck had wired Dr. Carroll Clark, Eiseley's future chairman, asking him to hold the slot until he could forward a letter of recommendation and the proper academic credentials. Speck composed a glowing, five-page testimonial the following day, virtually guaranteeing that Eiseley would complete his dissertation before June. According to Speck, no other anthropology student at an eastern university was "so ripe for energetic action and so well qualified by nature and training for engaging . . . in the commencement of his career." Indeed, "if our budget permitted it, he would be offered a rating and appointment here, similar to that which you have to offer at Kansas."[2] Eiseley wrote to Clark the same day, stressing the fact that he had earned some twenty-three credit hours in sociology in Nebraska that did not appear on his Penn transcript. During the next month at least six others wrote on his behalf, including Duncan Strong, Dwight Kirsch, James M. Reinhardt, and Lowry Wimberly, who described him as a young man possessed of a "striking personality, a good voice, and a sympathetic and loyal nature."[3]

By April, Clark was convinced that Loren Eiseley was his man. Unfortunately, the chairman's plans had hit a major snag. While conferring with the university chancellor about the position, Clark was told that adequate funds might not become available until the following year. Even under the best of circumstances, the most they would be able to offer Eiseley was two thousand dollars, some four hundred dollars less than originally discussed—"a fact I would blush to admit if it were not for the droughts, dust storms, crop failures, and other hardships suffered by the people of our state."[4] On May 1, following "heroic measures" by the administration, Eiseley was offered an assistant professorship at $2,100 for the academic year. Clark could make no promises beyond this, but if Eiseley could only hang on, the situation was bound to get better. "A single corn crop would make a tremendous improvement in the outlook."[5] Eiseley wired his acceptance two days later and began preparing to reenter the dust and gloom of the shifting landscape of the thirties.

In 1929 Kansans had earned an average per capita income of $535 a year; by 1933 this figure had been reduced to $251, or less than half. Though per capita income rose gradually during the rest of the decade, it never came within $100 of the 1929 figure. Annual rainfall averaged four and one-half inches less than in the twenties, and 1936 was the driest year in the history of record keeping. Blinding clouds of topsoil filled the air, chasing thousands of "busted" farmers all the way to California.

Those who remained behind were as depressed as the economy, and they vented their frustration at the polls. Kansas Governor Alfred "Alf" Landon, one of the few Republicans still in control of a state house, was mauled by Franklin Roosevelt in the 1936 presidential election, carrying only Maine and Vermont. Even more telltale was the massive inferiority complex evident throughout the state. Psychiatrist Karl A. Menninger, cofounder of the renowned Menninger Clinic in Topeka, revived painful memories of a violent past by giving them a new twist in an article titled "Bleeding Kansans." After returning from an extended visit to the coast, the author told of being stopped on the street by apologetic friends who spoke of how "hard" it must be for him to come back to the "drab monotony" of Kansas scenery. The brightest, most promising young Kansans were inclined to believe that their state possessed little, if anything, of cultural value.[6] To a newly minted Ph.D. with a chronic case of emotional hemophilia, such conditions would prove ideal.

II

The University of Kansas is situated atop Mount Oread, which was named in honor of Eli Thayer, organizer of the abolitionist Emigrant Aid Society and sponsor of the Oread Collegiate Institute in Worcester, Massachusetts. In Greek mythology the oreads were mountain nymphs, and if "the Hill," as it was commonly called, did not exactly qualify as a true mountain, its name was doubtless more pleasing to the educated ear than the colloquial Back Bone Ridge.[7]

In 1889 Kansas had the distinction of having the first academic department in the country designated "Sociology." However, like most other universities of the 1930s, it had yet to establish a separate department of anthropology, which meant that Eiseley was expected to teach in both fields. During his first year on campus, he offered six classes requiring five different preparations: Elements of Sociology I and II, General Anthropology, Cultural Anthropology, and The Evolution of Culture. Three more courses—The American Indian, Primitive Society, and Methods of Archaeology and Anthropology—were added the following year.[8] Matters were made more difficult by the fact that one large room on the second floor of the Administration Building served as the office for all eleven department members, the chairman included. Marston McCluggage, a young colleague of Eiseley, remembered that they would come in, get organized, go to class, and then head home immediately to get ready for the next day.[9]

Home for Eiseley was the University Club, a two-story stucco building nestled below the crest of Mount Oread. He occupied one of the twelve-by-fifteen-foot rooms in the bachelor dormitory, though whether in the basement or on the second floor, with its arresting view of the distant countryside, is unknown. When he grew restless, he had the use of a large commons on the first floor and could take his meals in a small dining area off the kitchen. He occasionally turned up in the evenings to watch his cigar-puffing colleagues play cards at portable wooden tables but rarely, if ever, joined in. Standing with his back against the wall and his hands in his pockets, he listened to every word and watched each movement with the alertness of a wary animal.

Mostly Eiseley studied beyond midnight, preparing outlines for the following day's classes. His teaching experience was limited to a few days of substituting for Speck. He remembered pacing nervously before his students that first semester, and likened himself to the proverbial Russian fleeing in a sleigh before a closing pack of wolves.[10] His anxiety notwithstanding, the thirty-year-old assistant professor made a favorable impression on most of his students, not least because of his physical attributes. One of his first female pupils at Kansas described him as "a great teacher. He also was a very handsome man and the coeds that year were all 'aflutter.' . . . Anthropology became very popular even though I suspect most of the girls didn't know what the word meant when they enrolled in the course!"[11]

Another former coed found him memorable for his low-key expertise and his almost offhand lecture style. "He spoke as he wrote, gracefully and literately. . . . I was fascinated by his ability to unwind some very complicated grammatical constructions." She also had the feeling that he was lecturing as much for his own benefit as for that of the students. "I sat next to a friend and we would sometimes nearly crack up at something he said completely dead-pan, and then we would see an answering gleam in his eye as he went on with what he had to say." When reading his autobiographical works years later, she was startled to learn of her professor's troubles. "When I knew him, I thought of him as [being] as close to the ideal humanist as I would ever get to know, a 20th century Renaissance man, and the model of what a professor should really be."[12]

Although their emotions did not run as high, Eiseley seems to have been equally popular among his male students. McCluggage, who was working on a Ph.D., took two of his colleague's anthropology classes. He remembered that Eiseley lectured from three-by-five-inch note cards and knew his material exceedingly well. Several of the lectures were tinged with the mystical. Morton Green, a native of New York City, was another of Eiseley's admirers. Green, who went on to a distinguished career as professor of paleontology at the South Dakota School of Mines and Technology, characterized him as "the fastest speaker in the West. He came in and he just started; he talked rapidly and we took voluminous notes." Green thought Eiseley a brilliant lecturer and a walking textbook rolled into one.[13]

Still, he did not please everyone. A future physician remembered him as the only professor he ever had who faced the blackboard, rarely turning around to look at the class. "I think he was a loner, rather dull and sombre, and rather eerie." The class breathed a collective sigh of relief when the semester was over: "we could go on to living life instead of being reminded of death five sessions a week, and being with a teacher who practiced dying while living."[14]

Whatever their particular angles of vision, all of Eiseley's students were in agreement about one thing: he was not interested in any form of dialogue, or in interacting with students outside the classroom. He never entered the room until the bell rang, and he gathered his lecture notes and was gone the moment it rang again. "If you wanted to ask him something after class, you had to grab your possessions any old way and RUN down the hall to catch him," one student remembered.[15] For Eiseley, teaching would prove a "lifelong battle" with anxiety. Yet the privileged few who gained his confidence found him even more interesting in conversation than when he was delivering a skillfully crafted lecture.

Too poor to afford an automobile, Eiseley walked almost everywhere, which meant that he was pretty much confined to the campus and the small business district stretching below Mount Oread. Mabel occasionally visited on weekends, sometimes driving down with the Schultzes; but the trip from Lincoln was a long one, and when Loren wanted to see his fiancée he usually flew up from Lawrence, much to the delight of Mabel's more romantic girlfriends. Still, there were some who remained skeptical of his intentions, since ten years of dating had not led to an exchange of marriage vows. Marguerite Lewis, librarian for the Department of Art at Lincoln, remembered an unmarried professor remarking that she was sure Loren was "like all of those men": he would let Mabel put him through school and then jilt her once he found a good position.[16]

Mabel, too, had experienced her private moments of doubt, but for reasons that had nothing to do with money. Dwight Kirsch's wife, Truby, to whom she had become quite close while Loren was studying in Philadelphia, sensed that something was amiss. "She told me," Mabel wrote Kirsch after Truby's untimely death in 1953, "quite spontaneously and in an unsolicited confidence, to pay no attention to [the] age difference between Loren and myself. She said that was an inconsequential detail in light of truly important considerations."[17]

Now there were difficulties of another kind. Mabel developed a "cyst" on her right breast and was told that she might have to undergo a mastectomy. Lacking confidence in the local medical community, she made arrangements to enter the Mayo Clinic in Rochester, Minnesota, where the growth was successfully removed without permanent disfiguration. However, the resulting medical bills, which she arranged to pay off in monthly installments, made it imperative that she keep her job for at least another year.[18]

The couple's financial problems were compounded by the growing irresponsibility of Eiseley's mother and widowed aunt. According to Lancaster County records, he had no sooner accepted the position in Kansas than Daisy sold the heavily mortgaged and rented family home, perhaps out of spite because she realized that her son would never return. Grace, without consulting her nephew, followed Daisy's example some months later, taking a heavy loss on her comfortable residence, which Buck had long since paid for, and forfeiting what little remained of her fading gentility. Hiring themselves out as housekeepers, the sisters depleted their meager savings while moving from one small apartment to another, each a bit more shabby than the last. At what point Eiseley first gave them money is uncertain, but the day inevitably arrived when he was providing much of their financial support.[19]

III

Dorothy Thomas had stayed on at La Casa Querida after Mary Austin's death while the trustees tried to find a way of preserving the house as a memorial, keeping intact its collection of manuscripts and other Austiniana. Plans were made to inter the writer's ashes in the garden, but a wealthy property owner living on the other side of the wall objected vehemently to the idea. The *gente*, or Spanish folk, talked in hushed voices of ghosts. Three years had passed with no final decision, while the urn containing Mary's ashes reposed in a local vault.

When word arrived that the mortuary was about to vacate its premises, the trustees had to act. On August 13, 1937, a cowboy, followed by two packhorses carrying a pick, shovel, trowel, and bag of cement, started toward a massive pyramid of sand and rock on the edge of the Sangre de Cristo Mountains east of Santa Fe. He was joined by a young friend and his wife; they rode the serpentine trail to the very top of the great mound known as Mount Picacho. There, on the outer rim of a world awash in white light, the ashes of Mary Hunter Austin were embedded forever in a rough-hewn sarcophagus of native granite.

Loren and Mabel were visiting Dorothy at the time. She told her rapt guests of Mary's abhorrence of those who "messed with her things." Mabel had been given the master bedroom, and Dorothy wanted to know if the thought of sleeping in Mary's bed frightened her.

"Why, yes," she replied, "but I look forward to the interesting experience."

Mabel's screams awakened Dorothy in the middle of the night. She came running from her room and encountered Loren barreling down the hall, his bathrobe and sleek, dark hair trailing behind, reminding her of an Indian. They reached Mabel simultaneously; she was sitting up in bed and trembling with fear.

"She stood right there, right there," Mabel blurted out, pointing at a bare spot on the floor. "And she said, 'Who do you think you are, sleeping in my bed? If you don't believe I'm here just open your eyes and look.' " It was at this point that Mabel had screamed.

"It wasn't a time to go to sleep again," Dorothy recalled. They gathered in the kitchen, where they lit a reassuring fire and drank strong coffee until sunrise.[20]

During lunch on the patio one day, the conversation turned to D. H. Lawrence and his widow, Frieda von Richthofen Lawrence, who was living on her ranch in the Sangre de Cristo range above Taos. Dorothy told of earlier meetings with Frieda and of an invitation from her to visit the ranch sometime. As Dorothy warmed to her subject, she proposed that they make the trip north the following morning. Fellow Nebraskan Lois Gerard agreed to join them, and the four set out in Dorothy's new Ford, a symbol of her growing success as a writer, shortly after dawn.

They arrived in Taos early enough to have a leisurely look around before eating lunch at the small inn. The experience was a new one for Lois, and she never forgot the colorful dresses of the girls working in the dining room, the soft shuffle of their leather sandals and moccasins. From Taos they drove some fifteen miles up into the mountains, the road eventually becoming little more than a wagon track before they passed a rude, sun-bleached sign, "Kiowa Ranch." Farther along they came to a tree bearing a painted phoenix. The road ended at the Lawrence yard in front of Frieda's three-room log cabin.

The others sat in the car while Dorothy went in alone. During her absence a distinguished-looking gentleman of aristocratic bearing passed a short distance away, turned his head slightly in their direction, and entered the cabin. This could only have been the mysterious Count Angelo Ravagli, Frieda's longtime companion and lover. He returned to show the others in. As Frieda waved them to chairs, she eased herself into a wooden rocker and with one foot set it to a gentle, comfortable rhythm.

This "powerful Valkyrie," as she was once described by a friend, seemed disarmingly peaceful and domestic. She wore a simple cotton housedress and much-laundered apron; on her feet were white, rubber-soled shoes of the type used for tennis. Her blond hair, once worn in a luxuriant upsweep, was now cut short and flecked with gray. Frieda's face was unlined and serene; traces of her German heritage were only slightly evident in her speech.

Mabel and Loren were charmed by their hostess, and she by them. However, Eiseley suffered some embarrassment when he attempted to discourse with Frieda in his faltering German, which she could not understand. At one point she left the room, returning a few moments later with a piece of Indian pottery in either hand, both of which she gave to the engaged couple as a wedding present. The next time Frieda saw Dorothy she remarked of Eiseley, "He has a noble German head; how it must have hurt his mother birthing him, but it was worth it."[21] She thought him not only handsome but brilliant and seemed positive that her notoriously difficult husband would have liked this fellow writer.

The afternoon at Kiowa Ranch ended with a short hike to the chapel containing Lawrence's ashes. The site had been chosen by Frieda, the structure planned and built by the count, with the help of some local workmen. They paused on the way to catch their breath and to take in the majestic view from nearly nine thousand feet up the side of Lobo Mountain. Behind them were the pines, climbing up and up and up; before them, the shimmering valley of Taos, stretching away to the dark crack that is the Rio Grande Canyon, with the river at its bottom. The sun's rays slanted through the open door of the sanctuary, rebounding off the whitewashed walls and simple altar. Fresh evergreen boughs and a small bouquet of wildflowers lay before the burial urn, a daily offering from neighboring Mexican families. Lois felt that she was indeed standing in a shrine—a place of peace for a man who had known so little of it in life.[22]

A final bright moment came when the four were at the car, saying their farewells. A tall man, his wife, and a lanky boy of twelve or thirteen rounded the corner of the house, heading toward one of the small guest cabins below. Both the man and the boy carried fishing poles, and the wife carried a small basket. Frieda motioned for them to come over and introduced Aldous Huxley, his wife, Maria, and their son. She asked Huxley how his writing had gone that day. He answered that it had gone well and that the fishing expedition had been undertaken as a celebration. As the friends drove away, Eiseley expressed sympathy for the youth, who carried the weight of both the Huxley and Arnold families on his small shoulders.

The following summer, in August 1938, after recovering from surgery at the Mayo Clinic, Mabel accompanied Eiseley to Albuquerque, where they stayed with Lou Korn and his wife, "Totsy." The Korns introduced them to their wide circle of friends, and Lou noted that Eiseley developed a particular fondness for the English-born novelist Eric Knight, author of *This Above All* and *The Flying Yorkshireman*. Knight died in a plane crash during the war, shortly after his *Lassie Come Home* was made into a successful motion picture. Eiseley also talked poetry with Paul Engle, a founder of the internationally acclaimed Writers' Workshop at the University of Iowa, and with Robert Lowe, a young professor of English at Purdue whom Dorothy had met at Yaddo, the writers' and artists' colony, during the summer of 1935.

It was Lou who began the good-natured teasing of his guests: "Gosh, you travel together and so forth, you just have to get married."[23] Totsy joined in, as did several of the couple's new friends. Eiseley sheepishly agreed, and the Korns happily made the arrangements. The wedding took place on Monday, August 29, at 2:30 in the afternoon. Since neither Loren nor Mabel wanted a religious service, the Korns rented a dining room in a local hotel and arranged for a probate judge to officiate. Lou agreed to serve as best man, and Dorothy drove down from Santa Fe to stand at Mabel's side. She was overjoyed when the call announcing the wedding came and smiled to herself on remembering that Mabel had once said, "I do not believe in long engagements."[24]

The bride wore high heels and a simple coffee-cream dress, making her appear even taller and more slender than usual; the groom chose a dark double-breasted suit, whose jacket he longed to remove in the stifling heat. Everyone in the small party was suffering and expected the service to be short and to the point. Somehow, though, the judge got wind of the fact that he had a promising writer standing before him and felt compelled to rise to the occasion. Dorothy remembered that he "swung right back into the Garden of Eden" and rhapsodized at great length. "He began with the first day and ended with the sixth day and [included] the evening and the morning" of every day in between. When God was done " 'He saw that it was good,' and we saw that it was good that [the judge] got there at last."[25]

Standing next to Mabel, Dorothy felt the vibrations of the unspoken message she was sending to the convulsed groom: "Loren Eiseley, evolutionist, if you dare burst out laughing before this man is done I shall never marry you again." A quaking Lou, on Eiseley's other side, was responding no better to Totsy's subtle commands. The time came at last to slip the gold band on Mabel's outstretched finger, but by now Eiseley was struggling so hard to contain himself that she had to help him.[26] When permission was finally given to "Kiss the bride," he wrapped his arms around Mabel, threw back his head, and rocked with laughter.

The newlyweds were toasted with iced champagne before the party drove to a nearby restaurant for the wedding dinner. Mabel later wrote that a good part of her honeymoon was spent "poking into caves and looking at all kinds of 'fascinating' archeological remains."[27] What she did not say is that her husband of only a few days foolishly drank some unboiled water in a Mexican village and came down with a severe case of what the locals called "Santa Fe–itis." The embarrassed bride telephoned Dorothy to ask if they could stay with her until Loren's dysentery subsided. Anxious to be of help, Dorothy told them to come ahead, and the rest of the Eiseley honeymoon was spent very quietly in the soothing confines of La Casa Querida.

IV

Financial considerations dictated that the newlyweds continue living as they had at least one more year. Eiseley returned to his bachelor quarters at the University Club, while Mabel went back to her parents' home in Lincoln to resume her duties as curator of the university art gallery.

The 1938–39 academic year began amid war and rumors of war. Because it was on a more human scale, the news Eiseley was receiving from his good friend Duke Tachibana proved especially distressing. Hoping to leave Japan for the United States, Duke had gone to a Tokyo bank to exchange his money for U.S. currency, only to be firmly refused. "Life here is not without its spice," he wrote with more than a touch of irony. "I found out that I have been trailed and shadowed first by the police and then by the army secret service, or whatever equivalent they have here." His neighbors had also been questioned concerning his movements and behavior. "All the letters, newspapers, and magazines I receive from the states have put me down as a marked man I guess. Anyhow," he joked, "I have the distinction of having good police protection even if I am not aware of it." Duke had taken Eiseley's advice and registered with the nearest consul, which made him feel "much better": "if the U.S. ever gets into a scrap with some foreign power—well, she has my name and address and you'll see Private Tachibana do some real fighting."[28] His words had a hollow ring to them, however, and both men knew it. Although Duke was a native-born American, there was not the slightest chance that Japanese officials would let him leave.

Autumn also brought a sharp reminder of another kind of loss. "Verily, we have both vanished into thin air," Harold Vinal wrote in October. "Can't you send me on some poems? It's been such a long time since a group of yours has been in the magazine."[29] Two and a half years to be exact. But Eiseley sent Vinal no more poems and, except for two short works published in the September 1939 issue of *Poetry*, wrote only for the *Prairie Schooner* until 1945, when he stopped composing verse altogether. His last "Crossroads" column, which featured a poem by his new friend Paul Engle, had appeared in the *Schooner*'s Spring 1938 issue.

For the time being Eiseley was preoccupied with teaching and the need to establish his credentials as a serious member of the anthropological community. In July 1937 he had spent a few weeks with the U.S. National Museum party at a Doniphan County dig in extreme northeastern Kansas. The invitation had been extended to him by Waldo R. Wedel, leader of the expedition and once a fellow student at Nebraska. Working along the high bluffs of the Missouri, the party unearthed a number of eighteenth-century Indian burials. The dead had been placed in a half-sitting position, and their graves covered with heavy slabs of limestone. Stained a deep green from copper ornaments, the bones were identified as belonging to members of a little-known tribe visited by early French explorers.[30]

Three months later Eiseley became convinced that he was on to something potentially far more important. Bernard Frazier, a sculptor and member of the Art Department, stopped by his office one afternoon. The artist had heard of the new anthropologist and had come to tell him of a deposit of ash and bone on the banks of Spring Creek in Smith County, about twenty miles below the Kansas-Nebraska border. Frazier and his cousins had grown up in the area and frequently played in the fields containing what he assumed was an ancient campsite. Preliminary investigations during weekends proved Frazier correct: burrowing through an overburden of ten feet, Eiseley discovered a thin "cultural layer" consisting of charcoal, fragmentary bison remains, flint chips, and other evidence of human occupation. Owing to its depth, the site represented at least a modest degree of antiquity, perhaps even the killing ground of the almost mythic Folsom man. Hoping to make certain, Eiseley asked the geologist H. T. U. Smith, a diminutive redhead with a Harvard Ph.D., to collaborate with him on the dig.

Thwarted by winter weather and a heavy teaching load, the two were unable to set out for north-central Kansas until early August 1938. They were joined by several students at Smith Center and, with the help of a local collector named Ivan Phetteplace, explored the site. The artifacts consisted mostly of scrapers and crude chert flakes, along with fragments of sandstone used as an abrasive. It was Phetteplace who found the single point that dashed Eiseley's hopes. The weapon was neither Folsom nor of any other Pleistocene type. What they had unearthed was a site between five thousand and seven thousand years old, well after the Ice Age but well before the spread of agriculture and ceramics into the region.[31]

This discovery, while of scientific importance, was not the "big find" of which Eiseley dreamed, in spite of his protestations to the contrary. "There was a kind of frenzy," he later reflected, "that seized men about the events of the terminal ice" during the 1920s and '30s—a frenzy that doubtless began when he was a youth, losing himself by the hour in adventure stories.[32] Eiseley had been fifteen when the world-renowned Egyptologist Howard Carter, working with Lord Carnarvon in Luxor's Valley of the Kings, discovered the treasure-laden tomb of the boy-ruler Tutankhamen. He read everything he could find about Carter and his excavations of other pharaonic tombs: Amenhotep I, Hatshepsut, and Thutmose IV. Equally indelible was Herbert Winlock's account of his discovery of the tomb of Meket-Re in Thebes, which, as a man approaching seventy, Eiseley vicariously incorporated into his own autobiography.[33]

What a story it would be if he were the first anthropologist to gaze upon the identifiable remains of an Ice Age man in North America. A site was uncovered by accident in southeastern Nebraska near the Platte River during steam shovel excavations for a huge navigation ditch. A fragmentary human skeleton and an accompanying charcoal stratum were exposed at the unusual depth of thirty-eight feet. Bert Schultz, who had recently been appointed assistant director of the Nebraska State Museum, called his friend in. After carefully examining the remains, Eiseley returned to Lawrence and made a grand pronouncement to the press in April 1939. The individual may have lived as long as fifteen thousand years ago, he began. "The find belongs to a much older period than the Smith County site upon which Dr. H. T. U. Smith and myself have been working. There are traces of extinct fauna," he continued, "and I feel confident that the site will be demonstrated to be of a high antiquity."[34]

Seeking to capitalize on their good fortune, Loren and Bert signed a contract with Macmillan for a book dealing with the history of Folsom man; it carried the working title "They Hunted the Mammoth: The Story of Ice Age Man." Each was to write a number of chapters aimed at a broad popular audience. Although the idea for the book went as far back as 1936, the two had just now gotten around to presenting it to a publisher. Both did a considerable amount of research and writing during the next two years, even though their "Pleistocene" skull ultimately failed to live up to Loren's extravagant billing. In 1941 an editor from Macmillan wrote Eiseley, informing him that the firm was no longer interested in the work. It was only a matter of time before the country would be at war with Japan, he explained, and in the midst of such a conflict few would presumably care about a book on the ancient hunters of mammoths.[35]

11

"A BIG, STRAPPING, FINE FELLOW"

I

In the studied photograph that appeared in the April 11, 1940, issue of the *Kansas City Journal*, Loren Eiseley is seated in a wicker chair before a cluttered bookshelf. The anthropologist gazes off into space, a large pipe dangling from the slightly curled fingers of his left hand. In the background, almost level with his chiseled countenance, a bleached human skull gapes blankly in the same direction. "K.U. Prof Gets $2,700 Fellowship" reads the bold-lettered caption. Other pictures and other articles trumpeting his success appeared throughout the state. According to the accompanying story, Eiseley had received notice of the prestigious award from the Social Science Research Council only a day before it made the papers. One of just ten recipients nationally, nine of whom were Ivy League Ph.D.'s like himself, he would soon apply for a leave of absence to undertake postdoctoral research in physical anthropology at Columbia University and the American Museum of Natural History in New York.

The publicity he received on this and other occasions suggests the presence of a sophisticated guiding hand. Eiseley's professional activities had been highlighted in the press as far back as 1936, when he loaned his African carving of a "mysterious" Negro woman—a gift from Frank Speck—to the fine arts gallery in Nebraska's Morrill Hall.[1] In May 1939 the *Lincoln Sunday Journal and Star* had carried an article on a special display of Robinson Jeffers's collected works at the University of Nebraska library. The exhibit had been planned with the help of Dr. Loren Eiseley, assistant professor of anthropology at the University of Kansas and Jeffers scholar. Readers were especially encouraged to view the letter and autographed picture sent to him by the solitary California genius, whom Eiseley was quoted as admiring above all modern writers because of their common heritage—"the poet and the scientist in one."[2] Shortly before leaving Philadelphia in 1937, Eiseley had written to Bert Schultz, who was still in New York: "Incidentally, do you have any trouble getting publicity about your stuff when you are away from home? If so tell me and I can tell Mabel to tip Mossholder [a Lincoln journalist] off about your forthcoming work."[3]

It was with mixed emotions that Mabel had given up her position at Nebraska in the summer of 1939 to join her husband of almost a year in Lawrence. Her boss, Dwight Kirsch, had become like an older brother to her; together they had built the university art collection into one of the finest of its kind. Mabel's services were deemed so valuable that she drove up from Lawrence during the early 1940s to help plan and promote the annual show. The former curator experienced no greater reward than when *Life* magazine announced its intention to do a feature story on the little known but distinguished gallery behind the cornstalk curtain.[4]

Eiseley left Kansas in June 1940 for New York City, where he took a small apartment at 107 West Seventy-sixth Street, not far from the American Museum of Natural History. Mabel stayed on in their rented house in Lawrence for a few weeks, then returned to Lincoln and her parents' home for the summer. Lacking formal training in physical anthropology, Eiseley had made arrangements to spend July and August reading intensively under the tutelage of Dr. Harry L. Shapiro, an urbane Harvard Ph.D. who held a joint appointment at Columbia and the American Museum. Shapiro also gave him free access to the museum's superb laboratory facilities while they pondered a more structured course of study for the fall.

By late July the ovenlike metropolis forced Eiseley to flee his apartment for the less oppressive surroundings of the New York Public Library. There he read from thick, dust-laden tomes of Hooton, Dixon, and Hrdlicka until his head dropped to his chest in the midsummer's torpor, only to return to his room to lie wide awake. After tossing and turning, sweat soaked, for hours, he arose before dawn to pace the floor or to catch up on his extensive correspondence. "Things are pretty lonesome here without Mabel," he confided to Carroll Clark, his understanding chairman. "In spite of my wandering tendencies I've gotten so thoroughly used to Lawrence and K.U. that I'm rather homesick at the thought of not showing up for the fall semester. . . . I find the East, in spite of libraries and all the intellectual facilities, less pleasing than it once was."[5]

The thought of ill-considered literary promises also nagged at him. In addition to the publishing agreement with Macmillan for the book on Folsom man, he had recently signed a contract with Thomas Y. Crowell to write a textbook on general anthropology.[6] Then, for good measure, he inked yet a third contract, this one also with Crowell. It called for him to produce a forty-thousand-word chapter for a text with the working title "Fundamentals of Sociology: A Situational Approach." The remaining chapters were to be written by his colleagues at Kansas, who included Seba Eldridge, professor of sociology and editor of Crowell's Social Science Series.[7]

Mabel arrived in September, and the couple headed up the New England coast to spend a few days with the Specks at their summer place in Gloucester, Massachusetts. Frank and Loren planned to put the finishing touches on an article they were preparing for the *Proceedings of the American Philosophical Society*.[8] The Specks' two daughters, teenagers Alberta and Virginia, saw their guests as the reincarnations of Lancelot and Guinevere. "Mabel was a tall, slim, beautifully dressed 'lady,' " Alberta recalled. "Loren literally filled the room with himself. He was tall and impressive in his tan suit and western-style hat—almost a cowboy hat. I can still hear Loren's voice, deep and serious, as he and my father discussed some important subjects at the dinner table."[9]

One of those subjects was almost certainly war. Hitler stood near the pinnacle of his career in the waning summer of 1940, a year that had seen democracy all but vanish from the continent that had invented it. Eiseley registered for the recently instituted draft at Columbia in October and fretted about a 10 percent drop in enrollments back in Kansas, which the administration attributed to conscription.[10] As the most recently hired member of his department, he would likely be the first to lose his position if the situation worsened. Rarely given to strong pronouncements on political issues, he nevertheless supported Clark's endorsement of President

Roosevelt's decision to oppose the isolationists in Congress by championing the Lend-Lease Act:

> I was pleased to find that we are in such hearty agreement on the war problem. There was a time . . . when I felt that the situation looked too hopeless to remedy and, after all, might prove to be no more than a European affair. Shortly after coming down here, however, my opinions changed. I think Britain has a good chance of holding on, and I furthermore think that her downfall would release endless international repercussions which would disastrously affect us. I do not believe I have any illusions about the war, about Britain, or about the dangers of another botched peace. But the other choice is immediate, and personally I am for all-out aid even to the point of war.[11]

In October the Eiseleys moved into a more spacious brownstone at 32 West Seventy-sixth Street, a block from Loren's summer quarters and only a short walk to Central Park. When the landlady told them that the second-floor apartment below theirs was vacant, Loren had Mabel telephone Dorothy Thomas, who had moved to New York in 1939, asking her to become their neighbor. Dorothy was so thrilled she broke her lease, forfeiting a month's rent and a hefty security deposit, and moved into what had once been a beautiful walnut-paneled library.

Although she rose at dawn to write, the attractive brunette also stayed up late, reading herself to sleep. Eiseley, who almost never retired until the small hours, would look out his window for the reflected light from Dorothy's bedroom. Upon seeing it, he would rap sharply on the steam pipes three times. "I would get up from bed and reach for slippers, and robe, and pocketbook," Dorothy remembered, "and run up those stairs. Loren would be waiting at the top . . . in his bathrobe to see me safely up. I would come in and the three of us would talk."[12]

In truth, Eiseley did most of the talking. "Loren, in his breathlessness, would get up and walk the floor. And he would stream-of-consciousness talk, like Noah walked and talked with God." Mabel, her stenographic pad at the ready, divided her attention between her midnight guest and her peripatetic spouse. "When Loren said something Mabel thought should be kept, she put it in her . . .

book. There are poems at which I was in on the conception—lines of poetry Loren said off the top of his head."[13] Their meetings sometimes lasted until the morning light. While she never complained, Mabel had difficulty keeping her eyes open, but Eiseley didn't seem to notice. "I don't think that Mabel was born a night person," Dorothy mused. "I think she was converted. As a girl marries into the Episcopal church, she was married into the night country."[14]

II

Dorothy made a concerted effort to take the Eiseleys out of themselves by introducing the couple to her diverse circle of friends. She arranged for them to attend a cocktail party given by Mary Hunter, the theater patron and socialite niece of Santa Fe's Mary Austin. The room buzzed when the beautiful Rita Hayworth made a grand entrance on the arm of her intense and imposing fiancé, Orson Welles, who was about to begin production on *Citizen Kane*. Yet "when Loren and Mabel walked into the room . . . there was a hush, and people looked up. Someone whispered to me, 'Who is that?' "[15] The arresting pair did not live up to first impressions, however, leading a somewhat disappointed but sympathetic Dorothy to the conclusion that her dear friends simply were not party people. "They didn't mingle; they just sat there together. . . . They didn't feel any belonging with social nonsense."[16]

There were times when Eiseley became so deeply depressed that he was "lugubrious." In an attempt to snap him out of it, Mabel would begin to poke and tease, calling him "Gloomy Gus" and "Jerry Jeremiah." If he responded as she hoped, he would spring from his chair and begin chasing her around the apartment, which was arranged so that they could trace a figure eight through the corridors. One night Dorothy was roused by an unusually violent hammering on the pipes. Alarmed, she ran upstairs to find the trembling couple clinging to each other, on the verge of tears. Gradually regaining his composure, Eiseley told of how he had been chasing Mabel when she slipped on a throw rug and nearly plunged headlong through a large open window in the hallway. Luckily, he had caught her by the ankles at the last second. "Everyone would have thought that I threw her out the window, that I killed Mabel!"[17]

On another evening, shortly after dusk, Eiseley rapped on Dorothy's apartment door to tell her that he had returned home to find

Mabel gone. He strode up and down "literally tearing at his hair in his anxiety over her being late, and the fear that something might have happened to her."[18] Dorothy suggested that he keep watch from the bay window facing the street. Mabel soon came up the front walk, and, like a relieved child, he raced down the remaining flight of stairs to meet her. She had worked later than usual at her part-time job, typing manuscripts for the detective-story writer Rex Stout, creator of the sedentary sleuth Nero Wolfe. From witnessing this and similar incidents, Dorothy, like Mabel's sister, Dollie, had not the slightest doubt which of the two was the dominant force in the marriage: "Mabel was his mother, his sister, his cousin, his friend; she was his stay."[19]

While they talked writing most of the time, Dorothy received a sharp reminder of Eiseley's reason for being in New York when she happened to mention a skull she had unearthed while picnicking with friends in the mountains above Taos. After considerable agonizing, she had given it to a friend in medical school rather than to the local museum. When Eiseley heard this, she recounted, "he looked at me as though I had utterly betrayed him." He rose and began his characteristic pacing of the floor. "A medical student, a medical student; what does he know of the value of a skull!" Dorothy began to believe that she had discarded the legendary missing link itself and was too crestfallen to tell him that the specimen had wound up as a pencil holder on her friend's desk. "It was the one time Loren was really mad at me."[20]

Her timing could not have been worse, for Eiseley was conducting research in the very time period associated with her random discovery. Following Shapiro's recommendation, he had enrolled in a class on the anatomy and anthropology of human dentition at Columbia. In addition, Shapiro had given him an opportunity to assist in the preparation and study of Ipiutak skeletal material recently collected around Point Barrow, Alaska, by a promising young anthropologist named Froelich Rainey. Then, from December 1940 to March 1941, Eiseley spent much of his time acquainting himself with the work of the biometric school of University College, London, including hands-on practice in the utilization of the "Lee-Pearson formulae" for computing cranial capacity.[21]

According to prevailing theory, quantitative differences must have existed between the various human strata in prehistoric America, as was true of other fossil materials being unearthed simultaneously in Europe, Africa, and Asia. It was thought that careful statistical analysis of these remains would enable anthropologists to establish the presence of distinct cultural horizons, casting new light on the much debated questions of diffusion, ecological adjustment, and migration. "If the economy of primitive groups is capable of profoundly affecting their physical type, this fact has modern social implications of a far-reaching order," Eiseley had written in his grant proposal. "If heredity sets sharp limits to such change, this, too, is of significance. And important, also, are the problems of mixture and dominance out of which secondary races are created." Of particular interest to him was the potential such a theory might hold when applied to human evolution on the Great Plains. "There exists, now, in Kansas, material which deserves such study, and which is accessible to me."[22] If, through statistical analysis, several distinct cultural horizons could be established between the disappearance of the Pleistocene hunters and the emergence of the Plains Indians, the scientific vision of the past would never be the same again.

As the final step in Eiseley's preparation, Shapiro arranged for him to undertake an intensive study of Basket Maker skeletons collected during the 1920s and 1930s by Earl Morris of the Carnegie Institution. These largely unexamined bones, which were thought to date from A.D. 200 to 500, had been excavated in Arizona's Canyons de Chelly and del Muerto and were, as far as Eiseley could ascertain, "the oldest large series capable of statistical manipulation on the continent."[23] Several months of painstaking labor with calipers and craniometer enabled him to advance only the most tentative of conclusions. Among the Basket Makers of Arizona mesocephaly or roundheadedness seems to have predominated: "This is somewhat at variance with earlier claims of delichocephaly [longheadedness] among this group." And contrary to statistical measurements of other racial types, the female skulls measured virtually the same in certain respects as those of their male counterparts, a possible effect of a "primitive" diet.[24]

Buoyed by his new learning, Eiseley suggested to Clark that the department seriously consider adding a course on physical anthropology to its offerings.[25] The chairman, who had recently secured field study and laboratory funds to support Eiseley's research after his return, heartily agreed; Introduction to Physical Anthropology became part of the regular curriculum during the 1941–42 academic year.[26] In passing, Eiseley also reported: "I don't believe I told you that at the Philadelphia meeting of the American Association for the Advancement of Science (January 1941) the Association elected me to fellowship 'in recognition of meritorious and outstanding contributions in the field of Anthropology.' "[27] Finally, before ending his New York visit in September, Eiseley wrote, "It occurs to me that . . . this fall you might like some kind of story about my activities here to pass along to the publicity department."[28]

III

"Do you realize, Mr. Hirohito, just what you have done?" the angry editors of the *University Daily Kansan* rhetorically asked the inscrutable emperor of Japan on December 10, 1941. "You have deliberately provoked war with the most powerful nation in the world. You have pitted your people and your scrawny resources against a nation with the greatest natural resources in the world, and the greatest determination in the world that this shall be a bitter fight to the finish. And that finish will not come until America is victorious. You can paste that in your hat, Mr. Hirohito."[29] Three days earlier members of the university community had been eating Sunday dinner when the fateful news of Pearl Harbor flooded the airwaves. Two former students had been killed during the first twenty-four hours of combat. "The Emergency," the popular name for the massive defense buildup of the previous nine months, had been transformed into all-out war.

The Eiseleys had probably heard the momentous news while passing what was described as a "beautiful, sunny day" in their apartment at 643 Tennessee. Their three rooms were on the ground floor of a grand old Victorian structure erected by one of Lawrence's most prosperous families, the Pennys, on land once laid bare by fire during Quantrill's Raid. Although the tiny kitchen was too small to eat in, there was a huge living room, whose marble fireplace and twelve-foot ceiling were accented by lavish amounts of hand-turned oak woodwork, with a parquet floor to match. The small bedroom, which faced the morning sun, was part of an enclosed porch whose large, side-by-side windows were hung with thick, dark curtains, giving it the somber look of a medieval bedchamber. Eiseley's burgeoning library, which had grown substantially during weekend visits to New York's secondhand bookstores, lined the apartment walls. "For local color," he wrote Wimberly, "I'll just add that my wife's tea friends are constantly being startled by the skulls which glare down at them from the top of one of my book cases! . . . I rescued them, treated their crumbling bones with alvar and now they're safe and warm till I, too, go my way into the darkness."[30]

These tangible symbols of death had taken on added meaning with the outbreak of hostilities. Eiseley was the last of a line that had volunteered for every major conflict since the Revolutionary War. "Perhaps it was foolish of me," he wrote in retrospect, "but I was still young and there was a family tradition. I wanted to go." At the same time, "My mother, I had come to know, was committable without the care and attention of my aunt. . . . Both women were totally dependent upon my support."[31]

Agonizing of a similar nature was taking place two blocks away in the household headed by Carroll Clark. A native of Minneapolis, Kansas, the forty-four-year-old department chairman had been a sergeant in the 53rd Coast Artillery Corps during World War I and had served with the American Expeditionary Forces in France. Clark and his wife, Pearl, had been "very much impressed" with Eiseley when he'd first arrived at the university and had sympathized when he told them how "hard up" he was financially. During the next few years Carroll did everything he could to improve Eiseley's salary, which rose from $2,100 in 1937 to $2,850 in 1942, the year Carroll went off to war a second time.[32] Mabel's arrival deepened the growing bond with the Clarks, and all were delighted when Pearl rented the nearby apartment for the Eiseleys shortly before their return from New York. Carroll, a gifted jazz musician who played for what he termed "occupational therapy," often teamed up with Mabel. "I feel," Eiseley wrote his former chairman many years later, "that in some invisible reality we have just put on our coats and started down the Hill together for an evening of good music, with Mabel at the keys of the piano and you playing the saxophone."[33]

Yet no matter what the social occasion, talk of the war always seemed to dominate. Of major concern was the fear that conscription, voluntary enlistments, and countless new jobs in the war industry would seriously cripple the university. Chancellor Deane W. Malott announced drastic changes in the academic calendar on January 16, 1942: Easter vacation was eliminated; summer session was lengthened from eight to twelve weeks so that students, by unbroken attendance, could receive their degrees in two and a half years. At Malott's request the governor issued a statement—drafted by the chancellor—announcing that the "most important contribution" the youth of Kansas could make to the war effort would be to continue with their education. Still, enrollments fell from a peak of 5,299 in 1940–41 to 3,800 in 1944–45, with women outnumbering men by more than three to one. The decline would have been even more precipitous had not Malott succeeded in having the university declared a center for the training of naval personnel, although this development did nothing to bolster sagging enrollments in either sociology or anthropology.[34]

In March 1942 came the announcement that construction on a huge munitions plant with the disarming name Sunflower Ordnance was about to begin a dozen miles outside town. Hundreds of job seekers poured in from the backwoods of the Ozarks and Oklahoma. Every vacant house, spare room, and unoccupied building was pressed into use, and many students had difficulty finding decent living quarters. Rent control—hitherto unknown on the sparsely populated plains—became familiar overnight. The pleasant, sleepy Lawrence that Eiseley had grown to like was suddenly an alien boomtown: "The change was mixed with many things in my life—a growing disillusionment with some aspects of scientific values, personal problems, abrasive administrators, humanity itself."[35]

IV

Pearl Clark remembered a spring evening in 1942 when her distraught husband came home from the university to tell her of the decision he had made after many weeks of deliberation: "They're putting the pressure on everybody in the department; they've got to get into the war effort. There aren't going to be any students here. I can't ask these young men to do something I won't do."

"I said all right, you go in then," she recounted.[36]

Approaching his forty-fifth birthday, Carroll had no illusions about his age or his physical condition, although he had shed some sixty pounds from his large frame since the debacle at Munich, believing that it would eventually become "our fracas" as much as Europe's. There was no question in his mind, however, that the armed forces would take a "big, strapping, fine fellow" like Loren.[37]

The two men met at the Clark home on a June morning, and Pearl, accompanied by the Clarks' two children, drove them to the depot, where they caught the train for Kansas City. There the two met with a recruiter for the Army Air Corps and told him of their decision to apply for commissions. After completing the required forms, they were sent to Fort Leavenworth to undergo physicals on June 27. Carroll, to his surprise, passed and was sent the final application papers the following day.[38] Eiseley was rejected because of his poor eyesight, which left him open to the dreaded prospect of being drafted as a common soldier.[39] Two months later Carroll, who eventually rose to the rank of major, left Lawrence for the remainder of the war, but not before seeing Eiseley promoted to associate professor. Pearl stopped by the Penny Apartments to visit the Eiseleys on September 18, three weeks after her husband's departure. Writing to Carroll that night, she described Eiseley as being "much unsettled" about the future. On September 29, Pearl found their situation even more depressing: "Loren is up for reclassification and expects to be leaving about December. . . . Both are pretty blue."[40]

It was during this period that Eiseley's scientific writing took a fundamental turn. Rather than complete the tedious study of Basket Maker craniology, he wrote a series of short, popular articles for *Scientific American*, based largely on material gathered for his collaborative efforts with Bert Schultz. He was paid thirty dollars for "The Folsom Mystery," which appeared in December 1942.[41] After discussing the little that is known about the Ice Age hunters of North America, Eiseley introduces his readers to a "peculiar" kind of mystery: whether the great bison pursued by Folsom man had perished during the glacial retreat or had trailed the ice northward, only to die out in the Canadian woodlands, perhaps as late as the nineteenth century. Supremely conservative regarding such matters, he refused to poke his head beyond the timber to advance a hypothesis of his own, nor did his writing measure up to the graceful prose of years to come. Yet *Scientific American*'s editor A. G. Ingalls had a certain feeling about the Kansas academic: "We get things from professors that, in their world, seem immense, yet to the average outsider—say a business or industrial executive—don't seem very important, and we have to take the readers as they are. . . . I have a suspicion, from studying this present story, that you have an instinct that tells you how to fling it at 'em. A lot depends on just that—a big lot."[42]

This was all the encouragement the praise-starved author needed; Eiseley was prepared to "fling it at 'em" at a rate unsuspected by Ingalls—another Eiseley article crossed the editor's desk only two weeks later, along with a cover letter proposing yet a third. "Pseudo-Fossil Man" was accepted in November of 1942 and appeared the following March. More characteristic of the writer to come, it begins with the trademark personal anecdote: "Some years ago, when the writer was engaged in archeological work near a small western town, a villager drew him aside and said: 'You should see Mrs. Jones. She is the widow of a doctor who used to collect fossils all over this country. She has some very wonderful things, and probably would be glad to dispose of them now.' " Though skeptical, the young scientist seeks out the widow and is ushered into a Victorian parlor containing the usual array of seashells, wicker, and dust-catching bric-a-brac. Following a proper interval of small talk, the hostess looks anxiously about before lowering her voice: "I have something very, very valuable. I have part of the skull of a primitive man." Her guest waits anxiously as the last wrapping falls away from a heavy, asymmetrical object, which is ceremoniously placed in his hand. His doubts flee: a human forehead with a massive ridge of bone above the eye orbits stares back at him—bone "such as is commonly found upon the skulls of the fossil men of the Ice Age."[43]

Moments later his emotional current is suddenly reversed when it is revealed that the good Dr. Jones obtained the specimen from a burial site in the same Indian village in which Eiseley is digging. The bone is not from the Ice Age, but is the five-hundred-year-old remains of an individual with an unusually primitive appearance. The talk shifts, final pleasantries are exchanged, the anthropologist leaves—he to contemplate what might have been, the disappointed widow to calculate her imagined monetary loss.

Ingalls had accepted Eiseley's third article and agreed to read a fourth when, suddenly, the bottom fell out. "As you know," he wrote Eiseley on June 15, "*Scientific American* will be changed to an industrial magazine beginning with the September number. . . . At the last minute, after we had prepared your story, . . . [we were] forced to pull out one from that issue." It was returned with an effusive apology and the usual check for thirty dollars.[44] While he must have been dispirited, it was clear that Eiseley's new expository style—shot through with the poetic qualities of mystery, pathos, and wonder—had touched a sympathetic nerve among educated lay readers, not to mention the sophisticated editor of a highly regarded monthly.

V

On September 18, 1942, the *Daily Kansan* had printed the names of forty males who had left their university positions to join the war effort. Scarcely a week passed when at least one former student was not officially listed as wounded, killed, or missing in action. On October 8 Chancellor Malott again asked each department to evaluate its faculty with a view to freeing able-bodied men for military service. Marston McCluggage, a father of four, became the next to go from the Sociology Department. The administration then began casting a questioning eye in the direction of Eiseley, whose well-knit frame and seemingly robust health made him all the more conspicuous.

His time with the Draft Board running low, Eiseley decided to approach the administration on his own behalf. Dr. Henry Tracy, the shorthanded chairman of the Anatomy Department, had offered him a position teaching that subject to first-year students in the School of Medicine. If Eiseley's superiors agreed to such a transfer, the Draft Board was almost certain to go along and defer him on the ground of essential service. He first met with Dean Paul B. Lawson. According to Eiseley's unpublished account of the meeting, he was treated no better than dirt. "He bellowed at me in the utter surety that I was an abject coward. . . . He was livid. The little bombastic terrorist who had lived all those years in first ministerial and then academic garb came frothing to the surface." Refusing to answer the man's "expletives," Eiseley promptly made an appointment to see the chancellor.[45] But he came away from his March 1943 meeting with Malott embittered. The chancellor was more cutting than Lawson had been: "I'll attend to you and the Draft Board. Make no mistake about it."[46] When he then requested a semester's leave to accept a visiting professorship at the University of Wisconsin, Malott, Eiseley informed Pearl Clark, became abusive: "I don't understand what your purpose is, personal advancement or deferment!"[47]

Obsessed by this humiliating memory, Eiseley later drew a melodramatic comparison between himself and a citizen of a totalitarian state, pouring forth the pent-up hostility of thirty years:

> From being, in 1940, the only post-doctoral research fellow selected by the Social Science Research Council from the state of

> Kansas, from receiving a personal letter of congratulation from the then governor of the state, I was being degraded and bullied like a man under the interrogation of the police. And they were so sure, so very sure, that this was the way to hold a restless faculty together. Terrify them. Terrify this humble creature about whose past in the black night they had no knowledge, nor of how many times he had already stared at death.[48]

The implication of cowardice was in all likelihood Eiseley's projection of his own deepest fears. A seeming exemplar of the traditional masculine virtues, he was the boxer who never fought a round, the westerner who loved horses but could not ride, the outdoors loner who never camped by himself, the fearless drifter on hurtling freights who nearly starved within days of leaving home.

He could not let matters rest, even if it only meant going through the motions to save face. He applied for a position in the Red Cross Foreign Service and received notice to go to Washington, D.C., for a preliminary interview. If accepted, he would serve behind the lines of battle, the financial problems associated with leaving the university taken care of. Whether he ever traveled east is not known, but he informed Pearl Clark that he had passed the physical, signing a waiver for his eyes and hay fever.[49] (An X ray taken at the university revealed no scarring of the lungs, casting doubt on his alleged struggle with tuberculosis.)[50] He also wrote of later applying for duty with the newly established military government in the islands of the Pacific. Supposedly rejected once more for physical reasons, he pointed another accusing finger at the hapless Daisy: "I have often wondered in the years since . . . whether it was actually the minor physical defects or the existing affidavits about my mother that made the difference."[51] If such papers existed, it was because the son had obtained them from a Lincoln physician; otherwise, the Draft Board could not have known of them. Looking back on this difficult time in her husband's life, Mabel noted gravely, "The less said about it the better."[52]

VI

Like phototropic moths, students and townspeople rushed to the Hill "by the thousands" to witness the demise of the Commons, a sprawling, one-story frame structure housing the Department of

Anatomy. The smoke and flames had been discovered by Sam Elliot, a custodian, at ten minutes after seven on the evening of March 3, 1943. Responding to Elliot's cries of "Fire!" sailors taking classes in Fowler Hall came running to the scene trailing a large canvas hose, only to discover that its threads did not match those of the nearby hydrant. By the time the fire trucks arrived, the building was engulfed; nothing could be done but keep the flames from spreading to the library and other campus structures.[53]

Eiseley was alerted by a telephone call from Malott's secretary, who had confused him somehow with C. Willet "Bill" Asling, a 1939 graduate of the University of Kansas Medical School and an assistant professor of anatomy. The anthropologist arrived in time to witness a Dantesque scene. In the basement of the disintegrating building were some fifty cadavers used for dissection by the medical students. All were sealed in steel tanks capable of withstanding the flames. A few more corpses were floating in a nonflammable phenol solution on the main floor, and when Asling arrived he directed the fire fighters to keep their hoses trained on them. Spotlights were later brought in to illuminate the smoldering ruin while the naked bodies were carried away by truck. A number of students became giddy in this surreal atmosphere: "The laughter, the ugly laughter," Eiseley wrote. As inappropriate as their behavior was, he sensed that the mockery represented a pitiful attempt at evading thoughts of their own mortality. "Death is a joke. We, we, are the immortals, the golden boys and girls," he imagined them saying.[54]

No one suffered a deeper personal loss in the conflagration than Dr. Henry Tracy, who had befriended Eiseley after their introduction by Carroll Clark in 1937 or '38. Virtually all of his notes, papers, and slides had gone up in smoke, along with what was believed to have been one of the finest private medical libraries in existence. The fire was but one in a string of recent tragedies that soon forced the onetime classical scholar to take up semipermanent residence in the local hospital. After suffering a life-threatening attack of bronchial asthma in 1942, Tracy watched his beloved son, Chapman, slip inexorably into schizophrenia and succumb in the State Mental Hospital at Topeka a year after being committed. His wife, Edith Chapman Tracy, a seemingly healthy woman, passed away suddenly within months of her only child's death. In constant need of adrenaline and related emergency medication, the exhausted chairman of anatomy had no choice but to take an extended leave of absence with partial pay.

Pearl Clark viewed Tracy's rapid decline with alarm, fearing almost as much for Eiseley's welfare as for that of his friend, whose "dark outlook" seemed to be spreading.[55] She may have been right, for Eiseley often mused over Tracy's bewildering fall from grace with the Fates:

> I knew . . . a scholar who had shifted in his last graduate days from the field of classics to the intricacies of zoology. A scintillating piece of research had rocked his profession, and he had marched steadily to the headship of a great department. He . . . was a graying, handsome man, with the world at his feet. He did not fail in health, his students loved him, and he loved them. The research died. His problem was more serious: he could not answer letters. His pupils could not depend upon him even to recommend them for posts or scholarships. Airmail letters lay unopened in his box. It was not that he was cruel. Anything a man could do by word of mouth he would do for his students, even if it meant the assumption of unpleasant tasks. Firm, upright, with a grave old-fashioned gallantry, in him . . . a door had closed forever. One never heard him speak of his family. Somewhere behind that door was a landscape we were never permitted to enter.[56]

Elsewhere Eiseley described how Tracy, who lived only a block or two away, frequently visited the Eiseley apartment after his wife died. They passed many stimulating hours discussing their wide-ranging interests—evolution, rare books, history, and, ironically for a man who became inert when faced by the blank page, writing. "His perception of my own literary ambitions was almost uncanny," Eiseley wrote.[57]

The day after the fire, Bill Asling was called in by Dr. H. R. Wahl, dean of the Medical School, to determine what should be done. With Tracy on the ropes and only one full-time anatomist on the staff besides himself, the normally optimistic assistant professor was dubious about keeping the program afloat, but he agreed to take charge and make an attempt to "patch up something." The department found a temporary home in the lower reaches of Haworth Hall, amid heavy-duty equipment used by the Geology and Mining Engineering departments. Out of deference to his superior, Bill maintained the pretense of Tracy's functioning as chairman by regularly driving back and forth to the hospital with the mail and a typist. "Tracy was coming up with new visionary schemes daily, including giant appropriations for supplies [and] equipment that had been off the civilian market for years by priority actions of the War Productions Board. I was desperate and out of my depth. I lunched a couple of times with Loren, just to have a chance to talk to someone reasonable."[58]

One day the two found themselves discussing Tracy's idea that Eiseley convert to the teaching of anatomy. Bill was teaching evening courses in Red Cross First Aid to the townspeople, who assembled in the parish hall of the Episcopal Church. He became good friends with the genial priest and learned that the cleric had been made a Draft Board member on the basis of his presumed expertise regarding conscientious objectors. While Eiseley had no religious scruples when it came to war, Bill explained his colleague's predicament at the university. "Board meetings were confidential so, of course, I don't really have knowledge of who helped to bring reason into the situation, but I'd guess, the priest. Within quite a short time Eiseley learned officially that . . . without reference to the University, the Board would delay any reclassification for a very reasonable period."[59] This was the breathing space he had been hoping for, time to begin serving in a civilian capacity deemed valuable to the national interest. Some months later Mabel informed Pearl Clark that Ogden Jones, another member of the Draft Board, had made arrangements for her husband to be placed on the essential services (2A) list in recognition of his new teaching responsibilities.[60]

Shortly after classes were over in the spring of 1943, Bill took his friend to the basement of Haworth Hall, where together they got out a cadaver and dissection guidebook. "Loren went at it full time all . . . summer, with me joining him in a borrowed lab whenever I could get there. He taught himself the whole of human gross anatomy basics—a tour de force of memory and concept."[61] The $475 he received for his labors also came in handy, for Eiseley's wages, like those of his colleagues, had been frozen the previous year, another casualty of war.[62]

Bill admired his friend's command when the time came for him to face his first class of some seventy-five junior-grade officers. Eiseley, who assumed the title of lecturer, moved among the dissection tables with seeming ease, patiently answering every question and posing others in an effort to stimulate critical thinking. Rather than prepare formal lectures, he preferred to teach "cadaver-side," surrounded by a host of craned necks and flashing pens. For some reason Eiseley reminded Bill of the great Flemish anatomist Andreas Vesalius, maybe because he thought of both as ideal Renaissance men.

Only later, after Eiseley wrote of a largely fictional experiment in anatomy, would Bill have reason to question his initial impression of his friend.

> It was a small death [Eiseley began] in that war now long since done. As it chanced, I was assisting one of my medical superiors in a cadaver dissection. He was a kind and able teacher, but a researcher hardened to the bitter necessities of his profession. He took the notion that a living demonstration of the venous flow through certain of the abdominal veins would be desirable. "Come with me to the animal house," he said. "We'll get a dog for the purpose." I followed him reluctantly.

His colleague, armed with a hypodermic, enters the pen amid "doleful barks and howlings." Selecting an intelligent-looking mongrel of "big terrier affinities," he quickly corners the friendly beast and shoots the needle home. The trusting animal takes a few steps before dropping to the floor comatose, never to open its eyes again.

After the procedure is completed, the students attend to their cadavers and straggle out into the slanting light of late afternoon. Eiseley stands by the window, a sentinel, viewing the last sunset in behalf of the now lifeless form. "I had been commanded. I knew that, even if I had not been in the animal house, the same thing would have happened that day or another. But he had looked at me with that unutterable expression. 'I do not know why I am here. Save me. I have seen other dogs fall and be carried away. Why do you do this? Why?' "[63] Eiseley himself had no answer: for reasons too deep to fathom, he believed himself chosen to bear the burden of a faith that has no institutional home.

Although his former colleague refrained from using names, Bill was certain that he was the "medical friend" alluded to in Eiseley's morality play. In truth, the Anatomy Department did very few live demonstrations, relying mostly on microscope slides, and kept no pen of mongrels such as the one Eiseley so vividly described. However, once each term Bill did perform an experiment that Tracy had designed to show students how quickly the body's defense system reacts when invaded by a foreign substance. The subject, a cat, is heavily sedated and cut open, after which a tiny bit of india ink is placed on the surface of the intestine, just beneath the protective membrane. Within seconds the ink is picked up and absorbed by the lymph nodes. As Bill described it, "What you are seeing is the fabulous rapidity with which foreign material is handled by a group of vessels which are invisible."[64] One of the nodes is then removed, cut into sections, and placed on slides so that students can view the still living cells ingesting the carbon particles.

"I don't know what it was, " Bill reflected, "that bothered Loren so much about it, but he felt, obviously, that the students didn't get anything out of it." Perhaps it was simply a matter of watching such a demonstration for the first time: "even forty years of it [doesn't] make you like taking the life of a creature."[65] But what Bill particularly objected to was Eiseley's unfounded remark "There is a man, a very great experimentalist, who has said to extend ethics to animals is unutterable folly."[66] After all, Bill pointed out, it was Eiseley himself who had been "terribly anxious" to enter anatomy and who, so far as anyone could tell, performed his required duties enthusiastically, without voicing a single scruple.

VII

One winter morning in early 1944, Bill was summoned to Chancellor Malott's office to settle some unfinished business. Almost a year had passed since fire had destroyed the old Commons building, yet the embalmed cadavers remained sealed in their half-buried tanks, the sides of which had been camouflaged with thick shrubs and other flora. Anxious to have the site leveled in time for spring commencement, the chancellor ordered Bill to remove the bodies so that a bulldozer could be brought in to finish the job. With storage at a premium, arrangements were made to construct a series of redwood tanks beneath the auditorium stage next to Haworth Hall. The plan was to remain top secret at all costs: "Imagine the drop-off in season ticket sales if the prospective audience knew about the [fifty] who were present in body but not in spirit," Bill quipped.[67]

After a futile attempt to rent the canvas-draped fences behind which the football team practiced the coming season's trick plays, Bill concluded that the job would have to be done at night. Grounds and Buildings agreed to provide floodlights and a hoist but drew the line when asked to supply the transportation. Finally, Claude Hibbard was prevailed upon to loan Bill one of the Dyche Museum trucks, a dilapidated old Dodge, which Eiseley agreed to drive. Bill also retained the services of a Negro hauler whose vehicle was in considerably better shape than the Dodge. It was decided that the technician who did the embalming for Anatomy would work at the original storage area loading the bodies, while Bill would wait at the rear of the auditorium to take delivery. Since the library closed at 9:50 P.M. and most of the lovers were out of the parking lots by 10:30—closing time for the women's dorms—they set 11:30 as "H [Haul]-Hour."

The intrepid party deployed at the appointed time, ignorant of the fact that an important detail had been omitted from their meticulous calculations. In Fowler Hall, just across the street from the buried tanks, machinist's mates were being trained for the navy around the clock. The brightly illuminated work site was wide open when some eighty noncoms were given their regular midnight break and filed out to smoke and shoot the bull. Bill recalled, "Loren pulled up his truck; the first cadaver rose on the hoist and at least 40 of the 80 machinist's mates raced for telephones." Within minutes cars filled with girlfriends, most of whom worked at the recently opened Sunflower Ordnance plant, began pulling up on the side street. "Each body rose, dripping, to the sound of cheers, and even though gently swung into the truck, the metallic bed gave off a hollow boom on contact which set off a chorus of groans. Loren," to whom it must have seemed like déjà vu, "pulled out, the head of a cortege, except that none of the following cars carried mourners."[68]

The Eiseleys were soon beset by a nightmare of a different order. Mabel discovered what she thought was another "cyst," this one in her left breast. An examination pointed to a less encouraging diagnosis. Wanting to be certain, Bill made an appointment for her with a specialist named Rumold in Kansas City, who confirmed that the growth was malignant and life threatening. He operated immediately, performing a radical mastectomy followed by postoperative X-ray therapy to destroy any remaining cancer cells. The medical bills were considerable, but less than they would have been had Bill not prevailed upon his colleague to extend Eiseley, now a member of the Medical School faculty, a professional courtesy.

Mabel's long and painful convalescence required that she reestablish her shoulder motion, which had been severely impaired by surgical damage to the muscle. She sat next to a paneled wall in the apartment for hours, finger-walking her left arm up and down its surface. Bill stopped by each day to change the dressings and to coach Loren, who took over his wife's physical therapy. "Loren was splendid in the way he saw her through."[69] During their private moments, though, the tables were sometimes reversed. "I had worried so much [over the first operation] that I couldn't worry anymore," Mabel related, "so I wasn't nearly as upset as Loren was; I made up my mind I had to live because I didn't think Loren could live without me."[70]

VIII

Slight of build, with the face of a mischievous Punch, Karl Mattern retained "a fleck" of his native German accent. He had immigrated to the United States as an adolescent, later entering the Chicago Art Institute to study under the noted painter and lithographer George Bellows, whose unself-conscious realism had a marked stylistic effect on his pupil. Moody at times, the painter, who joined the University of Kansas faculty in 1926, "would withdraw a little bit into a sort of sadness, but he was never away; he would come right back again."[71] Most often compared with Thomas Hart Benton, Grant Wood, and John Steuart Curry, "the Homer of Kansas," Mattern painted with a serious but rarely heavy hand, delighting in irony and satire. It was doubtless Mabel who had arranged for him to lecture on "Sense and Nonsense in Art" at the fiftieth annual exhibition of the Nebraska Art Association in March 1940, for which she also wrote the glowing publicity.[72]

Karl, Bill, and Loren were part of a small group, The Raconteurs, who squeezed into two cars every other Tuesday for a ten-mile drive into the country. Their destination was an unimpressive-looking lunchroom that served excellent steaks, fries, and draft beer. Although they were "all loyal and law-abiding supporters of the war effort," no one questioned why the proprietor never asked them to surrender a single ration stamp. After one such outing the group adjourned to the Mattern home on Louisiana Street. What they saw on being ushered into Karl's large wood-and-glass studio brought their collective frustrations to a stunning focus. On the opposite wall hung "All Steamed Up," a painting that had been displayed at the 1939 New York World's Fair. It depicts a great locomotive sitting in the middle of an endless golden wheat field on a piece of track with both ends curled up in the manner of sled runners. "You didn't need to be told anything," Bill recounted. "It was a terrible frustration; this was the story of the group. Everyone had things we [wanted to accomplish]. It wasn't just the war; it was the impossibility of overcoming the inertia, not laziness, but of overcoming the start because there wasn't room to start."[73]

While each man had his story to tell, it was the "Young Turks," as Bill labeled certain of his more disaffected colleagues, who harbored some hopes of changing the university before bailing out at war's end. Most of them were interested in pursuing major scientific research; Eiseley was among their number, along with Claude William "Hibby" Hibbard, Carl Schaeffer, Charlie Drake, Ed Taylor, and A. B. Leonard.

Word of the group's existence filtered up to Malott, who invited its members to dinner at the Chancellor's Mansion. The major topic of the evening's "gloves-off" discussion was to be the future of scientific research at the University of Kansas—or so the chancellor's guests were led to believe. After a decent but undistinguished meal, Malott opened the scheduled dialogue. He did not hold the floor for very long: the university was not about to become a place where faculty members "play at research." On occasion, a brief leave of absence in residence would be allowed for the purpose of looking more deeply into some specific question. But in those fields where the university's interests in research were deemed crucial, the administration planned to conduct national searches for distinguished scholars capable of attracting the best and brightest students. "The Chancellor," Bill quipped, "clearly had great skill as a conversation-stopper."[74] After a bit of diffident probing to make certain that they had heard correctly, the professors expressed their thank-yous and left in silence, never to meet as a group again. This may have been the very evening that Eiseley arrived at the apartment to exclaim repeatedly to a recuperating Mabel, "I've got to get out! I've got to get out!"[75] Writing to her husband following word of the denouement, a downcast Pearl Clark put the matter even more bluntly: "[Loren] hates Malott's very guts."[76]

IX

Bill Asling never forgot Eiseley's counsel on the subject of one's academic career: "Belong to your societies, go to meetings as much as possible, deal well with your associates; be sure to be registered, even with only a few lines, in the academic biographical reference sources." Then, "every two years, turn up a job offer elsewhere with either better rank or salary (preferably both) so that you have some negotiating tool in dealing with indifferent administrators." Most important of all, "be sure that the offer is one that you could accept if your local negotiations fail!"[77] Bill took Eiseley at his word, never doubting for a moment that it was no longer a question of whether his friend would be leaving Kansas, only when.

Meanwhile, the two found themselves spending much of their free time in the company of their fellow malcontent Hibby Hibbard, curator of vertebrate paleontology in the newly renovated Dyche Museum, who gave them the run of the place. They became enchanted by a fine collection of African wood carvings executed by the Mahone and Metabele peoples. All the male images were macrophallic—or had been until some prudish Kansas "wowser" had broken off the exaggerated genitals before the material first went on display about 1910. That reaction reminded Bill of Loren's comic description of those who visited the Eiseley apartment and were drawn to the books lining the walls. Their fingers drifted along until they reached Westermarck's *The History of Human Marriage* or Malinowski's *The Sexual Life of Savages in North-Western Melanesia* or Ellis's seven-volume *Studies in the Psychology of Sex*, at which point the work would be pulled from the shelf and examined furtively at some length.

At the time, any behavior deviating from heterosexuality or from the "missionary position" during intercourse was thought perverted by most of society and labeled pathological by much of the medical profession. When a two-volume study titled *Sex Variants* was published by the noted psychiatrist George Henry, Eiseley ordered the set for the Sociology Department and scanned it before having the librarian put it in the locked vault along with Burton's *Arabian*

Nights and Boccaccio's *Decameron*. "Loren's summary—indeed, his classification for most such works—was 'Scientific Pornography.' "[78]

He was no less adamant about the use of nonparlor language, especially in the presence of females. Records containing monologues laced with explicit sexual or scatological references were sometimes played at private faculty soirees. Eiseley could never understand where the pleasure came in having a phonograph dispense words that were not acceptable when uttered by the listeners themselves. Why use "son of a bitch," or worse, when "dolt" might do the job better? "We were fascinated," Bill mused, "by the depths of evil which Churchill conjured up when he called Hitler 'that bad man,' a faint drawl on the 'bad' for emphasis."[79]

Just as interesting to Bill was what he learned from his friend on the subject of race. Eiseley considered the fascist view of Aryan superiority the height of folly. Hitler's physical anthropologists had sold out by grossly distorting the existing data to bolster the Nazi party line. Bill, who had left an excellent teaching position at Nashville's Vanderbilt University, partly because of the South's blatant jim crowism, laughed along with Eiseley when he told of having been labeled Jewish by more than one educated Kansan who mistook his German name, prominent humped nose, and dusky complexion as prima facie evidence of Semitic origins.[80] Atop the hill overlooking the site of Quantrill's Raid on abolitionist Lawrence, amid a world war being waged against the tyranny of racism, not a single Negro or Jew was enrolled in the medical school. And had Duke Tachibana, who was a despised captive in his ancestral land, attempted by some quirk of fate to enter the university, he would have had the door shut in his face. The Board of Regents, over Chancellor Malott's strenuous objections, voted to deny admission to nisei students from the western United States until the end of the war.[81]

By mid-1944 many sensed the beginning of the end. American troops had completed the conquest of the Solomon and Marshall Islands, while Berlin was under almost daily assault by eight hundred Flying Fortresses. On June 4 Monte Cassino and Rome passed into Allied hands; two days later over seven hundred ships and four thousand landing craft battled an angry channel to discharge their burden on the Normandy coast. Hoping to delay the inevitable, Henry Tracy offered a restless Eiseley the opportunity to enter medical school but was gently refused. At age thirty-seven he felt that he was too old; nor did he believe himself capable of weathering the prolonged financial strain.[82] More important, the draft age had recently been lowered to twenty-six, removing the final constraint on his accepting another position. Writing on June 1 to Harry Shapiro of his "latest adventures in escaping from Kansas," Eiseley could barely contain himself: "Believe it or not the deed is done! I have recently been informed that I am head of the Department of Sociology at Oberlin College, Oberlin, Ohio, with carte blanche to develop anthropology. . . . You cannot imagine how relieved I am to get out."[83]

12

COUNTERPLAINT OF AN ANTHROPOLOGIST

I

As a young man working his way through Ohio State University on the eve of World War I, Carl Frederick Wittke barnstormed the Midwest with minstrel shows, donning blackface and singing folk music in a mellifluous baritone to his own accompaniment on an ancient but effective guitar. The Phi Beta Kappan and Harvard Ph.D. later authored fourteen books, including *Tambo and Bones: A History of the American Minstrel Stage.* A. Hunter Dupree, one of Wittke's most distinguished students at Oberlin College, remembered how his normally "gruff and forbidding" mentor would occasionally confound his history classes by giving impromptu demonstrations of minstrel routines.[1] Students were equally amazed to learn that the staid dean of the arts and sciences, who had turned fifty in 1942, played an aggressive game of softball, gave public lectures on such esoteric topics as "A Century of Baseball," and played a dozen musical instruments, including the violin, in the Oberlin Symphony Orchestra.

Oberlin was founded in 1833 by John Jay Shipherd and Philo Penfield Stewart, frustrated religious zealots determined to establish a sin-free Zion in the wilderness. They named their colony in honor of Johann Friedrich Oberlin, a European pastor who had turned a dying French village into a prosperous town of seemingly happy,

God-fearing souls. Those recruited by the founders had to sign the Oberlin Covenant, a list of twelve rigid demands prefaced by a jeremiad "lamenting the degeneracy of the Church and the deplorable condition of our perishing world."[2] When Oberlin Collegiate Institute first opened its doors in December 1833, fifteen of the forty-four students were women, giving it the distinction of being the first coeducational college or university in the nation. Three years later Oberlin became one of the first colleges to admit blacks, creating a haven for fugitive slaves and free people of color. By 1860 the proportion of blacks among the 2,100 citizens of the town of Oberlin was almost 20 percent and would continue to rise well into the twentieth century.[3]

When Newell Sims, chairman of sociology, announced his retirement in early 1944, Wittke saw his chance to upgrade a department whose curriculum reflected few of the sweeping changes taking place in the field. He was especially eager to add courses in anthropology, which, as one former student noted, "was succeeding sociology as the great scientific hope in the social sciences."[4] Many assumed that L. Guy Brown, an Oberlin professor since 1934, would be advanced to the chair, opening the way for a junior person capable of offering courses in both disciplines. But Wittke, who wanted no part of the old order, determined to bring in a new man to take charge. On March 10, 1944, he wrote to A. I. Hallowell, a professor at Penn, asking if he would be interested in the position. Hallowell had already accepted an offer from Northwestern, but he recommended three others, placing the name of a former graduate student at the top of the list. "He is an excellent teacher," Hallowell noted of Loren Eiseley, "and writes extremely well."[5]

Enter Paul Bigelow Sears, the middle-aged head of Oberlin's Department of Botany. A University of Chicago Ph.D., Sears taught at Nebraska from 1920 until 1927, when he became chairman of botany at the University of Oklahoma. Although his tenure in Lincoln overlapped Eiseley's early undergraduate years, the two do not seem to have met until the late 1930s. Sears remembered that Eiseley had sought him out during one of his frequent visits to the University of Kansas: "This was the real beginning of [a] life-long friendship."[6] It was Sears's books and popular articles, including one in an early issue of *Prairie Schooner*, that first attracted Eiseley to the older man. Almost from the moment Sears joined the Oberlin faculty in 1938, he urged Wittke, with whom he became very close, to hire an anthropologist. When the slot in sociology finally opened up, Sears hurried over to the dean's office to encourage him to seek Eiseley out.[7] Wittke, who had Hallowell's endorsement in hand, agreed, and the pursuit was on.

The dean's letter of inquiry reached Eiseley in early April. He replied immediately, expressing interest in the opening. However, his teaching duties in the Department of Anatomy presented problems. "I would be unable to terminate my position here before the summer of 1945," he wrote.[8] If, under the circumstances, Oberlin was still interested, he would be happy to submit a formal application. Undaunted by this turn of events, Wittke asked him to forward his credentials as soon as possible and to make plans for a visit to campus: "We shall make our appointment on the basis of a full professorship, and we want someone like yourself who represents a combination of sociology and cultural anthropology."[9] Eiseley responded on April 20, enclosing his vita but reiterating his position that any move before 1945 seemed out of the question.[10] Still, he agreed to travel to Oberlin by train, and the visit was subsequently scheduled for the first week of May.

The anthropologist returned to Lawrence jubilant. "I got a kind of 'bolstering' effect," he wrote Wittke on May 7, "from visiting a college which, even in these chaotic days, is going solidly about the business of educating students, believing in what it has to offer, and then not attempting to 'adjust' its courses to real or fancied demands of the times. This is very reassuring." Sounding much less disinterested than before, he cleverly broached the subject of salary: "I felt it advisable . . . to tell you of a substantial postwar position offered me by an eastern publisher of scientific work. . . . The salaries quoted—$4500 the first year and $5000 the second—are not static. In making any decision at this rather crucial stage of my career, then, I shall want to consider all sides of the question most thoroughly."[11] Apparently Eiseley had done some research of his own during his two-day visit, given the fact that $5000 was the going rate for new department chairmen recruited by Wittke.

The dean and the Committee on Appointments and Budget had one more candidate to interview. Meanwhile, an increasingly nervous Eiseley waited until May 18 for an answer, then wired Wittke in a virtual state of panic: "No present assurances to how long draft directive will last. To carry inquiries further without definite offer is to create potentially explosive situation with no adequate defense for myself. To rush matter in this way leaves no room for careful diplomacy and is regarded by all my friends as ill advised."[12] Fearing that the candidate was on the verge of withdrawing his application, the dean telegraphed a reply the following day, presumably after a hastily assembled meeting of the Committee on Appointments: "Happy to offer professorship and headship Department Sociology on two-year appointment salary five thousand. . . . Offer is absolutely contingent on being able to begin duties November of this year. Please wire decision collect as soon as possible."[13]

It was now Wittke's turn to wait while Eiseley looked to Henry Tracy for direction. Although he stood to suffer the most by Loren's departure, the convalescing chairman of Anatomy urged him to go. Then, "without a single suggestion from me," Eiseley wrote, "Tracy undertook to clear the way . . . with the University administration." Eiseley finally wired his acceptance to Wittke on May 26, then drafted a formal letter the next day.[14]

II

Even though Eiseley's salary was about to double and he was on the verge of leaving a place he had grown to detest, all was not well. The first hint of trouble surfaced in the letter he had written to Wittke following his visit to Oberlin. During the interview one or two individuals had implied that he might not enjoy teaching sociology, since anthropology constituted his major field. "If, for any reason, this impression should obtain, I should like to say that I have both enjoyed, and had an excellent following in, my sociology classes."[15] Wittke confirmed that Eiseley had cause to be suspicious. "The only hesitation the Committee had at any time," the dean wrote after locking up the appointment, "was whether the anthropological 'tail' might eventually wag the sociological 'dog.' "[16] Eiseley thought the metaphor amusing. "My own observation is that anthropologists on the whole have been altogether too heavily 'wagged' by sociologists. It will be a genuine achievement if, at Oberlin, we can create a situation in which tail is no more important than dog."[17]

By June matters had taken an ominous turn. Oberlin's cumbersome governing structure required that the recommendation of the Committee on Appointments and Budget proceed through the College Council, the General Appointments Committee, and then on up to the Board of Trustees for final action. Never had a decision of the Committee on Appointments and Budget been overturned, but when Wittke presented Eiseley's name to the College Council for approval on June 14, he encountered "determined opposition" spearheaded by Newell Sims, the outgoing chairman of sociology, and L. Guy Brown, Sims's disappointed heir presumptive. Both men argued that Eiseley was neither adequately prepared to offer advanced courses in sociology nor sufficiently experienced to head a department in which the emphasis on social work had always been paramount.[18]

The battle was fought out in two long council meetings during which Brown, a square-faced, balding little man, attacked with a ferocity that belied his weak chin and fragile, wire-rimmed spectacles. Besides making disparaging references to Eiseley's competence and alleged lack of interest in sociology, he charged that the chairman designate was narrowly trained as a physical anthropologist: "hardly more than a bone measurer" was Brown's characterization of his perceived rival, a thrust Wittke deftly parried by simply reading a description of the courses Eiseley had given in cultural anthropology at Kansas.[19]

Brown next produced a letter from Mabel A. Elliott, a University of Kansas sociologist, who had replied to what she described as his "cryptic request" concerning Eiseley's qualifications for the Oberlin post. Brown read aloud from the document, selectively omitting such passages as the following: "Few people on our campus possess anything resembling Dr. Eiseley's intellectual equipment. As you must know, he is an exceptionally well trained man with more than the usual range of qualifications."[20] What Brown did not know was that Professor Elliott had smelled a rat. She sent a copy of her reply to Wittke, doubtless after conferring with Eiseley, and the trap was set.[21] The dean waited for Brown to finish before exposing his fraud by reading the deleted passages to the council.[22] The sociologist's spurious case began to dissolve in the embarrassing silence that followed. The coup de grace was struck when Sims, a onetime supporter of Eiseley, claimed to have acquired "later information" about the anthropologist that rendered him unfit for the chairmanship. When asked by the council to make his knowledge available, Sims demurred on the ground of confidentiality.[23]

Several weeks later, however, after it appeared that the matter had been put to rest, Brown suddenly renewed his assault. He provided Wittke and Lloyd W. Taylor, a physicist and president of the

College Council, with typed copies of an article Eiseley had published in the *American Sociological Review* the previous December. Titled "What Price Glory? The Counterplaint of an Anthropologist," the semisatiric piece was written to rebut the charge of sociologist Adolph S. Tomars that Eiseley's discipline had no more lived up to its claim of scientific objectivity than had Tomars's own.[24] Eiseley admitted that anthropology had a long way to go in this regard, but he placed much of the blame at sociology's doorstep. The unwillingness of its practitioners to accept anthropology as a discipline in its own right had had a chilling effect: "the young anthropologist Ph.D.," he charged, "must seek his fortune . . . not within his own field, but outside of it." If, "as Dr. Tomars has so ably pleaded," the boundaries between sociology and anthropology are meaningless, "there is hope, then, for our forlorn division. It may be," he concluded tongue in cheek, "that we can teach sociology."[25]

Ignoring completely Eiseley's main theme that the distinctly inferior position of anthropology was not healthy for either discipline, Brown sought to convince Taylor that the article's final sentence was proof positive of the author's duplicity. The new department chairman's contempt for the teaching of sociology was as great as that for which he condemned the sociologists. But Taylor was having none of it, and he drafted a sharp letter of rebuke on August 19.

Taylor sent a copy to Wittke, who was in need of all the moral support he could muster from the faculty. Brown now turned his guns on the dean, unleashing a fusillade of abuse:

> I was surprised to hear a Jeffersonian democrat hide behind traditions after he had behaved in an undemocratic way. . . . There were persons in the Council who voted to get you out of a jam [for allegedly announcing the appointment prematurely] rather than on the merits of the case. . . . You sit by and let members of this faculty, who have not published anything, vote . . . on the careers of others who have made much more of a contribution. In a democracy one earns the right to be critical of others.

As for Brown's new superior:

> Oberlin College offered Mr. Eiseley a salary so far above his present salary that he is willing to come here and start a life of pre-

> tense. He does not want to teach sociology but he will have to pretend that he does. He has no respect for a college that appoints teachers to give text-book courses but he will have to pretend that he regards Oberlin College highly. He is very critical of college administrators—Presidents and Deans—who make such appointments but he will have to pretend that he has great respect for you and Mr. Wilkins. The members of the Appointments Committee will be treated with great politeness but underneath this front will be contempt. He was very articulate about appointments of this type when he talked with me and his article shows how keenly he objects to such a procedure.[26]

The following day Brown drafted yet another letter to Taylor, its three single-spaced pages undulating wildly between vitriol and self-pity. "In the Council meetings I discussed the real Eiseley, while the committee considered an imaginary person." Then, "you selected a colleague for me and did it in complete secrecy. Christian human beings do not treat each other that way. That sort of thing is not done on the janitorial level, let alone on the teaching level." Brown also suspected that Taylor and his fellow "conspirators" were meeting by twos and threes, "talking about me as a thoroughly undesirable person." Through it all, however, he claimed to have no ill feelings toward Eiseley personally: "I wrote him a friendly letter but have received no reply."[27]

III

Back in Lawrence, the Eiseleys were concerned about the housing situation in Oberlin and wanted to know if Wittke had any ideas. Eiseley described their needs as modest, but they were hoping to find something furnished. "We . . . have deliberately refrained from collecting anything beyond personal effects—books, pictures, dishes, and so on. Since we did not plan to remain in Kansas, this seemed sensible."[28] Wittke put them in touch with Alan B. Cole, a professor of history who was hoping to rent his house for the upcoming academic year. Located at 71 South Prospect, a pleasant fifteen-minute walk from campus, the two-story frame house was palatial compared with the cramped apartment in Lawrence. On the first floor were a large living room, dining room, huge kitchen, and another room off the kitchen well suited for use as a study. Upstairs, the

Eiseleys would have their choice of three bedrooms and the luxury of two baths. There was even an attic for additional storage, not that they needed it. Except for linens and a few kitchen utensils, the Coles planned to leave everything behind. Wittke considered the asking price of sixty-five dollars a month a bargain, and arrangements were made for Loren and Mabel to take possession during the last week of October.[29] They packed up their old Dodge coupe and headed east as the leaves were beginning to fall. According to Eiseley, Henry Tracy did him one last favor on the eve of their departure. "You will need some money to get there," Tracy volunteered. Eiseley nodded in agreement and insisted on making it legal by signing an I.O.U.[30]

The Cole house would have been the ideal place to start a family. Having celebrated her forty-fourth birthday in July, Mabel was fast approaching the time when she could no longer bear children. Yet it was one of life's milestones that both she and her husband were prepared to pass with few regrets. "I didn't really want a family," Mabel later confided. "I hope you're not shocked." She also knew Loren's limitations. Had there been children in the picture, "he wouldn't have gotten anything done."[31]

Of equal importance were the indelible impressions left by childhood, which neither looked back on with nostalgia. While Mabel denied that Loren's aversion to paternity was rooted in his self-proclaimed fear of the family madness, she had to admit that the Prices had remained childless for this very reason.[32] Nor can one overlook Loren's early pronouncements on the subject. Leah Dale, a high-school classmate, remembered his oft-repeated vow never to have offspring.[33] And when *All the Strange Hours* was published, Athena Spaulding was amazed by a passage in which her uncle pined for the family he never had. "Children spell trouble," he had told her repeatedly during their walks in Woodlands Cemetery.[34] Dorothy Thomas was equally certain that Loren's tormented home life played a major part in his thinking. Her sister Kenetha, who was also Mabel's friend, was told that Loren's children might inherit his mother's "craziness."[35] Whether Loren knew of his great-uncle Frederick Eiseley's descent into madness is open to conjecture. Daisy's tainted blood was deterrent enough: "she, and the whisperings in that old Victorian house of my aunt's, had done their work. I would run no gamble with the Shepard line. I would mark their last earthly appearance. Figments of fantasy I know them now to be, but thanks to my mother and her morbid kin they destroyed their own succession in the child who turned away."[36]

Mabel's story, albeit less traumatic, led her in the same direction. The perfect Victorian child, she had entered the world as a miniature adult, as stern of countenance and bearing as the parents with whom she was photographed as a toddler. Dollie, a tomboy, never once remembered her older sister playing with her or their younger brother, Charles, much less with any of the neighborhood children. "She was always going to the library getting books, reading; she would never climb a tree or anything like that. She never learned to swim and was very frail." Less serious minded than their sister, Dollie and Charles resented her intrusions into their boisterous world of make-believe: "[We] weren't too unhappy that she wasn't there to play with us." Fastidious as an old maid about her starched print dresses and ribboned hair, "Mabel had the quality of always wondering where her acts would lead; what the results would be if we went someplace or did something." The child's unusual maturity also earned her unusual privileges. Much of her time was spent in the kitchen doing "fancy cooking." She made beautiful cakes and other desserts, which, together with her skills at the piano, delighted a proud George Langdon. "Mabel was Father's real daughter."[37] What Dollie had not realized was that Mabel sometimes resented her role and the responsibility for watching over her siblings.

Always apart as children, neither of the Eiseleys felt the need to share their lives with anyone but each other.

IV

To make adjustments for wartime conditions, Oberlin, like Kansas, had substituted a three-term schedule for the traditional semester plan. Of the college's 1,220 undergraduates, 999 were women, and the Student Council had elected its first female president in the spring of 1944. An additional 407 males were on campus as part of the navy's V-12 program, raising the total enrollment to 1,627. The retirement of Sims and another resignation had reduced the Department of Sociology to a faculty of three, with only Eiseley and Brown available to teach. Frederick M. Zorbaugh, the third member of the department, had been called to active duty.

Eiseley entered the classroom at the beginning of the winter term, in early November, less than a week after he arrived in town. If nothing else, the department's limited offerings virtually guaranteed that the three courses he was to teach—Introduction to Sociology, General Anthropology, and Population Problems—would have healthy enrollments, but he was taking no chances. So anxious was he to even the score with Brown that when his classes reached their limits during registration, he refused to close them out. Instead, he requested that extra chairs be brought in from the library to handle the overflow, and no student was turned away, no matter his or her qualifications. "In this manner," Mabel quipped, "Loren got his revenge."[38]

So far as the visitor can tell, little has changed in Peters Hall since Eiseley last walked its creaking corridors: the hardwood floors, pedestal oak desks, and ancient blackboards remain untouched. The chairman occupied a tiny oak-trimmed office on the second floor of the massive Gothic bastion, a rough-hewn sandstone relic erected in the 1880s by the Akron firm of Weary and Kramer, whose letterhead described them as "specialists in court house, jail and prison architecture," an irony Eiseley would have appreciated. On either side of his office were classrooms from which the hourly vibrations set up by a hundred pairs of restless feet reminded him when it was his turn to hold forth.

As always, he arrived at the sound of the bell and exited the instant it rang again. He occasionally walked into the room and told the class that he had forgotten to bring his lecture notes. "As we . . . were about to pick up our notebooks and depart, he would start lecturing anyway, and go the whole 50 minutes without stopping."[39] When Piltdown man, a specimen supposed to have lived 200,000 to 1,000,000 years ago, was later discovered through fluorine testing to be a hoax, the revelation rang a bell with one of Eiseley's students, who dug out her old course notes to see what he had said on the subject. She found that he had dismissed the fossil with the statement that it didn't fit with any other prehistoric discoveries. "So he was not one of the anthropologists with egg on his face."[40]

Eiseley was finished with his classes by nine in the morning on Tuesdays, Thursdays, and Saturdays, and by eleven the other days of the week. Instead of remaining in his office, where he ran the risk of being cornered by talkative students, the chairman usually made a beeline for Carnegie Library. It was there that Carroll Newsom, the new head of physics, first encountered him while browsing in the stacks. Newsom had heard of the abuse heaped on his younger colleague, whom he viewed as a potential kindred spirit. He recalled, "I greeted him, but I didn't get much return. I soon began to realize that Loren was quite reticent; he didn't make friends easily, and it was quite a period of time before we had a conversation."[41] Eiseley gradually came around after Newsom told him of his keen interest in the cultural anthropology of the Indians of the Southwest. As his confidence in Newsom grew, it became obvious that Eiseley needed more emotional support than Mabel alone could provide. As had Wimberly, Speck, and Tracy, Carroll Newsom developed the kind of affection for Loren that a devoted father has for a son. "It was easy . . . since with respect to many of the basic problems of life he was not sufficient unto himself; he was almost a child in his need for support. His wife provided [him] with tremendous support, but he also needed to be sustained by a man."[42] Wittke, too, responded to this profound lack of security by nicknaming Eiseley "Junior."[43]

The anthropologist also had his charm, which was used to soften the normally cranky and acid-tongued Helen George Senour, head of the book order department. Incurable bibliophiles, the alienated intellectual and dour librarian were soon involved in an unlikely conspiracy of hearts. Eiseley had scrutinized Oberlin's collection during his interview and subsequently informed Wittke that there was "a serious lack" of anthropological literature, including both books and periodicals. He recommended that the major gaps be filled in as rapidly as possible: "From the standpoint of research and future activity in anthropology, I should like to make our library in that subject something to be proud of."[44] The dean concurred and forwarded Eiseley's extensive list of monographs to acquisitions, along with a cover letter instructing the staff to get cracking.

Eiseley spent a lot of time in the bookstores on Fourth Avenue during his occasional visits to New York. Senour gave him carte blanche to order anything he thought the library ought to have. In September 1945 he picked up twenty-nine volumes from the scholarly and rare books department of Barnes & Noble alone. Among these acquisitions was a little Victorian curiosity titled *Pins and Pincushions*, whose purchase he attributed to a childhood memory. "My grandmother had a wonderful pincushion. It . . . had blue ribbon strips across it and was embroidered with pink and red flowers. . . . Grandmother warned me never to put pins in my mouth, but she was always going around with them in her mouth when she was sewing."[45]

Eiseley kept track of his requests in a large box of file cards labeled "Lacks, Wants, & Orders." "Loren read everything and anything," Newsom mused. "He liked to roam through bookstores; whenever we took trips he went to [them] and rarely left without several books under his arm."[46] At some point during his three-year tenure at Oberlin, a wistful Eiseley hired a local printer to fashion a personalized bookplate picturing a sun-bleached bison skull and hoofprint silhouetted against a midnight background: "*Ex libris*, Loren Eiseley."[47]

While the poet daydreamed of the plains and the vanished buffalo, the scholar was beset by a nightmare of broken promises. He had been in Oberlin no more than a week before a letter arrived from William Mitchell, an editor with Thomas Y. Crowell. "We are now in the process of going over our plans for the coming year, and I note that it has been some time since we have heard anything from you regarding your manuscript on 'General Anthropology.' "[48] The contract had been inked in December 1939, and Mitchell, who had almost certainly been alerted to his author's departure from Kansas by fellow Crowell editor Seba Eldridge, wanted to know when he could expect a first draft. An embarrassed Eiseley lamely replied that he had been planning to write for many weeks, but the pressure of getting settled in his new position had interfered.

> This entire war period has been to me—as it has been to countless others—one of great strain. For a time I expected to go into the service, and made many adjustments of personal and family affairs. Then I was shifted by the University into a war speed-up program in the Medical School, because of an extensive background in anatomy. I ceased to have vacations—the period when I normally get my writing done. . . .
>
> You might think, since I am now heading a department of sociology, that my situation, so far as time for research is concerned, would be considerably improved. However this department is functioning under the handicap of a reduced staff, which means a heavy teaching load coupled with administrative problems. . . .
>
> Under the circumstances it might be much better for you to seek another anthropologist, less hindered by the turn of events than myself, to write the text which you require. . . . I . . . regret that

> my circumstances are such that it would be impossible for me to promise you even a first draft under the conditions which face me now.[49]

Despite the fact that Macmillan had long since backed out of its contract with Eiseley and Bert Schultz for "They Hunted the Mammoth: The Story of Ice Age Man," the longtime friends had not abandoned the project. In the vita Eiseley had prepared for Wittke, he had described the work as nearing completion, with a publisher arranged for.[50] By early 1943 Bert had tentatively arranged to publish the book with Appleton-Century Company, and Eiseley had agreed. Then Bert, who had replaced the aged Dr. Barbour as director of the Nebraska State Museum in 1941, thought better of the idea and decided instead to go with the University of Nebraska Press.[51] Having completed his part of the manuscript, he was stunned to learn that Eiseley had not done the same. Emily Schoessberger, a representative of the press, gave Bert the disheartening news on March 29, 1943: "Here you have his answer: it took a long time and is rather negative. It seems that he does not want to work on it right now, or that he is not favorably inclined towards us. Is it true that so much still remains to be done before the MS is finished?"[52] It seems doubtful that Eiseley had made any further progress on his part of the book during the year preceding his departure for Oberlin, at which point the project was abandoned. "I began to feel the urge to venture outside the domain of pure science once more," he later wrote of the episode. "The book which had been far advanced when the war came no longer appealed to me."[53] In October 1945, after a year at Oberlin, he was still promising Eldridge the forty-thousand-word chapter contracted for six years earlier.[54]

V

Thus far, Eiseley and L. Guy Brown had maintained an uneasy truce by intentionally avoiding each other. Ironically, it was their refusal to meet face to face that led to the inevitable showdown. Brown received a call from one of the college secretaries who, he claimed, was puzzled by the "complete shift" in his proposed teaching schedule for the 1945–46 academic year. Not only had his chairman assigned him six different classes, but fully half of them were scheduled to meet on Saturday mornings. Eiseley, by contrast, had given himself Saturdays off and hung up on Brown when he called to protest. Brown hastened to his typewriter and composed a lengthy chronicle of the indignities he had suffered at Eiseley's hands, ending by accusing the chairman of double-dealing: "You told Dean Wittke that the new courses had been talked over and agreed upon by the two members of the department. I did not know a thing about two of your courses until they were announced in the Curriculum Committee; and you know I didn't." The courses, both in anthropology, fulfilled his prophecy: "of course," he scoffed, "you were brought here with the understanding that you would 'teach more Sociology than Anthropology.' "[55]

Eiseley replied to Brown's letter two days later. He apologized for losing his temper, but he also refused to accept Brown's version of events. He recollected that he had consulted with Brown about his teaching schedule before carrying out the sociologist's wishes "to the letter." The business about Saturday classes was a misunderstanding, the result of a clerical error that Eiseley would have rectified if only "the secretary's office [had] called me instead of you." Although he was hesitant to broach the subject, Eiseley felt that there was something else Brown should know. "I have been under an exceedingly great strain for weeks because of a matter which has nothing to do with college affairs." He further confessed: "had I known all the difficulties involved, I would never have come to Oberlin to accept an offer which was presented officially in such attractive terms."[56] If Brown wished, he could phone and arrange a private meeting to thrash out their differences. The alternative was to remain at "each other's throats," and Oberlin wasn't big enough for that.

There was to be no accommodation save a return to the status quo of mutual avoidance. A female sociology major who graded papers for Eiseley remembered how sad he became. "Oh, Betty," he exclaimed one day, "it isn't that they just don't like me, they don't even like my wife!"[57] It seems that Mabel, ever the stylish dresser, had caused a stir among the more traditional faculty wives, who made catty remarks about her hats and exquisitely tailored suits. She, in turn, was no less contemptuous of her detractors. Oberlin's snobbishness had left a bad taste in her mouth from the beginning. Hearing the community referred to as "the Athens of the West," the obligatory cliché uttered at least half a dozen times on virtually every social occasion, was enough to drive her from the room. "That is one reason," she later remarked, "we left town in the summers."[58]

Loren made arrangements to teach at Penn during the summer of 1945, and the Eiseleys rented the upper floor of a duplex at 234 West Montgomery Avenue in the pleasant Main Line village of Haverford. Below them, it turned out, lived Mary Ellen Morris, and the Nebraska-born writer and photographer Wright Morris. The couples spent many evenings together on the front porch. A neighbor's dog usually appeared during the cocktail hour and left, like a proper guest, as the women were cleaning up. "In my opinion," Wright mused, "he loved Eiseley's deep voice, pitched to a subterranean rumble." Wright's cherubic face and mischievous, elfin eyes belied the fact that he, too, possessed a rich baritone timbre, much like Eiseley's father's voice. "Morris," he once said while dozing off, "when I listen to you go on and on, I can relax, knowing the world is in good hands."[59]

Listen he did, for Wright, who had been awarded the first of three Guggenheim Fellowships in 1942, had just published his second novel, *The Man Who Was There.* Mabel felt that their meeting was one of the best things that could have happened to Loren, because it made him concentrate on how to go about publishing.[60] The two men sometimes read their works aloud to each other while putting away generous slices of her banana cream pie. Wright found Mabel even more fascinating than her husband in some ways:

> Loren's wife, an Irish woman of the breed James Joyce had married, and bearing her some resemblance, had little patience with our speculations, but she enjoyed my jokes. Her own opinion of bone hunters and their reconstructions was frequently expressed with Irish directness and sarcasm, especially those fictions of Cro-Magnon and Piltdown man based on the molar of a missing jaw. Mabel put me in mind of one of Willa Cather's lost ladies who had found her escape as a professor's wife. Her taste in fiction ran to Henry James, who would have loved both her hats and her style. Loren took pride in her appearance, her independent spirit, and walked at her side with his hand cupped to her elbow, at ease in the role, the suits and the ties, that would have been appropriate to my father.[61]

Wright became aware of Eiseley's melancholy early on and dubbed him "Schmerzie"—short for *Weltschmerz*, or world pain. It reminded him of D. H. Lawrence: "In his silences it was the voices of the dead to which he was attentive."[62] The following summer Eiseley published an article in *Scientific American* titled "Men, Mastodons and Myth." On the cover of a reprint he scrawled: "To Wright and Mary Ellen from Weltschmerz."[63] Wright shared Mabel's concern for her husband's well-being when he drifted into one of his impenetrable blue funks.[64]

VI

A long blast from the powerhouse whistle plunged Oberlin into bedlam on Tuesday evening, August 14, 1945. The next thing anyone remembered was a woman running down Main Street screaming, "It's over, it's over!" Within seconds, hundreds of citizens were pouring into the streets; laughing and weeping at the same time, they hugged one another, danced impromptu jigs, and began parading through the town's center arm in arm. Children ran up and down the sidewalks throwing confetti and were promptly joined by college students who had evacuated Keep, Thompson, and May halls as if they were on fire. The delirious throng yielded temporarily to the Naval Unit Band, which marched triumphantly around Tappan Square before the servicemen headed, on liberty, for the brighter lights of Cleveland. A public-address system, mounted on a car at College and Main, blared out the news reports as they came in over the radio. Bells pealed in all the church steeples, adding to the general din. Then, without warning, a thunderstorm broke about nine o'clock. The outdoor celebration ended as suddenly as it began. Quiet reclaimed the town. The war was over.[65]

With their lease on the Cole house about to expire, the Eiseleys once again sought out a small one-bedroom apartment. Their new landlords were John and Margaret Haylor, owners of a downtown bookstore, who rented them the second floor of their rambling frame home at 128 Morgan Street, only a few doors from Paul and Marjorie Sears. Margaret Haylor grew fond of her new tenants. "The thing about Loren that fascinated me," she recalled, "is that he was interested in everything. You couldn't mention any subject at all that he wouldn't add a lot to it or inquire about."[66] He often stopped by the bookstore and took special pleasure in watching the antics of a gray squirrel through the back window.

Mabel stayed in the apartment and read most of the time, paying no heed to the midwestern convention of dropping by uninvited to chat. Her wan, aristocratic face seemed all the more pale as a result of prematurely graying hair, and she was not very strong physically. Only once, after several entreaties, was Margaret able to coax her into attending a social function. Mabel gave a well-received lecture on textiles to one of Oberlin's women's clubs but refused to have anything further to do with this or any other group.

According to the "Annual Report of the President, 1945–46," the single most important feature of Oberlin College life was the return of the veterans, whose numbers rose from 13 during summer term to 363 the following winter. Among them was an intense, dark-complexioned graduate student named Jacob Gruber, who had taken a bachelor's degree in classical archaeology before being drafted into the army in 1942. Lacking any background in the social sciences, Jake enrolled in one of Eiseley's sociology courses. He liked it well enough to take another and gradually became friends with his mentor, who occasionally invited the veteran, his wife, and a few others to the Morgan Street apartment for coffee. One day, late in the afternoon, a preoccupied Eiseley showed up at the Grubers' downtown apartment. He talked well past the dinner hour, attempting to persuade his student that he should change his field to anthropology and pursue a Ph.D. after leaving Oberlin. "It seemed reasonable to me," Jake reflected, "and so I decided to do it."[67]

Not long thereafter Jake became Eiseley's grader, a privileged position that enabled him to form a unique impression of the man:

> Loren was not a good teacher but a wonderful lecturer. His lectures were very, very effective—the style you find in his essays. He was a performer. Loren would come in just on the dot ten minutes after the hour, pick up from where he had left off the period before, talk for fifty minutes (there were never any questions), and then just as the hour ended, he would finish it off, turn around, and walk out. Now, when I say that he was not a good teacher, I think Loren was always very uncomfortable with students, and I think he was always very uncomfortable with people.[68]

Jake remembered a party he and his wife had given while they were in New York during the summer of 1946. The Eiseleys, who were also in the city, agreed to come, and the Grubers made certain that several of Loren's former pupils were present. Eiseley sat in the corner most of the evening, not sulking exactly, but saying very little. "Socially awkward" was the term used to describe him.[69]

In late February 1946, Eiseley wrote an unusually upbeat letter to Harry Shapiro, his friend and former teacher at the American Museum of Natural History:

> At the moment I am deriving a quiet satisfaction from the fact that my anthropology classes are growing in quality as well as numbers. Next semester I shall be devoting three-fourths of my actual teaching time to anthropology as compared with sociology, and as yet no criticism has been ventured! Naturally I have to take good care of my work in sociology. . . . But I do want very much . . . to till the soil for anthropology so that never again will there be such a furor raised as was raised when I was first brought here.[70]

Eiseley's optimism was well grounded. The Executive Committee of Oberlin's Board of Trustees met three weeks later, on March 9, granting him tenure effective the first of July. His only disappointment may have derived from the trustees' decision to do so "without [a] change in salary."[71]

The Eiseleys were in New York, where Loren was teaching a summer course on the races of man at Columbia, when he received startling news from Wittke. Frederick Zorbaugh, who had recently returned from the navy, had tendered his resignation on July 30. Eiseley made little attempt to disguise his feelings, since Zorbaugh was close to his nemesis Brown. "I am returning Zorbaugh's letter, as you requested. It has a slightly hurt sound, and I rather imagine that his leaving will be [in] the best interests of all concerned. I hope that we can do something better than merely 'replace' him."[72] Within days Wittke dropped a second bombshell: "Guy Brown was just in to say that he has received an offer from another institution and is taking it. This development is certainly startling, and it adds to your problems, but it also gives us a chance now to practically rebuild the department."[73]

When the Oberlin catalog appeared in the fall, Loren Eiseley was listed as chairman of the newly christened Department of Sociology and Anthropology.

VII

There had been little fieldwork during the war years, little time for reading in anthropology, especially after Eiseley had gained a place in the Department of Anatomy at Kansas. Writing to fellow anthropologist Clyde Kluckhohn in November 1944, he bemoaned his fate: "I envy you the amount of material you have been able to turn out during this period. . . . I find myself very rusty and will have to read assiduously to catch up on what is going on in anthro again."[74] Eiseley, who was nearing middle age, finally admitted to himself that "pure science" would never be his forte. "A long dormant aspect of my mind began to stir again," he wrote in an unpublished memoir. "There flitted before me the episodes of earlier years, the things that never go into scientific reports—emotional reactions, stories, anecdotes of birds and animals—all those things that had been piling up in my memory."[75] These he jotted down in a series of notebooks for future reference. Henceforth he would subtly relate his autobiography piece by piece, while using science as both metaphor and disguise. And though the medium was prose, the poet would play the final hand.

During an unpublished interview conducted long after he left Oberlin, Eiseley revealed that the essay style that made him famous had been inspired, and to a considerable extent shaped, by his onetime neighbor and fellow scientist Paul Sears. The author of two eloquent books and dozens of articles, the botanist took a classically humanistic approach to science and literature, and he encouraged his younger colleague to submit the essays with which he had been experimenting to various popular magazines.[76]

Eiseley turned first to Lowry Wimberly and the *Prairie Schooner*. His essay "There *Were* Giants" appeared in late 1945. Eiseley wrote, "Somehow in the jungles of a million years ago there roamed a mighty brother of the men from whom we seem to be descended. And of all the wild, incredible human faces which age by age have stared at their own reflections in the ancient drinking holes of the Solo River, none, surely, were more formidable than his."[77] An evocative, albeit untrue, picture. Although Eiseley's suspicions about Piltdown man were later proven correct, he sometimes threw caution to the wind when writing for a popular audience. No sooner was this article published than its subject, G. H. R. von Koenigswald, whom the author had all but given up for dead at the hands of the Japanese, surfaced from internment unharmed. The professor returned to his work to develop convincing proof that *Goliath javanicus* was no ancestor of man. He renamed the massive creature *Gigantopithecus* and traced its origins to the Middle Pleistocene. Von Koenigswald had discovered the skeletal remains of the greatest ape ever known.

Urged by Sears to test other waters, Eiseley submitted an article to *Harper's Magazine* at about the same time "There *Were* Giants" appeared in the *Schooner*. Jake Gruber and his wife, Shirley, happened to drop by the Eiseley apartment the day the letter of acceptance arrived, along with a check for $250. Eiseley broke out the bourbon and, as the word quickly spread, others joined the impromptu celebration, toasting the host and talking well into the night.[78]

Eiseley hearkened back to the style whose praises *Scientific American* editor A. G. Ingalls had first sung. "On the table before me lies a human skull of strange and unusual appearance. . . . There is a hint of Wells' *Time Machine* folk in it—those pathetic, childlike people whom Wells pictures as haunting earth's autumnal cities in the far future of the dying planet." It is at once the calcified remains of what we were and the futuristic shape of what we would become, "a mysterious prophecy and warning," which he dubbed "The Long-Ago Man of the Future."[79] The descriptions, Eiseley continued, of how man will look one day are never pessimistic. The lofty brow that distinguishes us from our simian cousins will swell even further to accommodate our expanding brain. Meanwhile, our face will shrink proportionally as the jaw shortens to compensate for the loss of our wisdom teeth. The man of the future, a creature of magnificent cranial endowment, with teeth that "could have nibbled sedately at the Waldorf," had actually walked the earth fifteen thousand years ago. Yet he had created no lasting civilization, leaving as his monument only the rubble of bleached bones. Perhaps the unloosed mechanism had run too fast: "these people may have been ill-equipped physically to compete against the onrush of more ferocious and less foetalized folk." Are the evolutionary forces searching for the right moment of his reappearance? Eiseley wonders. Or is his appearance itself destined always to mark the beginning of the extinction of a race? "Perhaps the strange interior clockwork that is here revealed [has] . . . set a limit to the human time it keeps. I wish I could be sure. I wish I knew."[80]

Some while after this piece appeared in *Harper's*, Eiseley wrote of receiving a letter that made his hand tremble. "I remember," its sender began, "all those squirmy things we collected in jars and buckets and took home to put in the aquariums you made."[81] Twenty-five years had passed since Jimmy Dawes, the closest of all Eiseley's boyhood friends, had simply vanished after they graduated from eighth grade. Now a successful officer in a major corporation, Jimmy had read the piece in *Harper's* and wrote to acknowledge his erstwhile companion's success. Eiseley jotted a reply on a postcard, saying that he was leaving Oberlin soon and would write once he was settled into his new position, but he never did. Jimmy had opened an old psychic wound by attempting to explain his sudden disappearance from Loren's life. His friend's father had determined that the time had come for his son to sever his ties with the pond-dipping child of a humble hardware salesman and mentally suspect mother. Eiseley asked himself,

> Could I say that I had long since accepted all that he had to tell me, and then ask him upon what impulse he had chosen to repeat what his father had said? And if you chose to forget your friend, the nagging thought persisted, why are you busy with this resurrection now? Am I made respectable at last by my printed name, because the *Atlantic Monthly* [*sic*] was taken and read in your father's house long ago?[82]

Wishing that he had been stronger, Eiseley folded the letter and put it away in a box of old correspondence, where it remained unread, if not forgotten, for another quarter century.

13

"THE TIME FOR CONFIDENCE AND PROMISES"

I

Frank Speck, whose health had begun to fail, was due to turn sixty-five in November 1946. Although he could continue teaching at Penn until age seventy, tradition dictated that he relinquish the chairmanship of anthropology. The administration saw this as a chance to pare the budget and formulated a plan to abolish the department after Speck's retirement. A. I. Hallowell, a founder of modern cultural anthropology, was promoted to full professor without a raise in pay, leaving him little choice but to accept a more lucrative position at Northwestern in 1944. D. S. Davidson, Eiseley's other major professor, also saw the writing on the wall and left for the University of Washington. Only Speck and a few graduate assistants, so-called acting instructors, remained.

In 1946, the director of the University Museum, George Valiant, committed suicide. A noted anthropologist from Yale, George Peter Murdoch, was called in to serve as an adviser during the search for Valiant's successor. Once Murdoch realized that the university that housed one of the truly great American museums in archaeology and ethnology planned to close its department of anthropology, he was horrified. Murdoch insisted that the university pledge support for the department before a new museum director was selected. Wishing to avoid public embarrassment, the administration yielded and anthropology was saved.[1]

Eiseley was summoned to Penn for an interview in November 1946, only four months after Frederick Zorbaugh and L. Guy Brown had tendered their resignations at Oberlin. Speck wanted Eiseley to succeed him, and it is likely that he conspired with Hallowell, who had high hopes of returning to Penn as part of the renaissance, to make certain that he got the job. When Glenn R. Morrow, dean of the College of Arts and Sciences, wrote asking Hallowell to assess Eiseley's qualifications, the anthropologist concluded his effusive letter of support by stating: "All in all, I believe that his appointment would be a happy thing for Pennsylvania in all respects, so that I hope soon positive action will be taken."[2]

The letter Eiseley had been waiting for arrived in late January 1947. "It gives me great pleasure," Morrow wrote, "to offer you the appointment to our faculty as Professor of Anthropology, at an annual salary of $6,500, beginning with the academic year 1947–48."[3] Eiseley wired his acceptance on February 3, but not before making absolutely certain that as chairman he would be allowed to recruit an additional professor of the "highest caliber." When Morrow assured him that he could, Eiseley wasted no time. Penn's Executive Board convened on February 18 and appointed A. I. Hallowell professor of anthropology at a salary of seven thousand dollars a year.[4]

Eiseley informed a disappointed but proud Wittke of his decision in early February. The dean wrote immediately to Morrow to congratulate Penn on its choice: "We have never made a better appointment. . . . I have not only developed respect for [Eiseley] as a man but a very deep affection which will follow him wherever he goes."[5] In a letter written many years later, Wittke, a victim of Parkinson's disease, thanked "Junior" for sending him a book whose title is not mentioned. "I appreciate the inscription," he wrote in a palsied hand, "though you give me more credit for getting you out of that damn swamp in Oberlin than I deserve."[6]

The Eiseleys lived for a time in suburban Rose Valley on Possom Hollow Road, well removed from their few friends and Loren's colleagues, most of whom favored Philadelphia's Main Line. Their small one-bedroom apartment was on the second floor of a stone house surrounded by the rolling hills and great hardwoods of what Mabel described as a "lovely country estate."[7] A balcony overlooked the hollow, enabling Loren to observe birds and small animals to his heart's content. When he wanted to view nature at closer range, he could descend an outside stairway to the backyard, which was crossed by a little brook.

Eiseley himself wrote that he and Mabel should have been happy there, but the stone house was "bleak and sunless," having been constructed on the dark side of a forested hill. However, the main problem was their landlady. Though a cultured woman, she consistently entered the apartment when the Eiseleys were away. "Finally, I missed a book or two, no doubt not intentionally stolen, but appropriated out of aimless curiosity, and forgotten."[8] A kind of paranoia descended upon the intensely private couple. They found themselves huddling more and more in the kitchen and bedroom, for their living room adjoined the "listening" corridor prowled by the too-attentive owner.

Jake Gruber, who had followed Eiseley to Penn, was now teaching anthropology and sociology at Temple while pursuing a Ph.D. He and his wife, Shirley, often took the commuter train out to Rose Valley, especially for Mabel's sake. She was even lonelier now than at Oberlin and seemed to have no life beyond her devotion to Loren. Yet Jake never had the sense that their bond was one between husband and wife, or even man and woman. "It seemed to me a kind of platonic relationship."[9] Bryn Mawr anthropologist Frederica de Laguna had similar feelings and watched in muted sympathy:

> It was almost as if Loren and his interests had squeezed Mabel out, and I think they did. I think what happened in that little apartment was typical. Every available inch had bookshelves. Loren had a tremendous collection of Westerns and science fiction, even over the doorway from the hall into the living room. The dining room became less and less a dining room and more and more a study. Mabel's corner of the apartment got smaller and smaller.[10]

Because Loren seemed unable to articulate his affection for Mabel, Jake felt that at least a part of his writing was undertaken to repay his debt to her.

II

"All things are possible," Eiseley began his address before the Philadelphia Anthropological Society on December 5, 1947. "My desk is new and uninitialed by the years. This of all times is the time for confidence and promises." Decrying the trend toward ever narrower specialization, the new chairman committed himself to a more ambitious goal: "the number of departments of anthropology which have equally distinguished reputations in physical anthropology, ethnology, linguistics, archaeology, and applied anthropology is very, very small. We intend to be one of those departments, and not the least among them."[11]

He reminded the assembled company of its extraordinary heritage, for Philadelphia had been home to many great disciplinary forebears, including native sons Joseph Leidy, Edward Drinker Cope, and David Garrison Brinton, who, in 1886, had offered the city's first course in anthropology at Penn. But there was another man—the most important of all to the story—"a man here tonight."

> To me, Frank Speck *is* Anthropology, as he has been to many hundreds. He carried the burden *and* the heat of the day in this institution. He made this department highly regarded from coast to coast, and he did more. By some indefinable essence of character, he made it so completely that the marks will not wear off in my time, nor in yours. The marks of a man, not an academician. . . . That, ladies and gentlemen, is why a large number of you are here tonight hoping for great things from Anthropology. Because of a strange stew, a witches' caldron of turtles, bear grease, and Indian masks that has been kept bubbling up in room 400 College Hall for the whole time I have been alive. That's why you're here. I feel a sense of repetition as I turn to the future.

Eiseley concluded by assuring his listeners that so long as he was chairman the department would continue to be "a place of eclecticism, of balance, of untrammeled exploration of the human drama. And I give my personal word of assurance to Dr. Speck; namely, that in my office, turtles as well as men will continue to be safe."[12]

This same enthusiasm marked Eiseley's private correspondence. "We are enjoying ourselves tremendously," he wrote to Carroll Clark in March 1948; "everything looks wonderful."[13] Wilton M. "Bill" Krogman, a professor of physical anthropology and anatomy at the

University of Chicago, had recently accepted a joint appointment in the Penn graduate schools of medicine and dentistry. An outstanding teacher and leader in the field of child growth and development, Bill accepted Eiseley's invitation to offer special courses in the Department of Anthropology. So did Carleton S. Coon, a Harvard professor and Ph.D. who had just been appointed curator of ethnology at the University Museum.

A third appointment, one that was to have a profound impact on Eiseley's life, involved the directorship of the University Museum. No matter who assumed the post, Speck would continue to feud, as he had with every museum director going back thirty-five years to George Byron Gordon, who had literally thrown Speck's possessions into the street. Eager to avoid conflict, Eiseley had accepted the chairmanship only after learning that his old friend Froelich "Fro" Rainey had been chosen to succeed George Valiant. Like Eiseley, Fro had studied with Speck, taking his M.A. in anthropology at Penn before heading off to Yale to complete a Ph.D. "We hit it off right away," although "we were entirely different," Fro mused. "He was really a very introspective fellow, and I'm very much the other way. I was always pushing him for decisions and pushing him for a sharp conclusion of his ideas."[14]

Eiseley and Fro's long collaboration began with a scheme to end the oldest feud on campus. With Bill Krogman, they created a series of titles for themselves and certain other members of their respective faculties. Eiseley became curator of early man at the University Museum, in addition to chairman and professor of anthropology. Fro, Bill, and Carleton Coon each assumed the impressive appellation of professor of anthropology. The added responsibilities were minimal, sometimes nonexistent, but the old barriers collapsed instantly while everyone's vita took on a more exalted tone. "Frank [Speck]," Fro fondly recalled, "moved back into the museum with great glee."[15]

III

Eiseley's first year at Penn went off without a hitch. Then in the fall of 1948, he awoke in the small hours, feverishly babbling a lecture to some unseen audience. A torrential rain beat against the bedroom window while lightning bolts sporadically pierced the night. He listened for the sound of thunder, but it never came. "I was deaf. . . . I was alone with that knowledge in the dark." He thought of Daisy, sleeping mutely some fifteen hundred miles away. "So now it was here, the thing so long feared, come in the night, creeping upon me in the midst of a fever."

Dawn found him pacing restlessly about the little apartment as Mabel, who had resorted to passing him notes, sought the services of a specialist by telephone. Eiseley wrote later, "I was a fully tenured professor but I had been at Penn for scarcely a year. What, after all, did they owe me? How could I expect to teach without hearing?" He descended the circular stairway and sat down on a stoop by the little brook; his mind flashed back to the derelicts he had seen waiting in the freight yards so long ago—society's outcasts.

The Eiseleys drove their ancient Dodge over to Ardmore on the Main Line to keep an appointment with Dr. Edwin Longaker, the balding and bespectacled head of the Department of Otolaryngology at Bryn Mawr Hospital. Eiseley's eardrums were carefully examined in a silver reflector. Then, a two-pronged fork was struck, and its vibrations were picked up by the auditory nerve. Dr. Ed, as his patients affectionately referred to him, pushed the reflector aside and scratched out his diagnosis in Latin: *otitis media*, infection of both middle ears. The eustachian tubes had closed, resulting in unequal pressure against the drums. Eiseley's hearing would return, but it could take as long as six months. "I saw my wife throw her arms around the doctor."

Others taught his classes while he minded the office and answered correspondence. "All around me chatting, laughing people on their way to work passed me like ghosts, only their gesticulating hands and moving lips proclaiming life without them."[16] Sound returned for a few bittersweet moments after each treatment, but then the curtain would descend once more.

While Eiseley floundered in silence, frightened and anxious for his livelihood and sanity, the editor of a "scientifically oriented magazine" supposedly reneged on his request for an article on human evolution. This blow plunged him even deeper into despair, but a despair that in saints and martyrs often gives rise to the moment of epiphany.

> Sitting alone at the kitchen table I tried to put into perspective the fears that still welled up frantically from my long ordeal. I had done a lot of work on this article, but since my market was

> gone, why not attempt a more literary venture? Why not turn it—here I was thinking consciously at last about something I had done unconsciously before—into what I termed the concealed essay, in which personal anecdote was allowed gently to bring under observation thoughts of a more purely scientific nature? . . . I had lived so long in a winter silence that from then on I would do and think as I chose. I was fond of my great sprawling subject, but I had learned not to love anything official too fondly, even high office. One had to stand aloof. Otherwise one was easily destroyed. . . .
>
> Perhaps I had begun to learn the independence among the mad Shepards, or freezing midnight streets, or listening to my father declaim "Spartacus to the Gladiators," or when he coiled his fist and made me shiver when he read from Shakespeare:
>
> *He was a kinde of Nothing*
> *Until he forged himself a name.*[17]

At last, while waiting for supper one March evening, Eiseley was distracted by a "soft sputtering" that seemed to emanate from the direction of the kitchen stove. He shouted to Mabel, who rushed in and confirmed that it was the sound of the flame under the kettle. Eiseley buried his face in his hands. "I will never be angry at noise again," he vowed.[18]

By the time of Eiseley's revelation, several articles compassing his new style had already appeared, including "Obituary of a Bone Hunter," his apologia for not spending more time in the field. Only three months after its publication, he stood before the Philadelphia Anthropological Society as a new department chairman, reasserting Penn's claim to scientific leadership in tracing the origins and cultural development of man. Eiseley's loss of hearing thus became his rationalization for taking a step fraught with relentless anxiety. He would lead a double life—being the prose poet and the scientist who had to pay the rent—also squeezing in the administrative duties to which he could never accustom himself. Wright Morris, whom he was seeing at least once a week, felt that Eiseley's preoccupation with his ears was "comically exaggerated," for he had suffered nothing worse than a nasty but persistent head cold.

> Both my wife at the time and myself perceived a classic instance of boyish characteristics in a man. There was a good deal of

> that. . . . The extent to which he actually suffered something and the manner in which he reported on it was more comical than anything else. He fell into periods which grew out of his anxiety, of where little else seemed to be on his mind and he would "me, me, me" himself through an evening.
>
> As we know in numerous instances when this particular type of misfortune occurs, almost anything that is latently neurotic in a person comes to the surface, and you get these exaggerated responses. Schmerzie was ideal for this sort of thing; he would suffer more, he would feel that he was going deaf. It was [part of] the basic tonic chords of his nature—his privacy, his sensitivity, his feeling that he was possibly selected out to suffer . . . more than usual. It doesn't take much from this point on to give you an absolutely first-rate hypochondriac.[19]

Far from indulging her husband, Mabel made "very short shrift of" such things, at least in the company of others. "Oh, come on Loren," was her typical response when a recitation of his grievances began to dampen the evening's conversation. Still, he could never desist for long. Stealing over to Wright's apartment alone, he confessed to the pleasure he took when they harangued each other on the foul state of the world. "Here the boy in the green bush can escape completely, for a time, from the toils and duties which seem to have fallen upon him through some incredible series of chances and events."[20]

Jake Gruber, who took over Eiseley's night class during his bout with the cold, said, "I was not aware until I read the autobiography that the deafness was there."[21] Furthermore, Eiseley traveled north to frigid Toronto in late December, the supposed midpoint of his six-month siege, to deliver a paper titled "Providence and the Death of Species" before the annual meeting of the American Anthropological Association. Frank Speck and A. I. Hallowell were also on the program, along with Ward H. Goodenough, a young instructor at the University of Wisconsin. The trio interviewed the young man for a new slot and, liking what they saw, invited the candidate to Penn in February. Put up in a hotel not far from the Eiseleys' apartment, Goodenough noted nothing unusual about his host's hearing during dinner, although it was obvious that he worried about his health: "He couldn't treat illness as a casual matter."[22]

IV

A wire sent by Paul Sears from southern Mexico arrived in mid-March 1948. The Oberlin botanist had been engaged in fieldwork near Tamazulápan, north of Oaxaca, when a party from the University of California chanced upon the partially exposed tusks of an ancient elephant. Further digging yielded a nearly perfect human skull and other skeletal remains. Sears, who had often spoken with Eiseley about the potential significance of such a find, persuaded the others to quit excavating until an expert on early man could be brought in.

Eiseley applied for emergency funding from Fro Rainey and left during Easter vacation for what he hoped would be a fateful rendezvous with Paleo-Indian man.[23] Sears met him at the Oaxaca airport, and they drove straight to the semiarid valley surrounded by the sheer granite walls of the Sierra Madre del Sur. Within a short time a discovery was made that crushed all visions of scientific immortality. Two inverted dishes, one large, the other small, lay next to the skeleton, civilized luxuries unknown to the hominids of the retreating ice.

Sears consoled his friend by encouraging him to see as much of the country as possible in the few days that remained, since Eiseley had never been so far south. As Sears remembered, "I assumed that, being a Westerner, Loren was familiar with horses. We got him on this animal, which was docile enough, and he went up the valley." Within minutes the workers were distracted by a "commotion" in the distance: "Loren was trying to get the horse to cross a little creek, and the animal had other ideas on the subject. It was quite a sight. All the [peasants] were so sympathetic; they stopped work and came over to help him . . . cross the creek and bring him back to headquarters. Apparently, he'd never been on a horse before."[24]

That same month Eiseley wrote to Carroll Clark of another trip—"my long-delayed African junket"—which he was hoping to take in the summer.[25] The idea may have first occurred to him as early as 1943, when he penned a letter to a then little-known anthropologist named Louis Seymour Bazett Leakey of Nairobi, asking for reprints of monographs on various anthropoids, including *Proconsul*, a Lower Miocene ape discovered by Leakey and his wife, Mary, near Lake Victoria in the thirties. The curator of the Coryndon Museum obliged and invited Eiseley to comment on the material once he had read and digested it.[26]

Whether Eiseley did so is impossible to say, but he was sufficiently interested in the anthropological revolution centered in East Africa to write five articles on the subject during the next six years. Most of his information was derived from the work of Raymond Dart, professor of anthropology at the University of Johannesburg, and Robert Broom, curator of the Transvaal Museum in Pretoria. Both were connected to discoveries of *Australopithecus*—the hominid ancestor of modern man.

In September 1946, a year before he resigned from Oberlin, Eiseley had submitted a grant proposal to Dr. Paul Fejos, the flamboyant director of the Viking Fund, a foundation for anthropological research established in 1941 by the dimly sinister Swedish industrialist Axel Wenner-Gren, who was then on the U.S. State Department blacklist for suspected collaboration with Hitler and Göring. Eiseley hoped that Viking would give him $3,500 for a "diplomatic field survey" of South and East Africa during the summer months of 1947. "In spite of local interest on the part of a few indefatigable and devoted workers like Dr. Broom, there seems to be no inclination on the part of South African institutions to devote extended attention to the unique paleontological and archaeological resources which lie in their section of the country." Broom, to whom Eiseley had already written, would serve as his primary contact. But time was of the essence. "He is old. He may return to England or he may not live many years longer. To delay is perhaps to sacrifice our single opportunity to make use of his advice and acquaintance with local people."[27]

Fejos, who was known for writing out generous checks at the drop of a hat, wasted no time. A draft for the full amount, payable to Oberlin College, was in Carl Wittke's hands in less than a month. The college immediately issued a press release trumpeting Eiseley's good fortune; it made not only the pages of the major state papers, but those of the *Christian Science Monitor*, the *New York Times*, and the *New York Herald Tribune*.[28] With almost a year remaining to complete travel arrangements and draw up an itinerary, the signs boded well for the summer of '47.

Word of the grant had barely reached Eiseley before he received a letter of congratulations from Sherwood L. Washburn, a brilliant young physical anthropologist on the faculty of Columbia Medical School. Eiseley had often stayed with "Sherry" when he visited New York City, and now it looked as if the two might be sharing quarters in a rather more exotic setting. "I'm off to Africa, too," his friend wrote, "also thanks to Viking. I'd like to collect monkeys and am undecided about just where to go. We will have to talk it all over this Xmas in Chicago."[29]

Although Eiseley had corresponded with Broom before applying for his grant, he had not, as he'd intimated to Fejos, broached the subject of visiting Africa personally. He now wrote immediately to the man whose help he most needed, telling him of his plans and asking for assistance in preparing an itinerary. Moreover, he intended to bring Mrs. Eiseley along, but, he hastened to add, "we would definitely not be 'tourists.' "[30]

The following March, Eiseley drafted a report to Fejos. "I have received no reply from [Broom] on the matter of my projected trip," though "I have reason to know that he received my letter, which he may simply have decided to ignore because of political commitments favoring the proposed expedition to South Africa by the University of California." Under the circumstances, the original plan would have to be revised. "That the trip could not have been undertaken this coming summer, in any case, has seemed discouragingly apparent for the past several weeks." Unreliable shipping conditions had made the passage over "literally impossible," to say nothing of the return voyage. His acceptance of the chairmanship at Penn also demanded that he remain in the States. Finally, he had just recovered from a "most troublesome siege" of flu.[31]

Fejos wrote what Eiseley described as a brief but cordial note, suggesting that they meet in New York to discuss his next move once the dust had settled at Penn. He also showed Eiseley's letter to a disappointed Sherry, who wrote to offer his regrets. Apparently Fejos had taken the news with less equanimity than Eiseley had thought, because Sherry felt it wise to include a friendly warning: "[Fejos] does not like to have idle funds tied up indefinitely. I got the impression that it would be best to turn the grant back to Viking and reapply later, unless you are absolutely sure that you can go a year later than planned." Eiseley's unconvincing excuse involving travel arrangements seems to have rankled as well. Sherry had checked the passenger ship schedule for South Africa: "Two weeks N.Y. to Cape Town."[32]

In June 1947, about the time the Eiseleys should have sailed, Eiseley instructed Wittke to return the funds entrusted to Oberlin, since his professional ties to the college had been severed. He promised Fejos that he would clarify his plans "as soon as possible," and the increasingly skeptical administrator agreed to issue a new check for $3,500 once Eiseley began teaching at Penn.[33] A month later Eiseley received some good news from Africa via Melville J. Herskovits, a colleague at Northwestern University. Van Rit Lowe, director of South Africa's Union Archaeological Survey, promised to meet him upon his arrival in Cape Town and introduce him to some of the top field men in the country.[34]

An effervescent Sherry, who had been forced to delay his sabbatical for a semester, did his best to coax Eiseley into making good his promise. He even offered to cut short his planned research in Kenya and come south if only his friend would agree to meet him at the end of July 1948. They could examine the local collections, especially Broom's, together, line up some sites for later fieldwork, and gather material for a joint paper on the Bushman and Negro pelvis, which Sherry had already outlined. Nor would Eiseley's literary talents go to waste: "If you did a paper of the sort you do so well for the Sci. Monthly, I might be able to aid. When will there be a better time to go? Africa HO!"[35]

"Your enthusiasm is so contagious," Eiseley replied on February 24, "that . . . I feel that I ought to hop on a plane right now and not wait until July." His initial desire to visit the continent was as strong as ever, but he pointed to "a number of problems" still to be thrashed out, "and not all of them are small." He promised to subject the matter to "intensive study" over the next few days and report again. "Africa HO yourself!"[36]

Wright Morris, who had been observing Schmerzie's irresolute behavior with a mixture of amusement and disbelief, grew increasingly impatient as the months passed. It was not altogether clear that Mabel, whose ticket and other expenses the Eiseleys would have to pay for out of their own modest savings, would be able to go. But leaving her home seemed out of the question; even short separations were fraught with tremendous anxiety on Eiseley's part. "If Mabel was not there at the end of the day; if she was not *there*, *there*. . . . You have to get clear back to where a boy is faced with a loss that is simply not bearable." It took Wright some time to grasp this and he often wondered aloud about Eiseley's strange capacity for equivocation: "What the hell is holding him up now?"[37]

Wright passed several evenings in the Eiseley apartment listening to guests who had been to Africa expound on the great scientific secrets coming to light almost weekly. Eiseley, who usually balked at entertaining strangers, was enthralled by the stories they had to tell. One of these men, an eloquent, self-confident Britisher, seemed to have tipped the scales. The visitor left with the unmistakable notion that he would be seeing Eiseley in a short time—in Africa. Wright remembered thinking, "Well if it's reached this stage, Schmerzie's finally going to do it."[38]

Sherry received the news he had been hoping for in mid-March. Both Loren and Mabel would be leaving by plane on July 15 and planned to join him in Johannesburg two days later. Their passport and visa applications had already been submitted. While they had not yet gone into any aspects of the trip after reaching Africa, their prestigious travel agent, Thomas Cook, would do that. Eiseley was also planning to see Paul Fejos at the end of the week to reconfirm the funding. Still, there were some uncertainties. "How," if it should become necessary, "shall we send letters or a cable?"[39]

"Everyone here is very helpful and friendly," an ebullient Sherry wrote from Johannesburg on April 15. "I have seen Broom's material. *Fantastic!* It is a true ape-man."[40] Far from contemplating retirement, the octogenarian "is a dynamo, one of the fastest and most likeable people I have ever met. He or his assistant goes to the quarries where the ape-men are found once a week. All the workers are on the lookout for fossils and save them." Sherry also visited Raymond Dart, who had recently found the partial skull of a new australopithecine. "He thinks it makes fire, but no one else here does."[41] His next stop was to be Kenya, where arrangements had been made to meet Leakey at the Coryndon Museum.

Eiseley replied that he and Mabel were going ahead with their plans. "The only apparent threat . . . is the family situation." The elderly aunt in charge of caring for his mother, whom he misleadingly described as "an invalid" in another letter, had fallen ill. "I mention this only because if any emergency should develop, I might have to check out completely."[42]

Sherry continued to bombard Eiseley with superlatives. "I'm at Kampala [Uganda], now," he wrote on June 6. "Had a wonderful time in Kenya and saw lots of Kikuyu and a few Masai. Leakey & MacInnes are very nice, and I went over their human and primate material. In one gorgeous morning I got a lot of new ideas on interpreting primate faces." Taken together, Kenya and Uganda were an anthropologist's paradise. "There is everything here and only a couple of people working. The opportunities are infinite. I only wish I was at least 3 right now! If only you were here!"[43]

As Eiseley related subsequent developments in a letter to Fejos, he had decided to cancel his travel plans on June 20. "That my disappointment was acute, I hardly need to mention." As department chairman, he had suddenly been confronted with the late resignations of two young instructors, both nontenured, who had decided to accept other positions. "It was unthinkable to absent myself at that point and leave certain decisions entirely to others."[44] While this development alone was sufficient cause for withdrawal in Eiseley's mind, he also wrote of the need to visit Nebraska and his bedridden mother in September.

Sherry, who was collecting monkeys in the bush, received a similar report. As always, he tried to put the best face on a bad situation: "You might be able to do a bigger trip in a year or two. Conditions should be better for travel by then. Do have a talk with Fejos."[45] But Eiseley knew better, and he was finally forced to admit as much to the Viking Fund's director: "it would be quite unrealistic to assume that I can count upon a 'free' summer in 1949. . . . Therefore I wish to relinquish the grant, with deep thanks for it again, in the hope that some other applicant who needs support for scientific work may be aided."[46]

V

That the decision to remain at home haunted Eiseley is apparent from the fact that he chose to broach the matter in the autobiography. Once again he blamed a callous administrator, who had angrily telephoned to denounce Eiseley's rejection of a candidate he had favored. "If you persist in your refusal to cooperate you will be called to explain yourself before the president, before myself, before—" The old phrase resurfaced in Eiseley's mind: "Men beat men." It was supposedly at this point that he decided the Viking grant would have to be returned: "Had I gone away from campus for any length of time, lurking forces would have sought to staff and commit the department to a course I deemed unwise. The responsibility was mine and mine alone."[47]

It is difficult to believe that a palace revolution could have taken place in six weeks, but the thought provided the rationalization Eiseley had been seeking. He had decided to reject the grant in mid-June, a full month before his and Mabel's planned departure, time enough to interview potential replacements for those who had resigned. So far as Nebraska was concerned, he had informed Fejos that he would not be going there until September. The Eiseleys' reservations called for them to be back in Philadelphia no later than the sixth of September.

Wright Morris was convinced that on one level, at least, Eiseley had truly wanted to go: "He was tremendously interested in those things. That he didn't do [them] must have been a source of the greatest strain to him because . . . his own involvement in what was being discovered was acute. He wanted to be the one there; he desperately wanted to make these judgments because he would feel, very appropriately, that he could do these things better than anybody else—or at least as well."[48]

Jake Gruber felt much the same and finally concluded that his mentor had been held back by some deep-seated fear of the unknown.[49] Eiseley might well have been writing of himself when he observed: "Thoreau, the physical stay-at-home, was an avid searcher of travel literature, but he was not a traveler in the body. Indeed, there are times when he seems to have regarded that labyrinth—for so he called it—with some of the same feeling he held toward a house—as a place to escape from."[50] As Wright Morris noted, "Schmerzie's world consisted of his mind, his office, and the commuter train."[51]

Eiseley also feared that if he went to Africa once, and it lived up to its anthropological potential, he might have to go again. The curator of early man at the University Museum wanted Sherry to understand that "I am by no means certain that if we landed the right sort of business out there that there might be implications for Penn."[52] One can only imagine what Eiseley's graduate students and colleagues, such as Fro Rainey and Bill Krogman, would have thought had they read this. It finally dawned on Sherry that his friend really didn't want to upset the quiet life he had created for himself, and he deeply felt the loss of not having Eiseley there to write about the findings.

As a professional writer, Wright Morris was also acutely conscious of this loss. He often reminded Eiseley that his early field experience fed the very best of his essays. "I felt the deprivation [of new material] was even more serious than he did." And as he feared, the time eventually came when Schmerzie exhausted the raw material of his youth, but by then it was too late. The imagination had to do too much, and the writer drifted into the sentimental. "He knew that he was subject to an embarrassing excess and that if somebody knew him they would hold him responsible for this sort of thing."[53]

Despite Sherry's warning that no one was taking seriously Dart's hypothesis concerning *Australopithecus prometheus*, the ape-man who made fire, Eiseley could not resist the temptation to spin a romantic yarn. The "assiduous bonehunter," as he was described in the byline of "The Fire Apes," which appeared in the September 1949 issue of *Harper's*, wrote that the discovery of these small and timid creatures "has shaken all our established notions of human cultural history." But how did this retiring species, which left no definitive evidence of having possessed even the simplest tools, acquire the forbidden magic of the gods? "Perhaps . . . they watched trembling behind a bush and learned from men the secret of fire." Whatever the answer, they were too late; the evolutionary pendulum had swept on, leaving them to perish in a fading world. "Theirs were the last furred hands and theirs the last half-animal voices to be seen and heard . . . before the pathway backward closed forever."[54] Once more, Eiseley had sketched a vivid and hauntingly beautiful picture. Had he gone to Africa to see for himself, he would have discovered that the truth was no less compelling than his fiction.

VI

Daisy, now seventy-three, and Grace, seventy-eight, continued to share an apartment on H Street in Lincoln. Mabel saw to their needs each summer when she returned to visit her own aging parents, who did their best to keep an eye on the strange-acting pair. A grudging Eiseley made the obligatory pilgrimage in late August or early September, after summer school was over.

Acceptance, if not understanding, usually comes with age, but in this instance there would be no gesture of reconciliation. Mabel put it as delicately as possible: "Loren had a very funny feeling toward his mother; he didn't really like her." As a devoted wife, she sided with her husband, but not without a certain guilt. The eccentric widow had developed an inexplicable attachment to her daughter-in-law and always treated Mabel very well. Matters grew worse about this time, for Daisy's fragile equilibrium seemed to be on the verge of collapse. "When letters would come from her," Mabel confided, "they were *so* painful. She never said anything very sensible except 'Why don't you get a job in California?' There was no appreciation of what [Loren] had already accomplished or what it took to do those things."[55] Dollie, Mabel's sister, referred to Daisy's correspondence less politely as "hate letters," which almost made Loren sick.[56]

Meanwhile, Eiseley's niece, Athena, had married and given birth to her first child, a daughter named Sandra. Having lost contact with her uncle since his graduate school days at Penn, she decided to write him at Oberlin in the summer of 1949, not knowing that he had returned to Philadelphia two years earlier. The letter eventually caught up with him in Berkeley, where he was teaching summer school at the University of California. His long, handwritten reply, dated July 26, is among the most psychologically revealing of the surviving letters. Weary and filled with self-pity, its author leaves the overwhelming impression of sadness, of a seemingly broken man in the shards of his career.

> Yes, I know, I could have got it [Athena's address] from other sources, but do you remember that conversation we had in which you said it was probably well for me that I was not in Philadelphia—permanently, I mean? Well ironically enough it happened. I have been there some time now and I know your father knows I am there because I live in the suburbs and my students occasionally phone the other Eiseleys by mistake. It is too bad, but we have never contacted them nor do I intend to. I think you should know this and judge it as you will.
>
> I simply felt that to avoid contact was the only way to avoid trouble later—the *only* way. It is too bad. I do not desire to hurt anyone. But as I told you that afternoon I had enough of family troubles as a child to know that enough is enough. My life has been troubled, painful and full of struggle. The peace I want is

very little—just to be let alone. I know from experience that that is hard to get. In fact my profession is strenuous and hard on the nerves, though this may sound strange to an outsider who sees only the romantic side of it.

So, in short, I have not gone to see the other Eiseleys, nor have they come to see us. It is good. I prefer it that way. I took the stand; there was nothing else that would have worked. I had seen enough to be sure. I think, moreover, that you will understand. My advice is just never to discuss it with them. Probably they will never bring it up of their own volition since apparently they had not told you I had moved.

I could say a good deal more—tell you that though an incorrigible non-letter writer, your uncle has thought of you often (do not smile, it is true) by campfires in lonely places in the mountains of Mexico and passing fast over your southland by air.

Now give the child a kiss for me since I have none and see that she goes to college and has the best of everything and is not spoiled. Maybe years from now she will want to know about me. You can tell her then—oh never mind. Just tell her he was a guy who had his troubles, was a poor letter writer, couldn't stand most of his relatives and died by himself and to hell with it. You can make one exception though—you can say he had a niece Athena—and that he found it hard to write to her because it stirred old things at the bottom of his heart. But you can say for all that she was a favorite of his.

"Only," you can go on to add, "the trouble with the guy was he was hard on all his favorites. And most of the time he just wasn't around. But he meant well." You can always say that last, you know. It'll see the thing through.

So long Miss 31
Loren[57]

On August 2 the Eiseleys left Oakland, California, by train. Two days later found them in Cody, Wyoming, where Eiseley was about to begin the last significant fieldwork of his career. The actual site was five miles northwest of town in the Absaroka Range, near the confluence of Lower Sage Creek and the Shoshone River. In 1939 Jimmy Allen, a local sheet-metal worker and amateur archaeologist, had found one of the more than two thousand arrowheads in his collection along the creek bank. Allen made a note of the place, but he did not return until the summer of 1948, when he found some odd-looking bones protruding from the surface. The collector risked embarrassment by telling his secret to a learned outsider, Glenn L. "Jep" Jepsen, Sinclair Professor of vertebrate paleontology at Princeton University, who was involved in some digging of his own at nearby Polecat Bench. Instead of dismissing the amateur, Jepsen was elated by what he saw and soon began formulating plans to return the following summer with a nine-man crew.

After returning to Princeton, Jepsen got in touch with his friend Fro Rainey to inquire whether Penn's University Museum might be interested in providing a consultant on early man once the digging began in earnest. Fro brought the matter before his Board of Managers, who agreed to appropriate the necessary travel funds. The museum director asked Eiseley to carry Penn's colors into the field, which he agreed to do, albeit reluctantly. He had to be in New York City on August 29 for a series of seminars sponsored by The Viking Fund, and family matters made it imperative that he stop off in Lincoln for a few days on his way back east. He had also promised the Wittkes that he and Mabel would pay them a visit in Cleveland, where Carl was now vice president and dean of the Graduate School at Western Reserve University, having stormed out of Oberlin after learning that he had been passed over for the college presidency.

Digging began immediately after the Eiseleys arrived. Within inches of the surface the party found a mass of moldering buffalo bones, their ends broken off for the purpose of extracting the protein-rich marrow. Mingled with the bones were over two hundred stone artifacts, including large numbers of beautifully shaped points, which had been fabricated by a complex technique Jepsen described as "horizontal parallel flaking." There was no question that Jimmy Allen had chanced on the slaughtering ground of the ancient nomadic culture known as Yuma.

After stalking and felling their prey, the hunters, who had inhabited the region around 5000 B.C., stripped the great beasts of their hides; they then built huge fires inside the carcasses and ate to their contentment. As the embers cooled inside the charred ribs and appetites returned, the uncooked meat was torn away to be roasted on fresh fires.

Covering some 2,500 square feet and containing the bones of at least 180 bison, the Lower Sage Creek site was soon determined to be the most valuable Yuma find on record, largely because of the abundance of implements and the many varieties of stone from which they were fashioned. One sharp-eyed excavator, equipped with a whisk broom and awl, uncovered four small piles of stone flakes, each different from the others and each consisting only of flakes from the same piece of stone. This rare discovery led Jepsen to hope that his team would eventually be able to match each pile of flakes to one of the finished projectiles from the digging—an archaeological first for North America if it could be done. In any case, the discarded chips had already challenged one long-established theory, that Yuma points were made with great individual effort over a period of days or even weeks. Instead, the findings suggested that the points were fashioned rapidly at a single sitting.[58] Yet most of the big questions remained unanswered. The few days Eiseley had planned to spend in Wyoming turned into nearly three weeks. Then, while the others stayed on to work the site, he headed east in late August, ideas of scientific articles briefly sketched in a spiral notebook.

He had barely arrived in New York for the Viking seminars in early September before granting an interview on the Wyoming project to Art Everett, a reporter with the Associated Press. Eiseley spoke of the campsite as "a find for which I have been waiting 20 years."[59] Neither Jepsen nor Princeton University figured prominently in the article, while Eiseley's credentials and affiliation with the University of Pennsylvania were well documented. Jepsen was understandably angered by his colleague's indiscretion, especially because they had agreed that no statement would be given to the national press until the excavation had been completed and the material subjected to laboratory analysis, a process that would take at least another year. "[Rainey's] secretary," an agitated Jepsen informed Eiseley, "writes that he holds an expectation that our material will be published in the U. of Pa. monograph series. Please straighten this out there. No final decisions have been made & I will not make them until we look into [the] format and authorship of the sections farther."[60] He concluded by asking that copies of all correspondence pertaining to the site be sent to his Princeton office.

A wounded Eiseley replied at length two weeks later, on November 6. So far as his correspondence on the dig was concerned, there was precious little, but Jepsen was "perfectly welcome" to it. "I do not have access to Rainey's files any more than he would have access to mine," Loren sniped, "but . . . I cannot imagine that he had indulged in much more correspondence about the site." He then sought to turn the tables by chiding Jepsen for treating him as an underling. "That Pennsylvania was given a 'consultant' position came as something of a surprise in view of the fact that we had assumed in the beginning that the project was to be a joint one." Although it was true that the term "consultant" had been used in his connection, was it not a bit unusual for an institution to furnish the services of an expert and then receive "nothing in return? . . . Had I thought that would be the case I could not, in all honesty, have remained; . . . the Museum had a right to expect something for its interest."[61]

Jepsen's six-page rejoinder contained a searing indictment of his colleague's past behavior and current accusations. "You seem not to have realized the extent of confusion and antagonism which resulted from your unexpected and unauthorized release of a story to the Associated Press in New York." Unbeknownst to Eiseley, a campaign was begun to prevent outsiders from "raiding Wyoming's treasures" as a direct result of the press release. "I was told that the University of Pennsylvania was through in Wyoming and probably in adjacent states." Only as a result of Jepsen's personal intervention was Eiseley spared "some extremely unpleasant situations."[62] If he and Fro still held hopes of developing other sites in the region, they would be wise to return and explain themselves to the angry citizens of Cody, and to the members of the local press.

The townspeople might have been more forgiving had Eiseley not treated them in a highhanded manner from the start. Those involved in the dig had asked Jepsen to speak about the project one Sunday afternoon. Wishing to put Eiseley at ease, Jepsen gave his friend the opportunity to address the group instead. The newcomer apparently donned what Sherry Washburn termed "his Methodist minister's guise," and it played poorly in the provinces. An amateur collector named Shelby approached Eiseley afterward to tell him that he had written everything the anthropologist said ten years previously. "That," Jepsen claimed, "was the most embarrassing incident in all my associations in cooperative research." Finally, it had been Jepsen's assumption that some of the artifacts from the dig would ultimately go to Penn until Fro Rainey, during a phone call on September 8, indicated that the university was not interested in receiving any. "You seem to have forgotten my report upon this to you," Jepsen wrote.[63]

Having more than met his match, Eiseley, who usually avoided conflict at all costs, drafted no reply, preferring to await Fro's return. As was to be expected, the plucky museum director took up the cudgel on Eiseley's behalf, as well as his own, but Jepsen refused to be swayed. The three finally agreed to meet in Princeton for lunch on December 22 in an attempt to thrash out their differences. Tempers were restrained, but neither did the holiday spirit prevail. On January 7, 1950, Fro wrote Jepsen that "Eiseley and I both feel that . . . there is no point in attempting to collaborate in this fog of confusion, recrimination and misunderstanding. The only sensible thing for us to do is withdraw the University Museum from the entire affair."[64] A copy of the letter was sent to Eiseley for his files, where it became an ironic postscript to the obituary of a bone hunter.

14

ANATOMY OF A *JOURNEY*

I

It was apparent to those who knew him well that Frank Speck's health was failing. In December 1948 his physician wrote Eiseley that the heart muscle was deteriorating, although it had not yet reached the point at which the patient need opt for retirement. He recommended, however, that the irreverent old eagle be forced out of his aerie atop College Hall.[1] "They have moved my office to the new place," a disgusted Speck wrote Eiseley the following summer, "but it is not yet put to rights. Some of the boys say they are going to try a bit of book arrangement there." Despite the onset of kidney disease, he refused to stay put. "I shall be off for a short trip soon to some N.E. Algonkian group, after the usual."[2]

During the final examination period at the end of January 1950, Speck, accompanied by his wife, Florence, journeyed to the Allegany reservation in western New York. Here the Seneca were to perform their midwinter rites, known as the Great Annual Renewal Ceremony, at Coldspring Long House, and Speck, as before, was welcomed as both observer and participant. The ethnologist had no sooner arrived than he suffered a seizure and collapsed. When her husband did not respond to the ministrations of the Seneca priests, Florence brought him back to Philadelphia's University Hospital, where he died on Tuesday, February 7, at age sixty-eight. The services were held at a funeral home in Media two days later, after which the body was taken by train to New York and laid to rest in the Hudson Valley.

Exactly how Eiseley took his mentor's passing is difficult to say. Speck's daughter, who was no longer in the area, wrote that "when my father was quite sick, Loren was very comforting."[3] And when, at the next meeting of the Philadelphia Anthropological Society, he was called upon to deliver Speck's eulogy, tears formed in his eyes. But the president of the society, a renowned Middle Eastern scholar and longtime colleague of Speck, was taken aback by this display of emotion, for it had never seemed to him that the two were particularly close.[4] John Witthoft, who was also in the audience, shrank as well when Eiseley became lachrymose. "Speck's attitude toward Eiseley was that toward myself or most of his other students—that of approval and encouragement up to the point where there was too much involvement."[5]

Eiseley had taken Jake Gruber out to meet Speck shortly after the Oberlin graduate came to Philadelphia. There was no question in Jake's mind that Speck was a "hero" in Eiseley's eyes, but it also seemed that the older man was becoming a source of embarrassment to the new department chairman. Penn had changed, but Speck's conduct in the classroom hadn't. Though still a fine teacher, "he gave the appearance of being a dunce of some sort. He wore the same jacket all the time, would engage in farting contests with his graduate students, used his knife to clean a turtle and then to cut his oranges, and so on." When Jake informed Eiseley that he was thinking of visiting Speck in the hospital before he died, he was surprised that he was told not to bother. "I think he dropped Frank Speck," he stated in retrospect. "I can't conceive of Mabel and Loren having a dinner party to which they would invite Frank and Florence."[6] Indeed, Mabel characterized Speck as "an eccentric—brusque, self-centered," but "popular with students."[7]

II

The Eiseleys had given up their Rose Valley apartment in the summer of 1949, after returning from California. They moved across the city to the tidy upper-middle-class suburb of Wynnewood on the Main Line, an easy fifteen-minute commute to Thirtieth Street Station, from which Eiseley walked the remaining mile to campus.

Their modest two-bedroom apartment was on the third floor of the Wyndon, a comfortable but architecturally undistinguished complex of red brick and wood set amid shaded grounds and quiet neighborhood streets. Although Mabel was exaggerating somewhat in describing the natural surroundings as "wild" when they first moved in, a nearby woods filled with the cardinals Eiseley loved had not yet been sacrificed for the shopping center that was soon to occupy the site.

More realistic than wistful, Mabel had long since given up the idea of having a house of her own, largely because she knew that the entire responsibility for its decoration and upkeep would have fallen on her shoulders. Anything and everything mechanical was alien to Loren. When their deteriorating car left the garage, an increasingly rare event, Mabel was almost always at the wheel, and it was she who saw to its maintenance. Loren, who wrote everything in longhand, never learned to use the typewriter, leaving to Mabel the task of preparing the final drafts of his work. Even the language he applied to modern technology was quaintly old-fashioned. The television set, which the Eiseleys never owned because Loren thought it a distractive influence, was "a machine," and the tape recorder an "electric recording device." They did keep a static-prone old radio, which Mabel always had tuned to a classical music station, that is, when it wasn't on the blink. Yard work appealed to Loren no more than applying a fresh coat of paint. As Marian Schultz observed, "Loren liked nature, so long as it was someone else's nature."[8]

The pretensions of Main Line society did not permeate the Eiseleys' interior world. On occasion Eiseley accompanied Wright Morris to the construction site of the Morrises' new home. After wandering about a bit, he would speak wistfully of the house he hoped to own one day, but Wright realized that his friend had "no interest in it whatsoever, except as a kind of fictive dream. It was quite American in a sense, quite touching."[9]

During his rambles about the neighborhood, Eiseley was fond of picking up almost any object he chanced upon, from cocoons, feathers, and unhatched eggs to rocks, glass insulators, and rusty bolts. This habit, in Wright's words, "was the source of the greatest vexation to Mabel. One could hardly touch on something where there was a more acute difference in their natures." More often than not, Mabel met Loren at the apartment door and, like the mother of a crestfallen little boy, made him empty his pockets of contraband before entering. For Christmas one year Mary Ellen Morris suggested that she and her husband give Eiseley a glass-encased ant colony, which Wright thought a wonderful idea. Schmerzie was enthralled, while a wordless Mabel looked at it from across the room with the jaundiced eye of her Irish forebears. "I would say," Wright recalled later, "that for several weeks there was some chance this relationship might be on the rocks. It was a little bit like giving a man who is subject to getting inebriated a case of brandy, when his wife has been trying to keep him on the wagon."[10] And just as one might have predicted, some of the insects escaped from their glass prison. The colony was snuffed out a short time later when Mabel issued an ultimatum.

There were also occasions when Mabel's censure of Loren took a less comic turn. Her ridicule could become fierce, causing Wright to puzzle over Eiseley's capacity to abide her cutting remarks without retaliating in kind. These storms passed quickly, however, and afterward Mabel returned to her normally amiable self. One of their few close friends felt certain that Eiseley was "afraid of Mabel."[11] Even Dollie had to admit that her sister could be ruthless on occasion. "If someone overstepped in some way she didn't like, that person was gone forever. It would take just one thing that she wouldn't discuss." And sometimes when the sisters went shopping together, Mabel acted "terribly" toward a clerk she thought had not been deferential enough. "She would make a point about it; she could be quite haughty."[12]

"I don't care how many books you buy or how much money you spend," Mabel often remarked to her bibliophile husband, "but where are we going to put them?"[13] Loren and Wright regularly hotfooted it in on the local to downtown Philadelphia, where they disappeared into the dimly lit confines of an establishment called Leary's, to emerge hours later, their clothes smudged with dust, arms straining under their weighty burdens of used books. After snacking at Schrafft's, they headed for Wynnewood, where Wright reluctantly stopped off to join his friend in facing the music.

> We brought the greatest sorrow to Mabel every time we came in. The apartment gradually became book crowded, which for Eiseley was a wonderfully satisfying thing, but for Mabel it was a massive pain in the derriere. There were books in the bedrooms, there were books in the dining room, there were books everywhere. This,

> too, was a controlling element in what Mabel felt she might be asked to do with the place. She did not, on any level, appreciate this particular type of decoration—on any level! I would often make excuses for Schmerzie, because I, too, was a sinner, so that we supported each other in this particular vice. . . . He had one of the authentic, beautiful, touching, poignant, and absolutely mad passions for books. He made mine [seem] quite minor.[14]

It was partly on Dwight Kirsch's recommendation that Mabel, in 1952, obtained a part-time position as secretary to Joseph T. Fraser, Jr., director of the Pennsylvania Academy of the Fine Arts. Located at Broad and Cherry streets in downtown Philadelphia, the Gothic Victorian structure, which first opened its doors in 1876, is best known for its superb collection of American artists, including Gilbert Stuart, the Peale family, Thomas Sully, William Rush, Thomas Eakins, Winslow Homer, and Edward Hopper. Mabel's tasks were varied, from answering correspondence and taking dictation to scheduling new exhibitions and writing copy for the accompanying catalogs. "I go there three, sometimes four days a week," she wrote their old friend Dorothy Thomas shortly after taking up her new duties, "and on the whole I enjoy the change from home-work very much. I can work . . . at my own dictation—the job being responsible and self-carried out. I plan my day, which is nice."[15]

Still, it was not as if the center of her universe had shifted in the slightest degree—or ever would:

> Things have gone along well enough for us. If it were not for the state of the world (remember Loren's woeful warnings?) I could put the case more positively, for we have a happy personal life, and are as snug as can be in our apartment.
>
> Loren grows more wonderful all the time, if that is possible. He is too busy and has too many burdens, but never so many that he can't read aloud to me and talk over all the things that interest us both.

As to his writing: "He is poring, now, over an article which he contracted to do, and which cannot be written in any other than a painstaking way: so many facts to be checked—so much care to be exercised in putting them together. Yet he never writes a *dull* article. I marvel!"[16]

Cavalryman Charles Frederick Eiseley, home from the Dakota Territory. *Courtesy of University Museum, University of Pennsylvania*

Charles Frederick Eiseley, American burgher. *Courtesy of Athena Virginia Spaulding*

Anna Barbara Enderly. *Courtesy of Athena Virginia Spaulding*

Clyde Eiseley and his second wife, Effie "Eva" Cearns. *Courtesy of Athena Virginia Spaulding*

Loren's half brother, Leo Eiseley, son of Clyde and Anna. *Courtesy of Athena Virginia Spaulding*

Great-grandmother Permila Shepard, a woman of "homicidal tendencies."
Courtesy of University Museum, University of Pennsylvania

Daisy Corey Eiseley. *Courtesy of University Museum, University of Pennsylvania*

Clyde Edwin Eiseley. *Courtesy of University Museum, University of Pennsylvania*

Loren Corey Eiseley at age three. *Courtesy of Dollie Langdon Hahn*

Uncle Buck—William Buchanan Price. *Courtesy of Nebraska State Historical Society*

Grace Corey Price. *Courtesy of Athena Virginia Spaulding*

Loren's maternal grandparents, Milo and Malvina Corey. *Courtesy of Athena Virginia Spaulding*

Loren, the little patriot. *Courtesy of Athena Virginia Spaulding*

Loren in his early teens. *Courtesy of Dollie Langdon Hahn*

Loren's "Harem." Alice Cave is first on the left, Mabel Langdon third. *Courtesy of Alice Cave*

LEFT: Loren hams it up for the ladies, spring 1932. *Courtesy of Alice Cave*
RIGHT: Loren and his best friend, Jac Cave. *Courtesy of Alice Cave*

“The Old Man,” Frank G. Speck in his favorite garb. *Courtesy of University Museum, University of Pennsylvania*

“The Doc,” Lowry C. Wimberly. *Courtesy of Wilbur Gaffney*

Mabel Langdon, Loren's fiancée. *Courtesy of University Museum, University of Pennsylvania*

Mabel and Loren in the California desert during his recuperation from "incipient tuberculosis." *Courtesy of Athena Virginia Spaulding*

The South Party, left to right: Bert Schultz, Mylan Stout, Emery Blue, Robert Long, Loren Eiseley, Eugene Vanderpool, and Frank Crabill. *Courtesy of C. Bertrand Schultz*

Loren (left) and Joseph Townsend, Jr., photographed from the mouth of Williams Cave in the Guadalupes, summer 1933. *Courtesy of University of Pennsylvania Archives*

A deeply tanned Loren in the main trench at Lindenmeier, summer 1935. *Courtesy of Athena Virginia Spaulding*

Loren and his niece Athena at his graduation (M.A.) from Penn in 1935. *Courtesy of Athena Virginia Spaulding*

Dorothy Thomas, Loren, and Mabel on the day they visited Frieda Lawrence at Kiowa Ranch in 1937. *Courtesy of Dorothy Thomas Buickerood/ Lois Gerard Clemens*

Loren Eiseley, associate professor of anthropology and sociology at the University of Kansas, c. 1943. *Courtesy of University of Kansas Archives*

"There was an eye that seemed torn from a photograph," Loren wrote, "but that looked through me as though it had already raced in vision up to the steep edge of nothingness and absorbed whatever terror lay in that abyss. . . . I knew the eye and the circumstance. It was my mother."
Courtesy of Athena Virginia Spaulding

Mabel Eiseley. *Courtesy of University of Pennsylvania Archives*

Loren in his office at Penn. *Courtesy of University Museum, University of Pennsylvania*

Loren Eiseley by Kappy Wells, Nebraska Hall of Fame, State Capitol, Lincoln. *Courtesy of Morrie Tuttle*

III

Eiseley's style had so captivated Harper editors Fred Allen, Russell Lynes, and Jack Fischer that they were publishing his articles twice a year while pressing him for even more material. "All of the Magazine people liked your piece, 'The Fire Apes,' just as much as I did," Fischer wrote in June 1949. "Although it is a little beyond our normal length, they feel it good enough to use without cutting—or, indeed, without change of any kind."[17]

"Buzby's Petrified Woman," published a few months earlier, had proved an affecting little yarn, which, according to the author's telltale note at the bottom of the title page, "is founded on an actual incident, but somehow has been expanded into what seems to be a sort of story." It begins with a preoccupied Eiseley sitting in the barber's chair of some one-horse town on the edge of the Badlands. The collecting season has been nothing short of a bust: "The institution for which we worked had received a total of one Oligocene turtle and a bag of rhinoceros bones. A rag picker could have done better. The luck had to change. Somewhere there had to be fossils."

His troubled reverie is suddenly interrupted by a voice coming from a back corner of the shop. "It's petrified! It's petrified I'm a-tellin' ya, a petrified woman, right out in that canyon! But he won't show it, not to nobody." Knowing full well that flesh does not turn to mineral as do wood and bone, the anthropologist is intrigued in spite of himself, for one could never tell what might turn up in the backcountry. Besides, "Old Man Buzby," its owner, "wasn't a feller to say it if it 'twern't so."

Eiseley writes down directions and asks Mack, a pseudonym for Emery Blue, to ride along. They drive for the better part of a day before the dirt road plays out, forcing them to proceed on foot into the overhang of hills surrounding Buzby's little tar-papered shack. Out the grizzled bachelor comes, forewarned by a pack of gaunt hounds, an air of faded dignity about him. Small and neat, he wears pince-nez spectacles behind which the horizon seems to linger in his deep gray eyes.

After engaging in some small talk and viewing Buzby's impressive collection of arrowheads, Eiseley and Mack finally broach the matter of the stone woman, hastening to add that it might be of great value to science. Their host becomes strangely silent and then, after a long interval, invites them to camp overnight in the yard. He will show them what they have come for in the morning, provided they promise to say nothing of its whereabouts on returning to town.

After daybreak, following a long and difficult scramble over boulder-strewn ridges, they find themselves standing next to Buzby at a niche under the wall of a canyon. He has removed his hat reverently and for a moment is oblivious to anything but the large object before them. It is just as Eiseley had suspected after seeing the ceaseless wind at work in those untold miles of scarred terrain. "There were some bumps in the right places, and a few marks that might be the face, if your imagination was strong." Suddenly Buzby breaks the silence with a heartrending plaint: "She—she's beautiful, isn't she?"

Getting redder by the moment as he looks sidelong at his no less embarrassed companion, Eiseley lies rather than destroy a lonely man's dream. "Mr. Buzby, that figure is astonishing. We must have it in the Museum." While the old man walks over to caress his mute goddess once more, Eiseley whispers to Mack, "It's okay. We won't have to pry the thing out. He'll never give her up."

Then, in an ironic twist worthy of O. Henry, Buzby sits down on a rock. "I think you're right," he blurts. "It's selfish of me. She'll be safer with you." Two days later an exhausted Eiseley and Mack are headed east by truck, the three-hundred-pound stone "woman" in the bed behind them. Mack pulls up beside the abutment of a bridge spanning a river gorge. "I took one end, and we heaved together. It's a long drop into the big Piney. I didn't look, but I heard it break on the stones."[18]

Emery, who participated in the incident that eventually gave rise to this article, did not remember it in "quite the same way" as his former tent mate. It was during the depths of the depression, and the two had stopped off to visit with the struggling owner of a freak show. Somehow, the man had obtained the mummy of an Indian child, which he believed to be very ancient and worth a considerable amount of money. "It wasn't our business to tell him that he was wrong," Emery reflected. "We simply heard him out and then moved on."[19]

Slowly the fan letters began to trickle in. A struggling California writer named Ray Bradbury, who was a year away from publishing a book called *The Martian Chronicles*, wrote both Harper and Eiseley. The young master of science fiction was especially drawn to "The Fire Apes" and "Buzby's Petrified Woman," the latter of which he later included in his anthology *The Circus of Dr. Lao and Other Improbable Stories*. As the title of the volume suggests, Bradbury recognized a fellow storyteller when he saw one. A science-fiction addict himself, Eiseley was deeply flattered by the attention. "I am discovering by degrees," he wrote Bradbury in October 1949, "that purely technical writing no longer satisfies me, and I am deriving a good deal of enjoyment from some of these recent endeavors. A reaction such as yours tempts me to steal a little more time for some arm chair wondering about the universe."[20]

As matters now stood, Eiseley was up to something more concrete than simply "arm chair wondering." In 1948 he had struck an unwritten agreement with Harper and Brothers to publish a book of his essays. "*Manhunt* is a much better title than any we had thought of," Jack Fischer wrote him in July. "Our enthusiasm for the book continues to rise, and I look forward to seeing the articles we discussed whenever you are ready to send them along."[21]

Nearly a year passed before Eiseley submitted a tentative outline. Finally, in August 1950, Fischer decided to broach the matter again. "We're now beginning to pull together our list for the spring of 1951, and if there is even an outside chance that your manuscript might be finished by, say, October 1, we'd like to reserve a place for it on our schedule." Obviously aware of his author's touchy disposition, the editor in chief apologized for making "a nuisance" of himself and hastened to add: "You will understand, I am sure, that I am not trying to hurry you. From our standpoint the book will be just as good in 1952 or 1953."[22]

Fischer's kid-glove approach elicited a polite but noncommittal reply, which later caused the editor to feel that he had given away too much. Eiseley responded, "I wish I could say that the end is in sight; it isn't, but I think I have made some progress. In the meantime I am glad that you understand so well that the kind of book I hope to do cannot be rushed."[23] While Harper continued to publish Eiseley's essays at a steady pace, little, if anything, was heard of the proposed book for another two years. In December 1952 Eiseley informed Fischer that he hoped to have a first draft ready by the end of the coming summer, if not sooner. He also noted that the work had taken a "philosophical twist," causing him great difficulties in terms of its organization. While much remained to be done, he had hit upon "a good scheme. It will demand, however, a much different title than our old one, *Manhunt.* I am inclined to favor '*The Great Deeps*,' " which was inspired by a quotation from St. Augustine: "Man himself . . . is a great deep."[24]

With publication now scheduled for early 1954, Fischer gave Eiseley another seven months to deliver the first three chapters, plus a synopsis of the remainder. In the meantime, an article titled "Is Man Alone in Space?" was rejected by the magazine division because of its length and complexity. The "magnificent piece," in the words of editor Fred Allen, would be "better as a chapter of your book." When Eiseley then appealed the decision to Fischer, he was told much the same thing.[25] In truth, Fischer had become dubious about Eiseley's ability to do what he had been promising for almost five years. While there was no question that he was a gifted essayist with a unique angle of vision, he seemed incapable of producing anything longer than fifteen pages. Yet Fischer wasn't even asking for this much, which doubtless explains why he hesitated to give up on his potential Thoreau. All he wanted Eiseley to do was forge his published material into a coherent whole.

Author and editor met at the latter's East Thirty-third Street office in early July 1953 to take up the question of the book's form once more. Determined to move beyond the status quo, Fischer took extensive notes based on their long, often discursive conversation. He later drew up a comprehensive outline composed of five sections and thirteen chapters, going so far as to suggest how each of the sections could be linked with the addition of a few transitional paragraphs.

To Fischer, the chief value of the book was its poetic and philosophical content. "It is one of the very few works in recent years which moves in the borderland between science, religion, philosophy, and poetry; this is terrain of the first importance, but it is difficult country and the reader needs to be led into it slowly and carefully." His proposal had the advantage of beginning with chapters that "can be made to appear fairly matter-of-fact, with the poetic and philosophical content increasing gradually as the book progresses. In that fashion we not only will avoid frightening the reader off with strange abstractions before he is prepared for them; we also ought to attain a greater degree of dramatic climax." Finally, the editor apologized if he had given Eiseley the wrong impression during their meeting. "I concentrated largely on the things which seemed to need fixing. . . . Perhaps I assumed too readily that you were aware of my enthusiasm."[26]

It so happened that Fischer's plea for movement coincided with the publication of "Is Man Alone in Space?" in the July issue of *Scientific American.* At the same time "The Flow of the River," a second Eiseley article recently turned down by Harper, was taken by *The American Scholar.* Whether, as Fischer hoped, Eiseley was aware of his enthusiasm does not seem to have mattered, for the Harper editor was to hear little from him concerning the book for another three years.

IV

The tools of Eiseley's trade were among the simplest a writer could ask for—a fountain pen, a bottle of black ink, a yellow legal pad of the extra long variety. He wrote on one side of the page only, often without pausing to indent for paragraphs, which were later marked by the insertion of the proofreader's symbol. His outlines usually consisted of nothing more than a short list of words jotted in the left-hand margin, a habit acquired during his student days when timed examinations dictated an economy of style. He spent considerable time revising rough drafts, for cancellations and insertions are a commonplace on almost every page; entire paragraphs were sometimes crossed out in disgust before being recast. When he was reasonably satisfied with the result, Mabel typed a second draft, which he reedited before having her type it a final time.

In a desultory fashion, he clipped newspaper articles and kept a variety of notebooks in which he jotted down the random insights that later became the basis of a lecture, an essay, or a poem:

> father and the rabbits, mother's paranoid aversion to pets, yet her objection to cruelty to horses, while at the same time her conduct was one long persecution of father.

> I was at the sea once—flat at Long Beach, Calif. It was not till the New England coast (harsh) that I recognized it.
>
> Lincoln contains my dead, the places where I wandered as a boy but its people are alien and aloof strangers to me. Once I thought of burial there but I shall not return—not there—the savor has gone from the salt.
>
> A good essay could also be written on animals living in holes, etc., and the dangers of going out into the world.[27]

Unlike many writers who can function only in isolation, Eiseley needed to have Mabel close at hand. "You probably remember his predilection for working on the dining room table," she wrote Dorothy Thomas in 1954, "the little 'do not disturb' piles of paper and books that he must use. . . . [I] sometimes picture the comfort that a small home might give us. One room will have to belong to the books and workshop."[28] Yet she knew that something fundamental would be lost if they were to make such a move. "I have learned . . . that it is much more important to hear all that Loren wants to tell me, and I sit while he reads aloud or wants a feeling of having things shared, than it is to go and rearrange a bureau drawer that might offend some irrelevant busy body, should that mythical person be on a tour of inspection."[29]

A certain amount of his writing was also done during sleepless hours in hotel rooms when Eiseley was on the road. The cost of meals and taxi fares occasionally crops up in the margins of an essay; stationery from establishments such as New York City's Barbizon Plaza, Indianapolis's Marriott, and Huntsville, Alabama's Red Roof Motor Inn substituted for the legal pad forgotten during the rush of packing.

Eiseley often thought better on his feet than when seated at a table or behind his desk. When Marguerite Lewis, a friend from Lincoln, visited the couple's apartment in the midfifties, she was shown the great circle he had worn in the carpet from miles of pacing. Mabel then summoned Loren from his study, and he proudly demonstrated his peripatetic ways, much to the delight of the admiring ladies.[30]

For Eiseley the ultimate test of word, sentence, and paragraph was not how they appeared on the printed page but how they played upon the ear. He once complained bitterly to a publisher about a fairly minor editorial change that offended his aural sensibilities: if the "barbaric, jangling awkwardness" was not rectified by restoring the original wording, he would have little choice but to demand that the manuscript be returned.[31] Not surprisingly, these are the very terms he used to describe his mother's abrasive voice. As a child Loren must have talked to himself all the time, while the spoken word took on totemic associations. As a grown man he was slow of tongue and had a farmer's long silences. Besides, he was a poet, and poets always read their works aloud. Although Mabel no longer sat at his feet as Dorothy remembered her doing in the old brownstone days in New York, she was never so busy that she couldn't be persuaded to "drop everything" to discuss an idea, or listen to a sentence fresh from Loren's pen.[32] It also pleased her to know that he was auditioning most of the pieces for Wright Morris in advance of sending them off to various publishers. And there was no question in Wright's mind that everything Schmerzie was composing had been turned on an orator's lathe.[33]

When they weren't reading to each other or ransacking the local bookstores, the two writers spent hours speculating about possible titles for their latest works. "It was one of our indoor substitutes for double-crosstics and charades," Wright mused. In fact, this activity became such an obsession that Wright once got his friend on the phone at two in the morning and said, "Listen to this one." There was a pause of several seconds before Eiseley finally replied, "It sounds good, but how about if I let you know after I wake up?"[34]

Eiseley inclined toward what Wright referred to as the "comprehensive metaphysical title": "He wanted to get that type exactly appropriate to his nature—something that would include everything and still have the poetic resonance. I would be sympathetic with that, but I would also be sensitive to the element of sentiment in it [which] I was a little bit suspicious of. . . . Both of us might go over a bit on one aspect or another, whatever it [was] we were attempting to state."[35] The surviving manuscripts bear out Wright's reflections. "The Snout," which appeared in the September 1950 issue of *Harper's*, had undergone at least nine title changes, and "The Flow of the River," published by *The American Scholar* in 1953, had been variously titled "Men, Snowflakes and Green Leaves," "I Remember My Green Extensions," and "The Shape of Water."[36] It is a tribute to Eiseley's sense of aesthetics that, almost invariably, the evolutionary process was for the better.

V

In 1951 Eiseley received the first in what became a series of ritualistic letters from Carl Wittke: "You have been recommended for the deanship of the Graduate School of the University of Colorado. I know nothing about the job, salary, or whether you would or should be interested if approached. All I say is that you have two strong supporters in Wilkins [Oberlin's retired president] & Wittke—if the boys at Colorado decide to move the leading primate from Philly to the West."[37]

Two months later, Eiseley was invited by Colorado's search committee to submit a formal letter of application. He complied with the request and sent a copy to his former dean. Wittke termed it an "admirable reply" but then ticked off all the reasons Eiseley should stay put. "Frankly, I doubt whether Colorado could offer you enough inducements . . . and you might become burdened with all kinds of administrative work which would irk you more than what you have to do now in Philadelphia." Why, then, had Wittke gone to the trouble of nominating his friend in the first place? Part of the answer is to be found in his closing paragraph, which says much about the historian's grasp of Eiseley's emotional makeup: "If nothing else comes of it, it is at least psychologically satisfying to be considered, not that you need it particularly in view of the many fine recognitions you get every year." He also congratulated Eiseley for receiving an invitation to teach at Harvard during the summer of 1952: "It brings Lillian's [Wittke's wife] prediction that you will eventually land there one step nearer."[38]

Eiseley played out the game by visiting Colorado. He reported in full on every detail once again, then waited for Wittke's final word on the subject, which was not long in coming. "My snap judgment is that you should not make the change. I know you have reasons to feel irked, . . . but so far you have won every battle, however bloody it may have been, and you have at least an even chance of keeping matters . . . under control."[39] Like a high-school beauty queen courted by many suitors, Eiseley was happy just to be asked, if only to refuse. He soon withdrew his name from further consideration and proceeded to wait for other offers, his proud father figure beaming in the background.

The appeal of his writing was such that the *Harper's* articles were being selected for college anthologies, for pocket books, and for reprinting in popular magazines like *Reader's Digest.* They had also won an enthusiastic following among the editors of certain New York publishing houses, several of whom attempted to woo Eiseley to their colophons. Ken McCormick, editor in chief of Doubleday and Company, was among the first. Writing from his Rockefeller Center office in July 1950, he praised "The Fire Apes," adding, "If you care to consider us as a publisher for a book of yours, we would be honored to discuss the matter with you."[40] In March 1953 an excited E. P. Swenson, senior editor at W. W. Norton and Company, wired Eiseley from New York: "Just read current Harper's article ["Little Men and Flying Saucers"] and congratulations too mild a word. If not already committed would be surprised but delighted to have chance to publish book by you will phone Wednesday."[41] Doubleday was also after him again, this time via a different editor. "Your articles in *Harper's* are so interesting," a young Jason Epstein wrote, "that I wonder if you won't consider publishing a book based on the same kind of material."[42] Finally, Kenneth Heuer, an editor of juvenile books at Viking Press, issued a similar appeal. But instead of citing Eiseley's work in *Harper's*, he praised a recent piece in *Scientific American*, "Man the Fire-Maker." "I would be very interested in seeing any of your work or talking to you about a projected book for high school age and up."[43] Though highly flattered by the attention, Eiseley declined all offers, citing his long-standing commitment to Harper and Brothers, as well as the heavy pressure of his administrative duties. Still, he promised to keep each of the publishers in mind, for one could never tell what "tricks" he might be up to in the future.

In addition to his other admirers, the author was being pursued by Hiram Haydn, a balding, somewhat melancholy-looking man with the elongated face and bearing of a Greek philosopher. The author of five novels, Haydn had received his Ph.D. from Columbia in 1942, specializing in seventeenth-century English literature. He then became editor of *The American Scholar*, the literary quarterly of Phi Beta Kappa, and was also editor in chief at Random House when Eiseley's essays first came to his attention. Two years had passed since Eiseley had made his initial appearance in the *Scholar*'s pages. After much cajoling, Haydn persuaded him to submit a second essay, "The Judgment of the Birds," in December 1955. Set among the towering pines and delicate ferns of some nameless mountain slope, it tells the moving story of an encounter with death in the wild.[44] The editor of William Styron, Wright Morris, William Faulkner, and Kenneth Keniston called the essay "the most beautiful piece of writing I have read in several years." Indeed, Haydn labeled it "a marvel." "What in the name of God do you mean 'I fear it may not suit'?"[45]

The essay led Haydn to raise an issue he had broached a time or two in their previous correspondence. "If I could dream up a book subject that would appeal to you, would you have any objection, if Harper's did not, to at least securing a release to do one book for us at Random House?" Not that Haydn, who had a reputation for absolute honesty, was interested in playing the part of the raider: "if you have a more or less permanent and contented relationship with as good a house as Harper's, I'll say nothing more."[46] Eiseley responded with a handwritten note on December 23, calling Haydn's reception "heart-warming" and "a most pleasant prelude to Christmas."[47] Although he could promise nothing at the moment, he saw no harm in their getting together for a friendly chat once the holidays had passed.

The meeting took place in the Madison Avenue offices of Random House early in the new year. Haydn later admitted to Eiseley that he had looked him over pretty carefully: "I still can't detect what it is about you that accounts for the magic of your writing. You seem to me to be a very decent and intelligent gentleman, but you didn't look a bit like Mozart and you didn't have a strange-shaped head, so I'll be damned if I understand it."[48] There were some other things about the author that Haydn found less appealing. These he kept mostly to himself until the posthumous publication of his autobiography, *Words and Faces*, many years later: "At our first meeting I was surprised at his heavy lugubrious manner, amazed at his circumlocutions. The master of that supple lyrical prose. In retrospect I find less to wonder at. The inner man of books and the outer one of social exchanges often do not resemble each other."[49] It would be some time before Haydn heard of Eiseley's nickname Schmerzie—or of another friend's less kind comparison to A. A. Milne's Eeyore the donkey.

The publication of "The Judgment of the Birds" resulted in what Haydn termed "a veritable waterfall of praise." No other article published during his twelve years at the *Scholar*'s helm had generated such unabashed enthusiasm. "You are rapidly reducing me to the status of an abject fan, a sort of bobby soxer. . . . Don't forget that when you finally write the book in this manner you have promised me first chance."[50]

So he had. Eiseley wrote to Jack Fischer in July to inform him of his decision. Since Harper's had turned down "The Judgment of the Birds" and had expressed no interest in publishing the other essays as they stood, it seemed a good time to part company as friends. Gracious to the end, Fischer agreed, yet left the door open on the off chance that Eiseley might change his mind. The editor concluded the final letter of their decade-long association by wishing Eiseley a pleasant summer, then added, "I hope that your family illnesses are now finally at an end."[51]

VI

Eiseley's first letter to Haydn about the book has a familiar ring. He suggests that the volume be called "The Great Deeps" and that the title page carry the appropriate quotation from St. Augustine.[52] He hoped that the manuscript, which he planned to have ready by mid-September, could be scheduled for publication in the spring of 1957.

Haydn returned to New York from a five-week vacation at his summer home on Martha's Vineyard to find Eiseley's manuscript waiting on his desk. He wrote a brief acknowledgment and promised a quick reading, but obviously anticipated no difficulties. "I'll be damned if I can remember what I told you you might hope for as an advance. Do remind me promptly for that would be a part of my conversation with the partner."[53] Eiseley replied that the amount discussed was one thousand dollars, with the possibility of another five hundred dollars in the event sales should exceed 3,500 copies. He was also toying with the idea of changing the title to "Bones and Searches" on the ground that it seemed "less pretentious."[54]

Things were going so nicely that Haydn sent a memo to the sales department on October 8, telling them to add "The Great Deeps" to the spring list. He, too, was unsettled about the title and asked for some feedback on three alternatives: "The Dark Side of the Planet," "The Crack in the Absolute," and "The Night Tide." In the meantime, he returned the manuscript to Eiseley for a bit of reworking and ordered the contracts department to proceed. The standard document was ready for the author's signature on October 12. It called for a manuscript of approximately 75,000 words, to be delivered not later than November 15. The straight advance of $1,250 was payable on demand. However, after consulting with Mabel, who handled the finances, Eiseley requested that it be held until the first of the year for income tax purposes. Colleague Ward Goodenough served as Eiseley's witness. "The Great Deeps" had yielded to "The Crack in the Absolute," which both author and editor thought an excellent compromise.[55]

Eiseley personally delivered the seventeen-chapter manuscript to Haydn's office on November 13, two days ahead of his contractual deadline. Because of recent "scientific changes," he had been forced to revise certain of the earlier articles, such as "The Fire Apes." The question of the title nagged him once more. Two weeks later, while scanning the autobiographical *Journal* of the Swiss professor and critic Henri Frédéric Amiel, he found exactly what he was looking for: "It is as though the humanity of our day had, like the migratory birds, an immense journey to make across space." Eiseley's only regret was that "The Immense Journey" would have been a perfect title for his own autobiography, which was yet to be written.[56]

Besides characterizing Eiseley as a lonely and diffident man who trusted and was comfortable with few, Haydn found him "very raw to the touch."[57] On several occasions Eiseley threatened to tear up his contract because one of Random House's employees had not shown him sufficient deference. The first such incident had occurred in early December 1956, when Eiseley returned to New York for what he hoped would be the final powwow on the manuscript. Someone in the permissions department approached him about obtaining a release so that one of his articles could be published in the Soviet Union by the United States Information Agency. Eiseley was in a foul mood and apparently sent the questioner scurrying. He wrote Haydn the following day in an attempt to explain himself. Not wishing either Mabel or his secretary to see what he was up to, he sent the original draft in his own hand and made no copy.

> I recognize that if you people have to have something more to protect yourselves . . . then it is my duty to get it . . . and I guess, perhaps through a morning devoted to other trying problems, that I had, without realizing it, got very close to the proverbial last straw. In some totally undefinable way, I found myself, going home on the train, shaking with the attempt to control an over stimu-

> lated endocrine system—suppressed rage that had flowered up out of nowhere over an incident of no importance except that it related to long intolerable strains throughout the last few months. . . . This case history may help you to know what goes on in the minds of rumpled authors trudging up these ecclesiastical stairs and being subdued and quiet little boys.[58]

In childhood Eiseley had been shamed into suppressing his emotions by a father who kept reminding him, "Your mother's not responsible for her actions." After Clyde passed from the scene, the Victorian man-child adopted an unending line of sympathetic surrogates, each of whom provided the constant reassurance he craved. When Haydn's indulgent reply—"Believe me, how well I understand your letter"[59]—contained all the right cues, Eiseley realized that he had found yet another. A second letter from his hand, elaborating on his personal woes, followed in short order.

> It had been a bad day before I reached you—one of those days in which all the accumulated bad luck of a year or more hits you in the space of a few hours. Problems involving the projected trip abroad, personal problems still looming ominously in connection with the hospitalized elderly relatives in the West, an ear infection which was troubling me—Lord, why go on? . . . It was just the wrong time—and I knew it afterward. No one can help that. I think we are about the same age, so you will know what I mean when I say that somewhere in here one begins to ask a lot of questions as one looks out a New York window at nightfall—and the answers are apt to be unpleasant or very few.

Indeed, at forty-nine, the two were exactly the same age, but the energetic Haydn had humored his friend by stating that he, too, often felt like an old man. "We can't have you reaching 75 so soon," Eiseley joked, "there's a great dearth of sensible people. And characters like me depend upon them to stay afloat."[60] With that the die was cast. "Little by little," Haydn reflected, "I . . . came to feel a strong sympathy for him. Eventually I realized that I shared more of his vulnerabilities than I wanted to believe."[61]

The worst was yet to come. Haydn had turned the manuscript over to Robert Linscott, "one of the best editors in the business," for a fresh reading. To begin with, Linscott felt that certain chapters were repetitious and should be cut. He next put his finger on the very problem that Jack Fischer had never been able to resolve. "I think it would make a better book if each of the four sections had . . . something to bind them together so [it] wouldn't seem so much a collection of separate essays on a rather vague theme." Finally, Linscott singled out flaws in several of the individual pieces. "The Places Below": "I'd omit this one. . . . I'm bothered by the imprecision and vagueness." "The Reaching Out": "I don't understand the incident of the 'Great Voyage.' He couldn't swim, yet he appears to have swum or floated down a river." "The Fire Apes": "The last two paragraphs are an example of how the author succumbs to the temptation of going anthropomorphic. It's cute but is it science?" It was after midnight when Linscott drafted his final paragraph, which, in the long run, would prove more telling than the rest of his observations combined: "As you see I've been much too literal, probably because, in a semi-scientific book, I anticipate more facts and fewer fancies—and passed quite over its good qualities. Disregard everything I've said; publish just as is, and you'll still have a book that quickens the imagination."[62]

Somewhat shaken by his colleague's analysis, Haydn postponed his next meeting with the author until another editor, Robert D. Loomis, could review the manuscript. Loomis's critique, which ran to four single-spaced pages, reached Haydn's desk in mid-January 1957. And like everyone else who had read the manuscript, Loomis was troubled by the absence of linkage, by the author's constant flip-flop between the roles of detached observer and emotional participant. "The book has a pattern, but it is a loose one, and there is bound to be some confusion and disappointment to the reader if he tries to read the book through as a book." He went on to suggest some drastic cutting and restructuring, advice that Haydn, who dubbed Loomis "the solid, reliable one," took to heart. Yet by the time Loomis had finished, he also realized that the work was equal to something more than the sum of its parts. "I think the author's real value is in his ability to make us aware, to shake up our egotistic complacency, of the unfathomable mystery of life and the wonder of the world."[63]

Eiseley met Haydn at the information desk in the main hall of Philadelphia's 30th Street Station on the morning of January 28. Together they returned to Wynnewood for an all-day session on the manuscript. The next morning, Mabel took a nasty fall on some ice outside the apartment door, injuring her left elbow and thigh. The X rays proved negative, but the pain was such that her doctor had to prescribe a sedative to enable her to sleep. Eiseley passed the next few nights anxiously watching over her while nursing his own psychic wounds. Taking pen in hand at 4:00 A.M., he drafted the longest of his surviving letters.

Claiming that he had no wish to burden Haydn with his personal troubles, he nevertheless filled three legal pages with a recital of them before coming to what he termed "*the* point":

> Individually I feel . . . a little befuddled that after some 25 years in this subject of evolution a house editor has to set me to rights about "other species of man," or to find that certain essays labelled "silly," "melodramatic," "ludicrous," are precisely ones which have been repeatedly requested for anthologies by staid English professors; this, however, does not lessen my now clear conviction that when two editors in a good house want to go out and retch in the street after reading the stuff that this ought to be enough. . . . If they want a "scientific" book in the usual sense—Fred Hoyle, John Pfeifer, etc. they know where to find these men. I even suggest they may like to see how scientific I can get when I choose to practice my profession!

What was the use of going on? The book had been removed from the spring list so that it could be quietly released in August, while people were on vacation, or projected into some "nebulous future" after Christmas. Therefore, Eiseley suggested that they tear up the contract. "Outside a little embarrassment, which I can easily survive, no harm has been done." He owed Haydn a great debt for allowing him to see that essays are on one side of the fence, science "forever" on the other. For too long he had been leading a divided life, reading and writing literary material when he should have kept to the bone trade. "Though it is late, I am strongly impelled to go back."[64]

VII

Having flexed his emotional muscle, Eiseley waited for a response from New York. Haydn telephoned immediately upon receiving the letter and tried to calm his friend down. He then let a few days go by before writing a brief note. The dark cloud had lifted by the time Eiseley, who was out of town when the letter arrived, penned a reply. Mabel's condition had improved to the point where she was about to return to work. Now that the ordeal was over, he was willing to give the manuscript one more try.

At Eiseley's insistence, the two agreed on a new deadline of March 1. Loath though he was to do it, the author abandoned the notion of sections and began jettisoning the chapters that had given both Linscott and Loomis the most trouble: "Big Eyes and Small Eyes," "The Places Below," "Toads and Men," "The Fire Apes," "The Serpent and the Bird," "Man Alone," and "The Brown Wasps." "The result, except for the three ending essays, will be less personal, more scientific but probably a little closer to what you want." The advance check had also arrived during his absence, but he would wait to hear from Haydn that "all is satisfactory" before cashing it. Moreover, he feared he might not make the deadline, "in which case I will assume the deal is off."[65]

The beleaguered editor in chief, who had displayed extraordinary patience for one not blessed with that virtue, now vented some frustrations on his own:

> Just let me say that I do wish you would stop talking about holding the check and—if I am not content with the new version—calling the whole deal off. Honest to goodness, Loren, how many times do I have to tell you that it's your book . . . and that as things stand now I'll take whatever you decide is the form you want it published in? . . . I am perfectly willing to go along with your intent of having it finished by March, but it just isn't rational to say, "Either this—or nothing." Please calm down, chief, and apply yourself with minimal serenity.
>
> P.S. I don't sound so damned serene to myself for that matter—rereading this."[66]

Eiseley met his self-imposed deadline by hand-delivering the manuscript on February 28. Haydn was not in his office, having been laid low by chronic sinusitis. The repentant author wrote to thank him for his patience under "what I know must have been great provocation." Mabel joined him in wishing Haydn well. "We have gone through so much of this kind of thing together and know so much of what it can mean in the way of worry—financially and otherwise—that we sincerely hope our hypochondriacal tendencies misread a cold or similar indisposition into something more serious. For God's sake take care of yourself." Haydn had heard Eiseley's "last snarl." It was to be "the quiet life" from now on. "About the book: If Random House should take it . . ."[67]

"Loren," the recovering editor shot back, "if you ever say to me again, 'If Random House should take the book!' "[68]

Because he was having "the devil's own time" characterizing the book in a single sentence, Haydn asked Eiseley to write his own jacket line. Eiseley responded with "In bone pits and through the night skies a solitary naturalist contemplates the eternal mystery behind man and nature." He explained that he had "deliberately avoided the word 'anthropologist' because so much of the book is not anthropological."[69] Haydn thanked him for trying but finally rejected the effort on the ground that the tone was too elegiac. After hearing nothing from Eiseley for almost a month, he wrote to apologize if he had inadvertently upset him.[70]

Haydn was not the only one having trouble describing the book. Hoping to obtain a quote for the dust jacket, he sent an advance copy to Marston Bates, a wiry University of Michigan zoologist who was known for serving his guests insect hors d'oeuvres with an anticipatory smile. "Sorry I can't think of anything neat or pointed to say," Bates wrote back; "if you want, I'll try again."[71] Wright Morris, who also heard from Haydn, had done little better: "A lot of feathered, as well as unfeathered friends, are going to like this book."[72] Haydn thanked the author but politely rejected the quote, citing the limitation of space as his reason. Paul Sears, who had since moved to Yale, was also unable to help, for his review copy arrived just as he was leaving on a trip. A desperate Patricia Rose, Random House's director of publicity, dashed down to the third floor and whisked Morris's reply from Haydn's desk for incorporation into the jacket after all.[73]

There were some good signs as well. Virginia Kirkus, founder of the prepublication review service for booksellers, called Rose to express her admiration for "a beautiful piece of writing." Her review of *The Immense Journey*, which arrived a week later, ended on a high note: "A book for grave pleasure, for contemplative and stimulating enjoyment, this is also happy in its elegance of style, and its underlying philosophy which denies materialism."[74] John Barkham, head of the popular syndicated service bearing his name, wrote to say that he hadn't been able to put it down—"and I mean that literally." "I wish I could convey the wealth of originality in this fascinating book," he wrote in the accompanying review. "It is a springboard for the reader's imagination: each page cries out to be quoted. . . . In my library it stands side by side with the great English naturalists."[75]

Dreading the moment of truth nonetheless, Eiseley was fast succumbing to an advanced case of publication jitters. He was especially worried about an old academic rivalry with a disappointed candidate for his job. "I am told," he wrote Haydn, "[that he] reviews a great deal for the *Times*."[76] Although he mentioned no names in writing, the person he had in mind was the widely read anthropologist Ashley Montagu. Bill Asling, who occasionally saw Eiseley at conventions after both had departed Kansas, remembered a conversation during which he spoke of Montagu's "anger" at him for seeking the chairmanship at Penn, a position Montagu, who was then teaching at Philadelphia's Hahnemann Medical College, also coveted.[77] Time, rather than healing this old wound, had only deepened it, for Eiseley's periodic reviews of Montagu's books were mostly of the negative variety. Now that the shoe was in danger of being placed on the other foot, Eiseley was hopeful that Haydn could do something, anything, to protect him: "I am simply anxious . . . that we are not handicapped by the sort of event which I have seen happen to colleagues whose work, by the happy accidents of book reviewing, has been handed over to their bitterest personal rival. Later on . . . [it] may not matter so much—for a first book I think it may, particularly in an organ like the *Times*."[78]

In spite of the enthusiasm shown by the early reviewers, Hiram Haydn was a deeply frustrated editor. He had ordered a first printing of five thousand copies and set the price at $3.50. Yet he could not persuade the powers at Random House, including its cherubic publisher, Bennett Cerf, that it would find an audience of any size. When Haydn's turn came to speak for the book at the summer sales conference, he launched into an impassioned presentation, only to be interrupted by Lew Miller, whom Haydn described as the most elegant sales manager he had ever known. Miller agreed that it was a fine work, indeed the best-written offering on the fall list, but predicted it would not sell for that very reason. "I jumped up again," Haydn recounted in his autobiography, "saying that there were some books, wonderfully written, that had unusual appeal and these transcended the formulae for best sellers."[79]

The advance orders of some one thousand copies at publication seemed to bear Miller out; the advertising budget was next to nonexistent. And despite Haydn's repeated pleas, neither Orville Prescott of the *Times* nor John K. Hutchens of the *Tribune* would agree to review it. On August 6, only three weeks before publication, Haydn sent a letter to Eiseley that barely concealed the fact that his hopes were flagging: "We have now firmly established in our own minds that . . . this is not likely a big seller"; however, the long-suffering editor in chief added, "it is a dark horse and must be watched carefully."[80]

15

THE GREATEST VICTIM OF ALL

I

Although Eiseley made plans to visit Europe on several occasions, he was never to set foot on the Continent. The closest he came was London sometime in late 1951. He remained in England just long enough to complete his business before flying home to Philadelphia and an anxious Mabel, whom he had telephoned every day.[1]

In September 1949 six prominent physical anthropologists had met at the University Club in New York City. Aside from Eiseley, those in attendance included Sherwood Washburn, who had moved from Columbia Medical School to the University of Chicago, and Paul Fejos of the Viking Fund, which was about to be rechristened the Wenner-Gren Foundation, now that the name of its benefactor had been removed from the State Department's blacklist. The six became charter members of the American Institute of Human Paleontology, of which Eiseley was unanimously elected president. According to Secretary Washburn's minutes, there was considerable discussion of the activities the institute might undertake, including the production of plaster casts and photographs for teaching and research.[2]

Eiseley was still president of the institute in November 1951 when an Englishman named Frank Oswell Barlow passed away at age seventy. Though Barlow had long earned his living as a mason, his name was as well known among paleoanthropologists as those of the greats with whom he regularly corresponded: Dart, Weidenreich, Broom, Keith, von Koenigswald, and Leakey. Like his father before him, Barlow was a virtuoso at casting and mounting vertebrate fossils for the British Museum of Natural History. Among his masterpieces is the first plaster rendering of the rara avis *Archaeopteryx*, the Jurassic bird that resembled a winged lizard.

Equally respected as a businessman, Barlow purchased the casting firm of R. F. Damon and Company. Retaining its well-established name, he acquired a virtual monopoly on the reproduction rights of the major fossil specimens from around the globe. A sampling of Damon and Company's last catalog, which was published just before Barlow's death, reads like a Who's Who of the anthropoid world: *Gigantopithecus blacki*, *Pithecanthropus erectus*, Swanscombe skull, *Sinanthropus pekinensis*, the Neanderthal men of Spy, Cro-Magnon man, and *Australopithecus*. Among the more popular offerings at ten pounds was *Eoanthropus dawsoni*, or Piltdown man, which was about to be exposed as a fraud.[3]

At the end of September 1951, a jaundiced and terminally ill Barlow began to settle his affairs. He was most concerned about his business, since no one in the family was interested in carrying on. Barlow dictated a letter of last resort to Eiseley in the hope that the American Institute of Human Paleontology might be interested in taking over. Eiseley, in turn, informed Paul Fejos, who agreed to put up £1,500 of Wenner-Gren Foundation money for the purchase of the casts, and to underwrite the cost of shipping them to the United States.

Shortly afterward Eiseley flew to London, whence he took the train to the Old Parsonage, Barlow's country house in West Sussex. There he viewed the scores of molds that had been stored on the shelves of a stable since 1941, the year their nervous creator removed them from a bomb-riddled London for safekeeping. The experience may have rekindled memories of Hagerty's barn and the little skulls Loren had left atop its dusty rafters. From the windows of the speeding train he glimpsed the moors that he and Bill Gaffney had imagined crossing as young poets hiking the outskirts of Lincoln.

Eiseley described Barlow as a man dying with great "nobility and bearing." He returned home a few days after their brief meeting, melancholy but triumphant. His coup failed to impress Fro Rainey, however, whose heart "sort of sank" when the shipment of casts reached Philadelphia. Fro had reluctantly agreed to reproduce the fossil models in the tomblike workrooms of Penn's University Museum, one of the few places in the country capable of maintaining Barlow's impeccable standards. "I have the feeling," Fro wrote Eiseley in a memorandum dated January 19, 1952, "that no one in your Institute [of Human Paleontology] fully understands the details of our casting operation. We must first make rubber molds which is a new and expensive process. . . . I should not be at all upset if you found some other institution to do it."[4]

Casting began in November 1952. During the next two years receipts from sales of 576 pieces totaled $7,947, while costs were estimated at $4,000.[5] "Obviously it did lots better than I thought," Fro chuckled in retrospect. "Loren was right; I had misgivings but it did pay off," mainly because of the huge growth in anthropology classes at the university level.[6] The museum continued this profitable operation through 1959, when the development of plastic extrusion techniques forced its transfer to a commercial manufacturer.

Along with the casts and business papers of R. F. Damon and Company came Barlow's nearly forty-year correspondence with the most famous and famous-to-be anthropologists in the world, some written from the very places of discovery. "If the pelvis and hind leg turn out to be as I suspect, *Australopithecus*," an ecstatic Robert Broom wrote Barlow from South Africa on November 9, 1936, "my discovery will be the second most important paleontological find of the century—only second in importance to *Sinanthropus* [Peking man]." Broom also sent a drawing of a portion of his female hominid and rhapsodized, like a smitten adolescent, over "her beautiful teeth."[7]

A few months before Broom's communication, a strapped and little known Louis Leakey had written Barlow on a less exalted note: "Can you let me know if there is any money due to me on royalties for casts. I am in urgent need of any money I can get just at the moment." Barlow jotted in the bottom margin, "Sent £6 Sept. 3."[8] By the time this material came into Eiseley's hands, the professional and economic fortunes of Leakey, who sold patent medicines tribe to tribe and ran guns for guerrillas operating against the Italians during World War II, had undergone a considerable change for the better. Having chosen not to go to Africa himself, Eiseley could only measure what he may have lost by reliving vicariously the experiences of other bone hunters.

II

According to Jake Gruber, the lectures his mentor gave in physical anthropology at Oberlin focused more on the history of evolution, with special emphasis on Darwin and his circle. "Even in the seminars at Penn, the same thing."[9] Jake, who chose as his subject St. George Jackson Mivart, F.R.S., was one of only two Ph.D. candidates, both in the history of science, who wrote dissertations under Eiseley's supervision. The remaining seventeen doctoral recipients during Eiseley's twelve years as chairman turned to other department members for guidance, particularly Ward Goodenough, whose fieldwork in such exotic climes as New Guinea, the Gilberts, and the Caroline Islands won the ethnographer an enthusiastic following.[10]

The Barlow materials were just about to arrive in Philadelphia when Eiseley received a prestigious appointment from the American Philosophical Society, an outgrowth of the junto formed by Benjamin Franklin in 1727. The society had recently acquired some 450 letters exchanged between Charles Darwin and Sir Charles Lyell, the gifted geologist whose division of the Tertiary period into the Eocene, Miocene, and Pliocene epochs facilitated the later acceptance of Darwin's theory of evolution. As library research associate, Eiseley purchased books by contemporaries of Darwin on any of the great man's ideas as well as acquired primary source materials in the form of letters or manuscript writings by Darwin and his correspondents. Finally, to commemorate the upcoming centennial of the *Origin of Species* in 1959, the Committee on Library charged him with producing a volume on "the reception of Darwinism in America," the research for which was to be based on the society's own books and papers.[11]

Delighted with his new responsibilities, the haunter of bookstores made countless trips on behalf of the society, sometimes with an enthusiastic Wright Morris in tow. From 1953 to 1954, over nine hundred volumes were added to the collection, along with a number of rare letters from Darwin to his old Cambridge schoolmate John Maurice Herbert.[12] What the society couldn't use Eiseley either carried home or hid in his office to avoid Mabel's detection.

Thanks mainly to Eiseley's seven-year quest, the library of the American Philosophical Society today houses the most complete collection of Darwiniana in America. Missing from its massive oak and metal shelves, however, is the centennial volume Eiseley had agreed to complete in time for publication in 1959. Instead, his enthusiasm had caused him to consent to an even more ambitious undertaking—the editorship of not one volume on Darwin but two. After many months of deliberation, it had been decided that the original theme of Darwin's reception in America should be scrapped. On December 20, 1955, the venerable Dr. George W. Corner, acting president of the society, wrote to inform Eiseley that he had been chosen to serve as general editor of two volumes of selected letters by Darwin and his contemporaries. The manuscript of *The Immense Journey*, or "The Great Deeps" as it was then known, was still far from finished, and Eiseley had committed himself to yet another major work. The recipient of a Wenner-Gren Foundation grant in the amount of four thousand dollars, he had taken a leave of absence with half pay for the academic year 1952–53 to begin research for a book dealing with what Paul Fejos, in his letter of approval, termed the "philosophical implications of human evolution."[13]

To facilitate his work with the society, Eiseley was awarded a grant of $1,800 from the Penrose Fund and given a one-year sabbatical with full pay by Penn, to begin in September 1956. Both awards were made with the explicit understanding that he would travel to England and, if necessary, the Continent in search of more rare books and manuscript collections.[14] He later implied, during a moment of pique, that Haydn's editorial demands had forced him to cancel his London reservations.[15] Haydn, of course, knew better and had cautioned his friend about "excavating possible books you might do . . . for years to come," although the editor admitted that he was hopeful of getting his share.[16] The pressure increased when, in November 1956, Corner informed Eiseley that two or three "elder members" of the society had raised certain questions about the magnitude of the undertaking. Two books at once seemed to them a very large order, raising the prospect that neither volume would be completed in time for the commemoration. Corner had come to Eiseley's defense by assuring his colleagues that all was well: "I told them that you are experienced in such matters and have a record of getting things done."[17]

In response Eiseley presented the Committee on Library with a counterproposal. He would still edit two volumes on Darwin, but only one on the correspondence, and its publication would likely be delayed until sometime after 1959. For the time being, he planned to concentrate on a collection of Darwin's "reprinted papers," which he promised to have ready on schedule. If the idea met with the committee's approval, he would remain in Philadelphia instead of going abroad. A flurry of letters and behind-the-scenes discussions resulted in the vote Eiseley had been hoping for. Apparently satisfied that their colleague would live up to his renewed commitment, the other members of the committee focused their attention on more pressing matters. As it turned out, Eiseley did the same.

Among the editors who had courted his favor was Jason Epstein of Doubleday and Company, who had first written to him in February 1953. Eiseley had thanked Epstein for his interest but cited his previous commitment to Jack Fischer at Harper's. Sometime later, before Haydn entered the picture, Eiseley had agreed to meet with Epstein to discuss the book he was doing on the Darwinian period. He remembered being taken to lunch in a noisy restaurant by the soft-spoken young man. Although four or more years had passed since his alleged loss of hearing, he claimed that he was still recovering from the ordeal.[18] "I pieced together the notion that an unusually well researched book was wanted," he wrote in a largely excised passage of the autobiography. "Looking back, I have to smile. I was dead serious, and I loved the subject. What had been wanted, I now suspect, was really what one might call a competent 'quickie.' " Overwhelmed with the confidence expressed in his abilities, he left New York resolved to do a two-volume work, the first of which would examine the history of evolutionary theory immediately before Darwin and after. The second volume, which he filed away in his mind, would address itself to the twentieth century.[19]

Since little of the prepublication correspondence with Epstein has survived, all that remains is Eiseley's autobiographical account of the struggle. Consummate bibliophile though he was, the Penn professor, who was approaching fifty, had never engaged in a research project requiring years of concentrated effort, nor would he do so again. The old Furness Library, a looming Neo-Gothic bastion of red sandstone topped by menacing gargoyles, was bulging at the seams with books whose covers were laden with the dust of a century. There was no air conditioning or photocopying machine. Eiseley described the lighting as so poor in some sections that the use of a miner's lamp would have been justified. As a fossil hunter, he had often experienced the unrelenting glare of the sun, but there had almost always been plenty of fresh air and a welcome breeze. "I think I have never endured more unpleasant conditions than those in the ancient library stacks . . . My experiences . . . were closer to the subterranean experiences of the Egyptian tomb robbers."[20]

Eiseley's metal files of note cards thickened as his promises to the American Philosophical Society languished, all but forgotten. "The Time Voyagers," as he had tentatively titled the Doubleday work, occupied almost every spare moment "in a way that would have astounded the brisk young editor. I was becoming insubstantial, the present with its publishing schedules a bothersome encumbrance."[21]

So much time had passed since the signing of the contract he felt certain that Epstein and his associates had given up hope of receiving a manuscript, let alone one written to coincide with the centenary of Darwin's masterpiece. Writing, in May 1957, to Haydn about some final changes in *The Immense Journey*, Eiseley added: "I am now in the last throes of my history of evolution book and trying desperately to make a June 1st deadline with it, a task which, I can assure you, is making me very peevish and sleepless."[22] He didn't quite meet the deadline, for on June 14 he wrote Epstein that "I am now one-third of the way through the final chapter and hope to have it completed over the weekend."[23] As was his custom, he hand-delivered the 383-page manuscript to his publisher's Madison Avenue offices a few days later, then proudly informed Haydn that Doubleday would probably be bringing it out about February.[24] "Great God man," the stunned editor in chief replied, ". . . you say that it has been accepted by Doubleday. Why Doubleday? I thought you were writing it for the Philosophical society—whatever it is called—but I didn't realize it was to go to a commercial publisher."[25]

III

None but the most perceptive reader of Eiseley's articles would have noticed the subtle transformation that had taken place on the cover of *The Immense Journey*. Before August 1957, the author had always used his middle initial, C. But from this point onward he would be known simply as Loren Eiseley—all trace of his mother excised from his name. He underscored his hatred of Daisy by dedicating the little work to the memory of Clyde Edwin Eiseley, "who lies in the grass of the prairie frontier but is not forgotten by his son." This retributory act concealed an added measure of revenge, for in a small notebook he had originally jotted: "is not forgotten by his sons."[26]

Publication day for *The Immense Journey*, Monday, August 26, found Eiseley in New York City doing radio broadcasts lined up in advance by Haydn. When sales failed to meet his expectations in the weeks that followed, he called to complain that Random House was not doing enough to promote the book. Haydn did some checking and found that the advertising budget was greater than either of them had thought, about the same as that for a work selling double the copies. "Mr. Cerf felt that we could not, as yet, order any new advertising." The good news concerned sales for the week ending September 15, which came close to two hundred volumes. To further allay Eiseley's suspicions, the editor cum psychiatrist asked him to catch the morning train to New York. "We could have an hour or more with the door shut and the phone off."[27]

In his handwritten reply, Eiseley apologized for being so suspicious but suggested that they meet friend to friend rather than editor to author. As always, he was well aware of the game he was playing yet couldn't break free of the syndrome.

> This is not said in bitterness but only with the full recognition that nothing stinks in a publishing house like a dead author and his book. . . . I see clearly that trying to be literary at my late age is hard on the blood pressure and leaves one about as ludicrously exposed as it is possible to be. Probably the whole thing was nothing but a reflex out of my youth, when I loved literature better than anything else in the world. Perhaps I still do, but if so I can manage to keep it to myself. . . . I will just come at the proper hour and perhaps we can have coffee and talk about the books of other people. This is a silly remark Hiram, but I don't believe I have felt like this since the first time I left home.[28]

Sometime in October the number of weekly orders began picking up; first by fifty, then a hundred, then more than two hundred. In mid-November Haydn wrote to say that a second printing of one thousand copies had been approved. The book had entered "that strange, mystic mid-world where it keeps on insisting that it's very much alive, but doesn't do it in sufficient numbers . . . that we can justify a larger printing as yet." The important thing, as Henry James used to say, "is that she's a 'movin'."[29] Haydn had also heard from British publisher Victor Gollancz. The English edition of *The Immense Journey* was scheduled for release in 1958.

The real turning point came in December, beginning with Dean Acheson's purchase of one thousand copies for Christmas presents. The former secretary of state had carried a volume to his winter retreat in Antigua, where he took turns with Archibald MacLeish reading aloud from it.[30] *Reader's Digest*, which then reached more homes than any other magazine, agreed to reprint one of the essays, and bookstore managers caught short in the holiday rush were frantically telephoning Random House in the hope of obtaining fresh stock. From Lincoln came a voice out of the past. "*The Immense Journey* is a masterpiece," an ailing Lowry Wimberly declared. "I just now finished reading it. I shall read it again. And then again."[31] Closer to home, Catherine Drinker Bowen, the author of such classic biographies as *Yankee from Olympus*, wrote from her residence in Bryn Mawr: "I don't know when I have read a book that put the heart back into me as this one. After all the slop, Norman Vincent Peale and everything so easy and fine if only we pray . . . and the jokes about the little men coming . . . how heartening to have a real writer look right AT it and say, NO!"[32] Deeply gratified, Eiseley had Bowen's letter copied for Haydn. "Naturally," he cautioned in all seriousness, "it is not for publicity."[33]

The week between Christmas and New Year's brought the best news of all. After ignoring Haydn's repeated request that they read the slender volume, John K. Hutchens of the *Herald Tribune* and Orville Prescott of the *Times* ran back-to-back reviews. Hutchens exposed one of the author's deepest fears: "Admirably intent on avoiding the laboratory's chilly jargon, Eiseley goes occasionally to the other extreme with somewhat transcendental daisies like 'the eternal pulse that lifts Himalayas,' and 'the green gloom of the mermaids' kingdom.' " Editors Linscott and Loomis had said as much in their lengthy memos to Haydn, but Hutchens also echoed their separate conclusions: "The heart is certainly in the right place."[34]

Prescott, who waxed even more enthusiastic, took an unprecedented step for a senior staff member of the nation's leading newspaper—he apologized to both author and editor in print. "When [the book] was published last August I was sure that I did not wish to read it, and this in spite of urgent recommendations from discriminating friends who had my best interests at heart. I was wrong and they were right." Not only had Eiseley succeeded in rendering the story of evolution comprehensible to laymen, but his "lyrically beautiful" prose had given Darwin's great insight an indefinable religious quality. "It would be possible to read [the essays] for their content alone and to be quite satisfied with Mr. Eiseley's ability to instruct. But it would be a dull clod indeed who would do so and the experience would be almost (but not quite) like reading Shelley for information about skylarks."[35]

Haydn was dancing a mental jig around his office desk. He scrawled "Amen!" after receiving both reviews, then hastened to reassure his author, "It may be late but it's not posthumous."[36] His spirits on the mend, Eiseley was ready to sit down and discuss two new books that had long been on his mind.

IV

Eiseley's poetry and prose present an odd nostalgia for the glacial ice of the Pleistocene, the skin-clad hunter and swirling blizzards of the snow wolf. His is the myth of the loner gazing down from the mountain slope, of the solitary hiker in the woods, of man against society giving permanent form to Thoreau's dream of turning his back on an impoverished world of polluted skies and teeming cities. Yet the finest of his essays, and the only one singled out by both Hutchens and Prescott, was not a paean to alienation but the lyrical, life-affirming "How Flowers Changed the World." "Even the great evolutionist, Charles Darwin, called [flowers] 'an abominable mystery,' because they appeared so suddenly and spread so fast." Because of the flowers, mammals had survived and were venturing into new domains, staking their claims to lands bereft of the godlike thunder lizards. Something else was also afoot, or at least nearly so:

> On the edge of the forest, a strange, old-fashioned animal still hesitated. His body was the body of a tree dweller, and though tough and knotty by human standards, he was, in terms of that world into which he gazed, a weakling. . . . He had a passion for lifting himself up to see about, in his restless, roving curiosity. He

would run a little stiffly and uncertainly, perhaps, on his hind legs, but only in those rare moments when he ventured out upon the ground. . . .

Apes were to become men, in the inscrutable wisdom of nature, because flowers had produced seeds and fruit in such tremendous quantities that a new and totally different store of energy had become available in concentrated form. . . . His limbs grew longer, he strode more purposefully over the grass. The stolen energy that would take man across the continents would fail him at last. The great Ice Age herds were destined to vanish. When they did so, another hand like the hand that grasped the stone by the river long ago would pluck a handful of grass seed and hold it contemplatively.

In that moment, the golden towers of man, his swarming millions, his turning wheels, the vast learning of his packed libraries, would glimmer dimly there in the ancestor of wheat, a few seeds held in a muddy hand. Without the gift of flowers and the infinite diversity of their fruits, man and bird, if they had continued to exist at all, would be today unrecognizable. Archaeopteryx, the lizard-bird, might still be snapping at beetles on a sequoia limb; man might still be a nocturnal insectivore. The weight of a petal has changed the face of the world and made it ours.[37]

In contrast to "How Flowers Changed the World," which had never before been published, Eiseley's second little masterpiece had been rejected by *Harper's* before Haydn had happily claimed it for *The American Scholar*. Set in the country so familiar to his pioneer grandfather, "The Flow of the River" tells of his solitary encounter with the magic contained in water, the planet's most abundant resource. One afternoon, while combing the banks of the Platte for fossils, Eiseley broke through a willow thicket and stumbled into ankle-deep water. He lay back, his face to the sky, and pushed off. Never mind the fact that he has just informed the reader, not once but twice, that he cannot swim, or that this particular river is "treacherous with holes and quicksands." Like the inexorably flowing waters beneath his outstretched body, the sheer force of the prose carries one away.

For an instant, as I bobbed into the main channel, I had the sensation of sliding down the vast tilted face of the continent. It was then that I felt the cold needles of the alpine springs at my fingertips, and the warmth of the Gulf pulling me southward. Moving

> with me, leaving its taste upon my mouth and spouting under me in dancing springs of sand, was the immense body of the continent itself, flowing like the river was flowing, grain by grain, mountain by mountain, down to the sea. I was streaming over ancient sea beds thrust aloft where giant reptiles had once sported; I was wearing down the face of time and trundling cloud-wreathed ranges into oblivion. I touched my margins with the delicacy of a crayfish's antennae, and felt great fishes glide about their work.

As the ages passed, like so many cottonwoods along the bank, form ultimately yielded to essence.

> I *was* water and the unspeakable alchemies that gestate and take shape in water, the slimy jellies that under the enormous magnification of the sun writhe and whip upward as great barbeled fish mouths, or sink indistinctly back into the murk out of which they arose. Turtle and fish and the pinpoint chirpings of individual frogs are all watery projections, concentrations—as man himself is a concentration—of that indescribable and liquid brew which is compounded in varying proportions of salt and sun and time. It has appearances, but at its heart lies water, and as I was finally edged gently against a sand bar and dropped like any log, I tottered as I rose. I knew once more the body's . . . reluctance to break contact with that mother element which still . . . brings into being nine tenths of everything alive.[38]

His was not, as many would argue, a fundamentally religious experience, nor did Eiseley himself believe it to be. He decried the "small and black and flame-licked" eternity that medieval Christianity had envisioned for the great mass of humanity, as well as the "small and black and . . . venomous" mind that had conceived it.[39] "Behind all religions lies nature," he wrote in one of the notebooks. "It lurked equally behind the burial cults of Neanderthal man, in Cro-Magnon hunting, in the questions of Job and in the answering voice from the whirlwind. In the end, it is the name for man's attempt to define and delimit his world, whether seen or unseen." But the human condition will not be improved by invoking such a doctrine, whether professed by shamans wearing animal skins or high priests clad in ermine-trimmed robes. If man is to find any measure of happiness, "He must dream with the dreaming greatness of the vast multicolored shape of life itself, not of man, nor of serpents, but of that enormous whole that contains them, as it contains a lover and the wandering stars and the enormous freedom to change."[40]

Eiseley rejected the dualism of disparate realms of being—good and evil, material and transcendent, universal and particular—and embraced instead a single, vast order containing all the levels and kinds of existence. At the center of this order is the One, an incomprehensible but all-sufficient unity. It was toward the unknowable One that he had metaphorically drifted on the sparkling river Platte that special afternoon. "I do not think" he wrote in the final paragraph of *The Immense Journey*, "if someone firmly twists the key successfully in the tiniest house of life, that many questions will be answered, or that the dark forces which create light in the deep sea . . . will be much if at all revealed." Rather, "I would say that if 'dead' matter has reared up this curious landscape of fiddling crickets, song sparrows, and wondering men, it must be plain even to the most devoted materialist that the matter of which he speaks contains amazing, if not dreadful powers, and may not impossibly be, as Hardy has suggested, 'but one mask of many worn by the Great Face behind.' "[41]

Wishing to avoid being mistaken for a self-proclaimed seer or mystic, he interrupts the narrative to set his readers straight: "Let it be understood that I am not the sort of man to whom is entrusted direct knowledge of great events and prophecies." At the same time, those who choose to accompany him on his immense journey, both forward and backward, need not look for science in the usual sense. "I have given the record of what one man thought as he pursued research and pressed his hands against the confining walls of [the] scientific method."[42]

The concept of the "balance of nature" was for Eiseley little more than a meaningless abstraction. Although he looked for unity, he also saw in nature an adversary relationship in which the diminutive are ever at the mercy of the aggressive and the powerful, albeit for him it was rarely the fittest that survived. A malevolent raven, a "sleek black monster," is condemned not by a jury of his peers but by the smaller birds of the forest for "murdering" a nestling; a bereaved hawk stands guard all night, then dances ecstatically on the wind when its caged mate is released by a sympathetic human spirit; a quivering mongrel pleads with its eyes to be allowed just one more sunset before it is sacrificed to the gods of science. Hapless creatures acted upon by a greater force. His father, the hoboes of the Great Depression, the prisoners fleeing to perish violently in the snow had been similar victims, but the greatest victim of all was Loren Eiseley.

V

"The Time Voyagers," which was scheduled for release in early 1958, had been retitled *Darwin's Century: Evolution and the Men Who Discovered It*. Eiseley repaid a debt by dedicating the work to Carl Frederick Wittke, "distinguished historian and friend of those whom history has forgotten."[43]

His editor, Jason Epstein, sent a copy of the bound galleys to Sir Gavin De Beer, editor of Darwin's notebooks on the transmutation of species. Eiseley became agitated when the British scholar criticized him for not having devoted enough space to the role of genetics in evolutionary change. "Important though the subject is," he wrote defensively to Epstein, "it is only one of several matters that I would want to explore in a second volume." He had already selected a title for the projected work, "Beyond Darwin's Century," and suggested that Epstein meet him for a quiet lunch to discuss the contract, but not before he had the chance to deal with his other editor. When Eiseley reminded Haydn that he had promised the book on evolution to Doubleday well before the two had met, Haydn apologized for being suspicious. But Eiseley's plan to sign a second contract with another publisher was bound to be met with strenuous objections from Random House. "As I told you earlier," Eiseley confided to Epstein, "the matter is one demanding some degree of tact and I will try and clear things up at the other end before contacting you."[44]

For some unexplained reason, publication of *Darwin's Century* was pushed back to the summer of 1958. When Eiseley informed the campus bookstore manager of this development, he was told that his would be an old book by fall, "and dead." He immediately fired off an angry letter to Epstein: "This, I do not take kindly to. . . . I[t] strikes me that a big outfit like Doubleday . . . is not very trustworthy on matters of this kind." All told, publication had been delayed by some six months—"enough time for me to have probably expanded the volume through the chapters suggested by De Beer! This may be an author's ritual frenzy but it is something I have not experienced from Random House."[45]

The first hardcover printing of five thousand copies, priced at five dollars, began arriving in the bookstores around July 1. This time Orville Prescott ran the first major review of the work on June 27. Expecting another offering in the vein of *The Immense Journey*, the *Times*'s critic was caught off balance by the sweep of Eiseley's scholarship: "This book is so immensely educational that it cannot be read to much purpose; it must be studied. Here and there in its dense pages are passages written with the grave elegance that makes 'The Immense Journey' so captivating, but these green oases in an arid land are few. Could it be that 'Darwin's Century' is a textbook in disguise?"[46] In an attempt to soothe his author's hurt feelings, Epstein accused the reviewer of being "at his worst" for refusing to "admit that Loren Eiseley is entitled to write a scholarly book on a serious subject. It is rather less than I expected from Prescott, who has seemed less foolish lately than he used to be. But," he added philosophically, "I don't think that it does any harm."[47]

Eiseley turned to a familiar quarter for solace. Writing to Haydn, he protested Prescott's assumption that his latest was intended to be light summer reading. "I was quite surprised that a man holding his professional position did not seem to be able to make this distinction—or at least did not wish to do so. I hope you will not feel under any obligation to read the book."[48] In his sympathetic reply, Haydn told his friend not to lose any sleep over the matter. "In a sort of a way it is a compliment—if a somewhat inverted one."[49]

The literary strategy employed in *Darwin's Century* is simple yet effective and once again demonstrates Eiseley's flair for the dramatic. Holding the central figure in the wings until page 140, he begins by charting the course of evolutionary thought from its roots in the Great Chain of Being, the fixed hierarchical concept of matter and spirit embraced by Thomas Aquinas and Dante Alighieri. At the dawn of the Age of Exploration and Discovery in the early 1500s, the secure little medieval domain, with its familiar plant and animal life fully accounted for in the Bible by God's saving grace and Noah's sturdy ark, found itself incapable of coming to grips theologically with the mounting discoveries of the oceangoing mariners. Though the voyagers set sail in quest of gold, glory, and adventure, they returned with bizarre fossils and biological specimens that piqued the curiosity of scholars even as they defied explanation according to traditional religious doctrine.

Enter the likes of George-Louis Leclerc, the comte de Buffon, whose many volumes of magisterial prose anticipated evolutionary theory—even Darwinism itself. Jean-Baptiste Lamarck, Buffon's contemporary, transformed the Chain of Being, or *Scala Naturae* as it was termed in the seventeenth and eighteenth centuries, into an escalator fed at the bottom by simple organisms spontaneously generated and propelled by an innate tendency toward perfection. Furthermore, both Lamarck and Erasmus Darwin, Charles's poetry-writing grandfather, postulated that when such life-forms are acted on by environmental changes, they develop not only new patterns of behavior but new organs and structures.

In spite of the ample credit given to his precursors, Darwin suffers no reduction in stature by comparison with them. If anything, the intellectual pace quickened when, in 1831, the frustrated student of medicine and theology, "rat catcher" his peeved father called him, stepped aboard the *Beagle* to join Captain Robert Fitzroy and crew, his head brimming with evolutionary suspicions that the continent of South America would confirm and the otherworldly Galápagos Islands would come very close to explaining. Transformed both physically and mentally by his five arduous years at sea, the globe-circling naturalist returned home to Down House in Kent, rarely venturing from its quiet precincts during the remainder of a sedentary life. It is from his journals, notebooks, and early articles that Eiseley traces the cumulative development of natural selection in the mind of genius, and through the various editions of the *Origin of Species* the modification of that theory once it had been subjected to scientific criticism. Of Darwin's legacy Eiseley concludes:

> Our world, in short, is a marred world, an imperfect world, a never totally adjusted world, for the simple reason that it is not static. The games are still in progress and all of us, in the words of Sir Arthur Keith, bear the wounds of evolution. Our backs hurt, we have muscles which no longer move, we have hair that is not functional. All of this bespeaks of another world, another game played far beyond us in the past. We are indeed the products of "descent with modification."[50]

VI

A short while after the publication of *The Immense Journey*, an intense young colleague had sought Eiseley out in his office. "He had paid me a call in order to correct my deviations and to lead me back to the proper road of scholarship. . . . He pointed out to me the time I had wasted—time which could have been properly expended upon my own field of scientific investigation."[51] Little did the unnamed visitor realize that he had struck the deepest of nerves. Eiseley, who had always been sensitive about his standing in the eyes of the scientific community, now believed himself to be under constant scrutiny.

It was at least partly for this reason that he had labored so hard to complete *Darwin's Century* on schedule. And, except for Prescott's unenthusiastic review in the *Times*, he was not to be disappointed by the judgment of the critics. John K. Hutchens deferred to his more scientifically astute colleague Maurice Dolbier, who understood perfectly what the author was trying to accomplish. Writing in the July 9 edition of the *Herald Tribune*, Dolbier concluded: "The soaring flights of imaginative prose that marked Mr. Eiseley's 'The Immense Journey' are necessarily less frequent in this less personal work, but they are here, too, keeping 'Darwin's Century' not only high above the level of a dry and difficult thesis, but also high above the patronizing tone of a mere popularization."[52]

Most gratifying of all was the praise from scholarly journals and respected figures such as William Irvine, author of *Apes, Angels, and Victorians*, the stylishly crafted dual biography of Darwin and Huxley. The Stanford University professor found little to quarrel with and much to admire. "Anyone interested in Darwin's great masterpiece . . . should read Mr. Eiseley's book."[53] *Darwin's Century* was among three works collectively reviewed in *Scientific American* and the only one to earn the anonymous reviewer's unqualified praise.[54] Marston Bates, who had been unable to think of anything "neat" to say for the dust jacket of *The Immense Journey*, penned a glowing, five-column review of *Darwin's Century* for *Science*.[55] Although he could never rest easy, Eiseley felt that at the very least he had bought himself some breathing space. As he later told an interviewer, *Darwin's Century* tended to dampen the criticism of those in the scientific community who had regarded him as a prodigal for expressing his personal views on birds, bones, spiders, and time.[56]

VII

A perceptive clerk working on the fifth floor of John Wanamaker's, Philadelphia's oldest and largest department store, might have noticed a graying, smartly dressed woman of aristocratic bearing regularly browsing the long rows of neatly displayed merchandise. What the new associate director of the Pennsylvania Academy of the Fine Arts was up to was first revealed in a letter her husband wrote to Hiram Haydn in October 1957, although he chose not to use her name. "I have noticed that copies of 'The Immense Journey' are no longer on display at Wanamaker's . . . and I thus assume that the last of their rather sizable stock has been sold." With Christmas only two months away, he wondered if the sales department could coax the retailer into placing "at least a small re-order."[57] A check by an assistant sales manager at Random House revealed that the work was not out of stock, but he succeeded in getting the order department to take an additional twenty-five copies nonetheless. A series of similar letters followed early in the new year, and each time Haydn dutifully communicated the author's concern to Richard H. Lieberman, the company's harried field representative. Finally, in July 1958, some unidentified sales executive wrote directly to Robert Hughitt, Wanamaker's book department manager, asking him to forgive his seeming impertinence for shipping fifteen copies of the work without authorization. "The author seems to be devoting the rest of his life to haunting your book department. For example, the latest communiqué from Eiseley tells me you have two copies in stock. Any time you want to hire yourself a good stock control man, I'll give you Eiseley's phone number!"[58]

Eiseley still owed his various publishers a total of five book-length manuscripts. The centenary of the *Origin of Species* had barely passed when he received an unsettling letter from William J. Robbins, executive officer of the American Philosophical Society. Eiseley had never claimed the remaining $1,200 of the travel grant awarded him in October 1956. "We are holding the balance at your disposal and would appreciate hearing from you on the status of the project."[59] It was only at the end of his long and convoluted reply that Eiseley summoned up the courage to address the central issue, evoking memories of a similar exchange with Paul Fejos concerning the ill-fated Africa trip: "The fact that the nature of the project as originally conceived was changed, and the added fact that I have been unable, because of a too-full schedule, to undertake some of the travel initially envisioned, means that the sum of $1800 will not be required. The remaining sum of $1200 can doubtless be immediately expended by the Society for worthy research, and I am glad that I shall not require it."[60] Although Eiseley still held out the vague hope that the volume containing reprints of Darwin's papers might someday be delivered, it is clear that the Committee on Library looked upon it as nothing more than a face-saving gesture. Nevertheless, Eiseley's long devotion to the society's superb collection of Darwiniana was not to go unrecognized. When the ballots for new fellows were counted in 1960, his name was added to the distinguished list of those in the humanities.

The impressive reviews that had marked the appearance of *Darwin's Century* were hardly mirrored in the volume's sales. Some 3,500 books had been shipped during the five months following publication, and Eiseley's royalty income, based on thirty-seven and one-half cents a copy, shrank to a mere $251.63 for the six-month period ending October 31, 1959. More disturbing still was the fact that Jason Epstein had parted company with Doubleday, leaving Eiseley with a new editor named Pyke Johnson, Jr., and a lengthening list of woes. Relations between the two were cordial but strained, owing largely to Johnson's growing concern for the balance sheet. "The Darwin market seems to be glutted," he wrote ominously in May 1959, "as sales of Gertrude Himmelfarb's volume are demonstrating."[61] A check of the other major houses indicated that everyone was in pretty much the same boat. In his reply the galled author took a parting shot at his previous editor: "I think it was wise that I urged Jason to get *Darwin's Century* out early and I am only sorry that he wasted six months in doing it." Then, bowing to the inevitable, he concluded, "I suppose this means that there is little use in bothering with a second volume to *Darwin's Century*. I will write it off the list therefore and turn to something else."[62]

Haydn was certain of what that something else should be—Eiseley's *Walden*. Unfortunately, his author had other ideas. Ever since the publication of *The Immense Journey*, Eiseley had been nagging Haydn with letters and phone calls about an anthology of naturalists he was hoping to edit for the Modern Library series, the kind of "quickie" supposedly discussed with Epstein during the early negotiations for *Darwin's Century*. Haydn considered the project a waste of talent and publishing resources, yet the editor in chief felt that he had little choice but to go along if he wanted Eiseley's signature on a second contract for an original work. He dutifully forwarded the outline and some sample chapters to the Modern Library editors for evaluation.

In the meantime, in an effort to boost Eiseley's self-confidence, Haydn had talked his friend into running for one of two openings on the editorial board of *The American Scholar*. The election, held in November 1957, nearly backfired. Journalist Richard Rovere took top honors with seventy-four votes, while Eiseley barely edged out Yale historian C. Vann Woodward, sixty-nine to sixty-eight, for second place.[63] He attended his first meeting in Washington, D.C., the following month, joining a company that included Jacques Barzun, Paul H. Douglas, John Kenneth Galbraith, Richard Hofstadter, Margaret Mead, and Harlow Shapley.

In early February 1958, Haydn persuaded Eiseley to pay him a visit in New York, apparently under false but nonsinister pretenses. "I came to your office unprepared for the discussion which emerged," Eiseley wrote on returning to Wynnewood. "I had naturally supposed that the anthology was the matter to be discussed." Instead, Haydn took the opportunity to convince him that the time had come to draw up a contract for the original prose work the two had been talking about for over a year. As usual, the title came first. For the time being, Eiseley was satisfied with "The Apparition" and suggested an advance of two thousand dollars. Yet his ambivalence toward signing his name on the bottom line could not have been more emphatically stated: *"At this point I should like to make it plain that I do not ask for anything."*[64] Choosing to ignore this disclaimer, Haydn expressed satisfaction with Eiseley's terms and instructed the contracts department to proceed.

Now that they were in agreement in principle, Eiseley relaxed a bit. *The Saturday Evening Post* was about to launch a prestigious series titled Adventures of the Mind and had asked him to write the first article.[65] When he learned from *Post* editor John Kobler that Haydn had "said some very kind things" about him, he wrote to express his gratitude. "I just wanted you to know that I am not unaware in my dour and gloomy fashion of what your support has meant to me."[66] Nevertheless, there were some things that even

Haydn could not bring himself to do on behalf of his friend. After many years of silence, Eiseley had suddenly been stirred by the voice of Euterpe. The resulting poem, which he sent to Haydn for possible inclusion in the *Scholar*, "simply spun itself out of my head the other morning partly before I awoke. . . . If it doesn't interest you, just throw it away."[67] Haydn did nothing of the kind, but neither did he publish it, citing a large backlog of verse as the reason. When Eiseley next tried his hand, Haydn's response was even less encouraging. "I suppose I have put [it] off this long because I think for you to have written a poem after an abstinence [of] many years must make you as tender about it as a mother about her babe. Let me keep it until you come on, for in all honesty I don't think it a good poem, but I do feel the thought and feeling behind it good and also a number of individual lines and phrases. Hope you don't feel bad about this."[68]

It had taken three months to draft a contract Eiseley was willing to sign. "The Apparition" was to be roughly the length of *The Immense Journey* and, despite its brevity, not to be delivered until November 1961. "My Lord," a staggered Haydn wrote when he learned that he would have to wait three and one-half years for some two hundred pages, "do you really mean November *1961*? Holy jumping beeswax!"[69] Eiseley meant just that, leaving his editor with little choice. It was also agreed that the advance would be held until January 1959, because income from the *Post* piece and other sources was threatening to push the Eiseleys into a higher tax bracket. With these matters finally settled, Haydn felt sufficiently confident to inform Eiseley of the bad news. After careful consideration it had been decided that the nature anthology was not for Random House. Of course, Loren was perfectly free to market this work elsewhere. "I will express just one hope, however, that if you do this it won't mean any delay in the delivery of your book now under contract with us."[70]

16

"AT SIXES AND SEVENS"

I

Lowry Wimberly's dying was a prolonged affair. His illness, which had first struck in December 1953, was not diagnosed as Parkinson's disease until three years later. When finally told that his condition was terminal, he promptly retired from the University of Nebraska at the age of sixty-six. Eiseley was in Lincoln in the summer of 1958, paying his annual visit to Daisy and Grace, when he heard that the Doc was sick. Unaware that Wimberly was dying, he got him on the telephone and was distressed at how aged and worn his voice had become. "I had the distinct impression that he did not really wish me to see him as he then was, but I had gotten deep enough into the conversation . . . that I could not very well withdraw from my intention any more than he could tell me not to come." Driving across town in a car borrowed from his in-laws, he promised himself to make the visit as short as possible. Wimberly met him alone, May having withdrawn to an upstairs bedroom, as was her custom whenever her husband had visitors. They sat in the parlor for a few minutes, chatting mostly of old times.

> After putting up some little defense before I came, he seemed genuinely glad to see me, . . . and when I went to the door showed me that he could still walk. . . . I think he wished not to be re-

> membered in this fashion. I respected him so much for feeling as he did that perhaps in the end I left more hastily than I should, but I was determined not to intrude upon his reserve. My situation was not an easy one, however, and I did not prolong it beyond a few moments.[1]

Wimberly died a year later, in July 1959.

Nowhere in his autobiography was Eiseley to mention either Wimberly or the little magazine in which he had gotten his start as a poet and essayist. In a handwritten letter to Martin S. Peterson, a friend and associate from the old *Prairie Schooner* days, he self-consciously observed of this omission, "As you doubtless have noted, I passed over U.N. pretty fast and it troubled me not to find a way of getting Wimberly in without delaying the forward drive of the narrative."[2] He went on to express the hope that he might still find a way of acknowledging his debt to his mentor elsewhere in print, something he never did.

A telegram was waiting for Eiseley when, accompanied by Mabel, he returned to Lincoln by train on the evening of November 29, 1959. "Our deepest love and sympathy to Grace. We are with you in spirit and may God sustain you all in this hour of trial."[3] It was signed Leo and Lola. A Mrs. Laws, who was in charge of the nursing home on Apple Street where Daisy was living, had telephoned two nights earlier to say that Daisy had passed away in her sleep. The eighty-four-year-old widow had been ill with a severe cold, yet the doctor summoned to treat her had not considered it life threatening. Death had been sudden and unexpected.

Mother and son had last seen each other the previous summer. According to Eiseley, their final meeting took place in front of the drab apartment house where Daisy and Grace were living before they entered separate nursing homes. His mother stood looking at her arm as though seeing it for the first time. "I wonder why that vein sticks out so," she suddenly exclaimed. "Why I believe I'm getting old. Do you think that's it? Old age?" Saying nothing, Eiseley shook his head and turned away, raising a hand in a combined gesture of despair and farewell. "The last I saw was the blue vein creeping down her arm as she repeated in a voice that seemed to emanate from another dimension, 'I'm old. I think I'm old.' "[4]

Arrangements were made for a private graveside service at Wyuka Cemetery. Eiseley refused to view the body. "I would not look at what lay at the end of the corridor. It was as though something was drawing me, something too earthbound to depart." As the hours crept by in leaden silence, he began to experience second thoughts. It was approaching midafternoon, almost time to leave for the cemetery, when he rose from his chair and entered the long hallway:

> I came to the place where she lay. I did not stand close. She slept forever now, that life of so much violence, the eyes closed that had looked upon the world through the narrowed slits of long deprivation into a world of utter silence. . . . I saw the high, full forehead, the profile that still possessed a strange unrealized beauty. I did not look at the mouth. I had seen it in its last years. I had seen it across my father's face, asking harshly about his insurance. It was only a moment that I stood there. She had had her way, as always, in the end.[5]

Daisy's belongings, which had dwindled with each successive move, were taken to the Langdons' for temporary storage. Among the boxes of papers and photographs was Daisy's certificate of marriage to Frank E. Myers, proof that Loren was well aware that his mother had been loved by another long before Clyde Eiseley had entered the picture.[6] Having come by train and timed his arrival so that he would be in Lincoln for as short a time as possible, Loren was anxious to leave. While waiting at the airport for his flight east, he rolled up a sleeve and discovered another part of his mixed legacy from Daisy. The disturbingly familiar "blue worm" was beginning to inch its way down his arm.[7]

II

Daisy Eiseley had lived just long enough to learn of her son's appointment to the office of provost at the University of Pennsylvania. During the first two centuries of its existence, Penn had no president, making the provost the highest ranking administrator. Following the creation of the presidency in 1923, however, the provost became the second in command, acting for the president during his absence and assuming primary responsibility for both the development of long-range planning and its implementation on a day-to-day basis. Eiseley's eighteen predecessors had held the prestigious office for an average of just over eleven years each; if he were to follow suit, retirement would be only two or three years away by the end of his tenure.

On the surface at least, Eiseley seemed perfectly suited for the post. To begin with, he was one of the cognoscenti, a Penn Ph.D. with fifteen years of administrative experience, twelve of them as a department chairman at his alma mater. He was also highly regarded as a classroom teacher, and word had just been received that *Darwin's Century* was the winner of the national Phi Beta Kappa Science Prize for 1959. Of equal importance was his standing among his colleagues. The anthropologist had been elected vice chairman of the faculty senate in 1955 and became Penn's faculty leader later in the academic year, when Jonathan E. Rhoads, a member of the university's school of medicine, resigned the senate chair to become provost. Indeed, the somewhat laconic surgeon, who had watched Eiseley follow in his footsteps with an approving eye, once quipped that he half-expected to look over his shoulder in the operating room and see Loren standing there, masked and gloved, ready to assist him.[8]

Penn's trustees voted overwhelmingly in favor of the appointment. When word of their decision was released to the press, the student editors of *The Daily Pennsylvanian* waxed enthusiastic over the selection: "As an understanding man, Dr. Eiseley can be expected to foster warm relations with the faculty and students. In our mind, we find Dr. Eiseley qualified in every respect. His appointment is an exciting event in which all students and faculty should take interest and pride."[9] Letters of congratulation were soon streaming in. Yet virtually every well-wisher felt compelled to leaven his enthusiasm with the hope that Eiseley would not stop writing.

In a letter to her boss, Joe Fraser, who was vacationing in Vermont, Mabel did little to hide her feelings on the matter. "I have a rather prayerful attitude toward the whole thing. Far from pushing Loren, I have (without being discouraging) tried to keep him from over-extending his energies. Having absolutely no social ambitions and liking a quiet life it is perhaps easy for me to be content." As the provost's wife, she would never be able to devote a full five days a week to her job.[10] While Mabel was willing to make such a sacrifice, her reservations extended beyond those of a woman who cared little for the social side of academics. Shortly after the appointment was announced, Otto Springer, the new dean of the College of Arts and Sciences, happened to drop by the apartment. The normally reserved professor of medieval German was both touched and a little embarrassed when Mabel suddenly placed her hand on his and whispered, "Would you give Loren all the help you can? I don't think he can quite handle the job."[11] It was a startling admission for one who was known for keeping her own counsel, and Springer left the Wyndon troubled. He could only guess at what Mabel was not to reveal until many years later: "I begged Loren not to take it."[12]

Mabel's fears were rooted in her husband's inability to make decisions affecting his own life, let alone the lives of others dependent on his leadership. The problem had manifested itself early in Eiseley's administrative career, after the resignations of Frederick Zorbaugh and L. Guy Brown had left him the only tenured member of Oberlin's Department of Sociology and Anthropology. With the new academic year less than two months away, a nervous Carl Wittke virtually pleaded with his chairman, who was teaching summer school at Columbia, to make at least one appointment before the start of fall classes. What the dean received instead was a series of rambling, collect telephone calls and a sheaf of turgid letters filled with endearing apologies. "It is too bad that you have to be troubled . . . when you should be having a vacation, but then I don't know what I should do if you weren't there! It makes all the difference in the world both to me and to Mabel."[13] After a month of getting nowhere, Wittke threw up his hands and made the appointment himself.

At Penn, Eiseley was chairing a department of less than half a dozen tenured professors, so his potential shortcomings as an administrator were not apparent to outsiders. Ward Goodenough praised him for his conscientiousness, but the young professor could not help but notice how anxious his chairman was. "Every little matter that came up he would tend to agonize over. . . . Making decisions relating to people was not easy for him. You couldn't bring a matter to him and get a quick decision; he had to lose some sleep over it first." Goodenough, whose office was adjacent to the chairman's, almost climbed the walls during the advisement period each semester. Students complained to him that Eiseley was rarely around; when they did catch him in, he anguished so over their class schedules that it was nearly impossible to obtain his signature. Choosing his moment carefully, the junior man offered to take some of the advisement burden off Eiseley's shoulders. "Oh would you?" the chairman exclaimed. "That's great!"[14]

Eiseley left much of the responsibility for hiring new faculty in the hands of his colleagues, especially Goodenough and A. I. Hallowell. Even the business of staffing the office with competent personnel gave him "fits." Somehow, the department had acquired the services of a secretary who could do nothing right. Things got so bad that the woman, who idolized the "wonderful Dr. Eiseley," was literally begging faculty members for work, which they would invariably have to redo themselves. Eiseley vacillated while the pressure from his department mounted. He finally had her transferred to another office.[15]

One may wonder why Eiseley, knowing that his problems would be magnified a hundredfold in the provost's office, opted to take the position. At least part of the answer is contained in a letter he wrote to William A. Caldwell, a friend of Hiram Haydn's and editor of the *Bergen Evening Post* in Hackensack, New Jersey:

> Your comments about Robert Frost as supervisor of building maintenance and Thoreau becoming inspector rather shook me up because I have been getting similar letters from other people. The one thing no one seems able to explain is how you provide for a group of aging relatives under any other happy, carefree Greenwich Village arrangement. The minute you have this problem solved, let me know, and I will come running.[16]

Mabel remembered Loren telling her much the same thing: the provostship represented a promotion and a substantial increase in salary.[17] She might well have added that her husband craved honors, although he worked hard at disguising this need.

III

Eiseley took office in October, then promptly departed for Cincinnati, Ohio, where he assumed the title of visiting professor of the philosophy of science in the University of Cincinnati's College of Medicine, a long-standing commitment from which he had been unable to extricate himself. Over the next three weeks he delivered six public lectures on the theme "Man's Quest for Certainty" to a packed auditorium. It was only after he returned to Penn and a

College Hall desk overflowing with paperwork that reality set in. Colleague Eliot Stellar, a future provost himself, put the matter simply: "It was only one month after he became provost that he knew he'd made a mistake."[18]

Eiseley immediately got bogged down in the endless swamp of administrative details, a deadly snare for one to whom seventeen deans, ten program directors, and a wide range of faculty committees reported. A slow and deliberate speaker, he would often take the floor and hold it for what seemed like hours on end. Fro Rainey, against his better judgment, had written a strong letter in support of his friend's candidacy, yet he was the first to admit that "the worst thing Loren did for himself was to become provost. . . . He was harassed from the word go! . . . It just got him at sixes and sevens. . . . At times I'd get impatient with Loren. We'd sit by the hour . . . and he'd come up with a conclusion and then he'd back off, and he'd come up again and back off. That's a curious mental quirk in somebody who is really so damned intelligent as Loren was."[19]

Robert E. Spiller, the distinguished nineteenth-century literary scholar and chairman of American civilization, saw Eiseley's predicament from a greater distance. There was "the melancholy man," the moody, introspective loner in touch with his own deepest feelings. Another Eiseley, who had only recently emerged, was a true stranger: "You would think he was a bank president, or the president of a college. . . . He had a tremendously impressive public personality. And I think that is really the tragedy of Loren Eiseley, because he loved that and he tried to become that. . . . A man of that kind is really afraid of himself." Once, when the various deans and department chairs were called by the provost to a meeting to discuss a major policy issue, Eiseley sat at the head of the long conference table, "looking like God Almighty but helpless as a child. The meeting got nowhere; he couldn't point up the issues; he couldn't pull it together; he couldn't direct the people there."[20]

Judging by the standard of Eiseley's predecessor, Jonathan Rhoads, and his successor, David Goddard, there was little communication between the new provost and President Gaylord P. Harnwell from the beginning—and even less as time wore on. Harnwell, like the more perceptive members of his faculty, was soon circumventing the provost's office to deal directly with the men bearing the brunt of Eiseley's burden, Vice Provosts Roy Franklin Nichols and E. Sculley Bradley. Fro Rainey, too, although he felt like something of a traitor, admitted that "even I, when I wanted to get a quick decision, would go to Sculley Bradley."[21]

IV

Eiseley remembered crying out in despair, after coming home from the university one evening, "I haven't read a book in two years."[22] The provostship was exacting a similar toll on his writing. He had penned but a single article during his first twelve months in office, though anyone perusing his vita would have had difficulty grasping this fact. From a literary point of view, Loren Eiseley was the ultimate conservationist, in terms of both his economy of style and his ability to recycle previously published material. Typical was the piece written for *The Saturday Evening Post* in 1958, "An Evolutionist Looks at Modern Man." The article, which underwent a number of title changes, subsequently appeared in eight anthologies and several magazines, including the U.S. Information Agency periodical *Ameryka.* So far as his reputation and bank statement were concerned, this was all to the good; but what, Eiseley kept asking himself, would he do when his reserves ran out?

He was increasingly haunted by a conversation that had taken place some time before he assumed the provost's mantle. A former colleague turned administrator suddenly became philosophical while the two were sharing drinks at a bar in Washington, D.C. "You know," he mused, "just two things happen to an academic. He finds he has administrative gifts and they pay better, so he . . . ceases to write as I have." Conversely, "you write in your field and you attend meetings and run errands until you are a pundit and are recognized at last as worthy of being president of a learned society. That is the choice. There is no other." After becoming provost, Eiseley had a chance encounter with his old friend, who, with a glint of amusement in his eye, welcomed him to the club. "In one more year," he quipped, "you'll never catch up in your profession. Tell me," he queried, twisting the knife a bit, "do you find time to write these days?"[23]

The irony of Eiseley's situation was accentuated by the fact that the personal honors were accumulating thick and fast. In addition to garnering its author the Phi Beta Kappa Prize of one thousand dollars, *Darwin's Century* was judged the best nonfiction book of the year (1958) by the Athenaeum of Philadelphia, a private research library specializing in works of literature, travel, and the decorative arts. At Western Reserve University, with a beaming Carl Wittke looking on, "Junior" was awarded an honorary doctorate of humane letters. A year later Eiseley walked across the stage at N.Y.U. and collected his second L.H.D.

Meanwhile, out in Lincoln, similar plans almost went awry. Bert Schultz had written secretly to Mabel, informing her of his decision to nominate Loren for an honorary degree at the University of Nebraska. However, when he suggested that the Anthropology Department serve as Eiseley's sponsor, its faculty balked on the ground that the nominee had not sufficiently distinguished himself in the discipline to warrant such an accolade. An angry but undaunted Bert then took his case to the English Department, where he received a more sympathetic hearing. "We have just held our breath since January," he wrote the Eiseleys right after the official announcement came. "So many members of the faculty are not in favor of such honors, but . . . before it was over everyone climbed on the bandwagon."[24] Not wishing to tarnish the moment, Bert left it up to the chancellor to inform Eiseley that his doctorate would be in humane letters rather than in science.

Although Eiseley had not written a single line of "The Apparition," his projected work for Random House, he suddenly found himself embroiled in a wrangle between Hiram Haydn and Bennett Cerf. Early in 1959 Haydn had decided to join fellow editors Alfred A. "Pat" Knopf, Jr., and Simon Michael Bessie in a new publishing venture that as yet had no name. During a conversation with Donald Klopfer, a high-ranking colleague at Random House, Haydn tipped his hand prematurely. Cerf, who happened to be out of town, stormed into Haydn's office three days later and told him off with "articulate heat." "I was guilty of a betrayal of trust and friendship, and he didn't want anything more to do with me. In fact, the sooner I got out the better." Things eventually calmed down, and Cerf later returned to his editor in chief's office with a tempting proposal. If Haydn would stay he could count on a vice presidency and stock options, as well as a number of other inducements. Though highly flattered, Haydn held firm and began clearing out his files a few weeks later.[25]

Some weeks after Cerf's outburst, he, Klopfer, and Haydn sat down to discuss the touchy issue of author affiliation. Everything was going well until Eiseley's name came up. "Of course we're not going to release Loren Eiseley!" Cerf exclaimed. "He stays with us."

Klopfer pulled the publisher up short. "Come on Bennett," he scolded. "We can't do that. Hiram faced us all down at the sales conference [by claiming] that *The Immense Journey* would sell forever. And that's what it promises to do. We all dragged our feet on it and we were wrong. Of course Hiram gets Eiseley, if Eiseley wants to go."[26]

The meeting concluded without further incident. Haydn immediately wrote to Eiseley, giving him the news. All the author needed to do was send a letter to Cerf asking that his contract be assigned to the new firm.[27] Eiseley complied a few days later. "My sole reason for requesting a transfer of contract is one which I believe you, as a publisher of long experience, would agree is valid: the fact that Hiram Haydn is an editor with whom I can work most satisfactorily, and with whom I wish to continue to work."[28] Still, the decision to leave what was arguably the top publisher in the country could not have been an easy one for any author, let alone an anxiety-ridden latecomer. In recognition of this, Haydn had resorted to his old stratagem of unvarnished flattery. The new house would be called Atheneum, after the Athenaeum Award Eiseley had recently won for a book published by a rival firm.[29]

During his administrative tenure of slightly less than two years, the briefest in Penn's history, Eiseley was absent from campus a total of at least five months. In addition to numerous speaking engagements, several lengthy vacations, and the usual bouts of hypochondria, he was fond of playing hooky. Instead of heading for his office after disembarking from the Paoli local at 30th Street Station, he would sometimes catch the early train to New York, where he would pass the day browsing the bookstores. Mabel, who was deeply concerned about her husband's peace of mind, proved a willing conspirator. These little junkets, she reflected, "substituted for the psychiatrist's couch."[30]

Meanwhile, Bessie, Knopf, and Haydn had set up shop at 162 East Thirty-eighth Street, where Eiseley became something of a familiar face. The "Poet and the Provost," as Haydn labeled him to point up the dichotomy between the inner man of books and the outer one of social exchanges, had a new project in mind. Eiseley wanted to be relieved of his present commitment so that he could concentrate on an autobiography with the working title "The Divine Animal." He met with the three partners to discuss the idea in October 1960 and afterward received a rave review from his editor. "Just a line to tell you again how wonderfully you did on Monday, how much I enjoyed our morning session and how pleased I was with your thoughtfulness in giving me a 'plug.' By all means," Haydn concluded, "full speed ahead on what sounds like a wonderful book, even if full speed means beginning sometime next year."[31] A contract was issued for the new work, though Eiseley refused the usual advance. With one stroke of his pen, *The Apparition* became just that.

V

"The provost," one of Eiseley's colleagues observed, "must have an elephant's hide, and Loren did not have an elephant's hide."[32] Fellow academic Richard Stonesifer came to the same conclusion: "I can't imagine Loren getting brutal in wordage with a dean who needed pepping up. He was just too nice a guy."[33] Instead, he turned the slights and grudges into emotional prose at three o'clock in the morning, ventilating the dark cellar of his psyche when no one else was about. Eiseley was equally lost when it came to the endless detail work required of his office. Never one to handle his correspondence with dispatch, he allowed the mail to pile up until the lack of space on his large walnut desk finally forced him to act. Mabel had handled every aspect of their personal finances, even seeing to it that Loren, who was oblivious to such things, had sufficient spending money before leaving the apartment each morning. When a horrified Harold Manley, the university comptroller, got wind of Eiseley's fiscal naiveté, he made a beeline for the president's office. On June 30, 1960, a memo bearing Eiseley's signature went out to all the deans and directors reporting to the provost. Dr. Arleigh Hess, Jr., a laconic, soft-spoken son of Penn who served the university in several capacities, had just been appointed to the newly created office of assistant to the provost for budgetary affairs.[34]

When once asked, "What did you do when you were provost?" Eiseley had his answer well rehearsed. He pointed in the direction of Bennett Hall, the site of his former office, and described how the corner of Thirty-fourth and Walnut streets projects in front of the building. The angle had once permitted fast-moving traffic to turn left without slowing down, posing a serious threat to the countless pedestrians who crossed the intersection each day. Eiseley had seen a half dozen accidents there himself, but it was the injury of a horse that moved him to have the angle changed to slow down the traffic.[35]

Never once, to the best of his office manager Mary Crooks's memory, did her boss lose his temper. Yet she noticed that he increasingly felt the need to get out of the office.[36] He usually headed for some secluded bench, where he nodded off in the afternoon sun or jotted down notes on the behavior of the small creatures he loved writing about. "Saw a pigeon on campus today . . . with an injured leg who used his wings to move when the other[s] walked. He used to rest in the sun with his wings spread out, lying on his side in an ungainly fashion but looking nevertheless well fed and managing to cope with his infirmity. Perhaps in winter he will suffer more. . . . Where he roosted and how, I had, of course, no idea. Sooner or later a cat . . ."[37] Robert Spiller happened to walk by during one such moment and debated with himself whether to intrude. "Loren was sitting on one end of the bench with a faraway look in his eyes, I suppose meditating, maybe brooding."[38]

Spiller also noticed that the provost had undergone a radical change of physique, and bluntly described Eiseley as "overstuffed." The tale of the tape is more precisely told in the orders various institutions placed for academic robes worn by the visiting provost. When he took office, Eiseley listed his height as five feet eleven inches and weight as 170 pounds. A year later he had ballooned to 200 pounds, causing him to rationalize by increasing his stature to an even six feet. While a suit coat or gown could hide much of the added poundage, his own bloated countenance betrayed him. The sculpted jaw of the Shepards expanded until his face became broader at the jowls than at the temples, an inversion of the normal rules of symmetry; the once severe chin first doubled, then tripled, until it hung over his shirt collar in folds, as did the thickening flesh of his bulging neck. A new wardrobe had to be purchased and glasses replaced with wider bows to prevent them from cutting into his sensitive skin.

This condition was the result partly of too many obligatory social engagements and partly of Eiseley's recently acquired habit of riding the bus back and forth to 30th Street Station. On occasion he still met Ward Goodenough for lunch at one of the campus cafeterias, as had been their custom when their offices were next door to each other in Anthropology. "He was an addict of vanilla ice cream," Goodenough recalled. "He'd go through line and get his meat and potatoes and then ponder whether to eat his ice cream plain or partake of pie à la mode. There was that streak in him of . . . self-indulgence."[39]

Conspicuous by her absence from all but the most important university functions, Mabel continued to fret behind the veil of a stoic. With Loren out of town and a March blizzard providing her with a "perfect excuse" for not going in to the academy, she unburdened herself in a long letter to her distant confidante, Dorothy Thomas:

> It isn't that one deliberately chooses to "go up in the world." Actually this is of little interest. We are, as you know, both simple people in our wants and tastes, and we have simply refused to play what is known as the "social game." I was afraid there might be more demands than are healthful, but we have continued to live in our same apartment and to do very much as we did before. Loren has a very realistic attitude toward his increased salary and prestige, and as for me I've made it clear from the first that this is to be no life sentence. I was happy with what we already had and most of all with Loren.
>
> But, Dorothy, one cannot pronounce or make ultimate decisions. *Loren is not completely a poet and dreamer.* He has a practical side (that kept him from trying to make a living as a poet!) and he gets a certain satisfaction out of employing some of his other talents. No one, I think, can, in one life, fully express all that is in him, or live the best-of-all-possible lives.
>
> This is not a sermon—if it is, it's but a poor one. I'm still trying to learn what the really important things are. Why does it take so long?[40]

Had Gaylord Harnwell been privy to these sentiments, he might never have offered the Eiseleys one of Penn's juicier perquisites. In February 1961 the president informed Eiseley that the so-called Provost's House on Pine Street near the campus was to be vacated at the end of April. The residence had recently been redecorated, and the departing occupant had even decided to leave his grand piano behind until other arrangements could be made for it. "While I do not know what the preferences of yourself and Mabel may be, it occurred to me that you might be interested in living in this house—

of course with no rent involved." For his part, Harnwell looked upon the prospective arrangement as a "happy" one and a gesture that would be "deeply appreciated by the faculty members in general."[41]

Or was it possible that the president knew more than he was letting on, using the offer of a house, which he suspected the intensely private couple would never accept, as a gambit to force the provost's hand? In any event, in April, with "the walls closing in on him," in Mabel's words, her husband submitted to Harnwell a brief letter of resignation, which the president accepted gracefully but without regret.[42] Some months later, after the burden of the provostship had been removed from his shoulders, Eiseley attempted to put his feelings about their failed partnership into words. "If we were a bit inarticulate with each other at times, I am sure that it was with a kind of speechlessness that comes upon men who share the same ideals, but who have come upon them along divergent paths. As we grow older our inner silences become, I find, harder to break."[43]

When Eiseley returned from his vacation in September, Mary Crooks cautioned him that he must remove the books overflowing the provost's office to make room for his successor. When he made no effort to do so, his office manager issued a sterner warning which also went unheeded. The impasse was not broken until one day she ordered her boss to get cracking. Eiseley closed the door to his office, and Mary heard nothing from him for several hours. Feeling a bit remorseful but determined to see the task through, she knocked on the door and walked in, expecting to find major progress. With few exceptions, all the volumes were still in place, while Eiseley was sprawled out on the carpeted floor amid a dozen empty cartons. He looked up at her with the guilty expression of a wayward child and held out the book in which he had become engrossed. "Mary," he said in a plaintive voice, "I didn't know I had this one."[44]

17

THE FIFTH HORSEMAN

I

While walking back to the apartment he and Mabel were temporarily renting on Ravenswood Avenue in Menlo Park, California, Eiseley suddenly experienced a pang of utter desolation recorded for possible inclusion in the autobiography: "Penn was no longer my home, nor Nebraska, nor this rose-pink California sky at evening. I was alone, alone, and I would die alone and it was too late anywhere in the universe to find refuge. I was lost no matter what. It came on me like a physical pain, like growing age, and I limped, my ankle hurt; what was I doing here in the gathering dark? Where was I to go?"[1]

According to Preston Cutler, assistant director of the Center for Advanced Study in the Behavioral Sciences, Eiseley had come to the institution in the fall of 1961, hoping to bind up the wounds he had sustained as provost.[2] Like the other forty-four fellows, he was free to do as he pleased—to read, to discuss, to reflect, or to write. Eiseley had even been spared the rigors of the formal selection process, which favors those actively involved in the training of graduate students. One day Carroll Newsom had received a call from Loren, who was never hesitant about asking the New York University president and one-time Oberlin colleague for a favor. He had long dreamed of spending a year on the West Coast and wondered if his friend knew anyone at the Center for Advanced Study. "I said, do you want me to work on it?" Newsom recalled, and Loren replied, "I'd appreciate it." The N.Y.U. president immediately telephoned Ralph Tyler, who was both the head of the center and a very close friend. After listening to Newsom extoll Eiseley's virtues for a few minutes, Tyler broke in, his mind already made up: "Carroll, I'm going to make the appointment."[3]

Instead of taking an apartment near the center, which is in Palo Alto, the Eiseleys sought to keep their usual distance by locating five miles away. They had planned to pick up an automobile, but, as Mabel related in a letter to Carroll and Pearl Clark back in Kansas, Loren decided that he preferred "the adventure" of walking.[4] It turned out that he got more of an adventure than he had bargained for. Ambling, alone and preoccupied, toward his office late one afternoon, he caught the toe of his shoe in a drain and went down, striking his face on the curb and breaking his nose. Blood began spurting from a gash in his forehead and collected in a bright red pool on the sidewalk. Impervious to the cries of solicitous passersby, he gazed down at the widening ring and exclaimed, "Oh, don't go. I'm sorry." These words, he later wrote,

> were not addressed to the crowd gathered about me. They were inside and spoken to no one but a part of myself. I was quite sane, only it was an oddly detached sanity, for I was addressing blood cells, phagocytes, platelets, all the crawling, living, independent wonder that had been part of me and now, through my folly and lack of care, were dying like beached fish on the hot pavement. A great wave of passionate contrition, even of adoration, swept through my mind, a sensation of love on a cosmic scale, for mark that this experience was, in its way, as vast a catastrophe as would be that of a galaxy consciously suffering through the loss of its solar systems.[5]

After recovering, he revisited the scene of the "crime," where a faint crimson discoloration still marked the sidewalk. "I shook my head, conscious of the brooding mystery that the poet Dante impelled into his great line: 'the love that moves the sun and other stars.' "[6] When he first asked Mabel to type up his account of the accident, she remembered thinking that it was the most moving passage he had ever written. Indeed, Mabel was so overcome that she rose from the typewriter, tears clouding her eyes, and told him how marvelous it was.[7]

In January 1962, Grace Price was taken to Lincoln General Hospital, where she lay near death for several days. Eiseley wrote his colleague A. I. Hallowell from Menlo Park that he and Mabel had been living "in a kind of poised-for-flight atmosphere." On the sixteenth, the doctor telephoned to say that Grace was much improved and could shortly go home. Then, about five o'clock the next morning, he telephoned again to inform them that she had died suddenly of heart failure. With the last of his familial links to Nebraska severed, Eiseley experienced a momentary sense of release bordering on the ebullient. "Life can be and often is beautiful here," he wrote Hallowell later that day. "At the Center I not only commune with some of the Great Minds to be found here, but also with lesser and equally engaging creatures—humming birds, lizards, black squirrels and a kind of honking toad. Now and then it strikes me as incredible that one can sit outside—in Mid-January—and drowse in the warm sunshine. But I must stop before I begin to sound like a Convinced Californian."[8]

Plane reservations were made, but only for one. Mabel flew to Lincoln the next day, where she was met at the airport by her brother Charles, who took her to the family home on D Street to stay with her recently widowed mother. Grace was buried at Wyuka Cemetery in the remaining space next to Buck on January 20, her flat gray stone—identical to those of her husband and sister—bearing only her name, birth and death dates, and a simply carved rose.

II

Many of those who came to the Center for Advanced Study were preceded by their reputations. According to Preston Cutler, Eiseley's was that of a "man with a golden pen." Hence, the assistant director was quite surprised when he met the former provost. "He spoke slowly, deliberately, with well chosen words, but conversation with him was not very exciting." Eiseley frequently came by Cutler's office, where he spent a great deal of time agonizing unnecessarily over alternative itineraries for the trips he was planning. "I was quite surprised by it. . . . I think one of his concerns was that his absences from the center should not become the cause of any undue comment." Eiseley's assertion to the contrary, there is little evidence to suggest that he engaged in much productive discussion with his peers. It was a common practice among the fellows to seek out those of similar interests for the purpose of organizing seminars, an activity in which he chose not to participate. Nor, when the opportunity came, did he follow tradition and make a formal presentation of his work to the group.[9]

Bill Asling, Eiseley's erstwhile conspirator in cadaver hauling atop Mount Oread, and Sherry Washburn, with whom he had twice planned to visit the Dark Continent, were both living in the San Francisco Bay area and teaching at Berkeley. Yet neither received so much as a call from him during his nine months' stay in Palo Alto. "He must have had some reason," a wistful Bill remarked.[10] Sherry just shook his head in retrospect and termed Eiseley's silence "a surprising thing."[11] The only one who did hear from the Eiseleys was Wright Morris, who had left Philadelphia in the late 1950s and settled, with his second wife, Jo, in the suburban community of Mill Valley, just to the north of San Francisco. However, it was Mabel rather than Schmerzie who made the first telephone call to the Morrises.[12]

These three men, their identities well disguised, were all to surface in Eiseley's writings in a negative manner. Bill Asling, who had shown Eiseley every kindness during their close association at the University of Kansas, was the unwitting villain whose commitment to medical science had supposedly blinded him to the animal suffering of the dissection chamber. Sherry Washburn was portrayed as the primatologist willing to shoot a baby monkey out of its mother's arms for the sake of some higher good. Wright Morris was singled out as displaying a more subtle but equally callous lack of sensitivity. In a notebook associated with *The Immense Journey*, Eiseley wrote: "The Story of Beadie, the water rat who had a penchant for getting into bottles. Beadie and Wright Morris."[13]

Beadie became "Conlin's rat" in the published version, "in order to protect the good name of a distinguished American novelist who was unaware of the low company he kept." On a lovely summer's evening, the fading light cast long shadows on the perfectly clipped lawns and hedges affordable only to the very rich and the very powerful. The novelist, clad in white from head to foot, had ushered his guests out onto the terrace. Holding a mint julep in his perfectly manicured hand, he gestured toward Eiseley. "Man," he pontificated, "will turn the whole earth into a garden for his own enjoyment. It is just a question of time. I admit the obstacles you have mentioned, but I have tremendous faith in man. He will win. I drink to him." As glasses were being raised all around, Eiseley happened to glance under his host's white canvas chair. There, outlined against the stuccoed wall behind him, was a sleek, dark rat, whiskers twitching with cynical contempt for the well-clothed party. While the supremely civilized "Conlin" persisted in his eloquent discourse, the rodent sniffed at his shoe and listened attentively, stretching to its full height. "He looked across at me, and it seemed best not to warn the company." The irreverent creature eventually disappeared into the drainpipe from which it had come. It seemed to Eiseley that the rat had addressed itself to him alone, "for I have never seen anything so perfectly appropriate."[14]

The writing, meanwhile, especially the autobiography, was not going well. "As for the book," a discouraged Eiseley wrote Haydn, "I am into it but not happy about anything just at the moment."[15] By June of 1962 he seemed ready to throw in the towel. Haydn met him for lunch in New York after one of his periodic flights back to the East Coast. There must have been some pretty blunt talk because, after speaking to her husband by telephone, Mabel wrote of "The Divine Animal": "Hiram unwilling to give up contract on this book." Relations continued to be strained when Eiseley visited Haydn's office a few days later. "Hiram advised against taking on too many outside assignments. Seemed somewhat upset & disgruntled."[16]

Eiseley was displaying every symptom of a man seduced by his own success. During this same visit to New York he discussed "literary matters" over lunch at Sardi's with *Holiday* editor Harry Bester; negotiated with the publisher Prentice-Hall, whose senior vice president was none other than Carroll Newsom, for a "full-time connection" as a writer-editor; conferred with the editors of *Ladies' Home Journal* about a projected article; arranged for an IBM executive to publish a shortened version of an essay in the company's periodical *Think*; and, finally, pressured Haydn to secure him an editorial slot with Atheneum—this after receiving an initially favorable response from Prentice-Hall.[17]

Before departing San Francisco for New York, he had spent the better part of a day closeted in a hotel room with four regents from the University of Hawaii, who had flown in from Honolulu to interview him for the presidency. After subsequently asking that his name be withdrawn from further consideration, he was offered, and accepted, a visiting professorship at the institution. Quickly repenting the folly of this action, he wrote to Leonard Mason, chairman of the Anthropology Department, pleading diminished capacity. "I am just recovering from an accident . . . during which I suffered a mild concussion, forehead injuries and a broken nose. I mention it only because, coming when and as it did, it interfered with clear thinking and an ability to make immediate decisions of more than usual complexity." It was with the deepest regret, he said, that he must resign the post. "I believe you will understand what it has cost me to send this letter and to say simply that I am sorry."[18]

A few months later found him back East at the Barbizon Plaza conferring with Provost Harry W. Porter about becoming president of the State University of New York at Stony Brook. In September, after he and Mabel had returned to Philadelphia, Eiseley arranged a conference with Atheneum's Marc Friedlaender in a last-ditch effort to obtain a contract for the much-traveled nature anthology, which Preston Cutler remembered him working on in California. The following morning he took a taxi to the offices of Macmillan to keep an appointment with a rising editor named Kenneth Heuer, who had long sought his services as an author, and who now wanted him to inaugurate a new scientific series.[19] The negotiations went so well that Eiseley soon received a contract for a short biography of the naturalist Alfred Russel Wallace.[20] He filed it away along with four successive versions of another contract recently negotiated with the Skokie, Illinois, firm of Rand McNally & Company. It was for a work tentatively titled "Introductory Anthropology," the book he dreamed would one day make him rich.[21]

III

Wishing neither to lose Eiseley nor to retain his services as provost, in April 1961 Penn President Gaylord Harnwell had taken an unprecedented step. "Though the University has not officially established any policy under which University-wide distinguished service professorships are recognized, we would be happy to propose [that] . . . you become a University Professor in the Life Sciences associated with the Department of Anthropology at the salary of

$22,500." The remaining details could be worked out during the final months of Eiseley's provostship, but Harnwell assured him that he could teach as much or as little as he liked, while allowing his intellect to range across the academic spectrum, "rather than be confined narrowly within a particular department."[22] After conferring with Mabel and a few intimates such as Carl Wittke and Carroll Newsom, a proud Eiseley drafted a formal letter of acceptance.[23] No announcement would be made until the following October, a little more than a week before Loren and Mabel boarded their train for the West Coast.

Upon his return to Penn in the fall of 1962, Eiseley quickly found his new dignity a mixed blessing. "I read as I pleased, and wrote for my own pleasure," he observed while warming himself in the memory of Clyde's letter describing him as a genius. In this respect, the sixties were "the happiest period of my life." At the same time, he was brought up short by a colleague who cursed the university professorship to his face.[24] But the thing that most upset Eiseley's critics was what one colleague, whose books and monographs fill several library shelves, labeled his "schizophrenia," the desire to be taken seriously as an anthropologist while living the life of a poet. By refusing to engage in original research or undertake the training of graduate students, he had not "earned" the right to occupy a distinguished chair, even though Penn was admittedly better known for his being there. In essence, this colleague felt, he was a man who could not measure up in his own field and had thus turned to another. An equally disaffected colleague, who had tried to read *The Immense Journey* five or six times without succeeding, dismissed it as a "disgusting hybrid" whose style reminded him of nothing so much as sentimental, old-fashioned oratory. Even Robert Spiller, who was no stranger to belles lettres, found fault with Eiseley's analytical skills, although he was fascinated by the man: "He was not a philosopher; system was one thing Loren Eiseley knew nothing about. . . . I would say he was a first-rate Loren Eiseley and let it go at that."[25]

Eiseley's favorite image of himself, and the one he projected repeatedly in his writings, was that of a humble, self-deprecating scholar who wanted only to be left to his own devices. "In practice," according to Ward Goodenough, "he was susceptible to the blandishments."[26] The incident that firmly convinced the younger man of this occurred while Goodenough was serving as department chairman during Eiseley's provostship. Anthropology had outgrown its quarters in Bennett Hall, and Goodenough, in concert with Fro Rainey, hatched a scheme to move the department into an uninhabited wing of the University Museum. The site Ward and Fro selected was an old ground-floor auditorium that had long since been converted into a storage room. At one end was a stage in the shape of a half-moon, with a series of large, ivy-ringed bay windows overlooking the lawn and a fountain gracing the museum's entrance. For their plan to succeed, however, they required two things: administrative approval and the allocation of funds for renovations.

After one of their lunches at the Faculty Cub, where Eiseley always requested the same corner table so that he could observe without being observed, Goodenough walked him over to the museum for a look around. The provost said little until they reached the chest-high stage, where Goodenough set his trap. Just imagine what an office this would make you, he exclaimed, his hand tracing a broad arc from floor to ceiling. All the contractor would have to do would be enclose the stage and build a series of bookshelves between the windows. Eiseley's face underwent a sudden change of expression. "I could really live in here," he beamed. "This is great; let's do it!"[27]

The remodeling was completed before the Eiseleys left for California, and Loren spent three days supervising the transfer of his hundreds of books from Bennett Hall to his new office, two blocks away. In conscious imitation of Frank Speck, he filled the remaining space with bison skulls, mastodon teeth, pickled mud skippers, human crania, and plaster casts taken from the Barlow molds. Jake Gruber, who by this time was a tenured professor of anthropology at nearby Temple University, noted, "Speck . . . had collected everything he had in his office and knew what they meant; Loren settled for trappings."[28]

Besides affording its new occupant more space, the museum office yielded an unexpected bonus. Its domed ceiling provided an ideal acoustic environment in which to test a newly written poem or bit of prose, much to the amusement of Eiseley's colleagues, who inhabited rather less sumptuous offices on the opposite side of the wall. The failed actor's son had at last found a haven beneath the proscenium arch.

IV

Although he was not a great student of the Bible, neither was Eiseley a stranger to Scripture. He had long been fascinated by the chilling Revelation of St. John, the mercurial, some say deranged, evangelist of Patmos: "And I looked, and behold a pale horse; and his name that sat on him was Death, and Hell followed with him. And power was given unto them over the fourth part of the earth, to kill with sword, and with hunger, and with pestilence, and with the beasts of the earth."[29] To forestall Death and his companions—War, Famine, and Plague—Eiseley visualized another rider, a metaphor for the modern age. Upon him rests the burden of warning our technological society that it must change its profligate ways. "All his life," wrote one who knew Eiseley well, "Loren felt the spur in his ribs. It was the spur of the Fifth Horseman."[30]

Eiseley's third book, a slender volume published by Atheneum in the summer of 1960, is made up of the six lectures he had delivered as visiting professor of the philosophy of science at the University of Cincinnati the previous year. Dissatisfied with the original title, "Man's Quest for Certainty," he turned to Shelley, his favorite Romantic poet, for another:

> *The splendours of the firmament of time*
> *May be eclipsed, but are extinguished not . . .*

"Man," *The Firmament of Time* begins, "is at heart a romantic. He believes in thunder, the destruction of worlds, the voice out of the whirlwind." But he is also a pragmatist and thinker: "Indeed, so restless is man's intellect that were he to penetrate to the secret of the universe tomorrow, the likelihood is that he would grow bored on the day after."[31] It is this Faustian drive that most concerns Eiseley in the early chapters of his little work and absorbed him throughout his life.

After paying homage to the likes of Copernicus, Bacon, Kepler, and Newton, the author recycles the material he treated at greater length in *Darwin's Century*, writing this time as a poet rather than a historian of science. His message is a simple one: for all its staggering achievements, Western science has done little to create better, more responsible human beings. Instead, the individual has been plunged into a vast maelstrom of technology, "consuming flesh, stones, soil, minerals, sucking down the lightning, wrenching power from the atom, until the ancient sounds of nature are drowned in a cacophony of something which is no longer nature."[32] Worse yet, he has ceased to have a conscience—the trait that above all others separates him from the animals. Such stability as survives, such graces as remain, are the remnants of the old Christian order, although the ethics of private interest groups are replacing those of society. A new metallic barbarism threatens to extinguish the species; some distant traveler may one day visit the silent ruins of what were once monuments to Western greatness.

Eiseley's strategy for survival rests with the educational system. "The whirlpool can be conquered, but only by placing it in proper perspective. . . . We must never accept utility as the sole reason for education." Education should be, in the end, a process more interested in the cultivation of noble minds than in change, for science is not enough for man. Progress that pursues only the next invention, that replaces thought with idle slogans, is not progress at all, much less the road leading back to the waiting Garden. Yet even as the Fifth Horseman contemplates the possibility of taking another road, the roar of jet planes, the ostentation of poorly designed automobiles, the clamor of overcrowded shopping centers shakes his Kierkegaardian faith in the eternal: "Perhaps God himself may rove in similar pain up the dark roads of his universe. Only how would it be, I wonder, to contain at once both the beginning and the end, and to hear, in helplessness perhaps, the fall of worlds in the night?"[33]

This melancholy credo found a responsive audience on both the Left and the Right. Atheneum partner Mike Bessie sent a copy of *The Firmament of Time* to the impish Boston-born and -educated journalist Theodore H. White, who was frantically assembling material for his Pulitzer Prize–winning *The Making of the President, 1960*. "I have been reading it now, in snatches," White wrote the author while trotting between Nixon and Kennedy headquarters in Washington. "Down here, living in politics, I find myself clutching for sanity. Your book is the most solid matter I have found to clutch."[34] Scientist Rachel Carson, an impeccable stylist whose best-selling *The Sea Around Us* was soon to be followed by *Silent Spring*, her devastating attack on the pesticide industry, was also impressed. "There are few writers of English prose who move me as deeply as Tomlinson," she wrote Eiseley from her home in Silver Spring,

Maryland, "but there are passages of yours that have much the same magical flavor."[35] "We seem to have read the same books!" he replied three weeks later, having just recovered from another in a long series of ear infections. "I am delighted that you, too, have admiration for H. M. Tomlinson."[36]

Eiseley also received a somewhat curious letter from the publisher William A. Rusher: "A gentleman who wishes to remain anonymous has asked us to institute in your name a gift subscription to *National Review*, which may already be familiar to you as America's leading secular journal of conservative opinion." Normally the gift would have been announced via a printed notice, but Rusher, like Eiseley's secret benefactor, had also read *The Firmament of Time* and wished to express the hope that "you will find in the *National Review* a viewpoint not inconsistent with that you expressed so eloquently."[37]

With few exceptions, the reviews of *The Firmament of Time* were as glowing as the fan letters. After going astray in his critique of *Darwin's Century*, Orville Prescott returned to the fold. He characterized Eiseley as a scientist "with a profound sense of reverent wonder before the mystery of life and the grandeur of the natural universe. His prose style is more graceful and embellished with more poetic figures of speech than that of most poets."[38] And for once it seemed that Eiseley's fellow scientists had set aside their objections to mixing metaphor and natural law. Calling the final pages of the book "close to a prayer," Morris E. Opler, a Cornell University anthropologist writing for the *New York Herald Tribune*, praised the author for a rare sensibility by which Shelley, Donne, and Shakespeare are made to "rub shoulders" with Bacon, Lyell, and Darwin.[39]

Sales increased steadily. Ten months after publication *The Firmament of Time* went into a third printing, thanks partly to a wave of publicity generated by a series of distinguished literary awards.[40] At ceremonies held in New York City on April 3, 1961, Eiseley became the twenty-sixth recipient of the John Burroughs Medal, the highest award granted for a popular book in the natural sciences, thereby joining a select company that included his childhood hero Ernest Thompson Seton, as well as contemporaries Rachel Carson, Edwin Way Teale, and Joseph Wood Krutch.[41] December brought him back to New York and the Rockefeller Institute's Founders Hall to receive the Pierre Lecomte du Nouy Foundation Award in the form of a silver medal and a one-thousand-dollar honorarium. The citation read in part: "to the author of the best essay, biography, autobiography or other work which is of particular interest for the spiritual life of our epoch and for the defense of human destiny."[42] "I am beginning to be awed," Haydn wrote Eiseley in all seriousness. "You know that I have never had any doubt about you, but when a friend moves up to the landing where the rest of the world says it too!"[43]

An important award that eluded Eiseley happened to be the one he coveted most, though he tried not to show it. "I have just received the news that *The Firmament of Time* is one of a very small group of books being considered for the National Book Award," he wrote Hélène Boussinesq, his French translator. "Let me make it clear that I do not expect . . . to achieve the final award, if for no other reason than that this is a political [election] year and also the anniversary of the beginning of the Civil War here in the United States."[44] Two weeks later his hopes were buoyed by a short article in *The New York Times Book Review*. "Although you never bet on any action by an award jury, unless you're the sole judge and lack conscience, the hottest shots . . . are these—Non-Fiction: *The Firmament of Time*, by Loren Eiseley, and *The Rise and Fall of the Third Reich*, by William L. Shirer."[45] While only the winners among the five finalists were announced in each category, Eiseley created a little fiction to soften the blow after Shirer's work carried the day. "*The Firmament* has done very well here," he wrote to his British publisher Victor Gollancz in October 1961, "and you may have heard that it was the final runner-up against *The Rise and Fall of the Third Reich.*"[46]

V

Rarely had Eiseley been in more distinguished intellectual company than when he spoke at the Faculty Club of the University of Pennsylvania on January 23, 1961, four centuries and one day after the birth of the English philosopher, essayist, and statesman Sir Francis Bacon. Eiseley, who was tapped to deliver the prestigious evening address, chose as his topic "Francis Bacon: His Role as Educator." He would soon redeliver this speech as well as another on Bacon at the University of Nebraska, where he was under contract to present the Montgomery Lectures on Contemporary Civilization. In addition to the attractive stipend of $1,500, he was guaranteed a percentage of the royalties accruing from the publication of the lectures by the University of Nebraska Press.[47]

The March lectures were well attended, and Eiseley returned to Philadelphia with the promise that his fourth book would be off the press by August. Some weeks later, Carroll Newsom, who had also taken part in the Bacon commemoration at Penn, received a "curious" telephone call from his friend. Eiseley's honorarium check from Nebraska had never come through, and he wanted some advice as to how he should handle the matter. Newsom recalled, "I said, 'Loren, that's too bad; why don't you write to them?' " "Oh, Carroll, I can't do that sort of thing; would you do it?" was the response he got. So Newsom placed a long-distance call to Clifford Hardin, chancellor of the university, and explained Eiseley's dilemma. The embarrassed official, who could not understand Eiseley's reticence to contact him personally, especially since they were on a first-name basis, saw to it that a check was in the mail within a week.[48]

There was worse to come. The manuscript of *Francis Bacon and the Modern Dilemma* was so slender that the press had requested him to add a third chapter; those based on the two lectures had already been typeset. It was at this point that Eiseley left for Palo Alto, forcing dismayed Nebraska editor Virginia Faulkner to delay publication by a year. "Will you please let me know . . . when we may expect the rest of the copy?" she wrote him in California in May 1962. "Galleys were sent you on June 13, 1961, and March 27, 1962. No galleys and no copy have been returned."[49] With Mabel at the typewriter, Eiseley dictated a sharp reply, stating that he was "well aware of the facts." If only Miss Faulkner had taken the time to check, she would have learned that he had been in contact by telephone with Bruce Nicoll, director of the press. Nicoll had approved his plan to add new Bacon material about to be published in the *Saturday Evening Post.* Everything, he promised, would be in the editor's hands by June 1.[50] This was when Eiseley took his nasty header on the sidewalks of Menlo Park, yet he managed to submit the revised manuscript by the deadline he had set for himself. He admitted that the circumstances under which the book had had to be completed were trying to everyone involved, but wrote, "It is my conviction that where alterations are necessary—and again I use *necessary* as a word meaningful to both parties—the cost is justified."[51]

Nicoll, who had rushed to meet the fall publication deadline, wired on September 7 that bound volumes were due from the printer within a week. Thus, Eiseley would be receiving no galleys. A stunned author telephoned Nebraska immediately, then followed up with a letter fraught with alarm: "The situation is most disquieting, and it will be necessary for me to see a final copy of the book as quickly as possible. In accordance with our conversation I will expect that no distribution of the publication, either commercial or non-commercial, will be made while the situation remains unclear."[52] After conferring with the senior members of his staff, a worried Nicoll again wired Eiseley, who was back in Wynnewood: "Copy of the book being shipped today. All copies being held pending word from you."[53]

It was even worse than Eiseley had imagined. Chapter 1, which had undergone little if any change since he'd read the early galleys, contained no printing errors, but the remaining sixty-seven pages were badly flawed. With Mabel's help, he compiled a list of fifteen corrections before reaching for the telephone to do for the sake of his art what he had been unable to do for money. Chancellor Hardin listened sympathetically and then requested that Eiseley draft a letter detailing his complaints, which he did the next day.

The entire blame, according to the aggrieved author, lay with the director of the university press, with whom it had "become impossible" to discuss any aspect of publication. Nicoll had implied that Eiseley was acting in a "vindictive" manner, but he would let that pass, having no desire to pursue the more unpleasant side of the situation. "We come now to the crux of the matter. . . . Unless there proves to be a way . . . of repairing the present edition—something which may, as we both fear—be too complicated and costly—I feel that the only other recourse left to us is to destroy the edition." If this were done, Eiseley would be willing to remit his $1,500 fee for the Montgomery Lectures in return for all rights to the material copyrighted by the press. "The loss of remuneration . . . troubles me less . . . than the dreadful expenditure of time, which is a dearly bought commodity on the part of anyone who must write when he can, and not when he would."[54]

"We are quite willing," a conciliatory Hardin replied, "to destroy the entire edition, but we feel that the Press should publish the volume." The marred pages would soon be reset and the proofs delivered to the author well in advance of the second printing. During the interim it might be better for all concerned if Eiseley directed his correspondence to Vice Chancellor A. C. Breckenridge, "who will then deal with Press representatives."[55]

Eiseley was about to write a letter expressing his satisfaction with Hardin's handling of the matter when he got a call from a librarian at Penn. She wanted him to know how pleased she was that the university had just received a copy of his new book from Nebraska. Bypassing Breckenridge, he sent Hardin a blistering indictment by special delivery. "I hesitate to accuse anyone of deliberate malice, but I must say that I am cynical at this point about the ethics of the Press."[56] Breckenridge did some checking and learned that the responsibility lay with the print shop, which automatically sent out copies of Nebraska books in exchange for those published by other university presses. The vice chancellor ordered that all such volumes be either recalled or destroyed, then wrote to assure Eiseley that "none will remain in circulation."[57] At last, on January 15, 1963, the new printing of *Francis Bacon and the Modern Dilemma*, consisting of seven hundred paperbound and one thousand hardback volumes encased in dust jackets of red and black, was ready for distribution, an equal number having been committed to the flames, including the copy the author had personally retrieved from Van Pelt Library.

VI

To
Francis Bacon
And Sir Thomas Meautys
his faithful secretary
who erected his monument
and chose in death
to lie at his feet
sharing honor and disgrace
this tribute
from one who
more than three centuries beyond their grave
is still seeking
the lost continent of their dream

Thus read the dedication of Eiseley's latest book. The author discovers so many points of identity with his subject that in describing him he describes himself, beginning with the first paragraph, "Sir Francis Bacon . . . was an Elizabethan stay-at-home destined all his life to hear the rumble of breakers upon unknown coasts," and ending with the last, "Across the midnight landscape he rides with his toppling burden of despair and hope, bearing with him the beast's face and the dream, but unable to cast off either or to believe in either." In between, and notwithstanding his disclaimer in the dedication, Eiseley, like Sir Francis, after thirty years of rebuff and cold indifference, had discovered an unknown continent, "not in the oceans of this world but in the vaster sea of time." Bacon, the changeling who opened the doorway to the modern world while keeping an eye out for some supernatural guidepost in the night, is an "incomparable inspiration" for the few endowed with the proclivity for mythmaking.[58]

From an Eiseleyan perspective, Bacon was also the very model of what a true scientist should be: "a man of both compassion and understanding," who had the ill fortune to live and die in an age he never truly inhabited. Though loved by such literary lights as Ben Jonson, the savant was dismissed by his contemporary William Harvey, the experimentalist renowned for his discovery of the circulation of the blood. Habitually inaccurate in much that he wrote on natural philosophy, Bacon sought to disarm his critics by metaphor: "I can not thridd needles so well."

While his temper had cooled somewhat, Eiseley was still smarting over the handling of *Francis Bacon and the Modern Dilemma* nine months after its publication. Writing in response to a friend's warm praise for the volume, he complained of "being forced" to publish with the University of Nebraska Press, "something that I would normally not have done. This in itself resulted in a certain obscurity, but to make things worse, they did not indicate that these were . . . lectures given at the occasion of the quadricentennial of Bacon's birth," creating the false impression that commercial publishers had lost confidence in his marketability. The work had also become confused in the public mind with Catherine Drinker Bowen's new biography, *Francis Bacon: The Temper of a Man*. "Some reviewers have reviewed the two books together as though they are the same kind of book—which they are not. The more pedantic have castigated me for things I never intended; namely, writing a complete study of the late 16th century!"[59] Eiseley's misplaced aggression was such that he never forgave his Bryn Mawr neighbor—whose letter praising *The Immense Journey* he had eagerly copied and sent to Haydn—for treading on hallowed ground. Richard Stonesifer, a friend and admirer of both writers, remarked that "Loren hated Kitty Bowen's guts."[60]

Eiseley took some solace from the comments of Robert C. Cowen, the reviewer for the *Christian Science Monitor*, who wrote that he looked on modern science with the moral insight of an Old Testament prophet. "The main impression left with the reader, and perhaps the outstanding value of this book, is an urgent challenge to think through the implications of the materialistic trend that this outlook has come to have today."[61] Dwight Pennington, a features editor for the *Kansas City Star*, saw the work as a renewal of the intense inner struggle between the man of science and the man of art. "The result is a victory for the artist."[62]

Just when it appeared that the dust had finally settled, Eiseley received a fan letter from the head of a New York law firm. He, too, was an admirer of the great Sir Francis, but had not Eiseley's tendency to hero worship blinded him to Bacon's questionable conduct as lord chancellor, namely, his alleged acceptance of bribes and the subsequent trial that led to his fall from grace? "I feel that the ugly features of a scoundrel should not be prettified in an account of his good deeds."[63]

"I was not writing a full-length biography," the author retorted. "I have said what I said and I retract none of it. I do not think there exists sufficient unbiased evidence to call one of the greatest minds in Western thought an ugly-featured scoundrel. You may, but I will not."[64]

VII

Although Eiseley may have been loath to admit it, indications are that he had profited from this disastrous publishing experience. The sixty proof pages of *The Mind as Nature*, which included a lengthy introduction by Arthur G. Wirth, publications chairman of the John Dewey Society for the Study of Education and Culture, reached him on May 26, 1962; he read, corrected, and returned them by mail to Harper & Row the following day, a far cry from his handling of the Bacon galleys. But someone had inserted his middle initial on the title page. The offending *C* would have to be stricken before the book went to press.[65]

Eiseley had delivered the annual John Dewey Lecture in Chicago three months earlier, flying out from Palo Alto with Mabel. Wirth, who handled the negotiations, described the society as a "labor of love, manned by volunteers who are not interested in apologetics for John Dewey, but in sponsoring inquiry—provoking ideas in the spirit of the man."[66] In other words, Eiseley was free to speak as he pleased, just as Ordway Tead, Oscar Handlin, Seymour Harris, and Gardner Murphy, his distinguished predecessors on the rostrum, had been. He accepted almost immediately, only to second-guess himself as the deadline approached a year later.

It was not the speech itself that troubled Eiseley, although he complained to Wirth of being "much harried" by unexpected events a month before its delivery, but the financial arrangements he had agreed to: a fee of $500, $250 of which would be paid at the lecture, with the balance due after publication.[67] Following the address, he began plying Wirth with letters of complaint. A well-known institution of higher education had recently paid him $1,500 for two lectures, in addition to tendering a standard publishing contract with an escalation clause, providing for even higher royalties should sales exceed expectations. While the "academic man" would expect a "routine academic sale" of the book, a professional writer and essayist had a right to expect more. After all, *The Firmament of Time* was approaching the fifteen thousand mark in sales, and this was only a fraction of the figures being generated by *The Immense Journey*. "I do not think that the modest honorarium involved in the address entirely covers this question."[68]

Eiseley had a point, but he was remiss for not having made it much earlier. A flummoxed Wirth replied that he was not sure how to proceed. He had negotiated with all past and future lecturers on the same terms as those Eiseley had accepted. So far, in spite of the quality of the four authors, not one of their books had sold as many as four thousand copies, and this figure included volumes sent to members of the society in return for their dues. "We do not want to be guilty of unfair exploitation," he wrote defensively, but his hands were tied, at least until the next meeting of the Executive Board in July.[69]

Indications are that Eiseley became embarrassed upon realizing that he had put the publication's director in an awkward position.

Nor did he relish the prospect of looking bad in the eyes of Wirth's fellow board members. "I had no intention of implying that my small publication is bound to exceed the sale of that registered by other lecturers. It may prove to be less in demand than the one, for example, by our mutual friend and eminent scholar Ordway Tead."[70] In an attempt to save face, he suggested a compromise. *Reader's Digest* was interested in publishing his speech in a shortened form. Thus, he would be satisfied with first serial rights and the promise that the book would be copyrighted in his name. A much relieved Wirth raised no objections to this modus vivendi and neither did the Executive Board. *The Mind as Nature* rolled off the press in August 1962 and bore an official publication date of October 10.

As a would-be autobiographer, Eiseley was having little success. "The Divine Animal" had been retitled "Acquainted with the Night" (doubtless after the poem by Robert Frost), but all attempts to generate a sustained narrative flow were proving futile. To a similarly occupied Lewis Mumford, with whom Eiseley had recently become acquainted while serving as a nonfiction judge for the National Book Awards, he wrote: "I share your qualms in the matter of autobiography. It is the most racking thing that I have ever attempted. Structuring it is always difficult and I am sure that a great deal will have to be reworded and thrown out before I manage to achieve anything satisfactory—assuming that I do."[71]

Hiram Haydn was also stepping up the pressure, if ever so gently. Of course, the editor understood the problems Eiseley claimed to be having with time, money, and family matters. "It is really only, Loren, my obsession (if you will) with the qualities of your creative work that has made me persistently keep after you." He was sorry if he had overdone it; "Atheneum will take you as you are."[72]

Eiseley poured what little he had managed to get down on paper into *The Mind as Nature*. Stepping out from behind the mask of Francis Bacon, the author became himself. "If I develop this little story of a personal experience as a kind of parable, it is because I believe that in one way or another we mirror in ourselves the universe with all its dark vacuity, and also its simultaneous urge to create anew, in each generation, the beauty and the terror of our mortal existence."[73] The narrator went on to describe in detail the strangest of his childhood and adolescent hours: the birth under the rolling yellow cloud of loess; the frantic signaling to a mother deaf to his emotional advances; the broken actor daydreaming of one more chance on cheap land in Arkansas; the fusion of his psyche with that of Melville's alter ago, Redburn; the alienation that would be his for life.

Only after he had returned the proofs did Eiseley give any thought to a dedication. Considering his audience, largely college teachers of education, and the fact that he had singled out none of his teachers for recognition in the text, he asked Mabel to write Letta May Clark, who was now living in retirement back in Lincoln. Would it be all right if Loren dedicated this forthcoming work to an old friend from T.C.H.S.? "How could I object?" the delighted spinster replied in an unsteady hand, "I am deeply touched and greatly honored."[74]

The scattered reviews of *The Mind as Nature*, which overlapped those of *Francis Bacon and the Modern Dilemma*, were as enthusiastic as the dust jacket blurbs by Joseph Wood Krutch and Carl Wittke. Yet a hidden time bomb, which had been ticking away for almost three years, suddenly detonated in June 1963, shattering Eiseley's fragile ego. John Beuttner-Janusch, a fiery young professor at Yale, published a devastating review of *The Firmament of Time* in the *American Anthropologist*. Beginning with the observation that the volume has been hailed as an iridescent study by *Newsweek* and two well-known litterateurs, Beuttner-Janusch, "a mere physical anthropologist, opened it with trepidation, even awe." He closed it, 183 pages later, with a poor impression of *Newsweek*'s judgment. "The style, the studied cadences of dramatic emphasis, the plays upon words, the conjuring up of picturesque images, suit the hortatory mode of the semi-popular lecture." B-J, as he was known to his friends and colleagues, then proceeded to shred the work chapter by chapter, unleashing such barbs as "sentimental," "trite," "verbal brambles," and "a series of moral parables on a somewhat higher level than those found in the repertory of a fundamentalist preacher." "As is already obvious," he wrote in mocking conclusion, "the reviewer is disappointed by this book," which was not, as it purported to be, an essay in the history of science but a "work of obscurantism. Science *is* exciting and absorbing because of what it is, and, even for undergraduates, we need not inject mystery, fevered prose, overblown metaphors, and sentimental twaddle into our subject."[75]

"B-J was an overactor in every sense," a colleague later mused. "He went through life trying to be outrageous."[76] Nevertheless, there it was for all the professional world to see—the very indictment that caused Eiseley, who had long feared such a development, to shrivel in the night. Worse still, Beuttner-Janusch's review of Ashley Montagu's *Man in Process*, which appeared on the same page as that of *Firmament of Time*, was ecstatic by comparison.

In Eiseley's case, to be intuitively forewarned was not to be forearmed. Hoping to mend the breach in his psychic defenses, he telephoned Bill Krogman, who listened sympathetically, then promised Eiseley that he would write a letter of rebuttal to W. C. Sturtevant, book review editor of the *American Anthropologist*.[77] Krogman wrote on July 15, denouncing the critique as a "gratuitously unkind and . . . unworthy piece of work." Neither was he above indulging in some polemics of his own. "B-J (whom I do not know personally) seems to have missed the spirit of this book. . . . I do hope the man is never asked to review The Book of Proverbs or the Song of Solomon!" Krogman concluded with the observation that Psalms 19:1 "is a good antidote to this opinionated, wisecracking 'review.' "[78]

The heavens declare the glory of God;
and the firmament showeth his hand work.

When Eiseley's copy of the letter arrived, he sat down immediately and penned Krogman a note of thanks. "You have spoken for *The Firmament of Time* as its author could not possibly have spoken. I am deeply grateful to you and so is Mabel."[79]

18

A DANCER IN THE RING

I

Since *The Mind as Nature* had provided Eiseley a toehold, he was anxious to finish the autobiographical work, and the lure of a Guggenheim Fellowship proved irresistible. Other than a sojourn in the plains to consult newspaper files and renew his acquaintance with the bone quarries of his youth, he planned to work mostly at home, beginning in September 1963 during another leave from Penn. His needs were modest; he requested only $4,700 for eight months' labor, all remaining expenses to be paid out of his own pocket. The references he compiled for the selection committee read like a who's who in the academic and publishing world. Old friends Carl Wittke, Hiram Haydn, and Marston Bates were joined on the list by more recent acquaintances Joseph Wood Krutch, Lewis Mumford, and John Kobler, the biographer and a contributing editor at the *Saturday Evening Post.*[1] Bates's letter of recommendation to Gordon N. Ray, a friend and director of the Guggenheim Foundation, contained only three sentences. "I should think Eiseley was distinguished enough both as a writer and a scientist to need no support from me or anyone else, but I suppose the forms should be observed," he concluded.[2] Of course, Bates also knew that Eiseley was close to Carroll Newsom and that the recently resigned president of

New York University was on the Guggenheim Foundation's board of directors.

A month after submitting his application, Eiseley was summoned to a meeting with Newsom in New York. They almost certainly discussed the fellowship, but Newsom had something more important on his mind. He had recently persuaded multimillionaire Richard Prentice Ettinger, chairman of the board of Prentice-Hall, Inc., to fund a new creative writing program at the Rockefeller Institute. Primary emphasis would be on interpreting the sciences for laymen, and a number of fellowships bearing the name of their benefactor had already been established to this end. Rockefeller's President Detlev Bronk, who according to Newsom "didn't do anything halfway," pledged a beautifully appointed office and a generous expense account to the yet-to-be named director.

As Newsom remembered, "Loren was fed up with things at the University of Pennsylvania, so he jumped at the chance" when offered the post.[3] But not before first arranging a meeting with Henry Moe, president of the Guggenheim Foundation, who told him in confidence that the decision on his application was favorable and would not be affected by any arrangements he might make with the Rockefeller Institute. Bronk, who had long been a member of Penn's Board of Trustees, persuaded Gaylord Harnwell to accept joint sponsorship of the program, along with James M. Hester, president of New York University. Eiseley would commute between Philadelphia and New York, and Mabel was welcome to accompany him as often as she pleased.

The Richard Prentice Ettinger Program for Creative Writing was officially announced on July 27, 1963, amid a media blitz designed to blanket the East Coast. Mabel declared the inauguration a personal triumph for her husband. "Loren [was] wonderful in his morning speech, as chairman at the afternoon session, and as chairman in the evening."[4] In his address, "The Illusion of Two Cultures," Eiseley expanded on the thesis first propounded by author and physicist C. P. Snow in the now famous 1959 Rede Lecture delivered at Cambridge University. The British peer had warned of the dire consequences likely to result from a sharply divided intellectual community: nonscientists share the impression that scientists "are shallowly optimistic and unaware of man's condition," while scientists see their literary contemporaries as "totally lacking in foresight, peculiarly unconcerned with their brother man . . . and anxious to restrict art and thought to the existential moment."[5] Having thought long and hard about the problem himself, Eiseley reached a somewhat different conclusion. "It is because these two types of creation—the artistic and the scientific—have sprung from the same being and have their points of contact even in division, that I have the temerity to assert that, in a sense, the two cultures are an illusion, that they are a product of unreasoning fear, professionalism and misunderstanding." That barriers exist is beyond question, but the greatest obstacle is the discipline of science itself—the "marked intolerance of those of its own membership who venture to pursue the way of letters."[6]

The concept of the Ettinger address may have been sparked by a prior invitation to speak before an even more glittering assembly. Lewis Mumford, the newly elected president of the American Academy of Arts and Letters, asked Eiseley to deliver the annual Blashfield Foundation address on May 22, 1963, during joint ceremonies with the National Institute of Arts and Letters in New York. "Your acceptance, dear Eiseley, would . . . help break down the deplorable gap between Snow's 'two worlds,' for you have demonstrated how arbitrary and factitious that break is."[7] During the luncheon preceding the midafternoon festivities, the Eiseleys shared a table with the Mumfords, Georgia O'Keeffe, the Van Wyck Brookses, and the John Herseys.[8] Sophia Mumford, who especially admired Eiseley's early essays, which she thought were less emotional than the later ones, remembered him gazing wistfully out the window in the direction of an old graveyard. Noticing this, Mabel volunteered that cemeteries held a fascination for Loren; he never could resist them. Sophia sensed an underlying tension as well. "He wasn't as relaxed and at ease . . . as his general demeanor." She had also read somewhere that he was an incurable insomniac and asked Mabel if this was so. "The only way he really gets any sleep," she replied, "is if I have some women in for a tea party; then he can come and curl up on the sofa while we chatter about him."[9]

Following the opening address by Mumford, which Mabel in a letter of appreciation described as "a movingly beautiful message which remains in one's consciousness,"[10] the black-tie audience of 1,600 watched while many of the country's leading intellectuals crossed the stage to receive their awards: Lillian Hellman, Bruce Catton, Joseph Heller, Samuel Eliot Morison, Robert Penn Warren, and Catherine Drinker Bowen in literature; Thomas Hart Benton,

Jacques Lipchitz, Leonard Baskin, and Georgia O'Keeffe in art; I. M. Pei, Buckminster Fuller, and Walter Gropius in architecture.

Eiseley then took the floor and delivered his twenty-minute address, "The Divine Animal," labeled with the recently discarded title of his stalled autobiography. He spoke not of the two cultures but of Banquo's ghost and the midnight world of Macbeth's three witches, of Delphic utterances and the gloom and night horrors of vast cemeteries he had known. "The terror that confronts our age is our own conception of ourselves."[11] Joseph and Isabel Fraser, who were among the Eiseleys' special guests, felt a tap on their shoulders during the speech. A friend leaned forward to say something about Eiseley, and there were tears running down his cheeks.[12] A few days later Mumford wrote to say that more than one academy member had made a point of telling him that it was the best Blashfield address he had ever heard: "I would go even further. . . . Every sentence stood for a whole chapter in a book that must, when your [autobiography] is done, be written."[13] In replying, Eiseley revealed that he had been toying with the idea "a little," but then admitted: "Why, oh why did I say I wanted nothing so much as a year which could be devoted solely to writing?"[14]

II

Seven years after the publication of *The Immense Journey*, Eiseley felt safe in saying that the book had become "something of a small American classic," selling in the tens of thousands each year.[15] One printing replaced the next so rapidly that he barely kept count. After sluggish sales in hardcover, *Darwin's Century* had also taken on a life of its own. The paperback edition was fast becoming a favorite with college professors, who were ordering it at the rate of two thousand copies a month by late 1963, stimulating wistful thoughts of the never-to-be-written second volume.[16]

Eiseley often talked publication with Richard Stonesifer, a former professor of English at Franklin and Marshall College who, through Eiseley's good graces, had joined the administrative staff of David Goddard, Eiseley's successor as provost. "Stony" noted that "Loren was immensely interested in the design of his own books . . . and in the bucks that they earned." And woe to the publisher who was ill prepared for the Christmas trade. The two were walking up Fifth Avenue in New York one day when they decided to take a quick look in Brentano's. After browsing a few minutes, Stonesifer encountered his friend rearranging two stacks of books. "I said, 'What are you doing?' to which Eiseley replied, 'They had my book under some others.' "[17]

Stonesifer, who had arranged for Eiseley to receive a third honorary degree in 1960, a doctor of science from Franklin and Marshall, watched in fascination while he scrambled to claim others. Eiseley was driven to Washington College in Chestertown, Maryland, on June 2, 1963, to give the commencement address and receive an honorary doctorate of humane letters. Bad weather grounded the private plane scheduled to return him to Philadelphia in time to deliver the baccalaureate address at Bryn Mawr later that same evening. He arrived by car just in time for dinner with President McBride and a few students before giving the address. Jonathan Rhoads brought him home and gave Mabel a glowing account of her harried husband's performance. The enthusiastic audience had clapped at the end of the speech—"unusual on such occasions," she noted.[18]

While many of the gifted shrink from the spotlight out of enervating timidity, Eiseley ascended podium after podium to keep the demons of self-doubt at bay. It was virtually impossible for him to turn down an offer of publication—or to deliver on all his promises. Behind the public image of a steady and wise master of the tongue hid the alienated youth longing for the anchor that would enable him to ride out the inner tempest. Once, during an unguarded moment, he admitted to leading a painful dual existence, beginning in childhood: "At home, inside the house, I played with toys and blocks perhaps farther into my growing up than some children do. This was a little private secret. I was consciously aware that if I invited other children beyond a certain age in to play with me that things got smashed, or that I might be laughed at. And so I [sometimes] went outside and played roughly in the streets as other boys did."[19] In addition to his earliest books, he preserved as many of his childhood playthings as he could—a small hammer, lead soldiers, a sword, a miniature flag, the stuffed lion with button eyes. More than mere objects of nostalgia, each was a tangible symbol that love, however twisted, was not wholly absent from the curtained house on Lincoln's South Street. Offers of important administrative posts, writing contracts, and speaking engagements became steeped in the same symbolism. Each was an affirmation of his worth, and, as he did with his toys, he gathered as many as he could around him.

Eiseley never stopped claiming illness and despair, the child's ways out, when his burdens became unendurable. "It always seemed to me," a perceptive Betsy Saunders wrote him from the offices of *The American Scholar*, "that anthropologists could arrange to experience ancient and magnificent diseases, those unknown to the rest of us."[20] He had no sooner settled in at the Rockefeller Institute than Haydn heard, via the usual handwritten method, "The dark years are beginning to gather, Hiram. I have a feeling that I shall not write very much more after this present task is done. . . . I feel as though I hadn't a line left in me or that I would bother to set it down if I had."[21]

The writer was at his most creative when addressing the editors of the *Encyclopaedia Britannica*, who were never to receive his long-promised article on some unspecified subject. The pressures of his new post were far greater than he had expected, and,

> I recently began to have trouble with vague pains in my jaw and neck with consequent loss of mobility in that area. After some time lost through inaccurate diagnosis the trouble now appears to be cervical displacement with arthritic manifestations which happily, I am informed, can be gotten under control. These, however, demand some special attention and exercise with appropriate apparatus—again time-consuming. I have been advised to ease up on engagements whenever possible and above all to avoid, temporarily, long hours of bending over a writing desk.[22]

The editors would surely understand. They should also know that he had been forced to withdraw from an expedition to the Galápagos Islands under the sponsorship of the Sierra Club. With nature photographer Eliot Porter, Eiseley was to have produced a book with the working title "The Immense Autumn: Darwin, Melville, and the Enchanted Isles."[23] Citing "dire pressures," he informed the trade department at Macmillan that he had no hope of writing the short biography of Alfred Russel Wallace negotiated two years earlier.[24]

Official notification that the Guggenheim was Eiseley's came in

April 1964; he promptly applied for and received another leave of absence from Penn. Mabel reduced her working schedule at the academy to be with her husband in New York, where they shared a rent-free dormitory apartment two or three days a week. Because the Ettinger Fellowships, only three of which had been awarded thus far, went only to well-established professionals, the program entailed no supervision of any kind. Scattered among Penn, New York University, and the Rockefeller, the recipients were provided with office space, housing, and the equivalent of a year's salary. Freed from overseeing the fellows, Eiseley was charged instead with publicizing the program, raising additional funds, and attracting talented writers with a scientific bent. With Mabel looking on, he interviewed a number of candidates for the position of his administrative assistant before they decided on Caroline E. Werkley, a widow with a teenage son.

From outward appearances, all seemed well with the Ettinger program. The Eiseleys attended a formal dinner at President Bronk's in May 1964, where they met and talked with Adlai Stevenson, U.S. ambassador to the United Nations. Some months later Eiseley was appointed to the President's Task Force on the Preservation of National Beauty and went to Washington for a press conference and face-to-face meeting with Lyndon Johnson.[25] In between, however, reports of dissatisfaction with his administrative performance began crossing Bronk's desk. It was decided that Carroll Newsom should write Eiseley a letter outlining the specific complaints, the most important having to do with his tendency to let things drift while pursuing his own interests. Eiseley responded with an intemperate blast in which he offered to resign. Newsom, whom Mabel described as "angry" in her diary, phoned the next day, warning his friend not to send such a letter to the Ettinger family. No one was asking for his resignation; they would meet soon and figure out a way to correct any deficiencies.[26] Thus they were able to patch over their differences for the moment, but relations were already strained from a bizarre incident that had occurred the previous February.

The Eiseleys often vacationed in Florida or the Caribbean during the winter and were delighted when Newsom learned of a newly opened resort in the Virgin Islands. The foursome flew from New York to San Juan, where they boarded a private plane for the flight to a little island whose only level spot had been converted into a makeshift runway. A fast motorboat then picked them up for the spray-soaked run to their destination. Everyone but Newsom quickly came down with a debilitating intestinal bug. The party eventually got back on its feet and salvaged a few halcyon days on the white sands. But when the time came to make the return flight, Newsom became ill with a dangerously high fever. He managed somehow to board the boat with the Eiseleys and four other couples for the forty-five-minute pounding back to the airstrip. This time two planes were waiting, but, according to the pilots, there was room for only eleven of the twelve passengers and none of their luggage. The Newsoms never would have believed what happened next had they not been eyewitnesses. "Women in their frenzy to reach the planes lost their shoes and discarded bothersome items of clothing, and men pulled their wives along so that they would not lose out in the race: the veneer of civilization suddenly vanished."[27] Among the five men racing wildly along the beach was a distinguished writer, a nationally known scientist, and three others with accomplishments justifying their inclusion in *Who's Who in America*.

A worried Frances Newsom begged her husband to get aboard, saying she would stay behind. He talked her out of that plan and soon found himself sitting alone, sweat soaked, on a boulder surrounded by a huge pile of luggage near the shore of an unpopulated isle, empathizing with Robinson Crusoe. Stripping down to his underwear, he waded into the ocean in the hope of lowering his temperature. Several hours passed before he reached San Juan, only to discover that, with the exception of his wife, no one was speaking to him. The terminal lacked air conditioning, and the authorities would allow none of the group to pass through customs without luggage. Carroll "joined us but very grumpy," Mabel wrote after their return to New York. "Bags terribly heavy."[28]

Although Eiseley was not aware of it, his period of probation ended in early October 1964, when Newsom wrote Bronk: "I feel some urgency about the Ettinger Program."[29] Both were convinced that the project was floundering and that its director must go if it was to have any chance of survival. Newsom gritted his teeth and scheduled a meeting with his old friend on November 4. Afterward, he wrote Bronk of the outcome. "Although my assignment was not a happy one, I must say that Loren showed a minimum of resentment." In fact, he seemed almost relieved. "There is little doubt in my mind that Loren should never again undertake an administrative position." The meeting concluded with Newson urging Eiseley to return to Penn and his writing.[30]

A day or two later Newsom received a call; he realized he was in trouble the moment he picked up the receiver. A furiously bitter Eiseley began by telling him to "go to hell" and ended by vowing to have nothing further to do with either him or his wife. Eiseley had been betrayed by one of the fathers and retaliated in the only way he knew how. A bit later Mabel telephoned Frances, with whom she was close, to reaffirm that "things were off between the two families" and were destined to remain so.[31]

III

In the upper-right-hand corner of a manuscript titled "Charles Darwin and the Mysterious Edward Blyth," Eiseley jotted a brief but important note: "In May of 1957 this paper's subject was discovered."[32] He was completing the final chapter of *Darwin's Century* and was tempted to hold up publication long enough to incorporate new material. But the work was already past deadline, and he had to be sure of his facts before venturing into print. What he had discovered could be published elsewhere, most likely in "Beyond Darwin's Century," the projected second volume of his evolutionary history.

It was the brief interval between the time the H.M.S. *Beagle*, a barnacle-encrusted brigantine, sailed into Falmouth Harbor in October 1836 and the beginning of Darwin's first notebook on the "species question" nine months later that so intrigued Eiseley. While researching the scientific literature of the period, he had come across three articles by one Edward Blyth, a gifted, self-trained naturalist who, in Eiseley's words, could "remember the color and shape of a darting bird or a fox going over a hedge."[33] Blyth, who was Darwin's junior by a year, moved to Calcutta for health reasons in 1841; there he became curator of the Museum of the Asiatic Society of Bengal. In India he wrote copiously, in the form of articles, museum reports, and letters to Darwin and his fellow naturalists. Although Blyth's obsession with detail may have been something of an impediment to his intellectual growth, it was a boon to the semi-incapacited master of Down House. Darwin cited the heavily bearded colonial in his early notebooks, in the various outlines leading up to the *Origin of Species*, in the *Origin* itself, and in his later works. But what the great man did not do was cite Blyth's essays published in *The Magazine of Natural History* between 1835 and 1837.

Few concepts as complex as that of evolution have a single parent, and Darwin himself never argued for absolute paternity. To his dying day he credited Thomas Robert Malthus, the English economist and pioneer in population study, with triggering his thoughts on the mechanism of species adaptation and change. Darwin did not begin reading Malthus until September 1838; the breakthrough in his thinking supposedly came a month later, as he was finishing Malthus's treatise. Furthermore, Darwin had excised the pages of his notebook from the period when he was reading Blyth a year earlier, and these were nowhere to be found. "Our thesis is somewhat startling," Eiseley observed, "namely, that Darwin made unacknowledged use of Blyth's work."[34] Or, to put it less graciously, which Eiseley was loath to do, Charles Darwin was an intellectual thief.

The first article in question appeared a short while before Darwin returned home, the second and third within months after the *Beagle* dropped anchor. Blyth began by reiterating what every perceptive farmer and goatherd has known since the Neolithic revolution: sheep, cattle, pigeons, and all other domestic species can be improved upon through human intervention in the reproductive process. The naturalist was prepared to extend his hypothesis beyond the barnyard gate, however, to include the birds and beasts of the field. "To what extent," he asked, "may not the same take place in wild nature, so that, in a few generations distinctive characteristics may be acquired, such as are recognized and indicative of specific diversity?" May not "a large proportion of what are considered species have descended from a common parentage?"[35] It is significant that these thoughts are expressed in the form of questions rather than in declarative sentences. After speculating a bit more, Blyth, like Kepler, kicked gravity away. Favorable variations occurring randomly in individuals are bound to be swamped by the whole; animals drifting into new territory because of overbreeding would have difficulty adapting and perish.

But Blyth, Eiseley argued, had not seen what Darwin had, and this was certainly true: bones of vanished species related to those of the present, pried from the earth with his own hands; finches with beaks specifically adapted to survival on a single Pacific atoll; flora and fauna advancing in waves to flourish in seemingly alien territory. Whereas one thinker speculated on the analogy between artificial and natural selection, the other translated theory into fact, yet in the process he concealed a great debt and thus secured for himself an even grander space in the pantheon housing the gods of modern science.

For those unwilling to accept such inconclusive evidence as the missing pages of a notebook, Eiseley supplied a brace of smoking pistols. He discovered the first of these in a single paragraph from the notebook of 1836, in which Darwin used the word *inosculate* not once, but twice. According to Eiseley, "It is not to be found in Darwin's vocabulary before this time." Conversely, *inosculate* (to have characteristics intermediate between those of similar or related taxonomic groups) was a working component of Blyth's scientific lexicon. Of the three papers under scrutiny, this "curious word" appears in those of 1836 and 1837.[36] The second notebook, penned during 1837, contains equally damaging evidence from Eiseley's point of view. Never intended for publication, it makes unequivocal reference to the Blyth article in which the author queries whether a large proportion of species have descended from common parentage.[37]

With the centennial of the *Origin* fast approaching, Eiseley grew restive. His name was linked to no scientific discovery of great moment, but here was a chance at immortality as a historical sleuth. Why delay publication for three or four years when he would soon be in a position to make his case while the spotlight was fixed on the icon himself? Eiseley accepted an invitation to publish his findings in a book edited by Bentley Glass and William Straus entitled *Early Forerunners of Darwin*. As the threads of the plot multiplied, however, it became obvious that the deadline could not be met; he therefore bowed out rather than inconvenience the other contributors. The bulging manuscript, well over a hundred pages with appendices, was finally completed in September 1958 and delivered to the American Philosophical Society for publication in its proceedings the following February. Though Eiseley harbored no illusions concerning Darwin's unassailable position in the history of science, neither could he foresee the consequences that lay in store; otherwise, he would almost certainly have drawn back. The author was about to become the major participant in a running battle from which, even in dying, he could not disengage himself.

Eiseley was not without his allies. Charles Coulston Gillispie, a historian of science at Princeton University, was putting the final touches on his much acclaimed *The Edge of Objectivity: A History of Scientific Ideas* when the Darwin essay reached him. Gillispie read it with great enthusiasm and wrote to tell Eiseley that he had made the year's most "interesting contribution" to Darwinian scholarship. Still, Gillispie wanted to give the matter some additional thought. Eiseley would surely agree that natural selection "*does*" more in Darwin than in Blyth or any other predecessor.[38] Others were less kind, though most of their letters were destroyed, along with much else that reflected negatively on Eiseley.

Certain biologists, including the great Theodosius Dobzhansky, whom Eiseley knew as "Doby" from the Rockefeller Institute, were convinced that Darwin's failure to acknowledge his predecessors was unconscious. Darwin had traveled so far, read so widely, concentrated so profoundly that he was incapable of separating the disparate intellectual threads commingled by his genius. This view Eiseley refused to accept. Until recently Coleridge's opium addiction had been accounted the source of his inspiration for "Kubla Khan," "The Rime of the Ancient Mariner," and that ethereal moonlight fragment "Christabel." But meticulous research by Werner W. Beyer, a Coleridge authority, clearly showed that unconscious metamorphosis was far from the whole story. Rather, Coleridge's translation of C. M. Wieland's tale *Oberon* held the key, just as Darwin's reading of Blyth had caused the mental tumblers to click. "It was from no memoryless dream that Darwin drew his illumination. It was more like being led across the stepping stones of a brook into an enchanted land from which the first intruder, Edward Blyth, had leaped safely back to 'reality.' "[39]

However beautifully the pieces may have fit, as fit they did for Eiseley, he would be proven wrong, and he knew so before he died. A lover of libraries but not of archives, he had neither wandered the silent precincts of Down House nor visited the Rare Manuscripts Room of Cambridge University Library to see the Darwin papers for himself.

In a letter to his professor, John Henslow, written from South America on November 24, 1832, Darwin employed the telltale word *inosculate* four years before reading it in Blyth. For this piece of information Eiseley would not even have had to go to England, since the pertinent section of the missive had been published as early as 1835 and republished without any deletions in 1903.[40] The missing pages from the first notebook were another matter. As is well known, Darwin was fond of removing notes from his early works and filing them with material he planned to incorporate into future writings. Such had been the fate of the "lost" pages Eiseley considered so incriminating. When the first notebook was reassembled at Cambridge in 1960 by Sir Gavin DeBeer and other scholars, it became apparent that the charge of plagiarism could not stand.[41] Darwin had indeed referred to Blyth, but never in such a way as to suggest paternity. It was as historians had long argued, even as Eiseley himself had argued in *Darwin's Century*: the concept of evolution arose from a wealth of sources and data, but it had been transformed into a grand symphony by a single hand.

Reflecting on Blyth only two years before his own passing, Eiseley reverted to his role as victim.

> Be at peace, Edward. The man you sought came. . . . I, who unearthed your whisper from the crumblings of the past, have been here and there excoriated by men who are willing to pursue evolutionary changes in solitary molar teeth but never the evolution of ideas. We still dance in rings, Edward. . . . We round back, we return. Suppose we were seated, like the tramps we are, at a fire by the railroad. What would we say as the dark closed in—Men beat men, verbally or physically—is that the most of it?
>
> No, not quite, Edward Blyth. For you see, I knew what would happen if I did not close the book upon you there in the catacomb. I reopened it for your sake, left it open for the world to read. And what happened afterward does not matter at all. . . . We are dancers in the ring.[42]

IV

Eiseley visited his Founders' Hall office for the last time on December 30, where, with Mrs. Werkley's assistance, he packed up the last of his papers and cleared the shelves of his books. Adding to his air of depression was a request just received from the director of archives at the University of Wyoming. Eiseley's "tremendous and brilliant role" in the field of Darwinian studies had not gone unnoticed in Laramie. Would he consider placing his papers in the university's Division of Rare Books and Special Collections?[43] Taken aback by this reminder of his own mortality, Eiseley pointed out that he still had use for much of the material: "I think in my case . . . such a decision is premature."[44]

His ineptitude as an administrator had been so benign that his reputation suffered little from his failure, enabling him to walk away in seeming triumph once more. With the new year came a boost for his flagging ego. President John Atherton of Pitzer College, one of the five loosely affiliated liberal arts and sciences institutions in Claremont, California, telephoned to inquire whether he would be interested in the position of dean of faculty. The candidate flew west a week later and returned with a firm offer. While mulling over the proposition, he was visited by a delegation of his students who wanted to know where their class was "heading." Several days after this disturbing turn of events, Eiseley received a letter from an anthropology major containing similar complaints and a personal attack, which he chose to ignore.[45] The problem may have had something to do with the fact that he was frequently absent from campus and rarely announced his plans in advance. Jane Goodale, a former graduate student who hung on her professor's every word, said, "We never knew whether he'd be giving a lecture or not. . . . We might be sitting there, and after a little while the secretary would come in and [tell us] he was not going to be there today."[46]

With the California offer in hand, Eiseley reverted to his proven strategy of playing both ends against the middle. In early March, President Atherton telephoned again, upping Pitzer's salary offer to $25,000, some $2,500 more than he was making at Penn. Thus armed, Eiseley made an appointment with Provost David Goddard to apply some pressure. Awkward to a fault when it came to such matters, he as much as admitted that the meeting turned into a fiasco. "Although I tried to say what was on my mind, our conference perhaps left us both a bit baffled." It had never been his practice to let Penn know when he was approached by another institution, even when the salary and fringe benefits were more attractive than those he was receiving. Pitzer, however, offered other inducements, not the least of which was a more dependable climate and accessibility to the mountains and canyons, with their beauty and wildlife. There was also the matter of secretarial assistance. Mabel's health was fragile at best, yet "she has had to assume the responsibility of caring for all the mail with which my pockets are stuffed when I arrive home. The simplest letter, if answered at my University office, . . . may have to be done over as many as three times." If

Goddard could see his way clear to provide him with a combination research assistant and secretary, as well as a raise commensurate with the salary promised at Claremont, the situation would almost certainly clarify itself. The provost should also know that it was largely at the urging of Mabel, who had developed a generous feeling of attachment for Penn, that he had drafted such a frank statement of his position.[47]

Eiseley received Goddard's answer the next day in a hand-delivered letter. As of July 1, his salary would be increased to $25,000 per year, the maximum amount paid to any professor in the university. Moreover, the budget for the upcoming fiscal year would contain a $6,000 appropriation for a research assistant. Goddard was not ignorant of southern California's natural charms, but "I also know your need of intellectual companionship and access to great libraries. . . . I think you also know how deeply you are admired by many of our faculty and students; if you were to leave the institution it would be a major loss."[48]

Still, the couple boarded a plane to Los Angeles on March 22. Eiseley missed another week of classes while they were wined, dined, and chauffeured about Claremont and its environs by the Athertons. Mabel even daydreamed a little by spending an afternoon with a real-estate agent. Eiseley joined her toward evening, and they revisited a house possessing what she described as "many desirable features." Finally, on April 1, after nearly two months of deliberation, Eiseley phoned Atherton to inform the president he would decline. "In all the years of my manhood," he wrote wistfully not long before he died, "I have never lived in a house."[49]

It was David Copperfield, speaking for his besieged creator, who observed: "My notoriety began to bring upon me an enormous quantity of letters from people of whom I had no knowledge—chiefly about nothing, and extremely difficult to answer." Upon entering Eiseley's university office for the first time, Caroline Werkley was astounded by what she saw. Not only was her new boss's desk awash in unanswered mail, but two long tables held undulating billows of the same gray and white flotsam, some of which was two years old. More boxes of correspondence flowed in each month, and the two would sometimes remain at the Eiseley apartment and work all day in a futile attempt to catch up. Mrs. Werkley, a petite, attractive redhead in her middle years, assumed the title research librarian, but she quickly became Eiseley's girl Friday, Saturday, and Sunday. Indeed, she was literally "on call" seven days a week, an arrangement facilitated by her having taken an apartment in her boss's complex. Even on social occasions, such as frequent dinners with Loren and Mabel at the Stouffer's restaurant nearby, she always carried a notebook to jot down Eiseley's musings for future reference. Besides enjoying their pleasant company, the widowed librarian was paid an extra one hundred dollars a month by the Eiseleys, which offset the cut in salary she had taken on leaving the Rockefeller Institute.[50] Having no television of their own, Loren and Mabel often walked across the parking lot to join Mrs. Werkley and her son, Christopher, in front of their set. Eiseley's love of used bookstores had never waned, and he reveled in the fact that he now had an automobile and chauffeur at his disposal. Mabel cheerfully packed the bibliophiles off on Saturday mornings, then went out to indulge a passion of her own—shopping for new clothes.

V

Hiram Haydn's prediction came true; Eiseley, who vented his spleen in midnight letters, never developed an ulcer, but Mabel did, and she spent much of her time in various doctors' offices trying to keep it under control. Her other ailments included heart palpitations, colitis, frequent colds, infections, and fluctuating blood pressure. She celebrated her sixty-fifth birthday in July 1965, a year marked by increasingly numerous medical entries in her desk diary: "M. not well. Stayed home from Academy."[51] Yet it was her husband who had received a stern warning from another of their physicians, one Dr. Spoont. At two hundred pounds Eiseley was considerably overweight and headed for trouble if he didn't slim down. Denying his sweet tooth, he cut out desserts and began walking on a regular basis for the first time in years. The weight came off with surprising ease, thirty pounds in three months. Robert Spiller, who was on sabbatical during this transformation, couldn't believe his eyes when Eiseley strode into the Faculty Club. "There came Loren, a totally different man in appearance. His suit just hung around him."[52] Even Dr. Spoont thought his patient was looking gaunt and might have overdone it a bit. He suggested that Eiseley regain five of the lost pounds, with, in Mabel's words, "restitutions of desserts, etc."[53]

As one who had been instrumental in bringing Richard Stonesifer to Penn, Eiseley also supported Stony's move to Drew University as dean of the College of Liberal Arts. He accepted President Robert Fisher Oxnam's invitation to speak at the installation ceremonies in October 1965 and was driven, along with Mabel, to the Madison, New Jersey, campus by David Goddard, for whom Stonesifer had worked at Penn. An artist in the audience was so inspired by Eiseley's talk, "Man: The Listener in the Web," that she painted an abstract titled "Primeval Dawn: A Thought for Loren Eiseley." "As far as I can make out," a teasing Stonesifer wrote, "things were very dark, with splotches of red and blue scattered about! I haven't the foggiest idea what you said that engendered this, . . . but I pass it on to alert you to the impact you are having on susceptible maidens of tender years."[54]

Eiseley found it difficult to replace a lost intimate: "It still continues to be lonely here without you," he confided to Drew's new dean. "I see Arleigh [Hess] occasionally, but his administrative duties are pressing."[55] Much of the void, however, was about to be filled by the arrival of an old friend but a new face on campus. The partnership at Atheneum had recently gone sour, plunging Hiram Haydn into depression. It was not long, though, before the resilient editor was back in action as copublisher at Harcourt, Brace & World.

It was often said of Haydn that he could never quite decide what he wanted to be—author, editor, or college professor. Apparently it never occurred to anyone that this student of the Renaissance wanted to be all three. Haydn got his wish in the fall of 1965, when he was appointed visiting professor at Penn's Annenberg School of Communications without having to relinquish his editorial duties or shelve his latest manuscript. In a letter of recommendation to George Gerbner, dean of the Annenberg School, Eiseley called his friend of almost ten years one of the two or three best editors in New York. He also mentioned that he had been with Haydn at three separate publishing houses during their long association.[56]

Haydn soon presented his friend with a new contract for the autobiography, which Eiseley had retitled "The Counting of the Days," to mark yet another beginning. William Jovanovich, president of Harcourt, Brace & World, was so elated over the signing that he published a private Christmas edition of *Man, Time, and Prophecy*, an address Eiseley had given at the University of Kansas Centennial Celebration in April 1966.[57] Most valued were the observations of Pulitzer Prize–winning historian and critic Van Wyck Brooks, whose posthumous autobiography had recently been issued by E. P. Dutton. Only the fact that intellectual urbanites control the literary climate can explain why the likes of Henry Beston, Rachel Carson, and Loren Eiseley are not more highly esteemed, Brooks lamented. "Why are these writers of natural history now called popularizers of science as if their style went for nothing, as if theirs were the bottom rung of the ladder of science instead of an upper rung of the ladder of art?"[58]

If literary recognition was to remain elusive, what of the money Eiseley felt he deserved? Mike Bessie remembered having heard Haydn and the author discuss this matter in terms of the anthropology textbook for which Eiseley had negotiated a series of unsigned contracts with Rand McNally in the early 1960s. "Given his situation," Bessie observed, "[Loren] must have been terribly tempted because . . . for most academic writers that is the sole possibility of fortune."[59]

To achieve this end, Eiseley retained the services of Joan Daves, a New York literary agent who, with her partner Marie Rodell, had once handled the European rights to *The Immense Journey.*[60] Eiseley conceived of the volume as a set of individual essays that could stand by themselves, although it was his intention to link them in "a satisfactory fashion. The idea would be to survey the major aspects of man's rise to dominance in the material world and, finally, the dangers that this dominance has brought with it."[61]

Daves lost no time in setting up an appointment at Harcourt with Haydn and an editor named Sims. The three worked out a contract proposal by which Eiseley would receive an advance of ten thousand dollars, plus a generous percentage of the sales of both the hardcover and paperback printings. Daves also managed to renegotiate the contract for "The Counting of the Days," although it was understood that she would receive no commission for this because Eiseley had made the original deal himself.[62] Before coming to a decision on the offer, he slipped into New York without his agent's knowledge to discuss it with Haydn and Jovanovich. Then, before getting back to Daves, he wrote Jovanovich: "I have reached the time of life when to curtail projects seems suddenly more desirable than to assume responsibility for new ones. I saw this clearly as we sat talking together. It is quite likely that your own sanity and very good judgment had something to do with this."[63]

That Eiseley had been less than aboveboard with his new agent and publisher is apparent from an entry in Mabel's diary. Gerard F. McCauley, an author's representative with the New York agency of Curtis Brown, Ltd., had recently been her husband's luncheon guest at the Faculty Club. McCauley had taken the train down to discuss the possibility of representing Eiseley in negotiations for the very book Daves was attempting to market.[64] They reached no agreement at the time, but subsequent letters suggest that the two had discussed figures far in excess of the advance offered by Harcourt. Indeed, McCauley would soon have Eiseley believing that $100,000 was not too much to demand.[65]

In addition to an excellent salary and steady royalty income, Eiseley was commanding healthy lecture fees, which threatened to push him into the 50 percent tax bracket. The payment for a sixty-minute address, $500 plus expenses in 1963, rose to $1,000 in 1967, climbed to $1,500 in 1972, and peaked at an even $2,000 in 1975. He balked at any request to lower his fee and rarely did so except if delivering a commencement address when he was the recipient of an honorary degree. According to the surviving records, which are by no means complete, he earned a total of $121,650 for his oratory.[66]

March and April, October and November were the months that saw Eiseley away from home the most. Since booking agents cost money, he left the arrangements in Mrs. Werkley's hands, a burden Mabel had gratefully passed on. It could take up to three years to firm up a lecture date, requiring the exchange of as many as two dozen letters. When multiplied by the scores of invitations Eiseley received, the final correspondence count must have reached into the hundreds, if not the thousands.

Harboring a well-grounded skepticism of institutional publicists, Eiseley wrote his own press releases in longhand. He was unalterably opposed to having his speeches taped or published, because almost everything he had to say was headed for the printer at some point in the future. He was more than willing to spend time at campus bookstores autographing his works, which were often ordered in large quantities in anticipation of his arrival. *The Immense Journey*, far and away his most popular book, sometimes sold as many as three hundred copies during the weeks preceding an address.

Eiseley's anxiety about money was apparent when the Carroll

Clarks hosted their longtime friend when he visited Lawrence in 1966 to share the podium with Buckminster Fuller, Karl Menninger, Arthur C. Clarke, and Deane W. Malott, the former University of Kansas chancellor whom Eiseley had blamed for so many of his troubles. Pearl recalled being awakened in the night by the smell of smoke, which, it turned out, was emanating from the guest room, where a sleepless Eiseley had lit up one of his large Cuban cigars. She could hear him pacing the floor and watched in dismay while he grew more restless and petulant as the week wore on. He seemed able to relax only during a leisurely breakfast, the nocturnal demons having vanished with the light. They talked of many things, including retirement and money. Pearl remembered him saying that he had never had any money to speak of; now that he did, he didn't know how to invest it.[67]

Like countless others of their generation, the Eiseleys had been frozen in a corridor of time called the Great Depression; no amount of recognition or income would convince them that they were more than a stone's throw from financial oblivion. They purchased no real estate and kept much of their money in low-interest savings certificates at local banks. The couple lived comfortably, but they were light-years away from the multimillionaire status bestowed upon them by friends who tended to believe that all successful writers are rich. Although *The Immense Journey* would sell over 500,000 copies before its author's death, the vast majority of these were paperbacks, yielding only a few cents each in royalties. Had the couple been willing to risk more by engaging a competent broker, they undoubtedly could have done much better. As it was, they were no more willing to trust an outsider with their money than they were an agent with one of Loren's publishing contracts. Excluding life insurance and retirement benefits, Mabel would become heir to an estate valued at $228,073, before legal fees and taxes.[68]

VI

The doubling, sometimes tripling, of their income through Loren's lecturing and writing did encourage the Eiseleys to make a much needed move to a larger apartment in the Wyndon. With the help of Chris Werkley, Eiseley began packing and hauling the scores of boxes containing his books to their new address, C-105 on the first floor. Waiting at the other end, Mabel and Mrs. Werkley opened the cartons and placed their contents on newly built shelves in the study, foyer, and living room. Hopeful of holding her ground this time, Mabel purchased several pieces of furniture and a beautiful Oriental rug for the large living area. A used but lovely Steinway spinet also caught her eye, and, after having it inspected for possible flaws, she wrote out a check for nine hundred dollars and took delivery two days later. Out came the sheet music of Scott Joplin, and Loren may well have danced an impromptu jig, as he was wont to do whenever he exceeded his quota of Wild Turkey, his favorite straight whiskey. Across from the long couch, where he liked to sit and read by the window, hung the huge painting of sunflowers Mabel had given him as a remembrance of things past; before it was a long coffee table bearing several prized volumes, including three autographed works by Wright Morris.[69]

Mabel's domestic burdens were eased considerably by Mary Smith, who commuted to Wynnewood from West Philadelphia on Thursdays to cook, clean, and do the household shopping. Ignorant of racial overtones, Mabel fondly referred to Mary as my "black angel" and was forever making condescending notes regarding her progress: "[Mary] shopped for me at grocer's & did a fine job."[70] Yet Mabel turned down many social invitations, especially those that threatened to make Loren the center of attention. He hated to be questioned, Mabel mused, especially on such things as "Is the skull of a negro thicker than that of a white?"[71]

Neither Mabel's resolve nor Mary's domestic magic were powerful enough to keep Loren in his place. The books and writing materials overflowed the new apartment. "People wonder why we don't entertain," Mabel once remarked wistfully to Caroline Werkley. It was not long before the omnipresent research assistant found herself hosting the Eiseleys' guests whenever Stouffer's restaurant would not do.

No sooner had they settled into their new apartment than Mabel received a call from her brother back in Lincoln. Their mother was seriously ill and had been scheduled for surgery. Mabel flew out to join Charles and Dollie in the deathwatch. Edith Langdon recognized her oldest child but believed they were back in their old home in Hastings. The ninety-one-year-old matriarch passed away the following morning.[72]

Eiseley often criticized his own mother and aunt for their careless handling of what had remained of the family possessions. He charged that some of the effects had been pilfered, others forgotten in attics and in basements while he had pleaded his case in vain. "I was less real than the janitor who could be bribed by rare old china to go to the grocery store."[73] Most distressing of all was the loss of his youthful correspondence and hundreds of photographs. Mabel's diary tells a rather different story, however. She returned to Lincoln in July 1966, three months after Edith's death, to tie up some loose ends. Sorting through the belongings left at her mother's house when Daisy and Grace had been placed in separate nursing homes, she came across boxes containing Loren's childhood toys, scores of family photographs, and "our correspondence." Mabel tore up many of the letters and sent two truckloads of other "discarded materials" to the dump. Grace's two scrapbooks of clippings about Buck's career were donated to the State Historical Society; a bow hewn by South American Indians went to the Nebraska State Museum. The remaining objects—a few dishes and one box of "miscellaneous material"—were shipped back to Philadelphia by Railway Express.[74] Neither had Daisy's destructive tendencies been quite so violent as her son alleged. In addition to a pair of matching bracelets, Milo Corey had presented his daughters with identical cameo brooches and gold lockets. Inheriting these after the sisters died, Mabel kept one set for herself and gave the other to Caroline Werkley.

Upon returning home in the early evening, Eiseley often glimpsed a solitary figure leaning against the apartment fence. It was "Willy," the Wyndon's aging black garage manager, who was slowly succumbing to cancer. "The fence, and it was a rickety affair, had begun for Willy to mark the boundary between life and death. He knew he was on the wrong side of the barrier, but there was nothing he could do about it." When it was finally over, Eiseley found that Willy refused to depart. "I doubt if anyone else remembers [him] now, but I do. . . . He exists in me, he watches."[75] In truth, Willy, a pseudonym for Ray Scott, was neither black nor terminally ill, although the Wyndon's garage manager had been crippled by a severe stroke. Both he and his wife returned to visit the Eiseleys the year of Edith Langdon's death, and Mabel wrote of her deep admiration for Ray's efforts to overcome his handicap.[76] The resident carpenter and handyman was dealt a similar fate at the poet's hands. Mabel and Mrs. Werkley secretly commissioned him to construct a Victorian dollhouse for Eiseley one Christmas, the kind he had often described Milo Corey as fashioning for the daughters of Lincoln's wealthy. The gesture so touched him that he wrote a poem commemorating the event.

> *Given to me long ago by a master carpenter now dead*
> *the old Victorian house sits on a table in my study.*[77]

When Mrs. Werkley showed the piece to the carpenter, he became upset, protesting his premature demise. She finally calmed him down by explaining that poets, unlike the rest of us, are not always to be taken at their word.[78]

Obsessed by thoughts and symbols of death, Eiseley came to an important decision in the autumn of 1966. He and Mabel were driven by friends to West Laurel Hill Cemetery in nearby Bala-Cynwyd, where they surveyed the 187 rolling acres of sugar maple, sweet gum, oak, and birch. A secluded section devoid of the stately mausoleums bearing the names of Philadelphia's leading families caught Eiseley's eye. He walked the tract and stopped beneath a great horse chestnut, whose burred fruit lay thickly on the ground. Mabel gave her assent and returned a few days later to complete the financial arrangements. Reflecting on what they had done in a letter to John Medelman, who was completing an article on him for *Esquire*, Eiseley wrote:

> I am traveling so constantly that I am now short of sleep and very, very weary. . . . Yesterday, persuaded by the power of your words, I went out and bought a cemetery lot. It was a good time. It is the last of autumn here with still a touch of golden light, and many of the leaves are down. I stood a long time looking at a squirrel with a nut at the door of a giant mausoleum. It seemed time to cast about for the winter coming. I tried to pick a good spot not far from a tree whose leaves were coming down all around me. For the moment it seemed that this was all my education had given me—an eye for a good place to rest. Perhaps it will do as much for you and that is enough.[79]

19

THE SECULAR PURITAN

I

Among the meager belongings the New Englander christened David Henry Thoreau carried to his cabin on Walden Pond was a looking glass. He who scolded his fellow man for excessive vanity loved peering into the little mirror on his wall and the giant mirror of the pond, listening, as Narcissus once had, to the intonations of the nymph Echo. Walter Whitman, who was born and died writing *Leaves of Grass*, generated a gallery of images, beginning with a daguerreotype posing him as a young man about town, sporting a cocked hat and garish necktie, the handle of his walking stick resting nonchalantly on a powerful shoulder. "I've been photographed, photographed, and photographed until the cameras are tired of me," Walt once exclaimed to Horace Traubel, his indefatigable Boswell.[1]

Like Whitman and Thoreau, Loren Corey Eiseley altered his name to suit his self-image and recreated past; like the author of *Leaves of Grass*, he yielded to the potent narcissism in his makeup by having his image reproduced as often as he could. Never did he seem happier as a child or young man than when posing for the camera from atop a hill, tree, or building. Later, Eiseley allied his granite visage with photographer Frank Ross, who took dozens of melodramatic publicity shots. On the dust jacket of *The Night Country*, the author stands under the stark light of a streetlamp, the frayed collar of his topcoat turned up against the nocturnal chill, like Mickey Spillane. Writer Kenneth Brower confessed that this photo made him want to laugh, despite the nobility of face. "To get the good out of any writer, one must put up with a little something or other, and with Eiseley that something is often the Grand Pose."[2]

On October 15, 1966, Eiseley launched the first program in his new television series, "Animal Secrets." Edward Stanley, director of public affairs at NBC, had broached the subject over lunch the previous February in New York. Hoping to capitalize on the success of the network's other nature series, "Wild Kingdom" and "Walt Disney's Wonderful World of Color," Stanley envisioned a format closely oriented to the elementary-school biology curriculum. Eiseley would serve as host, or teacher, appearing on camera to introduce the topic of the day before fading behind the scenes to narrate the remainder of the script, which would be filmed on location. Taking a central theme such as migration, each episode was designed to show how creatures in the wild are able to match or even exceed man's achievements with no aid beyond their natural endowment.

As with his publishing contracts, Eiseley prolonged negotiation for the series by questioning clause after clause of the proposed agreement. Instead of taking Stanley's advice and hiring a New York lawyer conversant with such matters, he retained the services of a local attorney who apparently knew nothing about broadcasting. He finally signed on July 14, accepting a fee of five hundred dollars per program. Stanley also agreed to submit each script in advance for Eiseley's approval, but the same privilege would not be allowed regarding publicity.[3]

Shooting began two weeks later at 7:30 A.M. atop Hawk Mountain, some forty-five miles northwest of Philadelphia. Mabel noted that her badly sunburned husband did not return home until late evening but that the day's work had gone well.[4] The Eiseleys refused to spend part of Loren's $7,500 in broadcast royalties on a television set of their own, so Saturday afternoons at 1:30 found them in Mrs. Werkley's living room, confronted, like 4 million other households, by the austere visage of a forbidding patriarch in black horn-rimmed glasses. Formally dressed and reading mechanically from cue cards while standing on a cliff, the naturalist seemed strangely out of time and place. Shortly after the series began, a receipt arrived for the fifteen-dollar check Eiseley had written in compliance with a provision of his contract. Clyde Eiseley's son was now an official member of the Screen Actors Guild.[5]

As a personality who was supposed to appeal most strongly to children, Eiseley proved no match for the avuncular Walt Disney and his galaxy of visual pyrotechnics, or, for that matter, the plodding but grandfatherly Marlin Perkins. "For god's sake, Loren," a frustrated Stanley once exclaimed, "can't you smile or gesture once in a while?" Eiseley later told the producer that he feared his teeth, which were slightly discolored, would make him look bad on camera.[6] The ratings for "Animal Secrets" never met expectations, and network officials decided to reduce the number of programs from fifteen to eight during the 1967–68 broadcast season. The series was also moved to late Sunday afternoons to take advantage of a substantially larger audience with a much heavier concentration of adult viewers. *New York Times* science editor Walter Sullivan was commissioned to do a number of the scripts; Margaret O. Hyde, a secondary-school teacher in Bryn Mawr and author of numerous science books for children, wrote the others. Eiseley, who was on sabbatical and away from the East most of the time, took a less active role, leaving much of the off-camera narration to others. Although "Animal Secrets" had garnered the Thomas Alva Edison Award as the best science television series for youth, production was discontinued, and the final program aired on May 18, 1968.

II

Mabel and Mrs. Werkley were both returning to empty apartments in the fall of 1967. Caroline Werkley's son, Chris, was now a sophomore at Drew University, where Dean Richard Stonesifer was keeping an eye on the youth at Eiseley's request. Stony speculated that the Eiseleys were paying at least part of Chris's expenses, a conjecture bolstered by an entry in Mabel's diary the previous autumn: "Chris Werkley came to say goodbye before taking off for college tomorrow. Brought L. some birthday cigars & made a nice little speech which L. appreciated very much."[7] When the youth graduated, Stonesifer received a five-hundred-dollar check from a grateful Eiseley, with instructions to find a suitable use for it at Drew.

Eiseley, in the meantime, packed his bags and headed in the opposite direction, having accepted a one-semester appointment as

Johnson Research Professor at the University of Wisconsin, thanks in large measure to his old friend Kenneth M. Setton, who had served as director of libraries at Penn from 1955 through 1964. When Setton announced his plans to leave Penn, Eiseley let it be known that he wanted to be considered for the vacant post. His love of books was obvious, but the thought of him returning to administration caused many of his colleagues to cringe. Stonesifer, whom Eiseley ragged endlessly about his fantasy, finally had enough. "I said, 'Loren, the University of Pennsylvania is at a point where they're going to have to . . . turn from this idea of having a towering scholar as a titular head and get themselves a professional librarian. The day is over when they can appoint somebody who is in love with books.' " Eiseley refused his friend's counsel, preferring to believe that Penn was slighting him again, just as he claimed it had by not commissioning his portrait as provost. "Loren," Stonesifer concluded, "wanted to be honored more than was seemly."[8]

With no responsibility other than a single public lecture at the end of his tenure, Eiseley had little to do at Wisconsin but read and write. From his office high up in the Old Observatory, a quaint sandstone artifact situated atop a hill overlooking Madison's Lake Mendota, he enjoyed the most spectacular view on campus, returning in the evenings to a comfortable apartment in the Claridge, a rambling three-story structure some two blocks from the state capitol. Yet he found little peace. Writing to Rudolph Umland, whom he had seen the previous year while lecturing in Kansas City, Eiseley characterized the depression generation from which both men had come as nothing but a memory. "I . . . feel increasingly alienated and remote from the turbulent student body which I now encounter."[9] He had seen the *Prairie Schooner* infrequently of late and found himself scanning the list of contributors in vain for familiar names. Doubts assailed him in the dark hours:

> Idly staring at an old Victorian house which I could see looming . . . from my study, I grew aware of something missing from my life. I considered the wisdom of a search, a search unlikely to yield tangible results. I was aware that I was growing old and that in spite of much travel and brooding I was a man trapped in the despair once alluded to by a devout writer as the hopeless fear confined to moderns that no miracle can ever happen.[10]

Eiseley's estrangement from the world was matched by a continuing alienation from what little remained of his family. Leo, who was now retired and living in Phoenix, had lost Lola, his third wife, to a stroke in 1960. Two years later found his half brother married once again, this time to Vera Cedargreen, a teacher of music and voice whom Leo proudly described as a "refined and cultured lady." Upon reading in the paper that Loren was scheduled to deliver a lecture in Phoenix in February 1966, Leo telephoned and arranged a meeting. Eiseley's feelings about the reunion may be deduced from a letter to Olgivanna Lloyd Wright, widow of the famous architect, who hosted a dinner for him at Taliesin West: "I have never encountered a more openhearted and kindly group of people. I felt this particularly because of certain business problems that were troubling me during my stay in Phoenix and which made it necessary for me to leave early—something I will always regret."[11]

Vera Eiseley's health, both physical and mental, declined rapidly during the ensuing months. She fell and fractured a hip, forcing her deeply worried husband to place her in a nursing home. Eiseley telephoned to let his brother know that he would be living in Madison until December 1967. "That's the first word I have heard from him for a year," Leo wrote his daughter Athena, a popular radio and television host in Honolulu. "He only called because he had received my letter about Vera; says he just has been too busy to write, so I wouldn't bother writing him. . . . I don't think he cares to hear from any of us too much as [he] doesn't want the trouble of answering mail."[12] Vera slipped into a coma and died of congestive heart failure the following spring.

During his stay at Wisconsin, Eiseley wrote in his notebooks of lying awake through the night or dozing fitfully during the small hours and then rising at the first blush of October light. "I cannot lay claim to being a profound student of the human psyche," he later wrote Dr. Vernon Brooks, executive director of the C. G. Jung Foundation for Analytical Psychiatry, "but . . . it should be of interest to the Society that some of these poems have arisen out of dreams so powerful that I have literally leaped out of bed, dashed to my study, and written them down in almost a frenzy before they departed."[13] Eiseley ascribed the process to the impulses and motivations of the subconscious. Elsewhere he attributed it to his "daemon in sleep."[14] During an interview with the critic and editor Edmund Fuller, he confided: "I do write from remembered experience, sometimes even from dreams."[15] Nor were his visions always of the night. He was still playing the Ouija board with Mabel as late as 1958, when *Darwin's Century* was released. The epigraph preceding chapter 3 is credited to one Max, who often communicated directly with Eiseley: "The locks are rusty; the keys no longer fit, in the mould of time they have become useless."[16] (Max, it seems, was a British medium, judging by the spelling of *mould*.) Mabel later refused to have anything more to do with the game, but Eiseley and Mrs. Werkley, an avid student of the occult, played on.

The precise cause of Eiseley's insomnia was never diagnosed, but it had begun shortly after Clyde's demise in 1928. In addition, there was his hypochondria, and his left hand trembled slightly when he took up the pen. Eiseley wrote a physician friend that the tremor also had come upon him when his father died.[17] A substantial body of clinical evidence suggests that many long-term insomniacs associate their condition with a vivid experience involving death.[18] They awaken at the slightest sound: the soft creaking of a floorboard, a faint breeze rustling a window shade, the chirping of a cricket, the wail of a siren. The perceived similarity of sleep to death fuses in the mind of the overly sensitive observer; fear of sleep becomes the fear of death, a marriage incorporated into early human thought. Darkness, too, is associated with death. Eiseley often napped soundly in the afternoon, preferably when there were others about. Night was for listening and for watching. As a young man working in the chicken hatchery, he condemned himself to a lifetime of perpetual vigilance.

On occasion Eiseley could be seen riding about Madison and the outlying country roads in a battered green Volkswagen with a cloth sunroof. His chauffeur was a soft-spoken young man of Welsh and Lebanese descent named Walter Hamady, an assistant professor of art as well as the founder and owner of The Perishable Press Limited. Eiseley's ability to evoke powerful visual images had long made him one of Hamady's heroes. Upon learning that Eiseley was coming to Wisconsin, the printer wrote to him in Philadelphia, offering to show him his operation and suggesting that he give serious consideration to publishing a small, high-quality work of limited circulation. Eiseley could not resist the temptation to "chat" about bookmaking and agreed to contact Hamady once he was settled.[19] He made good his promise by telephoning to ask if Hamady would like to have lunch. "Right from square one," Hamady reflected, "I started in on him, asking why he was such a big faker that he's gotta be writing scientific tracts when he's really a poet underneath it all?" One has to earn a living was Eiseley's reply. "It was very relaxed and lots of fun."[20]

Armed with topographical maps of the surrounding counties, the two rattled down twisting back roads in search of autumnal vistas and whatever else of nature they could observe from behind the windows of a noisy automobile, for Eiseley never once suggested that they get out and tramp around. Certain of Hamady's colleagues, one a highly regarded ornithologist, were somewhat skeptical of his new friend's standing as a scientist and naturalist. Hamady remembered Eiseley's sensitivity on this point and his remark that he had written *Darwin's Century* to staunch such criticism.

Hamady's colleagues had made a point. The construction of a shopping center next to the Wyndon during the midfifties had covered the last acres of green to which a footbound Eiseley had ready access. He tried to compensate by raising cacti in the living room and keeping an ample supply of sunflower seeds in the cardinal feeder next to the kitchen window. Besides giving him hours of pleasure, the feathered dependents qualified as a tax deduction after he purchased a twenty-dollar pair of binoculars to better observe their movements in connection with his nature writing.[21] Neither he nor Mabel would so much as kill a spider on the wall. "Leave them alone," Mrs. Werkley remembered both of them saying, "they won't hurt anyone."[22] The couple had once returned from Florida with a box of orchids, only to discover that a small tree frog had come along for the ride. Eiseley telephoned the Philadelphia Zoo and was told that the creature must be fed live insects. He called a taxi and carried the little fellow to the zoo himself on Washington's Birthday.[23] Many was the time he told Mrs. Werkley to stop the car so that he could tend to an injured animal or collect a stray dog in the hope of locating its owner. Far less the humanist than most of his readers gave him credit for, Eiseley wrote his friend and admirer Hal Borland: "I would place my hopes on life itself, without naming the form. As one theologian phrased it to me not long ago, I am biocentric rather than anthropocentric."[24]

Before leaving Madison, Eiseley gave the public address required in his contract. Hamady termed the occasion "absolutely spellbinding. The aisles were packed, the stage was packed all around him in the wings and the hallways. You could have heard a pin drop throughout the whole thing."[25] After they shared a last "seegar" and bottle of Guinness, Eiseley invited his young friend to visit him in Philadelphia during the upcoming Christmas vacation. Hamady accepted and was given the Eiseleys' bedroom so that a prowling Loren wouldn't disturb his sleep. During their forays into the Wisconsin countryside, Hamady had suspected that Eiseley possessed no sense of direction, a suspicion now confirmed. His host drew him a map of Philadelphia, which, if Hamady had followed it, would have taken him to West Virginia. Working together, Hamady learned, Mabel and Mrs. Werkley drafted Eiseley's daily itinerary; "otherwise, he was lost." One morning, as he was leaving the apartment, Hamady saw him turn to Mabel and ask, "Is where I'm going in my pocket?"[26]

III

Time, it seemed, had reversed itself. The sixty-one-year-old Eiseley was suddenly half his age, almost every physical characteristic down to the commanding baritone voice unchanged since the day he'd first set foot in Philadelphia. Had Ricky Faust or Duke Tachibana glimpsed the young man entering the Eiseleys' apartment in the fall of 1968, they could have come to but one reasonable conclusion: Loren was the father of a son who had grown into a ringer for the lanky, dark-featured Nebraskan they had roomed with some thirty years before.

James Hahn, or Jimmy, as Eiseley was fond of calling him, was indeed a relative, but their uncanny resemblance to each other was a matter of chance. Dollie Langdon's marriage to Lloyd Hahn, a former Olympian who once broke the great Paavo Nurmi's world records for both the mile and 1,500 meters, produced a daughter and a son. Born in 1938 during the week of Loren's marriage to Mabel, Jim was raised, along with his older sister, Mary Ann, on the Hahn family farm near Falls City, Nebraska, where his mother taught women's physical education in the public schools. Jim entered the navy in 1956, after graduating from high school, and saw a good deal of the world during his four years of service aboard the aircraft carrier U.S.S. *Hornet*. The GI Bill subsequently enabled him to complete a B.A. at the University of Colorado. Jim was now thirty and married, forced to abandon his slender hopes of becoming a doctor. Instead, he accepted Eiseley's invitation to come east and begin work toward a Ph.D. in physical anthropology at Penn.

With his wife, Elaine, Jim leased an apartment in Narberth, one stop down the Main Line from Wynnewood, enabling him to visit his aunt and uncle daily. It was not long before Jim began thinking of Eiseley as a "surrogate father," an attachment made all the easier by virtue of their shared good looks and affinities of temperament. Eiseley often motioned to his nephew to follow him across the hall, where they entered a second rented apartment filled with his overflowing library. Other than bookcases the only furnishings were a couple of dilapidated lawn chairs and a simple desk. Jim would sit down, prepared to read in silence until dawn if need be, while his equally silent but temporarily secure companion "worked and worked and agonized" over some manuscript. At other times Eiseley deserted his fountain pen and legal pad to read, like a man possessed, for days and nights on end. When his eyes grew tired he would lean back and remove his glasses. He once explained to Jim that his habit of sitting with his back to the wall had been born of a nearly fatal encounter. While he was riding the rails between Tucson and L.A. during the depression, a fellow traveler had stabbed him from behind with a knife.[27]

Nevertheless, Eiseley was fascinated by weapons; he was always bringing home an old gun or knife that had caught his eye in the window of a pawnshop or antique store. One fall evening, as Jim was walking across the parking lot behind the Wyndon with his aunt and uncle, his foot uncovered a .356 Magnum round hidden beneath some leaves. The men simultaneously dropped to their knees and discovered two more shells directly in front of a Salvation Army drop box. "We looked at each other and instantly evolved the truth." Ignoring the stenciled warning that illegal entrants would forever burn in hell, they found an old piece of iron and pried off the box's door. Jim climbed inside and began handing out the various contents, which Eiseley ransacked in search of the pistol. "It was *ours*, you know. All we needed was a little archaeology to produce the artifact." But before they could expose their prize, Mabel put a stop to the excavation. The two were berated like little boys and sent back to the apartment, where, Jim recalled, "we sheepishly assumed our position in the back room with elegant cigars. She brought us both tall glasses of Wild Turkey, and a few cookies. She did this reluctantly, and with a small lecture: 'Did You Boys Have Fun!'

Then her gentle voice broke to add, 'God, but you guys shouldn't really hang around together. It's an insult to culture and decency.' " Later that evening they listened while the collectors picked up the container. Eiseley looked mournfully at Jim and exclaimed, "Well, there it goes. Rats!"[28]

Once, when Charles Langdon visited Philadelphia, Eiseley and his brother-in-law decided to ham it up, western style, for the camera. The two combed their hair forward and sat down on Mabel's piano bench, each with a six-shooter in one hand, a glass of whiskey in the other, mugging like derelicts from Deadwood. Jim was somewhat surprised when his uncle told him that he never went unarmed into New York City. His choice of weapons on these occasions was a nine-inch forged-steel knife with a recurved hilt. "Knife, no. Not hardly, Jimmy, it's only a subway tool. After all, if we must go underground, it's best we be prepared. God knows what's down there."[29]

The campus office Eiseley so loved was also a source of great personal embarrassment. His fellow anthropologists, who were less sumptuously quartered, had to be passed whenever he headed for center stage. It finally got to the point where Jim was required to scout ahead, then telephone his uncle, who waited anxiously nearby, to tell him that the coast was clear. Even drinking had its pitfalls, for Eiseley refused to walk over to the neighborhood liquor store when his supply of bourbon ran low, sending Mabel or Mrs. Werkley instead. Whether this foible had anything to do with Buck's onetime alcoholism and the attendant family repercussions is difficult to say, but the women were not shy about scolding the secular Puritan for this contradiction of character.

Eiseley's sense of humor surfaced only when he was among relatives or with a small circle of intimates. Jim had a boyhood memory of his evolutionist uncle trying to get his fundamentalist mother's goat. Chewing on a toothpick, Eiseley suggested that man's ancestors had eaten wood to stay alive. Jim took the bait and went running to tell Dollie that Uncle Loren said that human beings were once termites. When Dollie protested, Eiseley feigned surprise and suggested that the lad had misunderstood, leaving his sister-in-law to stew. Once, during a visit to Stouffer's restaurant, Jim watched while Eiseley grew impatient at waiting in line. Afraid that he might lose his favorite corner seat, he hiked up his pants legs, broke ranks, and clambered over the furniture, tabletops and all, exclaiming,

"There, that's better!" Mabel was so angry and humiliated that she told him he would be going out alone in the future if he ever pulled such a childish stunt again.[30]

The couple loved to tell the story of their nearly disastrous first date. Eiseley had arranged to pick Mabel up at her parents' home on D Street. Arriving somewhat early, he met the man of the house and was asked to be seated. The minutes passed, but Mabel failed to appear, and small talk, which Eiseley was never good at, was wearing thin. Without warning a strange girl materialized on the stairwell and was shocked when confronted by an equally strange suitor. Eiseley had overshot his destination by a block, while Mabel, thinking she had been stood up, waited in anger. Years later she would poke him in the ribs and chide: "Fate led you directly to another, but no, not you. You didn't even have enough good sense to see it. Now look what you've got."[31]

Only once did Jim see his uncle cross the threshold of ribaldry. Eiseley was winding up his course on human paleontology, in which he had painstakingly explained the differences between man and the other primates, including the finer points of their sexual behavior. At exam time a coed wrote on her paper, "Man is sexually active at all times." Eiseley jotted in the margin, "I do not know who you have met, but he is a better man than I."[32]

Although often months behind, Eiseley made a conscientious attempt to answer all his fan mail, with one notable exception. Any letter written in brightly colored ink was dismissed on the ground that its author must be an oddball.[33] Others among his admirers requested a private audience for the purpose, in Mabel's words, of "touching the hem of his garment."[34] When Eiseley assented, arrangements were usually made to meet visitors in the corridor of the Anthropology Department, where he could readily size them up. Ill-matching socks, a strange hat, or other evidence of sartorial idiosyncrasy meant that the initial exchange of pleasantries would not be followed by more intimate conversation in Eiseley's sanctum sanctorum, the entry to which Mrs. Werkley protected with the single-mindedness of a Praetorian Guard. "Fame," Eiseley wrote a friend,

> brings trouble in its wake; people even on one's own campus who make up excuses to come and stare at you as though you were an animal in a cage, neurotics who wish you to endorse their unpub-

> lishable books which you have not solicited, mysterious phone calls from the lunatic fringe until one has to seek safety with an unlisted phone number, and people who seek to turn you into a "guru" at one of these odd institutions in California where people go to "explore" their minds.[35]

Upon returning from Topeka, Kansas, where he served a brief stint as Sloane Visiting Professor at The Menninger Foundation, Eiseley told Jim that *The Immense Journey* was being used as therapy, adding, "I hope the boys downstairs don't hear of this."[36]

Neither a seer nor a mystic, Eiseley was often mistaken for both—images conjured up by the poetry in his prose and by the talismans with which he surrounded himself. These included a "monster" figure from Africa, a number of magical appliances, and what Jim described as some "strange balls" of stone. His uncle had also acquired a crystal ball at one of the local antique shops, as well as a beautifully crafted Byzantine cross of the finest silver. This he wore around his neck on a handmade silver chain, not for religious reasons but because he admired it as a piece of art. Such objects, Jim recalled Eiseley confiding, "were used to his humor. He loved the guise of the mystic and yet he himself was not."[37] Jim felt that Eiseley was best characterized as an escape artist. Once, when the two were alone in the spare apartment, the conversation turned to the Apocalyptic Fifth Horseman. If there truly were such a rider, Jim queried, what color horse would he choose? "He in turn answered me with a question, 'What color is a chameleon?' "[38]

When his hand was forced, however, Eiseley spoke to the issue without equivocation, as in a holograph rebuttal to an aggravating review published in the *American Journal of Physical Anthropology* in 1956:

> In Russia, when the state for political reasons desires to destroy the public reputation of a writer, scientist, or official, one of the several epithets which may be used to convey the man's deviation from the party line is the word "mystic." . . . As an occasional student of the history of thought, I cannot resist the observation that this name-calling device occasionally emerges here in some few scientific quarters where there is an unconscious attachment to an extremely materialistic world view similar to that which broods with such intensity over the Russian landscape. One may write, for example, a nature essay in the purely literary tradition,

> expressing some feeling for the marvelous, or the wonder of life—things perfectly accepted when pursued in such old classics as Thoreau or Hudson, and then awake to discover that a certain element in the "union" regards one's activities in this totally separate field as "mystical" and "alien to the spirit of science." It was not so among the great Renaissance thinkers, but the growing compartmentalization of thought has contributed to a trade feeling that the shoemaker should stick to his last.[39]

Although the cant was missing, he said virtually the same thing in an interview with Edmund Fuller fifteen years later. "I know this term [mystic] has been sometimes applied to me as though I were lost in some kind of sectarian theology, which is outrageous."[40]

Yet it is easy to see why Eiseley earned such a reputation. He was neither an ideologue nor a polemicist, or, for that matter, an especially systematic thinker. The beauty of language was paramount to him, and he often contradicted himself for the sake of turning a phrase. Contradiction is, of course, commonplace in the writings of Thoreau and Whitman, but neither of them attempted credibility in science.

The artist in Eiseley bridled whenever a serious attempt was made to pin him down. A high-school teacher of English once visited his office hoping that he would explain certain passages in *The Immense Journey*, which she was using in one of her classes. Eiseley told her of Hawthorne's wife, Sophia Peabody, who attempted, without much success, to coax Melville into explaining *Moby-Dick*. Yeats, he went on to point out, also evaded such questions "rather neatly." "If you leave it open, people can then go on and create their own images and see things in their own way. . . . I am a man in flight; I have always been so, . . . and that is how I choose to remain."[41]

IV

While visiting the Southwest in the summer of 1967, Hiram Haydn had been felled by a heart attack. The peripatetic editor spent weeks flat on his back in a Santa Fe hospital before returning to his home on Martha's Vineyard, where he continued to recuperate. Rather than wait for his friend to recover, Eiseley chose this moment to write Haydn's boss, William Jovanovich, concerning one of his two publishing contracts with Harcourt, Brace & World. Citing the stress of academic pressures, he had decided to return the five-thousand-dollar advance on his intellectual autobiography. This, he hastened to add, did not mean that he had given up on the project, but "I think it best, and a matter of conscience, to return the money advanced and simply let our contract stand. . . . I have written Hiram but I have deliberately avoided intruding upon his rest by discussing these matters or calling him on the phone."[42] When informed of Eiseley's actions after coming back to work in November, Haydn wrote to say that he was perplexed: "Please straighten me out." Instead of writing, Eiseley jotted across the top of Haydn's query, "Answered by phone."[43] It was probably at this point that he first told Haydn the book would never be written and that it would be better for all concerned if the contract was nullified. Thinking this was just another of Eiseley's passing moods, Haydn consulted with Jovanovich, who agreed that they should wait for a break in the writer's inner weather.[44]

At the same time, work on the other volume, which Eiseley had decided to title "The Unexpected Universe," was giving him major problems. He wrote to Jovanovich of "a certain blockage" that had prevented him from meeting his projected deadline and suggested that they plan for publication in the fall of 1968.[45] But by late January of that year he estimated that the series of essays would not be finished for at least another six months. An old friend at the University of Wisconsin had lost his wife while Eiseley was in residence. "As a consequence," he wrote Haydn, "I spent a good deal of time with him in order to see him through." What he termed "social necessities" had also intruded heavily on his schedule.[46] He might have added that Mabel had not accompanied him to the Midwest, and her absence had removed a crucial factor from the equation. September 1968 and the familiar surroundings of Wynnewood found him closer to finishing, but once more he had been deserted by his Muse, a malady common to the writer of fiction. "Like the veriest amateur I have gone dry and am waiting for inspiration—if there is such a quantity. . . . In short, I grow old. This book, burdensome though it is, now threatens to be my swan song, rather than the autobiography. You cannot imagine how I yearn for retirement." Although he regretted the delay, he was now certain that "The Unexpected Universe" would not see the light of day until the fall of 1969. "I feel I have let you down and I do not know what to say about it."[47] But Haydn, as always, did: "Your publisher's belief in you will never wane."[48]

Things were rather less bleak on the other side of the ledger. *Life* magazine contracted to pay Eiseley $7,500 for the first serial rights to "The Angry Winter," an essay about his mythical shepherd named Wolf, which constituted chapter 5 of the yet unfinished manuscript. The editors hit a snag, however, when Eiseley became piqued at their decision to cut the piece in several places. They responded by sending a letter to Harcourt, stating that nothing would go to press without the author's consent. "I hope he will not fault me for trying," *Life*'s David Maness quipped, "he has nothing to lose but his temper."[49] When the article was slow to appear, a simmering Eiseley wrote the following in the margin of another letter from Maness: "answered longhand to the effect that it's *probably* February [1968] or nothing and that as Wolf's representative we have our pride and they can have their money back if they choose."[50] "There is no question," came the immediate reply. "We publish in February."[51]

Haydn took delivery of "The Unexpected Universe," minus one chapter, in February 1969 and promptly scheduled publication for October. A memo from Jovanovich termed the manuscript "simply *Great*," and its "wildly enthusiastic" reception by Harcourt's sales force caused the editor to go out on a limb and order a first printing of twenty thousand copies.[52]

Eiseley's usual prepublication jitters were fully fledged by June, especially the scars left by his psychic assassin, John Beuttner-Janusch. "My primary fear," he confided to Haydn, "is that the overemphasis upon me as an anthropologist will cause the book to be reviewed as such when it is in reality a kind of personal philosophy. . . . The danger is that the standard weeklies will have it reviewed by professional anthropologists who may be humorless in this connection. This I have had happen before." Yet neither did he wish the book to be labeled as "science for the layman." Better to advertise it as "a naturalist's personal encounter with the universe." He concluded by drafting a paragraph to be incorporated into the dust jacket, which Haydn did, no questions asked.[53]

Affecting nonchalance, Eiseley also wrote to Hilda Lindley, Haydn's assistant, about the publicity campaign. "I am very weary of the mass media and not particularly anxious to appear, but as I indicated to Hiram earlier in the spring, I would not object to a very few carefully selected appearances." It so happened that he knew someone with connections at NBC (doubtless Edward Stanley) who could arrange an interview on the "Today Show," which Eiseley himself had never seen. He had read in the *New York Times*, however, that such programs tend to make "a gull or clown out of the guest," but his reservations went deeper than this: "I spoke of my mother in 'The Star Thrower' under circumstances that I would not wish to elaborate further." The same was true of several other highly personal matters in the book.[54]

Indeed, the author had already experienced considerable discomfort as a result of his tendency to mythologize. Eiseley dedicated his latest literary effort to Wolf, "who sleeps forever with an ice age bone across his heart, the last gift of one who loved him." In the opening of "The Angry Winter," the beast is described as a big shepherd dog lying contentedly beside his bone-hunting master before a blazing hearth. On Eiseley's desk are the lance points of Pleistocene hunters and the massive leg bone of a fossil bison, a bone so mineralized that it rings when struck. As the night deepens, the fossil is absently placed on the floor. "A grating noise, a heavy rasping of teeth diverted me. I looked down." Wolf is mouthing the object with a fierce intensity. Eiseley tries to recover the fossil, but his efforts are met by a "low and steady rumbling . . . out of a long-gone midnight. . . . There is nothing in that bone to taste, but ancient shapes were moving in his mind and determining his utterance." Wolf's ferocity increases, the process of transformation seemingly irreversible: the rumbling has given way to a snarl, the flat head sways "low and wickedly as a reptile's above the floor." The most beloved object in the creature's universe is about to be sacrificed to primal memory.[55]

Fusing splinters from the past into fiction, Eiseley's Wolf was a combination of Frank and Linda Roberts's snuffling chow, Punky, and the black and tan German shepherd owned by Frank Denton, a fellow member of the old South Party. Eiseley's caption on a photograph taken in 1933 reads: "Frank Denton to whose roost I fled. Tough guy and crack shot, reserve officer, graduate in Geology. His dog Buster with whom I used to wrestle all evening."[56]

Eiseley had told the same story not only in *Life* magazine but in *Reader's Digest* as well, under the title "The Night the Shadows Whispered." A skeptical physician, who read the *Reader's Digest* version, wrote to ask the author how Wolf could identify a chunk of silica without a trace of organic matter in it. Eiseley postulated that "some kind of dim mental imprint of the shape may be carried in the germ plasm." Then, realizing that such a hypothesis might seem too farfetched to a fellow scientist, he qualified his remark: "The story was being used symbolically to open an account of man's Ice Age experience. The *Digest*, as you know, chops everything down considerably."[57]

Finer even than "The Angry Winter" is "The Star Thrower," a mythic venture set in a more hospitable clime—the spume-flecked beaches of an isle called Costabel. One frustrated reader confessed to having consulted three unabridged dictionaries, three atlases, several encyclopedias, and a number of other works to no avail: "Could it be that Costabel is a figment of your imagination, or is it simply a bend in the seashore which appears on no map?"[58] "The truth is," Eiseley replied, "that I like the sound of the name, that I picked it up by listening to a seashell many years ago somewhere on what has been sometimes called the coast of illusion."[59] He admitted, however, that the "hotel area" as described in the essay was real. Another admirer had already guessed the truth. Eiseley had padded noiselessly behind him on the beaches of Florida's Sanibel Island. "Sanibel, as you probably know, is a sheller's paradise, attracting at once the materialist pursuer of valuable shells and the somnolent seeker of truths. You capture the feeling well in 'The Star Thrower.' "[60]

Not only was the physical setting congenial but it gave the Eiseleys the opportunity to visit their old friend Lou Korn and his second wife, Dot, who lived just a few miles away in Fort Myers. Lou, a widower, had remarried in September 1965, giving Eiseley the opportunity to stand up with the man who had been at his and Mabel's side when they exchanged vows before a grandiloquent judge on that hot but hilarious August afternoon in 1938. Now that Carroll and Frances Newsom were out of the picture, the Eiseleys spent much of their vacation time in the Poconos, where Lou owned a summer home on Lake Wallenpaupack, just east of Scranton. There Eiseley wrote and strolled the wooded shoreline with Beau, the Korns' huge black poodle, who frequently stole into the back bedroom to lick his guests awake at dawn.[61] Some of the material for his television series, "Animal Secrets," was also filmed in the area, and in February 1968 the two couples traveled together by car to Sanibel, where a production crew from NBC awaited their arrival to begin shooting the final programs. Only after the filming was completed did Eiseley get down to the business of taking notes on his surroundings for the purposes of lecturing and writing.

V

Whenever one of his uncle's books was about to be released, Jim reflected, Eiseley literally ran for cover, holing up in the apartment for a few days until word got around and the first reviews were in hand. He need not have worried about *The Unexpected Universe*; the book took off like a rocket, propelled by reviews as glowing as the incoming sales figures.

Destined never to make the best-seller list, Eiseley came tantalizingly close in December 1969, when he appeared on the Nonfiction Runners-up list, along with author Gay Talese and soothsayer Jeane Dixon.[62] While conducting his ritual inventory of the local bookstores, he learned that his work had disappeared from most shelves a few days before Christmas. "Certainly it is very clear to me," he wrote angrily to Haydn, "that no book which is out of stock can be called a best seller, or is apt to recapture the initial impetus lost in this way."[63] Haydn credited Eiseley with possessing only about 5 percent of the truth. Owing to a delay at the printer's, Harcourt had been without books for no more than a week. "The chances are good that at any given time, one-half the books on the current best-seller list are out of stock. Despite every effort to gauge demand, this happens all the time." The editor advised Eiseley to relax.[64]

Still, one week later the author wrote Hal Borland to complain that his book had gone out of stock at the most critical time of the year. "If," on the other hand, "it continues to proceed at this rate I shall be in tax trouble."[65] Penn's chaplain, Rev. Stanley Johnson, remembered a train ride he had taken to New York City with Eiseley, who discussed his tax problems the whole way. The clergyman couldn't help smiling to himself, for he had once been a party to a similar conversation with author James Michener.[66]

In the meantime, praise for the book poured in. Princeton University physicist John A. Wheeler, who in 1968 gave black holes their name, wrote an eloquent tribute:

> Where else can one find such a perspective of "the second world"? . . . And how better than by poetry can one lay hold of this new universe and make it his own? . . . The Jersey meadowland dump, in fog and by night, with its fires gleaming, recalls the lotus flower and Buddha, beauty growing out of mud.
>
> Thank you for this wonderful book, a candidate if ever there was one for the du Nuoy prize—and written by a du Nuoy prizewinner whom I am always happy to see.[67]

Although they had had their differences over the relationship between Darwin and Edward Blyth, Theodosius Dobzhansky did not let Eiseley down. "Poetry and science are, it would seem, about as unmixable as oil and water," the geneticist wrote in the April 1971 issue of the *American Anthropologist*. "Yet there are exceptional scientists who succeed in making just such mixtures. Loren Eiseley is one of the exceptions."[68]

However, it was a poet by birth and by profession who fashioned the jewel in the crown. On February 21, 1970, W. H. Auden, whom Eiseley would soon be addressing by the affectionate "My dear Wystan," published a rambling seven-page review of *The Unexpected Universe* in *The New Yorker*. This great rumpled bear of a man, who always looked as though he had just emerged from hibernation, had first heard of the University of Pennsylvania professor at Oxford, where a student had given him a copy of *The Immense Journey*. Auden was enthralled, and from that time onward read everything by Eiseley he could lay his hands on. Auden concluded that Eiseley was a wanderer in danger of mental shipwreck "on the shore of Dejection." He saw Eiseley crying out, "I love the lost ones, the failures of the world." Although Auden, an Anglican convert, refused to believe in Chance, he was moved to his very marrow. "Thank God . . . Dr. Eiseley has reported . . . to me. Bravo! say I."[69]

Once again Eiseley found himself among the five finalists for a National Book Award, this time in the category of philosophy and religion. B. A. Bergman, book division editor of the *Philadelphia Bulletin*, felt so confident of his prospects that the following lead was typeset before word came down from the judges: "Dr. Eiseley of Penn Wins Award for Book 'Unexpected Universe.' " The body of the article, which was also cast in type, describes how Eiseley could have won just as easily in three other categories: arts and letters, history and biography, and poetry. When Erik H. Erikson won for *Gandhi's Truth* instead, Bergman sent Eiseley a copy of what might have been, along with his condolences.[70]

VI

Lost, or perhaps simply ignored, by critics and readers alike, was another message borne in this book from Penn's landlocked Odysseus. The new breed of student, he felt, was endangering the survival of the culture.

> In our streets and on our campuses there riots an extremist minority dedicated to the now, to the moment, however absurd, degrading, or irrelevant the moment may be. Such an atavism deliberately rejects the past and is determined to start life anew—indeed to reject the very institutions that feed, clothe, and sustain our swarming millions.
>
> A yearning for a life of noble savagery without the accumulated burden of history seems in danger of engulfing a whole generation, as it did the French *philosophes* and their eighteenth-century followers. Those individuals who persist in pursuing the mind-destroying drug of constant action have not alone confined themselves to an increasingly chaotic present—they are also, by the deliberate abandonment of their past, destroying the conceptual tools and values that are the means of introducing the rational into the oncoming future.[71]

"The hippies are a symptom of societal illness," Eiseley scrawled in one of his notebooks.[72] To old friends such as Carl Wittke, he lamented: "I find the increasing student chaos and erosion of standards distasteful. In short, I think we are going to hell in a hand basket." Of course, it was the prerogative of the "old boys" to say as much; "somewhere under all this hair, dirty feet, and odd clothing there no doubt still beats the true heart of America—at least I hope so."[73]

Elsewhere the agnostic invoked religious symbolism to underscore his sentiments. Speaking at Philadelphia's La Salle College, a Roman Catholic institution, after being awarded his twenty-second honorary degree, Eiseley beseeched his "brother scholars in Christ's name" not to turn their backs on the ancient robes and colors that represent the life of the mind. "They carry like old battleflags the loyalties and deaths of many men. Do not judge their meaning lightly, any more than you would judge lightly the cross that has sheltered all manner of sinful men and that has survived the tumult and violence of these 2,000 years."[74]

In 1968 Penn's trustees had voted to change Eiseley's title, along with that of his fellow University Professors, to Benjamin Franklin Professor, in honor of the institution's founder. Each of the five scholars so designated was freed from administrative responsibilities, but all were required to remain active in the classroom. The latitude was great, however, and Eiseley established a pattern of teaching only one course every other semester. Ruben "Ben" Reina, a native Argentinean who served as chairman of Anthropology from 1970 to 1975, often experienced difficulty when drawing up the schedule of course offerings. After committing himself to a particular class, Eiseley would withdraw once the schedule had gone to press, requiring the printer to insert the word *omitted* after his name if it was not too late.[75] Otherwise students got the bad news only after registration was under way.

One senior became so frustrated over this state of affairs that she wrote Eiseley to "blow off some steam"—and with good reason. The coed had transferred to Penn from another college after reading *The Immense Journey*, even changing her major in the hope of "sit[ting] at the feet of the master." Never once during her three years on campus had the professor offered a course she could take, and now she was about to graduate, unable to "achieve the dream of my academic career."[76] Eiseley wrote back to say that her heartfelt complaint had touched him, "because from where I sit I frequently feel that the younger generation is indifferent to the humanist values to which my life has been dedicated, and existence is lonely." He would be pleased to have the young woman as his guest for lunch, provided she could make the trip back to campus from her home in New Jersey, graduation exercises having taken place a month before he got around to sending his reply.[77]

Eiseley considered both himself and the campus besieged. The institution that had stood four-square behind Herbert Hoover and Alf Landon during his graduate-school days, and was still considered the most conservative of the Ivys, had suddenly gone berserk. In 1968 the student body had chosen to be addressed by Muhammad Ali, the Black Muslim and alleged draft dodger; by Tom Clark, former associate justice of the Supreme Court turned ultraliberal; by Madalyn Murray

O'Hair, shrill atheist and leader of the fight to ban Bible reading and prayer in the public schools; by Dr. Margaret Mead, staff-carrying guru of the left; by Harrison Salisbury, managing editor of the *New York Times*, who called for the United States to halt the bombing of North Vietnam; by Rev. William Sloane Coffin, Jr., Yale University chaplain and codefendant with Dr. Benjamin Spock in a suit brought by the federal government for counseling and abetting draft resisters; and by presidential hopeful Senator Eugene J. McCarthy, who promised an audience of ten thousand that, if elected, he would fire J. Edgar Hoover. Not to be outdone, rival candidate Robert F. Kennedy spoke in favor of the lottery over the draft, then fell to an assassin's bullet two months later, sharing the fate of Martin Luther King, whose murder sparked an antiracism march that led to the arrest of fifty-six students and faculty.

While the Vietnam Week Committee was planting eighty crosses on the lawn in front of College Hall, which Eiseley fondly remembered as once having been mowed by a horse-drawn sickle,[78] the staff of the 1969 *Record*, Penn's student yearbook, was plotting another coup. Protest pictures, including that of a naked man and woman on their knees in passionate embrace, upstaged the usual fare. The staff of the *Daily Pennsylvanian* chose to be photographed through the window of a gutted building, demonstrating their solidarity with the largely black and poor citizens of West Philadelphia. When one looks for the section called *Seniors* on page 369, one finds that there is no page 369 and no senior pictures either. Faced with the "hard reality" that traditional courses and curricula fail to hold any relevance, the newspaper had decided to sponsor a series of experimental seminars: "gradeless, creditless confrontations between faculty and students that serve to expand the minds and consciousness of both parties."[79] These offerings included McLuhan's Attempt to Crack the Nerve of the Square World, Confronting the Establishment, Political Victims in America, and The Campus Chef, which was "open to both sexes."

Doris Nicholas, one of the few graduate students close to Eiseley during this period, was surprised at her mentor's reaction to the campus upheaval. "He took it very personally, as if it were all directed at him. He was hurt in a way you wouldn't have thought this man could have been hurt. You would think he would have intellectualized it more, but he didn't."[80]

Eiseley had never been able to abide Margaret Mead, whose

"indecent" discussion of sexual practices in Samoa had caused him to censor his niece's reading material. The "incongruous wren," as Haydn referred to Mead in *Words and Faces,* had served with Eiseley on the board of *The American Scholar* before his resignation in 1966. Not only could she stop everyone in his tracks with a sally at once shocking, serious, and comic, but her radical politics and unconventional life-style drove Eiseley to distraction, as if the iconoclastic dowager had somehow been created for the singular purpose of antagonizing him. Almost everything about the woman was an affront to his rigid values, including Mead's three marriages and long-standing love affair with her mentor Ruth Benedict. When a fellow student of Doris Nicholas met with her committee to defend her dissertation, Eiseley stunned the assembly, and no doubt himself as well, by blurting out: "More sex and shit in a primitive society."[81]

If Eiseley is to be believed, the incident that most offended him occurred during one of his lectures, when he was interrupted by a heckling student with a covert sneer: "What is the relevance of evolution?" the youth demanded to know. "The relevance of evolution," Eiseley retorted, "lies only in whence you came and where you might be going. But perhaps you do not care."[82]

Although Eiseley and Fro Rainey had been friends too long to nurture grudges, their relationship became strained whenever the subject of student protesters came up. Fro remembered Eiseley's amazement when he invited a group of demonstrators to come inside the university museum and air their grievances in the auditorium. When he tried to explain that such a course was preferable to broken windows and bloodied faces, Eiseley just shook his head and ducked out.[83]

Eiseley became even more upset over the conduct of President Harnwell after an estimated four hundred demonstrators, led by Joe Mikuliak of the Students for a Democratic Society, occupied College Hall in February 1969. Protesting everything from the chopping down of trees to "Negro removal" in the wake of campus expansion, the students held their ground for six days, forcing the cancellation of classes. A number of faculty also got into the act, including the normally staid Otto Springer, former dean of Arts and Sciences, who went about, much to Harnwell's amusement, carrying branches like "Birnam Wood going to Dunsinane."[84] Mindful of the debacle that had taken place at Columbia over similar issues the previous spring, Harnwell succeeded in forging a compromise that saw the demonstrators emerge from the administration building singing, "Amen, Amen."

The blood remained in Eiseley's eye, and he fumed to Mabel, who, at age sixty-nine, had recently retired, that it was high time they get out of Philadelphia. He was further enraged when a stone came crashing through the window of his apartment study and landed in the chair in which he had been sitting only a few minutes before. Although there was nothing to connect the incident with the protest movement, Eiseley telephoned Bert Schultz in Lincoln to tell him that he wanted out. What was the local real estate market like? Bert did some checking for his old friend and learned that Maple Lodge Park, the great stone mansion whose incinerator Loren had scavenged as a boy, was for sale. Eiseley became very excited until Bert informed him that the disease he was hoping to escape had recently spread to the University of Nebraska campus.[85]

Eiseley vented his frustration by drafting a letter to Richard Nixon, who, ironically, owed his position in the White House to the massive antiwar demonstrations in Chicago during the 1968 Democratic National Convention. Decrying the erosion of America's resolve, he was counting on his president to set things to rights. "It appears to me that from Peru to Asia we are indeed beginning to justify the appellation 'paper tiger' with all the consequences present and to come that this invites." He realized that the president's job was being made more difficult by the widespread social unrest, which fit his conspiracy theory of history: "many people, particularly the young, are the more or less innocent dupes of unseen elements making use of the mass media for the purposes of propaganda." Nevertheless, he concluded by "pleading" with Nixon to do everything within his power "to retard this uncomfortable ebbing away of our power and purpose"; it "will be appreciated by at least one humble American who voted for you."[86]

On April 29, 1970, Robert Isaac White, the quiet gentleman-scholar who had become the sixth president of Kent State University in October 1963, drafted a letter to Eiseley. "I trust that none of the 'ruckuses' at the University of Pennsylvania . . . have brushed you. We have had our own problems and tensions but, so far, no traumatic eruption." However, it was impossible to tell what was going to happen "from one day to the next." Yet White's reason for writing had little to do with the campus unrest. The president simply wanted to inform Eiseley that the arrangements were all in place for his scheduled commencement address in June.[87]

The following day, during a nationally televised news conference, President Nixon informed the public of his decision to support a major South Vietnamese military sweep into Cambodia. American advisers were to accompany the troops, who were also promised heavy air and artillery support from U.S. forces. Campus reaction across the country was swift and furious. At Kent State rallying students tossed fire bombs into the rickety ROTC building and chanted slogans while it was reduced to a heap of charred timber. Mayor Leroy Satrom, his townspeople in an uproar and twenty-member police force on the verge of cracking, requested that Governor James Rhodes send in the National Guard. The governor was eager to oblige, having made campus demonstrations a key issue in his get-tough campaign for the U.S. Senate. On May 4 a salvo from guardsmen standing atop a knoll familiar to trysters as Blanket Hill left four students dead and another ten wounded, including a youth paralyzed from the waist down by a bullet in the spine. Some of the troops evidenced little if any regret: "It's about time we showed the bastards who's in charge," one told a reporter from *Newsweek*. Many of the citizens of Kent were similarly quoted.[88] When Eiseley, who would never give that year's commencement address, heard the news, he turned to a friend and remarked, "They got what they asked for."[89]

20

IMAGO

I

Joan Daves, the New York literary agent, quickly disappeared from the scene once it became clear to Eiseley that she could not obtain the money he wanted for his projected anthropology textbook. Gerard F. McCauley was summoned to make good on his claim that he could secure six figures. Working closely with Doubleday and Company executive editor Stewart Richardson, McCauley contracted for a fifty-thousand-dollar advance payable in five yearly installments of ten thousand dollars each, limiting his client's tax liability. Doubleday further agreed to take Eiseley's next book on the basis of only an outline, for which they would pay another advance of fifty thousand dollars, in addition to a royalty of 15 percent.[1]

The contract was ready for Eiseley's signature in June 1968. He lost no time in returning the document, which, to McCauley's chagrin, he left unsigned. Eiseley reminded the agent that their discussions had been based on the idea of a $100,000 advance for *one* book. "I am sorry that this confusion has somehow arisen, but I do not find in this contract the kind of protection that I was seeking. Under these circumstances Mabel and I prefer to drop the whole matter and to proceed in our own fashion." None of this, he added in a follow-up note, need affect anything that might arise in other areas, including another television program.[2]

Unbeknown to Hiram Haydn, Eiseley was being courted by Kenneth Heuer, director of the Science Book Department at Charles Scribner's Sons. A former lecturer at the Hayden Planetarium, Heuer had been pursuing Eiseley since 1954, when he was a fledgling science editor at Viking. The most he had been able to obtain thus far was a series of brief introductions and epilogues by Eiseley to works by Jack London, David Lindsay, and Thomas Henry Huxley.

Heuer was finally rewarded for his patience in early 1969. Armed with the offer from Doubleday, Eiseley met with Haydn and William Jovanovich concerning the textbook on anthropology. "Would [Harcourt, Brace & World] like to publish it?" he wanted to know. Both men replied in the affirmative. Eiseley then named his price, which was ten times the advance Daves had negotiated with Harcourt in 1965. Jovanovich explained that it was an unrealistic demand, and Eiseley left, obviously upset. Heuer took advantage of Eiseley's disenchantment with Haydn to make a deal. Man's footprints were about to be left on the surface of the moon, and the editor wanted Eiseley to be the first humanist to publish a philosophical account of the rocket century. "Depending on the author's views, it would give a sense of security (or insecurity) to the public. Your name also naturally comes to mind because you could put the moon shot in perspective with other explorations."[3]

Eiseley accepted in January 1969, waiting, as usual, until the tax man had cometh before taking delivery of the five-thousand-dollar advance. (Scribner's would doubtless have offered more had he not insisted on a clause limiting his income to five thousand dollars in any one calendar year.) As the author's representative, McCauley should have been the one handling the negotiations, but he knew nothing more about the deal than did Haydn, who was still hoping to hear that his old friend had settled down and returned to the autobiography.

On January 9, 1969, some two weeks before the contract was signed, NASA announced the names of the crew members who would attempt the first moon landing. Delays in the development of the lunar module had already made it clear that the honor would belong to the three men aboard *Apollo 11*, Neil Armstrong, Michael Collins, and Edwin Aldrin—simply the next in line by the luck of the draw. Nowhere in his book would Eiseley so much as mention them by name.

He had been in Dallas a month earlier to deliver an address before the annual meeting of the American Association for the Advancement of Science. Tom Johnson, a reporter for the *Dallas Morning News*, set up an interview during which Eiseley protested the resources that had already been expended on manned spaceflight. "Look at how much money and brains it took to get just three men around the moon. And look at the tremendous desolation they found when they got there." He agreed that the *Apollo 8* mission had been one of the great scientific journeys of all times, "but was it a search for knowledge only, and not wisdom?"[4]

The flack came thick and fast when Eiseley's fellow conventioneers read the article, which went out over the wire services. He immediately telephoned home to complain to Mabel that the reporter had "erroneously quoted" him.[5] Yet when Olivia Skinner of the *St. Louis Post-Dispatch* had asked him some of the same questions in March 1967, she had elicited an even more impassioned response. Eiseley characterized the space race to her as nothing but a giant potlatch held by Russia and the United States. "In developing science as we have, we have developed a vast invisible pyramid, comparable in terms of the existing wealth of our time to the Great Pyramid, the monument Cheops raised to himself. We, too, are falling under the lash of an overseer, increasing income tax and inflation."[6]

The seven essays that make up *The Invisible Pyramid*, the book for which Heuer contracted, were completed in a matter of months. Heuer received few if any of the troubled midnight letters that were a hallmark of the Eiseley-Haydn correspondence. Instead, the author telephoned almost daily, engaging his new editor in rambling, one-sided conversations. Eiseley went to New York as often as once a week to lunch and consult with Heuer. These junkets would sometimes terminate in visits to attractions of mutual interest, such as an Oriental gallery, a rare book shop, or the New York Stock Exchange. (Jim Hahn noted that his uncle read the *Wall Street Journal* faithfully but understood little or nothing of the market.)[7] Heuer never denied Eiseley the fundamental pleasure of a good listener.[8]

The slender manuscript was delivered on schedule in early 1970, with publication set for the fall. Eiseley agreed to provide an unusually detailed bibliography and, something rare for him, an index. "Make [it] as long as feasible," a concerned Heuer urged, "for I understand there is some room to move around in." Even so, the final product, whose first printing was set at 15,000 volumes, was only 173 pages and carried a list price of $6.95.[9]

The Invisible Pyramid was in press when Mabel went to the mailbox one morning and returned to the apartment aghast at what she had found. When her husband came home she met him at the door, ready to do battle. "Loren, look at this awful stuff that came in the mail!"

"What was that?"

"These filthy pictures of naked girls."

"Oh," he replied, "*Playboy* was going to show me what their magazine really looked like."[10]

The publishers had been attempting to lure Eiseley into print ever since 1964, when associate editor Murray Fisher wrote that "I rather imagine *Playboy* is among the last magazines from which you would have expected to receive a letter."[11] Fisher had guessed correctly. Eiseley rejected his offer of $1,500 for an article, as well as at least two others over the years. The financial stakes had become so attractive of late, however, that he was beginning to weaken. Leaving the negotiations to Heuer, he agreed to sign if the money was right. *Playboy* eventually made an offer of $3,500 for the rights to "The Last Magician," the concluding chapter of *The Invisible Pyramid*. This, together with the royalty checks he would be receiving for each of the other essays, all of which were contracted for by a wide range of periodicals, amounted to far more than the $5,000 advance he had taken from Scribner's. When Eiseley explained it in these terms, Mabel too began to have second thoughts and finally agreed that he should go ahead. "The Last Magician" appeared in *Playboy*'s August 1970 issue, along with "A Wild Pictorial on 'Myra Breckenridge,' " the "Bunnies of 1970," and a more sedate essay by environmentalist Rachel Carson. "I took a look at my graying hairs in the mirror," Eiseley wrote an amused Haydn, "and decided that if this was pornography I would keep on writing it. The ways of the literary world are wondrously peculiar and I find them more so every day."[12] Peculiar indeed: when William F. Buckley, Jr., editor of the ultraconservative *National Review*, came courting a few months later, Eiseley turned him down on the ground that he was too swamped to produce another essay.[13]

II

In September 1969 Eiseley wrote to astronomer Frank Bradshaw Wood in the hope of obtaining certain information on the progress of Halley's comet. "As you know," he explained, "some of my essays are of the personal variety and I have a point to make in all this which hopefully will dramatize a little better what I wish to say."[14] What he needed was the length of the comet's orbit and the year when it turned back toward the sun for its projected rendezvous in the mid-1980s. This was not the first time Eiseley had called on a colleague to provide him with such background material. William L. Straus of Johns Hopkins had been asked a similar favor when Eiseley was writing "How Flowers Changed the World," the superb essay on angiosperms from *The Immense Journey.*[15]

Wood did "a little computing" and came up with an orbit of eighteen astronomical units, or 1,674,000,000 miles. "It headed back this way probably in 1948." The intrigued astronomer speculated on Eiseley's plans for the data: "The Russians blockaded Berlin and Halley's comet turned in its orbit; Harry Truman was elected President and Halley's comet headed for Earth."[16] Wood's hypothesis proved wrong, but Eiseley was so taken by the historical connections that he incorporated the material into the opening essay of *The Invisible Pyramid*, heightening its dramatic effect.

Rather, it was his personal bond with the comet that he wanted to stress, forged in 1910 by Clyde's command that he watch for it a second time and remember the one who'd loved him best as a child. There it was in a nutshell—the pitiful life span of a man against aeons of inconceivable antiquity, the cold nothingness of the zero against the stars' eternal drift. "I was too young to have known that the old abandoned house in which I played was the universe. I would play for man more fiercely if the years would take me back." At some point in the not very distant future Loren Corey Eiseley was going to die: "it is in the [comet's] destiny as well as mine. I lie awake once more on the dark bed. I feel my heart beating, and wait for the hurrying light."[17]

Man, John Donne once observed, lives in a close prison, yet its bars are dear to him. At the same time, he is a dreamer whose mind transcends the confines of body, time, and space: "my thought is with the Sunne and beyond the Sunne, overtakes the Sunne, and overgoes the Sunne in one pace, one steppe, everywhere." Eiseley lauded the exploits of the great terrestrial nomads—Lewis and Clark, Frémont, Cook, Frobisher, the desk-bound Francis Bacon, and the mythical Odysseus—while impugning the motives of those who venture beyond the earth's maternal rim. He saw them as little more than technological drones rather than true adventurers playing alone against the odds. But it was the hubris of the astronauts and a gullible public that troubled him the most: just where do we think we are going?

The life span of a man is that of a mayfly compared with the distances he wishes to travel. Light, moving at a speed of 186,000 miles a second, takes something like 100,000 years to complete its journey across our own undistinguished galaxy, the Milky Way. Alpha Centauri, also called Proxima Centauri because it is the closest star to Earth, is 4.28 light-years distant. Yet to reach it at the present rate of space travel would require a time equal to the whole existence of *Homo sapiens* on the planet. Increase our present rocket speed by a factor of one hundred, and generations would still pass before the object could be reached. Civilization might well have vanished before the first message was received.

As much as Eiseley admired *The Martian Chronicles* and the other wonderful yarns spun by the Ray Bradburys of the world, he confessed a deep skepticism concerning the chances that we would encounter sentient beings in our forlorn little corner of the cosmos. "There are far more stars in the heavens than there are men upon the earth. The waste to be searched is too great for the powers we possess. In gambling terms, the percentage lies all with the house, or rather with the universe."[18]

In sum, the scientific culture made possible by the invention of the zero has been stymied by the ancient diminutive whorls of the Hindus and the Maya. The eternal conflict that pits the microcosm against the macrocosm has revealed to humankind that it is locked inside a cosmic prison from which there is no escape through physical flight. The restraints were little eased by a 240,000-mile journey in a cramped and primitive capsule to a dead satellite.

The society that hewed Ozymandias from rock and geometrized the Valley of the Kings also evidenced a curious penchant for the erasure of human memory. The monotheist Akhenaton decreed that the names of his idolatrous predecessors be stricken from stele and tablet with hammer and chisel. Upon the pharaoh's death, Sakere evened the score when he ordered that the son of Aton's capital at

Tel el Amarna be defaced and abandoned. Rome did as much to Carthage, Robespierre to the Christian calendar, Stalin to the intelligentsia of the Soviet state. The *damnatio memoriae* Eiseley called it, and he complained that his students literally refused to read anything more than five years old. As "time effacers" they cared only about the future. "Plot gives way to episode. The existential world of the hippy provokes sensate experience but does not demand dramatic continuity." This, he believed, was the onset of chaos in which social order might well disappear in the faceless cities of the Western world. "Make the revolution," they shout à la the Jacobins. "Afterwards we will decide what to do about it."[19] If one cannot efface the past, one can at least pretend that history has never been.

In his own way, Eiseley was no less a protester than the youth whose confrontational tactics caused him to move furtively about campus, slipping in and out of back doors. Ostensibly a work of social criticism, *The Invisible Pyramid* is more an aging poet's fugue, the eternal question of human existence set in counterpoint against the flight of *Apollo 11*: "At my death I will look my last upon a nation which, save for some linguistic continuity, will seem increasingly alien and remote. It will be as though I peered upon my youth through misty centuries. I will not be merely old; I will be a genuine fossil embedded in onrushing man-made time before my actual death."[20] A protector of the human spirit like his fellow poets, Eiseley compared himself to a crab who is born wary and is frequently in retreat. In the time of the world eaters his kind was threatened not with obsolescence but with being hunted to extinction.

III

Haydn heard through the publishing grapevine that Eiseley had signed a contract with Scribner's. When he asked the author what this meant, Eiseley assured him that it was a "special case," which would have no bearing on their long-standing relationship. Besides, Harcourt had no option clause on his next book. Haydn agreed, but he could not help feeling disappointed after all the years the two had spent together.[21] With *The Invisible Pyramid* due for release in three months, Eiseley wrote to state once more that it was his intention to return the five-thousand-dollar advance for what he termed "the originally planned autobiography."[22] "Why do you refer to . . . [it as] the *originally planned* autobiography?" Haydn wanted to know. "Don't you still plan to do it?"[23]

In his reply, Eiseley began by lamenting his economic fate. He was well within sight of retirement but without satisfactory financial protection in the light of ongoing inflation. What was Mabel to do if anything should happen to him? Haydn would doubtless remember the anthropology text for which he had sought a one-hundred-thousand-dollar advance. "Since that time I have been proffered an advance in six figures for the same work and I have accepted. I am sure you will understand that there is nothing personal about this except as it relates to distributed monies for my retirement." Furthermore, the "meddlesome curiosity" he had encountered over certain personal incidents in *The Unexpected Universe* had given him second thoughts about the work. "Perhaps you will deem me oversensitive, but I have to go around in public and be asked all sorts of questions, and since I feel deeply over some of these episodes of the past I do not enjoy some of the social situations which I encounter." He could see no other recourse than to abandon the project and cancel the contract in a manner agreeable to Harcourt. "In conclusion, let me add that these thoughts have been troubling me over the last several years. . . . At long last I grow conscious of mortality."[24]

This decision, Haydn wrote in his memoirs, came "like a flash storm." He consulted with William Jovanovich, who told him to do as he thought best. Feeling the situation to be hopeless, the weary editor gave Eiseley his release, bringing down the final curtain on an association of fifteen years. The victim of another massive heart attack in December 1973, Haydn went to his grave believing that Eiseley had felt rejected the day Jovanovich did not offer him the huge amount of money he wanted.[25] He may well have been right. Just before Eiseley's own death, he wrote a grateful letter to Anne Freegood, an executive editor at Random House. After twenty years the firm had decided to increase the percentage of his paperback royalties on *The Immense Journey*. "My then editor [Haydn], who professed to be my friend, did not warn me. It was not until long after that I found I had been used."[26]

Whether Eiseley truly accepted a one-hundred-thousand-dollar advance is an open question; no signed contract for this amount survives among his papers. However, the proposal was supposedly mentioned during lunch with Heuer at a restaurant overlooking the skating rink at Rockefeller Center. Heuer later wrote that he tried gently to persuade Eiseley to write his own books in his own way; the financial rewards would be just as good in the end. Eiseley merely needed someone else to put into words that which he already knew.[27]

Perhaps, but Heuer's motives were hardly as pure as Pleistocene snow. One week after Eiseley wrote Haydn to tell him that his decision concerning the autobiography was final, Heuer telephoned Eiseley with a major proposal. Scribner's wanted to rewrite the contract for *The Invisible Pyramid* by merging the work with Eiseley's next two books. The three-volume package would yield him a minimum advance of $55,000. The first installment of $5,000 had already been paid under the contract for the forthcoming work. There would be five additional installments of $10,000 each, beginning on January 1, 1971, and continuing through January 1, 1975; any additional earnings would be paid in successive calendar years.[28]

Eiseley thought the proposition over for nearly two weeks before replying. Had Heuer forgotten the "textbook," which, when completed, could very easily propel him into the 50 percent tax bracket? His duties at Penn were also showing signs of intensifying, because of both the upcoming bicentennial celebration and the Philadelphia meeting of the American Association for the Advancement of Science in 1971. After serious discussions with his wife and lawyer, he had come to the realization that to promise so much would be foolish at the present time. Still, things might look quite different in a year or two. "In the meantime we can see how sales go on *The Invisible Pyramid*, and both of us may be able to assess the situation in more realistic terms."[29]

The first week of November 1970 found Eiseley in New York, making the now familiar rounds of radio and television talk shows.[30] The first reviews of *The Invisible Pyramid* were already in, and they contained little to complain about.

Rex Stout, with whom Eiseley had carried on a desultory correspondence over the years, wrote that he would be turning to his friend's latest as soon as he could complete Albert Speer's *Inside the Third Reich*. "What a contrast! A poison and an antidote."[31] Whether the creator of Nero Wolfe discovered the remedy he was seeking is difficult to say. Few readers or reviewers did, partly because of the affecting prose, partly because Eiseley did not suggest one. Sir Julian Huxley, the noted biologist and science writer, took the author to task for this shortcoming. "Although I agree with Eiseley that we must get to know ourselves better, we've tried for over 2,000 years but with little effect." The idea that man must make peace with his animal host is hardly enough; "birth control and conservation are the greatest needs of today"; it is essential that man properly order his own abilities, thoughts and likes.[32]

At Christmas, Wright Morris wrote his annual greeting from California and could not resist poking a little fun at Scribner's latest find.

> Dear Schmerzie:
>
> I . . . was interested—as they say in the trade—to see that Brer Eiseley is now a Scribner author, with personal access to the oak-framed offices on the 5th floor. Or has that all changed? I rather hope not; having fond memories of my moments with [Max] Perkins. Who are the great and fruitful minds in attendance at the moment? How do you like the Gent's facilities? If they have the same elevator service, I suggest you ride UP—but walk down.[33]

Schmerzie had already done this and more. Charles Scribner, Jr., was elated to have Eiseley aboard and honored him at a luncheon celebration. The occasion lasted for several hours, leading the publisher to believe that they had come to a genuine meeting of the minds. At last, it was time for Eiseley to take his leave. Turning to Scribner, he exclaimed, "I really am delighted to have had this chance to get to know you. Goodbye, Henry."[34]

IV

After running the gamut of titles from "The Uncompleted Man" to "The Night Tide," Eiseley finally decided to call his second offering with Scribner's *The Night Country*. The "interim book" was released in late 1971, only a year after *The Invisible Pyramid*, as explained in a letter to a friend. "I say an interim book because it is really a collection of a number of my older essays and uncollected pieces, most of them of a somewhat personal character for which I get rather constant requests."[35] As befit the title, he dedicated the work to his fellow insomniac Malvina McKee Corey, "who sleeps as all my people sleep by the ways of the westward crossing."

So wide was Eiseley's latitude at Scribner's that he unabashedly composed his own dust jacket copy, which survives in holograph in the publisher's files:

> *The Night Tide [Country]* is the meditative summation of the experiences of a professional archaeologist and bone hunter. It moves easily from solitary childhood cave experiences and the wanderings of young manhood into the profound meditations of an adult humanistic scholar. Throughout, the book is characterized by that feeling for penetrating anecdote and scientific range of experience that has made Loren Eiseley's name so widely known beyond his discipline.[36]

Eiseley's purpose in *The Night Country* was to claim a time and make it forever his own. Through the mind of the grizzled fox flits the memory of the clairvoyant Malvina, standing at the window, whispering to no one but herself. When Eiseley drew close he could overhear a dialogue at two levels of consciousness—one of the day, one of the night. During nocturnal solitudes he finds himself rising to walk over and stare out the window in his turn. "Now I talk of life and death, and the stream begins once more to divide irrevocably within my head."[37]

For a man to be remembered, he must have done memorable things or, failing that, create the impression of having done them. Eiseley's compulsion to fictionalize was a means of scratching his initials more deeply than others. Though clever about concealing his spoor, the mythographer left unmistakable imprints in one of the notebooks meant for burning at his demise.

A long entry, dated April 14, 1956, concerns the essay titled "Big Eyes and Small Eyes," which was published twice before its inclusion in *The Night Country.* In addition to the tale of Wright Morris and the irreverent rat Beadie, the essay tells the story of a harrowing night dating back to Eiseley's years as a drifter during the Great Depression. The author is alone, on an endless blue plain, bound for an unnamed city that lies below a distant white-capped peak. He crosses a barbed-wire fence and begins walking toward the silhouetted mountain in the moonlight. The thought gradually occurs to him that he is being followed. "I stopped abruptly and listened. Something, several things, stopped with me. Dead silence." Calling out, he receives no answer. The pattern is repeated, and it is obvious from the sound that the number of pursuers is growing and closing in by degrees. The youth can either throw caution to the wind and run, inviting headlong pursuit and the possibility of serious injury in unfamiliar terrain, or turn around and confront the creatures of the dark. He gropes in vain for some type of weapon before challenging the enemy, screaming all the way. The wide-eyed cattle yield little ground, and he goes limp at the moment of recognition.

After composing himself, Eiseley renews his quest for the horizon, but the game continues. "Range cattle, something spelled out in my mind—wild, used to horsemen—what are they like to a man on foot in the dark?" Will they stampede? With his nerves about to crack again, Eiseley catches a glint of wire in the distance. The race is on against a backdrop of thundering hooves. He vaults the fence, landing several feet down in the soft sand of a streambed, while the bovine cavalry wheels off into the night.

The adrenaline is flowing; rather than hole up and continue his trek at dawn, he pushes on, only to be threatened a second time—this too by the very animals he loves. With the night lights of the city beckoning below, he begins the perilous descent into the valley on whose rim he has emerged. But the hero has unwittingly chosen to come down in the middle of a mining operation guarded by two huge dogs, which are alerted to his presence by falling stones. The sound and the fury of the slavering beasts is enough to wake the dead. Trapped above them on a small ledge, he awaits the appearance of a night watchman, but none materializes. It is becoming difficult to hang on. If he should fall, he might no longer have the strength to fight them off. Slowly he works his way down into their midst, speaking all the while in a controlled tone. "I held an arm over my throat and stood stark-still. They came up to me warily, but one made a small woofing sound in his throat and I could see the motion of his tail in the dark." Orpheus has lulled Cerberus with the lyre of human kindness. "When I come to the Final Pit in which they howl, I shall, without too great a show of confidence, put out my hand and speak once more."[38]

The notes for the essay tell a different but no less interesting tale:

> There must be dogs barking at the bottom of chaos—great hoarse hounds whose voices bounce eternally against falling rock and echo and reecho in the crevices of the night. Only a dog's voice out of

> the deep abysses carries the proper menace and at the same time preserves the weird objectivity and indifference which is part of the hunting pack. . . .
>
> Start . . . with the night journey, mention Thoreau's mysterious Walden dogs, perhaps the dog gnawing human bones beside me. . . . Discuss how domestic animals get out of hand at night—you can use the cattle episode here. Why was I not riding to the city on the plain? Because it was the years of the depression and I had no money. Build up the fear atmosphere right to the doggy climax. This fear can be built on the idea that the mind inside is bigger than the outside.[39]

Officially released on November 10, 1971, *The Night Country* was instantly recognized by many as Eiseley's finest work since *The Immense Journey.* The Athenaeum of Philadelphia, which had chosen *Darwin's Century* the city's best nonfiction book of 1958, broke "an unwritten rule" by bestowing its highest honor on the author a second time.[40] In a passage singled out by Eiseley himself, William R. MacKaye of the *Washington Post* wrote, "This is a wise, eloquent, noble book by a man whose learning and whose use of it is a gift to all of us."[41] Thomas Lask of the rival *New York Times* suggested that scientists might not find the essays rigorous or meaty enough, "but they are not really for them. They are for the rest of us who enjoy thoughtful talk, lucid argument and a mind tough enough to serve as a whetstone for our own insights."[42] Similar sentiments were echoed in *Time, The Atlantic Monthly, Life, The New Yorker,* and many more.

V

Eiseley's popularity was never greater. Scribner's had no option on his next book, but Heuer had discovered the formula for keeping his temperamental author happy. In 1969 Walter Hamady, the young artist and bookmaker from Madison, Wisconsin, published a limited edition of three Eiseley essays titled *The Brown Wasps.* Hand-set in the elegant typeface Palatino and printed on handmade rag paper imported from England, the book was chosen one of the year's fifty best by the American Institute of Graphic Arts and became a collector's item. Publisher and author corresponded regularly over the ensuing years, and in March 1972 Hamady wrote to ask what had happened to Eiseley's poems. "Lose your nerve? We are still very interested in doing anything you might have us do, that is if you can ever permit such a twiddle diddle edition, what with all this fame and glory stuff you are indulging yourself in."[43]

A third Scribner's contract, this for Eiseley's first book of poems, was inked within three weeks of Hamady's latest query.[44] But as Eiseley told it, the subject had come up during a casual conversation over lunch with Heuer. "All on his own, without being in the literary end of the House, he first persuaded me of his genuine interest and then Mr. Scribner."[45] The head of the firm later observed that he took the risk first because Eiseley was selling so well, and second because his writing so integrated the genres of poetry and prose that one could hardly tell the difference.[46] Dedicated to Mabel, who was at his side when the poems were written over the years, *Notes of an Alchemist* (aka *Fox Curse*) made its belated appearance in November 1972, after Eiseley's carping about the illustrator had forced Heuer to fire him and hire another.[47] When the first printing of 7,500 copies disappeared from the bookstores just two weeks before Christmas, the poet complained to a friend: "This can be infuriating but there is always caution with a first book of poetry and apparently they underestimated the demand."[48]

Hamady's interest in the poetry was less of a threat at Scribner's than the anthropology textbook, which was still hanging fire. Glencoe Press, a division of the Macmillan Company located in Beverly Hills, had drafted a contract that seemed to fulfill Eiseley's every demand. In return for a four-hundred-page manuscript and some one hundred illustrations to be delivered in March 1975, Glencoe agreed to pay the one hundred thousand dollars Eiseley had long been seeking. Having achieved his dream, he could now face reality, although he lacked the courage to deliver the bad news in person. "My life is simply subject to too many vicissitudes and pressures and it stands to add to them. In this Mrs. Eiseley concurs. This letter, then, is to tell you that I do not wish to reopen negotiations and that my decision on this score is adamant and not subject to persuasion or reversal."[49]

Gerard McCauley, Eiseley's putative agent, had been kept in the dark concerning the publishing arrangements with Scribner's. Nor was he consulted during the negotiations with Glencoe. Indeed, it was a jubilant Heuer, not Eiseley, who informed McCauley of Scribner's *Notes of an Alchemist* coup. Since McCauley had nothing in writing, there was little he could do except complain bitterly. The time and money he had invested in trying to obtain generous contracts were considerable to say the least, yet the writer seemed never to take their relationship seriously, as evidenced by his repeated dealings behind the agent's back.

If Eiseley had any lingering doubts about Scribner's commitment to him, these were dispelled by a development similar to that which gave rise to his first book of poetry. It began with a letter from John Scott Mahon, an associate editor at the University of Michigan Press, who had written to Nebraska to find out who owned the paperback rights to *Francis Bacon and the Modern Dilemma*. Having learned that they had long since reverted to the author, Mahon offered to reissue the work for a five-hundred-dollar advance against a royalty of 6 percent.[50] Eiseley replied that he would have to think it over, which meant that he made a beeline for Scribner's Fifth Avenue offices. Although the untested *Notes of an Alchemist* was still in production, Heuer unflinchingly drafted another contract, which Eiseley signed in early November 1972. The first ten thousand volumes of *The Man Who Saw Through Time*, complete with a new first chapter, were ready for shipment to booksellers the following April. Not only did Eiseley receive an advance four times that offered by Michigan, but he lived to see the work pass through six printings, which were followed by two more after his death.[51]

VI

Martin Meyerson, Gaylord Harnwell's successor as president of Penn, was among the first to congratulate Eiseley when it was announced that he had been elected to membership in the National Institute of Arts and Letters, in March 1971. "It is a kind of Walter Mitty dream come home to me in my last years," Eiseley replied, "for there was a time when I was a young man when I must confess that I dreamed more of poetry and literature than I did of science."[52] It was in his youth that he had headed out to the California coast for the express purpose of gaining an introduction to his idol Robinson Jeffers, the only writer, according to Jim Hahn, that his reticent uncle ever sought out.[53]

Word from the National Institute had no sooner arrived than Eiseley received a letter from Dr. David Sachs of the Philadelphia Association for Psychoanalysis. W. H. Auden was scheduled to deliver the organization's annual Freud Memorial Lecture and specifically requested that Eiseley be invited to the dinner preceding his talk. The crowded affair gave the poets little chance to take each other's measure, but, since Auden was living in New York, Eiseley invited him to lunch at the University Club, his favorite haunt when doing business with his publisher or making the rounds of the used bookstores. Eiseley admitted to having been intimidated by the rutted visage, reminiscent of a topographical map of the Badlands, staring back at him from across the table. He was also careful about what he said. "I . . . kept discreetly away from the matter of contingency and the indeterminacy principle in the universe, not wishing to offend Auden's religious sensibilities," he wrote to a friend.[54] He wondered aloud to Jim as well about the possible repercussions of dining in public with an acknowledged homosexual.[55]

The two spoke of seemingly inconsequential matters. "What public event do you remember first from childhood?" Auden wanted to know. "I think for me, the Titanic disaster."

Eiseley might have said the same, since both were born in 1907. But he recalled another event of the same year—1912—instead. It concerned a penitentiary, a murdered warden, a frantic escape into a blizzard, an armed posse and death. "We never made it," he blurted out unconsciously, drawing a curious look from his guest.[56] The incident was fresh in Eiseley's mind, for he had recently returned from Nebraska, where he had taken notes from old newspaper accounts of the prison break.[57] He had written his own name on the sign-out slip for the microfilm, but on another slip, crumpled up in his pocket, he claimed to have scrawled Tom Murray, an alias of ringleader Charles Taylor, in an unexplainable gesture of defiance.[58]

Eiseley was invited to attend Auden's sixty-fifth birthday party at The Coffee House in February 1972. Unfortunately, he was scheduled to deliver a speech in the Southwest, and the two never met again. There followed a brief and mostly lopsided correspondence, Eiseley writing paragraphs and pages, Auden hastily scratching out a few lines. What might be called the "My dear Wystan letters" contain, by Eiseley's own admission, nothing of literary importance.[59]

In a note from Oxford dated November 23, 1972, Auden wrote, "I must tell you how much I have been enjoying *Notes of an Alchemist*. . . . On principle, I disapprove of Free Verse, but, in your case, I think you are absolutely right to use it."[60] Soon after, Auden asked Eiseley's permission to dedicate a poem to him in *The New Yorker*.[61] The honoree was quick to return the favor. He had just delivered a draft of his second book of poetry, *The Innocent Assassins*, to Scribner's. "And as for Man," a melancholy reflection on a seemingly doomed New York City, bears Auden's name in the dedication. Six months later the English bear was felled by a heart attack in his Vienna hotel room.

The only other poet of renown attracted to Eiseley's verse was Howard Nemerov, the gnomic denizen of St. Louis, who was inching his way toward a Pulitzer Prize in one-hundred-degree heat, while fending off a pack of boisterous progeny. As did Auden, Nemerov made the first move. He and Eiseley composed scandalously effusive blurbs for each other's dust jackets and stumbled over themselves laying on epistolary compliments. Nemerov, too, published a poem for Eiseley in *The New Yorker*, which left no question about his place in the then pecking order of bards. Unlike Auden, Nemerov was told that no dedication would be allowed, forcing him to preface the piece with a line from *The Unexpected Universe*, to which he cleverly attached Eiseley's name.[62] Hoping to return the favor, Eiseley, a member of the National Institute of Arts and Letters Awards Committee, nominated Nemerov for a major poetry prize, only to learn that he had already received it.

Conversely, Eiseley's conduct toward an unknown amateur naturalist named Annie Dillard bordered on the inexcusable. Twenty-eight years old and living by a creek near Hollins, Virginia, with her husband, the poet and professor R. H. W. Dillard, she was about to have her first book published by Harper's, which was also serializing the manuscript. An awestricken Dillard sent Eiseley a copy of the first installment and sheepishly asked if he might be willing to read the galleys with a view to providing a line or two for the dust jacket. "Wright Morris was here a year ago," she added. "He not only spoke of you *fondly*, but was also very good-natured at my insistence that he speak of you *constantly*."[63]

One might think that Eiseley's nostalgia over his own success with *Harper's Magazine* would have made him a soft touch, especially where a young writer was concerned. Instead, he drafted a long reply, lecturing Dillard about the intricacies and etiquette of the publishing game without even so much as skimming her article. In any case, he was too burdened with his own work to take on this onerous task. But when William McPherson, editor of the *Washington Post Book World*, later contacted him, he accepted an invitation to review *Pilgrim at Tinker Creek*. While Eiseley enjoyed some of the author's unusual descriptions and unique insights, he criticized her too frequent use of slang words, such as *pizzazz*. According to him, she also committed the unforgivable sin of attributing to Joseph Wood Krutch an obscure incident about a parasitic worm that Eiseley himself had mentioned in *The Unexpected Universe*.[64] The old purist who still admired Job did not believe the literary torch had yet been passed to a new generation of nature writers; perhaps it never would. Caroline Werkley remembered that Eiseley was roundly criticized for nit-picking, especially after *Pilgrim at Tinker Creek* was awarded a Pulitzer Prize.[65]

VII

Hard it is on earth . . .
Ax time, sword-time . . .
Wind-time, wolf-time, ere the world falls
Nor ever shall men each other spare.[66]

These lines are from an Old Norse Edda that Eiseley was fond of quoting, and they had taken on an even deeper meaning now that he was recording notes for "The Snow Wolf," a science-fiction novel set in the next great ice.

The return of the Pleistocene has been triggered by an electronic device planted in a pyramid by the Russians, who have discovered the secret of controlling the world's weather. Its unnamed inventor has been silenced in a Siberian labor camp. But the final revenge is to be his. The scientist has fooled his superiors into thinking the device is continent specific when it is not. Disillusioned by man, he wants to wipe the slate clean and start over, as nature did in the Cambrian period.[67]

Like the paranoid inventor, another will soon come to know that all men's hands are against him, except that he will suffer from no delusion. For the moment, however, Big Foot (or Big Paws) plays innocently with his doomed brothers and sisters beside a cave in the Sierra Madre, members of the dying breed of lobo wolves, the great, gray range killers of the *llano estacado*. Rags, the cubs' mother, is both deaf and mad. "Suddenly, so suddenly that it startled her mate, she leaped agilely into the air and twisted and snapped sideways at nothing." Hers is the fey madness of the changeling seer who exists speechless, "the terrible insanity that is both wrong and right."

Not only are Big Foot's feet exceptionally large for a lobo wolf, but he towers over his siblings like a floating white ghost from the past. Some fantastic accident in the germ plasm of the cub's parents has produced a living fossil. Big Foot is the reincarnation of *Canis dirus*, the dire wolf, fearsome predator of the Pleistocene. All his life Big Foot will dream dim Ice Age dreams of sweeping tundras, long-horned bison and stalking cats with six-inch fangs, hulking mammoths and snows no living being has seen.

The rest of the pack is killed by rifle, trap, or strychnine, and Big Foot heads south, where the ice is also certain to form. He hides in cemeteries throughout Mexico and Central America, for the sign of the cross is avoided by men. After traversing the Isthmus of Panama, the great creature takes a mate, a dog called Sleek Foot, whose rawhide tether he severs with his jaws. Together they vanish into the Venezuelan moonlight, heading for the Andes and the end of a five-thousand-mile journey.

In time men call him the Snow Wolf and cross themselves when they speak his name. Only when summoned to bury their dead will they venture near the real crosses of wood inside his range. They wait anxiously for some sign that his numbers are increasing, but to no avail. He is the first and the last, a gift, or a curse, of God.

Enter General Armstrong with his repeating rifle and telescopic sight, the finest money can buy. Like his quarry, Armstrong is an anachronism, a much decorated career officer whose fighting skills are quite useless to a British Empire that is no more. Onward and upward the great white hunter comes, relentless, unemotional, deterred by neither the billowing snows nor the empty darkness on the ramparts. After days of giving chase, a bullet strikes home, mortally wounding Big Foot, who tastes his own blood. He waits patiently behind a large cross, his vacant yellow eyes and sensitive nose aligned in the direction his pursuer must come, while Sleek Foot watches from above. As the snow swirls, the dire wolf bounds forward, its shearing carnassials tearing headlong through the cloth and leather at Armstrong's throat. Alien blood is mixed with Big Foot's own. In an instant, ten thousand years have come and gone as, once more, snow fills the channels of a dying fossil brain.[68]

It is not difficult to understand why "The Snow Wolf" was never completed. Perceptive critics would have seen it for what it was, a sentimental gloss on Eiseley's own life, which he seemed unable to write about without first shifting into animal form or assuming an alias. While he had not given up entirely on the autobiography, as he had led Haydn to believe, the moment for a final decision was at hand.

Eiseley had been forced to vacate his beloved office, with its ivy-ringed bay windows, and move into Penn's new anthropology wing in 1972. His sweeping view of the museum grounds was abruptly replaced by that of a littered parking lot, oil refineries, and scaling railroad viaduct. The single advantage of the new arrangement was the separate outer office provided for Mrs. Werkley, who could now intercept unwelcome visitors before they reached her boss's door. Since Jim Hahn had gone to live in Nome, Alaska, Eiseley had gotten into the habit of summoning his assistant in the small hours to take down his nocturnal musings. Some looked upon him as her "guru," while others referred to her as his "office wife." Many puzzled over this symbiotic relationship and wondered at Mabel's tolerance. Never once did the lady let her composure slip, for she had known from the beginning that Loren needed all the help he could get. But after his passing she wrote in a frank letter to a nun captivated by her husband's books, "Mrs. Werkley . . . did not know *everything*."[69]

Otto Springer saw his longtime acquaintance on the railroad platform one day looking haggard and depressed. Eiseley had just returned from a series of speaking engagements. "If only they would leave me alone," he complained. Springer could not help thinking that Eiseley had gotten caught up in the public eye and did not have the will to step back. A certain pomposity was beginning to overshadow his better self. "He gave you the feeling he knew who was talking, even on light matters."[70]

And talk he did. Eiseley's monologues on the inconsequential were capable of transforming department meetings into the verbal equivalent of the Chinese water torture. Even the most innocent of remarks by a colleague, especially if it concerned research, would cause him to sit bolt upright and launch into a convoluted apologia that soon had everyone gazing wistfully at the door.[71] Fellow writer Wallace Stegner, who served with Eiseley on the National Park Service Advisory Board in the 1970s, recalled him delivering a subcommittee report on a small matter but sounding for all the world like Isaiah. Listeners snickered behind their hands. "Reading a dry report as if it held the secrets of life *was* a little funny."[72]

The interminable one-sided telephone calls became more frequent in the final years. Little given to small talk at the office, Eiseley would have Mabel dial Penn colleagues Solomon Katz, Arleigh Hess, Jr., or Ruben Reina, whom he proceeded to address without the least regard for time. Though all admired him greatly, they ducked calls on occasion, especially when the phone rang around dinnertime and their wives could not hold the meal for two or three hours. Reina noted Eiseley's growing compulsion to deal with every angle and consequence of the smallest problem, sometimes requiring "a lot more weighing" than Reina had patience for. And Eiseley talked about his health far more than "I wanted to hear."[73] Richard Stonesifer noticed that, even more than in the past, his friend's writing was becoming death haunted, almost like John Donne posing in his own coffin.[74]

Little anyone did in Eiseley's behalf seemed to please him. After years of coaxing by Fro Rainey, he finally agreed to accompany the museum director on an expedition to Fro's native Montana in the summer of 1973. It was Eiseley's first venture into the field since his early days as Anthropology chairman. They headquartered at what was once the Rainey family ranch near Glendive and leisurely went about their ten-day search for evidence of early man. It turned into more of a nostalgic junket by two aging westerners than a scientific enterprise; a few Yuma points came to light but little else. Eiseley returned home and wrote Howard Nemerov to complain about the rifles with telescopic sights that had become fixtures in the air-conditioned cabs of the great harvesting machines. The prairie-dog towns of his youth were poisoned out, and a beautiful red fox that he saw running through the sage had caused their guide to remark, " 'I will remember and come back with a trap this fall. The pelts are better then.' It is all so sad and beautiful and hopeless that one's heart aches."[75] All the while Fro thought Eiseley was having the time of his life.

Eiseley also made his first and only visit to Walden Pond that summer. He walked its circumference with his host, Dr. Malcolm Ferguson, president of the Lyceum in Concord, but became distracted from his purpose by flotsam bobbing in the blue: "It occurred to me [that] . . . a few refuse receptacles placed along the shore might at least encourage some people to deposit their trash rather than throw it into the Pond."[76] Then, when he made the solitary trek to Thoreau's grave, the anticipated communion between the writer of light and the one of shadows was thwarted by hippies squinting at the outline of the tombstone through the misty dawn.

Eiseley resigned his membership in New York City's prestigious Century Club in August 1973, citing financial difficulties and family illness. In what was fast becoming a standard benediction, he informed President Russell Lynes that he expected soon to be vanishing into the western landscape. "Do you remember that old bit of Americana that speaks of those golden days when an easterner who had fallen upon hard luck could just put a sign on his office door, 'Gone to Texas,' mount a horse and disappear?"[77]

Friends from his youth in Nebraska waited expectantly for the return of their fellow bone hunter, only to be disappointed. In March 1968 Bert Schultz wrote Eiseley that he would soon have a tiny fossil oreodont named after him. In addition to *Hadroleptauchenia eiseleyi*, there would also be a *bluei, crabilli, vanderpooli,* and *stouti*. "Oh yes, there will be a *marianae* too." Bert suggested that the old South Party re-form at Fort Robinson to reminisce.[78] Three years later everyone made it except Eiseley, who begged off because of a bad tooth. However, he redeemed himself by dedicating *The Innocent Assassins* to his fellow bone hunters and to C. Bertrand Schultz, "in memory of the unreturning days."

The group planned to meet again in June 1975, and this time Eiseley promised to be among them. People flew into Chadron airport from all over; one colleague living in Malaysia held a special gift of a delicate butterfly on his lap the whole way. But, as before, Eiseley failed to show up and gave no clear explanation for his absence.[79]

On September 18, 1974, Eiseley became the twelfth recipient of the Distinguished Nebraskan Award. The gala presentation was held at the John F. Kennedy Center for the Performing Arts in Washington, D.C., and attended by dignitaries of every stripe, from senators to university presidents. The Eiseleys and the Schultzes stayed within two doors of each other at the Watergate. The four were walking down the corridor together conversing when Eiseley suddenly stopped and put a finger to his lips. "Shh!" he whispered. "The walls have ears." Startled at first, they all broke into laughter.[80] Unfortunately, his good humor was about to sour, dampening the august occasion. One of the speakers was Dr. Steven B. Sample, an administrator at the University of Nebraska. Sample had decided to go over Eiseley's undergraduate transcript, perhaps because he knew so little about him. What happened next is related in a letter Eiseley wrote to Patrick Young, a reporter with the *National Observer*, who was also present: "I was amused at the Watergate atmosphere in which the Vice Chancellor of the University of Nebraska was careful to announce . . . that I had failed a class in Spanish. If I had had the time I could have pursued that train of invective a lot farther than he did. Probably there were more people at the gathering who will remember that I once flunked Spanish than that I received the Eminent Nebraskan Award."[81]

The "to hell in a hand basket" letters also continued to mount, which, of course, was nothing new. The difference is that, at age sixty-seven, Eiseley had fallen victim to his own cant, believing everything he wrote.

> There must have been intelligent men in the last days of the Roman empire who knew very well it would collapse but who were utterly helpless when it came to turning the great juggernaut aside from its path. I have come to believe, with Spengler, that one can only try to endure with a certain stoicism what one sees as fated, and give all oneself and pass on what little love and sense of duty one small ephemeral body may possess.[82]

Mortality was beginning to catch up with his friends; Claude Hibbard and Carl Wittke had recently passed from the scene, not to mention Haydn and Auden. Eiseley made an appointment with Provost Eliot Stellar to discuss his retirement and the disposition of his papers designated for preservation. (These would not include such things as the haunting query from boyhood friend Jimmy Dawes, which had lately resurfaced while Eiseley was gleaning his files.) Having pronounced his grave site "not so bad" after trying it out under a brilliant summer sky, he signed his last will and testament on August 8, 1974. It was beginning to look as though he would be breaking a very old promise after all, but through no fault of his own. "I will try my best to keep that date with the returning star," he wrote an admirer. "But one does grow tired."[83]

VIII

In August 1974, Eiseley made the following entry in one of his notebooks: "Time. What did it matter now, it was breaking apart like disjointed memories."[84] He had just received a letter from Edwin Way Teale, who was pleased to know that his fellow nature writer was at least "nibbling" at the idea of an autobiography. Teale went on to describe two methods of approaching the task. The first, or "inclusive way," has the author commencing at the beginning and progressing, in chronological order, to the end, like a motion picture. But Teale intimated that a second approach, what he called the "selective way," would work better for Eiseley. The special days and times are set down in sharply focused vignettes, like a sequence of still pictures recorded by electronic flash. This was how Teale's own life played back with abnormal clarity on those nights when sleep refused to come.[85] With this communication, the psychological logjam that had been building for fifteen years suddenly burst. References to a "selective biography" began surfacing almost immediately in Eiseley's correspondence.

Three months later found him writing all-out. Not only did an excited Kenneth Heuer want to see what he had down on paper but the editor offered to draft a contract on the spot. Both invitations were declined. "All autobiographies are difficult and it is barely possible . . . that, in the end, I may decide not to risk it."[86] The manuscript pages were piling up so rapidly, however, that Eiseley was soon ready to discuss a contract for "The Other Player." The document was drawn up and signed on February 4, 1975. He decided on an advance of ten thousand dollars and insisted that the option clause for his next book be stricken.[87] The title was changed to *All the Strange Hours*, from a line in Swinburne's "Ave Atque Vale" ("Hail and Farewell").

Eiseley considered dedicating the work to Wright Morris, who had done the same for him, but such a decision would have required that he discuss their long friendship, something he was not prepared to do. The honor ultimately went to Charles Frederick Eiseley, "cavalryman in the Grand Army of the Republic," and to William Buchanan Price, "without whose help my life would have been different beyond imagining." It was one of the few times, here or elsewhere, that Eiseley openly admitted being indebted to anyone.

Reading *All the Strange Hours* is akin to viewing a surrealist painting. Rarely are the portraits strewn across Eiseley's inner landscape placed in chronological order. Some are slightly askew, while others—such as those of the murderous outlaw Tom Murray and Eiseley's well-meaning professor Orin Stepanek, who arranged for his stay in the California desert—are hung upside down, standing truth on its head. "Like a shape summoned up from among the erratic twisters of the dust bowl days, Eiseley can only be himself," the author had written for the jacket, a line Heuer or someone else excised before the copy went to press.[88]

It can be fairly argued that *All the Strange Hours* is among the longest chronicles of an individual death in literary history, spanning almost seventy years. The work begins with the zero and ends with it, and the cipher overshadows every other stage of Eiseley's existence as well, from childhood to Shakespeare's seventh age of man. Death and Chance are one and the same to him, the inscrutable "Other Player," the "laughing puppet," who must inevitably win the final hand.

But what of the hours that were not so strange? Where are the captain of the high-school football team and president of his senior class? Where are Jac Cave and Bill Gaffney and Rudolph Umland, Dorothy Thomas, Lowry Wimberly, Hiram Haydn, and a knowing woman named Mabel Langdon? Where are the dates, the names, and the documentation normally associated with a scientist, especially one who kept a number of notebooks over the years? Eiseley's own excuse that he wanted to keep the narrative moving hardly convinces. The writer was not only creating a unique history to satisfy the fundamental need to make his life come out right in the end, but also carefully setting the stage for future generations. "If our heroes prove to be immortal," wrote Anatole France, "then so—perhaps—are we." Like the priests of Akhenaton he decried, Eiseley practiced his own form of *damnatio memoriae*, beating the time effacers at their game by becoming his own most memorable creation.

The Romans placed a wax portrait mask on a patrician corpse before displaying it in the Forum. They called it an imago, or image. Both Freud and Jung applied this term to a personal prototype formed in childhood against whom all others are measured in later life. For some the imago becomes a compulsion from which escape is impossible, and Eiseley fell victim to this psychological trap: the constant search for a father who could measure up to his every fictional ideal of a vanished Clyde, the craving of love and comfort from women who treated him as a vulnerable hero and child. The enclosed world of his Nebraska youth proved so crucial imaginatively that it set limits on the degree of his maturity, barring his full entry into man's estate. The Odyssean status he so craved was an impossibility, given his failure to surrender to something larger and grander than himself.

Yet in his prose, as in his profession, Eiseley labored in behalf of the poetic rather than a literal truth. Eschewing structure, he created a series of scenes reminiscent of shadows that dissolve and re-form, rousing intense emotions. Most affecting are those whose setting is the natural world but whose ultimate concern is human arrogance—the minuteness of the species against the vast perspective of cosmic drift. Recognition flows like an underground stream through Eiseley's pages, an aching nostalgia tinged with dread of the dark and dust, which is almost everything we have and are, save the mysterious incandescent fire of the chromosomes. Eiseley's pilgrimage, like that of the New England ruminants who were his literary forefathers, constitutes a variation on the ancient myth of man's fall from grace—the quest of a scientist at odds with his calling. Fear, anger, sorrow, elation, and rejection are as much a part of his writing as the Darwinian revolution, the genetic code, or the sun-varnished bones of the early mammals.

The many who read him and wrote mentioned always his capacity to stir some previously unfathomed sentiment, to serve as a trigger for their own deepest yearnings. Favorite passages were read and reread in the gloom of a stormy afternoon or the silence of a sleepless night, words transforming time and place, images emerging, memories summoned, the spirit transported. Unspeakable loneliness and melancholy were for Eiseley a part of the natural order. "I am every man and no man, and will be so to the end," he wrote.[89] It is a long and honored journey—stretching from Beowulf to Edgar Allan Poe to Isak Dinesen and Jorge Luis Borges. Eiseley's vision, like theirs, is not so much pessimistic as resigned.

The autobiography, like his many other works, must be viewed primarily as literature rather than as a historical document. In it Eiseley's deficiencies as a man are transformed into the personal myths that garnered him fitting acclaim as a writer. For just as he was able to imagine and bring to reality an original literary style—"the concealed essay"—so he believed that he could re-create his life story to accord with a self-determined vision of his place in the universe. While the autobiography is rife with distortions, fantasies, and illusions, it will forever be the most vivid and, in some essential sense, veracious evocation of its chimerical subject and author. As he wrote,

> I did not care for taxonomic definitions, that was the truth of it. I did not care to be a man, only a being. I lifted the huge bone meditatively. The dream had faded; there was no way to ask the Player to recast the dice. To do so always ended with Tom Murray, because Tom Murray had died as a hunted man yet still defined as human. I had inadvertently joined him, identified with him. But in that greater winter where I sought retreat, Tom Murray could lead me no further.[90]

IX

Mabel was enjoying her best health in years, but Loren was experiencing greater stress than usual over the release of his latest work. "This is not a 'kiss and tell' sort of a book," Mabel wrote Mary Mattern, a friend from the Kansas days, "and anyone looking for sex exploits will be disappointed. Nor am I more than briefly referred to." She saw no reason to take the public too intimately into their private domain. "Also I felt that the story should be Loren's."[91]

Eiseley's anxiety increased not just because he was publishing an autobiography; a recent confrontation with the editorial staff of *Philadelphia Magazine* had left him deeply unsettled. A former student of his had submitted an article on her professor's philosophy, concentrating on "The Last Magician," the *Playboy* essay from *The Invisible Pyramid*, which recalls a strange encounter in New York's Pennsylvania Station. Eiseley, who was then about fifty, became aware of a man loitering in the distance. They began moving toward each other on a broad stairway. Phantom or genetic twin, Frank Speck, who had been dead for several years, passed by his successor without any sign of acknowledgement. "The blind eye turned sideways was not, in truth, fixed upon me."[92] The author of the article on Eiseley took this encounter for a supernatural revelation that he should resign his administrative post and complete the work he was intended to do.

After reading the piece in manuscript, Eiseley wrote Art Spikol,

Philadelphia Magazine's executive editor, that, if published, it would damage his professional reputation. "I am aghast at the implication that I received the spectacle of a man closely resembling Frank Speck as the actual incarnation of my former teacher."[93] The article was rejected posthaste, but not without further cost. Its wounded author wrote Eiseley to express her regrets and strike a well-placed blow of her own. "I am surprised that you object to my conclusion. . . . In all honesty, I do not know how it can be interpreted otherwise, and I am merely one among many of your loyal followers who have been so affected." She could not conceive that Eiseley's "mystical side—the facet you apparently did not realize that you project—in any way detracts from your reputation as an evolutionist."[94]

All the Strange Hours reached the bookstores in late October, but then, despite a third printing, promptly went out of stock the week before Christmas, adding to its author's string of bad luck. Bemoaning his financial loss and exclusion from the best-seller list again, Eiseley, in a letter to Ray Bradbury, branded the book business "a chaotic gamble."[95] He had canceled his subscription to the *New York Times* because of the cost and had been rushing to the newsstand every morning in anticipation of what he termed the "make-or-break" review. When it finally appeared on December 18, the agony of waiting was replaced by an equally familiar form of psychic torture. Alden Whitman compared the prose to a bottle of Cliquot Club ginger ale: "full of fizz and bubbles, it goes down with a tang. But let the carbonation work off, and it is very chancy stuff indeed." Whitman labeled the author's teleology "a quagmire." Seeming to argue for chance and design simultaneously, Eiseley left the reader to wonder just where this eminent anthropologist stood on evolution.[96]

Mabel was almost as shaken as her husband. Fortunately for them, Edmund Fuller's review happened to appear the same day in the *Wall Street Journal.* His high praise eventually found its way onto the cover of the paperback edition. "[Eiseley] is one of the most remarkable individual minds among us. There is no comfort in him but often a great, brooding beauty. He inhabits sometimes the landscape of King Lear."[97]

Kenneth Heuer had termed Eiseley "very promotable" in the background report required on all books published by Scribner's, and so he was. Included among his television appearances was an interview by the Chicago-based critic Robert Cromie on his nationally syndicated program "Book Beat." The fix was in; with Cromie's acquiescence, Eiseley spent the entire half hour rambling on about Madeline and Night Country, two cats whose stories remind one of charming little fables or the affecting homilies of an eloquent priest. But the program had no sooner aired than letters began arriving that churned up some bittersweet memories.

A morose Eiseley had written that the old International House on Fortieth and Spruce had long since been demolished. "The wreckers, it sometimes seems to me, always follow fast upon my heels."[98] But the grand old mansion, little altered in appearance on the outside, had not succumbed to progress, and he must have walked past it a hundred times during his several decades at Penn. Richard Faust, Ricky of bygone days, had not forgotten and wrote to him. "First of all, let me assure you that I—'Ricky'—am alive and well, as the saying goes, and living in Raleigh. . . . What a flood of memories [the autobiography] evoked!" He was relieved to hear that Duke Tachibana had made it safely through the war.[99]

Jac Cave, the class jester who'd drifted down the Missouri and out of Eiseley's life, had also tuned in. "I believe you can understand how a man of seventy years can read a book with lumps in his throat, and how he must stop at times to rub away the unexpected tears." Jac had called for Loren on more than one occasion, and Loren had been there to help. "Could not I in turn have been of some help to you in your dark hours?" All the while Jac had thought his best friend was "blissfully" continuing his higher studies.[100]

Writing to Heuer a few months before his editor came to a parting of the ways with Scribner's in December 1975, a seemingly stoic Eiseley professed to being cleansed of "an old midnight bitterness." The act of writing *All the Strange Hours* had had a deeply cathartic effect.[101] He was saddened by Heuer's leaving, but Charles Scribner, Jr., wrote to reassure him that the firm's commitment to his work was in no sense compromised. To be Eiseley's publisher was an "extraordinary honor."[102]

As the author withdrew to contemplate what next to write, his public acclaim mounted. The autobiography was into its fifth printing by May 1976, and the first twenty thousand paperback copies were on order, with tens of thousands more to come. Eiseley received the Christopher Award for *All the Strange Hours* in February and went up to the Boston Museum of Science on October 18 to accept the Bradford Washburn Award, consisting of a gold medal and a stipend of five thousand dollars in recognition of his contribution toward the public understanding of science. Later that month the Humane Society of the United States awarded him the Joseph Wood Krutch Medal for defending life on Earth. Invitations to speak threatened to overwhelm Mrs. Werkley. At this stage of his life, Eiseley preferred to read his poetry rather than lecture for an hour; he even cut his fee for those willing to take the bard over the professor, not that the content or the style differed substantially.

In early 1976 Eiseley was approached by Kappy Wells, a young New York sculptor who had studied under Jacques Lipchitz. Up to this point most of her work had been concerned with animals, but occasionally a human face and compelling spirit caused her to write the type of letter Eiseley received. The project she had in mind was a bust that would require only a few sittings of about an hour each, and she could come to Philadelphia if he found it more convenient. His initial reaction was negative, but both Mabel and Mrs. Werkley liked the enclosed photographs of the artist's work. Recognizing that protest was futile, Eiseley yielded, but it took some months for the sittings to be arranged. Dollie Hahn happened to be in Wynnewood on her annual visit when her brother-in-law walked in the door one afternoon, visibly upset. "Well, girls, the old man is on his way out!" The newly completed bust had fallen from its shelf onto a concrete floor, shattering into a hundred pieces. Everyone laughed but a brooding Eiseley, who refused to sit again, forcing Wells to execute a second bust from photographs and memory.[103]

Shortly thereafter Eiseley began experiencing some physical discomfort. Following an examination he was scheduled for surgery on an enlarged prostate gland in late September. This condition was not uncommon for a man his age, and he was soon out of the hospital and apparently headed for a complete recovery. Then came the low-grade temperature and jaundice, which were first diagnosed as hepatitis, later as a disorder of the gall bladder. His appetite disappeared, and he began dropping weight all too rapidly. Several medications were prescribed, but his condition worsened, requiring a gaunt Eiseley to reenter the hospital in Bryn Mawr the day after Christmas. Exploratory surgery was scheduled for the morning of December 28, and the finding could hardly have been worse. The doctors discovered a large tumor on the bile duct at the top of the pancreas, which they diagnosed as malignant and inoperable. Mabel "crumpled," and the new year dawned with Eiseley knowing it would be his last.

There were other doctors, of course, but none better than Jonathan Rhoads, Eiseley's longtime colleague at Penn. Could his old friend at least buy him some extra time, he wanted to know? Rhoads was skeptical, but he agreed to perform a pancreatectomy, or Whipple's procedure, which involves removal of the gland and part of the duodenum. Success, which was far from assured, would mean an additional year of life, perhaps two, during which the patient would have to take pancreatic enzymes with his food as well as insulin injections. The rare operation, lasting several hours, was performed at the University of Pennsylvania Hospital by Rhoads and Dr. Julius Mackie, Jr., another old acquaintance, on January 27, 1977. Eiseley would not leave the premises for six weeks.

Nothing he had ever experienced could rival the loss of dignity he suffered while in intensive care. This most private of men could do nothing for himself. He lay motionless for days, his body and facial cavities invaded by tubes and monitored by hissing cyclopian beasts that never slept. White walls, white gowns, white lights, a technological Pleistocene in which, paradoxically, all hope of escape was abandoned. On February 22 Mabel wrote a friend that Dr. Rhoads said Loren was looking better. "But they keep doing things to him—he's had innumerable x-rays and the like."[104] Nearing her seventy-seventh birthday, she was spending several hours at the hospital each day. How could she leave, even to protect her own fragile health, when Loren's unrelenting insomnia released him only when he sensed her presence in the room? Nor was Mrs. Werkley ever far away.

Eiseley finally walked down the hospital steps into a wintry March, shrunken and hunched, barely able to hold the fading embers of his life together. Like Clyde, he was a victim of nature's ultimate betrayal, the body attacking and destroying itself. Neither he nor Mabel could bring themselves to use the word cancer. Loren had undergone abdominal surgery, serious to be sure, but that was all.

The telephone bills between Alaska and Philadelphia skyrocketed. Eiseley talked to Jim Hahn sometimes twice a day, attempting to convince both himself and his heartsick nephew that he could defy medical science by surviving indefinitely with a proper diet and medication. Colleague Ruben Reina, who occasionally took Eiseley on leisurely drives to a suburban park between the rounds of hospitalization, sensed his underlying fear and was surprised that a man who had written so incisively of death was not better prepared to meet it. When Ricky Faust came to town and decided to look up his old college roommate, he was met by a "stone wall." Even the Schultzes, who had been friends with the Eiseleys longer than anyone, would know virtually nothing until the end. Stanley Johnson, the Penn chaplain, was one of Eiseley's most faithful hospital visitors, but the two discussed neither theology nor death. The chaplain soon realized that Eiseley was more comfortable with the silences and left it at that.

The Eiseleys' roller-coaster hopes took another turn almost immediately following Loren's release from the hospital. The jaundice, accompanied by vomiting, recurred, and he was readmitted on March 14. Massive doses of penicillin and round-the-clock nursing care enabled him to return home two weeks later; there he dozed on the couch and attempted to keep up with his correspondence by dictating to Mrs. Werkley. He wrote his eighty-three-year-old half brother in April that his symptoms were somewhat similar to those of malaria. "It has been a hard grueling episode over which I do not care to dwell unnecessarily." Loren closed by advising Leo to take care of himself, as well as the cats and dog.[105]

On May 26, Athena called to say that her father had died of heart failure the previous evening. Whether Eiseley would have gone to Leo's funeral had he not been dying himself will never be known; he did promise to keep in closer contact in the future. Athena knew only that her long-estranged uncle was quite ill, and she began to dream of him, jotting down the few symbolic fragments she could remember in the morning: "On my awakening—[Loren] has possibly discovered all former thinkings have exploded."[106]

Scribner's, who had been told that Eiseley had contracted "a mysterious bug," mailed him the galleys of *Another Kind of Autumn* in mid-April. This, his third book of poetry, was dedicated first to Caroline Hutton Elsea and then equally to her three daughters, of whom Mrs. Werkley was discreetly named last, but doubtless only after gaining Mabel's imprimatur. The title, derived from the volume's first poem, had become a metaphor for Eiseley's existence over the last few months.

the mountain is gone and this fragment
lies on my desk imperishable and waiting for me in turn
to be gone.[107]

He also completed the outline for "The Loren Eiseley Sampler," a major anthology of his poetry and prose. Scribner's was anxious to publish the book, but it never came to light because of posthumous contractual differences with Mabel.[108]

The old physical symptoms flared up again in early June, and into the hospital Eiseley went for another two-week stay. Released on the seventeenth, he was home only four days before having to take the too-familiar taxi ride back to campus; it was his last. Beneath the inescapable glare of the blinding white lights, he began to slip away, swimming in and out of consciousness among the splinters of memory. The surgeons went back in on July 5, just to be sure, and found that the tumor had recurred, hopelessly blocking the intestine.

Jim, who was staying with his parents in Colorado while getting his pilot's license, came east to be there at the end. Mabel turned seventy-seven on July 9, and Mrs. Werkley prepared her usual champagne dinner in an effort to make the occasion as special as possible. The three had visited Loren that afternoon, but he remained unconscious the whole time. Earlier in the week, however, when Mrs. Werkley was discussing the upcoming celebration, he had suddenly opened his eyes and asked plaintively, "What about me?" Deeply torn, they promised to toast him when the time came.

The three were drinking champagne in Mrs. Werkley's living room when the telephone rang around six o'clock. When the caller identified himself as Dr. Rhoads and asked for Mabel, everyone knew what was coming. A persistent dream has meaning and is sometimes fulfilled. Death's posse had finally got its man.

EPILOGUE

The rough-hewn crescent of stone Loren and Mabel would share was already in place under the buckeye tree, its inscription taken from "The Little Treasures," a poem in *Another Kind of Autumn*: "We loved the earth but could not stay." They both preferred cremation and were decided on this course well before Eiseley's final illness. But when Mabel, by her own account, happened to mention the subject to her sister one day, Dollie became deeply upset. The Scriptures, she protested, were quite clear on this point: to defy them by choosing anything but a traditional burial would constitute a sacrilege. Realizing that it would be futile to debate the question, Mabel broached the matter with her husband. After a few moments of thought, he replied, " 'Well, I don't want to hurt Dollie's feelings. You and I know that it doesn't really matter, either way, but under the circumstances perhaps a conventional funeral would be best.' "[1]

Jim had his uncle's direct orders and little time to carry them out before the service, which was scheduled for 2:00 P.M. Wednesday, July 13, at the Oliver H. Blair Funeral Home on Chestnut Street. Feeling very much like the thief he was about to become, he headed toward Penn in a borrowed car, wondering how it would look if he was imprisoned on the day of the funeral.

The object of his larcenous intent was Skeleton No. 4989, or Eddie, who had been a whimsical fixture in Eiseley's office for a decade. In truth, these bones constituted the earthly remains of Dr. Edward Drinker Cope, the native Philadelphian who had become the most distinguished of nineteenth-century paleontologists. Ranging from the marl pits of New Jersey to the Badlands where the South Party had once roamed, the University of Pennsylvania professor discovered over one thousand new species of extinct vertebrates, including many of the dinosaurs, before his untimely death at age fifty-six, in 1897. Cope's skeleton, together with other miscellaneous materials, was donated to the University Museum by the Wistar Institute of Anatomy and Biology in 1966. The carton of distinguished bones immediately caught Eiseley's eye. After scribbling a note that read "Gone to lunch—Edward Drinker Cope," he removed the eminent newcomer from the anthropology laboratory for "safekeeping."

A rearticulated Eddie sometimes rested on a long desk in Eiseley's office. Fro Rainey often came by for lunch, and the two were fond of toasting what remained of their spiritual forebear with shots of Wild Turkey, Cope having liked his alcohol better than most. At Christmas Mrs. Werkley draped the compliant guest with garlands and tinsel; dried flowers were tucked into his carton the other months of the year, a rite first performed by the Neanderthals of Shanidar. Then, sometime in the mid-1970s, an artist from the Museum of Natural History requested permission to borrow the doctor's cranium as a model for a bust he was doing in conjunction with a special exhibition. Cope's skull was unusual for a number of reasons, not the least of which was its hammer-driven gold fillings. Eiseley let it go, much to his subsequent anger, for it disappeared without a trace. It was after this episode that he called Jim in Alaska to begin plotting Eddie's final disposition.

Jim first tried taping the bones to his own arms and legs, but he was sweating profusely in the July heat and had visions of "falling apart" before the eyes of a museum guard. The skeleton would have to be carried out in its box, disguised as books from his uncle's office. This simple deception was accomplished without a hitch. Jim then headed for the funeral home, where only Mabel, Mrs. Werkley, her son, Christopher, and himself were authorized to view the body. Not having taken into account the fact that the polished birch casket had a single lid as opposed to the split type, he wilted upon realizing that the mortician soon would discover the stowaway and thwart the plot, leaving him no choice but to smuggle Cope's skeleton back into the museum. Eiseley would go out with only two things of this earth—his silver Byzantine cross and his stuffed lion with shoe-button eyes.[2]

More touching than the funeral to Mabel was the memorial service held at the University Museum in November. Rev. Stanley Johnson delivered the invocation and ended the tribute by reading from *The Immense Journey*. In between, several old friends—Eliot Stellar, Jonathan Rhoads, Ward Goodenough, Bert Schultz, Paul Sears—bid Eiseley a public farewell while music was provided by the Philadelphia Piano Quartet. But the most eloquent remembrance of all had come from one who could not be present.

July 28, 1977

Dear Mabel:
Beginning with the beginning, the first meeting in Haverford, the summer evenings (with the dog!) on the terrace, the snapshots of the men folks in the Victory garden, decked out in hats supplied by the ladies, the sound effects courtesy of the Paoli local, the dunked ice cubes, the free-flowing gabble, beginning with such beginnings without end I've been reliving my life with the Eiseleys.

No Leary's *that* summer: although books, and a globe of the world, were carted back from whatshisname's junk and antiques on the pike, also a platform rocker, upholstered in green train-seat satin, the property of THE cat, now nameless, famous for the swig he took from the dregs of cocktail glasses. Then the affluent suburbs, the weedy terrace with the garden statuary and the pith helmet rakishly worn by academes, planning safaris, or telling risqué jokes to displaced ladies, one a master of the homemade and packed peanut brittle, reserved for Xmas., and the banana cream pie, reserved for Eiseley and Morris, followed by the siesta of Master Eiseley while Morris gabbled (I feel the world's in safe hands, quoth Eiseley) and so they fared westward, where camp was established for wild and tame life observation, neighbors, cats, birds and chipmunks, lured to the carport by creature-feeling bodies slack in the sling chairs, spirits ascending, underfoot the primal ooze of the Morris-Eiseley tar pits, the like of which was there none for bone storing, truth retrieval, grist to the mill of feathered, forked and fanged observers, their eyes gleaming in the privet, their natures tuned to the hum and vibrations of the Master, hammocked in a sling chair, the glow of his rum-soaked crook a friendly beacon, the sound of his baritone a comforter, a life-enhancer, the purr of his nature a reminder that here, if nowhere

> else, all of God's chilluns were in safe hands, even the cat Sour Mash. From this composte dreams sprouted, the bubbling and greenish spring water was bottled (for emergencies prophesied on the potsherds) many were boldly encouraged and a few were chosen, fevers and storms were survived, trees toppled and felled, lawns unevenly mowed, yet nothing took the place of the pachysandra, seasons creaked and rolled, ties loosened, the crack of heat lightning signalled early departures, the curdling of half-and-half in the cat's dish, the sound of alarms, the smoke of burning leaves, all of it once, twice, thrice forever and the last time.
>
> O Mabel dear for those who were there it was a good rich life, savory as peanut brittle, deserving of our affection and celebration, the pleasures and torments of our emotions. We think of you, we love you, and we continue to cherish our much shared lives.
>
> Wright[3]

There was one more promise to be kept. Jim went down into the basement of the Wyndon, where the tenants were allotted storage space, and began hauling out the heavy boxes Eiseley had asked him to destroy. These he reduced to ashes in a literary rite as old as paper itself, claiming not to have examined the contents before the sacrifice. Eiseley had referred to Hemingway's fate at the hands of biographers when exacting Jim's pledge.

The surviving correspondence attests to the fact that there were several who aspired to write Eiseley's life, but with one exception he managed to keep them all at arm's length. The shell formed in childhood had thickened and grown encrusted over the years; it rarely opened and closed quickly. It was one thing if Eiseley himself chose to reveal certain secrets from his past, but revelation was forbidden to anyone else. He thought of biography, when he thought of it at all, in nineteenth-century terms—the Victorian lionization of the public man: preserve the encomiums, purge the rest. The new biography was simply more than he could tolerate, with its obsession with sex, fascination for idle gossip, and dime-store psychoanalysis. It was another product of "permissive society," amounting to little more than removing someone's clothes before a gaping public. Finally, there was the pride of the thinking man—the belief that no one could possibly capture his essence on the flat plain of the printed page.

Scholarly articles, dissertations, even book-length literary studies were another matter. In these cases Eiseley was almost always willing to lend a hand. But when E. Fred Carlisle, a professor of English and Whitman scholar at the University of Michigan, got too close by seeking interviews with longtime friends and former colleagues, Eiseley, with Mabel's help, brutally slammed the door. "I sincerely hope," he wrote a crestfallen Carlisle three months before his death, "that if you are a friend of mine you will understand my motivation and try, if you must write a critique, to leave the author out of it."[4]

Mrs. Werkley stayed on for two more years, sorting and cataloging what remained of the papers and manuscripts, disposing of others with Mabel's approval. When this job was finally completed, she returned to Moberly, Missouri, and the red Victorian cottage of her childhood on "The Hollow." There the "good dragon," as her boss had sometimes referred to her, still writes of gnomes and goblins and beasties and things that go bump in the night, communing all the while with the ghosts of Donne, Marlowe, Montaigne, and Sir Thomas Browne.

After returning to Alaska, where he lived among the native Eskimos in Barrow until 1985, Jim headed south in search of a warmer clime. He found it among the Hopi up on Third Mesa, where the deer and the antelope still roam.

Mabel, frail but gritty as the loess of the rolling yellow cloud, stayed on at the Wyndon until the end, keeping everything, with the help of Mary Smith and a series of live-in companions, just as it was when Loren had last walked out the door. When I finally met and interviewed her for the first time in September 1984, I was stunned by the similarity between her aspect and the vision of old age projected in "Twilight Musing," her *Schooner* poem written fifty-six years earlier. The white hair was indeed waved, low-knotted by a bright ribbon at the neck. And, as she had predicted, her hands remained soft and lovely through the years. The only things missing were the tapers in their silver candlesticks for casting faint shadows on the wall. The voice was weak, and I rose from the sofa where Eiseley had often sat gazing at the painted sunflowers and placed a chair next to hers. She took a deep breath, looked me squarely in the eyes, and said, "Well, tell me what you want to know."

NOTES

CHAPTER 1: PROGENITORS

1. *IP*, 1–2.
2. EFH. Also see *Norfolk Daily News*, Feb. 4, 1918, 5.
3. *Nebraska: A Guide to the Cornhusker State*, compiled and written by the Federal Writers' Project of the Works Progress Administration (New York: Viking Press, 1939), 6.
4. Willa Cather, *My Antonia* (New York: Houghton Mifflin Company, 1918), 5.
5. *Norfolk Press*, Sept. 14, 1916, 1.
6. NARSF (Pension Records).
7. James C. Olson, *History of Nebraska*, 2nd ed. (Lincoln: University of Nebraska Press, 1966), 125.
8. NARSF (Pension Records); Logan Valley Cemetery Records, Winslow, NE.
9. EFH; *The Story of Koxie Comie, 1866–1966, Norfolk, Nebraska Centennial Booklet*, ed. Norfolk, Nebraska, Centennial Committee (Norfolk: Norfolk Junior Chamber of Commerce, 1966), 22, 32, 36, 38.
10. EFH; *Norfolk Daily News* Feb. 10, 1896, 3, Mar. 7, 1896, 5.
11. EFH; Clyde's Shakespeare is now in the UPA.
12. Prospect Hill Cemetery Association Records, Norfolk, NE, Burial 342.
13. *Norfolk Daily News*, Nov. 1, 1890, 1.
14. EFH; *The Story of Koxie Comie*, 50–52; *Norfolk Daily News*, Nov. 1, 1890, 1.

15. EFH.
16. *Anoka Herald*, May 8, 1903, 8. Also see Boyd County Court House Marriage Records, Butte, NE, license no. 668, May 4, 1903.
17. Boyd County District Court Records, Butte, NE, Clyde E. Eiseley vs. Eva Eiseley, July 22, 1905; EFH.
18. Woodbury County Court House, Sioux City, IA, Certificate of marriage, Clyde E. Eiseley and Daisy E. Corey, Nov. 10, 1906; EFH.
19. NSHS, Daughters of the American Revolution Application Papers, Grace Corey Price, 929.1351, N272da, v. 5, 229–232; *Dyersville, Iowa Centennial: Official History and Program, 1972* (Dyersville, 1972), n. pag.
20. Interview with M.E., Apr. 2, 1985.
21. NSHS, Daughters of the American Revolution Application Papers, v. 5, 229–32; *Dyersville, Iowa Centennial: Official History and Program*; UPT 50, E36, Box 48 contains the Eiseley family Bible and a letter (Box 5) on Eiseley genealogy written by one Wirt McKee to Grace Corey Price on May 3, 1921. For additional information see UNA, *Alumni Assoc.*, Loren Corey Eiseley Papers, 40/5, Box 1, f. Cor., 1921–1976.
22. NSHS, MS. no. 507, Price, William B. This entry consists of two scrapbooks, both unpaged, of newspaper clippings, pamphlets, and other memorabilia collected by Grace Corey Price. It was later given to the historical society by Loren and Mabel Eiseley. Also see *Who's Who in Lincoln, 1928*, 179.
23. UPT 50, E36, Box 50. Daisy's paint box is also in this carton, along with much additional memorabilia.
24. NSHS, RG 207, Lancaster County, Lincoln, NE, Marriage Records, v. 15, 531; *Lincoln Evening Journal*, Oct. 14, 1895, 5.
25. NSHS, Lancaster County, Lincoln NE, District Court Divorce Petitions, v. 30, 41.
26. EFH.

CHAPTER 2: "A HOUSE OF GESTURE"

1. Grace Price to L. and M.E., Apr. 3, 1956, UNA, *Alumni Assoc.*, Loren Corey Eiseley Papers, 40/5, Box 1, f. Cor., 1921–1976.
2. *MN*, 19.
3. State of Nebraska, Bureau of Vital Statistics, Lincoln, NE, Certificate of Birth no. 125–452–07, Loren C. Eiseley; EFH.
4. Interview with A.V.S., Apr. 1, 1985.
5. EFH. *The Fremont City Directory, 1910–1911*, 79, lists Leo Eiseley as a boarder in his father's house.

6. UPT 50, E36, Box 5, f. The Nebraska Society of Washington, D.C., 2.
7. UPT 50, E36, Box 20, f. 16, *NC*, 53.
8. *UU*, 86; *NA*, 23–25; *ASH*, 25–29; Interview with M.E., Apr. 21, 1985.
9. UPT 50, E36, Box 25, f. 4, *All the Strange Hours*, 53.
10. Edmund Critchley, "Language Development of Hearing Children in a Deaf Environment," *Developmental Medicine and Child Neurology* 9, no. 3 (1967), 274–80. Also see Rachel Mayberry, "An Assessment of Some Oral and Manual-Language Skills of Hearing Children of Deaf Parents," *American Annals of the Deaf* 121 (October 1976), 507–12.
11. *ASH*, 172–73; UPT 50, E36, Box 40, f. 9, Midcentury Authors.
12. *Lincoln Daily Star*, Mar. 14, 1912, 1.
13. *Aurora Republican*, Aug. 25, 1911, 1; *Lincoln Daily Star*, Mar. 15, 1912, 5.
14. *ASH*, 174.
15. *Lincoln Daily Star*, Mar. 9, 1912, 1.
16. *Lincoln Daily Star*, Mar. 15, 1912, 5.
17. R.U. to G.C., Dec. 11, 1984.
18. *Lincoln Daily Star*, Mar. 16, 1912, 4.
19. *Lincoln Daily Star*, Mar. 17, 1912, 6; Mar. 19, 1912, 1; *Gretna Breeze*, Mar. 22, 1912, 5.
20. *ASH*, 174.
21. Ibid., 172.
22. UPT 50, E36, Box 40, f. 61, "An Interview with Loren Eiseley," 8; *MN*, 58.
23. UPT 50, E36, Box 51.
24. *NC*, 5–6.
25. L.E. to Joe B. Frantz, Jan. 14, 1970, UPT 50, E36, Box 1, f. F.
26. *MN*, 21.
27. Trinity Methodist Church Membership Record: 1887–1899, Lincoln, NE, n. pag.
28. *MN*, 22.
29. Aurora Public Schools, Aurora, NE, Grade School Record, Loren Eiseley, Sept. 10, 1917, to May 31, 1918.
30. *NC*, 19–20.
31. L.E., "Underground," *Nebraska Alumnus* 33, no. 8 (October 1937), 10.
32. *ASH*, 33–34.
33. Ibid., 30–31.
34. Ibid., 32.
35. Ibid., 233.
36. Ibid., 29.

37. NSHS, MS. no. 507, Price, William B.
38. UPT 50, E36, Box 5, f. The Nebraska Society of Washington, D.C., 1.
39. *NC*, 95.
40. *ASH*, 171.
41. *Norfolk Daily News*, Feb. 4, 1918, 5.
42. *IA*, 68–70; *Lincoln Daily Star*, Dec. 13, 1918, 2.
43. *ASH*, 79; UPT 50, E36, Box 26, f. Chicago Tribune; *Philadelphia Inquirer, Today Magazine*, Jan. 27, 1974, 16. Several volumes from E.'s childhood library are preserved in the BML and UPA.
44. R.U. to G.C., Dec. 11, 1984.
45. *ASH*, 160.

CHAPTER 3: T.C.H.S.

1. EFH.
2. *MN*, 19.
3. UPT 50, E36, Box 8, f. Lengthier Biography, 1.
4. UNA, R.G. 27/4/9.
5. L.E. to Mamie Harms Eiseley, Oct. 22, 1922 (courtesy of A.V.S.).
6. *ASH*, 79; Interview with M.E., Apr. 21, 1985.
7. *NC*, 7.
8. *ASH*, 16.
9. L.E. "Whiskers," Nov. 27, 1923, EE.
10. UNA, R.G. 27/4/9.
11. *Philadelphia Inquirer, Today Magazine*, Jan. 27, 1974, 18.
12. "An Interview with Loren Eiseley," *Exploration 1974*, 8.
13. *UU*, 216–18.
14. EFH.
15. *UU*, 80.
16. *ASH*, 233.
17. *ST*, 175; *ASH*, 5.
18. Agnes Graham Isaacson to L.E., Aug. 20, 1958, UPT 50, E36, Box 1, f. I.
19. UPT 50, E36, Box 8, f. Lengthier Biography, 2.
20. Interview with Leah Dale Masters, Nov. 3, 1984. For a more detailed description of this method see Lucius Adelno Sherman, *Analytics of Literature: A Manual for the Objective Study of English Prose and Poetry* (Boston: Ginn and Company, 1901).
21. Interview with Georgia Everett Kiffin, Sept. 12, 1984.
22. Interview with Helen Hopt Kleven, Sept. 19, 1985.
23. Alice Cave to G.C., Mar. 12, 1984, May 18, 1984.
24. The playbill, graduation program, class prophecy, and will were given to G.C. by Georgia Everett Kiffin.

25. Interview with Leah Dale Masters, Nov. 3, 1984.
26. Interview with Arthella Gadd Anderson, Nov. 12, 1984.
27. Junior-Senior Banquet Speech, May 1, 1925, EE.
28. The account of the California trip was derived from the following letters to G.C.: Gladys L. Cave, widow of Jac Cave, Feb. 15, 1984; Alice Cave, Mar. 12, 1984; Faye Munden, Mar. 26, 1984, May 7, 1984.
29. *UU*, 173–74.

CHAPTER 4: "SOME DESTINY NOT DECIDED"

1. Robert Manley and R. McLaran Sawyer, *Centennial History of the University of Nebraska*, 2 vols. (Lincoln: University of Nebraska Press, 1969–1973), II, 34–39.
2. Ibid., I, 215.
3. Ibid., II, 38–39, 43.
4. Jac Cave to L.E., undated, UPT 50, E36, Box 1, f. C.
5. *ASH*, 77.
6. UPT 50, E36, Box 8, f. Lengthier Biography, 2.
7. UNA, R.G. 27/4/1. A typed copy of Eiseley's university transcript, lacking certain written annotations, is in UPT 50, E36, Box 1.
8. UPT 50, E36, Box 8, f. Lengthier Biography, 2.
9. *ASH*, 80.
10. Interview with Mrs. Arnold Barager, Sept. 14, 1984.
11. UNA, R.G. 27/4/1. In place of a grade the letter *D* appears on the transcript; it means, "Delinquent at time of withdrawal," apparently a face-saving sanction demanded by the unknown professor.
12. Ibid.
13. *ANW*, 87.
14. Interview with A.V.S., Apr. 3, 1985.
15. L.E., "Riding the Peddlers," *Prairie Schooner* 7, no. 1 (Winter 1933), 45.
16. Ibid., 50.
17. BML.
18. R.U. to G.C., Jan. 14, 1985.
19. UPT 50, E36, Caroline E. Werkley, "Report of Loren Eiseley Collection," rev. ed., Sept. 1978, 16.
20. Interviews with M.E., Sept. 8, 1984, Sept. 19, 1985.
21. Interview with M.E., Apr. 21, 1985.
22. Interview with Marian Schultz, Nov. 14, 1984.
23. *Daily Nebraskan*, Apr. 3, 1925, 1.
24. Interview with M.E., Sept. 8, 1984.

25. M.E. to D.T.B., Aug. 11, 1980 (courtesy of D.T.B.).
26. M.E. to D.T.B., July 31, 1980.
27. UPT 50, E36, Werkley, "Report of Loren Eiseley Collection," 17. This inscription, in slightly altered form, was later used as the dedication for *ANW*.
28. R.U., "The Ghost of Lowry Wimberly," *Prairie Schooner* 41, no. 3 (Fall 1967), 329.
29. For a more detailed account of the birth and development of the periodical see Paul R. Stewart, *The Prairie Schooner Story: A Little Magazine's First 25 Years* (Lincoln: University of Nebraska Press, 1955).
30. Leon Edel, *Henry D. Thoreau*, University of Minnesota Pamphlets on American Writers, no. 10 (Minneapolis: University of Minnesota Press, 1970), 14.
31. R.U., "Looking Back at the Wimberly Years," unpub. ms, BML, 32–33.
32. Interview with M.E., Apr. 21, 1985; L.E. to R.U., Jan. 26, 1967 (courtesy of R.U.).
33. L.E., "There Is No Peace," *The Freshman Scrapbook* 1, no. 4 (July 1927), 11. The only available issues of this publication are in the UNA. Also see *Prairie Schooner* 1, no. 3 (July 1927), supp.
34. L.E., "Night in a Graveyard," *The Freshman Scrapbook* 1, no. 4 (July 1927), 32.
35. L.E., "Autumn—A Memory," *Prairie Schooner* 1, no. 4 (October 1927), 238–39 (ellipses E.'s).
36. Interview with W.G., May 21, 1984.
37. Ibid.
38. R.U. to G.C., Dec. 11, 1984.
39. Interview with W.G., May 21, 1984.
40. R.U., "Lowry Wimberly and Others: Recollections of a Beerdrinker," *Prairie Schooner* 51, no. 1 (Spring 1977), 27.
41. L.E. to R.U., Jan. 26, 1967 (courtesy of R.U.). Umland was planning to write a memoir of the early Wimberly circle and wished to include some personal information about the Doc's more successful students. Though polite, Eiseley did not wish to become involved. Yet on being nominated for the honorary post of poet laureate of Nebraska in 1975, he directed his research assistant to write the following: "He [Eiseley] was interested to learn that you were the editor of the *Prairie Schooner* and a former pupil of Lowry Wimberly, who was also one of his teachers and a good friend." UPT 50, E36, Box 3, f. Poet Laureate, Caroline E. Werkley to Bernice Slote, Dec. 15, 1975.
42. R.U., "Looking Back at the Wimberly Years," 17; Interview with W.G., May 21, 1984.
43. Interview with W.G., May 21, 1984.

44. L.E. to R.U., Jan. 26, 1967.
45. *ASH*, 77.
46. Ibid., 79.
47. *MN*, 40–41.
48. *ANW*, 3. When Eiseley's poems were republished, I have used the collected works.
49. R.U. to Pamela Gossin, May 24, 1982, BML.

CHAPTER 5: DEATH OF A SALESMAN

1. *ASH*, 8–9, 17.
2. EFH; *Norfolk Daily News*, Mar. 31, 1928, 2.
3. *ASH*, 17.
4. Ibid; *UU*, 206, 211.
5. *ASH*, 15.
6. State of NE, Bureau of Vital Statistics, Lincoln, NE, Standard Certificate of Death, no. 3116, Clyde E. Eiseley.
7. EFH; *MN*, 22.
8. *ASH*, 176.
9. Geoffrey Wolff, "Minor Lives," in *Telling Lives: The Biographer's Art*, ed. Marc Pachter (Washington, D.C.: New Republic Books, 1979), 68.
10. *NC*, 170–71.
11. UPT 50, E36, Box 25, f. 2, *All the Strange Hours*.
12. *ASH*, 229, 231.
13. UPT 50, E36, Box 25, f. 4, *All the Strange Hours*.
14. R.U. to G.C., Dec. 11, 1984.
15. *ASH*, 18.
16. L.E. to Lila Wyman Graves, BML. This letter, which contains numerous deletions and interlinear corrections, has been reproduced in as close to the final form as possible.
17. The account of Lila was derived from many sources, most notably interviews with her niece, Marian Rivett Myers, Jan. 13, 1986, and nephew, Robert Wyman Rivett, Jan. 17, 1986.
18. R.U., "Looking Back at the Wimberly Years," unpub. ms, BML, 22.
19. *ASH*, 79.
20. UNA, R.G. 27/4/1.
21. *MN*, 33.
22. Faye Munden to G.C., May 7, 1984.
23. *Poetry: A Magazine of Verse* 35 (December 1929), 142–43. For the original manuscript see UPT 50, E36, Box 39, f. "The Deserted Homestead."

24. *MN*, 22; *ASH*, 17.
25. *ASH*, 20.
26. UPT, 50, E36, Box 33, f. Guggenheim Fellowship, b.
27. *ASH*, 22.
28. NSHS MS. no. 507, Price, William B.
29. *ASH*, 22.
30. Ibid., 38–40. Aware that he might have been stretching his readers' credulity, Eiseley insisted that this "strange-sounding upper-class name of Goodcrown was genuine" (38). However, a search of the Detroit police records under the Michigan Freedom of Information Act yielded no such name.
31. Interview with M.E., Sept. 8, 1984.
32. *ASH*, 45–46.
33. Ibid., 46.
34. Friedrich Wilhelm Nietzsche, *Ecce Homo: How One Becomes What One Is*, trans. R. J. Hollingdale (New York: Penguin Books, 1979), 37.
35. *ASH*, 64–69.
36. Ibid., 9–12.
37. UPT 50, E36, Box 24, f. 24, *All the Strange Hours*.
38. L.E., "The Mop to K.C.," *Prairie Schooner* 9, no. 1 (Winter 1935), 36, 38.
39. *ASH*, 52–53.
40. W.G. to Pamela Gossin, June 22, 1982, BML.
41. R.U. to G.C., Dec. 11, 1984.
42. William Ellery Channing, *Thoreau: The Poet-Naturalist* (Boston: C. E. Goodspeed, 1902), 18.
43. R.U. to G.C., Dec. 11, 1984.

CHAPTER 6: ''THE TEARSTAINS OF REMEMBERING''

1. UPT 50, E36, Box 3, f. L.C.E. Student at University of Nebraska.
2. *Lincoln Sunday Journal*, May 10, 1931, sec. 5-C.
3. It is possible that Eiseley and "the Russian poet" were one and the same. Preston Holder, who circulated among the anthropologists and later became one himself, occasionally remarked that Eiseley was as "mad as a Russian." R.U. to G.C., Mar. 6, 1986. Holder also described him as a "morose, romantic and somehow doomed figure from some 19th-century Russian novel." Preston Holder to R.U., Oct. 28, 1978 (courtesy of R.U.).
4. Interview with Flavia Waters Champe, Nov. 12, 1984.

5. Interview with C.B.S., May 21, 1984.
6. My discussion of the background and history of the Nebraska State Museum owes much to ch. 4 of Edwin H. Colbert's *A Fossil Hunter's Notebook: My Life with Dinosaurs and Other Friends* (New York: E.P. Dutton, 1980).
7. *ASH*, 87.
8. C.B.S., "Field Notes of the South Party, 1931," NSMA, 56, 64, 136; "Acquisition Records: South Party, 1931," NSMA, 14–8–31 SP.
9. C.B.S., "Field Notes of the South Party, 1931." NSMA, 63, 127; "Acquisition Records: South Party, 1931," NSMA, 15–8–31 SP.
10. *NC*, 119–120.
11. Interview with Emery Blue, May 21, 1984.
12. C.B.S., Loren Eiseley Memorial Convocation, UNA, Feb. 22, 1978.
13. *NC*, 122.
14. C.B.S., "Field Notes of the South Party, 1931," NSMA, 98.
15. *Lincoln Sunday Star*, May 3, 1931, 1.
16. M.E., "The Cathedral," *Prairie Schooner* 2, no. 1 (Winter 1928), 15.
17. M.E., "Autumnals," *Prairie Schooner* 3, no. 4 (Fall 1929), 201.
18. M.E., "Twilight Musing," *Prairie Schooner* 2, no. 3 (Summer 1928), 194.
19. This account is based on Interview with Helen Hopt Kleven, Sept. 19, 1985; Kleven to G.C., Jan. 23, 1986.
20. Kleven to G.C., Jan. 23, 1986.
21. Ibid.
22. L.E. to Helen Hopt, Sept. 15, 1931 (courtesy of H.H.K.).
23. L.E. to Hopt, Oct. 26, 1931 (Courtesy of H.H.K.).
24. W.G. to Pamela Gossin, June 22, 1982, BML.
25. D.T.B., Friends of Loren Eiseley Celebration, UNA, Sept. 13, 1984.
26. Ibid.
27. Mari Sandoz, "I Remember Lincoln," *Lincoln Journal*, Centennial Series, no. 6, May 8, 1959.
28. R.U., "Looking Back at the Wimberly Years," unpub. ms, BML, 24.
29. "Lizard's Eye" was given to W.G. by Kenneth Forward's widow. Gaffney, in turn, made the poem and background material available to me. W.G. to G.C., Feb. 24, 1985.
30. Thomas Henry Huxley, *On a Piece of Chalk*, ed. with an introduction and notes by Loren Eiseley (New York: Charles Scribner's Sons, 1967), 13.
31. Thomas Henry Huxley, *Discourses: Biological and Geological Essays* (New York and London: D. Appleton and Company, 1925), 30, 32.
32. R.U., "Looking Back at the Wimberly Years," 17.

CHAPTER 7: *LES MAUVAISES TERRES*

1. C.B.S., "Field Notes of the South Party, 1932," NSMA, 3–4.
2. UNA R.G. 27/4/1.
3. Interview with C.B.S., Nov. 15, 1984.
4. Ibid.
5. *IJ*, 186–192.
6. C.B.S., "Field Notes of the South Party, 1932," NSMA, 9–20.
7. Ibid., 30.
8. C.B.S., Loren Eiseley Memorial Convocation, UNA, Feb. 22, 1978.
9. Interview with C.B.S., Nov. 13, 1984.
10. L.E. to W.G., May 20, 1932, BML.
11. Interview with C.B.S., Nov. 15, 1984.
12. "Acquisition Records: South Party, 1932," NSMA, 113–27–6–32 SP, 149–1–7–32 SP.
13. *NA*, 119.
14. "Acquisition Records: South Party, 1932," NSMA, 1–16–6–32 SP.
15. Frank Denton, "Field Notes of the South Party, 1932," NSMA, 27.
16. Interview with Emery Blue, June 7, 1985.
17. Edwin H. Colbert, *A Fossil Hunter's Notebook: My Life with Dinosaurs and Other Friends* (New York: E.P. Dutton, 1980), 64.
18. Interview with C.B.S., June 12, 1984.
19. Interview with C.B.S. and Marian Schultz, Nov. 13, 1984.
20. Emery Blue, "Field Notes of the South Party, 1932," NSMA, 14, 18.
21. Ibid., 40–43.
22. *UU*, 220–21.
23. Ibid., 221–23, 226.
24. Emery Blue, "Field Notes of the South Party, 1932," NSMA, 43. Entry dated July 23, 1932.
25. L.E. to Erwin Barbour, July 16, 1932, NSMA, 32/1/1, f. Barbour, Erwin, Cor., 1932, E.
26. L.E. to W.G., Apr. 23, 1932 (courtesy of W.G.).
27. Erwin Barbour to Frank D. Frankenthal, Feb. 19, 1932, NSMA, 32/1/1, f. Barbour, Erwin, Cor., 1932, F.
28. Interview with C.B.S., Nov. 15, 1984; Erwin Barbour and C.B.S., "The Scottsbluff Bison Quarry and Its Artifacts," *Bulletin of the Nebraska State Museum* 1, no. 34 (Dec. 1932), 283–86; C.B.S. and L.E., "Paleontological Evidence for the Antiquity of the Scottsbluff Bison Quarry and Its Associated Artifacts," *American Anthropologist* 37 (April–June 1935), 306–19.
29. Interview with C.B.S., May 21, 1984.
30. Neal Copple, *Tower on the Plains: Lincoln's Centennial History, 1859–1959* (Lincoln: University of Nebraska Press, 1959), 136–37.

31. James C. Olson, *History of Nebraska*, 2nd ed. (Lincoln: University of Nebraska Press, 1966), 290.
32. Copple, *Tower on the Plains*, 141–42.
33. Interview with W.G., May 21, 1984.
34. UPT 50, E36, Box 25, f. 4, *All the Strange Hours*.
35. These works hang above the desk in the LER.
36. L.E., "Music of the Mountain," *Voices*, no. 67 (December 1932–January 1933), 46–47.
37. *Prairie Schooner* 3, no. 2 (Spring 1929), 167–78.
38. Robert Manley and R. McLaran Sawyer, *Centennial History of the University of Nebraska*, 2 vols. (Lincoln: Centennial Press, 1969–1973), II, 59.
39. *ASH*, 78.
40. UNA R.G. 27/4/1.
41. L.E. to Lowry Wimberly, June 22, 1933, UNA, *Prairie Schooner* Archives, 12/10/16, f. Ea–Fz (Eiseley's ellipses).
42. Interview with Emery Blue, May 21, 1984.
43. Interview with Mylan Stout, June 15, 1985.
44. Interview with Frank Crabill, Sept. 21, 1984.
45. *ASH*, 87.
46. *FT*, 89.
47. *NA*, 76–79.
48. Interview with C.B.S., Nov. 15, 1984.
49. C.B.S., "Field Notes of the South Party, 1933," NSMA, 54; "Acquisition Records: South Party, 1933," NSMA, 14–17–78.
50. *IA*, 81; Interview with Frank Crabill, Sept. 21, 1984. Whether by intent or lapse of memory, Eiseley wrote that the cat's tooth had pierced the scapula of its rival.
51. Interview with Robert Long, June 12, 1986.
52. Interview with Emery Blue, June 21, 1984.
53. Interview with Mylan Stout, June 5, 1985.

CHAPTER 8: MASKS

1. UPT 50, E36, Box 3; *ASH*, 87–88.
2. Interview with M.E., Sept. 8, 1984.
3. Ibid.
4. *ASH*, 89–90.
5. UPT 50, E36, Box 34, f. F: "The Future of Anthropology in Philadelphia," 2–3; Interview with M.E., Sept. 8, 1984.
6. Interview with Lewis "Lou" Korn, July 16, 1986.
7. *ASH*, 90–91.

8. APS, 572.97 Sp3, 6B1, Box 6, Speck Misc. Notes.
9. *UU*, 62.
10. A. I. Hallowell, "Frank Gouldsmith Speck, 1881–1950," *American Anthropologist* 53, no. 1 (January–March 1951), 75–76. For additional background on Speck see John Witthoft, "Frank Gouldsmith Speck," *Dictionary of American Biography*, supp. 4, 1946–1950 (New York: Charles Scribner's Sons, 1974), 761–63; and Ralph W. Dexter, "On Field Trips with Frank G. Speck, American Ethnologist," *The Biologist* 36 (1954), 13–17.
11. L.E. to C.B.S., Nov. 9, 1933, NSMA, 32/1/2, f. Schultz, C. Bertrand, Cor., 1933, A–F.
12. L.E. to Lowry Wimberly, Nov. 14, 1933; UNA, *Prairie Schooner* Archives, 12/10/16, f. Ea–Fz.
13. Ibid.
14. *ASH*, 111.
15. Interview with M.E., Sept. 8, 1984.
16. M.E. to D.T.B., Sept. 22, 1980 (courtesy of D.T.B.).
17. *Philadelphia City Directory, 1935–36*. Leo later moved to an apartment at nearby 4742 Pine Street. EFH.
18. Interview with C.B.S., May 21, 1984.
19. APS, 572.97 Sp3, Box 29, L.E., "A Tribute to Frank Speck," May 1, 1938, 4.
20. Interview with John Witthoft, Sept. 18, 1984.
21. APS, 572.97 Sp3, Box 29, L.E., "A Tribute to Frank Speck," 4.
22. "Fox Curse," *ANW*, 42.
23. *IP*, 137–38.
24. *ASH*, 112.
25. Ibid.
26. Interview with Virginia Tomlin Cotter, June 30, 1984.
27. *Daily Nebraskan*, June 19, 1934, 1.
28. UPT 50, E36, Box 51, "Eiseley's Archaeological Notebook." With the exception of two pages, the entire "notebook" is given over to a mundane listing of field expenses.
29. Interview with Joseph B. Townsend, Jr., July 17, 1984.
30. UPT 50, E36, Box 51, "Eiseley's Archaeological Notebook."
31. See Mary Youngerman Ayer, "The Archaeological and Faunal Material from Williams Cave, Guadalupe Mountains, Texas," *Proceedings of the Academy of Natural Sciences of Philadelphia* 58 (December 1936), 559–618; E. B. Howard and Ernst Antevs, "Studies on Antiquity of Man in America," *Carnegie Institution of Washington Year Book*, no. 33 (1934), 309–11; Book Review, *American Antiquity* 3 (1939), 291–93.
32. *ASH*, 98.

33. Ibid., 99.
34. E. B. Howard to H. F. Jayne, Aug. 11, 1934, UM, f. E. B. Howard, Cor., 1930–1944.
35. *ASH*, 99.
36. Interview with Joseph B. Townsend, Jr., July 17, 1984.
37. Interview with Lewis Korn, July 16, 1986.
38. L.E., "Underground," *Nebraska Alumnus* 33, no. 8 (October 1937), 10–11, 14.
39. *ASH*, 107–10; L.E. to Joseph Townsend, Jr., July 23, 1975, UPT 50, E36, Box 1, f. T.
40. Interview with Joseph B. Townsend, Jr., July 17, 1984.
41. Peggy Pond Church to L.E., July 19, 1968, Aug. 20, 1968; L.E. to Church, Aug. 14, 27, 1968, UPT 50, E36, Box 1, f. C.
42. Only the last stanza of "Requiem for Mary Austin" is printed here. See Thomas Matthews Pearce, *The Beloved House* (Caldwell, ID: The Caxton Printers, Ltd., 1940), 215–16.
43. Interview with Macklin Thomas, Sept. 22, 1984.
44. Interview with Marguerite Lewis, Sept. 12, 1984.
45. D.T.B., Friends of Loren Eiseley Celebration, UNA, Sept. 13, 1984.
46. Interview with D.T.B., Sept. 14, 1984.
47. L.E. to E. Fred Carlisle, Mar. 23, 1974 (courtesy of E.F.C.). Eiseley employed this metaphor on many other occasions. See, for example, L.E. to Etta May Van Tassel, Feb. 3, 1972, UPT 50, E36, Box 1, f. V; L.E. to Louis Zara, Oct. 18, 1969, UPT 50, E36, Box 1, f. X-Y-Z; *UU*, 140.

CHAPTER 9: THE HUNTERS AND THE HUNTED

1. Richard Allen Faust to G.C., Feb. 24, 1984.
2. *The Pennsylvanian*, Sept. 16, 1933, 6.
3. *The Pennsylvanian*, Mar. 8, 1934.
4. Francis Tachibana to M.E., July 22, 1977, UPT 50, E36, Box 1, f. T.
5. UPT 50, E36, Box 3, f. University of Pennsylvania, L.C.E. as Student.
6. APS, 572.97 Sp3, Box 29, L.E., "A Tribute to Frank Speck," May 1, 1938, 3–4.
7. Interview with Lewis Korn, July 16, 1986.
8. *ASH*, 114.
9. Richard Allen Faust to G.C., Feb. 24, 1984.
10. *ASH*, 114–15.
11. Interview with A.V.S., Apr. 2, 1985.
12. Ibid.

13. Ibid.
14. UPT 50, E36, Box 8, f. Lengthier Biography, 3; Interview with M.E., Sept. 8, 1984, Sept. 19, 1985.
15. Interview with A.V.S., Apr. 2, 1985.
16. UPT 50, E36, Box 3, f. L.C.E. as Student at the University of Nebraska. This misfiled seminar paper was written while Eiseley was at Penn. His thesis is available at VPL.
17. L.E. to C.B.S., c. Feb. 1935, NSMA, 32/1/2, f. Schultz, C. Bertrand, Cor., 1934, Eiseley, L.
18. C.B.S. and L.E., "Paleontological Evidence for the Antiquity of the Scottsbluff Bison Quarry and Its Associated Artifacts," *American Anthropologist* 37 (April–June 1935), 317–18.
19. C.B.S. and L.E., "An Added Note on the Scottsbluff Quarry," *American Anthropologist* 38 (July–September 1936), 521–24.
20. *University of Pennyslvania Catalogue, 1933–1934*, 168, 173.
21. L.E. to C.B.S., c. Dec. 1934, NSMA, 32/1/2, f. Schultz, C. Bertrand, Cor., 1934, Eiseley, L.
22. L.E. to Lowry Wimberly, c. early May 1935, UNA, *Prairie Schooner* Archives, 12/10/16, f. Ea–Fz.
23. *ASH*, 115, 119. Also see "The Tiger Chooses," *IA*, 60–62.
24. Edwin N. Wilmsen and Frank H. H. Roberts, Jr., "Lindenmeier, 1934–1974: Concluding Report on Investigations," *Smithsonian Contributions to Anthropology*, no. 24 (Washington, D.C.: Smithsonian Institution Press, 1978), 1; Edwin N. Wilmsen, *Lindenmeier: A Pleistocene Hunting Society* (New York: Harper & Row, 1974), 22–23.
25. L.E. to C.B.S., c. Jan. 1935, NSMA, 32/1/2, f. Schultz, C. Bertrand, Cor., 1935, D–E.
26. L.E. to C.B.S., Feb. 4, 1935, NSMA.
27. L.E. to Erwin Barbour, June 14, 1935, NSMA, 32/1/1, f. Barbour, Erwin H., Cor., 1935, D–E.
28. Wilmsen and Roberts, "Lindenmeier, 1934–1974," 17; photos in UPT 50, E36, Box 3, f. L.C.E. Student at University of Nebraska.
29. L.E. to Dr. Edwin N. Wilmsen, Nov. 19, 1968, UPT 50, E36, Box 1, f. W; "Centered, Loren C. Eiseley," *Pennsylvania Triangle* 54, no. 4 (February 1967), 24; Frank H. H. Roberts, Jr., "Additional Information on the Folsom Complex," *Smithsonian Miscellaneous Collections* 95, no. 10, 1936, 14.
30. Interview with John L. Cotter, June 19, 1984.
31. L.E. to Frank Roberts, Sept. 9, 1935, NMNH, MS. Coll. no. 4951, Frank H. H. Roberts, Jr., Papers, Box 13, f. Cor., Incoming, Loren Eiseley.
32. *Lincoln Journal*, Aug. 20, 1935, 1.
33. NSHS, MS. no. 507, Price, William B.

34. *ASH*, 84, 85.
35. Interview with Dollie Langdon Hahn, Sept. 24, 1986.
36. UNA, R.G. 27/4/1.
37. D.T.B. to G.C., Feb. 14, 1985.
38. UPT, Alumni Transcript File, f. Eiseley, Loren Corey.
39. L.E. to C.B.S., Dec. 31, 1935, NSMA, 32/1/2, f. Schultz, C. Bertrand, Cor., 1935, Eiseley, L.
40. L.E. to C.B.S., Jan. 28, 1936, Feb. 12, 1936, June 30, 1936, NSMA.
41. L.E. to C.B.S., Jan. 7, 1936, NSMA.
42. R.U., "Lowry Wimberly and Others; Recollections of a Beerdrinker, *Prairie Schooner* 51, no. 1 (Spring 1977), 28–29. The story of the Writers' Project in Lincoln is told by Jerre Mangione, *The Dream and the Deal* (New York: Little, Brown, 1972), 109–16.
43. R.U. to Pamela Gossin, May 24, 1982, BML.
44. R.U. to G.C., Dec. 11, 1984.
45. R.U. to G.C., Jan. 14, 1985.
46. R.U. to G.C., Dec. 11, 1984.
47. R.U. to Pamela Gossin, May 24, 1982, BML.
48. R.U. to G.C., Apr. 19, 1985.
49. L.E. to Lowry Wimberly, June 22, 1933, UNA, *Prairie Schooner* Archives, 12/10/16, f. Ea–Fz.
50. Interview with Dollie Langdon Hahn, Sept. 24, 1986.
51. Ibid.
52. Ibid.
53. D. S. Davidson to L.E., Apr. 22, 1936, UPT 50, E36, Box 2, f. D. S. Davidson; *University of Pennsylvania Catalogue, 1933–1934*, 169–70.
54. Jacques Chambrun to L.E., July 9, 1936, UPT 50, E36, Box 35, f. M.
55. L.E. to C.B.S., Aug. 18, 1936, NSMA, 32/1/2, f. Schultz, C. Bertrand, Cor., 1936, Eiseley, L.
56. Interview with D.T.B., Sept. 14, 1984.
57. *ASH*, 122–30.
58. UPT 50, E36, Box 8, f. Lengthier Biography, 3–4.
59. UPT 50, E36, Box 33, f. Guggenheim Fellowship, c.
60. "Significance of Hunting Territories of the Algonkian in Social Theory," *American Anthropologist* 41, no. 2 (April–June 1939), 269–80; "Montagnais-Naskapi Bands and Family Hunting Districts of the Central and Southeastern Labrador Peninsula," *Proceedings of the American Philosophical Society* 85, no. 2 (January 1942), 215–42.
61. Interview with Lewis Korn, July 16, 1986.
62. *ASH*, 88.
63. Ibid., 91–92.

64. Ibid., 94–95.
65. Ibid., 120; *NC*, 170; *Lincoln Star*, Dec. 17, 1936.
66. L.E. to C.B.S., Mar. 1937, NSMA, 32/1/2, f. Schultz, C. Bertrand, Cor. 1937, Eiseley, Loren.
67. F. G. Speck to H. L. Crosby, Apr. 30, 1937, UPT 50, E36, Box 3, f. L.C.E. Thesis.
68. Joan B. Anderson, Reference Librarian, to George J. Custandi, Sept. 8, 1983, UPT 50, E36, Box 3, f. L.C.E. Thesis. The Penn Library contains neither of the two dissertation copies required of all Ph.D. candidates. The fifty-one other dissertations completed in 1937, each in alphabetical order and numbered consecutively, are to be found in the stacks. Neither lost nor pilfered, Eiseley's work was never received, although it appears in the card catalog.
69. The two articles are "Index Mollusca and Their Bearing on Certain Problems of Prehistory: A Critique," *Twenty-fifth Anniversary Studies of the Philadelphia Anthropological Society*, ed. D. S. Davidson (Philadelphia: University of Pennsylvania Press, 1937), 77–93; "Pollen Analysis and Its Bearing upon American Prehistory: A Critique," *American Antiquity* 5, no. 2 (October 1939), 115–40.
70. Interview with M.E., Sept. 8, 1984.
71. "Index Mollusca and Their Bearing on Certain Problems of Prehistory," 89.
72. UPB (University of Pennsylvania Archives) 7.74, f. Presenter: Prof. Frank G. Speck.
73. *ASH*, 130.

CHAPTER 10: MOUNT OREAD

1. *ASH*, 62.
2. Frank Speck to Carroll Clark, Feb. 20, 1937, UKA, Carroll Clark Papers, Cor., Eiseley, 1937–1978, PP/1, Box 4.
3. Duncan Strong, Dwight Kirsch, James Reinhardt, and Lowry Wimberly to Carroll Clark, UKA.
4. Carroll Clark to L.E., Apr. 20, 1937, UKA.
5. Carroll Clark to L.E., May 1, 1937, UKA.
6. Karl A. Menninger, "Bleeding Kansans," *Kansas Magazine* (1939), 3–6.
7. Clyde Kenneth Hyder, *Snow of Kansas* (Lawrence: University of Kansas Press, 1953), 103.
8. *Annual Catalogue of the University of Kansas: 1937–1938* 39, no. 5 (March 1938), 170–73; 40, no. 5 (March 1939), 168–71.
9. Interview with Marston McCluggage, June 14, 1985.

10. *ASH*, 136.
11. Velma M. Baldwin to G.C., Sept. 16, 1985.
12. Rachel Dyal to G.C., Sept. 19, 1985.
13. Interviews with Marston McCluggage, June 14, 1985; Morton Green, June 13, 1985.
14. Harry L. Goldberg to G.C., July 18, 1985.
15. Rachel Dyal to G.C., Sept. 19, 1985.
16. Interview with Marguerite Lewis, Sept. 12, 1984.
17. M.E. to Dwight Kirsch, Feb. 28, 1953 (courtesy of Jo Ann Kelly Alexander).
18. Interview with M.E., Apr. 21, 1985.
19. *Lincoln City Directories, 1938–1958*; Interview with Dollie Langdon Hahn, Sept. 24, 1986; *ASH*, 147.
20. Interview with D.T.B., Sept. 14, 1984.
21. Interview with D.T.B., June 17, 1984.
22. Lois Gerard Clemens to G.C., Jan. 28, 1985. My account of the day's events owes much to this memoir.
23. Interview with Lewis Korn, July 16, 1986.
24. D.T.B., Friends of L.E. Celebration, UNA, Sept. 13, 1984.
25. Ibid.; Interview with D.T.B., June 17, 1984.
26. M.E. to D.T.B., Aug. 22, 1954 (courtesy of D.T.B.).
27. M.E. to Helen Staenble, Mar. 23, 1948, UPT 50, E36, Box 9, f. 6, *The Immense Journey*.
28. Francis Tachibana to L.E., Oct. 9, 1938, UPT 50, E36, Box 1.
29. Harold Vinal to L.E., Oct. 11, 1938, UPT 50, E36, Box 2, f. Harold Vinal.
30. *University Daily Kansan*, News Bureau Biographical File—Loren Eiseley, July 28, 1937.
31. *University Daily Kansan*, May 25, 1938, 1; L.E., "Evidence of a Pre-Ceramic Cultural Horizon in Smith County Kansas," *Science* 89, no. 2306 (Mar. 10, 1939), 221.
32. *ASH*, 105.
33. Ibid., 101–10.
34. *University Daily Kansan*, Apr. 16, 1939, 1.
35. Interview with C.B.S., May 21, 1984. For the publishing contract see NSMA, 32/1/2, f. Schultz, C. Bertrand, Cor., D–G, 1938. (This misfiled document is dated 1939.)

CHAPTER 11: "A BIG, STRAPPING, FINE FELLOW"

1. *Daily Nebraskan*, Nov. 5, 1936, 1.
2. *Lincoln Journal and Star*, May 7, 1939.

3. L.E. to C.B.S., c. Mar.–Apr. 1937, NSMA, 32/1/2, f. Schultz, C. Bertrand, Cor., 1937, Eiseley, Loren.
4. Interview with M.E., Sept. 8, 1984; M.E. to Mr. Heady, c. Apr. 1940, UKA, News Bureau Biographical File—Karl Mattern.
5. L.E. to Carroll Clark, July 23, 1940, UKA, Carroll Clark Papers, Cor., Eiseley, 1937–1978, PP/1, Box 4.
6. UPT 50, E36, Box 26, f. Crowell-Collier.
7. Ibid.
8. Frank Speck and L.E., "Montagnais-Naskapi Bands, and Family Hunting Districts of the Central and Southeastern Labrador Peninsula," *Proceedings of the American Philosophical Society* 85, no. 2 (January 1942), 215–42.
9. Alberta Hartmann Speck to G.C., May 14, 1984.
10. L.E. to Carroll Clark, Oct. 3, 1940; Clark to L.E., Oct. 5, 1940; L.E. to Clark, Oct. 30, 1940, UKA, Carroll Clark Papers, Cor., Eiseley, 1937–1978, PP/1, Box 4.
11. L.E. to Clark, Apr. 5, 1941, UKA.
12. Interview with D.T.B., June 17, 1984.
13. Ibid.
14. Interview with D.T.B., Sept. 14, 1984.
15. Ibid.
16. Interview with D.T.B., June 17, 1984.
17. Ibid.
18. D.T.B. to G.C., Mar. 13, 1986.
19. Interview with D.T.B., Sept. 14, 1984.
20. Ibid.
21. UPT 50, E36, Box 3, f. Social Science Research Grant—1941, 1.
22. Ibid., 2.
23. L.E. to Carroll Clark, Apr. 11, 1941, UKA, Carroll Clark Papers, Cor., Eiseley, 1937–1978, PP/1, Box 4.
24. UPT 50, E36, Box 3, f. Social Science Research Grant—1941, Report for Third Quarter, 1–2; L.E., "Racial and Phylogenetic Distinctions in the Intertemporal Interangular Index," *Transactions of the Kansas Academy of Science* 46 (1943), 63, 65.
25. L.E. to Carroll Clark, Mar. 18, 1941, UKA, Carroll Clark Papers, Cor., Eiseley, 1937–1978, PP/1, Box 4.
26. Clark to L.E., Feb. 7, 1941, Mar. 21, 1941, UKA; *Annual Catalogue of the University of Kansas: 1941–1942* 43, no. 10 (May 1942), 217.
27. L.E. to Clark, Apr. 11, 1941, UKA, Carroll Clark Papers, Cor., Eiseley, 1937–1978, PP/1, Box 4.
28. L.E. to Clark, Mar. 18, 1941, UKA.
29. *University Daily Kansan*, Dec. 10, 1941, 1.

30. L.E. to Lowry Wimberly, Sept. 1, 1944, UNA, *Prairie Schooner* Archives, 12/10/6, f. Ea–Fz.
31. *ASH*, 147.
32. UKA, Academic Employment Records, Eiseley, Loren.
33. L.E. to Carroll Clark, Dec. 12, 1967, UPT 50, E36, Box 1, f. C.
34. Clifford S. Griffin, *The University of Kansas: A History* (Lawrence, Manhattan, Wichita: University Press of Kansas, 1974), 487–88.
35. *ASH*, 146.
36. Interview with Pearl Clark, June 9, 1985.
37. Ibid.
38. UKA, Carroll Clark Papers, Biographical, PP/1, f. Headquarters of the Army Air Force.
39. Interviews with Pearl Clark, June 9, 12, 1985.
40. War letters quoted here and later were recorded during interviews with Pearl Clark, June 9, 12, 1985.
41. L.E., "The Folsom Mystery," *Scientific American* 167, no. 6 (December 1942), 260–61.
42. A. G. Ingalls to L.E., Oct. 14, 1942, UPT 50, E36, Box 3, f. Misc. Cor., 1938–1977.
43. L.E., "Pseudo-Fossil Man," *Scientific American* 168, no. 3 (March 1943), 118.
44. A. G. Ingalls to L.E., June 15, 1943, UPT 50, E36, Box 3, f. Misc. Cor., 1938–1977.
45. UPT 50, E36, Box 24, f. 14, *All the Strange Hours*, 3.
46. Ibid., 4.
47. Interview with Pearl Clark, June 9, 1985.
48. UPT 50, E36, Box 24, f. 14, *All the Strange Hours*, 4.
49. Interview with Pearl Clark, June 9, 1985.
50. UPT 50, E36, Box 3.
51. *ASH*, 148.
52. Interview with M.E., Apr. 21, 1985.
53. *University Daily Kansan*, Extra Edition, Mar. 3, 1943, 1; Mar. 4, 1943, 1.
54. *ASH*, 151–52.
55. Interview with Pearl Clark, June 9, 1985.
56. *MN*, 31–32.
57. L.E. to Paul Roofe, Feb. 4, 1976, UPT 50, E36, Box 1, f. R; Interview with Pearl Clark, June 9, 1985.
58. C. Willet Asling to G.C., Apr. 8, 1985, 14.
59. Ibid., 12–13.
60. Interview with Pearl Clark, June 9, 1985.
61. C. Willet Asling to G.C., Apr. 8, 1985, 14.
62. UKA, Academic Affairs Employment Records, Eiseley, Loren.

63. *ASH*, 148, 149.
64. Interview with C. Willet Asling, May 17, 1985.
65. Ibid.
66. *ASH*, 150.
67. C. Willet Asling to G.C., Apr. 27, 1985, 3.
68. Ibid.
69. Ibid., 7.
70. Interview with M.E., Apr. 21, 1985.
71. Interview with C. Willet Asling, May 17, 1985.
72. *Lincoln Journal and Star*, Mar. 17, 1940; UKA, News Bureau Biographical File—Karl Mattern.
73. Interview with C. Willet Asling, May 17, 1985; Asling to G.C., Apr. 8, 1985.
74. C. Willet Asling to G.C., Apr. 8, 1985, 11.
75. Interview with M.E., Sept. 8, 1984.
76. Interview with Pearl Clark, June 9, 1985.
77. C. Willet Asling to G.C., Apr. 21, 1985, 6–7.
78. Ibid., 5–6.
79. Ibid., 5.
80. Interview with C. Willet Asling, May 17, 1985.
81. Griffin, *The University of Kansas*, 497.
82. *ASH*, 151; Interview with Pearl Clark, June 12, 1985.
83. L.E. to H. L. Shapiro, June 1, 1944, AMNH, Cor. Pertaining to Loren Eiseley, 1941–1948.

CHAPTER 12: COUNTERPLAINT OF AN ANTHROPOLOGIST

1. A. Hunter Dupree to G.C., Dec. 7, 1985.
2. *Oberlin Community History*, ed. Allan Patterson (State College, PA: Josten's Publications, 1981), 70.
3. Geoffrey Blodgett, *Oberlin Architecture, College and Town: A Guide to Its Social History* (Oberlin, OH: Oberlin College, 1985), xvi.
4. Interview with Jacob Gruber, Sept. 20, 1984.
5. A. I. Hallowell to Carl Wittke, Mar. 24, 1944, OCA 9/1/4, Card 2, Box 7, f. Loren C. Eiseley, 1944–47.
6. Paul B. Sears to G.C., Aug. 13, 1985.
7. Interview with Paul B. Sears, July 21, 1984.
8. L.E. to Carl Wittke, Apr. 8, 1944, UPT 50, E36, Box 3, f. L.C.E. at Oberlin College (Ohio).
9. Wittke to L.E., Apr. 18, 1944, UPT.
10. L.E. to Wittke, Apr. 20, 1944, OCA, 9/1/4, Card 2, Box 7, f. Loren C. Eiseley, 1944–47.
11. L.E. to Wittke, May 7, 1944, OCA.

12. L.E. to Wittke, May 18, 1944, OCA.
13. Wittke to L.E., May 19, 1944, OCA.
14. L.E. to Wittke, May 27, 1944, OCA.
15. L.E. to Wittke, May 7, 1944, OCA.
16. Wittke to L.E., May 19, 1944, UPT 50, E36, Box 3, f. L.C.E. at Oberlin College (Ohio).
17. L.E. to Wittke, May 27, 1944, OCA, 9/1/4, Card 2, Box 7, f. Loren C. Eiseley, 1944–47.
18. Wittke to L.E., June 21, 1944, OCA.
19. Ibid.
20. Mabel A. Elliott to L. Guy Brown, June 16, 1944, OCA.
21. Elliott to Carl Wittke, June 16, 1944, OCA.
22. Wittke to Elliott, June 22, 1944, OCA.
23. An extensive report on parts of these proceedings is contained in the Eiseley file at Oberlin.
24. Adolph S. Tomars, "Some Problems in the Sociologist's Use of Anthropology," *American Sociological Review* 8, no. 6 (December 1943), 625–34. For Eiseley's rejoinder see 635–37.
25. L.E., "Counterplaint of an Anthropologist," 637.
26. L. Guy Brown to Carl Wittke, Aug. 20, 1944, OCA, 9/1/4, Card 2, Box 7, f. Loren C. Eiseley, 1944–47.
27. Brown to Lloyd W. Taylor, Aug. 21, 1944, OCA.
28. L.E. to Carl Wittke, May 27, 1944, OCA.
29. Wittke to L.E., July 12, 1944; L.E. to Wittke, July 24, 1944, OCA.
30. *ASH*, 151.
31. Interview with M.E., Apr. 21, 1985.
32. Ibid.
33. Interview with Leah Dale Masters, Nov. 3, 1984.
34. Interview with A.V.S., Apr. 2, 1985.
35. Interview with D.T.B., June 24, 1984.
36. *ASH*, 229.
37. Interview with Dollie Langdon Hahn, Sept. 24, 1986.
38. Interview with M.E., Sept. 8, 1984.
39. Mary Jeanne Astier Kalb to G.C., Feb. 3, 1986.
40. Kalb to G.C., Oct. 26, 1985.
41. Interview with Carroll V. Newsom, Nov. 3, 1984.
42. Carroll V. Newsom, *Problems Are for Solving: An Autobiography* (Bryn Mawr: Dorrance & Company, 1983), 290.
43. See, for example, the Eiseley-Wittke cor. in UPT 50, E36, Box 1, f. W.
44. L.E. to Carl Wittke, June 7, 1944, OCA, 9/1/4, Card 2, Box 7, f. Loren C. Eiseley, 1944–47.
45. Caroline E. Werkley, "Lost Pumas, Pincushions, and Gypsies," *Journal of Library History* 11 (Oct. 1969), 350–51.

46. Interview with Carroll V. Newsom, Nov. 3, 1984.
47. UPT 50, E36, Box 50.
48. William H. Mitchell to L.E., Nov. 3, 1944, UPT 50, E36, Box 26, f. Crowell-Collier.
49. L.E. to Mitchell, Nov. 19, 1944, UPT.
50. OCA, 9/1/4, Card 2, Box 7, f. Loren C. Eiseley, 1944–1947.
51. C.B.S. to Emily Schoessberger, Jan. 22, 1943, NSMA, 32/1/2, f. Schultz, C. Bertrand, Cor., 1943, S.
52. Schossberger to C.B.S., Mar. 29, 1943, NSMA.
53. UPT 50, E36, Box 8, f. Lengthier Biography, 5.
54. L.E. to Seba Eldridge, Oct. 6, 1945, UKA, Carroll Clark Papers, Cor., Eiseley, 1937–1978, PP/1, Box 4.
55. L. Guy Brown to L.E., Apr. 26, 1945, OCA, 9/1/4, Card 2, Box 7, f. Loren C. Eiseley, 1944–47.
56. L.E. to Brown, Apr. 28, 1945, OCA.
57. Interview, May 19, 1986.
58. Interview with M.E., Sept. 8, 1984.
59. Wright Morris, *A Cloak of Light: Writing My Life* (New York: Harper & Row, 1985), 111.
60. Interview with M.E., Sept. 17, 1984.
61. Morris, *A Cloak of Light*, 111–12.
62. Ibid., 112.
63. UPT 50, E36, Box 35, f. M.
64. Interview with Wright Morris, Aug. 14, 1984.
65. *Oberlin Review*, Aug. 17, 1945, 1.
66. Interview with Margaret G. Haylor, June 4, 1986.
67. Interview with Jacob Gruber, Sept. 20, 1984.
68. Ibid.
69. Ibid.
70. L.E. to H. L. Shapiro, Feb. 24, 1946. AMNH, Cor. Pertaining to Loren Eiseley, 1941–1948.
71. Ernest Hatch Wilkins to L.E., Mar. 12, 1946, OCA, 28/3, Box 21, f. Eiseley, Loren C.
72. L.E. to Carl Wittke, July 31, 1946, OCA, 9/1/4, Card 2, Box 7, f. Loren C. Eiseley, 1944–47.
73. Wittke to L.E., Aug. 4, 1946, OCA.
74. L.E. to Clyde Kluckhohn, Nov. 19, 1944, HUA, HUG 4490.3, Clyde Kluckhohn Papers, 1938–1947 (D–H).
75. UPT 50, E36, Box 8, f. Lengthier Biography, 5.
76. UPT 50, E36, Box 40, f. 47, 6.
77. L.E., "There *Were* Giants," *Prairie Schooner* 19, no. 3 (Fall 1945), 193.
78. Interview with Jacob Gruber, Sept. 20, 1984.

79. L.E., "The Long-Ago Man of the Future," *Harper's Magazine* 194 (January 1947), 93.
80. Ibid., 96.
81. *ASH*, 164–65.
82. Ibid., 166–67.

CHAPTER 13: "THE TIME FOR CONFIDENCE AND PROMISES"

1. Interviews with Ward H. Goodenough, July 13, 1984; Froelich Rainey, Aug. 2, 1984.
2. A. I. Hallowell to Glenn R. Morrow, Oct. 25, 1946, APS, MS. Coll. no. 26, A. I. Hallowell Papers, f. Pennsylvania: University (1922–1963).
3. Glenn R. Morrow to L.E., Jan. 23, 1947, UPT 50, E36, Box 3, f. L.C.E. appointed to University of Pennsylvania.
4. UPA 6.4, Provost's Papers, Box 21, f. Anthropology, 1948–1971.
5. Carl Wittke to Glenn R. Morrow, OCA 9/1/4, Card 2, Box 7, f. Loren C. Eiseley, 1944–1947.
6. Wittke to L.E., Feb. 23, 197[?], UPT 50, E36, Box 1, f. W.
7. Interview with Mabel Eiseley, Oct. 2, 1984.
8. *ASH*, 177.
9. Interview with Jacob Gruber, Sept. 20, 1984.
10. Interview with Frederica de Laguna, Sept. 27, 1984.
11. UPT 50, E36, Box 34, f. F, The Future of Anthropology in Philadelphia, 1, 5.
12. Ibid., 3, 9.
13. L.E. to Carroll Clark, Mar. 12, 1948, UKA, Carroll Clark Papers, Cor., Eiseley, 1937–1978, PP/1, Box 4.
14. Interview with Froelich Rainey, Aug. 2, 1985.
15. Ibid.
16. *ASH*, 178–81.
17. Ibid., 182–83.
18. Ibid., 184.
19. Interview with Wright Morris, Aug. 14, 1984.
20. UPT 50, E36, Box 8, f. Lengthier Biography, 6.
21. Interview with Jacob Gruber, Sept. 20, 1984.
22. Interview with Ward H. Goodenough, July 13, 1984.
23. L.E. to Froelich Rainey, Aug. 16, 1948, UM, f. North America: Early Man Project, 1948. Also see M.E. to Helen Staenble, Mar. 23, 1948, UPT 50, E36, Box 9, f. 6, *The Immense Journey.*
24. Interview with Paul B. Sears, July 21, 1984.
25. L.E. to Carroll Clark, Mar. 12, 1948, UKA, Carroll Clark Papers, Cor., Eiseley, 1937–1978, PP/1, Box 4.

26. L.S.B. Leakey to L.E., Feb. 11, 1944, UPT 50, E36, Box 2.
27. L.E. to Paul Fejos, Sept. 2, 1946, 2, 3, UPT 50, E36, Box 2, f. Fejos, Paul.
28. OCA, 28/3, Box 21, f. Eiseley, Loren C.
29. Sherwood Washburn to L.E., Nov. 20, 1946, UPT 50, E36, Box 2, f. Fejos, Paul.
30. L.E. to Robert Broom, Nov. 7, 1946, UPT.
31. L.E. to Paul Fejos, Mar. 4, 1947, UPT.
32. Sherwood Washburn to L.E., Mar. 31, 1947, UPT.
33. L.E. to Paul Fejos, June 7, 1947; Fejos to L.E., June 11, 1947, UPT.
34. Melville J. Herskovits to L.E., July 21, 1947, UPT.
35. Sherwood Washburn to L.E., Feb. 12, 1948, UPT.
36. L.E. to Washburn, Feb. 24, 1948, UPT.
37. Interview with Wright Morris, Aug. 14, 1984.
38. Ibid.
39. L.E. to Sherwood Washburn, Mar. 13, 1948, UPT 50, E36, Box 2, f. Fejos, Paul.
40. Washburn to L.E., Apr. 15, 1948, UPT.
41. Washburn to Paul Fejos, Apr. 23, 1948, UPT. Copies of this correspondence were sent to Eiseley in Philadelphia.
42. L.E. to Washburn, Apr. 23, 1948, UPT.
43. Washburn to L.E., June 6, 1948, UPT.
44. L.E. to Paul Fejos, Sept. 22, 1948, UPT.
45. Sherwood Washburn to L.E., July 6, 1948, UPT.
46. L.E. to Paul Fejos, Sept. 22, 1948, UPT.
47. *ASH*, 203–4.
48. Interview with Wright Morris, Aug. 14, 1984.
49. Interview with Jacob Gruber, Sept. 20, 1984.
50. *UU*, 140.
51. Interview with Wright Morris, Aug. 14, 1984.
52. L.E. to Sherwood Washburn, Feb. 24, 1948, UPT 50, E36, Box 2, f. Fejos, Paul.
53. Interview with Wright Morris, Aug. 14, 1984.
54. L.E., "The Fire Apes," *Harper's Magazine* 199 (September 1949), 55.
55. Interview with M.E., Apr. 21, 1985.
56. Interview with Dollie Langdon Hahn, Sept. 24, 1986.
57. L.E. to A.V.S., July 26, 1949 (courtesy of A.V.S.). "Miss 31" is a reference to Athena's age at the time.
58. *Casper Tribune Herald*, Sept. 18, 1949, 5; *Cody Times*, Sept. 8, 1949, 15; Glenn L. Jepsen, "Ancient Buffalo Hunters in Wyoming," *Archaeological Society of New Jersey Newsletter*, no. 24 (July 1951), 22–24.
59. UPT 50, E36, Box 3, f. Cody, Wyoming Project, AP release, Sept. 2, 1949.

60. Glenn L. Jepsen to L.E., Oct. 22, 1949, UPT.
61. L.E. to Jepsen, Nov. 6, 1949, UPT 50, E36, Box 1, f. J.
62. Jepsen to L.E., Nov. 30, 1942, UPT.
63. Ibid.
64. Froelich Rainey to Jepsen, Jan. 7, 1950, UM, f. North America: Early Man Project, 1949–1950.

CHAPTER 14: ANATOMY OF A *JOURNEY*

1. Eugene Underhill to L.E., Dec. 28, 1948, UPT 50, E36, Box 2, f. Speck, Frank.
2. Frank Speck to L.E., July 23, 1949, UPT.
3. Alberta Hartmann Speck to G.C., May 14, 1984.
4. Interview, Sept. 25, 1984.
5. Interview with John Witthoft, Sept. 18, 1984.
6. Interview with Jacob Gruber, Sept. 20, 1984.
7. Interview with M.E., Sept. 8, 1984.
8. Interview with Marian Schultz, May 19, 1983.
9. Interview with Wright Morris, Aug. 14, 1984.
10. Ibid.
11. Interview with Caroline Werkley, June 10, 1984.
12. Interview with Dollie Langdon Hahn, Sept. 24, 1986.
13. Interview with M.E., Sept. 8, 1984.
14. Interview with Wright Morris, Aug. 14, 1984.
15. M.E. to D.T.B., Mar. 7, 1952 (courtesy of D.T.B.).
16. Ibid. (emphasis M.'s).
17. John C. Fischer to L.E., June 6, 1949, UPT 50, E36, Box 29, f. 8, *The Star Thrower.*
18. L.E., "Buzby's Petrified Woman," *Harper's Magazine* 197 (November 1948), 76, 78, 79.
19. Interview with Emery Blue, May 21, 1984.
20. L.E. to Ray Bradbury, Oct. 9, 1949 (courtesy of R.B.).
21. Jack Fischer to L.E., July 19, 1948, UPT 50, E36, Box 9, f. 6, *The Immense Journey.*
22. Fischer to L.E., Aug. 3, 1950, UPT.
23. L.E. to Fischer, Aug. 8, 1950, UPT.
24. L.E. to Fischer, Dec. 23, 1952, UPT 50, E36, Box 1, f. F.
25. Fischer to L.E., Apr. 20, 1953, UPT 50, E36, Box 9, f. 6, *The Immense Journey.*
26. Fischer to L.E., July 14, 1953, UPT.
27. UPT 50, E36, Box 25, f. 2, *All the Strange Hours*; Box 20, f. 16, *The Night Country*; Box 9, f. 20, *The Immense Journey*; *The Lost Note-*

books of Loren Eiseley, ed. Kenneth Heuer (Boston: Little, Brown and Company, 1987), 90.

28. M.E. to D.T.B., Apr. 6, 1954 (courtesy of D.T.B.).
29. M.E. to D.T.B., Feb. 28, 1953.
30. Interview with Marguerite Lewis, Sept. 12, 1984.
31. L.E. to E. Light, Feb. 29, 1968, UPT 50, E36, Box 6, f. F, "Race: The Reflections of a Biological Historian."
32. Interview with M.E., Sept. 17, 1984.
33. Interview with Wright Morris, Aug. 14, 1984.
34. Ibid.
35. Ibid.
36. UPT 50, E36, Box 8, f. *The Immense Journey.*
37. Carl Wittke to L.E., Sept. 12, 1951, UPT 50, E36, Box 3, f. Colorado, University of—offer of post.
38. Wittke to L.E., Nov. 21, 1951, UPT.
39. Wittke to L.E., Mar. 14, 1952, UPT.
40. Ken McCormick to L.E., July 14, 1950, UPT 50, E36, Box 9, f. 8a, *The Immense Journey.*
41. E. P. Swenson to L.E., Mar. 10, 1953, CUL, Spec. MS Coll., Norton, f. Eiseley, Loren Corey.
42. Jason Epstein to L.E., Feb. 16, 1953, UPT 50, E36, Box 9, f. 8a, *The Immense Journey.*
43. Kenneth Heuer to L.E., Sept. 1, 1954, UPT 50, E36, Box 2, f. Heuer, Kenneth.
44. L.E., "The Judgment of the Birds," *The American Scholar* 25, no. 2 (Spring 1956), 158.
45. H.H. to L.E., Dec. 20, 1955, UPT 50, E36, Box 9, f. *The Immense Journey.*
46. Ibid.
47. L.E. to H.H., Dec. 23, 1955, LC, *American Scholar* Author File, Series B, Box 66, f. E.
48. H.H. to L.E., Feb. 24, 1956, UPT 50, E36, Box 2, f. Haydn, Hiram.
49. H.H., *Words and Faces* (New York: Harcourt Brace Jovanovich, 1974), 282.
50. H.H. to L.E., Feb. 24, 1956, Apr. 9, 1956, UPT 50, E36, Box 2, f. Haydn, Hiram.
51. Jack Fischer to L.E., Aug. 9, 1956, UPT 50, E36, Box 9, f. 6, *The Immense Journey.*
52. L.E. to H.H., Aug. 17, 1956, CUL, Random House, Box 432, f. Eiseley.
53. H.H. to L.E., Sept. 25, 1956, CUL.
54. L.E. to H.H., Sept. 26, 1956, CUL.

55. For the contract see UPT 50, E36, Box 9, f. 7, *The Immense Journey.*
56. L.E. to H.H., Dec. 2, 1956, UPT 50, E36, Box 9, f. 7, *The Immense Journey.*
57. H.H., *Words and Faces*, 282.
58. L.E. to H.H., Dec. 8, 1956, CUL, Random House, Box 432, f. Eiseley.
59. H.H. to L.E., Dec. 10, 1956, CUL.
60. L.E. to H.H., Dec. 13, 1956, CUL.
61. H.H., *Words and Faces*, 283.
62. R. N. Linscott to H.H., Dec. 20, 1956, CUL, Random House, Box 432, f. Eiseley.
63. Robert D. Loomis to H.H., Jan. 15, 1957, CUL.
64. L.E. to H.H., Jan. 30, 1957, CUL.
65. L.E. to H.H., Feb. 10, 1957, CUL.
66. H.H. to L.E., Feb. 15, 1957, UPT 50, E36, Box 9, f. 6, *The Immense Journey.*
67. L.E. to H.H., c. Mar. 1, 1957, CUL, Random House, Box 432, f. Eiseley.
68. H.H. to L.E., Mar. 5, 1957, CUL.
69. L.E. to H.H., Apr. 6, 1957, CUL.
70. H.H. to L.E., May 6, 1957, CUL.
71. Marston Bates to H.H., June 24, 1957, CUL.
72. Wright Morris to H.H., June 13, 1957, CUL.
73. Patricia Rose to L.E., June 18, 1957, CUL.
74. Rose to L.E., June 15, 1957, CUL.
75. John Barkham to Rose, May 21, 1957, CUL.
76. L.E. to H.H., Mar. 25, 1957, CUL.
77. Interview with C. Willet Asling, May 5, 1985.
78. L.E. to H.H., Mar. 25, 1957, CUL, Random House, Box 432, f. Eiseley.
79. H.H., *Words and Faces*, 283.
80. H.H. to L.E., Aug. 6, 1957, CUL, Random House, Box 432, f. Eiseley.

CHAPTER 15: THE GREATEST VICTIM OF ALL

1. Interview with Wright Morris, Aug. 14, 1984.
2. UPT 50, E36, Box 28, The Barlow File, f. Human Paleontology.
3. UPT 50, E36, Box 28, f. London.
4. Froelich Rainey to L.E., Jan. 19, 1952, UPT 50, E36, Box 28, f. Human Paleontology.
5. Emily Pettinos to L.E., Mar. 30, 1955, UPT 50, E36, Box 28, The Barlow File, f. Casts.

6. Interview with Froelich Rainey, Aug. 2, 1984.
7. Robert Broom to F. O. Barlow, Nov. 9, 1936, UPT 50, E36, Box 28, The Barlow File, f. Broom, Robert.
8. Louis Leakey to Barlow, Sept. 1, 1936, UPT 50, E36, Box 28, The Barlow File, f. Leakey.
9. Interview with Jacob Gruber, Sept. 20, 1984.
10. The nineteen dissertations completed between 1947 and 1959 are available at VPL.
11. APS, Committee on Library Minutes, 1951–1962, Archives 8, 22, Dec. 18, 1952, 1–2; L.E., "The Program of the Darwin Collection in the Library," *Proceedings of the American Philosophical Society* 98, no. 6 (December 1954), 449–52.
12. Thomas A. Horrocks, "The Evolution of a Collection: Charles Darwin and the Library of the American Philosophical Society," unpub. ms. (courtesy of T.A.H.).
13. Paul Fejos to L.E., Jan. 29, 1952, UPA 6.4, Provost's Papers, Box 21, f. Anthropology, 1948–1971. Also see Glenn R. Morrow to Edwin B. Williams, Feb. 12, 1952, UPA 6.5, f. Provost's Staff Conference Files.
14. L.E. to Lloyd W. Daly, Jan. 9, 1956; Daly to Edwin B. Williams, Jan. 27, 1956, UPA 6.5, Provost's Papers, Box 11, f. Provost's Staff Conference Faculty Files; L. P. Eisenhart to L.E., June 5, 1956, UPT 50, E36, Box 4, f. American Philosophical Society—General no. 2.
15. L.E. to H.H., June 30, 1957, CUL, Random House, Box 432, f. Eiseley.
16. H.H. to L.E., Oct. 23, 1956, CUL.
17. George W. Corner to L.E., Nov. 20, 1956, UPT 50, E36, Box 4, f. American Philosophical Society—General no. 2.
18. *ASH*, 187.
19. UPT 50, E36, Box 24, f. 18, *All the Strange Hours*.
20. *ASH*, 188.
21. Ibid., 189.
22. L.E. to H.H., May 23, 1957, CUL, Random House, Box 432, f. Eiseley.
23. L.E. to Jason Epstein, June 14, 1957, UPT 50, E36, Box 11, *Darwin's Century*, f. 13.
24. L.E. to H.H., June 19, 1957, CUL, Random House, Box 432, f. Eiseley.
25. H.H. to L.E., July 1, 1957, CUL.
26. UPT 50, E36, Box 9, f. 2, *The Immense Journey*.
27. H.H. to L.E., Sept. 19, 1957, CUL, Random House, Box 432, f. Eiseley.
28. L.E. to H.H., Sept. 21, 1957, CUL.

29. H.H. to L.E., Nov. 11, 1957, CUL.
30. H.H., *Words and Faces* (New York: Harcourt Brace Jovanovich, 1974), 283; *The Lost Notebooks of Loren Eiseley*, ed. Kenneth Heuer (Boston: Little, Brown, 1987), 133.
31. Lowry Wimberly to L.E., Dec. 13, 1957, UPT 50, E36, Box 2, f. Wimberly, Lowry.
32. Catherine Drinker Bowen to L.E., Dec. 15, 1957, UPT 50, E36, Box 2, f. Bowen, Catherine Drinker.
33. L.E. to H.H., Dec. 18, 1957, CUL, Random House, Box 432, f. Eiseley.
34. *New York Herald Tribune*, Dec. 26, 1957, 17.
35. *New York Times*, Dec. 27, 1957, 17.
36. H.H. to L.E., Dec. 27, 1957, CUL, Random House, Box 432, f. Eiseley.
37. *IJ*, 74–77.
38. Ibid., 19–20.
39. *The Lost Notebooks of Loren Eiseley*, 113.
40. Ibid., 152–53, 113.
41. *IJ*, 210.
42. Ibid., 164, 13.
43. L.E. to Jason Epstein, June 29, 1957, UPT 50, E36, Box 11, *Darwin's Century*, f. 13.
44. Jan. 28, 1957, UPT.
45. May 14, 1958, UPT.
46. *New York Times*, June 27, 1958, 23.
47. Jason Epstein to L.E., June 27, 1958, UPT 50, E36, Box 11, *Darwin's Century*.
48. L.E. to H.H., July 8, 1958, CUL, Random House, Box 432, f. Eiseley.
49. H.H. to L.E., July 15, 1958, CUL.
50. *DC*, 197.
51. *FBMD*, 80.
52. *New York Herald Tribune*, July 9, 1958, 15.
53. William Irvine, "Evolution of the Theory," *New York Times Book Review*, June 29, 1958, 4.
54. *Scientific American* 202, no. 1 (January 1960), 178.
55. *Science* 127, no. 3 (June 1958), 1493–94.
56. *Philadelphia Inquirer*, *Today Magazine*, Jan. 27, 1974, 19.
57. L.E. to H.H., Oct. 30, 1957, CUL, Random House, Box 432, f. Eiseley.
58. L.E. to H.H., July 15, 1958, CUL.
59. William J. Robbins to L.E., Jan. 28, 1960, UPT 50, E36, Box 4, American Philosophical Society–General no. 2.

60. L.E. to Robbins, Feb. 2, 1960, UPT.
61. Pyke Johnson, Jr., to L.E., May 25, 1959, UPT 50, E36, Box 11, f. 13, *Darwin's Century.*
62. L.E. to Johnson, May 26, 1959, UPT.
63. H.H. to the Members of the Editorial Board, Nov. 5, 1957, LC, *American Scholar*, Editorial File, Box 68, f. Board Elections.
64. L.E. to H.H., Feb. 9, 1958, CUL, Random House, Box 432, f. Eiseley (emphasis E.'s).
65. See L.E., "An Evolutionist Looks at Modern Man," *Saturday Evening Post* 230, no. 43 (April 26, 1958), 28–31.
66. L.E. to H.H., Feb. 20, 1958, CUL, Random House, Box 432, f. Eiseley.
67. L.E. to H.H., July 8, 1958, CUL.
68. H.H. to L.E., Nov. 21, 1961, LC, *American Scholar*, Editorial File, Box 115, f. Board Members—Expired Terms 1966.
69. H.H. to L.E., Apr. 14, 1958, CUL, Random House, Box 432, f. Eiseley (emphasis H.'s).
70. H.H. to L.E., June 9, 1958, CUL.

CHAPTER 16: "AT SIXES AND SEVENS"

1. L.E. to R.U., Jan. 26, 1967 (courtesy of R.U.).
2. L.E. to Martin Peterson, Feb. 27, 1976 (courtesy of M.P.).
3. UNA, *Alumni Association*, Loren Corey Eiseley Papers, 1921–1976, 40/5—1933, Box 1, f. Cor., 1921–1976.
4. *ASH*, 228–29.
5. Ibid., 230–31.
6. UNA, *Alumni Association*, Loren Corey Eiseley Papers, 1921–1976, 40/5—1933, Box 1, f. Genealogical Materials.
7. *ASH*, 228.
8. Interview with Jonathan Rhoads, Aug. 1, 1984.
9. *Daily Pennsylvanian*, Sept. 30, 1959, 2.
10. M.E. to Joseph T. Fraser, Jr., Aug. 12, 1959 (courtesy of J.T.F.).
11. Interview with Otto Springer, Aug. 30, 1984.
12. Interview with M.E., Sept. 8, 1984.
13. L.E. to Carl Wittke, Aug. 8, 1946, OCA 9/1/4, Card 2, Box 7, f. Loren C. Eiseley, 1944–1947.
14. Interview with Ward Goodenough, July 13, 1984.
15. Ibid.
16. L.E. to William A. Caldwell, Apr. 18, 1960, UPT 50, E36, Box 1, f. C.
17. Interview with M.E., Sept. 8, 1984.
18. Interview with Eliot Stellar, July 23, 1984.
19. Froelich Rainey to Malcolm Preston, c. May, 1959, UPA 4, Office of

the President: Papers, Box 101, f. Provost, Selection of, 1955–1960; Interview with Froelich Rainey, Aug. 2, 1984.
20. Interview with Robert E. Spiller, Sept. 7, 1984.
21. Interview with Froelich Rainey, Aug. 2, 1984.
22. *ASH*, 205.
23. Ibid., 203, 205–6.
24. C.B.S. to L.E., Apr. 21, 1960, UPT 50, E36, Box 5, f. Nebraska, University of—honorary degree.
25. H.H., *Words and Faces* (New York: Harcourt Brace Jovanovich, 1974), 101–2.
26. Ibid., 102.
27. H.H. to L.E., Apr. 6, 1959, UPT 50, E36, Box 9, f. 7, *The Immense Journey*.
28. L.E. to Bennett Cerf, Apr. 6, 1959, UPT.
29. H.H., *Words and Faces*, 122. Haydn and his partners dropped the second *a* in *Athenaeum* to simplify the spelling.
30. Interview with M.E., Sept. 8, 1984.
31. H.H. to L.E., Oct. 14, 1960, UPT 50, E36, Box 26, f. Atheneum.
32. Interview, Sept. 25, 1984.
33. Interview with Richard Stonesifer, Nov. 4, 1987.
34. UPA 4, Office of the President: Papers, Box 101, f. Provost's Office, 1955–1960, June 30, 1960.
35. *ASH*, 209–10.
36. Interview with Mary Crooks, Sept. 8, 1984.
37. *The Lost Notebooks of Loren Eiseley*, ed. Kenneth Heuer (Boston: Little, Brown, 1987), 93.
38. Interview with Robert E. Spiller, Sept. 7, 1984.
39. Interview with Ward Goodenough, July 13, 1984.
40. M.E. to D.T.B., Mar. 4, 1960 (emphasis M.'s; courtesy of D.T.B.).
41. Gaylord Harnwell to L.E., Feb. 20, 1961, UPA 4, Office of the President Papers, Box 143, f. Provost's Papers, 1960–1965.
42. Interview with M.E., Sept. 17, 1984.
43. L.E. to Harnwell, Oct. 21, 1961, UPT 50, E36, Box 3, f. Benjamin Franklin Professors.
44. Interview with Richard Stonesifer, Nov. 4, 1987.

CHAPTER 17: THE FIFTH HORSEMAN

1. Ledger II, 66, EE.
2. Interview with Preston Cutler, May 23, 1985.
3. Interview with Carroll V. Newsom, Nov. 3, 1984.
4. M.E. to Pearl and Carroll Clark, Dec. 17, 1961, UKA, Carroll Clark Papers, Cor., Eiseley, 1937–1978, PP/1, Box 4.

5. *UU*, 177–78.
6. Ibid., 178–79.
7. Interview with M.E., Sept. 17, 1984.
8. L.E. to A. I. Hallowell, Jan. 17, 1962, APS, MS Coll. no. 26, Hallowell Papers, f. Eiseley, Loren C.
9. Interview with Preston Cutler, May 23, 1985.
10. Interview with C. Willet Asling, May 17, 1985.
11. Interview with Sherwood Washburn, May 17, 1985.
12. Interview with Wright Morris, Aug. 14, 1984.
13. UPT 50, E36, Box 9, f. 2, *The Immense Journey*, 14.
14. *NC*, 34–35. For another version of this story see *The Lost Notebooks of Loren Eiseley*, ed. Kenneth Heuer (Boston: Little, Brown, 1987), 96.
15. L.E. to H.H., Jan. 11, 1962, LC, *American Scholar* Editorial File, Box 115, f. Board Members–Expired Terms, 1966.
16. M.E., Desk Diary, 1962, June 9, 12, EE.
17. Ibid., June 8–12.
18. L.E. to Leonard Mason, June 22, 1962, UPT 50, E36, Box 3, f. Hawaii, University of.
19. M.E., Desk Diary, 1962, Feb. 21, Aug. 8, Sept. 20–24, EE.
20. UPT 50, E36, Box 27, f. Macmillan Company.
21. UPT 50, E36, Box 27, f. Rand McNally.
22. Gaylord Harnwell to L.E., Apr. 17, 1961, UPA 4, Office of the President Papers, Box 143, f. Provost's Office—Selection of Provost, 1960–1965.
23. L.E. to Harnwell, May 15, 1961, UPA.
24. *ASH*, 207–8.
25. Interview with Robert E. Spiller, Sept. 7, 1984.
26. Interview with Ward Goodenough, July 17, 1984.
27. Ibid.
28. Interview with Jacob Gruber, Sept. 20, 1984.
29. Revelation 6:8.
30. James Hahn to G.C., Nov. 21, 1987.
31. *FT*, 1, 4–5.
32. Ibid., 124.
33. Ibid., 146, 166.
34. *The Lost Notebooks of Loren Eiseley*, 133.
35. Rachel Carson to L.E., Nov. 4, 1960, UPT 50, E36, Box 2, f. Carson, Rachel.
36. L.E. to Carson, Nov. 23, 1960, UPT.
37. William A. Rusher to L.E., Oct. 14, 1960, UPT 50, E36, Box 27.
38. *New York Times*, Aug. 31, 1960, 27.
39. *New York Herald Tribune*, July 24, 1960, sec. 6, 4.

40. H.H. to L.E., Apr. 4, 1962, UPT 50, E36, Box 12, f. 6, *The Firmament of Time.*
41. UPT 50, E36, Box 4, f. John Burroughs Award, 1961.
42. UPT 50, E36, Box 4, f. Du Nouy Award, 1961, for *The Firmament of Time.*
43. H.H. to L.E., Dec. 7, 1960, UPT 50, E36, Box 6, f. *The Immense Journey.*
44. L.E. to Hélène Boussincsq, Fcb. 27, 1961, UPT 50, E36, Box 9, f. 9, *The Immense Journey.*
45. *New York Times Book Review*, Mar. 12, 1961, 8.
46. L.E. to Victor Gollancz, Oct. 23, 1961, UPT 50, E36, Box 26, f. English Publishers.
47. John C. Weaver to L. E., Feb. 24, 1960, UPT 50, E36, Box 5, f. Nebraska, University of; L.E. to Arthur G. Wirth, May 9, 1962, UPT 50, E36, Box 14, f. S, *The Mind as Nature.*
48. Interview with Carroll V. Newsom, Nov. 3, 1984.
49. Virginia Faulkner to L.E., May 2, 1962, UPT 50, E36, Box 13, f. 3, *Francis Bacon and the Modern Dilemma.*
50. L.E. to Faulkner, May 5, 1962, UPT.
51. L.E. to Harry Kaste, June 17, 1962, UPT (emphasis E.'s).
52. L.E. to Bruce Nicoll, Sept. 10, 1962, UPT.
53. Nicoll to L.E., Sept. 18, 1962, UPT.
54. L.E. to Clifford Hardin, Sept. 29, 1962, UPT.
55. Hardin to L.E., Oct. 9, 1962, UPT.
56. L.E. to Hardin, Oct. 15, 1962, UPT.
57. A. C. Breckenridge to L.E., Oct. 16, 1962, UPT.
58. *FBMD*, 3, 95, 4.
59. L.E. to Howard Selsam, Oct. 11, 1963, CUL, Spec. MS Coll., Selsam.
60. Interview with Richard Stonesifer, Nov. 4, 1987.
61. *Christian Science Monitor*, June 27, 1963, 11.
62. *Kansas City Star*, June 26, 1963, 30.
63. UPT 50, E36, Box 1, f. D, Feb. 18, 1964.
64. UPT 50, E36, Box 1, f. D, Feb. 28, 1964.
65. L.E. to Elizabeth Pace Barnes, May 27, 1962, UPT 50, E36, Box 14, f. 5, *The Mind as Nature.*
66. Arthur G. Wirth to L.E., Dec. 20, 1960, UPT.
67. Ibid.
68. L.E. to Wirth, Mar. 31, 1962, UPT.
69. Wirth to L.E., Apr. 27, 1962, UPT.
70. L.E. to Wirth, May 9, 1962, UPT.
71. L.E. to Lewis Mumford, Sept. 28, 1962, VPL, Lewis Mumford Papers, f. 1395.

72. H.H. to L.E., Jan. 31, 1962, UPT 50, E36, Box 12, f. 6, *The Firmament of Time*.
73. *MN*, 17–18.
74. Letta May Clark to M.E., June 14, 1962, UPT 50, E36, Box 2, f. Clark, Letta May.
75. *American Anthropologist* 65 (1963), 693–94.
76. Interview with William Davenport, Sept. 18, 1984.
77. L.E. to W. M. Krogman, July 16, 1963, UPT 50, E36, Box 1, f. K.
78. Krogman to W. C. Sturtevant, July 15, 1963, UPT.
79. L.E. to Krogman, July 16, 1963, UPT.

CHAPTER 18: A DANCER IN THE RING

1. UPT 50, E36, Box 33, f. Guggenheim Fellowship.
2. Marston Bates to Gordon N. Ray, Oct. 9, 1962, UPT.
3. Interview with Carroll V. Newsom, Nov. 3, 1984.
4. M.E., Desk Diary, 1963, Oct. 29, EE.
5. C. P. Snow, *The Two Cultures* (Cambridge: Cambridge University Press, 1959), 5–6.
6. L.E., "The Illusion of Two Cultures," *The American Scholar* 33, no. 3 (Summer 1964), 396.
7. Lewis Mumford to L.E., Jan. 14, 1963, UPT 50, E36, Box 4, f. American Academy of Arts and Letters.
8. M.E., Desk Diary, 1963, May 22, EE.
9. Interview with Sophia Mumford, July 21, 1984.
10. M.E. to Lewis Mumford, May 23, 1963, VPL, Lewis Mumford Papers, f. 1395.
11. *NC*, 54–55. The Blashfield address was republished at least four times under as many titles. It appears as "Instruments of Darkness" in *NC*.
12. Interview with Isabel and Joseph Fraser, Jr., Sept. 7, 1984.
13. Lewis Mumford to L.E., May 26, 1963, UPT 50, E36, Box 4, f. American Academy of Arts and Sciences.
14. L.E. to Mumford, June 1, 1963, VPL, Lewis Mumford Papers, f. 1395.
15. L.E. to Hélène Boussinesq, Dec. 8, 1964, UPT, 50, E36, Box 9, f. 9, *The Firmament of Time*.
16. Pyke Johnson, Jr., to L.E., Oct. 25, 1963, UPT 50, E36, Box 11, f. 13, *Darwin's Century*.
17. Interview with Richard Stonesifer, Nov. 11, 1987.
18. M.E., Desk Diary, 1963, June 2, EE.

19. Interview of L.E. by Edmund Fuller, Oct. 20, 1971, BUSC, Edmund Fuller Collection.
20. Betsy Saunders to L.E., Apr. 21, 1960, UPT 50, E36, Box 26, f. *The American Scholar.*
21. L.E. to H.H., Oct. 21, 1963, LC, *American Scholar*, Editorial File, Box 115, f. Board Members—Expired Terms 1966.
22. L.E. to Warren E. Preece, Dec. 7, 1963, UPT 50, E36, Box 26, f. Encyclopaedia Britannica.
23. David Brower to L.E., July 28, 1963, Aug. 4, 1963, UPT 50, E36, Box 27, f. Sierra Club.
24. L.E. to Arthur Gregor, Jan. 20, 1964, UPT 50, E36, Box 27, f. Macmillan Company.
25. M.E., Desk Diary, 1963, May 26, July 30, EE; UPT 50, E36, Box 3, f. White House Task Force (Natural Beauty and Conservation).
26. M.E., Desk Diary, 1963, June 22–23, EE.
27. Carroll V. Newsom to G.C., Oct. 25, 1984.
28. M.E., Desk Diary, 1964, Feb. 24, EE.
29. Carroll V. Newsom to Detlev W. Bronk, Oct. 8, 1964, RUA, f. Richard Prentice Ettinger Program for Creative Writing.
30. Newsom to Bronk, Nov. 12, 1964, RUA.
31. Interview with Carroll V. Newsom, Nov. 3, 1984; Newsom, *Problems Are for Solving: An Autobiography* (Bryn Mawr: Dorrance & Company, 1983), 292.
32. UPT 50, E36, Box 32, f. 4, *Darwin and the Mysterious Mr. X.*
33. L.E., "Charles Darwin, Edward Blyth, and the Theory of Natural Selection," *Proceedings of the American Philosophical Society* 103, no. 1 (February 1959), 97. This article and others relating to the subject are reproduced in Eiseley's posthumous work *DMX*.
34. L.E., "Charles Darwin, Edward Blyth, and the Theory of Natural Selection," 102–3.
35. Edward Blyth, "On Psychological Distinctions Between Man and All Other Animals; and the Consequent Diversity of Human Influence over the Inferior Ranks of Creation, from Any Mutual and Reciprocal Influence Exercised Among the Latter," *Magazine of Natural History* 1 (1837), 135.
36. L.E., "Charles Darwin, Edward Blyth, and the Theory of Natural Selection," 100.
37. L.E., "Darwin, Coleridge, and the Theory of Unconscious Creation," *Daedalus* 94, no. 3 (Summer 1965), 590.
38. Charles C. Gillispie to L.E., July 16, 1959, UPT 50, E36, Box 2, Gillispie, Charles C. (emphasis G.'s).
39. L.E., "Darwin, Coleridge, and the Theory of Unconscious Creation," 595.

40. See *More Letters of Charles Darwin*, ed. Francis Darwin, I (New York: D. Appleton, 1903), 12. The passage reads, in part: "So much for the dead, and now for the living: there is a poor specimen of a bird which to my unornithological eyes appears to be a happy mixture of a lark pigeon and snipe. Mr. MacLeay himself never imagined such an inosculating creature." Nora Barlow, Darwin's descendant, wrote to inform Eiseley of this very point: Barlow to L.E., Feb. 20, 1963, EE. Also see Joel S. Schwartz, "Charles Darwin's Debt to Malthus and Edward Blyth," *Journal of the History of Biology* 7, no. 2 (Fall 1974), 301–18.
41. "Darwin's Notebooks on Transmutation of Species," ed. Gavin De-Beer, *Bulletin of the British Museum* in (*Natural History*) Historical Ser., 2 (1959–60), 23–73.
42. *ASH*, 200.
43. Gene M. Gressley to L.E., Dec. 18, 1964, UPT 50, E36, Box 1, f. G.
44. L.E. to Gressley, UPT.
45. M.E., Desk Diary, 1964, Feb. 9, 21, 22, Mar. 3, EE.
46. Interview with Jane Goodale, Sept. 26, 1984.
47. L.E. to David R. Goddard, Mar. 29, 1965, UPT 50, E36, Box 3, f. Pitzer College (Miscel.).
48. Goddard to L.E., Mar. 30, 1965, UPT.
49. Box 24, f. 2, *All the Strange Hours*.
50. M.E., Desk Diary, 1965, July 14, Aug. 4, EE.
51. Ibid., Apr. 27.
52. Interview with Robert E. Spiller, Sept. 7, 1984.
53. M.E., Desk Diary, 1965, May 3, EE.
54. Richard Stonesifer to L.E., Jan. 6, 1966, UPT 50, E36, Box 5, f. Drew University.
55. L.E. to Stonesifer, Nov. 22, 1965, UPT.
56. L.E. to George Gerbner, May 11, 1965, UPT 50, E36, Box 2, f. Haydn, Hiram.
57. The contents of the little book were later reprinted in *Man and the Future*, ed. James E. Gunn (Lawrence: University Press of Kansas, 1968), 18–37.
58. Van Wyck Brooks, *An Autobiography* (New York: E. P. Dutton, 1965), 471.
59. Interview with Simon Michael Bessie, Mar. 10, 1985.
60. H.H. to L.E., Apr. 4, 1962, UPT 50, E36, Box 12, f. 6, *The Firmament of Time*.
61. L.E. to Joan Daves, Mar. 15, 1965, UPT 50, E36, Box 26, f. Harcourt, Brace & World.
62. Daves to L.E., May 4, 1965, UPT.

63. L.E. to William Jovanovich, June 12, 1965, UPT.
64. M.E., Desk Diary, 1965, Apr. 14, EE.
65. UPT 50, E36, Box 26, f. Doubleday and Co., Inc.
66. UPT 50, E36, Boxes 5 and 6, f. Doubleday and Co. The more likely figure is nearer $200,000.
67. Interview with Pearl Clark, June 12, 1984.
68. Register of Wills, Montgomery County Courthouse, Norristown, PA, Last Will and Testament of Loren Corey Eiseley, reel 392, 510–518; Inventory and Appraisement Report, reel 150, 165–90.
69. M.E., Desk Diary, 1966, EE.
70. M.E., Desk Diary, 1966, Jan. 27, EE.
71. Interview with M.E., Sept. 8, 1984.
72. M.E., Desk Diary, 1966, Apr. 2–24, EE.
73. *ASH*, 227.
74. M.E., Desk Diary, 1966, July 7, 12–13, EE.
75. *ASH*, 162–63.
76. M.E., Desk Diary, 1966, Oct. 30, EE.
77. *AKA*, 82.
78. Interviews with Caroline E. Werkley, June 10–11, 1984.
79. L.E. to John Medelman, Oct. 31, 1966, UPT 50, E36, Box 26, f. *Esquire*.

CHAPTER 19: THE SECULAR PURITAN

1. Justin Kaplan, *Walt Whitman: A Life* (New York: Simon and Schuster, 1980), 38.
2. Kenneth Brower, "The Bone Hunter," *Omni* 1, no. 12 (September 1979), 139.
3. UPT 50, E36, Box 27, f. NBC—Animal Secrets.
4. M.E., Desk Diary, 1966, July 30, EE.
5. Screen Actors Guild to L.E., Nov. 1, 1967, UPT 50, E36, Box 27, f. NBC—Animal Secrets.
6. Interview with Edward Stanley, Mar. 31, 1985.
7. M.E., Desk Diary, 1966, Sept. 5, EE.
8. Interview with Richard Stonesifer, Nov. 4, 1987.
9. L.E. to R.U., Dec. 15, 1967, UPT 50, E36, Box 1, f. U.
10. Ledger II, Dec. 7, 1967, EE.
11. L.E. to Olgivanna Lloyd Wright, May 3, 1966, UPT 50, E36, Box 1, f. W.
12. Leo Eiseley to A.V.S., Sept. 26, 1967 (courtesy of A.V.S.).
13. L.E. to Vernon Brooks, Sept. 4, 1973, UPT 50, E36, Box 5, f. Jung Foundation.
14. UPT 50, E36, Box 18, f. 4, *The Invisible Pyramid*.

15. Interview of L.E. by Edmund Fuller, Oct. 20, 1971, BUSC, Edmund Fuller Collection.
16. *DC*, 57.
17. L.E. to William Gooddy, June 14, 1974, EE.
18. See, for example, Alice Kuhn Schwartz and Norma S. Aaron, *Somniquest* (New York: Harmony Books, 1979), ch. 7. Also see *UU*, 64–65.
19. Walter S. Hamady to L.E., July 17, 1967; L.E. to Hamady, July 31, 1967, UPT 50, E36, Box 2, f. Hamady, Walter S.
20. Interview with Walter Hamady, Dec. 15, 1987.
21. M.E., Desk Diary, 1958, Mar. 10, EE.
22. Interviews with Caroline Werkley, June 10–11, 1984.
23. M.E., Desk Diary, 1960, Feb. 22, EE.
24. L.E. to Hal Borland, Aug. 5, 1969, EE.
25. Interview with Walter S. Hamady, Dec. 15, 1987.
26. Ibid.
27. Interviews with James Hahn, Sept. 27, 1987, Dec. 1, 1987.
28. James Hahn to G.C., Oct. 4, 1987.
29. Hahn to G.C., Nov. 10, 1987.
30. Interview with Hahn, Sept. 27, 1987.
31. Hahn to G.C., Nov. 5, 1987.
32. Hahn to G.C., Nov. 4, 1987.
33. Interview with Hahn, Sept. 27, 1987.
34. M.E. to Richard Stonesifer, Nov. 10, 1977 (courtesy of R.S.).
35. L.E. to William Gooddy, Jan. 19, 1971, EE.
36. Interview with James Hahn, Sept. 27, 1987.
37. Hahn to G.C., Nov. 6, 1987.
38. Hahn to G.C., Dec. 12, 1987.
39. " 'Deviation' in Physical Anthropology," EE. See also *The Lost Notebooks of Loren Eiseley*, ed. Kenneth Heuer (Boston: Little, Brown, 1987), 98–99.
40. Interview of L.E. by Fuller, BUSC.
41. Ibid.
42. L.E. to William Jovanovich, Sept. 13, 1967, UPT 50, E36, Box 16, f. 10, *The Unexpected Universe*.
43. H.H. to L.E., Nov. 1, 1967, UPT.
44. H.H., *Words and Faces* (New York: Harcourt Brace Jovanovich, 1974), 284.
45. L.E. to William Jovanovich, Sept. 13, 1967, UPT 50, E36, f. 10, *The Unexpected Universe*.
46. L.E. to H.H., Jan. 30, 1968, UPT 50, E36, Box 16, f. 10, *The Unexpected Universe*.
47. L.E. to H.H., Sept. 10, 1968, UPT.

48. H.H. to L.E., Sept. 16, 1968, UPT.
49. David Maness to Hilda L. Lindley, Feb. 21, 1967, UPT.
50. L.E. to Maness, Oct. 27, 1967, UPT 50, E36, Box 27, f. *Life* magazine.
51. Maness to L.E., Nov. 21, 1967, UPT.
52. Memo from William Jovanovich to H.H., undated, UPT 50, E36, Box 16, f. 10, *The Unexpected Universes* (emphasis J.'s).
53. L.E. to H.H., June 30, 1969, UPT.
54. L.E. to Hilda Lindley, July 1, 1969, UPT.
55. *UU*, 93–95.
56. UPT.
57. L.E. to Leo Reich, May 16, 1968, UPT 50, E36, Box 1, f. R.
58. W. H. Frey to L.E., June 30, 1970, UPT 50, E36, Box 1, f. F.
59. L.E. to Frey, July 6, 1970, UPT.
60. Hugh A. Gilmore to L.E., Mar. 6, 1970, UPT 50, E36, Box 1, f. G.
61. For Eiseley's poignant tribute to the beast see *AKA*, 43–44.
62. UPT 50, E36, Box 16, f. 10, Best Sellers, *The Unexpected Universe.*
63. L.E. to H.H., Jan 16, 1970, UPT.
64. H.H. to L.E., Jan. 30, 1970, UPT.
65. L.E. to Hal Borland, Jan. 29, 1970, EE.
66. Interview with Stanley Johnson, Oct. 1, 1984.
67. John A. Wheeler to L.E., Nov. 7, 1969, EE.
68. *American Anthropologist* 73, no. 2 (April 1971), 305.
69. *The New Yorker* (February 21, 1970), 125.
70. B. A. Bergman to L.E., Mar. 5, 1970, UPT 50, E36, Box 27, f. *Philadelphia Bulletin.*
71. *UU*, 6.
72. UPT 50, E36, Box 40.
73. L.E. to Carl Wittke, Apr. 17, 1969, UPT 50, E36, Box 1, f. W.
74. UPT 50, E36, Box 5, f. La Salle College.
75. Interview with Ruben Reina, Sept. 20, 1984.
76. UPT 50, E36, Box 1, f. C (undated).
77. Ibid., July 2, 1968.
78. *NA*, 100.
79. *Daily Pennsylvanian*, Sept. 19, 1968, 5.
80. Interview with Doris Nicholas, Oct. 2, 1984.
81. Ibid.
82. *The Shape of Likelihood: Relevance and the University*, with an introduction by L.E. (Auburn, AL: Auburn University Press, 1971), 7.
83. Interview with Froelich Rainey, Aug. 2, 1984.
84. *Pennsylvania Gazette*, June 1970, 7.
85. Interview with C.B.S., Nov. 13, 1984.
86. L.E. to Richard Nixon, Apr. 16, 1969, EE.

87. Robert I. White to L.E., Apr. 29, 1970, UPT 50, E36, Box 5, f. Kent State University.
88. *Newsweek*, May 18, 1970, 32.
89. *Philadelphia Inquirer*, July 11, 1977, 4-A.

CHAPTER 20: *IMAGO*

1. Gerard McCauley to L.E., June 17, 1968, UPT 50, E36, Box 26, f. Doubleday.
2. L.E. to McCauley, June 24, 25, 1968, UPT.
3. Kenneth Heuer to L.E., Dec. 13, 1968, UPT 50, E36, Box 18, f. 9, *The Invisible Pyramid*.
4. UPT 50, E36, Box 4, AAAS—Dallas, Dec. 27, 1968.
5. M.E., Desk Diary, 1968, Dec. 27, EE.
6. UPT 50, E36, Box 40, f. 32, Mar. 28, 1967.
7. Interview with James Hahn, Dec. 1, 1987.
8. *The Lost Notebooks of Loren Eiseley*, ed. Kenneth Heuer (Boston: Little, Brown, 1987), 162–63.
9. SCR, f. Eiseley, Loren, *The Invisible Pyramid*.
10. Interview with Richard Stonesifer, Nov. 4, 1987.
11. Murray Fisher to L.E., July 10, 1964, UPT 50, E36, Box 27, f. *Playboy* magazine.
12. L.E. to H.H., Aug. 12, 1970, UPT 50, E36, Box 16, f. 10, *The Unexpected Universe*.
13. William F. Buckley, Jr., to L.E., Mar. 25, 1971; L.E. to Buckley, Apr. 2, 1971, UPT 50, E36, Box 27, f. National Review.
14. L.E. to Frank Bradshaw Wood, Sept. 19, 1969, UPT 50, E36, Box 1, f. W.
15. L.E. to William L. Straus, May 18, 1955, EE.
16. Frank Bradshaw Wood to L.E., Sept. 30, 1969, UPT 50, E36, Box 1, f. W.
17. *IP*, 3, 12.
18. Ibid., 79.
19. Ibid., 109.
20. Ibid., 22.
21. H.H., *Words and Faces* (New York: Harcourt Brace Jovanovich, 1974), 284.
22. L.E. to H.H., Aug. 12, 1970, UPT 50, E36, Box 16, f. 10, *The Unexpected Universe*.
23. H.H. to L.E., Aug. 21, 1970, UPT (emphasis H.'s).
24. L.E. to H.H., Aug. 26, 1970, UPT.
25. H.H., *Words and Faces*, 285.

26. UPT 50, E36, Box 27, f. Random House, Apr. 22, 1977.
27. *The Lost Notebooks of Loren Eiseley*, 162.
28. SCR, f. Eiseley, Loren, *The Invisible Pyramid.*
29. L.E. to Kenneth Heuer, Sept. 16, 1970, UPT 50, E36, Box 18, f. 9, *The Invisible Pyramid.*
30. SCR, f. Eiseley, Loren, *The Invisible Pyramid.*
31. Rex Stout to M. and L.E., Dec. 8, 1970, EE.
32. *Playboy* 17, no. 11 (November 1970), 12.
33. Wright Morris to L.E., Dec. 21, 1970 (courtesy of W. M.).
34. Interview with Charles Scribner, Jr., Jan. 17, 1988.
35. L.E. to Earl W. Count, July 26, 1971, UPT 50, E36, Box 1, f. C.
36. SCR, f. Eiseley, Loren, *The Night Country.* Slight alterations were made in Eiseley's draft before printing.
37. UPT 50, E36, Box 20, f. *The Night Country.*
38. *NC*, 39–43.
39. Ledger I, 18–19, EE.
40. Nathaniel Burt to L.E., Dec. 11, 1972, UPT 50, E36, Box 4, f. Athenaeum Award.
41. *Washington Post*, Dec. 14, 1971, B1.
42. *New York Times*, Nov. 10, 1971, 45.
43. Walter Hamady to L.E., Mar. 12, 1972, SUNY, SB.
44. SCR, f. Eiseley, Loren, *Notes of an Alchemist.*
45. L.E. to Howard Nemerov, Jan. 18, 1973, EE.
46. Interview with Charles Scribner, Jr., Jan. 17, 1988.
47. SCR, f. Eiseley, Loren, *Notes of an Alchemist.*
48. L.E. to Fletcher McCord, Dec. 7, 1972, UPT 50, E36, Box 1, f. M.
49. L.E. to John Gallagher, Feb. 5, 1972, UPT 50, E36, Box 26, f. Glencoe Press.
50. John Scott Mahon to L.E., Sept. 8, 28, 1972, UPT 50, E36, Box 27, f. University of Michigan Press.
51. SCR, f. Eiseley, Loren, *The Man Who Saw Through Time.*
52. L.E. to Martin Meyerson, Mar. 23, 1971, UPT 50, E36, Box 4, f. The National Institute of Arts and Letters.
53. Interview with James Hahn, Dec. 1, 1987.
54. L.E. to Mrs. David Walrath, June 4, 1976, EE.
55. Interview with James Hahn, Apr. 5, 1988.
56. *ASH*, 27–28.
57. UPT 50, E36, Box 24, f. 24, *All the Strange Hours.*
58. *ASH*, 264.
59. L.E. to Mrs. David Walrath, June 4, 1976, EE.
60. W. H. Auden to L.E., Nov. 23, 1972, EE.
61. *The New Yorker*, Apr. 14, 1973, 40.

62. *The New Yorker*, Dec. 18, 1971, 36.
63. Annie Dillard to L.E., Aug. 3, 1973, UPT 50, E36, Box 2, f. Dillard, Annie (emphasis D.'s).
64. *Washington Post Book World*, Mar. 31, 1974, 3.
65. Interview with Caroline E. Werkley, June 10, 1985.
66. *UU*, 143.
67. "Notes for Operation Snow Wolf," EE.
68. Ledger II, 1–30, EE. Much of the original manuscript material is reproduced in *The Lost Notebooks of Loren Eiseley*, 193–99, 202–08.
69. M.E. to Sister Janet Moore, June 10, 1980, UPT 50, E36 (unfiled) (emphasis M.'s).
70. Interview with Otto Springer, Aug. 30, 1984.
71. Interviews with Anthony Wallace, Aug. 12, 1984; William Davenport, Sept. 18, 1984.
72. Wallace Stegner to G.C., May 14, 1986 (emphasis S.'s).
73. Interviews with Solomon Katz, Sept. 6, 1984; Arleigh Hess, Jr., July 29, 1984; Ruben Reina, Sept. 20, 25, 1984.
74. Interview with Richard Stonesifer, Nov. 4, 1987.
75. L.E. to Nemerov, Aug. 16, 1973, EE.
76. L.E. to Malcolm M. Ferguson, Sept. 4, 1973, UPT 50, E36, Box 1, f. F.
77. L.E. to Russell Lynes, Aug. 6, 1973, UPT 50, E36, Box 4, f. Century Club.
78. C.B.S. to L.E., Mar. 12, 1968, EE.
79. Interview with C.B.S., May 21, 1984.
80. Ibid.
81. L.E. to Patrick Young, Nov. 26, 1974, UPT 50, E36, Box 1, f. X-Y-Z.
82. L.E. to Fredrick R. Abrams, Jan. 3, 1974, UPT 50, E36, Box 1, f. A.
83. L.E. to Mary Van Tassel, Feb. 3, 1972, UPT 50, E36, Box 1, f. 51.
84. UPT 50, E36, Box 25, f. 4, *All the Strange Hours*, 2.
85. Edwin Way Teale to L.E., Aug. 23, 1974, EE.
86. SCR, f. Eiseley, Loren, *All the Strange Hours*.
87. Ibid.
88. Ibid.
89. UPT 50, E36, Box 25, f. 5, *All the Strange Hours*.
90. *ASH*, 272–73.
91. M.E. to Mary Mattern, Sept. 11, 1975, BML.
92. *IP*, 138.
93. L.E. to Art Spikol, Apr. 12, 1975, UPT 50, E36, Box 27, f. *Philadelphia Magazine*.

94. L.E. to Art Spikol, Apr. 17, 1975, UPT.
95. L.E. to Ray Bradbury, Apr. 1, 1976, EE.
96. *New York Times*, Dec. 18, 1975, 43.
97. *Wall Street Journal*, Dec. 18, 1975, 16.
98. *ASH*, 113–14.
99. Richard Allen Faust to L.E., Dec. 9, 1975, UPT 50, E36, Box 1, f. F.
100. Jac Cave to L.E., UPT 50, E36, Box 1, f. C. This letter is undated but Eiseley replied on Mar. 26, 1976.
101. SCR, f. Eiseley, Loren, *All the Strange Hours*.
102. Ibid.
103. Interview with Dollie Langdon Hahn, Sept. 24, 1986. The second bust is now in the capitol building at Lincoln, where Eiseley was inducted into the Nebraska Hall of Fame on September 3, 1987, commemorating the eightieth anniversary of his birth.
104. M.E. to Dwight Kirsch, Feb. 22, 1977, UPT 50, E36 (unfiled).
105. L.E. to Leo Eiseley, Apr. 4, 1977 (courtesy of A.V.S).
106. A.V.S. to G.C., undated.
107. *AKA*, 15.
108. SCR, f. Eiseley, Loren—1977–78.

EPILOGUE

1. M.E. to Sister Janet Moore, Sept. 30, 1981, UPT 50, E36 (unfiled).
2. James Hahn to G.C., Nov. 25, 1987. Also see Caroline E. Werkley, "Professor Cope, Not Alive But Well," *Smithsonian* 6, no. 5 (Aug. 1975), 72–75.
3. Wright Morris to M.E., July 28, 1977 (courtesy of W.M.).
4. E. Fred Carlisle, *Loren Eiseley: The Development of a Writer* (Urbana, Chicago, London: University of Illinois Press, 1983), xiii.

BIBLIOGRAPHY AND ABBREVIATIONS OF FREQUENTLY USED SOURCES

The reader seeking a more exhaustive bibliographical treatment than this one is referred to Jeanne DePalma Gallagher's 236-page *Bibliographic Card Catalog Index for the Writings of Loren Eiseley*, available through the University of Pennsylvania Archives, Philadelphia.

BOOKS BY LOREN EISELEY

ASH — *All the Strange Hours: The Excavation of a Life*. New York: Charles Scribner's Sons, 1975. Prose.

The Brown Wasps (private edition). Mount Horeb, WI: The Perishable Press Ltd., 1969. Prose.

DC — *Darwin's Century: Evolution and the Men Who Discovered It*. New York: Doubleday and Co., 1958. Prose.

FBMD — *Francis Bacon and the Modern Dilemma*. Lincoln: University of Nebraska Press, 1962. Prose.

FT — *The Firmament of Time*. New York: Atheneum Publishers, 1960. Prose.

IA — *The Innocent Assassins*. New York: Charles Scribner's Sons, 1973. Poetry.

IJ — *The Immense Journey*. New York: Random House, 1957. Prose.

IP *The Invisible Pyramid.* New York: Charles Scribner's Sons, 1970. Prose.

MN *The Mind as Nature.* New York, Evanston, London: Harper & Row, 1962. Prose.

The Man Who Saw Through Time (revised and enlarged edition of *Francis Bacon and the Modern Dilemma*). New York: Charles Scribner's Sons, 1973. Prose.

Man, Time, and Prophecy (private Christmas edition). New York: Harcourt, Brace & World, 1966. Prose.

NA *Notes of an Alchemist.* New York: Charles Scribner's Sons, 1972. Poetry.

NC *The Night Country.* New York: Charles Scribner's Sons, 1971. Prose.

UU *The Unexpected Universe.* New York: Harcourt, Brace & World, 1969. Prose.

POSTHUMOUS BOOKS BY EISELEY

AKA *Another Kind of Autumn.* New York: Charles Scribner's Sons, 1977. Poetry.

ANW *All the Night Wings.* New York: Times Books, 1980. Poetry.

DMX *Darwin and the Mysterious Mr. X: New Light on the Evolutionists.* New York: E. P. Dutton, 1979. Prose.

ST *The Star Thrower.* New York: Times Books, 1978. Poetry and prose.

MANUSCRIPT COLLECTIONS AND ARCHIVES

AMNH American Museum of Natural History, New York, New York

APS American Philosophical Society, Philadelphia, Pennsylvania

BML Bennett Martin Public Library, Heritage Room, Lincoln, Nebraska

BUSC Boston University Special Collections, Boston, Massachusetts

CUL Columbia University Library Archives, New York, New York

HUA	Harvard University Archives, Cambridge, Massachusetts
LC	Library of Congress, Washington, D.C.
LER	Loren Eiseley Seminar Room, University of Pennsylvania, Philadelphia, Pennsylvania
NARSF	National Archives and Records Service Files, Washington, D.C.
NMNH	National Museum of Natural History, Smithsonian Institution, Washington, D.C.
NSHS	Nebraska State Historical Society, Lincoln, Nebraska
NSMA	Nebraska State Museum Archives, University of Nebraska, Lincoln, Nebraska
OCA	Oberlin College Archives, Oberlin, Ohio
RUA	Rockefeller University Archives, New York, New York
SCR	Charles Scribner's Sons, New York, New York
SUNY, SB	The Perishable Press Ltd. Collection, Department of Special Collections, Library, State University of New York, Stony Brook, New York
UKA	University of Kansas Archives, Lawrence, Kansas
UM	University Museum, University of Pennsylvania, Philadelphia, Pennsylvania
UNA	University of Nebraska Archives, Lincoln, Nebraska
UPA *or* UPT	University of Pennsylvania Archives, Philadelphia, Pennsylvania
VPL	Van Pelt Library (Rare Books), University of Pennsylvania, Philadelphia, Pennsylvania

OTHER SOURCES

EE	Eiseley Estate
EFH	Eiseley Family History. Compiled and written by Leo Eiseley, Loren's half brother, during the 1950s and 1960s. Courtesy of A.V.S.
A.V.S.	Athena Virginia Spaulding
C.B.S.	C. Bertrand Schultz
D.T.B.	Dorothy Thomas Buickerood
H.H.	Hiram Haydn
L.E.	Loren Eiseley
M.E.	Mabel Eiseley

R.U.	Rudolph Umland
W.G.	Wilbur Gaffney

BOOKS

Angyl, Andrew J. *Loren Eiseley*. Boston: Twayne Publishers, 1983.

Carlisle, E. Fred. *Loren Eiseley: The Development of a Writer*. Urbana, Chicago, London: University of Illinois Press, 1983.

Gerber, Leslie E., and Margaret McFadden. *Loren Eiseley*. New York: Frederick Ungar Publishing Co., 1983.

Haydn, Hiram. *Words and Faces*. New York: Harcourt Brace Jovanovich, 1974.

Heuer, Kenneth, ed. *The Lost Notebooks of Loren Eiseley*. Boston: Little, Brown, 1987.

Morris, Wright. *A Cloak of Light*. New York: Harper & Row, 1985.

Newsom, Carroll V. *Problems Are for Solving: An Autobiography*. Bryn Mawr: Dorrance & Company, 1983.

Stewart, Paul R. *The Prairie Schooner Story*. Lincoln: University of Nebraska Press, 1955.

ARTICLES ABOUT EISELEY

Auden, W. H. "Concerning the Unpredictable." *The New Yorker* (Feb. 21, 1970), 118–25.

Brill, Naomi. "Loren Eiseley and the Human Condition." *Prairie Schooner* 61, no. 3 (Fall 1987), 64–69.

Carlisle, E. Fred. "The Heretical Science of Loren Eiseley." *Centennial Review* 18 (Fall 1974), 354–77.

———. "The Literary Achievement of Loren Eiseley." *Prairie Schooner* 61, no. 3 (Fall 1987) 1, 38–45.

———. "The Poetic Achievement of Loren Eiseley." *Prairie Schooner* 51, no. 2 (Summer 1977), 111–29.

Christensen, Erleen. "Loren Eiseley, Student of Time." *Prairie Schooner* 61, no. 3 (Fall 1987), 28–37.

Christianson, Gale E. "Loren Eiseley: A Poet in the White River Badlands." *Nineteenth Annual Dakota History Conference Pa-*

pers, ed. Herbert W. Blakely. (Vermillion, SD: 1987), 23.A3–23.A7.
———. "Loren Eiseley and Lowry Wimberly: Companions in Alienation." *Heritage of the Great Plains* 20, no. 3 (Summer 1987), 21–27.
———. "Loren Eiseley in Lincoln: Two Poems and a Remembrance." *Prairie Schooner* 61, no. 3 (Fall 1987), 9–27.
———. "Loren Eiseley: Sentinel of the West," *The Nebraska Humanist*, 1989, 67–73.
———. "Nebraskans Loren Eiseley and Wright Morris: A Literary Friendship." *Magazine of the Midlands*, December 17, 1989, 7–8
———. "The Masks of Loren Eiseley." *Biography* 13, no. 4 (Fall 1990), 317—27.
———. "Widow's Pique." *Philadelphia Magazine* 81, no. 8 (August 1990), 141–46.
Heidtmann, Peter. "An Artist of Autumn: An Essay." *Prairie Schooner* 61, no. 3 (Fall 1987), 46–56.
———. "Locating Loren Eiseley." *Biography* 7, no. 3 (Summer 1984), 206–12.
Howard, Ben. "Loren Eiseley and the State of Grace." *Prairie Schooner* 61, no. 3 (Fall 1987), 57–59.
Nemerov, Howard. "Loren Eiseley, 1907–1977." *Prairie Schooner* 61, no. 3 (Fall 1987), 5–8.
Schwartz, James M. "Loren Eiseley: The Scientist as Literary Artist." *Georgia Review* 31 (Winter 1977), 855–71.
Umland, Rudolph. "The Ghost of Lowry Wimberly." *Prairie Schooner* 41, no. 3 (Fall 1967), 325–38.
———. "Looking Back at the Wimberly Years." Unpublished MS, Heritage Room, Bennett Martin Public Library, Lincoln, NE. 39 pp.
———. "Lowry Wimberly and Others: Recollection of a Beerdrinker." *Prairie Schooner* 51, no. 1 (Spring 1977), 17–51.
———. "More Beerdrinking with Wimberly." Unpublished MS, Heritage Room, Bennett Martin Public Library, Lincoln, NE. 40 pp.
Werkley, Caroline E. "Eiseley and Enchantment." *Prairie Schooner* 61, no. 3 (Fall 1987), 60–63.
———. "Lost Pumas, Pincushions, and Gypsies." *Journal of Library History* 11 (Oct. 1969), 188–96.

———. "Of Skulls, Spiders and Small Libraries." *Wilson Library Bulletin* 44 (Oct. 1969), 188–96.

———. "Professor Cope, Not Alive But Well." *Smithsonian* 6, no. 5 (Aug. 1975), 72–75.

DISSERTATIONS

Appel, George F. *Modern Masters and Archaic Motifs of the Animal Poem.* University of Minnesota, 1973.

Christensen, Erleen. *Loren Eiseley: Modern Shaman.* University of Kansas, 1984.

Kassebaum, L. Harvey. *To Survive Our Century: The Narrative Voice of Loren Eiseley.* Indiana University, 1979.

Schwartz, James M. *The "Immense Journey" of an Artist: The Literary Techniques and Style of Loren Eiseley.* Ohio University, 1977.

ACKNOWLEDGMENTS

The author of any work of nonfiction, especially one that has taken the better part of five years to complete, inevitably becomes indebted to many individuals and institutions. This writer is certainly no exception. During my time in Nebraska, I was offered help and hospitality at every turn, but I wish to thank especially C. Bertrand and Marian Schultz, Rudolph Umland, Ruth Thone, and The Friends of Loren Eiseley, who were there at the beginning when I needed them most. For sharing their personal recollections of Loren Eiseley with me I am grateful to the following for favors both large and small: Faye Munden, Alice Cave, Leah Dale Masters, Lois Gerard Clemens, Georgia Everett Kiffin, Arthella Gadd Anderson, Helen Barager, Helen Hopt Kleven, Mylan and Eunice Stout, Frank W. Crabill, Robert S. Long, Marguerite Lewis, Macklin Thomas, and Viola Hasskarl. Sadly, Wilbur Gaffney and Emery Blue have recently departed the scene—grand gentlemen both and not forgotten. No one could have been more accommodating than the staffs of the University of Nebraska State Museum, the Bennett Martin Public Library, the Archives of the University of Nebraska, and the Nebraska State Historical Society. I am particularly indebted to staff members Hugh H. Genoways, Carol J. Connor, James Gulick, Ann Rineart, Joseph G. Svoboda, Elsie V. Thomas, and Sherrill F. Daniels.

I was received with equal grace in Lawrence, Kansas, where Pearl Clark took me in tow, making the depression and war years come alive. That same hospitality was forthcoming from Marston McCluggage, Morton Green, L. R. Lind, and John Nugent, head of the University of Kansas

Archives. No individual contributed more to my understanding of Eiseley in his middle years than did his Kansas colleague and close friend Dr. C. Willet Asling, whose detailed memoir and interviews of the period will long remain invaluable to Eiseley scholars.

The Oberlin years would be far more obscure were it not for the incisive observations and background provided by Jacob Gruber, who later followed Eiseley to Penn to complete his Ph.D. Equally important in this regard are the reflections of Carroll V. Newsom, one of the few who remained close to Eiseley over the years. Paul B. Sears, A. Hunter Dupree, Margaret Haylor, Mary Jeanne Astier Kalb, and George Simpson also contributed to my knowledge of the period, as did the document collection in the Oberlin College Archives, which was made available to me through the good offices of Roland M. Baumann.

Eiseley's friends, colleagues, and former students in and around Philadelphia were generous to a person. Few knew him as well or contributed more to this volume than his fellow Nebraskan and author Wright Morris. Of those who taught with him at Penn, I must single out Froelich Rainey, Ward Goodenough, Ruben Reina, William Davenport, John L. Cotter, John S. Witthoft, John Pritchard, Anthony F. C. Wallace, Murray G. Murphey, and Solomon Katz. I am further indebted to Eliot Stellar, Caroline Werkley, Thomas Ehrlich, Jonathan E. Rhoads, Julius Mackie, John A. Eichman III, Francis E. Johnston, Arleigh P. Hess, Jeanne DePalma Gallagher, Mary Crooks, Stanley Johnson, Mr. and Mrs. Joseph C. Fraser, Jr., Walter Hamady, Virginia Cotter, Richard Allen Faust, Lewis Korn, Frederica de Laguna, Jane Goodale, Janet M. Biddle, Sheldon Judson, Lewis and Sophia Mumford, Preston Cutler, and Doris Nicholas. The late Robert Spiller, Otto Springer, and Joseph E. Townsend, Jr., were equally helpful.

The archives in which I spent the most time are those of the University of Pennsylvania, located beneath the stands of venerable old Franklin Field. I can only say that every scholar should be as fortunate. My incessant demands spanning several months did nothing to dampen the good humor of Mark Frazier Lloyd and his excellent staff, anchored by Hamilton Elliot, Maryellen Kaminsky, and Curtiss Ayers. Hats off to all of them! I also wish to thank Robert H. Dyson, director of the University Museum, and archivist Douglas M. Haller and staff for their many kindnesses. Beth Carroll-Horrocks, manuscripts librarian of the American Philosophical Society, facilitated my labors at that august institution; Whitfield Bell, Jr., and Bentley Glass provided keen insights into its inner workings. Thomas A. Horrocks of the Library of the College of Physicians of Philadelphia generously allowed me to quote from an unpublished article he authored.

Dorothy Thomas Buickerood, now ninety, who knew both Loren

and Mabel Eiseley long before fame came calling, provided me with not only much to write about but the will to persist during those dog days of composition that beset every author. Thank you, dear Dorothy; may your own elegant pen continue to skim across the page as it has for most of this century. Thanks are also due to writers Ray Bradbury and Wallace Stegner, and to writer and reviewer Edmund Fuller.

Richard J. Stonesifer is deserving of special mention for his perceptive reflections on Eiseley, as are Alberta Hartmann Speck, daughter of Eiseley's mentor, and Sherwood Washburn, who never did get Eiseley to go to Africa. E. Fred Carlisle, the author of a fine literary study of Eiseley, generously gave me access to his considerable personal archives, including his extensive correspondence with our mutual subject.

Few, if any, writers have been associated with finer publishers than was Loren Eiseley, a fact to which I can personally attest. I am especially grateful to Simon Michael Bessie, Charles Scribner, Jr., Charles Scribner III, and to Random House, Macmillan, Atheneum, and Harcourt Brace Jovanovich for their scholarly assistance and permission to quote from Eiseley's works.

In addition to the institutions already noted, I would like to thank the following: the American Museum of Natural History, Boston University Special Collections, Columbia University Library Archives, Harvard University Archives, the Library of Congress, the National Archives, the National Museum of Natural History, Rockefeller University Archives, Department of Special Collections at the State University of New York at Stony Brook, the University of Pennsylvania's Van Pelt Library, and Cunningham Memorial Library at Indiana State University.

To colleague Rebecca Shepherd Shoemaker, who read and helped edit the manuscript, goes a special gesture of tribute for what must have often seemed an endless and thankless task. And to my literary agent, Michael Congdon, who was with me all the way, kudos.

Funding for research was generously provided by the American Council of Learned Societies, the National Endowment for the Humanities, and the Faculty Research Committee of Indiana State University. I am also grateful to the university for the sabbatical during which much of this research was conducted.

Finally, I must express my unreserved gratitude to the relatives of Loren Eiseley. Athena Virginia Spaulding gave me access to a previously unknown family history and photographs once the property of her father, Leo Eiseley, Loren's half brother. Her own knowledge of the family and youthful associations with Loren aided me in filling in otherwise inexplicable gaps. Dollie Langdon Hahn, Mabel Eiseley's sister, and her son, James, who drew close to his writer-uncle during the years of fame, opened equally important windows from the other side. Their willingness to grant me access to the estate papers was a gesture of trust I shall never forget. I am pleased to note that they took their cue from Mabel Eiseley herself, who, after several fits and starts, agreed to a series of interviews beginning in the late summer of 1984. Although her health was failing, her memory and spirit remained strong, enabling me to learn many details of the private life she and Loren had guarded so tenaciously through the years. It was through Mabel's good graces that I was put in contact with others who only agreed to speak after she gave the signal. I like to think that there is much in this biography that would have pleased her, including the recognition she so richly deserves for seeing a shy, somewhat backward Nebraska boy down the path to literary glory. My final thanks to a most elegant lady.

As always, however, it is the members of one's own household who see one through. Thanks be to Laurie and to our bulldog, Mambo Manny, who sends melancholy scurrying with one wiggle of his ample behind.

INDEX